SIMON & SCHUSTER MEGA CROSSWORD PUZZLE BOOK

Series 20

300 never-before-published crosswords

Edited by John M. Samson

 Gallery Books

New York   London   Toronto   Sydney   New Delhi

Gallery Books
An Imprint of Simon & Schuster, Inc.
1230 Avenue of the Americas
New York, NY 10020

First Gallery Books trade paperback edition September 2020

GALLERY BOOKS and colophon are registered trademarks
of Simon & Schuster, Inc.

For information about special discounts for bulk purchases,
please contact Simon & Schuster Special Sales at
1-866-506-1949 or business@simonandschuster.com.

The Simon & Schuster Speakers Bureau can bring authors to your live event.
For more information or to book an event, contact the Simon & Schuster
Speakers Bureau at 1-866-248-3049 or visit our website at
www.simonspeakers.com.

Designed by Sam Bellotto Jr.

Manufactured in the United States of America

10 9 8 7

ISBN 978-1-9821-3038-1

COMPLETE ANSWERS WILL BE FOUND AT THE BACK.

FOREWORD

"YOUR MOVE!" by Greg Johnson ... a bonus puzzle for starters.

ACROSS

1 Coffee option

5 Google Talk, informally

10 Ice-cream type

14 Glass separated by muntins

15 Windy City hub

16 Stomach, playfully

17 Resolves

18 VW compact

19 Minuscule amount

20 Abandon

22 Fact-checking site

24 Raw sea delicacy

25 Thunderbird degree

28 Make a typo

29 Stirring or blending

32 Trendy foam footwear

35 Swept the series

36 Beantown pros, to fans

37 Vitamin brand

39 Summer mo.

40 Mother of Sean Lennon

41 14th Greek letters

42 WWW address

43 Hanky alternatives

47 Jupiter's mother

48 Fleshy mushroom

49 Proclamation

50 Moss of "Mad Men"

52 Tugboat's service

53 Costa ___ Sol

54 Image quality, briefly

55 Honker

58 Wheels for Woody and Buzz

62 Crossword cookie

63 Like most people

66 Riding

67 Road shoulder

68 Tubular pasta

69 Kunis of "Family Guy"

70 Alluring

71 Fires

72 Sinuous shockers

DOWN

1 Apple's ___ Touch

2 Breeze-catching garment

3 Start of a two-part message regarding the diagram's center

4 Autocrat

5 Berry in some facial creams

6 Oven-baked cereal snack

7 Milliner's product

8 Nature imitator

9 Earl and Lady Grey

10 Annabella of "The Sopranos"

11 End of message

12 It may be tempted

13 Yuletide poem beginning

21 TV show's sophomore run

23 Needed

26 Go a few rounds

27 Year in Spain

29 Not out

30 Dick Tracy's creator

31 Timbre

33 Inverted "v" mark

34 Air spirit of myth

38 Bites a bit

44 Airline seating class

45 Crossed (out)

46 Bullring "bravo!"

47 Storage for a heating system

51 Morphed into

55 Shows sadness

56 Native Canadian

57 Hits with a "Bzzzzt!"

59 Change for a five

60 Rock's partner

61 Places for pampering

64 Blue on a map

65 Business brief?

The Margaret Award winner is BIG APPLE HOT SPOT by Pam Klawitter.

John M. Samson

1 DEAL ME IN   by Lee Taylor
Alternate clue for 51 Across: Arizona tourist attraction.

ACROSS

1 Dark suit
7 Menial laborer
11 Droop like an old mattress
14 Geisha garment
15 Pearl Harbor island
16 Pool stick
17 Enters data
18 High school gala
19 Washington bill
20 They're fixed in the song "Handy Man"
23 A bit teary-eyed
26 Drano ingredient
27 "Wash, ___, repeat"
28 Drive-through conveniences
29 Pantomime character
31 CBS forensics drama
32 Affectionate
33 Pained cries
37 Travel website
39 Tiny aperture
40 Available for the job
41 Angel costume accessory
42 Put the kibosh on
43 Hassles
45 Mother ___
46 Declivitous
49 "___ for Alibi": Grafton
50 Shown on TV
51 Thames River crossing
54 Sendak's "Where the Wild Things ___"
55 Leafy green vegetable
56 Short foot races
60 Exclamation from Emeril
61 Summers, in Marseille
62 Clothing
63 Like shrinking violets
64 Goes bad
65 Royal guards

DOWN

1 Hit the slopes
2 Lapel adornment
3 Rock concert equipment
4 Has suspicions
5 Sweepstakes submission
6 Fair to middling
7 With bulging peepers
8 Breadmaker
9 "We've got trouble"
10 Big kahuna
11 Treat with contempt
12 Women in a tree?
13 Gaggle members
21 Kevin in "De-Lovely"
22 Capital of Hawaii?
23 Aggressively male
24 "___ the house!"
25 Maggie in "Downton Abbey"
29 Skin or leaf openings
30 Stirs up
32 Part of a hearth tool set
34 School roll
35 Say "y'all" or "cap'n"
36 Health class, for short
38 Ran a towel over
39 Zoroastrian
41 Athina Onassis, notably
44 iPad or Nook
45 Misleads
46 Hefty slices
47 Bar Mitzvah scroll
48 Tom Riddle, to Harry Potter
50 Striped marble
52 Western alliance since 1949
53 WW2 turning point
57 That guy
58 Before, to Shelley
59 Cambodian coin

2 TWIN CITIES   by Richard Silvestri
You can include "sailors" in the clue for 33 Down.

ACROSS

1 Hymn singers
6 Pointed tool
9 Cuff
14 "Stormy Weather" singer
15 Far from forward
16 Book read in a mosque
17 Peach or pumpkin, e.g.
19 More or less
20 Cal. zone
21 At deuce
22 Tours of duty
23 "Tristram Shandy" author
25 Wooden rod
27 Neutral color
29 Courtroom conference
33 Hard to lift
36 Head of the class?
38 Wheels for a big wheel
39 Bar on a car
40 Words of wisdom
41 Date at the Forum
42 Stadium level
43 Sneaky guy?
44 Nancy Drew creator
45 Harder to climb
47 Performed a cappella
49 Oktoberfest fare
51 It has its ups and downs
55 National Guard building
58 Sound of amusement
60 Greek vowel
61 River through Nantes
62 "Love that bowler!"
64 1040 and others
65 Mess up
66 Perrier alternative
67 Alamogordo event
68 Tribute in verse
69 Beatrice's adorer

DOWN

1 Musical talent
2 Actor Buchholz
3 Speechify
4 Rural hotel
5 Interim government
6 Rue the run
7 Dressing spot
8 Corrosive substance
9 Enjoyed the rink
10 Feudal lord who gets around?
11 Club for Bethpage
12 Lacking slack
13 Tolkien tree creatures
18 At any time
22 Sty dwellers
24 Think the world of nightcrawlers?
26 Some Missouri natives
28 Milk suppliers
30 Wait patiently
31 Communicant's response
32 Bloomer with hips
33 Boaters and bowlers
34 Leave the stage
35 Sheltered, at sea
37 Nosh
40 Imitative behavior
44 Worked dough
46 Least adulterated
48 U.S. Open stadium
50 Show place?
52 European finch
53 Chance to hit
54 Bruce of Gotham City
55 ___ Romeo (Italian auto)
56 Dig like a pig
57 Swampy ground
59 43,560 square feet
62 "The Matrix" hero
63 Little Stowe girl

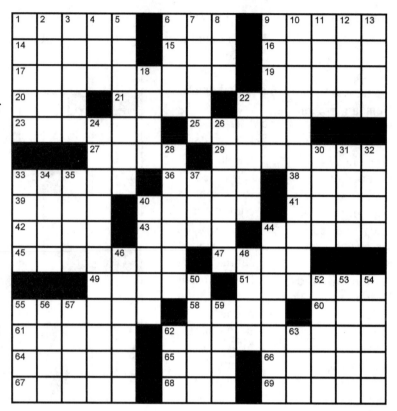

3 BROADWAY MELODIES   by Todd Gross
Dorothy Loudon sang 21 Across in the original 1977 Broadway production.

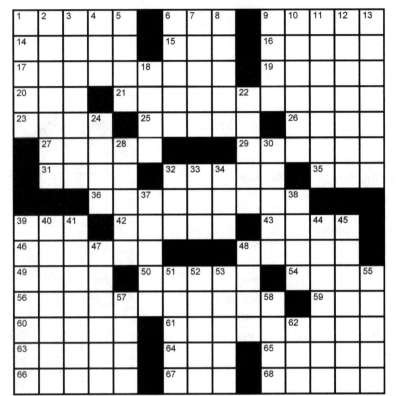

ACROSS

1 Blows smoke
6 Latin noun gen.
9 Group of Boy Scouts
14 Japanese dog breed
15 "I ___ Killer" (Netflix series)
16 Temporary tattoo ink
17 "Fiddler on the Roof" number
19 Earth pigment
20 Came down with
21 "Annie" number
23 Puts on the dog?
25 "I thought ___ never leave!"
26 Notarization proof
27 "Wrong!"
29 Not fit to stand trial
31 Older brother of Isaac
32 Eldest Marx brother
35 Answer sheet
36 "No, No, Nanette" number
39 Louis and Lucia: Abbr.
42 Overhead camera
43 Epps of "ER"
46 Texas poker
48 Award for achievement
49 English horn's family
50 Yemenite's neighbor
54 Spit out
56 "Billy Elliot the Musical" number
59 Liberace's nickname
60 Hospital communication device
61 "The Pajama Game" number

63 Alkaline compound
64 Hockey sportscaster Emrick
65 Reach its end
66 Small change
67 Hematite, e.g.
68 Famed photographer Adams

DOWN

1 Ways of the jungle
2 Kharkiv locale
3 Debacles
4 Bouquet business since 1910
5 Hoist the main
6 Belief without proof
7 Chew the scenery
8 Macho
9 Roughneck
10 Derelict in one's duties
11 Taking five
12 Like some rural roads
13 Dinner garnish
18 Former Yugoslav leader
22 Official order
24 Right away, to an RN
28 Glove fabric
30 "It's ___ Never": Presley
32 Corp. money mgr.
33 Sweetie
34 Rage
37 Knight suit
38 Drop
39 Waterproof boot
40 Responsible (for)
41 Plum liqueur
44 Masters Tournament blooms

45 Let off the hook
47 Not too bad
48 Falafel bread
51 Make a mess of
52 One with a role to play
53 Sister's daughter
55 ___ One vodka
57 Uno, dos, ___
58 Hit by the Village People
62 Lady lobster

ACROSS

1 More together
6 Advances in cribbage
10 Area opposite the Adam's apple
14 Where to find class in Paris
15 Member of the Adams family
16 Disappearing Sea
17 Flash stick
19 Oscar-winning Beatty film
20 Thermostat, for one
21 Legal precedent
23 Good or bad reaction
25 Santa Fe Trail town
26 Get cracking
31 Kitchen scrubbers (with 12-D)
34 Playing with matches, say
35 "East of Eden" housekeeper
36 Swift literary style
38 Wiser partner
40 Rapper ___ Wayne
42 Mustached Seuss character
43 Busy
45 "___ for Silence": Grafton
47 Hawaiian goose
48 Sun. speech
49 Coachella Valley resort
52 Uruguayan coin
53 Three Stooges projectile
54 Joltin' joe?
58 Was revolting?
63 "Ship ___!"
64 Stocked/TITLE
66 Hershey candy
67 It borders Buffalo
68 Run ___ brick wall
69 Colleague
70 River of Flanders
71 Sound condition?

DOWN

1 Shooting sites
2 Sore spot
3 Adjective, oddly enough
4 Spreading trees
5 Change flights
6 Part of mph
7 Doctor documents
8 Bestow upon
9 Goes back and forth
10 They make horse collars
11 You might find this in geometry
12 See 31 Across
13 "You're something ___!"
18 Wilde-ly entertaining
22 Unlike Berg's "Wozzeck"
24 Dirtbag
26 Landing of TV
27 "It's the truth, I swear!"
28 Sedated
29 Like most colleges
30 Jefferson's religion
31 Luring lady of Greek mythology
32 Shaggy ape
33 "Battle of the ___" (2017)
37 Singer Braxton
39 Mumbai money
41 Have trouble with esses
44 It opens many doors
46 Hubert's VP successor
50 Hapless lot
51 Put the brakes on
52 Wilder's costar in "Stir Crazy"
54 Dodge City lawman
55 "If it fits, wear it" item
56 Word before vault or after utility
57 Jax's friend on "Sons of Anarchy"
59 "Yipes!"
60 Jacques in "Mon Oncle"
61 Mireille in "World War Z"
62 June 6, 1944
65 Painter Gerard ___ Borch

5 KEYBOARD KEYS by Karen Motyka
"The Emerald Archer" is one alias of 10 Down.

ACROSS

1. Pet shelter letters
5. Sound at a fun house
9. Veep who resigned in 1973
14. Roger Miller's "Chug-___"
15. Narcissus adorer
16. "1984" laborer
17. "Grease 2" star
19. Sword of Damocles
20. Regained control, as a ship
21. Abounded (with)
22. Total flop
23. "Doctor Zhivago" director
24. Ray-Bans, slangily
28. Game with hand signals
32. Henry VIII's house
33. Edible seeds
34. Kapoor of "Crossing Jordan"
35. Vivacity
36. Showing strain
37. Uncivil disobedience
38. Cookie Monster's pal
39. Alita portrayer Salazar
40. "The Lawrence Welk Show" dance
41. Table
43. Becky Thatcher's love
44. "Beverly Hillbillies" daughter
45. Measure of an A/C
46. Secret passage, perhaps
49. Exchange of ideas
54. Shark in "West Side Story"
55. Graveyard or swing
56. Things to whistle
57. Prado hangings
58. Pearl Jam's "___ ID"
59. Love, Italian-style
60. Gridiron cheers
61. Seine tributary

DOWN

1. Crossword exams?
2. Surveyor's map
3. Sugar form
4. Turkish commander
5. Da Vinci, for one
6. Had a part in
7. She ___
8. "¡___ favor, señor!"
9. Pop up
10. Oliver Queen's alter ego
11. It's what's to be expected
12. "Night" author Wiesel
13. Fuse with a blowtorch
18. Holstein feature
21. Ruffle the hair
23. Norbulingka site
24. Precipitous
25. Londoner's greeting
26. "The Hitchhiker's Guide to the Galaxy" author
27. Unwelcome sign
28. Burn myrrh
29. Regular paper
30. Bring back memories
31. Harrison's "Norwegian Wood" instrument
33. Indiana's state flower
36. Bridge guarder of folklore
40. Anka and Newman
42. Word from Miss Manners
43. Things to pull up
45. Blessed event
46. Sheffield farewell
47. "E pluribus ___"
48. Boy of Mexico
49. Copperfield's first wife
50. One of Pittsburgh's three rivers
51. Fernandez of tennis
52. Unexplained sightings
53. Diminutive suffix
55. It was hell, to Sherman

6 COCKTAIL HOUR*   by Brenda Cox

The cocktail at 20 Across is sometimes called a vodka buck.

ACROSS

1 Elder penguin in "Happy Feet"
5 Flint
10 Queequeg's captain
14 All-encompassing prefix
15 Brickyard 400 entrant
16 First capital of Japan
17 Grp. marching around campus
18 Pianist Claudio
19 Curry and Coulter
20 Kremlin drug smuggler?*
22 Some De La Hoya wins
23 It has a hub at ORD
24 Like cornflakes sitting in milk
26 September stone
31 Tree frog
34 Colgate-endorsing org.
35 Open up
37 "I Was ___ War Bride" (1949)
38 One way to travel
40 Leg of lamb
42 Italian news agency
43 Former UN head Kofi
45 MLB commissioner (1998–2015)
47 Joke around
48 More contrived
50 Ran a tape back
52 Bump on a log
54 Tavern
55 Leek, for one
57 Rain forest avian*
63 Chili pot
64 Hirsch in "Milk"
65 Award given Rajiv Joseph
66 First floor apt.
67 UFC champ McGregor
68 Chapeau holder
69 Lemke of baseball
70 Course hazards
71 Magic wand tip

DOWN

1 Regular at Cheers
2 Melville's Tahitian tale
3 Myrmecology's study
4 Drunken sound
5 Bar hopping (with 54-A)
6 Ruin
7 Suede shade
8 War, to Mars
9 Make even
10 Bête noire
11 Funny business*
12 Pisa's river
13 What McCartney played
21 Home of Hawaii's Pipeline
25 Birthplace of Venus
26 ___ Jessica Parker
27 Hersey title town
28 Analgesic*
29 Pete Rose's 1,314
30 Full of oomph
32 Programmer on "Westworld"
33 Double-check a sum
36 Cheney, to Bale
39 Easygoing
41 Bar fixtures?
44 "___ Blu Dipinto di Blu"
46 Gun filler
49 Unwanted item
51 Friar's Club bigwigs
53 Bit of gossip
55 Microphone type
56 Arm part
58 ABBA ballerina
59 Mess hall mess
60 Skeptic's rejoinder
61 "All Time High" singer Coolidge
62 Some bucks

7 JUNIORS by John M. Samson
32 Down is nicknamed "The Iron Man."

ACROSS

1 Steak sauce brand
5 Hall Johnson ___
10 Porcine repast
14 Kiss, in British slang
15 "Peg Woffington" novelist
16 Newcastle redundancy
17 Junior in the MLB Hall of Fame
19 Theater org.
20 Self-centered person
21 FX's "Sons of ___"
23 Latin noun case
24 Cry of pain
25 Badlands rise
27 Before
30 Spud sieve
33 Semisoft cheese
35 San Francisco valley
36 Lab gel
37 Some kings
38 John in "Bumblebee"
39 Down with a bug
40 By and by
41 "Pyramids" singer John
42 Promote growth in
44 First lady's son
46 Skye in "River's Edge"
47 Jazz fan?
51 Unlucky
54 Clownfish
55 Sommer in "The Oscar"
56 Junior member of the Rat Pack
58 Wished otherwise
59 Plant swelling
60 Musical symbol
61 Football coach Babers
62 American-born saint
63 Wraths

DOWN

1 Set a price
2 European lake
3 "___ that one, the other one!"
4 Gadget for a hard-boiled cook?
5 Pivotal periods
6 Lift a weight
7 Klutzy fellow
8 It's a thought
9 Ryan in "R.I.P.D."
10 Like cabs on a rainy day?
11 Junior of horror films
12 Imprecation
13 Dull Jack's lack
18 Lethe, for one
22 Star quality
26 Banded quartz
27 McDonald in "Ricki and the Flash"
28 Cooked
29 Check number
30 It ruins a dry spell
31 Inuit word for "house"
32 Junior in the MLB Hall of Fame
34 Cuprite, e.g.
37 Treats lovingly
38 Trattoria entrée
40 Lille moon
41 Doled, with "out"
43 Great Lakes port
45 "The Pilgrim's Progress" author
48 Hang suspended
49 Biscotto flavoring
50 They're out on a limb
51 Buffalo bunch
52 His, to Jacques
53 "The Sweetest Taboo" singer
54 Rounds
57 Player on a Queens bench

INGREDIENTS I   by John M. Samson
"Numen Lumen" is the motto of 48 Across.

ACROSS

1 Butter measure: Abbr.
5 Swing states?
10 "Liquid sunshine"
14 EPA-banned spray
15 Negate
16 "Scandal" novelist Shusaku
17 Hollandaise sauce ingredient
19 Bill of Rights advocacy grp.
20 Taxi squad members
21 Gordon Ramsay's domain
23 Shout targets
24 Cancún cat
25 Does lacework
27 Fagin's gang members
30 Not slowing down a bit
33 VIP's vessel
35 Grave
36 More than vexation
37 "Hamilton" star Phillipa
38 Syracuse–Albany dir.
39 Thelma in "The Maltese Falcon"
41 A. Sullivan's "The Lost ___"
43 River in a 1914 battle
44 Trading places
46 Gulf of Finland tributary
48 University of crossword puzzles
49 Jeanie Bueller's brother
53 Tacit
56 Lush with vegetation
57 White-bearded Smurf
58 Russian dressing ingredient
60 Suffix with team or young
61 Go wide of
62 "Octopussy" director
63 Lifeboat pair
64 Delights, in slang
65 Start of Idaho's motto

DOWN

1 Scented powders
2 Merino sound
3 Festival dance of Brazil
4 Integrity
5 Grandeur
6 Cross to bear
7 Naval spy org.
8 Canard à l'orange ingredient
9 ___ of hand (magic)
10 Responded to
11 Worcestershire sauce ingredients
12 Lazing around
13 Verb, for example
18 Foch of "Spartacus"
22 Randy's skating partner
26 "Fierce" alter ego of Beyoncé
27 Side issue?
28 Enya's language
29 Carson's Carnac, for one
30 Construction zone
31 Dance with a queen
32 Buffalo wings ingredient
34 Affectionate sound
40 "A Fistful of ___"
41 Movie houses
42 Protects
43 Gridiron gain
45 Louis XIV, for one
47 Country singer Gosdin
50 Garage door tracks
51 Garment trim
52 Minutes taker
53 ___ jure
54 Miss Bond in "Casino Royale"
55 Bryan of Bon Jovi
56 Word on a sample check
59 Over there, to bards

9 INGREDIENTS II by John M. Samson
Orange juice is another ingredient of 11 Down.

ACROSS

1 Carpet features
5 Trig symbol
10 Fraud
14 ___-bodied seaman
15 Singer Neville
16 Confucian dynasty
17 Reuben sandwich ingredient
19 Put up a print
20 Accumulated over time
21 Spiral flower clusters
23 Equates
24 Bus. entity
25 Store in a hold
27 Tacks, at sea
30 Mr. Slate, to Fred
33 Battery type
35 Wolfish look
36 Reset setting
37 Bagel go-with
38 Frost bite
39 Slight
41 Dispassionate
43 Something to pay down
44 V8 juice ingredients
46 ___ City, Baghdad
48 NFL quarterback Derek
49 Wood stock
53 August birthstone
56 Real
57 Explorer Tasman
58 Butterscotch ingredient
60 Frosty's eyes
61 "Embraced by the Light" author
62 Meat on a kabob, maybe
63 "My treat!"
64 "Ivanhoe" author
65 "Oh, were it not true!"

DOWN

1 Like some medicinal sprays
2 Primitive counters
3 Spunk
4 One with foresight
5 Accepts the challenge
6 Alcoholic
7 ___ of Good Feelings
8 Escorted trip
9 Sodium bicarbonate, e.g.
10 "Moonlight Sonata" movement
11 Mimosa ingredient
12 Top-drawer
13 Ceramic gift-shop items
18 Peewee
22 Small piece of a machine
26 Languishes
27 3-D graph line
28 Smooth-talking
29 Back-to-school mo.
30 Russet pear variety
31 Chaplin on "Game of Thrones"
32 Beef stroganoff ingredient
34 Bird cry
40 Raised writing
41 Disco lights
42 Advisory council
43 Risky one to neck with?
45 Baggage tag for O'Hare
47 Puts on apparel
50 Imperial
51 Kind of queen
52 Belgrade people
53 Couturier Rabanne
54 Black, poetically
55 Gillette razor name
56 "M*A*S*H" Emmy winner
59 "Deep Space Nine" changeling

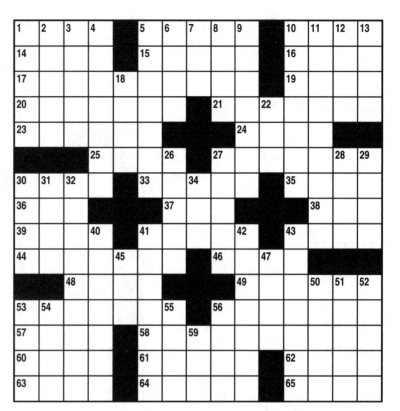

COVER-UP by Pam Klawitter
In 2003, 22 Down was inducted into the Robot Hall of Fame.

ACROSS

1 Do a bit of boxing
5 "I can't ___ thing"
9 Many a reggae artist
14 Tackle box item
15 Unlike Godiva
16 Sister-in-law of Ruth
17 Miner's quests
18 Word form for "both"
19 It's where the action is
20 Veranda with a panoramic view
23 Tolkien tree creatures
24 Clamming center?
25 Crunchy-skinned sides
32 Neighbor of Sicily
33 On the fence?
34 Maze runner
35 Second of a Latin trio
36 Sled dog with a statue in Central Park
38 Traditional Hindu music
39 NFL animal
40 Tart plum
41 Unit of length
42 Hugger-mugger
46 Stock holder
47 Hermione portrayer
48 New England seaside abode
55 Pulitzer winner for "John Brown's Body"
56 Ride in a glider
57 London trolley
58 They might be up your sleeves
59 Belly-wash
60 Theater opening
61 Outlaw, Beatle, or Packer
62 Ex-hurler Hershiser
63 Kaput

DOWN

1 Like a boat to China?
2 Satisfied sound
3 You find it in geometry
4 They're paid at memorials
5 32-card card game
6 Practically
7 "Forbidden fragrance" perfume
8 Tennis score
9 Waze display
10 Make a collar
11 A bit of a job
12 Fish or gas follower
13 "Gotcha!"
21 "My Way" lyricist
22 "Star Wars" droid Artoo-___
25 Malcolm-___ Warner
26 Memorable shrine
27 Turned white
28 Giant of crosswords
29 Pontificate
30 Type of beaver
31 Rating symbol
32 Salsa artist Anthony
36 Chenin ___ grape
37 Center of Chicago
38 Sailing club events
40 Poison-pen journalist for the "Daily Prophet"
41 They're in charge: Abbr.
43 Show one's face
44 The 60s or 70s
45 Without scruples
48 Sixer rival
49 Princess of Arendelle
50 ___ buco (veal dish)
51 It's a way in
52 The world's tallest is in St. Louis
53 Cat, in Catalonia
54 Shine
55 Touring singer's home away from home

11 OFFICE OXYMORONS by Pam Klawitter
"So which is it?"

ACROSS

1 Tell all
5 Powhatan's son-in-law
10 Command to Rover
14 Do an HGTV job
15 Make immune to
16 Jumped down from the saddle
17 He grew up on "Toy Story"
18 Alpine region
19 Afternoon dos
20 Adhesive . . . or not?
23 Apple leftover
24 "Exodus" setting
28 "All together now . . ."
30 Movie set shot
32 Magnon starter
33 Correction fluid . . . or not?
35 She's got milk
36 In ___ (going nowhere)
37 Trauma spots, briefly
38 Give up formally
39 Defunct carrier: Abbr.
40 Organized . . . or not?
44 Once owned
45 Still life prop
46 Blunt blades
47 Part of GPS
49 Jenna Bush's "___ Story"
50 A duplicate . . . or not?
56 Like the Beatles' Mr. Mustard
59 Sudoku skill
60 "Cosmo" rival
61 Online read
62 Lasso loop
63 Coward of the theater
64 Cries from a head slapper
65 Old politico Kefauver
66 Lint catcher

DOWN

1 Muffin flavor
2 Fallon's predecessor
3 Bldng. annex
4 "The Last ___" (1991 Willis film)
5 Like Berra's uniform number
6 In the cooler
7 Hang back in the shadows
8 Throat problem
9 Slippery and sinuous
10 Serve a bar mitzvah
11 Paul Bunyan's cook
12 "Mamma ___"
13 They're out of this world
21 Morrison or Braxton
22 App addict
25 Give in to
26 Wears down
27 Bring down
28 Windpipe, e.g.
29 Gridiron groups
30 Naptime in Navarra
31 Tsang ___ dog
33 Plaster strips
34 Pittsburgh pucksters
38 Waning moon
40 Campground enthusiast, briefly
41 "Bear of little brain" creator
42 Threatens
43 Gem cut in slabs
48 Grilling utensil
49 Biscotti flavoring
51 Baby patter
52 "___ a Feeling": Ricky Nelson
53 Odette's genus
54 Bargaining result, maybe
55 Business review site
56 Club with resort villages
57 Second-largest bird
58 Spa sound

12 DECISION MAKING   by Patti M. Walker
. . . according to Sheldon Cooper.

ACROSS

1 José Altuve's team
7 TV-sked abbr.
10 Walgreens competitor
13 Ziploc again
14 Magazines might be full of them
16 Short straw, perhaps
17 Golden Oldies successor
19 Bit of eHarmony info
20 Bollywood attire
21 School for King's Scholars
22 It's up for debate
24 Doodle pad
27 Bloodline
30 Subj. for newcomers
31 HBO competitor
32 Watch a Netflix flick
37 Icelandic epic
41 Chef's tool for cutting herbs
44 Baseball's "Slammin' Sammy"
45 Give the go-ahead
46 Pizzeria chain
47 Dorm monitors
49 Baseball's Hammerin' Hank
51 Barfly of sorts

58 At sixes and sevens
59 It really stinks
60 Stage award
64 Cowgirl's cry
65 "Live long and prosper" speaker
68 Test for college srs.
69 It's found in geometry
70 It often comes with sides
71 Word of belonging
72 Bit of work
73 How neglected gardens go

DOWN

1 Semicircles
2 Ward of "FBI"
3 Bygone ruler
4 Join a protest
5 ___ in "Oscar"
6 More conniving
7 Pack to the future
8 Wild ride
9 "Into the Badlands" network
10 Jewelry fastener
11 Fashionista's read
12 Head in a herd
15 Jumps bail
18 Windy City rail initials
23 Pitching goals

25 Plastic alternative
26 Surround
27 Shows curiosity
28 Home of the Buckeye Nation
29 Withers on the vine
33 Hint at
34 Workers with rounds
35 Stationary front
36 Cause for a 19th-hole buying
38 Gloomy
39 James Bond foe

40 Jimmy Buffett's "Son of ___ of a Sailor"
42 Menu word with asada
43 Ratings symbol
48 Tropical lizard
50 Gets a shelter dog
51 James Bond foe
52 Japanese beer or city
53 Stadium employee
54 Hard-luck case
55 Wildlife tracker

56 Saldana of "Avatar"
57 Gendarme's cry
61 Tiresome type
62 Frozen treat at Burger King
63 Barely managed, with "out"
66 Choler
67 Nestlé's ___-Caps

13 "DOUBLE ROOM, PLEASE"   by Patti M. Walker

24-A is home to the only surviving 19th-century American wooden whaling ship.

ACROSS

1 Late bloomers
5 Pool opener?
9 Get a clean slate
14 Noted Israeli statesman
15 Radisson rival
16 Ways of doing
17 Lost clownfish of film
18 Fidel's hermano
19 They can be loaded and stolen
20 When starting over, this is the place to go
23 Gate guesses at ATL
24 Rasputin, for one
28 Part of NPR
30 Bruin nickname of old
32 Part of many a clash
33 Home Ec staple
35 It's in your makeup
36 "Gimme a break!"
37 Prefix for puncture
38 Uruguay uncles
39 It's all good
40 Where custody might be awarded
44 GPS suggestion
45 MLB 2003 AL MVP
46 Wonderland directive
47 Largest of the Finger Lakes
49 Winningham of "Casa Valentina"
50 Part of a sports break
56 Burrito topper
59 Stephen A. Smith's network
60 Skin soother
61 The Chicago Picasso makeup
62 "Vogue" shelfmate
63 Monster of the west
64 Horse holders
65 Music store purchase
66 Lee or Tucci

DOWN

1 Fix a fence
2 Ride-sharing app
3 Call from the crib
4 Trapped in a ski chalet
5 Frank on a stick
6 Some Kindle selections
7 Give the cold-shoulder treatment
8 Rural skyline sight
9 Sonogram sights
10 TripTik info
11 They might pop up
12 "Told ya so!"
13 End of days
21 Put-writing filler
22 Roadie's load
25 Extreme boredom
26 Give the cold-shoulder treatment
27 Take it easy
28 In the middle of nowhere
29 No longer sleeping
30 1961 Heston movie
31 "Breaking Bad" lawyer Goodman
33 Some are emotional
34 Guerilla garb
38 Beach carryalls
40 Spa offerings
41 Nearly dried-up sea
42 Hankered for
43 All-occasion item
48 Buddy in "Born to Dance"
49 "Curly" wood
51 Not a good look
52 Getaway spot
53 Came back to earth
54 "Kinky Boots" drag queen
55 ___ Cuisine
56 Armenia, once
57 Finished off
58 May 1 honoree, in Hawaii

14 AQUARIUS by Harvey Estes
The clue at 20 Across could be a bit misleading.

ACROSS

1 Charlie Parker biopic
5 Poland Spring rival
9 Hoodwinks
14 Area east of the Urals
15 Somalian supermodel
16 "No, thanks"
17 Good time
18 Rant's partner
19 Underground vault
20 Starbuck's agreement
23 Center-to-perimeter line
24 Warns about a sting, e.g.
27 Hock
30 Sevastopol locale
31 Tanning trigram
34 Hyena's hideaway
36 Everything ___ place
37 Clive Christian No. 1, for one
40 Rock singer Apple
41 Interstate rumbler
42 '60s radical org.
43 Put in a chip
45 Races the engine
47 Far out from the coast
49 Giving relief to
54 Diviner's goal
57 Up and at 'em
59 "___ La Douce"
60 Highly unusual
61 NBA venue
62 Loses force
63 Middle name at Menlo Park
64 Arranges
65 Mailed out
66 Nikita's no

DOWN

1 Kiddie-lit elephant
2 "___ Little Prayer": Warwick
3 Het up
4 ___ Lama
5 Clearance event
6 Apple of a sort
7 Morning cupful, in slang
8 Lacking the knack
9 "Catch Me If You Can" star
10 Revolting developments
11 "Ignore it!"
12 Medium strength
13 Retired jet
21 Rebuttal to "nope"
22 Eccentricity
25 Elaborate parties
26 Scale notes
28 Channels
29 Less naughty
31 Book back
32 Sit-in sitter
33 Subtle detail
35 Red cooking apple
38 Pauses in speech
39 Party hardy
40 Hot trend
44 Aachen article
46 Carpenter's cutter
48 Mylanta targets
50 Plastic wrap brand
51 Europe's "boot"
52 Gumption
53 Like Johnson's Society
55 Buffalo's lake
56 Black cat, for one
57 Smallish batteries
58 Sign of a Broadway hit

15

A&Q   by Marie Langley

1 Across was a regular panelist on the show "Match Game."

ACROSS

1 "Fried Green Tomatoes . . ." author
6 Did a take-off on
10 Heavy mists
14 Brief role
15 "South Pacific" isle ___ Ha'i
16 Standing in the military
17 List divider
18 Skewed view
19 All right
20 **Start of the answer**
23 Armistice mo.
24 Cursive curlicue
25 Conked on the bean
29 Major blood carriers
33 Restroom, for short
34 **End of the answer**
37 Fateful March day
39 Deighton of spy thrillers
40 Colleges, in Australia
41 **Start of the question**
46 Language ending
47 "Friends," for one
48 Gay duds of a carol
50 Hot under the collar
53 Tried to get elected
54 **End of the question**
59 Part of Hawaii
60 Book after 2 Chronicles
61 Mob scenes
63 Creole veggie
64 Company with a reptile logo
65 Diary bit
66 Protein source
67 Model Banks
68 Anesthesia of old

DOWN

1 Broadcast-regulating org.
2 Thailand neighbor
3 Bullets and shells
4 Spacecraft for two astronauts
5 Say "Fine by me!"
6 Pop palindrome
7 Sets of socks
8 Cheer up
9 Counter cleaner
10 Overly elaborate
11 Former acorns
12 Small biter
13 Pilot's domain
21 Word before "after"
22 Christian in fashion
25 Seventh heaven
26 Hub-to-rim lines
27 Prevent, as danger
28 Havarti additive
30 Piano adjuster
31 Licorice-flavored plant
32 Car in "Peggy Sue Got Married"
35 Voice of Bugs
36 New Age music superstar
38 Thick-crust pizza style
42 Operate properly
43 Triumphant cry
44 Grand Ole ___
45 In hot water
49 Rub with oil
51 Flustered state
52 Trial's partner
54 Income at a casino
55 Vital glow
56 Syllables of triumph
57 Closet pest
58 "To be" to Henri
59 Unruly gathering
62 Neighbor of Leb.

16 THEMELESS by Harvey Estes
20 Across is Ariel's BFF (best fish friend).

ACROSS

1 Floored
6 Early VCR format
10 King who married Jezebel
14 Source of green energy from a yellow star
16 Retro style
17 A person
18 A person
19 "Yer dern ___!"
20 "The Little Mermaid" character
22 They're kept in pens
24 Moderate paces
25 Home to many Kurds
28 Swenson of sitcoms
31 Stand on a corner
33 Merciless foe of Flash Gordon
34 Clairvoyant
35 Dickens's Drood
36 Direct deposit (abbr.)
37 Where buoy meets gull?
39 Mount Rushmore prez
40 Englert in "Beautiful Creatures"
42 Ukraine urban area
43 Perry and Della's creator
44 Kathmandu's land
45 Yahoo.com, e.g.
46 Sugary drinks
47 Thinner, as air
49 Allowance after tare
51 "Field of Dreams" sport
54 Law school subject
58 Cough (up)
59 Leave before Eminem takes the stage?
61 "Firebird" composer Stravinsky
62 Like a liar that can't stop lying
63 Minus
64 "Rebel Without a Cause" star
65 Fix a button

DOWN

1 ". . . or ___ just me?"
2 Denial for Nanette
3 Ray of "The Green Berets"
4 Queued up
5 Watergate senator Sam
6 Like Leroy Brown
7 Sufficient, to Moonbeam McSwine
8 Pond duck
9 Set aside
10 Uvula neighbor
11 Move in the direction of
12 Easy to get into
13 Quantum physicist Niels
15 Peachy, in a sense
21 "Family Matters" nerd
23 Casual footwear
25 "Let me say it another way . . ."
26 Where many go ballistic?
27 Italian appetizers
29 Mythical wish granters
30 Will of "Arrested Development"
32 Quadrupeds have four
37 A-list member
38 "O Brother, Where Art Thou?" hero
41 Chosen pursuits
43 Greasy spoon sign
48 Like overwrought fans
50 Old anesthetic
51 Something to post
52 Everest climber Gammelgaard
53 Cone material
55 S&L assets
56 Blanchett of "Elizabeth"
57 Spit out
60 Midmorning hour

17 THEMELESS by Harvey Estes
25 Across and the two clues that follow share a curious relationship.

ACROSS

1 Crest container
5 "Hägar the Horrible" dog
10 Agape
14 Schick competitor
15 Chlorine's pool target
16 Tiresome talker
17 Pressure source, perhaps
18 "For a Few Dollars More" director
19 "Let It ___": Everly Brothers
20 Crime lab study
21 Unbending
22 "The Wizard ___"
23 Justin Verlander, for one
25 "There Is Nothin' Like a Dame," e.g.
27 "There is nothing" philosophy
30 Like a dame
31 Like mild weather
32 Saturn or Mercury
33 Crucial element
34 Winner of a race
39 Resistance unit
40 Pitcher's activity
41 Gum tree
45 Narrow flag
46 Easter egg hunters
48 Uttered obscenities
49 Polo of "The Fosters"
50 Horse handlers
53 Campers, for short
54 Be specific about
55 Lose ground
56 In order (to)
57 Storefront sign
58 Moves like the Blob
59 Trumpet muffler
60 "I ___ tell!"
61 Sassy
62 Puts to work

DOWN

1 Gregory Hines specialty
2 Flatware
3 Hyper-ventilates
4 Attention
5 Shaker filler
6 NY Met, e.g.
7 Self-centeredness
8 Dressing choice
9 One who passes the bar?
10 Costello's partner
11 "Knight of the ___ Countenance"
12 Expensive wrap
13 Signed over
21 Magnetic coil
24 Ancient Mariner's verse
26 A mouse may be this
28 Responsible for
29 Dam up
32 "___ la vie!"
35 Kind of hammer
36 Afraid
37 Drain of energy
38 Ways to go
41 TV ad directive
42 Bargain-basement
43 Some aces
44 Sam Sheppard, to Bailey
45 Drop off
47 Trial partner
51 Thomas Gray poems
52 Holey fabric
56 Mustangs' school

18 ON HIS SATANIC MAJESTY'S REQUEST   by Theresa Yves
... not to be confused with a similarly titled Rolling Stones album.

ACROSS

1 What the mouse did to the clock
6 Low pitch source
10 Pull a switch
14 Hot under the collar
15 Masseuse's target
16 Singer Vikki
17 Corny side
18 Christian in fashion
19 Johnson of "Laugh-In" fame
20 Outcry against Satan's arrest? (with 51-A)
23 Words before lightly
24 Hot to the max
25 Do a critic's job
26 Early Briton
29 "Cool beans!"
30 Eskimo transport
31 "Aquarius" musical
32 English forest
33 Mean
35 Bob Marley, for one
39 Host after Carson
40 Hawkeye Pierce portrayer
44 Tear producer
45 And so
46 In a minute
47 "Dr. No" actress
49 Is overwhelmed
51 See 20 Across
54 Steinbeck title rodents
55 Stronghold in a western
56 Get together
57 Slightly
58 Chop shop casuality
59 Like a lot
60 Firebug, for short
61 Resign, with "down"
62 Basin pitchers

DOWN

1 Oil field worker
2 Airport event
3 Lack of sophistication
4 Put into words
5 Pains in the neck
6 Expressed, as farewell
7 Biting, as wit
8 Thin French fry
9 Court opening
10 Freshwater eels vis-à-vis marine eels
11 Tip of 38 Down
12 Public performer
13 Robert of "The Music Man"
21 ___ Minh City
22 "Forget it!"
27 Holder of 21 merit badges
28 Eye makeup
33 More together
34 Ham and eggs
35 CoPilot display
36 Yearly payoff
37 Brandy cocktail
38 Undersea weapon
40 At this point in time
41 Creep
42 Blood bank visitor
43 Back section of a puzzle book
48 Couch potatoes' perches
50 It leaves you red in the face
52 "Place de l'Opera" artist
53 Cry to a thief

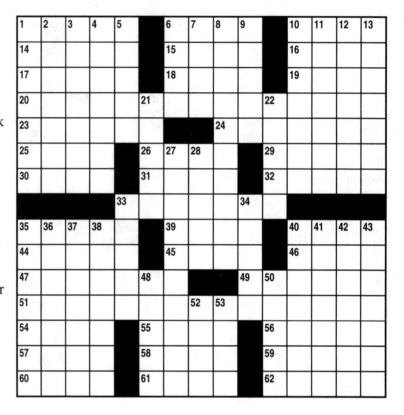

19 THEMELESS by Harvey Estes
"The Ghost Who Walks" is the nickname of 35 Across.

ACROSS

1 "Jabberwocky" laugh
8 Went ballistic
15 Turns in
16 Herb shelf label
17 Like a Thomas Gray work
18 Build an arbor around
19 Fallen Russian orbiter
20 Mireille of "World War Z"
22 Collars
23 Preplanned funeral?
26 Like a barefoot cowboy
27 Pre-Lenten carnival site
30 "Come ___ are"
33 "The Joker's Wild" network
34 Road imperfection
35 Lee Falk superhero
38 Rum Tum Tugger's creator
40 Balanced
41 Sitcom aunt
43 "Over There" soldiers
44 Fabergé objet d'art
45 Vessels take them
48 "Goodnight Moon" is one
52 Bounty stopover
55 Prefix for pilot
56 "That's all ___ wrote!"
57 Put on a pedestal
59 Alley X's
61 Comment over a clean plate
62 Improve spiritually
63 Examines again
64 They may be just

DOWN

1 Either side of de la
2 Spiral shape
3 Funny Cheri
4 Fix, as an election
5 Auditions
6 Digs in the woods
7 Accompany
8 Till
9 Airplane seat features
10 Makes a better program
11 Torment
12 Cornfield din
13 "The ___ Love": R.E.M.
14 Needing patches
21 Shaker filler
24 Porterhouse, for one
25 Caterpillar creation
27 Rack's partner
28 "Are you hurt?" response
29 Makes a pick
30 Vaulted room
31 Chase flies
32 Cristina of "Grey's Anatomy"
34 Wild time
36 Following orders
37 Cold cuts, e.g.
39 Landscape blots
42 Lamb pen name
45 Donnybrooks
46 Evoked laughter, perhaps
47 Irritate
48 Part of a hull
49 Painter Kokoschka
50 Butler of film
51 Positive reactions
52 Duct drop
53 Toll unit
54 Obey the sentry
58 Some big NFL guys
60 "Now ___ seen everything!"

56 ACROSS   by Pam Klawitter
The name for 52 Across was originally registered in the Netherlands in 1942.

ACROSS

1 Spanish suns
5 Go for ___ (swim)
9 "Underboss" penner
13 Andrea Bocelli album
14 Where to visit Morro Castle
15 Part of TAE
16 Evaporate, as an opportunity
19 Mark Harmon series
20 Scraps of cloth
22 Brew the Lipton
24 Some farm youngsters
25 Elton's john
26 Stinging remarks?
27 Ortiz of "Ugly Betty"
28 Trompe ___ (optical trick)
30 Unceremoniously shown out
35 Sheltered on the sea
36 Resort near Lake Tahoe
37 Teen flick sweetheart
44 Horse trait?
45 Fertility lab supply
46 21st Greek letter
47 Meal starter
48 Sol-do bridge
50 Apple handles
52 Battlefield board game
55 Superhero with a hammer
56 Small, seedy nightspots/ TITLE
60 "Shooter" star Omar
61 Final Four initials
62 Bachelor chaser?
63 Liquor store group
64 Decent chap
65 "___ we forget"

DOWN

1 Give in to gravity
2 Geraldo's gold
3 Pride Lands female
4 Barbecue ___
5 "Hamilton" parts
6 Doltish interjection
7 Spain's peninsula
8 Wasn't gentle with
9 Educator Horace
10 Alan in "Flash of Genius"
11 "Anne of Green Gables" setting
12 Took care of the problem
17 Iceberg indicator
18 Brief web chats
21 Lonesome fish?
22 What to do with wild oats?
23 Bygone airline
24 Prepare to be dubbed
27 Say it and mean it
28 40-day observance
29 Hymn opener
31 "SNL" staples
32 First name in Romanian tennis
33 Fontana in Roma
34 Six: Prefix
37 General ___ chicken
38 Flower of Scotland
39 Leaning toward chaos
40 Zero instances
41 Be at the controls
42 Bit of resistance
43 "___ for Ricochet": Grafton
48 Chopin's "___ Sylphides"
49 Key to good spirits
50 Noted seashell seller
51 As it dries, it gets wetter
53 View from Lyon
54 Actress Harper
55 "Can you beat ___?"
57 Beach shade
58 OTS grads
59 Tennis re-serve

EXTRA LARGE   by Pam Klawitter
9-D is home to North America's largest parking structure under a single roof.

ACROSS

1 Make like a hoarder
6 RSVP encl.
9 Bar in the bathtub
13 Tab grabber's words
14 Little boxers
16 "Inner" prefix
17 Don Draper et al.
18 Cut and splice
19 They're often about nothing
20 Farming science that fell the times?
23 More toned
26 Slacks off
27 "I always arrange my Tupperware tops by size!"
30 Bring to a boil
31 Verb type: Abbr.
32 Take a closer look
33 Wedding proclamation
35 "Rosanna" group
39 Duesenberg, e.g.
40 One with longings
41 "If you boys don't stop running through my flower bed . . ."
45 Slangy weather word
47 Milieu of martens
48 Like the self-centered toy block master builder?

51 Say it and mean it
52 Abram from "This Old House"
53 Did some carpentry
57 Part of TVA
58 Whoopi in "Captain Planet and the Planeteers"
59 Harden to
60 Chrysler contemporary
61 ___ G BIV (color code)
62 Convertible alternative

DOWN

1 Waikiki's ___ Wai Canal
2 Rx item
3 It takes a PIN
4 More malodorous
5 Capitol Hill VIP
6 They make Top-Siders
7 Porsche competitor
8 Grand in scale
9 Northwest hub
10 Walking a beat, say
11 Hold precious
12 Sits for a shot
15 Some royal Scots
21 Some appliances
22 Shelf bracket
23 Word before dash or happy
24 Kiwi, for one
25 Stropping result
28 Curtain fabric

29 Ted Turner creation
33 Demolition derby skill?
34 Essandoh in "Django Unchained"
35 Spot for a Facebook "happy birthday!"
36 Change for a five
37 It might be pitched outside
38 Bits for Spot
39 Miner's access
40 Some are coined
41 Tall tale
42 Squirrel's horde
43 "Please, allow me . . ."
44 Part of SSN: Abbr.

45 Aristotle's teacher
46 Party hearty
49 Ride in a glider
50 Lady Antebellum, e.g.
54 You won't get a bang out of it
55 RE/MAX competitor
56 Home of the cubs

FIGHT BACK   by Sarah Daniels
15-A received more than 100 honorary degrees from colleges around the world.

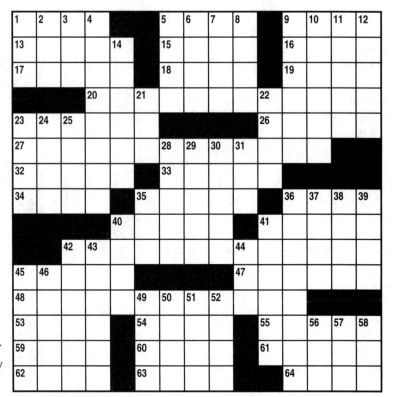

ACROSS

1 Sophia's home
5 Belgrade native
9 Tiny bit
13 Big names in Hollywood
15 "Night" writer Wiesel
16 Fastest shark
17 Dreadlocks wearer
18 Bull or buck
19 Part of the program
20 Daunting task
23 Small burger
26 Baton race
27 Fight for control
32 He was Sheriff Lobo
33 Lacks options
34 Small fortune
35 Graduation party rentals
36 Some business card abbrs.
40 Party boat
41 Transports
42 Hand-to-hand engagement, perhaps
45 All fired up
47 Most "Andi Mack" watchers
48 What foreign exchange students may encounter
53 A bit of QED
54 Baseball brothers
55 Humana rival
59 Give an Amazon review
60 Daybreak to a poet
61 Odie's output
62 Squeezed every cent from
63 Pantyhose problem
64 Art Deco master

DOWN

1 Big-ticket item on "The Price Is Right"
2 Chicken-king connection
3 Sib nickname
4 Teacher's pet, usually
5 18-wheeler
6 Star of David airline
7 Little stream
8 "Call the Midwife" network, informally
9 Dutch beer
10 Snitch on
11 Cub Scout leader
12 Beardless Disney dwarf
14 Some holiday lighting
21 Mins. upon mins.
22 Cornstarch brand
23 Junk email
24 Norse god of mischief
25 "Heads ___, tails you lose!"
28 Unit of heat
29 Where the antelope play
30 "¿Como esta ___?"
31 Porsche models
35 Sitar string
36 "Me too!"
37 Sled alternative
38 Joie de vivre
39 Speedy jets of yore
40 Neo-soul singer Erykah
41 "That's a pity!"
42 Burning the midnight oil
43 Took home
44 Windy City transit org.
45 Very tart
46 Sistine Chapel work
49 Fordham team
50 SpaceX founder Musk
51 Lady Crawley on "Downton Abbey"
52 Chest organ
56 Blue Jays, on a scoreboard
57 "I Am ___ Spock": Nimoy
58 Brewpub quaff

ACROSS

1 Goddesses of destiny
6 What hoarders do
11 Adjust a skirt
14 Binky Urban, for one
15 Home of many Indians
16 Cole Porter, collegiately
17 Visibly ashamed Crusoe?
19 It means nothing at all
20 Some breadless sandwiches
21 Rationale
23 Showy perennials
26 Edited heavily
27 Old Spanish coins
28 MoMA section
29 Uris hero
30 Fine fiddle, briefly
32 Cheats in a track meet
35 Balsam and Douglas
37 "Nights in White ___": Moody Blues
39 Dirt dauber
40 Some are taken orally
42 Lists of options
44 Short way to go?
45 Topped on eBay
47 Hand holder
49 Leather workers
51 Passed along
52 Seeks out in an emergency
53 They're a pain
54 "Ready Player ___" (2018)
55 Gloria's "Sunset Blvd." number?
60 Hairy Addams cousin
61 Davis of "Grumpy Old Men"
62 You believe in it
63 Part of TBS: Abbr.
64 Flicker flats
65 Change places?

DOWN

1 Near partner
2 What Endymion never did
3 2012 Seth MacFarlane film
4 Join formally
5 They're connected by flights
6 Sonora sign-off
7 Department store section
8 Roker and Gore
9 Reinforced, with "up"
10 Muscular
11 Muppet birthday bash?
12 "The Waste Land" poet
13 "Now We Are Six" author
18 "Fantastic ___ and Where to Find Them" (2016)
22 Mouse pointer
23 Sloppy copy
24 John Denver album
25 Poems about Rapunzel?
26 French sculptor
28 Lost to Deep Blue
31 "Groundhog Day" director
33 Floral Lauder fragrance
34 Use up
36 Delivers shocking news
38 Uno is one
41 Mountie hat
43 Early film fare
46 Window-shop
48 Stocking-cap feature
49 Toulouse trio
50 Family nickname
51 Orb's 2013 prize
53 Steamy state
56 Silly sort
57 "Ask the Dragon" songwriter
58 Aquarium tool
59 Sporty Mustangs

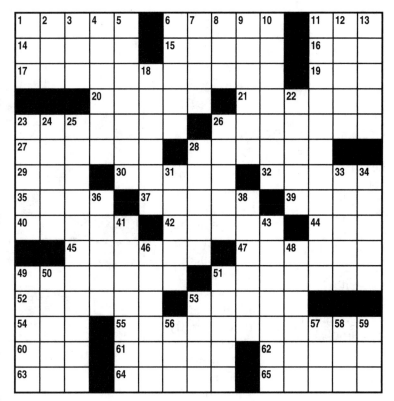

24 STACK ATTACK   by Bonnie L. Gentry
Hopefully you won't say 67 Across after completing this puzzle.

ACROSS

1 "No more wasting time!"
16 Where "The Rachel Maddow Show" began
17 Referred to the "see" notation in an encyclopedia
18 They're caught in pots
19 App with a microphone button
20 Common MLB injury
21 Trust with, temporarily
24 Carriage named for an English county
27 Tops in wariness
31 End of Rick Blaine's toast
32 "Man of Steel" star (with 35-D)
33 Jazz greats?
36 Be off the mark
38 Humanitarian agency created by JFK
39 Ray of fast-food fame
43 The moral route
46 "Barefoot Contessa" host Garten
47 180 degrees from norte
48 Gilligan's shipwrecked ship
50 Banded gemstones
53 Freeway byproduct
54 Rapa ___ (Easter Island, to locals)
55 Junker of a car
59 Citizen Kane's Rosebud
62 Powder-keg environment
67 "Huh?"
68 Tumblers, e.g.

DOWN

1 Common wedding gown feature
2 Home to the sport of hurling
3 San Francisco conveyances
4 Smart mouth
5 Contacts privately on Twitter, briefly
6 "The Star-Spangled Banner" contraction
7 Versailles "very"
8 Old platters player
9 Bakery artist
10 Bollywood garments
11 Little Italian number
12 "The Force Awakens" role
13 A bouncer might check it
14 Wedding flower girl, often
15 Like the devout
22 "Winter of Artifice" author
23 Remove spying devices
25 Former USSR constituent
26 What insurers insure against
27 Felonious flight
28 Queen's record label
29 Miss America wear
30 Godunov and Romanov
34 Catalonian uncles
35 See 32 Across
37 Boarded up
40 Shirley Temple hair features
41 John Lennon's adopted middle name
42 Call from a crow's nest
44 Emotion of the miffed
45 ___ sum (Cantonese cuisine)
47 Canonized French lady
49 Snacks between meals
50 The no crowd
51 Nameless network user
52 Rock made into flagstones
56 Figs. used with gate closings
57 Israeli writer Oz
58 Beer ___ (bar game)
60 Pennsylvania port
61 SFPD investigators
63 iPhone card
64 Perpendicular extension
65 Cardinal's cap monogram
66 Sports org. with a tour

ACROSS

1 #MeToo, for one
16 Uncle Sam's income
17 Ability to outperform
18 Granny ___
19 "Red Solo Cup" singer Keith
20 Chinese zodiac animal
21 Passion in fashion
24 Awards won by Stephen King
27 It can lead to an indictment
31 Brain-scan inits.
32 "Unforgettable" King Cole
33 Like some guesses
36 Automaker Ferrari
38 Prefix with sphere
39 Massage therapist hirers
43 Reference citer, in a manuscript
46 They're hypothetical
47 Lombardi Trophy org.
48 Gilbert and Sullivan specialty
50 Orators' perches
53 "Gosh darn it!"
54 Lob trajectory
55 Put on the computer
59 Succulent lobster piece
62 Leads up to a dramatic conclusion
67 South Pole's latitude
68 Aaron Judge's 2017 honor

DOWN

1 Many a "Li'l Abner" character
2 Not right now
3 1948 Winter Olympics site
4 Set of seven
5 Quattro preceder
6 Industrious Aesopian character
7 Equestrian's concern
8 Deep-voiced, for a woman
9 Monitored bed
10 Zero's "Fiddler on the Roof" role
11 "___ grown accustomed to . . ."
12 Sign flashed by Churchill
13 How Hoffman played Tootsie
14 Beet or cane extract
15 Swimming events
22 Kid's word of wonderment
23 Put an ___ (stop)
25 Unwelcome grade
26 Sheepskin alternatives, for short
27 Lansing–Flint dir.
28 It might move you
29 Rudely brief
30 Start of some budget brand names
34 Per unit, informally
35 Lugged along
37 Ices, mob-style
40 Paltry amount
41 Area for a boat's name
42 FICA funds it
44 Yucatán "yay!"
45 Bobble a grounder
47 Considerate of
49 Foodie's hangout
50 African capital whose name means "tamarind tree"
51 "There ___ free lunches"
52 Bad shot on the links
56 Seeing right through
57 "Yeah, right!"
58 All-purpose tape
60 Sorna in "Jurassic Park III"
61 Eye suggestively
63 LPGA Tour player Se Ri ___
64 Hindu term of respect
65 Org. with .edu addresses
66 Cobbler

HOLDING COMPANY by Jim Holland
17 Across won the Bram Stoker Award for Best Novel in 1998.

ACROSS

1 "Too bad"
5 Type of buddy
10 "Brandenburg Concertos" composer
14 Given life
15 "99.44% pure" soap
16 Competent
17 1998 Stephen King work
19 Koontz's "___ to December"
20 Lacking principles
21 One-armed bandit
23 Skater Shoma ___
24 Some Ivy Leaguers
26 Completed one's defense, say
28 Keebler character
31 Unplanned event
34 Rosary part
36 "Rule, Britannia!" composer
37 Desert springs
41 Really fun bunch
44 Make a successful stab at
45 "Dianetics" author Hubbard
46 Anon partner
47 Pumps up
50 Type of curve
51 Propeller cap
54 Newts
56 Yellowstone bugler
57 They can be tight or loose
60 Cyclones of Ames, briefly
64 ___ avis
66 Unforeseen trouble
68 Capt. Hook's alma mater
69 "Silas Marner" author
70 "Movin' ___" ("The Jeffersons" theme)
71 Big top
72 Uncool
73 Holiday quaffs

DOWN

1 "Dancing Queen" group
2 Rich soil
3 Jason's ship
4 Dagwood's "SKNXX-X!"
5 Like the Pentateuch
6 Lacto-___
7 Miller dramatized his
8 City founded by Ivan IV
9 Palace city of SW India
10 Good term, paradoxically
11 More or less
12 "Jurassic Park" creature, e.g.
13 "Great" king of Judea
18 FDR's terrier
22 Mortise partner
25 Use a sidebar
27 Vampire hunter's weapon
28 Recedes
29 ___ of faith
30 Charge
32 Prefix for structure
33 Take down a peg
35 Exhaust
38 Golf great Ballesteros
39 "My ___ Adored You"
40 CCCP states
42 Bert's buddy
43 Ten of two
48 Dealt with hot stuff
49 Pack away
51 Left Bank cap
52 Send over the moon
53 Goodyear headquarters
55 Faint
58 Melting watch artist
59 Salon sound
61 River under the Ponte Vecchio
62 Self-satisfied
63 Cooking amts.
65 Farm creature
67 Caveman of comics

WORD SEARCH by Jim Holland
. . . and that word is revealed at 63 Across.

ACROSS
1 "Chantilly ___": Big Bopper
5 Facebook activity
10 Pulverize
14 Mosque prayer leader
15 "I don't give ___"
16 Prefix for eight
17 First job, often
19 Western Native Americans
20 Gave a dazzling performance
21 Take a shortcut
23 Throw down the gauntlet
26 Rachel's sister
27 Eagles in uniform
31 Pops
35 It can be thin at times
36 Poi source
37 Paint a picture in a way
38 End end which becomes no end
40 ___ Cristo
42 "Twin Peaks" actress Sherilyn
43 They're for turning things around
45 Sends out Morse
47 "Hop on the bus" guy in a Simon song
48 Nose around
49 Roald Amundsen got there first
51 ___ no good
53 What "you" used to be
54 Got mushy
58 "Zounds!"
62 "So sorry"
63 Getting to the bottom
66 "Dennis the Menace" girl
67 Become accustomed to
68 "The Samurai" novelist Shusaku
69 Pants part
70 Heads of France
71 Bottomless

DOWN
1 ChapStick targets
2 Asian nurse
3 Mob muckety-muck
4 Corrects a text
5 Koepka breaks it often
6 Surprised reaction
7 Type of chef
8 Completely wrecks
9 Jobs or Wozniak
10 Sass
11 West End opener
12 Type of cell
13 Hydrant hook-on
18 Do a double take
22 Bed of roses
24 Goes meandering
25 Irish bread?
27 "Post No ___"
28 Huge amount
29 "Say ___ the Dress" (TLC series)
30 Kemo Sabe's friend
32 Klattenhoff of "The Blacklist"
33 Invalidate
34 Word after common or horse
37 Forty fathoms, for one
39 Hollers
41 Lacking slack
44 "House" actor Omar
46 Patina
49 "He's___" (Chiffons hit)
50 Narrowed, as pants
52 Levi's Shrink ___ jeans
54 Jokers
55 Fashion designer Saab
56 Granny
57 U-bolt cousin
59 Top-notch
60 Guy
61 Cry to a thief
64 Dr. with a "Detox" album
65 How more than one party ends?

ACROSS

1 Birdcage swing
6 Hardly husky
11 Tech with a space segment
14 Steel identified from the end
15 Friend in the 'hood
16 "I knew it!"
17 Source of troubles
19 Set up, as a rock-climbing harness
20 Studied closely
21 "Bambi" aunt
22 Little lump
24 "Capiche?"
27 ". . . two, if by ___": Longfellow
28 Spill-proof vessel for tots
30 English cousin of "Zut alors!"
33 Piglet's parent
35 High five
37 Auto prefix with diesel
38 Map line charting similar temperatures
41 911 car
43 Like Tide in 1946
44 Parodied
46 Gives the nod
47 Like many Miami Beach buildings
49 Kitchen counter container
52 Civil War general
54 Adding a "D" changes it from feminine to masculine
55 Knitted gift for baby
58 Turkey
59 "To Sir, With Love" singer
63 "___ My Why": Beatles
64 "Stop talking!" (and a theme hint)
67 Ship pronoun
68 Hair or eye color, e.g.
69 Offer input
70 Mr. Potato Head piece
71 Goddesses of the seasons
72 Thumb-types

DOWN

1 Popeye's tooter
2 "Buy it now" site
3 Monsieur Descartes
4 Looper's profession
5 Healthcare choice
6 Beer-lemonade drink
7 Inlaid tile designs
8 Embassy VIP
9 Stuffed Tour de France animal
10 "Experience Amazing" car
11 Home of a Muppet grouch
12 PGA lefty Mickelson
13 Grayish green
18 Sign for another tour of duty
23 Speller's showcase
25 Occasion for special glasses
26 Drink and then some
28 Crockpot
29 Kung ___ shrimp
31 In need of a hot tub
32 Pulls off
33 Object to
34 "Makes sense"
36 Voyager 1, for one
39 "Calling all cars!"
40 Blackbird
42 Bunny hill, for one
45 Radio station no-no
48 Table scrap
50 Voting crowd
51 Conn who was Frenchy in "Grease"
53 Swimming pool info
55 Ammonia, chemically
56 Workers' rights agcy.
57 Monaco money
60 OS developed at Bell Labs
61 Dryer detritus
62 SUVs
65 Sigma's succeeder
66 Printer's bullet

29 "GET BENT!"   by Greg Johnson
A clever challenger from this Pennsylvanian puzzler.

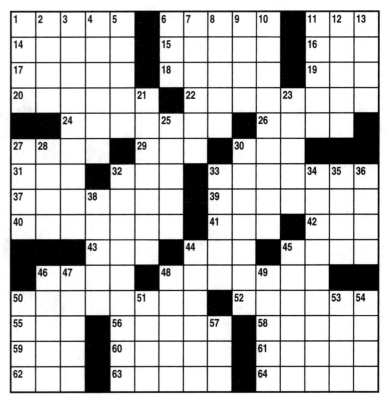

ACROSS

1 Jeering insults
6 Handheld toy . . .
11 Corp. officers
14 Indian ___
15 Get every test question right
16 Bedridden Adrian's plea to Rocky
17 Painter's base layer
18 BBQ picker-uppers
19 What the herder heard
20 . . . types
22 Like set traps
24 With coldness and darkness
26 "Othello" manipulator
27 Frat letters
29 Ready to blow
30 Network launched 6/1/80
31 Put two and two together
32 According to
33 Engage in mixology
37 Between high- and low-water marks
39 Not good, not bad
40 Miso ingredient
41 Title given to Paul McCartney
42 Zero, in World Cup
43 Hazardous for walking
44 Push-up muscle
45 Big Apple fashion label
46 Fairy-tale monster
48 Available to work
50 Fun journey in a car
52 Full of . . .
55 CPR pro
56 Desqueaked
58 Deck with 78 cards
59 Furry Halloween costume
60 Prankster-to-victim cry
61 "OED" 2015 Word of the Year
62 Educational career goal
63 . . . out
64 Karaoke words

DOWN

1 Type-A . . .
2 Rapper who plays a TV cop
3 BFF
4 Stands for painting
5 Be disruptive while asleep
6 Beef marbling
7 "___ a tale unfold . . .": Shak.
8 Laine of the Moody Blues
9 Band bookings
10 . . . with a ball bearing
11 Beetle
12 Its keys unlock nothing
13 Acquire, informally
21 Express delivery promise
23 Much-needed vacay
25 Mrs. Pence
27 Rasta headwear
28 "Grazie ___!" ("Thank God!" in Italian)
30 Raw fish served in citrus juice
32 Figure . . .
33 It's a stunner
34 One will affect your account balance
35 Not fer
36 Count (on)
38 "Fun, Fun, Fun" car
44 Salty Robin Williams role
45 Teen idol description
46 Get-up-and-go
47 Like upscale communities
48 Dirty stuff
49 Military 411
50 Cradle grain
51 Reason for a 10-34 police alert
53 Trendy berry from China
54 . . . pep
57 ___ el Beida (Casablanca)

ACROSS

1 Portmanteau for a male bond
9 Place of rapid growth
15 Adopt a healthy lifestyle
16 Vague warning
17 Campus life
18 Five Nations tribe
19 Supermarket feature
20 Quarterfinal groups
22 Gum unit
23 Think piece
25 Osculate
26 One-liner, perhaps
27 Like some herds
29 Willem of "The Grand Budapest Hotel"
30 Hopeful
34 Calf component
35 Not upright
36 Lopsided court result
37 Put at risk
38 Like dangerous drivers
39 Paddle
40 Thirsty cry
41 Behavior researcher Shere
42 Bandleader Arnaz
43 Hayek in "Everly"
48 Partner census of monogamy
49 Alter
51 Leave port
52 More like a fairy-tale duckling
54 Wet blanket, in slang
56 Fodder enjoying fermentation
57 "Diving Into the Wreck" poet Rich
58 Win the heart of
59 Atlantic hue

DOWN

1 Lawn bit
2 Prepares potatoes, in a way
3 Racing paths
4 Kind of blitz
5 Humbling feeling
6 Film fish
7 Mouse use
8 Raising spirits
9 Fallon and Kimmel
10 Tram loads
11 Midmorning
12 Went ape
13 Salad green varieties
14 Freeloaders
21 Sudan suffix
24 Deadhead in "Hamlet"?
26 Old Testament tower site
28 Arbor feature
29 Wetsuit crew
30 Shelter for those without means
31 Penetrating slowly
32 Long cigar
33 Totally absurd
34 Links warning
36 Wiggle room
38 Melons with white flesh
40 Allowing alcohol
42 Engraver Albrecht
44 Curious one
45 Singer Cleo
46 "Now We Are Six" author
47 Type of wrench
49 "Let ___!"
50 Metrical Pound
53 Cartesian conclusion
55 Quick turn

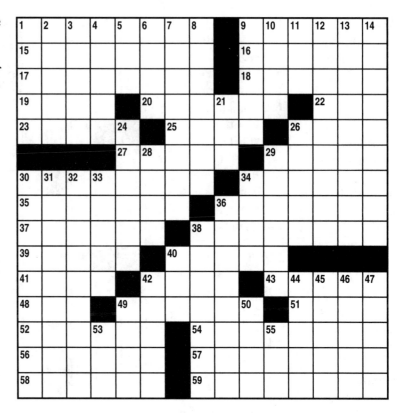

31 THEMELESS by Harvey Estes
Officials have banned 33 Down from some public events.

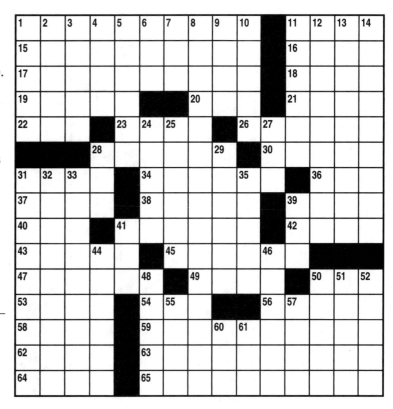

ACROSS

1 Where to buy an auto repair shop?
11 Site of unseeing eyes
15 Part of HUAC
16 Flying fisher
17 "Don't change this"
18 Flag throwers, at times
19 Belief statement
20 To God, to carolers
21 Snack on the trail
22 Taken in
23 Do a slow burn
26 "The ___ Queene": Spenser
28 Home style
30 Ageement addendum
31 Seedy joint
34 Pickling juices
36 Prefix with Baptist
37 "No mo'!"
38 S&L units
39 "Wizard of the Sea" pirate
40 Little john?
41 Battery terminals
42 Start of many words
43 Treat badly
45 Commander's wife in "The Handmaid's Tale"
47 Potter, for one
49 Auctioneer's cry
50 Like Humpty Dumpty
53 "Shake ___!"
54 Neighbor of Leb.
56 Memorable mission
58 Tick off
59 Histrionic
62 Athenian aitches
63 Obey the rules
64 Pt. of DOS
65 Time past

DOWN

1 Mean neighbor of Aunt Em
2 Beginning of ___ (watershed moment)
3 Had status
4 Enclosed in
5 Board opposite
6 Hesitation sounds
7 Obedience school command
8 Bachelor holdings
9 Part of a basketball court
10 "I'm at the ___ my rope!"
11 Pianist Rachmaninoff
12 Set the future in stone
13 Banishes from a social network
14 Eagles classic
24 Like some legends
25 Polo and more
27 Start of MGM's motto
28 WW1 troop group
29 Visceral prefix
31 Some Algonquian Indians
32 Lack of capacity
33 Plastic horns
35 City on the Ruhr
39 Soul for the road
41 Ireland's ___ Lingus
44 Most prudent
46 Less remote
48 Simple song
50 Prima ___
51 Big name in air conditioning
52 Sidney of Charlie Chan films
55 Pump, for one
57 Kind of pad
60 Courtroom fig.
61 Café alternative

THEMELESS   by Steve Russell
The clue at 41 Across can be taken two ways.

ACROSS

1 What one wishes were so
11 Full-house component
15 In a sensible way
16 "___ with an E" (Netflix series)
17 Encroachment
18 Not much
19 Variety of poker
20 GI mail drop
21 Talk like Harvey Fierstein
22 Suede source
25 Bussing on a bus, e.g.
27 Fam. reunion attendee
28 Way to be feelin' in a Paul Simon song
30 Gathering point
32 Linen trigram
35 "See ya!"
36 Lie atop
37 Teetering between two choices
41 Number of days in four months
42 Cruising locale
43 Ill. clock setting
44 Gondola guy
45 Big shot
48 Partner census of monogamy
49 College web address suffix
51 Colbert, who coined 1 Across
55 Small fry
57 "Thank God ___ Country Boy"
59 Forestall, with "off"
60 Johnson of "Laugh-In" fame
61 Accounts
64 Jessica Rabbit, for one
65 Band booking
66 Spirit ___ Louis
67 Sure and Dove

DOWN

1 Sherman Act target
2 Bob Marley, for example
3 One-eighty
4 Likely to lead to exhaustion
5 "A Bug's Life" villain
6 Suffix with concert
7 D.C. team member
8 "On the Waterfront" director Kazan
9 Slipshod
10 Meeting of the rite-minded people?
11 Early late-night name
12 Emperor penguin's domain
13 Not now, but soon
14 Martian moniker
23 Benson of "Ice Castles"
24 Show instability
26 Pt. of ABC
29 Left-hand page
31 Night school subj.
32 Topic best avoided
33 Recognizing
34 High heels
36 Push back, perhaps
38 Charlemagne's domain: Abbr.
39 French I verb
40 Retreats
45 Society type
46 A wearer
47 Kia sedan
50 Had the main meal
52 Port in a storm
53 Happening
54 Fits together
56 Dispatched
58 2012 Affleck flick
62 Way cool
63 In the past

33 THEMELESS   by Steve Russell

33 Down was Oxford American Dictionary's 2007 Word of the Year.

ACROSS

1 Saloon stock
5 Long tales
10 Cracker's target
14 Immense flock
16 Go bad
17 Boniness
18 Put the finger on
19 No-win situation
20 Auto outings
21 Rather, informally
22 Water down
24 Seasoned hands
28 Wilde play about a dancer
30 One with merchants for customers
35 Met number
36 Capital of France?
37 Milan's Teatro alla ___
38 No-win situations
39 Idle on the set
40 Minimally
42 Marvelous, in slang
44 Minuteman container
45 Play the market
47 Fritter away
52 A literary Bell
53 Tanked up
57 Locks out of Rapunzel's tower
58 Osculation location
59 Ben Stiller's mom
60 Fifty-fifty
61 Does a dog trick
62 Vice follower
63 March Madness trophies

DOWN

1 Gather up
2 Slowly, in scores
3 Samantha of "Doctor Dolittle"
4 ___ Ste. Marie
5 Not the real thing
6 Certain something
7 Sandpaper coating
8 Took steps
9 Retiring
10 Require as part of the agreement
11 Hear here
12 Nadal and Federer, e.g.
13 Pair in a line
15 Stick or split
20 Radical '70s gp.
23 Plain of Sharon locale
25 Bacon pieces
26 Some lies
27 Bed supports
29 All-star game side
30 Herbicide target
31 One-eyed monster of nature
32 Giving directions
33 Supporters of farmers markets
34 Designed for all grades
41 Like a winning golf score
43 John's sign
46 Treasure cache
48 NBA legend Iverson
49 Controlled computer
50 Group belief
51 Unspoiled spots
52 Patrick Stewart's "Moby Dick" role
54 Penultimate fairy-tale word
55 Peaty areas
56 Bear with us at night
58 Bk. after Exodus

MISSING FANS by Jim Page
... and those fans can be found at 35 Across.

ACROSS

1 Golden
6 Lawn pest
10 Sun and moon
14 Gregg specialist
15 Emperor tutored by Seneca
16 British car trunk
17 Qumran Caves discoveries
19 Site of Vulcan's forge
20 "Mercy!"
21 More morose
22 "The Way of Love" singer
24 Opposed to
27 ___ Novo (Benin capital)
29 Moon Unit, to Dweezil
30 Expected in
31 On one's feet
32 "The Giving Tree" tree
34 Auto financing abbr.
35 "Touch of Grey" fans missing in four answers
38 NPR creator
41 Admirer
42 OWN chairman
46 El Dorado treasure
47 Camelot knight
48 Watts in "Diana"
49 1995 Sean Penn film
54 "Playbill" players
55 Youth
56 Alphabetized
58 Tech support caller
59 Like a sailboat on a windless day
63 Barclays Center team
64 2018 "Star Wars" film
65 "___ at the office"
66 ___ quam videri
67 Do a slow boil
68 Mesquite locale

DOWN

1 Mule's father
2 Chief Ouray's tribe
3 Book buyers
4 Stuffed envelopes
5 ___-Cola
6 Troll
7 Rent anew
8 Domain name locale
9 Ox genus
10 Division signs
11 Large Capitol room
12 Crams for exams
13 Track official
18 B&O and C&O
21 Derived from
22 Red Cross skill
23 ___ polloi
25 Tremulous tree
26 Arizona river
28 Not-so-great rating
32 "It was ___ and stormy . . ."
33 Upsilon follower
36 Wanted soldier
37 It started with Sputnik
38 Kibbutz, for one
39 Pats on the back
40 Easter wear
43 Turnpike toll, basically
44 Prelunch hrs.
45 "Job" for the Sopranos
50 Better antonym
51 Yucca fiber
52 "When pigs fly!"
53 Grad school test
57 Buffoon
59 Mir successor
60 "We will ___ be undersold!"
61 Perón or Braun
62 Low-___ graphics

35 THEMELESS   by Jim Page
Alternate clue for 29 Down: Kitchen request.

ACROSS

1 Used a sled
5 Up to snuff
9 Settle on
14 Currency adopted by Estonia on 1/1/11
15 Bumper ___
16 Outlandish
17 Hyena's hideout
18 French film
19 Round the bend
20 Persnickety one
23 I-95 and I-81
24 Blarney talk?
25 Becomes baggy
27 Sonnet's last six lines
30 Sewn-on decoration
34 Key below Z
35 "Road ___" (Hope/Crosby film)
37 Creamer of the LPGA
38 Enter
40 Church song
42 D.C. nine
43 Sous-chef wear
45 Written in base 8
47 "Forgot About ___": Eminem
48 Book value
50 Jayhawker's home
52 Lepus americanus
53 Utah's lily
54 ___ Poupon mustard
56 Nonsense
62 Bank recoveries
64 Bushy hairdo
65 Picked straws
66 More or less
67 MGM cofounder
68 Eleventh-hour
69 Off-the-wall
70 "Olly, olly ___ free!"
71 Ghostbuster Spengler

DOWN

1 Number one
2 Island feast
3 Crocus cousin
4 ___ Horn sheep
5 Get used to
6 Bouquet tosser
7 Protracted
8 Sword with a fuller
9 Cobbler's tool
10 Peach State native
11 Tear gas deployers
12 Aquatic bird
13 Häagen-Dazs rival
21 Maverick played by Garner
22 Robitussin meas.
26 Cloud-capped peak
27 Astronomer Carl
28 Marry away
29 Sow discord
30 Beethoven's fifth?
31 Kay Ryan, notably
32 Extreme
33 Abates
36 Licorice, e.g.
39 1987 Kevin Costner film
41 Dismantle
44 Neither correlative
46 Lombardy lake
49 Tennis official
51 Pool plaything
53 Shopaholic's thrill
54 Take hurriedly
55 Singer McEntire
57 Film composer Schifrin
58 Sly as ___
59 Straightaway race
60 Apollo's mother
61 Bremner in "Wonder Woman"
63 Wallowing place

36 PARK PLACE by Eva Finney
The park at 17 Across was used as a location for "Back to the Future."

ACROSS

1 Bus. entity
5 Sushi eel
10 Lacking panache
14 Barrister Clooney
15 Wind pants material
16 Start of a Welk countdown
17 Griffith Park place
19 Diego in "Frida"
20 Imitator
21 Solar timepiece
23 Like Olympians
24 Factors in weather forecasts
25 Denounced
29 Indigenous group
32 Golfer Mickelson
33 Hinder
35 Pheasant brood
36 Cyclotron particle
37 Monastery address
38 59, in the Forum
39 Simpatico
41 Paint layers
43 Frankfurt's ___ Oper
44 Pancake house fixture
46 Draft horse gear
48 "The Lion King" role
49 Common cover-up?
50 Be composed of
53 Vulgar
57 Unfatty
58 Brackenridge Park place
60 Up-front stake
61 Bruin's no-no

62 Belief systems
63 Film ___
64 Cuban line dance
65 Rx label info

DOWN

1 Higher math, for short
2 Melville tale of Tahiti
3 Grating voice
4 Frolicsome
5 Like communities without HOA fees
6 Nabokov's "nope"
7 Every last iota
8 Wends
9 Cut off
10 "30 Rock" star
11 Cherokee Park place
12 Whistler's mother
13 Time can do it
18 Mark Harmon series
22 "___ a peep!"
25 Mimicry
26 Carol singers
27 Ault Park place
28 "Roxana" author
29 Not atop
30 Proof jobs
31 "Battle of the ___" (2017)
34 Carefree syllable
40 "Lou Grant" star
41 Definitive opus
42 Lea of "Miss Saigon" fame
43 Robot that looks human
45 MCII ÷ II

47 Public outbreak
50 Kith and kin
51 Wine, in combinations
52 Food served with frijoles
53 Pow!
54 "Not ___ many words . . ."
55 Jazzman Zoot
56 Watering aid
59 "Ladders to Fire" author

ARENAS by Eva Finney
1st Mariner Arena was a previous name of 32 Down.

ACROSS

1 Chamonix peaks
5 One Bush had two
10 "The ___ lama . . .": Nash
14 Straight up, at the bar
15 Don Draper, e.g.
16 Cause of ruin
17 Golden 1 Center site
19 Hyphenated IDs
20 "Reach" singer Gloria
21 Flambeaux
23 Close up like before
24 Ukraine's "Mother of Cities"
25 Trucker's allowance
27 Like the MGM logo
30 Streisand, familiarly
33 Man of the casa
35 "Numen Lumen" university
36 Sky altar
37 Letters on Boot Hill
38 Secular
39 Tiny stream
41 Paid for a hand
43 Disaster relief org.
44 Election night data
46 Use a rotary phone
48 "O.G. Original Gangster" rapper
49 Christian in "Bobby"
53 Laughable
56 Visualize
57 Novello in "Gosford Park"
58 Capital One Arena site
60 Alpine pool
61 Geometric calculations
62 "Enchanted" Hathaway role
63 Robert on Traveler
64 Clarinet and oboe
65 Do a twenty-one job

DOWN

1 Snow goose genus
2 Temporary contract
3 Summit goals
4 Avenue crossers
5 Burrito cousins
6 Bob Dylan's "Gates of ___"
7 LBJ's VP predecessor
8 Olympic swimmer Biondi
9 Put one over on
10 Offensive, as an amount of money
11 Bridgestone Arena site
12 Non-PC suffix
13 Smaller amount
18 Light years off
22 Copacabana city
26 Migratory seabirds
27 Cantered
28 "Failed States" author Chomsky
29 "The Memory of Trees" singer
30 Mueller report releaser
31 Indy driver Luyendyk
32 Royal Farms Arena site
34 College hoop tourney
40 Swiss lake
41 Like many '60s protests
42 Send packing
43 Signaled to stop
45 Primary color
47 Pianist Feinberg
50 Threepeater's prize
51 "Waterworld" orphan
52 Kidney artery
53 Put in a footnote
54 Spoon-shaped
55 Custody
56 "___ no idea!"
59 Meet

ACROSS

1 Willie Sutton's target
5 Seniors, say
10 Harbor pirates
14 Perry's lake
15 Anne in "Volcano"
16 Italian wine
17 L.A. lady in an Elton John song
19 "___ the Sun in the Morning"
20 Spices up
21 Hard not to like
23 Dress (out)
24 DFW posting
25 Crayoned in
29 U2 guitarist
33 Claude of "B. J. and the Bear"
34 Silva in "Skyfall"
36 Protrude
37 Delayed
38 John Lennon song
39 "Gee!"
40 First Response rival
41 Cut grass
42 Zubin who conducted the Three Tenors
43 Huge number
45 Limerick river
47 Cologne article
48 Words of tribute
49 How stock pumpers act
53 Without heat
57 Manicurist's case
58 Scary trucker in "Pee-wee's Big Adventure"
60 Red-tag event
61 Vis-à-vis exams
62 Akin to aqua
63 That being so
64 ___ larceny
65 Braithwaite of "Downton Abbey"

DOWN

1 Trifecta and exacta
2 "Acoustic Soul" singer India.___
3 Hirschfeld hidden name
4 Heinz logo
5 Shape-shift
6 Monocle glass
7 UVA's conference
8 Whigham of "Boardwalk Empire"
9 Peasant of old Russia
10 Fly
11 1961 Jimmy Dean hit
12 Organic compound
13 Bag with handles
18 Some revolvers
22 Intuitive ability
25 Aron's "East of Eden" twin
26 Striped animal in a zoo
27 Girl of classic comics
28 Flood
29 Amphibious hoppers
30 Goth foe
31 Fervor
32 Hawke in "Juliet, Naked"
35 Rosemary Clooney's "Botch-___"
38 What swains pitch
39 Originate
41 Pint-size
42 Word heard in fine stores
44 Easter flowers
46 Square-shooting
49 Defeat or excel
50 "Industry" state
51 Pig's feed
52 Chinese zodiac animal
53 Large, sweet fruit
54 Outspoken equine
55 Richard in "Pollyanna"
56 Crème ___ crème
59 Chinese zodiac animal

AWARD RECIPIENTS   by John M. Samson
The race at 34 Across is first leg of the U.S. Triple Tiara.

ACROSS

1 Miz Beaver's friend
5 Antenna alternative
10 Sweet on
14 Pagan icon
15 Edmonton center?
16 Ishmael's son-in-law
17 Actor with a stage award?
19 Ranch unit
20 Bad vibrations
21 Allure
23 "___ for Peril": Grafton
24 2013 Rooney Mara film
25 First editor of "Ms."
29 Forward movement
33 Garcia and La Douce
34 Pre-Belmont fillies stakes race
36 Debussy's key?
37 Outline
38 Prep for a match
39 Famous pen name
40 Some
41 Ark groups
42 Tires in the homestretch
43 Popular steak
45 The Pirate Bay download
47 ___-pah-pah band
48 Ward heeler
49 Smutty
53 Next year's alumnae
57 McGwire's 1998 rival
58 Painter with a literary award?
60 Doltish dude
61 Saffron's "Ab Fab" mother
62 Buttonhole
63 Treater's words
64 Claire in "Les Misérables"
65 Twenty make two hundred

DOWN

1 Penn State rival
2 Gas leak indicator
3 Out of the picture
4 2020 Tokyo athlete
5 Where it's legal to shoot eagles
6 Snootiness
7 Crispy sandwich
8 Darth's daughter
9 Originally, once
10 Redoubtable
11 Playwright with a film award?
12 Meth lab raider
13 Sugarland song
18 Fountain finds
22 "This is bigger___ big!"
25 "The Da Vinci Code" albino
26 "Lemon Tree" singer Lopez
27 Actress with a TV award?
28 Sausalito's county
29 Elevate
30 Predatory seabird
31 The Doctor, for one
32 Dough raiser
35 Hole-in-one prize, at times
38 Clavell's "___-Pan"
39 First to arrive
41 Apple or pear
42 Hart's-tongue leaf
44 Get hold of
46 Bayreuth stagings
49 Munch Museum site
50 Blessing
51 "A friend in ___ . . ."
52 Source of Wagner's "Ring Cycle"
53 Rational
54 Make eyes at
55 Drop from the sky
56 Pre-2004 boomers
59 Cotton machine

40 ANAGRAM PAIRS* by Brian E. Paquin
15 Across was the lunar module pilot on that mission.

ACROSS

1 Fanfare
5 Towel a spill
10 Baby seals
14 Taxi alternative
15 Apollo 13 astronaut
16 Seed pod
17 The Eternal City
18 Ed in "Too Big to Fail"
19 Spanish boy
20 Like safe-sailing waters*
22 Source of cash in a NYC subway*
24 Builds on
26 Sneezy word
27 Hahn of "Grey's Anatomy"
30 On the double
32 Stare at
33 Global misogynist?*
38 "Long, long ___ . . ."
39 Biological pouch
40 Morning goddess
41 Threshold
42 Room in need of a cleaning?*
45 Pool table cushion
46 Big name in chips
47 Astronaut Schirra
48 Pic
51 Pony player's strategy
54 Pathetic personals?*
56 Con game that can't fail?*

60 In good time
61 Davis in "Do the Right Thing"
63 Kentucky border river
64 Alan heard in "Toy Story 4"
65 Running battles
66 Worf portrayer Michael
67 Unspec. category
68 Relieves
69 "___ So Cold": Rolling Stones

DOWN

1 Run like a top
2 Symphony reed
3 Internet image
4 Foreword
5 Glass fragment
6 Palm Springs and Medina
7 Baseball bat stickum
8 Put to work
9 Hairy wave
10 Universal remedy
11 Bathsheba's first mate
12 Speckled bean
13 Sports replay speed
21 Rx watchdog
23 Dash gauges
25 Elected (to)
27 Elizabethan expletive
28 Prego competitor
29 NYSE debuts
31 Nautical greeting
33 Dawn's direction
34 Paris play parts
35 River duck
36 Diabolical
37 ___ on (trust)

39 Church council
43 Best Picture of 1997
44 James Joyce classic
45 Musket loaders
47 Teensy
48 Sacred song
49 John McCain's POW place
50 Aromas
52 Musical opus
53 Lock of hair
55 Not all
57 "Trouble ahead!"
58 Royal address
59 Long stretches of time
62 Home to many schools

41 SWARM OF BEES   by Brian E. Paquin

21 Across is also the title of a Bruce Springsteen song.

ACROSS

1 Puffs
6 Fictional whaler
10 Marsh wader
14 ___ nous (between us)
15 Gaucho's weapon
16 Nursemaid
17 Option for some future homeowners
19 Recipe amt.
20 Sluggers' stats
21 Basset hound's facial feature
23 Jessica in "Dark Angel"
26 Bill or Hillary, briefly
28 "Woman With a Pearl" painter
29 Break in the action
31 Achieve
33 Badlands scenery
34 Canyon sound
35 2016 Lloyd's Banking Group acquisition
38 Scarfed down
39 Hubbub
42 Not 'neath
43 Hatch
45 Frost work
46 Calculators of yore
48 Amboy Dukes guitarist Ted
50 Fast-food utensils
51 Daisy Mae's man
52 "What's that?"
54 Store gds.
55 Flowering shrubs
57 Internet novice
59 Measuring stick
60 Economic extremes
65 Internet locations
66 Jailbird with a cool hand
67 Uncovered
68 Fiasco
69 Once, once
70 Lines up

DOWN

1 Arachnid abode
2 Shiba ___ (Japanese dog)
3 Pig's digs
4 Divided fairly
5 Novak Djokovic, for one
6 Mistreat
7 ___ polloi
8 Shakespeare title start
9 Mean critter
10 Provisional
11 Caution sign for a car's rear window
12 Map within a map
13 Exhausts
18 Makes an offer
22 ER status
23 Sportscaster Rashad
24 Deceive
25 Easy trip to first
27 Scottish king killed by MacDuff
30 Computer connection
32 Those people
34 Very dark black
36 Head turners
37 Come up
40 Surgically fixable
41 Mouth, slangily
44 Like an unproductive inning
47 B-2 Spirit feature
49 "Golly ___!"
50 "Git!"
51 Sky blue
53 Like some ambitious goals
55 Calla lily
56 Curdled
58 Ghostly forms
61 Rubber stamps
62 Vase
63 Dry, like wine
64 Six-pointers

42 BODY AND SOUL by Anna Carson

An insight into the mind of a melodrama casting director.

ACROSS

1 Whip around in the wind
5 Penguins pass them around
10 Earring piece
14 Vegetable soup bean
15 Classic dentifrice
16 Counting-out word
17 Rep. Ilhan ___
18 Wedge-shaped mark
19 Play in a kiddie pool
20 **Start of a casting director's quip**
23 Rose color
24 Dictator's aides
25 Knot-tying site
27 **More of quip**
32 Fliers mil. post
35 Type of history
36 Online marketing
37 Run up the flagpole
40 Sung syllable
41 Joanna of "Growing Pains"
42 Kabuki performer
43 Bean toppers
45 Driving area
46 **More of quip**
50 Old defense pact
51 Brought back into play
55 Clingy seedpod
56 **End of quip**
60 Hairy copiers
62 Try to deceive
63 Made tracks
64 Monastery man
65 Corby of "The Waltons"
66 "On the Waterfront" director Kazan
67 Pop artist Warhol
68 Presses the sustain pedal
69 Sax player's purchase

DOWN

1 Avoid gum disease
2 Fishing cap
3 Blow away
4 Babysitter's employer
5 "The Old Guitarist" painter
6 Words before arms
7 Golfer's transport
8 Kind of socks
9 Petty potentate
10 Use the Singer
11 Split
12 Emphasize with ink
13 Like Easter eggs
21 Bossy utterance
22 Lean and lovely
26 Schlep
28 Garden products brand
29 French Revolution leader
30 Ancient Gulf of Aqaba port
31 Additional
32 Arab of song
33 Deal primarily with
34 Unhappy outcome
38 Reading place
39 Meadowlands races
44 Service deliveries
47 Stirred up
48 Stephen in "Breakfast on Pluto"
49 "Sons of Anarchy" creator Kurt
52 Ripped off
53 Frightfully strange
54 Hate the thought of
55 Crimson Tide, for short
57 Arizona river
58 Skipper's spot
59 Part of a dance routine
61 Wild blue yonder

43 CLUE BUILDER by Harvey Estes
The answer to 48 Across can be found in the back of the book.

ACROSS

1 Limerick man
5 Wielded a bat
10 "The Highwayman" singer Phil
14 Humdinger
15 Bert's annoyer
16 Koala nail
17 Country in a Beatle song
18 Period on the throne
19 Collette of "The Hours"
20 CLUE 1
23 Roth offerings
24 Moving people are in this
25 Traffic light
28 Delta asset
29 Treasured violin
30 Come-on
31 One of the Village People
34 CLUE 2
38 Alf and others
39 Dessert cheese
40 Erie and Huron
41 "Playbill" listings
43 Greeley's advice
44 One way to accept things
47 Teetotalers
48 CLUE 1 + CLUE 2
53 "___ hungry I could. . ."
54 Scrabble one-pointers
55 Minnesota neighbor
56 HBO political comedy series
57 Dog among the stars
58 Send tumbling
59 Water whirled
60 Make a swap
61 Some volleyball hits

DOWN

1 In addition
2 Remove from office
3 "Frozen" queen
4 Become
5 "Game of Thrones," for one
6 Small songbirds
7 Hospital division
8 Fun after sundown
9 Crank out
10 A number of pumps
11 Satiates
12 Vietnam capital
13 Fleet of foot
21 Center of a sink
22 Ghostly pale
25 Cruel marquis
26 "Da Doo Ron Ron" opening
27 Talks a blue streak
28 Stade Roland Garros site
30 Medicare eligibilty factor
31 Orange Vanilla soda
32 Is indebted to
33 "Hey, over here!"
35 Different from objects of nature
36 The elder Bridges
37 Court confrontations
41 Parachute part
42 Helping hand
43 Kvetch
44 Green fruit
45 Identified as
46 Stuck together
47 Sci-fi extra
49 Colada fruit
50 Center of the earth
51 Foolish fellow
52 Drains, as energy

ACROSS

1 Bowler's edge
5 Brokerage name
10 Heroic deed
14 "Tonight Show" host for 22 years
15 Hospital caution
16 On top of that
17 **Start of an entomology joke**
20 Under-the-gun spot
21 Naive
22 Crew tool
23 Bank contents
24 **More of joke**
31 Stretched out
32 Prickly
33 Dick of "Bewitched"
35 Lab eggs
36 Boat for pairs
37 "Agnus ___" (Mass prayer)
38 **More of joke**
45 Rolling stock
46 Attacks
47 Streamlined shapes
51 Way to show approval
54 1969 Super Bowl
55 They give a hoot
59 **End of joke**
64 Like available books
65 Every last dollar?
66 Attached with glue
67 Tower of London guards

DOWN

1 Prosaic
2 Major at Little Bighorn
3 "What's ___ for me?"
4 Asian rainstorm
5 Checkerboard shapes
6 Neighbor of Ger.
7 Op. ___
8 Queen of Olympus
9 Cook in a wok
10 Big fan of autumn?
11 Additional
12 Dangerous nestful
13 Playpen pile
18 Big bargain
19 Proton place
24 Relish the relish
25 Royal headpiece
26 On ___ with
27 Prometheus stole it
28 Like a GI peeling spuds
29 Mine bonanzas
30 NBA venue
31 Choir perch
34 "Santa Baby" singer Eartha
39 One of the crowd, perhaps
40 Single, in Paris
41 Fed. oversight group
42 Psyche division
43 Chop off
44 Enclave of South Africa
48 Run amok
49 "What's the ___?"
50 Teeming (with)
51 China problem
52 "Stormy Weather" singer Horne
53 Turns up the boom box
56 "To ___ it may . . ."

57 Place for waiters
58 Chevy LUV successor
60 Las Vegas roller
61 Put a halt to
62 Modus operandi
63 Cutty Sark cutter

45 LIVE TO SERVE   by Marie Langley
For those who want to help.

ACROSS

1 Booted
5 "Frozen" queen
9 Sites for studs
14 Singular
15 Blades of grass
16 Springer's sister of Sherlock
17 First homicide victim
18 In the sack
19 Star in Perseus
20 Kiwanis, 4-H, etc.
23 "Gimme ___" (Stones hit)
24 Cruising
25 Bring up the rear
28 Small wound
30 Shared coin
31 Feels
32 Hawaiian staple
35 Enrollment documents for 20-A (with 37-A)
37 See 35 Across
39 Cold-weather prefix
40 Gordon in "Oklahoma!"
44 Obscure
45 Shoot at the garden
46 Obtuse
47 High point
50 Set the dial to
52 Hallway with 35/37 Across?
57 Vital vessel
58 Scissor sound
59 Kind of ranch
60 Bill attachment
61 French 101 verb
62 ___ Scott Decision
63 Helped with dishes

64 Where they yell, "Cut!"
65 Confessional list

DOWN

1 Pole, for one
2 Transient
3 First-year law student
4 Inaccurate conception
5 Cause to beam
6 "Lady Marmalade" singer Patti
7 Add to the pot
8 Ursula in "Dr. No"
9 Cordelia's dad
10 Borrowed
11 Like a three-dollar bill
12 Save on wedding bills
13 Taco topping
21 Flyers org.
22 Winning QB of Super Bowl VII
25 Hardy female
26 Totally botch
27 Affleck flick
29 Kyrgyzstan city
31 "In the Heat of the Night" locale
32 Round end
33 Lex Luthor's henchman
34 Iwo Jima, e.g.
36 World Series figure
38 Toss-up ratio
41 Courtroom figure
42 Chance upon
43 Groveled
45 Soft seat

46 "What's the ___?"
47 Edgar, to mystery writers
48 Loft group
49 Tuesday, in Tours
51 Knuckleheads
53 Ask for ID
54 Cosmonaut Gagarin
55 Heaven on earth
56 Some wines

46 GOING MY WAY   by Gary Larson
41 Across is home to more than two million olive trees.

ACROSS

1 Show follower
4 Kind of song
8 Secure
14 College URL suffix
15 Present
16 Insulation measurement
17 Short time
18 Symphony member
19 Flings
20 Scammed
22 Postal machines
23 Level
24 Bedrock pet
25 Literature Nobelist Kertesz
27 Square measure
29 Painting surface
34 Unruly crowd
35 Frock wearer
36 Movie units
37 Low life?
39 ATM maker
40 Father of Manat
41 Greek island
42 Reservation
44 Tell tall tales
45 Katey of "Sons of Anarchy"
46 Armbone
47 Coffee from Mauna Loa
48 Ed Sheeran's "___ Team"
50 "Knock it off!"
52 Drops the ball
56 Kind of bliss
59 2006 Wimbledon singles champion Mauresmo
60 Learned one
61 Hotel freebie
62 Far from shore
63 "Thinking Ahead" reader
64 Dolt
65 Church contributions
66 Sheller's focus
67 Louse-to-be

DOWN

1 Whip
2 Mental flash
3 Markdown on Facebook?
4 Excelled
5 Online workshop
6 "East of Eden" brother
7 Family tree word
8 Torcher's misdeed
9 Showdown in Hollywood?
10 Like some apples
11 Toward the sheltered side
12 Stage coach
13 Big name in oil
21 BBC America's "Killing ___"
22 Lake Tahoe native
24 Countdown in Transylvania?
25 Apple offerings
26 Jason in "Aquaman"
28 Fives, in Florence
30 Electrifying swimmer
31 Putdown on Wall Street?
32 Done in
33 Milo of "Ulysses"
35 Crackdown in San Andreas?
38 Graphic designer's deg.
43 Ristorante entrée
47 Japanese carp
49 Pays attention to
51 Corners
52 Enticement
53 Old Dodge model
54 Boxing prize
55 Dull
56 Buddy
57 Smoothie fruit
58 Took a powder
60 Banquet

ACROSS

1 Commits a faux pas
5 Early lessons
9 Like a good cake
14 Moon landing, notably
15 Gather up
16 Hammer in "The Lone Ranger"
17 "Swapping hogs at the county expo, I made a ___"
19 Email button
20 Mrs. Hughes of "Downton Abbey"
21 "Way We ___ Be": Jim Croce
23 Soccer shoes
25 502 on a monument
26 Lego inventor Christiansen
29 Cobb and Johnson
30 Nino who scored "La Strada"
33 Shoots from cover
35 "Reaching for the calamine lotion, I made a ___"
37 Tall Corn State
40 O'Hare initials
41 Oahu goose
42 "Choosing between ginger cookies, I made a ___"
47 Explorer Frobisher
48 Pamplona pronoun
49 West Coast hrs.
52 Inkless pen
53 The All-Knowing
55 Fly
57 Contend
60 "One for My Baby" composer
61 Susan Lucci's vamp
64 "Styling a coif out of bushy hair, I made a ___"
66 Mist up
67 Castle tower
68 "The Coldest Rapper" rapper
69 Super Bowl XX winners
70 Belly-wash
71 Highlands loch

DOWN

1 Upshot
2 "Indeed!"
3 Lifts
4 Narrow ridge
5 Abbr. on a bus schedule
6 Belle's caller
7 Blackguards
8 It can kill on the road
9 E.B. White's "elixir of quietude"
10 Android operating system
11 Babysitter's bane
12 Part of RSVP
13 Mystery author Josephine
18 Neon fish
22 Reversi piece
24 Shipwreck signal
26 Andy Taylor's son
27 "QB VII" author Uris
28 Serf of yore
31 More than a plop
32 "Crime doesn't pay," e.g.
34 "Small world, ___ it?"
35 Spellbound
36 Spreading trees
37 Belief systems
38 Go ___ great length
39 Chary
43 Picture puzzles
44 Some, in Seville
45 Cockpit prediction
46 Rival of Rafa and Roger
49 Fontainebleau attraction
50 Jobs and Wozniak
51 Doctrines
54 City room fixtures
56 Broom-Hilda's friend
57 Computer brand
58 Prefix meaning "flow"
59 Nailed at a slant
61 Subside
62 "Pioneer Woman" Drummond
63 Violinist Kavafian
65 Tax preparer

A CASE OF THE BLUES   by Linda Gould
The title of the album at 58 Across is taken from the lyrics of "Purple Haze."

ACROSS

1 Nabob's nursemaid
5 North Pole coat
10 Stile member
14 Powers in "Rage at Dawn"
15 One born in late March
16 "Yipes!"
17 Garth Brooks song
19 City in "Folsom Prison Blues"
20 Ceramic aerophone
21 Uncommitted
23 New Guinea port
24 Automotive classic
25 Is contingent
29 "Sleepless in Seattle" star
33 Cropped up
34 Water slide
36 Capp's quaff
37 Ski lifts
38 Voice of Scar in "The Lion King"
39 Fruit for flavoring gin
40 Apocrypha bk.
41 Unfeeling
42 Crowed
43 Churned as if boiling
45 Shoulder belt
47 Plato's P
48 Potato eye, e.g.
49 Keep in check
53 Least complicated
57 His, in Marseille
58 Jimi Hendrix album
60 Scrap

61 Hopping mad
62 Come by
63 Like some restaurant openings
64 Ancient Persians
65 River into the Seine

DOWN

1 Buckshot
2 Anthony in "El Cantante"
3 "Deadwood" heroine
4 Like Sphynx cats
5 Given a one-star review
6 "Un bel di" is one
7 Tamper with
8 "It Had to Be You" lyricist
9 Feed the kitty
10 Postal machine
11 Majestic plural
12 Sicilian city
13 Hotel amenity
18 "Jack & ___": Mellencamp
22 Promote
25 Calendar circles
26 Irregularly edged
27 Makeup item
28 Menu fish
29 Chew loudly
30 Little green men
31 Fugard's "A Lesson From ___"
32 Demands
35 ___ polloi (common folk)
38 Graph add-on
39 La Jolla locale

41 Clodhopper
42 Orange drink
44 Frugality
46 Dies down
49 Sinatra's pack pals?
50 "Call Me by Your Name" hero
51 Alternative to whole
52 Uncle Mo, to Nyquist
53 90° from norte
54 Morales of "Caprica"
55 Hits the slopes
56 Newcastle river
59 Singing the blues

51 RECORD HOLDERS   by Linda Gould
51 Across can reach a maximum speed of 240 mph.

ACROSS

1 Cartoon flapper
5 It might be rigged
9 King in "The Iliad"
14 Place to hang Christmas lights
15 Time for giving
16 "Anybody home?"
17 "Let this stand"
18 Knock senseless
19 Bungling
20 World's slowest animals
23 Sabermetrics stat
24 DNA or fingerprints, e.g.
25 Aretha Franklin hit
29 Stifle
33 "MacGyver" actor Dana
34 Eugene climbed it in "Tangled"
36 Pass at Daytona
37 Largest primate
41 LAPD alert
42 Unexpected complication
43 Source of rings
44 Schroeder's gang
47 Unkempt ones
49 Cenozoic is one
50 Prefix meaning "the same"
51 Fastest animal on earth
60 Up the ante
61 Email status
62 Wang the designer
63 Sweater synthetic
64 Betray nervousness
65 Sweet-milk cheese
66 Out of energy
67 Musher's transport
68 Remove a word

DOWN

1 How father knows?
2 Hippocratic ___
3 CB sign-off
4 "I've Gotta Crow" singer
5 William Blake, for example
6 Taurus, e.g.
7 Turn sharply
8 Keep an eye on
9 "The Fair" French king
10 French Impressionist
11 "___ My Mind Wander": Willie Nelson
12 Xanadu's river
13 Verbal gems
21 Thumbs-up critic
22 Dum spiro ___
25 Amend an atlas section
26 Hitch and run
27 Explore the reef
28 Nabisco Wheat ___
29 "Battle of the Sexes" role
30 J.R.'s mother in "Dallas"
31 Literary soirée
32 Straddles
35 "Suburgatory" actress Gasteyer
38 "___ Is Born" (2018)
39 Apollo 14 astronaut Stuart
40 In a relationship
45 Liam in "Kinsey"
46 Like ASAP memos
48 Picked a pocket or two

51 They're in it for the money
52 Masterson contemporary
53 Get to, so to speak
54 AOL et al.
55 Patricia of "The Subject Was Roses"
56 Suffix for differ
57 Homophone for seed
58 Graduate exam
59 Put a handle on

52 ONLY ON TV by Pam Klawitter
56 Across is the only child of two Muggle dentists.

ACROSS

1 Take a surprise shot at
6 Lat. noun gender
10 Cool and collected partner
14 Word with wave or pool
15 He aims for the heart
16 Olive genus
17 Only child of a Beverly Hills millionaire
20 Gardeners, at times
21 Homicide evidence
22 D-backs on a scoreboard
23 Boomer babies
24 Roman historian
27 Only child of an "FYI" news anchor
33 Starting square
34 Prepare for
35 Craggy home
36 "All sales ___"
38 Call on the court
40 Avoid wedding costs
41 Old Greek market
42 Jungle sound
44 Glass in "Charade"
45 Only child of a Mel's Diner waitress
48 "Glee" actor Monteith
49 "The Hustler" game
50 "Why ___ Me?" ("Shendandoah" song)
52 Predisposed toward

56 Hermione of Hogwarts
60 Only child of a Fairfield housekeeper
62 Flimflam
63 "Field of Dreams" setting
64 With force
65 North Sea feeder
66 Kay Ryan, notably
67 Went up the creek

DOWN

1 Oyster ___
2 Lake Nasser source
3 Hanging out
4 When you get what's coming to you
5 Dr. Hartman of "Family Guy"
6 Willie in the Hall
7 "NOS4A2" network
8 Metal binder
9 Crevice
10 Cairo Christian
11 Homer's "On ___ Shore"
12 "Why don't we?"
13 Marshal Dillon
18 Windows typeface
19 1935 loser to Braddock
23 Cornwallis, for one
24 Lite, on a label
25 Montoya in "The Princess Bride"
26 "Spider-Man 3" villain
28 Horse transport
29 Little faith?

30 Down East college town
31 Windshield blade
32 In dire straits
34 Baby cage
37 Type of wrestling
39 Preschooler
43 Big name in arcade games
46 Tout's whispering
47 "Anybody home?"
48 Screening locale
51 Blu in "Rio"
52 "Hey, pal!"
53 Quite blue
54 Middle East gulf
55 Handle
56 Exam for a Wharton applicant
57 Animated
58 "The Fifth Son" author Wiesel

59 Lemon zest, e.g.
61 Overpower

53 OPENING REMARKS by Pam Klawitter

Samuel L. Jackson became the first celebrity voice of 30 Down in 2019.

ACROSS

1 Shot of Scotch
5 Too snug
10 ABC's "Celebrity Wife ___"
14 Dwelling
15 Postponed
16 Lunar ring
17 "Well, look who's here!"
20 They're left behind
21 Witherspoon in "Penelope"
22 Grad-student jobs
23 Langläufer's gear
25 "I don't want to hear it!"
33 Engage in rhetoric
34 Wall Street symbol
35 Card game with forfeits
36 "Read my ___!": Bush
37 Noted shock jock
39 Computer display
40 Make do (with "out")
41 "Ah, me!"
42 Office transmission option
43 Observe a September 19th "holiday"
47 Leather finish
48 Legged it
49 Feel the same
52 Tropical lizards
56 Use your magic words for mommy
60 Point of cutlery
61 Fine thread
62 Rose holder
63 Yankee or Oriole, briefly
64 Waiting room
65 Relaxation

DOWN

1 Nonfielding hitters: Abbr.
2 Hitchcock film
3 City near Des Moines
4 Smokehouse product
5 Honk a hello
6 Swarm in
7 Amscrays
8 FDR's predecessor
9 Concert shirt
10 "Enough already!"
11 Ocean swell
12 Start of Oregon's motto
13 Cracow citizen
18 "___ bar the door!"
19 Not as humid
23 Dump closure
24 Bond villain Kamal
25 "Rent me" sign
26 Wachter of MSG Networks
27 Boutonniere's place
28 USMA grads
29 Beyond plump
30 Amazon Echo assistant
31 Opus for an ennead
32 Immerse
37 Buttonhole, say
38 Choose
39 Scratch the surface
41 Do some tailoring
42 Concluding
44 Lighthouse custodian
45 Sweater pattern
46 Church mouse, for one
49 1930s movie dog
50 "Passages" author Sheehy
51 Cub legend Sandberg
52 "The ___-bitsy spider . . ."
53 Campbell in "Skyscraper"
54 Narrow shoe width
55 Leak sound
57 Dobby, for one
58 Raul's uncle
59 Wide shoe width

THEMELESS by Harvey Estes
Once prevalent, 18 Down are now on the endangered species list.

ACROSS

1 Hot food in husks
8 Gunpowder containers
15 It's heard before some hockey games
16 All over the place
17 One who frames his customers
19 Ballet bends
20 Club fees
21 "___ match?"
22 First Family member in 1964
24 Water hazard
26 Atlas page
27 Summer, in Montréal
28 Democratic Donkey creator
30 Mark up with graffiti
32 Menial, in a medieval milieu
34 ___ sci
36 Takes a hit on a stock's price
37 Where to gratify your shellfish desires
40 '70s hot spot
43 Skunk warning
44 "ER" actor La Salle
48 Different from
50 Till section
52 Former Burmese leader
53 U-turn from NNW
54 Airing
56 Tao founder
58 "How do you like ___ apples?"
60 Very, in Vichy
62 Wood-shop tool
63 Perform a 12/31 custom
66 Far out expanse
67 "Come or you'll regret it!"
68 Went over carefully
69 Boils over

DOWN

1 Removes from power
2 Candlelight mood setter at church
3 Spacecraft sent to Mercury
4 Paid to get in
5 "Rent" composer
6 Childcare writer LeShan
7 Aforementioned
8 Portable home
9 Did blackboard duty
10 The D'backs, on scoreboards
11 Hunger sign
12 Hassock
13 Pin for dressing up
14 De-ices a windshield
18 Avian Christmas gifts
23 Carpet features
25 Greek salad cheese
29 "Ice Age" sabertooth
31 Hack's customer
33 Central points
35 Blast furnace output
38 John's "Double Fantasy" album collaborator
39 Composer Jacques
40 Floor cleaner
41 Of sound body
42 More smooth
45 More like a rough wagon path
46 Coming from the sea
47 Promoted a pawn
49 Way in
51 Pay tribute to
55 Flight part
57 Swear words
59 Dish list
61 Laments aloud
64 Balaam's beast
65 Appomattox figure

55 THEMELESS by Harvey Estes
1 Across was named as Cambridge Dictionary's 2018 word of the year.

ACROSS

1 Fear of being without your phone
11 Scrunches up
15 They relieve pain
16 Big name in chemicals
17 Flushed
18 Friendly red monster
19 Normandy port
20 Shepard on "Ally McBeal"
21 Think obsessively
22 Radial need
23 Oscars, mostly
25 Manger contents
26 Australian football defenders
30 Ate into
32 2010 vampire film
33 Bubble maker
35 Open up ___ of worms
36 1987 Masters winner
37 Proceeds
41 Antenna housings
44 Ambulance equipment
45 Noted
46 U-turn from NNW
47 RN offering
48 Monkey suit, briefly
49 "Java" trumpeter Al
51 Stand by a nude, perhaps
53 Make ___ dash for it
57 Theater award
58 Marianne cocktail ingredient
60 Additional
61 How old tape may wind
62 Some volleyball hits
63 Where the paperwork piles up

DOWN

1 Pusher chaser
2 Most fit for the draft
3 Like neat beds
4 Buck heroine
5 Mag. leafs
6 Bad guys on the stage
7 Daredevil Super Dave _____
8 Baudelaire's well
9 Summer refresher
10 He danced in "Silk Stockings"
11 Trials and tribulations
12 Habitually
13 Easily gotten
14 Like a winter wonderland
22 Increase, with "up"
24 Mail carrier's conjunction
26 Baylor mascot
27 Like people who are easy to talk to
28 Keyboard player
29 Baseball great Ralph
31 Matt of "The Martian"
34 Observe the Sabbath
38 Surfing site
39 Forget
40 Bloodhound's quarry
41 Goes through again
42 Sources of good fortune, some say
43 Social reformer Dorothea
46 Pumps and such
50 Links supporters
52 Throw out
53 It's all around you
54 Bearing
55 Got an A on
56 Singers Reeves and Shannon
59 Speck

ACROSS

1 "Let justice roll down" book
5 Hike
10 Luxury fleet
14 Join
16 "Lawrence of Arabia" director
17 French verse form, or a character in 52 Across
18 Bone by the radius
19 Casual conversation
20 Old stringed instrument
21 Guitar master Paul
22 Fabric on the table
23 Left for cash
27 Regard
29 George, who was Mary Ann
30 In more favorable circumstances
33 Men behaving badly
34 Comer who plays 17 Across
35 Angelina's tomb-raiding role
36 Short trousers
38 More discerning
39 Den purchase
40 Easy gait
41 Broad neckwear
43 Durable wood
44 Liza's sister
45 Meringue maker
51 Android operating system
52 Spy-action thriller series with Sandra Oh
53 Steams up
54 Leaves in the bowl
55 Since, to Burns
56 Diving hazard, with "the"
57 Gambling city

DOWN

1 Off-roadsters
2 Hurt badly
3 Ark. neighbor
4 Bear growl?
5 Sounded off
6 Geometry calculations
7 "___ never fly!"
8 Parachute material
9 Hydrocarbon ending
10 Large game fish
11 Crisp named after an opera star
12 Fades away
13 Bag of chips, maybe
15 Small platform
20 Don Juan, for one
22 Express fondness, with "on"
23 Kiss, barely
24 Cumming of the stage
25 Letterbox cousin
26 Like a Maori greeting
27 Resulted in
28 Porter's regretful miss
30 Off-white
31 Off the hook
32 Klinger portrayer
34 Rattles
37 Antifur org.
38 Comes to
40 Cruise ship compartments
41 Neurologist Alzheimer
42 "Pardon me"
43 Made eyes at
45 Limerick land
46 Secluded vale
47 Jelling agent
48 Prefix with prompter
49 Hunter of good books
50 Change the décor of
52 Putin's onetime org.

57 THEMELESS by Anna Carson
The clue at 58 Across deserves a question mark.

ACROSS

1 Analyze this
8 Shows up
15 Relating to high-tech flight
16 Clear up
17 Toiletry item
18 McBride of country
19 Farthest
20 Snide one
21 Island gifts
23 Least serene
24 U.S. budgetary financial crisis of 1/1/ 2013
29 Hawke of "Training Day"
30 For all practical purposes
35 Get an eyeful
36 Slender candle
38 Fictional hunchback
39 Price offsetters
41 Empathetic response
42 Fed head linked to the phrase at 24 Across
45 New York team
49 Part of YSL
50 "My" Willa Cather character
52 Refined form of bauxite
57 Din in the alley, perhaps
58 Responded like a pupil
59 Board of art school
60 Thrown out
61 Speaker arrangements
62 Space probe equipment

DOWN

1 100-meter, for one
2 River to the Severn
3 Out of control
4 Dire destiny
5 Luanda dweller
6 Holiday glitter
7 Sour
8 Draws a bead
9 Switch schools
10 Removed at the perforated line
11 Pass the threshold
12 Color of a bête
13 Hilly, sandy area
14 Turn on
22 Evades the guards, e.g.
24 Intuited
25 Sinus, e.g.
26 Whigham of "Boardwalk Empire"
27 Part of a hand
28 End for Benedict
31 Paycheck abbr.
32 Richard of "A Summer Place"
33 Stopper
34 Fam diagram
36 Connects with
37 Reinking in "Micki + Maude"
40 It's vulcanized
41 Kind of shot
43 Skirts
44 Go through again
45 Places for tents
46 ___ a time
47 Shoulder warmer
48 Lawn care tool
51 A long, long time
53 Some rainwear
54 "Suffice ___ say . . ."
55 Adverb in verse
56 Makes sense, with "up"

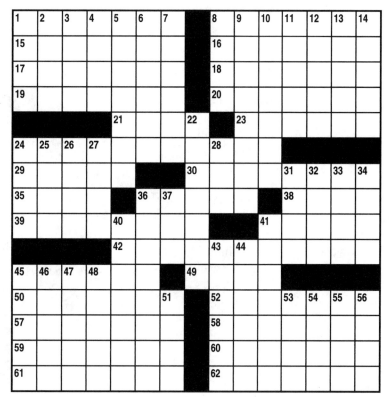

58 THEMELESS   by Harvey Estes
The opposite of 35 Across is a more familiar term to most.

ACROSS

1 Tommy Roe hit named for a legume
9 "Open" author Andre
15 Batman is a caped one
16 Took the plunge
17 Paper vehicle
18 Rasta locks
19 Western director Sergio
20 Price phrase
22 Needing towels
23 Unproven ability
24 Jill in "Diamonds Are Forever"
27 "Deck the Halls" phrase
28 Wineglass feature
30 Calls the game
31 Offer to a hitchhiker
32 Pernod flavoring
34 Pop, for one
35 They once were "riche"
39 Chipped in
40 São ___, Brazil
41 Overturn
42 Waikiki souvenirs
43 Feint
47 Sun shades
48 Noble partner
50 School org.
51 1040 senders
52 Lean
53 Bengay targets
55 Like a Slinky
57 White expanse
60 Contend
61 Offer a greeting
62 Course portion
63 "Grease" actress

DOWN

1 Piano practice
2 Most amusingly ironic
3 Continent without a desert
4 Channel of armchair athletes
5 Raconteur's repertoire
6 Palm Pilot, e.g.
7 Ending for velvet
8 Forte
9 Extra charge
10 Hiker's snack
11 NYC's Park ___
12 Natural saline solution
13 Put on the bench
14 Split seconds
21 Acidity nos.
25 C-E-G in C, e.g.
26 "___, Joy of Man's Desiring"
27 Fire in the belly
29 Self-styled experts
31 Ancient European region
33 Cry out for
34 YouTube button
35 Kind of mile
36 Conditionally released
37 Mess kit items
38 Tylenol target
42 "Viva ___ Vegas" (1964)
44 Supported
45 "Fifty Shades of Grey" protagonist
46 City N of Philadelphia
48 First State statesman
49 Obama daughter
52 Interlocking block
54 Grammy winner for "Believe"
56 Guitarist Paul
58 Cleveland cager, briefly
59 Potato spot

THEMELESS   by Harvey Estes
Punny clue for 18 Down: McCartney's banded guitar?

ACROSS

1 Party down
8 Crown jewels, scepter, and such
15 "From your lips to God's ears!"
16 Ham activity
17 Cold turkey
19 Potato spot
20 Gentle rhythm
21 President known as "Dutch"
22 Corrida combatant
24 Flower killer
25 Out of kilter
28 "The Lion King" hero
30 Give a hard time
32 Union demand
37 Company with cars
38 Turn away
40 Not even close
41 "Take a load off"
43 Part of ERA
45 Leave alone
47 Wanting
48 Library volume
52 Diet lunches
54 Stay out of sight
56 Min. parts
57 1.0, for one
60 Wagon train member
63 Jazz diggers
64 After the bell
65 Green lights
66 Hyundai fleet

DOWN

1 Behavior researcher Shere
2 Call for a mate
3 Use a ballot
4 Clean air gov't grp.
5 Chaps
6 Carrier of old
7 Kings and queens, but not aces
8 Pt. of AARP
9 Gulf leader
10 Went to the top
11 What one may shed
12 Specialized speech
13 Onetime pyramid builders
14 Star's rep
18 Rockfish
22 Mock playfully
23 "A loaf of bread . . ." poet
25 Obsessive whaler
26 File command
27 Letang of the Penguins
29 Collection of bits
31 Stuff to the gills
33 Green TV units
34 Skye on the screen
35 Arctic Cat, for one
36 Water whirled
39 Seasoned hands
42 "Close but no cigar" type
44 (No need for details)
46 Chooses
48 Kind of male
49 Wears down
50 Bounds' partner
51 Suffragist Paul
53 Cold response?
55 Skater Katarina
57 Small biter
58 Anti-fur org.
59 Greek war deity
61 Three dots, in Morse
62 Suffix with plug

63 ACROSS   by Greg Johnson
Here's one for those who like a good challenge.

ACROSS

1 Cracked, as a door
5 1978 was BMW's first one
9 "Grease" greaser
14 Recital numbers
15 Hershey candy in a cylindrical wrap
16 Currency of Pakistan
17 "My mistake, you are correct . . ."
19 Departing words
20 Adams of western pictures
21 Man who made a 2016 farewell speech
23 Watch the rugrats
24 Soldier at Cold Harbor
26 In the slightest
28 "Thinking back upon that . . ."
33 Cape near Boston
35 GP's gp.
36 Ambassador appointed by the prez
37 Element used in batteries
40 Guest at a synagogue
42 April Fools' Day sign
43 Sound engineer's concern
44 ___-rare (steak order)
45 "She looks familiar but . . ."
50 Did a stable job
51 Acapulco gold
52 Online help source
55 Type of committee
57 Words of surrender
61 Words of resignation
63 Owing money
65 Four in a deck
66 Early copter
67 Hiding from MPs
68 Musical membranophone
69 Guardpost warning
70 License plates, in the language

DOWN

1 One of earth's seven
2 English version of Ian
3 Cry of dismay
4 Cleveland's 1969 Cuyahoga tragedy, e.g.
5 "Wind in the Willows" weasel battler
6 "Papa Loves Mambo" singer
7 "Arabian Nights" woodcutter
8 Go round
9 Shakedown cruise
10 Hit up for a smoke
11 Wall St. tech announcements
12 Home debtor's option, briefly
13 Skillfully dexterous

18 First sch. for many
22 Abbr. equated with 3
25 Spark
27 Dryer buildup that's a fire hazard
28 Their flag has a wheel in the center
29 "Deeeee-lish!"
30 Ronald McDonald's purple pal
31 Prefix for port
32 Did a Halloween prank
33 Berry with three vowels
34 Undercover buster
38 Department selling boxers
39 "Oh, really?"
40 Shout for a pest to leave
41 Similar statement
43 Landlocked country bordering Greece
46 Seed damage preventer
47 Bethlehem university
48 Keystone State county
49 "Slow Ride" '70s rockers
52 Hall-of-Fame catcher Carlton
53 Sky or sea shade
54 Teacher's "surprise"
56 Key for shortcuts
58 State with many cornfields
59 YouTube journal
60 Slithery swimmers
62 Judge in the 1995 news
64 All the rage

WEIGHTS AND MEASURES by Jim Holland

71 Across was inducted into the American Theater Hall of Fame in 2018.

ACROSS

1 Utah ski resort
5 Original Garden Stater?
9 Play the coquette
14 Evening, in Paris
15 Jack Bauer's "24" wife
16 Dental tool
17 Fools the shortstop
20 Protein acid
21 Nursery "piggy"
22 Verb, ironically
23 Reunion goer
26 Caused a chemical change
28 Suffices for the time being
32 The works
33 Aromatic garnish
34 Type of chair or car
38 Kopa's leonine mother
40 Style hair in a way
43 "¿Quien ___?" ("Who knows?")
44 Seaman's shout
46 Alliance formed in 1949
48 Deighton or Dawson
49 Breaks out of a gloomy mood
53 "What Lies ___" (2000)
56 "Frozen" queen
57 Twitter cofounder Williams
58 Slugger Williams
60 "101" title word
64 Text messages, old-school
68 Be bombastic
69 Word before pads or socks
70 Land of the leprechauns
71 Cicely in "Sounder"
72 Install, in a fashion
73 Spotted horse

DOWN

1 Charles family member
2 Rich soil
3 Pool party torch
4 Event forums
5 ___ snail's pace
6 Young socialite
7 What the suspicious might smell
8 Skater Ito
9 Waitress on "Alice"
10 Gets underway
11 "Failure ___ an option"
12 Prompt again
13 Zogby's concern
18 Very dependable
19 "How've you ___?"
24 Military group
25 Emu egg sitter
27 Coolers, briefly
28 Perino of Fox News
29 Norway's St. ___ Festival
30 Grasso or Raines
31 Springboard
35 "Apparition du Visage" artist
36 Second son
37 Pacific goose
39 Reach in rising fashion
41 MS. accompanier
42 And more, briefly
45 Song syllable
47 Davis in "Grumpy Old Men"
50 "A Bug's Life" princess
51 They take bad bounces, at times
52 Feeding trough
53 Stupefy
54 "___ Breath You Take": Sting
55 Grannies
59 Aarhus native
61 The Bee Gees, e.g.
62 ___ avis (nonpareil)
63 Comet, to some
65 B. Obama, in 2005
66 "___ Clown": Porter
67 Find a tenant

62 THEMELESS by Eva Finney
Alternate clue for 41 Down: Kind of pine.

ACROSS
1 Fishing derby fish
5 Sticker
8 "Yond Cassius has ___ ...": Shak.
13 Mexican pastry
15 Russian newspaper
16 Hostile
17 Online broker
18 Bridge blunderer
19 Game stick with a netted pocket
20 Cyberspace discussion system
21 The jolt in Jolt
23 Roofing man
24 All there
25 Christie's bids
26 Help
29 Velour feature
30 Mens ___ in corpore sano
31 "___ tête, Alouette!"
33 AWACS landing spot
36 Furnace fuel
40 Sea inlets
42 Hardly hardy
43 Sanskrit's language group
45 Fishes, in a way
47 Better half
48 Clare ___ Luce
49 Inconveniences
50 Syracuse transit org.
51 Roundheads
52 Like some quilt blocks
53 Begins brawling
54 ___ drop of a hat
55 Active Japanese volcano
56 Michael in "Superbad"

DOWN
1 Mideast capital
2 No sense of history
3 Rubylike gems
4 Uniformity
5 "Don't play" on scores
6 Feast of Esther month
7 Gadot in "Wonder Woman"
8 Bach's "The ___ Fugue"
9 "The Sea Wolf" captain
10 Dodger's forte
11 Book supplement
12 Shetland negative
14 Ibadan native
15 Race track bet
19 Spam source?
21 Motorist org. of Toronto
22 Cassandra's curse
24 Part of a canon
27 Polaroid
28 Mark of omission
32 Noncommittal, in a way
33 Jack Russell's remark
34 Hazelnut
35 M-16 adjunct
37 Us, in Essen
38 Hero-worship
39 Assent from an hombre
41 Rusty Nail ingredient
44 Private plane
46 "Based on ___ story"
47 Painter Andrea del ___
49 Colors
50 Auditor, for short
51 Steve Stricker's org.

63 DAY IN, DAY OUT by Jonathan O'Rourke
"Spend the money quickly, Mister Bond." — 4 Down

ACROSS
1 Mardi Gras wear
6 Best Buy buy
10 Ivan the Terrible, for one
14 Dominant male
15 Met show-stopper
16 Glowing review
17 Be a bad winner
18 [Uh-oh!]
19 Pinnacle
20 Flowering vine
23 Flabbergast
24 Fa-la link
25 Perches
29 4 pm Manchester meal
32 Grant in "Monkey Business"
34 Lie adjacent to
35 Start of the yr.
36 Hoodlum
37 Epsilon followers
39 It's not kosher
40 URL suffix
41 Worker's compensation?
42 Texas Hold'em bullets
43 White tie
47 Bill Clinton memoir
48 Feedbag morsel
49 Singer DiFranco
52 German mutant in "Dark Phoenix"
56 Pilgrimage to Mecca
59 Castle
60 Start of a wish
61 Light bulb, in comics
62 Black, to Blake
63 Irish tenor Tynan
64 Maintains the yard
65 Join, as farm animals
66 Two under par

DOWN
1 Earth's core
2 Green-light
3 Future fungus
4 "Octopussy" villain Kamal
5 Hit the spot
6 Dicker
7 Ke$ha's "Your Love Is My ___"
8 Work the soil
9 Hazy
10 Preschooler's utensil
11 Use a ray gun
12 "Hail, Caesar!"
13 King of old Rome?
21 "___ to worry!"
22 Carrot or radish
26 Missouri city, informally
27 "___ in Heaven": Clapton
28 Made a putt
29 Genesis vessel
30 Given an "R"
31 Wizards' org.
32 Like the road up Pikes Peak
33 Tannenbaum topper
36 Words from Wordsworth
37 "Riders of the Purple Sage" author
38 French toast ingredient
39 Alternatives to Macs
41 Starbucks freebie
42 "Top Hat" dancer
44 Masked Japanese fighters
45 George Gipp's coach
46 Musical knack
49 "___ came a spider . . ."
50 Mount Dhaulagiri locale
51 One of the Horae
53 One for the road
54 Pocketed
55 "Hold your horses!"
56 That guy
57 Foofaraw
58 Yom Kippur observer

64 JUST A FEW QUESTIONS by Brian E. Paquin
8 Down is the first Mets player to hit 50 or more home runs in a season.

ACROSS
1 Like some excuses
5 Smashing pumpkin sound
10 Gusto
14 Sarah McLachlan hit
15 With anger
16 Competitive advantage
17 Streisand-O'Neal comedy
19 River islands
20 Incapable of
21 Superlative for Brutus
23 Vista
24 Since
25 Baseball sketch in "The Naughty Nineties"
32 Experience nausea
36 Range
37 Like some bloomers
38 Shanty
41 Israel's first UN delegate
42 Took the bull by the horns
44 Most eerie
46 Handford puzzle book
49 Remote button
50 Bed parts
55 To the point
59 Manual dexterity
61 Faithful action?
62 Taco Bell slogan
64 First name in mystery
65 Enlighten
66 Stereotypical lab assistant
67 Marvel mutants
68 Werner in "Ship of Fools"
69 Alice, in a Nevil Shute novel

DOWN
1 Places for sprinklers
2 Off-the-cuff
3 Mazda roadster
4 Go nuts over
5 Not ajar
6 The heat
7 Canadian cousin of inc.
8 Mets player nicknamed "Polar Bear"
9 Business baron
10 Fervor
11 "Desperate Housewives" character
12 DI's, often
13 Dry run
18 Emits
22 Close buds
24 "Shoot!"
26 One of two matching items
27 Gaelic "Oh my!"
28 Treated (a sprain)
29 Pre-fight garb
30 Whirlpools
31 Revival shelter
32 Glitch
33 Apiece
34 Sermon ender
35 Lustful look
39 "Snow White" collectible
40 Nanny's little one
43 Wonka portrayer
45 Grier of the "Fearsome Foursome"
47 "He that is ___ anger . . .": Prov. 16:32
48 Does the laundry
51 Hinder
52 To the max, in the '60s
53 Take to the air on Super Sunday
54 Unyielding
55 Ovechkin of hockey
56 Wave not meant for surfing
57 Stethoscope sound
58 Make the first bet
59 Rover rescuer
60 He had a lion's lines
63 It's milked in Tibet

SOUPED UP   by Brian E. Paquin
Alternate clue for 20 Across: "Everyone leave!"

ACROSS

1 "The Beeb"
4 Saintly devotion
9 "Chocolat" actress Lena
13 Jeff Lynne's group
14 Eisenhower opponent Stevenson
15 Cheap cigar
16 Just so-so
18 Bald raptor
19 Pursue intently
20 The utmost
22 Harebrained
24 "Give You Up" singer
25 Vivacity
28 Head starter
30 Draw off
34 Home facelift, briefly
35 NCIS employee
37 Like some arts
38 Envelope abbr.
39 One of Zsa Zsa's sisters
40 Warning to heed
41 Small songbird
42 Harvard and Yale
44 Pouting expression
45 Surprisingly
47 Wall St. subj.
48 Concert gear
49 Civil War cap
51 MacLachlan on "Desperate Housewives"
53 Mocking
57 Born in Baghdad
61 Watch for
62 Downsizing events
64 Post-punk types
65 Ruckus

66 Competitive standoff
67 One of the Baldwins
68 Coal
69 Unlatch, to a poet

DOWN

1 Plays the ponies
2 Blemish
3 Rum mixer
4 Arctic wear
5 Nev. neighbor
6 Souped-up menu choice
7 Like unlikely tales
8 Capitulate
9 Souped-up menu choice
10 Letterhead pic
11 Ice dome
12 "No way, Nikita!"
15 Not swanky
17 Souped-up menu choice
21 Heart of the matter
23 Italian monk
25 It's trumped by brains
26 So-o-o last decade
27 Info about the enemy
29 Evil one
31 Sign held up in a televised audience
32 Outwit
33 Baby boys from Barcelona
36 Souped-up menu choice

42 Verizon and Mediacom, e.g.
43 Salty sauce
46 Pants parts
50 "Who's there?" reply
52 Permanent resident of the big house
53 Epic tale
54 Soldier status
55 Evaluate
56 News story
58 Biography starter
59 Ear opener
60 "Got it!"
63 Bank charge

66 THEMELESS by Theresa Yves
The role of 37 Across is usually played a man.

ACROSS

1 Every minute
11 Yuppie wheels
15 Job source in "Poldark"
16 Sudden transition
17 The fleeting character of life
18 Goad
19 Richard Branson's title
20 Gymnastics event
21 Start of a Tony Orlando song title
22 PR person
24 Vocal critic
26 Rodeo need
29 Nobelist Wiesel
31 "Foiled again!"
32 Checkout count
33 Make changes to
34 "You ___ what you eat"
35 Russian news service
36 Diet guru Jenny
37 "Hairspray" mom
38 News source, for short
39 Sheepskin word
40 Beat by a whisker
41 B&O et al.
42 Estimating words
43 McDonald's equipment
44 Understands
46 Grimm beasts
48 "___ my wit's end!"
49 Ghana capital
51 Louis Quatorze, for one
54 Asian prefix
55 Putting on paper
58 Nip and ___
59 Holes 11–13 at Augusta National
60 Hook ally
61 Helps to unwind

DOWN

1 Pursues thespianism
2 Convex moldings
3 On ___ with
4 Hosp. aide's superior
5 Guitarist Paul
6 Hot-dish holder
7 Conversational filler
8 American ICBM
9 Letter abbr.
10 All worked up
11 Wooer of Olive Oyl
12 Scout's honor
13 W-2 form recipient
14 Pioneers a movement
22 Draws a bead
23 Surfing wipeout
25 Brit. word ref
26 Pastors' assistants
27 In short supply
28 The good guys in WW2 France
30 Darth's daughter
33 2012 Affleck flick
36 Bach wrote over 200
37 Ice cream brand
39 Miss Piggy's self-reference
40 Before, in the past
43 Lingua ___
45 Stir up
47 Looks amused
50 Revived, with "to"
51 "Class Reunion" novelist Jaffe
52 Comes up short
53 Memo starter
56 Survived, with "by"
57 Beats by ___

67 THEMELESS by Theresa Yves

A restaurateur said that 17 Across was "The best 25 customers I ever had."

ACROSS

1 "The Piano Lesson" artist
8 Mozart's rival
15 Brought to bear
16 Like an electrical plug
17 Gilded Age tycoon and bon vivant
19 Holocaust hero Schindler
20 Lively card game
21 Matinee figure
22 He rubs you the right way
26 About
30 Gave support to
35 Like some roofs
37 Humana rival
38 FICA tax, for one
41 Shaw of swing
42 Increase sevenfold
43 Bad-mouth
46 Little green edibles
47 Manhattan's Russian ___
49 Oahu carving material
53 Subordinate of a maj.
54 Thoreau work
59 Chance to start over
63 Not prepared
64 No tape-breaker
65 Scrolls found in the Qumran Caves
66 Sickle swingers

DOWN

1 "What would you have ___?"
2 Center of revolution
3 Durable East Indian wood
4 Hogwarts librarian Pince
5 Blackout cause
6 State rep.
7 Teaching deg.
8 Upright piano
9 Camelot knight wear
10 Soft toss
11 Icon letters
12 "My stars!"
13 Change the décor of
14 Pastoral work
18 Comeuppance
23 In a competent manner
24 Sought damages
25 Fail to keep a poker face
26 Syrian leader
27 Lamb Chop's friend
28 Pinball fouls
29 TV studio sign
31 Arrangement
32 R.E.M. vocalist Michael
33 Atoll girl in "Waterworld"
34 Claire in "Homeland"
36 Say "hi!" to
39 Geometric art style
40 Capable of performing
44 Leave the Union
45 Yellow fruit
48 Where to have a meeting of the minds?
49 Sing the praises of
50 "Snowbird" singer Murray
51 Norm's wife on "Cheers"
52 Flabbergasted
55 Hogwash
56 Scat Daddy, to Justify
57 Some miles away
58 Driving needs
60 Vegas opening
61 Attention
62 Soccer chant word

THEMELESS **by Ben Gibbs**

Richie Havens performed 17 Across at Woodstock in 1969.

ACROSS

1 "At Wit's End" author Bombeck
5 Tourist magnet
10 Heels
14 Milk marks, in Manchester
16 "I'm just ___ for the money"
17 "Sometimes I Feel Like a ___ Child"
18 Gillette razor product
19 Finish, in a wine tasting
20 Univ. marchers
21 Glove behind the plate
22 Change
24 Review applicants
28 One of Charlie's angels
30 Winning
31 ___ Green Giant
32 Drop the ball
34 Substance
35 Chewy treat
36 "Don't Throw Bouquets ___ "
37 Grand ___ Opry
38 Shepard on "Ally McBeal"
39 Referred to
40 Running things
42 Haying machines
43 Woman's shoe style
44 Malted beverages
46 "___ Rock": Simon song
47 When?
53 Carpenters song
54 Dramatic
55 Accutane treats it
56 Sagebrusher
57 "I'm game!"
58 Teri on "Desperate Housewives"
59 Chevy LUV successor

DOWN

1 Flaubert heroine
2 Mouth part
3 Heinz hound
4 Queens stadium name
5 NHL goalie Brodeur
6 Ostentatious display
7 Dressers
8 "___ la vie!"
9 School gathering
10 Dante translator John
11 Kirsten Dunst title role of 2006
12 One close to the soil
13 Lewis of the LPGA
15 Designated
23 Access add-on
24 Palm starch
25 Spicy condiment
26 Hostile feeling
27 Put away
29 Sports car, briefly
31 Unidentified Doe
33 Wine list subheading
35 Riverside trails
36 Be laid up
38 Govt. broadcaster
39 Street in San Francisco
41 Gibber-jabbers
42 Like meringue
43 Of ebb and flow
45 Tibet city
48 Quaker's pronoun
49 Asparagus serving
50 "Johnny Mnemonic" rapper
51 Filly, later on
52 Panache

69 THEMELESS by Ben Gibbs

56 Across conducted the Philly Pops from 1979 to 2013.

ACROSS

1 Once again
5 Rushed
9 Judicial agenda
14 Pulsar emission
16 Bar garnish
17 Italian chain
18 "In ___ days a glimpse of stocking . . ."
19 Employee in a safe place?
20 Laments
21 Friendly nation
22 Contrivance
23 Gives a break
27 Govt. code breakers
29 Sheep follower
30 Pertaining to the fleet
31 Part of Batman's garb
32 Strong ___ ox
34 Some nest eggs
35 "In your dreams!"
36 StarKist's Charlie
37 Postwar agreement
38 Passable
39 Gray hardwood tree
40 Abner's partner
41 Carson or Franklin
42 Ornery individuals
43 Thrashes about
45 Acapulco Almighty
47 United Healthcare rival
48 Factor in voter analysis
53 Virgil's Troy
54 "Step on it!"
55 Part of a designer name
56 "Theme from Summer of '42" pianist
57 Cube's dozen
58 Linear
59 Get a move on

DOWN

1 Oman man
2 Big wine valley
3 Carl Sagan's dragon locale
4 Flirty gesture
5 Doesn't just sip
6 "Doonesbury" segment
7 Intermittently
8 PC place
9 Sam who sang "Cupid"
10 Takes the edge off
11 Secondary problems
12 Toss-up
13 Become aware of
15 Standing by
22 Tim on "Madam Secretary"
23 Barber's stroke
24 Corresponded to
25 Fire drill activity
26 Just under the wire
28 Influence
31 Blast furnace fuel
33 Nope and such
35 Loaded Londoners
39 Not as quiet
42 Hit on the head
43 Savoir-___
44 High priests of Tibet
46 "10 Things ___ About You" (1999)
48 Famed Bruin's nickname
49 Recyclable items
50 "___ the Music Speak": ABBA
51 Bond girl Hatcher
52 "Son of Frankenstein" blacksmith

ACROSS

1 Data center workhorses
11 "Who's the Boss?" character
15 Herb that restores health
16 Aspirin is one
17 2004 Cruise/Foxx film
18 Darn, maybe
19 Emphatic denial
20 Genetic info carrier
21 Jethro Bodine portrayer Max
22 Fought dirty
24 Poet translated by Ciardi
25 Irritate, with "on"
29 Look of disdain
31 Article written by Cervantes
32 Nielsen stats
34 Popular cruise port
35 Uncertainties
36 Celi in "Thunderball"
37 Country singer Milsap
39 Stage Magic, to Justify
40 Tolkien creature
42 Replace an ace
43 Ocean State sch.
44 Eye-popping paintings
46 Merchandise
47 Like rainbows
49 Low man at the Met
51 Call at camp
52 Directional ending
53 Runs on
58 Part of an OK
59 Garnish request
61 Harass visually
62 FrieslandCampina product
63 No way, old way
64 Observes

DOWN

1 Speed of sound
2 Skin moisturizer
3 "___ never work!"
4 Dudley Do-Right's gal
5 GMO fare
6 Turn informant
7 Eroded, with "away"
8 Helen of "The Queen"
9 Heavyweight Holyfield
10 Ward of "Sisters"
11 Deadly African snake
12 Queen Mary, for one
13 1980 Lily Tomlin film
14 Deals with
23 Curve shape
24 Like the aroma of a bakery, informally
25 Where caps are thrown
26 ATC coverage area
27 Reactor
28 "___ There Was You"
30 Cork's country
33 High-energy snack
38 2019 Miss America Franklin
41 Hack's service
42 ACLU concern: Abbr.
45 Attack verbally
48 Fruity-smelling compound
50 Elbow room
52 Members of the flock
54 "Just ___ deoch an doris . . .": Lauder
55 Evens the score
56 Canadian gas brand
57 British carbine
60 Bounty letters

71 THEMELESS by Harvey Estes

38 Across was once home to over 1,100 islands.

ACROSS

1 Area free from harassment
10 Harmful aspects
15 Beauty spot
16 Night watch
17 Worn out
18 Solar-treated material
19 Ready for press
20 Seesaw sitter of verse
21 Stuffed to the gills
22 Granada gentleman
24 New Haven alum
26 JFK info
27 "As ___ saying . . ."
31 Studebaker sports car
33 Make an embarrassed gesture
37 Half a lover's quarrel
38 One-time "Sea of Islands"
39 "Cosmicomics" author Calvino
41 Hook ally
42 Curtain materials
44 Result of a first workout
46 Clenched fist, e.g.
47 "The Kingfish" Long
48 Province east of NB
49 AOL, e.g.
51 TV host known for pranks
56 About
58 Karen Carpenter, for one
62 Kind of office
63 Labor leader Chavez
64 Inferior stuff, in slang
66 Act badly
67 Like jewels in scabbards
68 Force units
69 Search targets

DOWN

1 Acts skittish
2 TNT alternative
3 Get along
4 Muse for Millay
5 2005 Prince hit
6 Jewelless crown
7 Malt beverages
8 Mrs. Dithers of "Blondie"
9 Come next
10 Hard to nail down
11 "Livin' la ___ Loca": Ricky Martin
12 Jim Croce song
13 First Amendment quintet
14 Trips without wheels
23 Light into
25 Pakistani metropolis
28 Reducing concerns
29 Flight ht.
30 Big hit
32 Grp. or org.
33 Like action films
34 Harley Quinn, to Batman
35 Acts foolishly
36 Novelist Wiesel
40 Reed or Rawls
43 École employees
45 Kind of teeth
50 Caressed like a collie
52 Dalai Lama's traditional seat
53 Ill-mannered oafs
54 Show host
55 Cries out for
57 Peter on "Six Feet Under"
59 Capp hyena
60 White lie, sometimes
61 Creole veggie
65 Deli hero

AQUARIANS* **by Jean Peterson**
Traits: Progressive, original, independent, humanitarian.

ACROSS

1 "Sabre Dance" composer Khachaturian
5 Lady's love
10 Native Canadian
14 Pale-green moth
15 Onetime Van Halen lead singer
16 Take a few days off
17 Lake Tahoe lift
18 Become hardened to
19 A big fan of
20 "Girl on Fire" singer*
22 Typical high schooler
23 Abstain from
24 Texas longhorn
26 Obtains justly
29 Sudden charge
32 David Muir's network
35 Get in touch with
37 Usher's beat
38 He had a lion's lines
40 Vermont product
42 Argento in "Marie Antoinette"
43 Had a brain freeze
45 Golden
47 Giant with 511 homers
48 Cuban Missile ___
50 Flower
52 Whale tracker
54 Annoying sounds
58 Rock pioneer Perkins

60 "Blue Bloods" star*
63 "___ Ben Adhem"
64 Itinerary
65 Rochon in "Waiting to Exhale"
66 Subgroup
67 Indignation
68 Coup d' ___
69 Sommer in "Jenny's War"
70 Insecticide targets
71 Learning method

DOWN

1 Union station?
2 Russian coin
3 Diarist Nin
4 "Peanuts" girl with glasses
5 West End houses
6 What privates never pull?
7 Flu symptom
8 "The Bells of St. ___" (1945)
9 Magician's cry
10 Standards
11 "Get Shorty" star*
12 East, to Celia Cruz
13 Public school near Windsor Castle
21 River in Austria
25 Wife of Alfonso XIII
27 "Glee" star Rivera
28 Cancel a launch
30 Cufflink's spot

31 2006 NBA champs
32 Le Carré spy Leamas
33 Mueller report reviewer
34 "Down to Earth" star*
36 Pitch
39 Determined
41 Trailblazers
44 Deafening noise
46 Put in the fridge
49 Petty despot
51 "Chug-A-Lug" singer Roger
53 "Nightline" creator Arledge
55 Look after
56 Renown
57 Oceanic ray
58 Beer buy

59 "Green Mansions" hero
61 Cups with slogans
62 Proofer's "never mind"

73 PISCEANS* by Jean Peterson
Traits: Compassionate, artistic, intuitive, wise, musical.

ACROSS

1 Break off suddenly
5 Tsarist edict
10 Spreadsheet unit
14 Going rate?
15 Vivid yellow
16 Jai ___
17 "The Times They ___-Changin' ": Dylan
18 Rainbow fish
19 ___-flam
20 "Forrest Gump" star*
22 Cheese you can crumble
23 Admire
24 Shakespearean forest
26 "Put your hands up!"
29 Pinched
32 Hide ___ hair
35 Beefer
37 Empty-headed
38 Over
40 Elsie the Cow's hubby
42 Spengler played by Harold Ramis
43 Skimpy skirts
45 Crest containers
47 Culbertson of bridge
48 Hollow replies
50 AMC model in "Cars 2"
52 "___ jolly swagman . . ."
54 Scenes of action
58 Rob in "Killing Kennedy"
60 "The Voice" coach*
63 "Dies ___ " (funeral hymn)
64 Locker room item
65 "Picnic" playwright
66 "It Must Be Him" singer
67 Slowly wear away, as a cliff face
68 Word heard at an auction
69 Teaching degrees
70 Edited out
71 Nephew of Cain

DOWN

1 Part of a playhouse
2 Ephron and Charles
3 Warning that's often red
4 Golf legend Gary
5 Extreme
6 "Ol' Man River" composer
7 Mine, in Menton
8 "Semper Fidelis" composer
9 Registers
10 Excedrin ingredient
11 "Inception" star*
12 Café additive
13 South American capital
21 Escorts
25 Highway felony
27 Highland Scot
28 Shorten a skirt
30 Hydroxyl compound
31 Answer in the negative
32 Form request
33 Of the ear
34 "Frost/Nixon" director*
36 McEntire of country
39 Homesteaders
41 Looked back on
44 Blink of an eye
46 Like the Kalahari
49 At the table
51 Update
53 Slobber over
55 Curtain material
56 Part of WASP
57 Bird food
58 Parasitic pests
59 Toward the mouth
61 Gone from the company, in a sense
62 Persian of yore

74 ARIANS* by Jean Peterson
Traits: Courageous, confident, optimistic, honest, passionate.

ACROSS

1 Hail Mary, e.g.
5 Lively jazz tune
10 Desert formation
14 UAE belongs to it
15 Flynn who swashbuckled
16 Pandora's boxful
17 Mudslinger, maybe
18 Terra ___
19 Dele's negator
20 "Almost Famous" star*
22 Club or cream follower
23 Alex Trebek offering
24 Sandarac, e.g.
26 Sound of skepticism
29 Computer virus
32 Is holding
35 Stone pillar
37 Part of an X-ray machine
38 Sir Guinness
40 College classes
42 It's over a foot
43 Thin and graceful
45 Menus, essentially
47 Scots denial
48 Not us
50 Ferber's "Giant" ranch
52 Ganja smoker
54 Davidovich in "Hollywood Homicide"
58 Place for a token
60 "Noah" star*
63 1958 Leslie Caron movie
64 One of two in a typical string octet
65 Morales in "La Bamba"
66 12th grader, e.g.
67 Acid salt
68 Brown shade
69 Performed by a choir
70 It may be shorted at summer camp
71 Harper Lee's "Go ___ Watchman"

DOWN

1 "The Beer Barrel ___"
2 Like royal jelly
3 NYSE members
4 They have threads and heads
5 Type of deposit
6 Trampled
7 Bowser's breakfast
8 Moped feature
9 Venus namesake
10 Ethan Hunt's "impossible" tasks
11 "Your Song" singer*
12 Wintertime transportation
13 "The Thin Man" dog
21 She-lobsters
25 Lady of Spain: Abbr.
27 Poke around
28 Natural aptitude
30 Sarah McLachlan hit
31 Leakes of "Glee"
32 Toroidal shape
33 Made a touchdown?
34 "Steve Jobs" star*
36 Scots Gaelic
39 Card sharp's practice
41 Firm
44 49 endings
46 Athenian portico
49 Martin and McQueen
51 Modifies
53 Mennonite group
55 Magazine number
56 Best man's proposal
57 Baker or Loos
58 Pepper and Snorkel: Abbr.
59 "In ___ of flowers . . ."
61 Speck of dust
62 Not aweather

75 TAUREANS* by Jean Peterson
Traits: Reliable, patient, devoted, practical, stable.

ACROSS

1 Jam
5 Artificial jewelry
10 Hankering
14 Large moth
15 Dana of "MacGyver"
16 "The Phantom Tollbooth" hero
17 Prayerful approval
18 Brownish gray
19 Chinese border river
20 "Pulp Fiction" star*
22 Feds
23 Mideast desert
24 "America's Drive-In" chain
26 Bad tee shot
29 Get through trickery
32 Ecclesiastical deg.
35 Biblical matriarch
37 "Evita" subject
38 Next in line
40 Bob of "Surviving Suburbia"
42 Spanish surrealist
43 "The Age of Innocence" heroine
45 Blue state
47 Little lump
48 Croquet stick
50 Shakespearean actor Booth
52 Chiliad's 1,000
54 Chair's list
58 ___ vu
60 "Aquaman" star*
63 "Time" singer Tori
64 Did a deck job
65 Face with two hands
66 "Peter Pan" pirate
67 "Guitar Town" singer Steve
68 Summer camp setting
69 Clutched
70 Regard with awe
71 Fulda River tributary

DOWN

1 North Pole surname
2 Card game with melds
3 Lend ___ (heed)
4 Praying insect
5 Funnel-shaped flowers
6 Banned apple spray
7 Lowlife
8 Spanish snacks
9 Before, to bards
10 Dreamed up
11 "Cowboy in Me" singer*
12 Whodunit board game
13 Didgeridoo, for one
21 "The Merry Drinker" painter
25 Forty winks
27 Maryland menu item
28 Quarter bird
30 "Kinky Boots" drag queen
31 Oklahoma city
32 Noah's eldest son
33 Honduras seaport
34 "Allentown" singer*
36 Chief
39 Gave out for publication
41 Stymied
44 Org. that founded Poetry Out Loud
46 Breathe loudly
49 Sent to another team
51 Stylus
53 Smudge
55 Aquatic nymph
56 "Headlines" rapper
57 De Niro's drama coach
58 Sprint
59 Noted plus-size model
61 Without a stitch
62 Scat singer Fitzgerald

76 GEMINIS* by Jean Peterson
Traits: Gentle, affectionate, curious, adaptable.

ACROSS

1 "As it ___, it ain't": Carroll
5 Monastery head
10 Mideast gulf
14 What a caboose brings up
15 Subdue
16 Harley
17 H-hour, theatrically
18 Daughter of Helios
19 Trim down
20 Seven-time Wimbledon winner*
22 Greek goddess of wine
23 Schoolboy
24 Fulminates
26 Beyond help
31 In demand
34 Hour, in Firenze
35 "The Third Man Theme" composer Karas
37 Shopworn
38 Rebuke
40 Bar mixer
42 Devilish
43 Hale's ex-patriot
45 Potpourri scent
47 Testee's dream
48 Emphatic type
50 They hold bows when taking bows
52 Pakistani God
54 Geological period
55 Olivia in "Wayne's World 2"
57 "Fantastic Beasts" star*
63 ___-European languages
64 Knoll nymph
65 Mystery writer Drummond
66 Bowl over
67 Doodlebug, for one
68 Rowlands in "The Brink's Job"
69 "Gypsy Girl" painter
70 One to be respected
71 Composer Speaks

DOWN

1 Pension rollovers
2 Broken-off branch
3 ___ the Great (boy detective)
4 Triviality
5 Fender bender, e.g.
6 Enterprise detention area
7 "Hamilton" role
8 Award for "Green Book"
9 Lauren Bacall film
10 Behind the times
11 Cool jazzman*
12 Similar
13 Marlin and Coral's son
21 FDR's terrier
25 Y's transformation
26 Egyptian president Mubarak
27 End of Ripley's slogan
28 "Rush Rush" singer*
29 Convertiplane
30 ___ boom
32 "Adam Bede" novelist
33 Temple of Apollo site
36 Pale aqua
39 Puffs out
41 It opens in January
44 Naught
46 Weary by excess
49 Wheedle
51 Rainbow color
53 Hourly
55 Hollowware item
56 Rectangular pilaster
58 Puncher's bunch
59 Basilica area
60 Robert Craig Knievel
61 Cornbread
62 Appeal to

77 CANCERIANS* by Jean Peterson
Traits: Tenacious, imaginative, loyal, sympathetic, persuasive.

ACROSS

1 Trouser turnup
5 Poison oak, for one
10 Say with conviction
14 "___ Want to Do": Sugarland
15 Like one of the flock
16 Like black olives
17 Pulled thread
18 Whiz group
19 Make baby booties
20 "Misery" Oscar winner*
22 Fruit drinks
23 Irish dog
24 Téa in "Bad Boys"
26 Iditarod racers
29 Hot spot
32 Small portion
35 Bath buggies
37 Conspicuously chic
38 Screen fave
40 Hatred
42 Look for
43 Send payment
45 Haggard's Quatermain
47 Marvin in "The Dirty Dozen"
48 Courtroom schedule
50 Swiss mathematician (1707–83)
52 Bit of museum treasure
54 Sparta's rival
58 Satyrlike deity
60 "You're So Vain" singer*
63 Jim Davis dog
64 Prayer bones
65 Legal plea, briefly
66 Gaelic girl
67 Hawaiian island
68 Conductor Klemperer
69 Does some batiking
70 Kim's "Fifty Shades Darker" role
71 Ooze through

DOWN

1 Sherry barrels
2 Arm bones
3 Bluegrass partner of Scruggs
4 Scuffles
5 Poncho's hat
6 Eye layer containing the iris
7 In pristine condition
8 Conservationist Adams
9 Let up
10 Land of Opportunity
11 "Riddick" star*
12 Boy of Mayberry
13 Volstead Act opponents
21 Sound of distress
25 UK lexicon
27 Man Ray's art
28 Pleased look
30 Glenn of "The Walking Dead"
31 Young'un
32 Kookaburra, e.g.
33 Lead-in for graph or gram
34 "Edge of Tomorrow" star*
36 "Star Trek" chief navigator
39 Portraitist's goal
41 Kuala Lumpur's country
44 ___ Aviv
46 Barclays Center cagers
49 Cause to giggle
51 Heavy herbivores
53 Gondolier's locale
55 Get melodramatic
56 Nick in "Noah"
57 Buttinsky
58 Bend
59 "___ Without Rain": Enya
61 Lacoste of Lacoste
62 Almost fat-free

78 LEOS* by Jean Peterson
Traits: Creative, passionate, generous, warm-hearted, humorous.

ACROSS

1 Clothes consumer
5 Handbag holder
10 Brainless
14 Double Stuf cookie
15 "___ be next?"
16 "Of course!"
17 Monk's room
18 Circe's island
19 Matching
20 "Cloud Atlas" star*
22 Street fight
23 Condense on a surface
24 Part of a dovetail joint
26 Spot for a spare tire
29 Military decoration
32 Uris novel (with "The")
35 World's most wired city
37 Freetown coin
38 BPOE members
40 Crack of dawn
42 Dish with fish
43 Ecofriendly Seuss character
45 Roberts of "Fawlty Towers"
47 Mining explosive
48 November meteor shower
50 "Deathtrap" actor
52 Henry VIII's eight
54 Low mountain crests
58 Brewer's grain
60 "A Star Is Born" star*
63 Prima donna's song
64 Piano study piece
65 Pacific salmon
66 Budget item
67 Heeds the alarm
68 Tropical hardwood
69 "Raising Arizona" star
70 Babysitters, often
71 Ago, in a seasonal song

DOWN

1 Starbucks order
2 Knoll nymph
3 Poker giveaways
4 Adjective for bamboo
5 Tars
6 "How Do I Love ___?": Browning
7 Katy Perry song
8 Heads-up
9 Significant participant
10 Sheds duds
11 2008's "Fastest Man Alive"*
12 Office communiqué
13 Veggie in V8
21 Eventful time periods
25 Zero, in soccer
27 Whiskey ___
28 He works on pianos
30 King's "Faithful" coauthor
31 Cauldron beastie
32 ___ or high water
33 Skin-soothing additive
34 Hogwarts School architect*
36 French moon
39 Clean
41 Unrivaled
44 Louis ___ ("the Sun King")
46 Apt anagram of vile
49 Most of Libya
51 Commands
53 "Trois Gnossiennes" composer
55 Like caramel sauce
56 Allen at Ticonderoga
57 Feed the fire
58 Alaimo of "Star Trek: DS9"
59 Region
61 Guiding spirit
62 Fall garden?

79 VIRGOS* by Jean Peterson
Traits: Loyal, analytical, kind, hardworking, practical.

ACROSS

1 Biting quality
5 Absolute minimum
10 Cradle grain
14 Online person
15 View from the Himalayas
16 She plays Harry's friend Hermione
17 Kunis of "Jupiter Ascending"
18 Knot on a trunk
19 Full of oneself
20 "Frida" star*
22 Viking crematory
23 L.A. clock setting
24 Andalucía address
26 Potent potable
31 Signal
34 "What ___ to do?"
35 Big name in computer chips
37 Malty black tea
38 Formal affair
40 Altar boy?
42 To be, in Latin class
43 Was all leers
45 Adams exhibited at MoMA
47 Bull Halsey's org.
48 Shark's hitchhiker
50 Watched a Netflix flick
52 Surprising political move
54 Spanish national hero
55 Venetian evening
57 "NCIS" star*
63 Maine Coon sound
64 Eric Trump's mother
65 Wife of Charlie Chaplin
66 Towards the mouth
67 Totally consumed
68 Fateful March date
69 Stocking stuffers
70 Wintry glaze
71 Graded item

DOWN

1 Mylanta rival
2 Mother of Prometheus
3 Mrs. Chester A. Arthur
4 Dad's dad
5 Photographer's concern
6 City in Sicily
7 "___ in the Life": Beatles
8 WinStar Farm breeders
9 Had a heart-to-heart
10 Knee-jerk ___
11 "Beautiful Creatures" star*
12 Siberian river
13 Google cofounder
21 A spot of bubbling wine
25 Teachers' union
26 September honoree
27 JPEG file content
28 "Groundhog Day" star*
29 Another, in Aragon
30 The Strip lights
32 Cannes cup
33 Improve upon
36 In need of a map, maybe
39 Aerobics attire
41 Shopkeeper
44 Joanne in "Red River"
46 Jabba the Hutt's captive
49 Units in the board game Risk
51 Nimble
53 Maritime
55 The Munsters' pet
56 Monaco money
58 Interest factor
59 Dandling joint
60 Customary usage
61 Aces
62 Anti-Greeley cartoonist

80 LIBRAS* by Jean Peterson
Traits: Cooperative, diplomatic, gracious, fair-minded, social.

ACROSS
1 Pear variety
5 Kirsten in "Spider-Man"
10 Egg drinks
14 Norse deity who defeated Thor
15 Emulate Gable and Lombard
16 Without delay, for short
17 Seaweed extract
18 Running mate of 2008
19 "Daily Bruin" publisher
20 "Hit the Road Jack" singer*
22 Sumos throw it
23 Roman household diety
24 Haggadah reading time
26 Truly grand
31 Cash register part
34 "Deep Space Nine" changeling
35 Greek slave
37 Of some purpose
38 1939 Garland costar
40 "Blues Queen" Washington
42 Scarlett O'Hara's daughter
43 Building wing
45 Range units
47 Decline
48 Like cookie dough
50 Unable to cope
52 Facilitated
54 Get the point
55 Engine puff
57 "The Book of Henry" star*
63 Indian queen

64 "Rich Man, Poor Man" novelist Shaw
65 Opie's aunt
66 Switch or buck add-on
67 Smart-___ (wise guy)
68 Fail to name
69 Teller's partner
70 Islands veranda
71 Hurricane handle

DOWN
1 Tough test, informally
2 Olympian Korbut
3 Dispatch a dragon
4 Compass creation
5 Took leave
6 Suffix for mod
7 Winning coach of Super Bowl X
8 Operatives
9 Stiffened
10 Sicken
11 "Lady Windermere's Fan" playwright*
12 Vex
13 Row
21 Day-after dish
25 R&B group ___ Hill
26 Elephant tooth
27 Hersey bell town
28 Strawberry Fields dedicatee*
29 Mother of Romulus
30 Triton's trumpet
32 Immigration Museum island
33 Harvests

36 Allowance for waste
39 Tie-in
41 Capital of Finland
44 Handwritten kisses
46 Emulate Etna
49 Renunciation
51 Arm-twist
53 Child actress Hood
55 Attend Exeter
56 Interlaken river
58 Wilson in "The Darjeeling Limited"
59 Flaky mineral
60 Tony Musante cop show
61 Cut fat
62 Fill to the brim

81 SCORPIOS* by Jean Peterson
Traits: Resourceful, brave, passionate, stubborn, loyal.

ACROSS

1 Weeps audibly
5 Rapper's entourage
10 November 13, e.g.
14 Cruel storybook character
15 "Neapolitan Novels" author Ferrante
16 Homophone of 38 Across
17 Appreciate a performance
18 Apple processor
19 Valentine's Day matchmaker
20 "Somebody Like You" singer
22 Torres of "Suits"
23 Trial by fire
24 Stonewashed fabric
26 Clichéd
29 Names seen on Smithsonian walls
32 Yellowstone bugler
35 Alfalfa's gal
37 Ducksoo Palace site
38 Potatoes go-with
40 Early violin cousin
42 Ian Fleming villain
43 The I of IV
45 Bar Mitzvah scroll
47 Really big shoe
48 Tiers
50 Carl Kahler's "My ___ Lovers"
52 Certain button
54 Melee
58 "Mr. Guitar" Atkins
60 Jefferson Airplane lead*
63 Mata of espionage
64 Painter Matisse
65 Nastase of tennis
66 Memo heading
67 Nomadic buffalo hunter
68 Pheasant brood
69 Forks over
70 Errant golf shot
71 90° on the compass

DOWN

1 Terrific, in "Variety"
2 Unwanted observer
3 Hair twist
4 Singing group
5 Funny
6 Genus of whistling swans
7 Belgrade citizen
8 Ben Hogan rival
9 ERA leader
10 Dreamed up
11 "Very Good Girls" star*
12 College founded in 1440
13 Word repeated in a Doris Day song
21 Unlike a gut course
25 Discouraging words
27 Tare's relative at the weigh station
28 Plumbing pipe
30 Old Norse character
31 Tart jam flavor
32 Napoleon biographer Ludwig
33 Capp's ___ the Hyena
34 "Roar" singer*
36 Atmosphere: Comb. form
39 Peace compacts
41 5-hour Energy ingredient
44 Prince Valiant's son
46 Embroidered possessive
49 They're worth seeing
51 IV solution
53 Angler's accessory
55 Eyelashes
56 Etchers' needs
57 Shotgun sport
58 Snack in a bag
59 Mandlikova of the court
61 Histamine opener
62 Spongy shoe

SAGITTARIANS* by Jean Peterson
Traits: Generous, idealistic, friendly, energetic, open, sincere.

ACROSS

1 Jakarta's island
5 Harmonica parts
10 Show keepsake
14 "Shake ___!"
15 Page of "Inception"
16 Spot for studs
17 Rooney in "Mary Magdalene"
18 Hawaii's ___ Kea
19 Word with rule or pricing
20 "Night at the Museum" star*
22 Bit of pepper
23 Respectful term in Japan
24 Sire
26 Nonplus
31 Bratislava river
34 Alternative to a 401K
35 If it breaks, things get wet
37 Georgia's Lake ___ Thurmond
38 Buds
40 "The Silence of the Lambs" director
42 Uppish one
43 Hermione Granger's Patronus
45 Not street smart
47 Nautical heading
48 Sandy Koufax was a great one
50 Ready ahead of time
52 Drive forward
54 ___ Tin Tin

55 Pianist von Alpenheim
57 "Wrecking Ball" singer*
63 "Buddenbrooks" novelist
64 Attach a codicil
65 Remove from office
66 "Without ___" (Grateful Dead album)
67 Where Elsa was born free
68 Hawaiian honker
69 "___ who?"
70 Susan Sontag piece
71 Toponymic cheese

DOWN

1 What a door is in
2 Wings
3 "Trading Spaces" designer Yip
4 Andre of tennis
5 Jogged the memory
6 Lod Airport carrier
7 Jewish month
8 Star in Cygnus
9 Caught in a trap
10 Dorm dwellers
11 "Proud Mary" singer*
12 Author of "The Haj"
13 "Little Women" woman
21 Like Tacko Fall
25 Furnace fuel
26 Two-legged stand
27 Muse of poets

28 Mickey Mouse's first voice*
29 Equivalent
30 Update an atlas
32 "Moody River" singer
33 Firmly fix
36 VIP of UAE
39 Bits and pieces
41 Buddy Holly hit
44 Dem. rival
46 "Lawrence of Arabia," for one
49 Updated version
51 "Do I have a volunteer?"
53 Gimlet fruits
55 "Look at me, ___ helpless . . ."
56 Smallville girl
58 Capture on film
59 "Orinoco Flow" singer
60 Deeply regretted
61 J. McCain's alma mater
62 Pipe part

83 CAPRICORNS*   by Jean Peterson
Traits: Ambitious, persistent, realistic, sensitive, disciplined.

ACROSS

1 Liquid asset
5 Big bargain
10 Enterprise-D android
14 Pot chip
15 One who cries "uncle"
16 Birds raised for food
17 Marquee name
18 Perfume base
19 Combat vehicle
20 4-time Masters winner*
22 Mallard genus
23 Dictionary thumb-guide
24 Favor, in slang
26 Vote-winning group
31 McDonald's clown
34 Conductor de Waart
35 Acted human
37 Home on the range
38 "Fantastic Mr. Fox" author
40 Treated to a night out
42 Target of a bang-up job?
43 Veep elected in 1968
45 Toss, as confetti
47 It starts in juin
48 Accounts book
50 Genealogist's concern
52 Avidly accept
54 "General Hospital" network
55 "___ It Romantic?"
57 "Changes" singer*
63 Pew locale
64 Obliterate
65 Cedar home?
66 Unrestrained
67 Yellow finch
68 Morning star's locale
69 Boater's blades
70 Romantic rendezvous
71 Blackthorn fruit

DOWN

1 Dramatis personae
2 2016 Rihanna album
3 Male caribou
4 "From ___ Eternity" (1953)
5 Winter Floridian
6 Newcastle novice
7 Architect Saarinen
8 Low-pH liquids
9 Landlord
10 Held back
11 "Brockmire" star*
12 Sushi fish
13 Quotes, as a price
21 Like a super blood wolf moon
25 Subdivision part
26 Winner's award
27 "Crime doesn't pay," e.g.
28 "Rocky Mountain High" singer*
29 Speaker at Cooperstown
30 Busybody
32 Slow, at the Met
33 Scare off
36 Bruce in "The Cowboys"
39 Will subjects
41 Hedonistic
44 Freshly painted
46 "Up, Up and Away" composer
49 Most churlish
51 Scottish biscuits
53 Carrot cleaner
55 Airport desk offering
56 Ramirez of "Grey's Anatomy"
58 Fluctuate
59 Tut's fertility goddess
60 Prosperity
61 Childish retort
62 Kitchen annex

84 THEMELESS by Victor Fleming
45 Across is illegal in some countries, although serious injuries are rare.

ACROSS

1 Water, facetiously
9 Exams for future DA's
14 Immobilized
15 Humorous term for a cigar
17 EEG oscillation
18 Alley of song?
19 Stern counterpart
20 "___ Sutra"
22 BFG in "The BFG"
23 Dr. Seuss classic
26 Merrie Melodies Martian
29 Gain a lap
30 First name in diarists
31 Frizzle
33 Park vehicle
37 Recreational angling
40 Major add-on
41 Lyft alternative
42 Like "Sleep No More"
43 Enfant terrible
44 Most minimal
45 Rock concert craze after a stage dive
51 Souvenir of the past
52 Legal start
53 New mortgage deal, briefly
57 "Soon . . ."
59 Poison-free
61 The rest, to Caesar
62 Prince Harry and Meghan, e.g.
63 Hospital divisions
64 Pert and Prell

DOWN

1 BOLO and ATL
2 Downsizing plan
3 Poker money
4 Don Johnson series
5 Shoat's mom
6 Luke and Leia's father
7 "Roots" star Burton
8 Swell condition?
9 Permit
10 Thin as a rail
11 Becker of "L.A. Law"
12 November gem
13 "Alphabet City" star Vincent
16 Not taken in by
21 Aziz of "Master of None"
24 Moorish idol, for one
25 Bridgestone product
26 Nutmeg spice
27 Henry Gray's subj.
28 "Round and Round" group
31 Buy quickly
32 Nonprofit online course provider
33 Pressure source
34 Seldom encountered
35 Caveat on eBay
36 Track and field competition
38 Cash sources
39 Pastrami preference
43 Checkpoint request
44 "Kiss Me Kate" sister
45 Swamp creature, for short
46 Extend a note
47 "Get Here" singer Adams
48 Dentist's request
49 Wives of rajahs
50 Lather
54 Mitsubishi model
55 Greek pastry
56 Cold desserts
58 ___ in yak
60 Cat's pa

85 THEMELESS by Victor Fleming
Re: 7 Down, Vic once left one reading: "Next time leave me a can opener!"

ACROSS
1 Gaslight era carriage
7 In silence
15 Mustang-like
16 Some Western Europeans
17 Streamlet
18 Regardless of
19 Relapse
21 Hummingbird hums
22 Mutton ___
23 Walkie-talkie button
24 Light remark during a black moment
29 "The Mill on the Floss" author
30 TaylorMade club
31 Query
34 NBA alum Yao
35 Support the economy
37 Side by side?
38 Waited in the waiting room
39 Furnish with a lining
40 Pass bills
41 Marketing goal
44 Berlin bride
46 The Supreme Court, e.g.
47 Key partner
48 Klutzy mea culpa
52 "Tell them you did it!" response
54 Paste in a can
55 Hit with a fine
56 Comes up
57 Comes prior to
58 Find a new lead

DOWN
1 Savory, e.g.
2 Pastel shade
3 Now, for Cicero
4 Need for a plumber
5 Single attempt
6 Full-flavored
7 Memos seen on parked cars
8 Instrument with metal keys
9 Dreaming phenomenon
10 Taps a reserve
11 More supple
12 Dine cheaply
13 McCarthy era figure?
14 Pre-1991 republics: Abbr.
20 Tape recorder speed: Abbr.
24 Don't throw these stones
25 Shawkat of "Arrested Development"
26 Pocket fuzz
27 Burial receptacle
28 Chic, in the '60s
31 Subject of the film "Delta Blues" (with 35-D)
32 Faith-based offshoot
33 "Roar" singer Perry
35 See 31 Down
36 Attach, in a way
37 Like Henry Gray's textbook
39 De Vil in "101 Dalmatians"
40 Overgrown weed lot, e.g.
41 Lyricist's product

42 Take off the top
43 GM tracking service
44 Less
45 Reims royal
47 Lou Gehrig's mentor Wally
48 Get through, but slowly
49 Tabula ___
50 Some map nos.
51 Royals manager Ned
53 Lousy egg?

CELESTIAL TRAVELERS by Gene Newman
"Stupid is as stupid does." — 26 Down

ACROSS

1 M&M's inventor
5 Senior NCO
9 Gags
14 Burr, to Princeton
15 Pack tightly
16 Release
17 George W. Bush vis-à-vis John Roberts
19 "Rush Rush" singer Abdul
20 Nasal partitions
21 Keats subject
22 Drive forward
23 Hasten
25 Chariot horses
26 "Wow!"
29 Perlman in "Hellboy"
30 Cambodian currency
31 Father of the Titans
33 Makes filthy
37 Oscar winner Sorvino
38 Planter fill
40 "Blame It on the Bossa ___"
41 Moon shadow
43 Spanish English
45 Candidate's goal
46 Crime-lab evidence
47 Half a fly
48 "La Traviata" heroine
51 Clear reasoning
53 Pelvic artery
54 Poker table note
55 Goddess of love
59 Niger-Congo language group
60 Between a genus and a species
62 Middle East chieftan
63 Wight, e.g.
64 Russian news agendy
65 Chemist who discovered isotopes
66 Abound
67 Latin Amer. ladies

DOWN

1 "The Rich ___ Wife" (1996)
2 "Wake Me Up" singer Blacc
3 Between the loin and the round
4 Mormon Church founder
5 Wharton School deg.
6 Former GM subsidiary
7 Magnificence
8 Gull's cousin
9 Tiger Woods' island
10 Cloisonné technique
11 Dimwit
12 Like some shower floors
13 Elite Navy group
18 Tiny republic in Micronesia
24 Rhododendron
25 Sounding wistful
26 Winston Groom character
27 Clinton's canal
28 Come by
30 Like Hank Aaron's no.
32 Sickened
33 Bikini part
34 Shed
35 First lady's namesakes
36 MS submittal need
39 Gumby creator Clokey
42 Quicksilver
44 Ingenuous
46 Two-bagger
48 Aura
49 "Remember the ___!"
50 Hit sharply to left field
51 Cootie
52 Coins almost all zinc
54 Denver's "___ Love?"
56 At hand
57 "Superman II" villainess
58 Impudence
61 Baguette

87 CONFUSION REIGNS by Gene Newman

In spite of the fact Sheena rides one, the clue at 53 Across is true.

ACROSS

1 Diplomacy
5 "Frozen" snowman
9 Rowing team
14 Nautical marker
15 Cover a dice bet
16 Tennis score
17 Dumbfounded
19 Prefix for structure
20 Puffy pastries
21 Mallet golf club
22 Culminate
23 "___ Fly With Me"
24 Beach
28 ___-color pasta
29 Country singer McEntire
33 Kool-Aid holders
34 Pechora's mountains
35 Prince Valiant's son
36 At sixes and sevens
40 Rickenbacker, for one
41 Runyon's markers
42 Mertens of tennis
43 Captures
45 Cicero's lang.
46 Swoons
47 Surveyor's map
49 "It's Raining ___" (1982 hit)
50 Mine danger
53 What zebras aren't
58 Swiftly
59 Confused
60 Pine product
61 "The Kite Runner" boy
62 Seedy bar
63 Kefauver of 1950s politics
64 Blue Lagoon and Bath
65 Kind of doctor

DOWN

1 Dosage: Abbr.
2 Prefix for pilot
3 Sudden takeover
4 Here's an exemple
5 Exit point on a diving board
6 Land-rich Scot
7 Summer quaffs
8 Did a zoo job
9 Aversion
10 Snap specialist
11 Milkweed coma
12 0.405 hectares
13 Expensive
18 In spite of that
21 Battle of Verdun defender
23 Complains
24 Borne chair
25 ___-baked potato
26 Corrective button
27 Circumference part
28 Piscine rainbow
30 Cancel the cookout
31 Treaty of ___-Litovsk
32 4,300-mile range
34 "Das Boot" vessel
37 La Scala city
38 Was off kilter
39 It means "champion" in Arabic
44 Coins
46 Longest human bones
48 Claims on property
49 Group pledged to omertà
50 Geneva-based welfare org.
51 Barbary residents
52 Enormous
53 Office fill-in
54 Does the math
55 Short crisp sound
56 Moses' grandfather
57 Adam's apple spot
59 Liberal arts awards

HISTORIC SIEGE   by Gene Newman
A monument commemorating 20 Across is in Colonial National Historical Park.

ACROSS

1 Sky one to the outfield
5 Pleasant or crazy
10 Merino mommies
14 Having cast off
15 Being home to certain vines
16 A jack or a tom
17 Lowland or highland
18 Hired enforcers
19 24 Across, e.g.
20 Siege site of 1781
22 Medieval language
23 GI sacks
24 Where Tiberius died
26 Talkative flyers
29 It makes the heart grow fonder
32 Prefix for mentioned
33 Out of the ballpark
35 Zounds alternative
36 Cannes cocktail
37 General who accepted the sword of surrender at 20-A
40 Ship hauler
41 White-tailed eagles
43 Evaluate
44 Heeded the alarm
46 Returns to square one
48 Courtesy car
49 Some Pennsylvania Dutch
50 Starbucks espresso drink size
51 Pie-eyed
53 Victorious battalion commander at 20-A
57 Equestrian sport
58 Where "Aïda" premiered
60 Roused from sleep
61 Artemis, to Apollo
62 Nash who wrote "A Word to Husbands"
63 Biblical animal namer
64 Freelancer's encl.
65 Missing necessities
66 Walk-the-dog toy

DOWN

1 Of delicate construction
2 "Hedda Gabler" setting
3 Four Freedoms subject
4 Rail carrier
5 Prejudiced ones
6 Takes an oath
7 Stuffed Tour de France animal
8 Sadie Hawkins Day catches
9 What a "zebra" steps off: Abbr.
10 Einstein was a famous one
11 Victor at 20-A
12 "A-Tisket, A-Tasket" singer
13 Appear

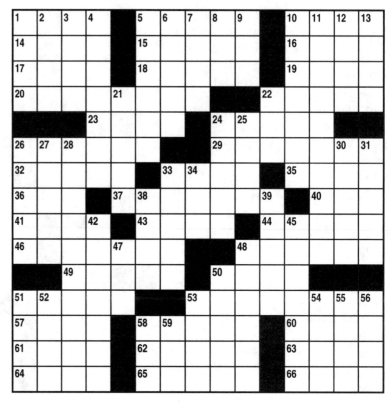

21 Terrycloth accessory
22 Saturn's wife
24 Lightweight vessel
25 Son of 63 Across
26 Creator
27 Greatly excited
28 General defeated at 20-A
30 Effectuate
31 Lawn tool
33 Grind
34 Columbus Day mo.
38 Annoys
39 Scott in "Aladdin"
42 Indefinite person
45 Scenic transport
47 Do away with
48 Arizona fruits
50 Challenged
51 Makes a pick
52 Tall Corn State
53 Camouflage
54 Fuss and feathers
55 "It's a deal"
56 Animated clownfish
58 Joint tenant
59 Balsamic vinegar price factor

"ZIP-A-DEE-DOO-DAH" by Gene Newman
Gene was waiting in line at the post office when this theme came to him.

ACROSS

1 It's a long story
5 It passes the bucks
8 "No Country for ___" (2007)
14 A certain age
15 Film noir classic of 1950
16 Fool's gold
17 They're no longer useful (also SD 57732)
19 "I Go to ___": Peter & Gordon
20 Prominent
21 Superlative for the Nile
22 Accounts receivable (also MT 59101)
24 Inquire
27 African scourge source
28 Blood bank abbr.
31 Because of
33 Monte Cristo, e.g. (also MA 02563)
36 Concurred
38 Seance event
39 Perfect place (also MI 49768)
42 Weltschmerz
43 Attempt
44 Ra or Sol
47 Covenant receptacle
48 Dealing partner (also WV 26003)
50 Strategic withdrawal
53 Life jacket
58 City torched by Xerxes
59 Water main cleaning (also NY11351)
60 Charming, e.g.
61 Risk taken on an outcome
62 ". . . ___ saw Elba"
63 Grammar studies
64 Japanese statesman
65 EPA's sister org.

DOWN

1 Caesar and Vicious
2 Code type
3 Objective
4 "You ___": Lady Gaga
5 Mortal lover of Aphrodite
6 Play the flute
7 Like Jekyll
8 Rival
9 Supine
10 Bottom of the barrel contents
11 Mickey and Minnie, e.g.
12 Vacation times in Versailles
13 Follows machine gun or love
18 Like the platypus
21 Only child of Elvis
23 Sgts. salute them
24 Go with the flow
25 Marilyn's role in "Some Like it Hot"
26 Tralee's county
28 Feather, e.g.
29 Happen
30 Arab chieftain
32 Rose type
34 Searches deeply
35 Ashen
37 Maladies
40 Bird feeder content
41 An 8×10, briefly
45 Gin drink
46 Using cruise control, for short
48 Old World warblers
49 Therefore
50 Wholly absorbed
51 Bordeaux being
52 Like some alibis
54 A question of timing
55 Cliffs of Moher locale
56 Ko-Ko's dagger
57 Payday cry
59 Dillinger's nemesis

90 YE OLDE WORDS I*   by John M. Samson

Trumpeters and trombonists know 11 Down in a different sense.

ACROSS

1 Feathery neckwear
5 "Pogo" setting
10 Michelle's mother
14 Line on a Swiss map
15 Sword of Damocles
16 Caesar's love
17 Grammy winner for "Believe"
18 Spurious wing
19 Way up a hill
20 Farmer*
22 A dog's age
23 Publican's place
24 Jacket worn by Sammy Davis Jr.
26 Holiday
31 Retreats
34 Orinoco tributary
35 Lake Titicaca's backdrop
37 Taj of blues
38 Job privilege
40 Hopscotch hoppers
42 Slatch
43 Ran its course
45 Works in the cutting room
47 Aussie bush bounder
48 Aunt Polly's charge
50 Vociferous
52 Jennifer Saunders sitcom
54 Odysseus' rescuer
55 Billboard award
57 Scoundrel*
63 Frog genus
64 Gideons' gift
65 Con ___ (with vigor)
66 State emphatically
67 Acquire (debt)
68 Lanky
69 Political district
70 Ocean motions
71 Lighten

DOWN

1 "Fiddle Fugue" composer
2 "Hawaii Five-O" setting
3 Aphrodite's consort
4 Novak Djokovic's homeland
5 Crossing over
6 Join metal to metal
7 Jack-in-the-pulpit family
8 Brera Palace site
9 Airmada members
10 Nurturing
11 River mouth*
12 Stallion shade
13 Boots one
21 Stage org.
25 Breakfast meat
26 Puffs on an e-cigarette
27 Bradley Center, e.g.
28 Shoemaker*
29 Drooling comic canine
30 Squares
32 Owl's weapon
33 Parcel out
36 Jacket feature
39 Computer peripheral
41 They walk the line
44 Rock's ___ Leppard
46 Lilt
49 Chinese zodiac animal
51 Binary
53 Russian crepes
55 Jay's stomach
56 Flowing rock
58 Multiple choice choices
59 Sherlock's find
60 Field
61 River inlets
62 Cooked through

YE OLDE WORDS II*   by John M. Samson
34 Down is usually partnered with "fire."

ACROSS

1 Super Bowl LIII winners
5 Kane in "Pearl"
10 Mumtaz Mahal's tomb site
14 "___ a Kick Out of You"
15 De la Garza of "Beyond Borders"
16 Nice Nellie
17 Brasil '66 singer Hall
18 Restore
19 Seine-et-___
20 Pharmacist*
22 Pirate known to Wendy
23 Pasture barriers
24 Partitions, as in fruits
26 "___ la vista, baby!"
29 Hall-of-Fame pitcher Fingers
32 2013 Kentucky Derby winner
35 Emmy winner Gibbons
37 Black tea called orange
38 Bitter
40 Item in a bank
42 Place for a cooling pie
43 "In the doghouse" is one
45 Himalayan antelope
47 Marshal at Waterloo
48 Two in 1,000,000?
50 Spanish port
52 "The Crucible" town
54 Unfathomable thing
58 Baryshnikov, by birth
60 Giraffe*
63 Buck chaser
64 Small African antelope
65 Nike rival
66 Outfielder's call
67 Drapery fabric
68 Novelist Hostovsky
69 Honey bunch
70 Active
71 Floor model

DOWN

1 Armenian rice dish
2 With a dropped jaw
3 Part of a dovetail
4 Saver of nine
5 Fondled
6 A Baldwin brother
7 Bullfrog genus
8 Rare birds
9 Grisham's Mitch McDeere, e.g.
10 Last Supper attendees
11 Cat*
12 Stand up
13 "The African Queen" screenwriter
21 Recuperate
25 Taylor Swift's music
27 Social gatherings
28 Nahuatl speaker
30 Archery prize of Heracles
31 Hard to grasp
32 Of the ear
33 Swiss watch name
34 Sulfur*
36 Mystique
39 Marinara ingredients
41 Adriana Lima's profession
44 Bad start?
46 Souse
49 Jackie Robinson's base
51 Went quickly
53 Novelist Puzo
55 Calibrate
56 1983 Michael Keaton film
57 Literary town that needed a bell
58 Meek creature
59 Canal of song
61 Diminutive
62 Black

YE OLDE WORDS III* by John M. Samson
Lou Gehrig and Alan Ameche were nicknamed 11 Down.

ACROSS

1 "Diary of ___ Housewife" (1970)
5 Ryan on "Sons of Anarchy"
10 Under the weather
14 Barn topper
15 Wahine ta-ta
16 Islands on the Arafura
17 Goldie's "Laugh-In" costar
18 Like an oboe's sound
19 Poly preceder
20 Rascal*
22 Literary tidbits
23 El Greco's city
24 Jewish appetizer
26 Sweet orange
29 Battalion members
32 Romano on "Mad Men"
35 Excellence
37 Part of some purses
38 1960s orbiting chimp
40 Moves skyward
42 Argento in "Marie Antoinette"
43 Blacksmith's tool
45 Like a Stan Lee film appearance
47 Summer hrs. in CT
48 Totter
50 Stimulate the economy
52 Winter fisherman's drill
54 Annette's "Bikini Beach" role

58 "___ Loves Mambo"
60 Clothing*
63 Mesmerized
64 Well-worn words
65 Miranda in "I, Frankenstein"
66 Behold amorously
67 Foal fathers
68 Prom goer
69 Calls the bet
70 Soupçons
71 Types a typo

DOWN

1 Corsair's call
2 ___ Polo
3 Conductor Dorati
4 Dig more
5 Bachelor party aftermath
6 Suffix for gland
7 Italian landscapist
8 Crude cabin
9 It's a gift
10 City on Florida's Gulf Coast
11 Steam locomotive*
12 Beverage choice
13 "Fallin' " singer
21 Red-coated cheese
25 Its job is taxing
27 Schmidt of Google
28 Hartman and Bonet
30 Coughed up
31 Quarrel
32 Usher
33 Queen of 1,000 days
34 Tomato*

36 Day-to-day employee
39 Puts in place
41 Like 26 Across
44 Drumstick
46 Coldplay's "___ Love"
49 Beat a dead horse
51 Break
53 Diameter halves
55 Get in the way of
56 Stage direction
57 Berkshire jackets
58 Champions Tour members
59 Opera singer Haugland
61 Rural structure
62 "When ___ Home": Beatles

YE OLDE WORDS IV*   **by John M. Samson**
60 Across is a stock commedia dell'arte character.

ACROSS

1 Vinegar is a mild one
5 "Dynasty" actress Emma
10 Word for Homer's works
14 Green Hornet's valet
15 Like sandalwood
16 Tenderfoot
17 Muslim republic
18 Casa grande
19 Catchall abbr.
20 Red-hot iron*
22 Flightless bird of Chile
23 Like booty
24 Musical repetition mark
26 Kitchen lady of song
29 New Orleans team
32 Ninny
35 Speeder's nemesis
37 Cordwood measure
38 Splinter group
40 Wrack and ruin
42 Nieuwport river
43 Phillips who played Neelix
45 Employee reading
47 Mount a diamond
48 Made things right
50 Mailing list items
52 Rick Nelson's dad
54 Squash must
58 Marchmill of "Wessex Tales"
60 Cowardly buffoon*

63 Last word from Rhett Butler
64 Wished (for)
65 Disney lion queen
66 Antioxidant berry
67 Spokescow since 1938
68 Sparkle
69 Suvari in "American Beauty"
70 Sunflower edibles
71 Suffice

DOWN

1 Parts of SWAK
2 Gemologist's weight
3 Fashion designer Zucchelli
4 Huey Duck's uncle
5 Georgia's oldest city
6 Z ___ zebra
7 Salsa option
8 Maned lions
9 Entangled
10 Forever and a day
11 Female soothsayer*
12 "Dies ___" (hymn)
13 Designated driver's drink
21 Israeli premier (1969–74)
25 Reason for a pit stop
27 Driver in "The Last Jedi"
28 Place of refuge

30 Tire swing support
31 Rockefeller Center muralist
32 No longer docked
33 Badger's burrow
34 Scholastic*
36 Trevi Fountain locale
39 Kenya neighbor
41 Allies
44 Pince-___ glasses
46 Coal stratum
49 Some chinaware
51 Brunch biscuits
53 French school
55 ___ Lumpur, Malaysia
56 Great applause
57 Scottish clan chief
58 Netherlands cheese

59 Alençon specialty
61 Cathedral section
62 Tara in "The Big Lebowski"

94 STATES OF MATTER by Emma Avery

5 Down's stage name is a portmanteau of his first and last birth names.

ACROSS

1 To-do list item
5 iTunes purchase
10 Many an iPhone app
14 When to hear "Aaron Burr, Sir"
15 Like some cannons
16 Live a nomadic life
17 Track event
18 Meted out medicine
19 Part of AKA
20 Outmoded TV choice
23 Big name in car repair
24 Flip-flop
27 Teamsters president
31 Sorta kin
33 Letters that make you lose sleep
36 Great spot to build a house
39 Plains tribe
41 Polite turndown
42 Tandoor-baked flatbread
43 Eco-taxed cars
46 Mrs. in Mexico
47 Jarrett of Fox News
48 Ford heir
50 Big name in modern astronomy
53 "Hinterland" setting
57 They're easily cashed in
61 Durango domicile
64 Betting option
65 Harry Potter's Patronus
66 Opposed, in Dogpatch
67 "Knock ___!"
68 Shout heard in tag
69 Top-notch
70 Facebook comments
71 Popular seafood of Tokyo

DOWN

1 Busch Gardens city
2 Amtrak speedster
3 Geyser output
4 Many tourist-trap buys
5 Clear+Vivid podcaster
6 "Gigi" playwright
7 Anjou relative
8 Geek squad customers
9 Mythological sorceress
10 Doted-on relative
11 MSN alternative
12 More, in Mexicali
13 Music with angst
21 Bossy remarks?
22 Part of DOE
25 Seaside shades
26 Like the Sea of Serenity
28 Sitcom dude in a black leather jacket
29 Letters on a soft drink can
30 Airline seat request
32 Pulitzer Prize–winning Ferber
33 Rapper Snoop
34 House in "Game of Thrones"
35 "Move along, nothing ___ here!"
37 Gave up the ghost
38 Pound warnings
40 Fried veggie
44 Tangelo relative
45 Stitches up
49 Rin Tin Tin rival
51 Accouter
52 Make a dash for
54 "Please, I insist!"
55 Cyber Monday commerce
56 Some NCOs
58 Knot-tying words
59 Not clumsy
60 Pound sounds
61 Uber alternative
62 Time of your life
63 007's org.

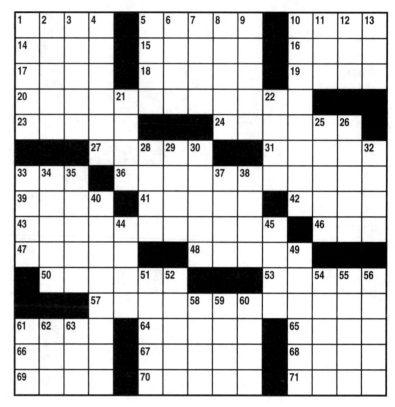

INSIDE MEASUREMENTS by Emma Avery
25 Across was once home to a saloon built by Wyatt Earp.

ACROSS

1 Course in a bowl
5 Hamlet's soliloquy starter
9 No Oscar winners, these
13 Part of the choir
15 Met highlight
16 First name at Tesla
17 Out-of-stock certificates
19 "Five-O" nickname
20 Union founded by George Meany
21 Stay in a game of musical chairs
22 Work on a bone
23 Mortar holders
25 Iditarod destination
27 With a bit of whimsy
32 Ramone's wife in "Cars"
34 "As ___ on TV"
35 Major artery
36 Clark and Acuff
38 A "look at me" walk
41 Singer Stefani
42 Musical reeds
44 Like Nash's lama
46 Final finish
47 It has many peaks and valleys
51 Limits for politicians
52 In ___ (bogged down)
53 Villain in "The Lion King"
56 LAPD alert
58 It's dropped and weighed
62 Chicago mayor Lightfoot
63 Original idea
65 Give a nudge
66 They carry a charge
67 Gabler of fiction
68 Early road runners
69 Dow Jones stats: Abbr.
70 Odd conclusion?

DOWN

1 "Nobody doesn't like ___ Lee"
2 Snoopy's misfit brother
3 One of Monopoly's two: Abbr.
4 Rainy day wear
5 Word with bo or kwon do
6 Tolkien brutes
7 ___ Bottom (SpongeBob's city)
8 Sheena of song
9 Mrs. Tiggy-Winkle, for one
10 Rickman of "Harry Potter" films
11 Lisa in the Louvre
12 Winter coat
14 Some old Toyotas
18 Dodgers great Gil
24 Feeder fodder
26 Old Elton John label
27 "Here's ___, Mrs. Robinson . . ."
28 "The Crooked E" company
29 "Desert Fox" Rommel
30 Some seasons on the Seine
31 Philosopher Immanuel
32 Email header
33 Gray wolf
37 They're on the lookout
39 Donald Duck, to Huey
40 See 55 Down
43 ___ Anne de Beaupré
45 SpaceX event
48 Oil-rich peninsula
49 Ad-lib comedy
50 Hankered for
53 Speak like a sot
54 Apple detritus
55 Affleck thriller set in 40 Down
57 Word in a Jim Parsons sitcom title
59 Half a kid-hunting game
60 Ye ___ Tea Shoppe
61 Food label specs: Abbr.
64 NASA budget item

1 Down was originally called "Peppo" to compete with Dr Pepper.

ACROSS

1 Free ride
5 They have handles
10 Begin to cure
14 "Oh, sure!"
15 Where living is high
16 Tabloid fodder
17 Morning soap opera?
20 Securer of locks
21 It shows ownership
22 Ducky color?
23 First Bond film
25 Unfavorable review of the pasta?
30 It's hair-raising
32 Pedigree competitor
33 "This ___ test"
34 Bargain bin letters
35 Vampire teeth
37 Exhausting trip
38 Part of UNLV
39 Hospital helper
40 Tractor handle
41 Slogan in the busy bakery?
45 "What ___ around comes around"
46 Got off at the ranch
47 It may smell like a rose
50 Casualties of global warming
54 Something all herbalists must learn?
57 Castilian canape
58 Former SeaWorld orca
59 Of an important period
60 Greek warrior
61 "Cinq Grimaces" composer
62 Quite ordinary

DOWN

1 Mr. of soft drinks
2 Start of a spell
3 One with a vision?
4 Track officials
5 Meryl's was golden in "The Post"
6 Fab Four member
7 It's heard in the Highlands
8 Henrietta, NY campus
9 Parisian possessive
10 20 minutes of hockey
11 A way out
12 Shuffle follow-up
13 Speck in the sea
18 Nancy Drew pseudonym
19 Lab burners
23 Pull along
24 Sleep phenomena
25 Analyze grammatically
26 Guy Fieri hangout
27 Given the gate
28 Software buyer
29 Como, for instance
30 Corn tuft
31 Word on some Ocean Spray products

35 Mayberry deputy
36 They're often about nothing
37 Links appointments
39 Hold precious
40 Do a runway job
42 Brightly-colored lizards
43 Sub meat
44 Biblical blight
47 "___ girl!"
48 "___ she blows!"
49 Use a keyboard
50 Swarm member
51 Gateway Arch's Saarinen
52 Genetic strands
53 D-Day town
55 Editor's stack: Abbr.
56 "Gotcha!"

LITERARY ORPHANS* by Pam Klawitter

27 Across and moon pies were a popular workingman's lunch in the 1950s South.

ACROSS

1 Shore scavenger
5 "Dude!"
8 Part of NPR
13 Mother of Prometheus
14 It's often compared to golf balls
15 Yankee candle asset
16 Sherilyn of "S.W.A.T."
17 Craving
18 Tiny bits
19 Nine-fingered ringbearer*
22 Work on a popsicle
23 Jenna and Barbara, to Jeb
27 Pepsi alternative
30 "Absolutely!"
32 Current concern
33 "The boy who lived"*
35 Blue Jays, on scoreboards
36 Touch, for one
37 Half of a corny variety show
38 "___ boy!"
39 "ASAP!"
40 Bosom friend of Diana Barry*
44 Most common point value in Scrabble
45 Queen dowager of Jordan
46 They're fire proof
47 "Gossip Girl" girl
49 PDI ___-Hands
50 He lived with aunts Spiker and Sponge*
56 "E! News" figure
59 Home of Iowa State
60 Spanish capital
61 Gabrielle of volleyball
62 Dispatched
63 Ballpark stats
64 Streisand film
65 Tandem number
66 Looks both ways?

DOWN

1 Fishing hook
2 One with a password
3 De Niro's "Shark Tale" role
4 Flat minder
5 Onetime Israeli PM Ehud
6 Diana of "Game of Thrones"
7 Russian skater Protopopov
8 Cascade peak
9 Got up
10 Stipple
11 "___ little teapot . . ."
12 Western alliance letters
14 Often stolen car item
20 Greasy
21 Memo words
24 Stock purchase?
25 He who acts badly?
26 Attacks, skunklike
27 Endangered grazers
28 1920s rival of O'Bannion
29 Braggart
30 Use the tiller
31 Chief Ouray's tribe
34 "That's terrible!"
38 Settlers
40 Lee who lived by the sea
41 Author Chomsky
42 San Simeon family
43 "___ Angel" (Mae West film)
48 Kick out
49 Court reporter
51 Wicked Witch of the ___
52 Saw-billed duck
53 London underground
54 Sandusky's lake
55 "The Hunger Games" director
56 Faith Hill album
57 Width for Bigfoot
58 Cariou in "About Schmidt"

98 MEDICAL MISGIVING by Linda Gould
If laughter is the best medicine, then why do people die laughing?

ACROSS

1 Dallas cagers
5 Some sculptures
10 Partly open
14 Home to billions
15 Jamaican sorcery
16 Akebono's sport
17 **Medical misgiving: Part 1**
20 Strike back
21 Miniscule
22 Pluto, for one
23 Emulated Jack Horner
24 Hero of a Virgil epic
28 USA, in Ryder Cup play
30 Almighty in "Evan Almighty"
33 Pelvic artery
34 Kitchen scraps
35 "The Way We ___" (1973)
36 **Medical misgiving: Part 2**
39 Where to get the scores
40 On Easy Street
41 Hackneyed
42 Bengal mascot Who ___
43 Be without
44 "You're welcome, Miguel!"
45 Cry out loud
46 Round Table knight
47 End position of a winner
50 Besmirches
56 **Medical misgiving: Part 3**
58 Paul in "The Good Earth"
59 ___ Cologne
60 Villainess from Krypton
61 Meat loaf serving
62 Bare-bones displays
63 Math subj.

DOWN

1 Bryn ___ College
2 Arthur ___ Courage Award
3 Hanoi citizen
4 Capital of Yemen
5 Some are heavenly
6 WW2 Atlantic menace
7 Zen, for one
8 "The Help" director Taylor
9 Movie channel
10 No liability
11 Evita's husband
12 Adams and Schumer
13 Like cheeks in cold weather
18 Wool-bearing mammal
19 Make orange juice
23 Freelancer's enc.
24 Looked through the crosshairs
25 Knox in "The Mummy's Tomb"
26 With a chill in the air
27 Deserve
28 Halloween choice
29 Aquatint
30 "Angie" star Davis
31 Echo, for one
32 "The Gift of the Magi" heroine
34 Auricular
35 Aptly named NYC sports radio station
37 Disagreeable one
38 Spain and Portugal
43 Rich source
44 Transplant patients
45 Respectful address in colonial India
46 Pete's wife on "Mad Men"
47 "Present ___!"
48 Semi load
49 European volcano
50 Russian royalty, once
51 Sea-green
52 Annoyingly self-confident
53 Put to work
54 "Happiness is a quick-starting car" sloganeer
55 Pillow cover
57 "Toy Story" dino

99 RICE GUYS FINISH LAST by Harvey Estes
. . . with apologies to a Houston team.

ACROSS

1 Elephant king
6 Fraternal address
10 Ems and Baden-Baden
14 Kate's sitcom companion
15 Top-flight
16 Rick's old flame
17 Fender bender close calls?
19 Brest milk
20 UNC is in it
21 Auction stipulation
22 Très chic
24 "De-Lovely" star Kevin
26 Key in again
27 White elephant, e.g.
29 Humongous
30 Roof problem
31 Inadvertent witnesses
35 Chalky white
36 Like Swiss cheese
37 Suffix in pathology
38 Rupture
40 Stadium portal
41 Heavy volumes
42 "Fight Fiercely, Harvard" songwriter
44 Zany trio
47 Arno bridge
48 "You got it, bro!"
49 Cattle encourager
50 Society page figure
53 Gulf leader
54 How the Battle of Barnet was fought?
57 Major at Little Bighorn
58 Auction site
59 Atkinson in "Bean"
60 Cut calories
61 Wags
62 Comics orphan

DOWN

1 Silents star Theda
2 Meg's "Prelude to a Kiss" costar
3 Ban from a group
4 Volleyball center
5 Sit tight
6 "One O'Clock Jump" composer
7 Antarctic sea
8 Hydrocarbon ending
9 "Don't worry"
10 Miranda Warning entitlement, e.g.?
11 Mole, maybe
12 Stage comment
13 Deity with goat's feet
18 "Ignorance ___ excuse"
23 Magritte or Russo
25 Ultimate ultimatum?
26 Out of bed
27 Swiss mounts
28 Jump up
29 Strong winds
31 Vatican VIPs
32 Intimidate without a sound
33 Remembrance of Dracula
34 River near Dunkirk
36 Domestic beer?
39 Like some lunch orders
42 Stolen goods
43 "Bewitched" mother
44 McCarthy's trunkmate
45 "My Cousin Vinny" actress
46 Put in your two cent's worth
47 Emulates raptors
49 Pre-coll. exam
51 Morales of "Bad Boys"
52 Nota ___
55 Sci-fi contemporary of Ani
56 Bryce Dallas Howard's dad

BAR NONE by Erik Agard
Lateral symmetry and a tricky theme highlight this Marylander's challenger.

ACROSS

1 Gin mixer
6 Fine mist
11 Johnny who threw for the Colts
13 Horse house
14 Tackled a job
16 Some are bottled
17 Listened in on
19 Hawaiian hand gesture
22 Cube root of XXVII
23 Boston Dynamics creation
27 Kalahari stopover
28 ASME members
29 Blown away
30 In the uppermost echelon
31 T. Gabbard's party
32 Group with a bass named Bass
33 Sch. near Monticello
34 It's banned in Central Park
37 Comedian DeLaria
38 Melodic format in Indian music
40 Like tableside Cristal
41 Any ___ in a storm
42 Ultra sound?
44 Hard to come by
46 President from Plains*
50 Angela Davis goal found in clue* answers
56 Rihanna's nickname
57 Winnow down
58 Gaffe to avoid
59 A. Laffer, for one
60 Magritte and Lalique
61 Mas who baa
62 Belt
63 Part of GPS
64 Impetuous

DOWN

1 Subtle pull
2 Alabama island near Florida
3 Baby bug
4 Lifter's admission
5 Mantel pieces*
6 Band of gold*
7 FDR granted 3,687
8 Stats for 18 Down
9 ___-metal (rock genre)
10 Bobbing fist, in ASL
12 "Sprechen ___ Deutsch?"
13 Hot tub
15 Checked for fit
16 Earthshaking
18 2009 World Series MVP Matsui
19 French nuns
20 Turkish candy
21 Crumbly Italian cheese
24 University in Waco
25 ___ manual
26 Mexican beer
35 One in black
36 Snuggles up
39 Inverse math function
41 Half a couple
43 ___ Te Ching
45 Charlottetown's prov.
47 Cuts costs
48 Piano key wood
49 Junctions
50 Veep picker
51 It's part of PR
52 Metaphor for strength
53 Big Sioux River state
54 Bulk of a Michigan bankroll
55 Snack

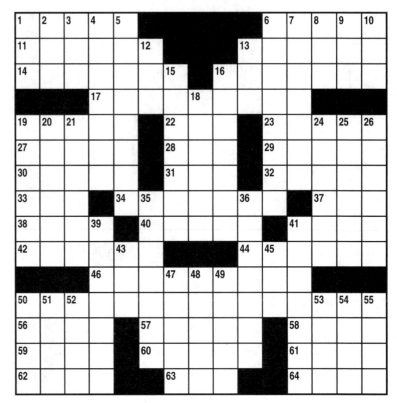

101 X MARKS THE SPOT   by Erik Agard

There's a buried treasure under these X's. Start digging DOWN!

ACROSS

1 Pagan religion
6 Is, pro tempore
12 Man of Rio
13 African expanse
14 Small ripple
16 "Let's do this!"
17 Four Corners state
18 Tested for fit
19 Yoga accessory
20 Guitars, slangily
22 Kia compact SUV
23 Skeptical remark
25 Things to mind
28 "Star Wars" baddies
29 Deli meat
31 Golden Gloves sport
33 "___ a Hole": Beatles
37 Solidified (with "up")
39 Burn a burger
41 Pygmalion's love
44 Idris in "Thor"
45 Headquarters
46 Egress
49 Husky, for one
50 Onslaught
53 Trapdoor hider
56 "Oh yeah? Watch me!"
57 Some viruses
58 Untapped
59 Malnourished
60 Black suit
61 Scrumptious

DOWN

1 Advice for a lobster lover
2 Ask along for
3 Word in café names
4 Four Corners st.
5 Pepsi Center, for one
6 "Spine tingle"
7 ESPN anchor Champion
8 "Case closed"
9 R&B Grammy winner Raphael
10 Passions
11 Decline
12 Turbaned sages
15 Playground game
16 "The coast is clear"
21 Colombian guerrilla group
24 Even if, briefly
26 Amongst
27 Nothing
29 Bad mood
30 Accept
32 "___ tree falls in the forest . . ."
34 NASA lunar discovery
35 Big event for Jack Hughes in 2019
36 "Precious" star Sidibe
38 Like a March hare
40 Frayed and worn
41 Tank top
42 Godmother of Tupac Shakur
43 Was inclined?
45 Posts bond
47 Nimoy's "___ Not Spock"
48 Facet
51 ___ Reader
52 A ton
54 Jazz legend Fitzgerald
55 Leathercraft tools

THEMELESS   by Alyssa Brooke
5 Down is derived partly from a vegetable that begins with a Z.

ACROSS
1 Hell of a guy?
10 Leftover
15 Bond's field
16 Drawing in brown
17 Green lights
18 Defeatist phrase
19 Did a med nurse's job
20 Stock page abbr.
22 Fin change
23 Chap
26 Plumbs the depths
28 Prepare for a sales pitch
33 Deep inside
35 Army volunteers, for example
37 Messing around the "Will & Grace" set
38 Hoosier Bayh
39 Uncomplaining
41 Bay in SW Oregon
42 Certain ball wear
44 Pitched poorly
46 "Judgment at Nuremberg" star
48 Ceased
49 Good with one's hands
51 "___ Antonio Rose"
52 RDU guesstimates
53 Press for payment
55 Native American abode
60 Supermodel Evangelista
62 "Step back!"
65 It makes all stops
66 Cloakroom sights
67 Opposing force
68 Gold Cup entrant

DOWN
1 Wampum unit
2 Bruin nickname
3 "Shooter" star Omar
4 Former Capri currency
5 Vegetable strips that resemble pasta
6 Pt. of SASE
7 Ovine entreaty
8 Rough on the eyes
9 Outdoes
10 CBS forensic drama
11 Gets back together
12 Ambulatory
13 Ristorante soup
14 Ball clubs
21 "And how!"
24 Hill builders
25 Caused by
27 Deutschland article
28 Appears
29 Like some American in Paris?
30 Movie starring Jennifer Beals
31 Worthless thing
32 Like a new parent
34 Let up
36 Internet destinations
40 ___ Nostra
43 Roadside warning sign
45 Credit Karma's sector
47 Jar part
50 Literacy volunteer, e.g.
52 Fanning in "3 Generations"
54 Chevy of yore
56 Switch attachment
57 Nectar flavor
58 Bolts down
59 Highland dialect
61 One of the Khans
63 Gumshoe, for short
64 Ancient pol. entity

103 THEMELESS by Alyssa Brooke

The raft at 1 Down was named in honor of the Inca god Viracocha.

ACROSS

1 Making designer genes?
11 Summer hire
15 Shirley Temple Black was one
16 Blue hue
17 Honor Garbo's request?
18 Songwriter Bacharach
19 Matching
20 Dana of "The Sting"
22 Rhine feeder
23 Not digital
26 Moor drama from the Bard
28 Dorothy's visit to Oz, e.g.
31 Sup at home
32 Contradicted
36 Come up with
37 Dodge of old
38 Combined
40 Some lifesavers
41 High-protein seed
43 Give a new value to
45 Fingerboard ridges
46 Wolf's warning
47 Most lean and sinewy
49 "Who cares?"
54 Former RR regulator
55 Pockets
58 Green target
59 Place of honor
61 Orderly
64 Enlightened about
65 Amtrak accident
66 "Let me count the ___"
67 Stemware for 007's martinis?

DOWN

1 Kon-Tiki wood
2 Clarification starter
3 Sotomayor's nominator
4 Czech chief Vaclav
5 Wall St. group
6 Country of Ft. Sumter
7 Crinkly cabbage
8 Matinee figure
9 Corporal or sergeant
10 Like Johnson's Society
11 Bar bill
12 Opportunity to respond
13 Diego Rivera and others
14 Isabella or Anne Bass, e.g.
21 Onetime Korean president
24 "___ bodkins!"
25 Quest object
27 Icicle supports
29 Berliner's article
30 Gild the lily
32 Type of abandoned spouse
33 Revolutionary War maps, e.g.
34 Old urban area
35 Al Capone's "Enforcer"
36 They're beloved
39 Three R's supporter
42 "That makes sense"
44 Roadside warning sign
46 "Kramer vs. Kramer" Oscar winner
48 Imploded Las Vegas casino
50 Impact sounds
51 Optimists have high ones
52 Dress shape
53 Big tops
56 Word before "a soul"
57 Hartford Insurance symbol
60 It's tapped out in desperation
62 Feel badly
63 P. Hearst's abductors

104 THEMELESS by Betty Lopez

Ctrl+Alt+Del is one keyboard combo to 1 Across.

ACROSS

1 Shut down a problem app
10 Frame again
15 Under
16 Give the slip
17 Pains in the neck
18 Our planet, in sci-fi tales
19 Night-school subj.
20 Radical '60s org.
21 Verbal bully
23 Leaves for a drink
24 Doing a "shake 'n' bake" move
25 Where you sip by the sidewalks
28 Servant of Dios
29 Rd. service providers
30 Regulation
31 It's passed in revivals
32 Romantic interludes
34 Berkshire institution
35 Tear producer
37 Wallach and Whitney
38 Along the back
40 Joke that can go either way?
41 Gnu feature
42 Carp relative
43 Come and go
45 Cried like a kitten
46 Pharmacy solution
48 Jennings of "Jeopardy!" fame
49 Indian bean tree
50 Broadbent in "Iris"
51 India's smallest state
54 Dress shape
55 Grocery providers for the needy
58 Leases digs
59 Apple with a bite taken out, e.g.
60 Kind of rehearsal
61 Madrid maidens

DOWN

1 Civil punishment
2 The heavens, to Atlas
3 Fencing piece
4 Dollar divs.
5 Strikes out
6 Lecture follow-up
7 Dad's bros
8 Frozen dessert
9 Tried out
10 Made a grand sound grander
11 Decathlon division
12 Emergency imposition
13 Shot for severe allergic reactions
14 Quelled a riot
22 Exposure to public view
23 Troubled times, often
24 Exhaustion
25 It has your number
26 Telemarketing tool
27 Served with spinach
28 Kind of Pizza Hut pizza
31 Stay out of sight
33 Red Sea nation
36 Crew tool
39 Without guile
44 Basketweaving and such
45 Clubber
47 Beveled edges
48 Familiar address
50 Folk singer Baez
51 Summer pest
52 Creole veggie
53 Sets a price
56 Vein hope
57 Montreal mate

THEMELESS by Betty Lopez
Lawrence is the birth name of 61 Across, but no one ever called him that.

ACROSS

1 Makes a wake on a lake
5 "El Condor ___": Simon & Garfunkel
9 UFO
14 Alarm hater
16 Cocoon creator
17 Back in the day
18 ". . . rained many ___": Shak.
19 Babies of the '90s and '00s
21 Put a halt to
22 Green center
23 Some are human
25 Galápagos lizards
29 Scuffle
30 Paternal mates
31 Walk stiffly
33 Get wind of
35 Man of Oman
37 Wintry road hazard
39 Charles portrayer Scott
40 Michael of "The Cider House Rules"
42 Insignificant individual
44 Letters of forensic dramas
45 Like a verdant field
47 China cabinet displays
49 Makes new alterations to
50 Butterfield of "Ender's Game"
51 That to Juan
52 It's good luck for all but the original owner
59 Hooded pullover
61 He caught Don Larsen's perfect game
62 Loren-Heston film
63 Coral reef, e.g.
64 Thelma in "Thelma & Louise"
65 Fill up
66 Throw in a salad bowl

DOWN

1 Smelting refuse
2 McKinnon of "Saturday Night Live"
3 Words after pass
4 Five Nations tribe
5 Rainy day sounds
6 Be that ___ may
7 Interstate rumbler
8 Mars, in combinations
9 Coats with crests
10 Stable staple
11 "Save the Whales" group
12 Elmer Gantry, e.g.
13 Where suburban kids play
15 They've been aired before
20 "The Enemy Within" network
24 Fraction of a meter
25 Apple Store purchase
26 White elephant purge
27 Wright-Patterson org.
28 Slightly blue
29 Shotgun sport
32 Kareem, orginally
34 Superman's love
36 ___ B'rith
38 Dissertation
41 "CHiPs" star
43 Elapse
46 Fed. benefits agency
48 Least risky
49 Fasten anew
53 Advantages of top seeds
54 Florida city, informally
55 "___ the Sun in the Morning"
56 "Here, ___ go?"
57 Vein contents
58 Highland hats
60 Folks

106 A HELLO TO ARMS by Harvey Estes
Harvey needed a concealed carry permit to construct this one.

ACROSS

1 Eight, in Essen
5 Ontario and Michigan
10 Moscow news agency
14 Gin fruit
15 Segal or Fromm
16 Black and white (or golden) cookie
17 Bono with an alluring lady?
20 Reserved
21 Manner of speech
22 Slangy one-eighty
23 Appomattox figure
24 Where we live
25 Wasn't completely honest
27 Plug up
29 Gallery objects
30 Autobahn auto
31 Courtly dance
33 The Pied Piper's tunes?
38 Blue "Yellow Submarine" cad
39 Commonly cited auth.
41 Courtroom VIPs
44 Competes
45 Gets the heck out of Dodge
47 Come by
49 Toothpaste style
50 Site for three men in a tub
51 Clarinets and flutes
52 Support for a ground force
55 Old Dominion's most friendly region?
58 Peekaboo words
59 Hot under the collar
60 "Hey, over here!"
61 Vegas sight
62 Doest preserve?
63 Are apparently

DOWN

1 Balaam's mount
2 Many selfies
3 Melon that sounds like a list
4 Caterpillar construction
5 Like many company cars
6 Nickname of a links legend
7 Scottish pirate
8 Pilate's "Behold!"
9 Library sound
10 Trunk without a lid
11 Fleet attack group
12 "Turn! Turn! Turn!" songwriter
13 Most angry
18 Lock manufacturer
19 Extra-rare, at the steak house
22 Radar anomaly
24 Homecoming figure
26 David Bowie's genre
27 "Done!"
28 "Glory in the Flower" playwright
31 Sub sinker
32 Former Russian despot
34 Make corrections
35 Paramount
36 Kind of
37 Make up
40 Govt. intelligence org.
41 "On the Origin of Species" author
42 Drill command
43 Quad predecessor
45 Skeleton in the closet, e.g.
46 Plug up
48 Pitchers
49 Southern dish
52 Pivoting shaver
53 Juan, in Moscow
54 The rich and famous
56 K-9 attack command
57 Long green dispenser

TALL TAIL   by Harvey Estes
This one is beyond the pail.

ACROSS

1 Comfy spot
5 Break protectors
10 Kamal in "Octopussy"
14 Track shape
15 Diary bit
16 Parrot in "Aladdin"
17 "Ach!"?
19 Barcelona boy
20 Pooh-poohs
21 Works in a soup kitchen
23 "What's ___ problem?"
24 "Hit the road!"
25 Layers of bricks
28 Unload
29 Brass, for one
30 Refs' decisions
31 Overdressed dude
34 Resign, with "down"
35 "On the Beach" author
36 Willing to take part
37 Burnt ___ crisp
38 "___ bells!"
39 Stage salesman
40 Gung-ho guy
42 Some train cars
43 Clinically clean
45 Requiring extra innings
46 Shady places
47 Humanitarian, to scoffers
51 Cold-blooded killer of flies
52 Get dumped?
54 Eurythmics' "Would ___ to You?"
55 Four pairs
56 Sherman Hemsley religious sitcom
57 Conduit bends
58 Takes a load off
59 Mailed out

DOWN

1 Turns on the waterworks
2 Pizzeria appliance
3 Get along
4 Basketball hoop play
5 Population count
6 Nobelist Sadat
7 Sports page number
8 Prefix with corn
9 Part of a word
10 Somewhat
11 Legendary winter storm?
12 Endora portrayer on "Bewitched"
13 Grafton's "N Is for ___"
18 O. Henry device
22 Pop singer Tori
24 Juice units
25 Crow's-nest site
26 Kind of sax
27 Surety money for a lowlife?
28 Tennis misstep
30 Sevigny in "Boys Don't Cry"
32 Epps of "House"
33 Ink dispensers
35 Fetches, in a sense
36 Venetian vessels
38 Bad ___ day
39 Rest atop
41 Breaks down
42 Finger and toe
43 Debussy contemporary Erik
44 Source of online conflict
45 Vacancy notice
47 Some Morse taps
48 Taj Mahal feature
49 Uniform
50 Patronize Alamo
53 Score on a serve

ACROSS

1 Symbol of Eire
5 "Midnight Cowboy" antihero
10 Fifth-year exams at Hogwarts
14 Genus of trumpeter swans
15 Wax eloquent
16 You, amongst Friends
17 46 calories (1 cup)
19 Fourth dimension
20 They come to terms for terms
21 Placed
23 Egypt (1961–71)
24 Leave open-mouthed
25 Rug treatment
29 Beverage
33 Runs
34 50-50 test guess
36 Leia's son Kylo
37 Mischievous ones
38 Walk proudly
39 "Beowulf" beverage
40 "___ Blu Dipinto di Blu"
41 Select group
42 Italian table wine
43 Enlarge
45 Made a hot impression on?
47 ___-Magnon
48 Unsure syllables
49 They're puzzling
53 Emulated Mme. Defarge
57 Junction point
58 6 calories (1 large)
60 Poe's raven, e.g.
61 Waikiki welcome
62 Tabula ___
63 Muralist friend of Dali
64 Osmond or Most
65 Ran

DOWN

1 Werewolf's call
2 Winged parts
3 Gets spoiled
4 Makes conjectures
5 "Creepshow" director
6 Trojan ally in the "Iliad"
7 Jazz guitarist Farlow
8 Quark's "DS9" cousin
9 Greek goddess of wine
10 City in Kansas or Ontario
11 79 calories (1 large slice)
12 Togo's chief port
13 Sought damages
18 Brings in at harvest time
22 Blanchett in "The Aviator"
25 David's weapon
26 Seascape master
27 114 calories (1 cup)
28 In many cases
29 Take a sounding
30 East, in Essen
31 Liberty
32 Drew to a close
35 Coach Parseghian
38 ___ Anne de Beaupré
39 Loves of teratophiles
41 Source of nuclear energy
42 Address in "Gunga Din"
44 Silvery
46 Airstrip
49 Nephew of Cain
50 Iditarod Trail city
51 "Take ___ song and make it better . . ."
52 1944 battle site
53 Madeline in "Paper Moon"
54 Pitfall
55 Language of Cork
56 Doublet
59 Howard or Perlman

109 CALORIE COUNTING II by John M. Samson
Four desserts are calorie-counted below.

ACROSS

1 Self-help program part
5 Put a handle on
10 Vodka brand
14 Desdemona's enemy
15 "Orfeo" is one
16 Black Rock architect Saarinen
17 256 calories (1 cup)
19 Pitcher with 5,714 lifetime strikeouts
20 Summer attire
21 "Golden Girl" Getty
23 Eden evictee
24 Hush-hush maritime org.
25 Affectionate salutation
29 Boxer with a grill
33 Kick out of school
34 "Ring My Bell" singer Ward
36 Summer in Nice
37 Org. for Lt. Columbo
38 Plastering pole
39 Sweat shops?
40 "___ be a monkey's uncle!"
41 Beach vacation souvenir
42 Buff
43 ___ trunk
45 Military builders
47 Gulager in "The Tall Man"
48 Julius Erving's nickname
49 Some sale sites
53 Calls the shots?
57 Blarney locale
58 401 calories (1 piece)
60 Virna in "Arabella"
61 Lionel Richie song
62 Sulky race
63 Military lights-out call
64 Like England's Coronation Chair
65 Brat's specialty

DOWN

1 Sasha and Malia, e.g.
2 Plantation near Twelve Oaks
3 Designer von Furstenberg
4 Like some sugar
5 Titled ones
6 Pongids, e.g.
7 Convened
8 "Harper's Bazaar" cover illustrator
9 Fortnight's fourteen
10 Pacific
11 450 calories (1 slice)
12 Face-to-face test
13 Solitary
18 Bellybutton
22 One third a 1970 epic war film
25 Sub stations
26 Place on a pedestal
27 228 calories (0.5 cup)
28 Snuffy Smith's child
29 Packs it in
30 Giant with 511 homers
31 "___ told by an idiot . . .": Shak.
32 Mudlarks have muddy ones
35 Without value
38 Haggard novel
39 All the king's men?
41 Quite pleased with oneself
42 Exercise handrail
44 "You Oughta Know" singer Morissette
46 Cofounder of GE
49 Hanukkah gift
50 Solo delivered at the Met
51 Nymph rejected by Narcissus
52 1975 home of four sports teams
53 Editor's notation
54 Buono of "The Sopranos"
55 Octagon stoppages
56 Gets firm
59 Large cervid

BEST PICTURE LINES   by Linda Gould
The line at 17 Across was spoken by Clint Eastwood in that Oscar-winning film.

ACROSS

1 Gander gender
5 ___ yokel
10 Urban brume
14 Erelong
15 Post of propriety
16 Sgt. Carter's nemesis
17 **"I seen the angel of death, he's got snake eyes."**
19 At a good distance
20 Home of Ford Field
21 Emulate Dürer
23 Shanghai's Jin ___ Tower
24 "Softly ___ Leave You"
25 "One of Us" singer Joan
29 Tom Swifty words
33 Computer invader
34 Don't dissent
36 Fill a flat
37 "Look at me, ___ helpless . . ."
38 Doll up
39 It's no anecdote
40 Election Day mo.
41 Mellow
42 Training student
43 Former friends
45 Church candle lighter
47 Falstaff's prince
48 Singer Grande, familiarly
49 Like Tiger's 2019 Masters play
53 Drudgery
57 West Virginia resource
58 **"Was that cannon fire, or is it my heart pounding?"**
60 Nightmarish boss
61 Water prefix
62 Come out even
63 Bulb measure
64 Düsseldorf neighbor
65 Lord High Everything ___

DOWN

1 Adams in "Octopussy"
2 Henry VIII's second/fourth wife
3 TriBeCa pad
4 Like Godzilla
5 Roman army unit
6 Leave on the editing room floor
7 Cicero's 104
8 Not windward
9 Redgrave in "Georgy Girl"
10 Thinly scattered
11 **"She's an owl, sickened by a few days of my sunshine."**
12 Fifth king of Norway
13 Richard in "Chicago"
18 Pride sounds
22 "I ___ at the office"
25 Like a jumbuck
26 "Biloxi Blues" playwright
27 **"Every man dies, not every man really lives."**
28 O.K. Corral brothers
29 The Dean Dome, e.g.
30 Room with comfy seating
31 Give rise to
32 MSU center
35 Scrabble two-pointer
38 Dessert often served a la mode
39 Emulate Pavlov's dog
41 Creek
42 Antigua essentially
44 Xylophonist's need
46 Atomic number 6
49 Boat that's towed
50 Roman raiment
51 What Aleve may relieve
52 Tampa Bay squad
53 Gross minus net
54 Blue dye
55 Tops a cinnamon roll
56 Haul aboard
59 Radical '60s org.

111 POMPEY'S PUN by Chris Carter

The joke below is old as the hills—all seven of them!

ACROSS

1 Spur-of-the-moment
5 Complains
10 Popular Hasbro dolls
14 Tennis name of fame
15 Start of a Neapolitan song
16 Doesn't give ___
17 **Start of a pun by Pompey**
19 Nest of pheasants
20 Weedy rye grass
21 Ristorante liqueur
23 Current flow measures
25 **More of pun**
26 Fragrant perennials
28 Lord Wimsey's creator
29 Spam, mostly
30 Album songs
32 Shot of Scotch
33 **More of pun**
36 DNA kit tool
38 Bath and Baden
39 Ecdysiast's prop
42 Trunk tires
44 Pinching pennies
47 **More of pun**
49 Large snake mackerel
50 Quandaries
52 Tax on commodities
53 "By the power vested ___ . . ."
54 **End of pun**
56 "Prayer for the Dying" singer
57 Like a land baron
58 Night, in Nantes
59 Recipe abbrs.
60 Rebellion of 1786
61 ___ buco (veal dish)

DOWN

1 Numbers yet to be crunched
2 Feeling such a fool
3 Himalayan guides
4 Marilu of "Taxi"
5 Join together
6 Peer Gynt's mom
7 Salazar in "Alita: Battle Angel"
8 Spruce Goose, e.g.
9 Yellow finches
10 Rochester's love
11 Sudan neighbor
12 October exam
13 Streaks
18 King mackerel
22 Köln or Nürnberg
24 "If I Ran the Zoo" author
27 Rome's Spanish ___
31 Despicable person
33 Blue Devils' rivals
34 Letter-shaped girder
35 "In my opinion . . ."
36 Thin strips
37 Where the world is flat?
39 Ill-humored
40 Founder of Olympic Airlines
41 Consent
42 Sicko
43 "The Lion King 2: ___ Pride" (1998)
45 1140, to Flavius
46 Quaker State mountains
48 Cabinet wood
51 "Ice Age" sabertooth
55 Asian automaker

112 DOWNBEAT by John M. Samson
The official elevation of 45 Across is 29,029 feet.

ACROSS

1 Dinner checks
5 Serve as helmsman
10 Eight: Comb. form
14 Four Corners corner
15 Toyota rival
16 "Eragon" storyteller
17 Elvis Presley film
19 Brontë's Jane
20 Without direction
21 Contest forms
23 It's a blast
24 Heyerdahl's ___-Tiki
25 Powder room?
29 Mooched
33 Wonder Woman's crown
34 Sackcloth and ___
36 Car song of 1964
37 Automaker Ransom
38 Caper
39 Horsehair
40 Beak
41 Africa's third-longest river
42 "Last of the Red Hot ___"
43 Brief
45 Highest mountain above sea level
47 "Don't ___ this at home"
48 Gerund suffix
49 Crafter
53 Magnify
57 Construct
58 Tales of woe
60 Lecher
61 "King of the Hill" beer
62 Guesstimates at SFO
63 "Book of ___": Confucius
64 Host holder
65 Poi ingredient

DOWN

1 Oompah-band instrument
2 Brother of Brynhild
3 Tin Man's creator
4 Homes for the homeless
5 It erupted in 1786
6 Ski lifts
7 She reigned in Spain
8 Uma's "Be Cool" role
9 Picnic spoiler
10 Uranus moon
11 Stephen Rea film (with "The")
12 Went like lightning
13 "Rag Mop" brothers
18 Auburn hair dye
22 Stats for Ivan Drago
25 Do community service
26 Upset
27 Unfortunately the case
28 "Tootsie" Oscar winner Jessica
29 Middle Earth region
30 Short chest muscle
31 Certain lab equipment, formerly
32 Archaic verb
35 Envelope abbr.
38 Small island
39 Elizabeth II's sister
41 Part of a vote tally
42 "Park" in Silicon Valley
44 Misdemeanors
46 "Mr. Lonely" singer
49 Hendrix hairdo
50 40 square rods
51 PDQ relative
52 Gaylord Ravenal's love
53 Carlisle Cullen's wife
54 Hayworth in "Salome"
55 Rig
56 Calgary's ___ Plaza
59 "Casey at the ___"

113 UPBEAT by John M. Samson
17 Across was designed by Harvey Ball in 1973.

ACROSS

1 Inkling
5 Emulated Rip
10 Run off
14 Sunshine Hydrox alternative
15 Churchill trademark
16 Hunter and Holm
17 Most popular emoticon
19 Rapier relative
20 Like prodigies
21 Chatty bird
23 Three cheers, perhaps
24 Theatre of Dublin
25 Make a meaningful connection
28 Soapstone, mostly
29 Hem and ___
32 High society
33 Treaded things
34 ___ trial basis
35 Squire-to-be
36 Churchly council
37 Hallway runners
38 Biblical verb ending
39 "Inception" director
40 Left Bank cap
41 Reason to serve again
42 Good War cards
43 Bother
44 Prickly shrub
46 Lowest in rank
47 "Strange Interlude" playwright
49 Court-martial candidate
53 "Freebie and the ___" (1974)
54 The Beau Brummels hit
56 Basic beliefs
57 Nutritionist Krieger
58 "Glory in the Flower" playwright
59 To be, in ancient Rome
60 No honor students they
61 LPGA golfer Hataoka

DOWN

1 Ball thrower
2 Madam in "The Balcony"
3 Diamond, for one
4 Permit
5 Grain cutter
6 "___ but a walking shadow . . .": Shak.
7 Falstaffian oath
8 War chest funder
9 Shook in fear
10 "Dog Day Afternoon" event
11 "Special" times at the bar
12 "Finally ___ know!"
13 Hosea, in the Douay Bible
18 Maternal relation
22 Alphabet
24 Homophone name of Erin
25 Fight off
26 Send sky-high
27 Sunny grins?
28 Brown and Turner
30 David Boreanaz series
31 Trifle away
33 10th President
36 Popularly termed
37 Check
39 Tenterhook
40 Roger Federer's birthplace
43 Talks (over)
45 Wash off
46 Aboveboard
47 Legitimate award
48 Highlands loch
49 Drab
50 Prickly pear
51 Hollandaise ingredients
52 Seehorn in "Better Call Saul"
55 Rio phone greeting

114 MEDITERRANEAN SHORES   by Layla E. Palmer
Asterisked clues relate to 50 Across.

ACROSS

1 Sullivan's was "really big"
5 Start of a notable palindrome
9 Staff at sea
13 Stag or stud
14 Don's family
16 Like a fire pit
17 Swan genus
18 Second course?
19 Sack attachment
20 Wandered off the path*
22 Gateway Arch architect Saarinen
23 Sweater letters
24 States of panic
26 Common carry-on
30 Pears for poaching
32 You find them in math class
33 Result of oversleeping
37 Watered-down
38 Yeltsin of Russia
39 You can see right through it
40 Outdoor airs
42 Big Apple cager
43 "Time ___ Time": Lauper
44 They can be twisted or turned
45 Judd of "Taxi"
48 Schooner contents
49 Getting the job done
50 Cradle of Western civilization
57 Wildly enthusiastic
58 "Hello" hitmaker
59 LSU tiger mascot
60 Who wrote that?: Abbr.
61 Wine variety
62 '60s TV sidekick
63 Socially clueless one
64 Half a dozen habaneros
65 Shipboard assents

DOWN

1 Urban cover
2 Sire of Sunday Silence
3 PayPal founder Musk
4 "If wishes ___ horses . . ."
5 Energizes the crowd
6 Soda-shop treats
7 Worshipper's spot
8 Dobrev of "The Vampire Diaries"
9 Sound off*
10 Ed in "Too Big to Fail"
11 Play nice
12 Key glitches?
15 They're the pits
21 "Boys for Pele" singer
25 IV units
26 Congressional output
27 Korean golfer ___ Song
28 Tree for a partridge
29 Commit oneself*
30 More like Godiva
31 Frequent Mayberry jail occupant
33 Find at the mine
34 Litchi nut feature
35 Paella ingredient
36 Sounds from a scolder
38 It gets wet while you get dry
41 NY Giants are in it
42 Joint with a cap
44 Strike sites
45 Hulk in the ring
46 Totally ridiculous
47 Demanding standard
48 Two-time loser to Ike
51 Ringing words?
52 Hockey fake-out
53 Watson in "Beauty and the Beast"
54 Breezy
55 Start of a carnival game
56 Cruz and Nugent

115 NEW BEGINNINGS by Layla E. Palmer
43 Down is also the name of a noted Paris fashion house.

ACROSS

1. Like molasses in January
5. "C'est la vie!"
9. Sounds of shock
14. Buono of "The Sopranos"
15. Strike out
16. Make confetti of
17. Aphorism that most put stock in?
20. "Scary" Spice Girl
21. Some are fine
22. Dethrones
23. Worried-sounding guitar part
24. Stroller pusher
25. Debatable factors of big-rig shipping?
32. FDR and JFK
33. Greek characters
34. Trim a tree
35. Tent furnishings
36. Hugh Laurie role
38. DC rejection
39. Squeeze out
40. Midi length
41. Barbecue spot
42. Cabinet chicanery?
46. Ballad endings
47. Meadow musings
48. Wasn't well
50. PC key
51. Pop-up nuisances
54. Online destination for loners?
57. Ridiculous
58. "___ goes to the runner"
59. Ratted on
60. Colorful cardinals
61. Big Apple letters
62. Hook sycophant

DOWN

1. Ponzi scheme
2. Work on the docks
3. Viva voce
4. Wit
5. Smitten one
6. Bequeathed
7. Some handouts
8. Home to many schools
9. Coffee dregs
10. Alveolus
11. Rotisserie part
12. Calls' companions
13. Undercover guy
18. O.K. Corral brothers
19. Erin Moran TV role
23. Dovetails
24. Yup opposites
25. Command to a police dog
26. Japanese mushroom
27. Little bitty biters
28. Mar a shine
29. "Get Here" singer Adams
30. "___ I can help it!"
31. Bit of improv
36. Bob or bun
37. Chihuahua cheers
38. Distillery vessels
40. Big wheels in the deli
41. Song of David
43. "Unison" singer Dion
44. Lay hands on
45. "The Black Stallion" novelist
48. Paquin of "True Blood"
49. Crooked type, briefly
50. It's made of blocks
51. Kylo Ren player Driver
52. It goes with wine
53. Sapient
54. Use a crosshair
55. Recyclable item
56. Stop start

116 THE WHOLE NINE YARDS by Pam Klawitter
39 Down was inducted into the Songwriters Hall of Fame in 1995.

ACROSS

1 Alerts from 5 Down
5 Stands the test of time
10 First lady after Eleanor
14 Sugarland number
15 Western quaker
16 Sorna in "Jurassic Park III"
17 ___ 'acte
18 Words on a check
19 Amazing, slangily
20 Car safety feature
23 Plan parts
24 Part of IBM: Abbr.
25 Catch at the theater
26 Greek N's
27 Young socialite
30 Mother's Day mailing
32 Boys on the brae
34 One who keeps at it
38 Butt of jokes
42 Roll call lists
43 Early offering from 67 Across
45 Haying machine
48 Landing stat: Abbr.
50 Word in a bride's bio
51 When it's hot in Le Havre
52 Prefix for tarsal
56 Walks and waits
58 Competitor of Williams-Sonoma or Pier 1 Imports
62 Bright and breezy
63 Bilbao bulls
64 Six-petaled flower
66 Jazz flutist Herbie
67 Video game company
68 Periodic table info: Abbr.
69 Apart from this
70 Lauren on "The Love Boat"
71 Blue bird of Twitter, e.g.

DOWN

1 "Toni Erdmann" director
2 Right on time
3 Home of Walter Reed Medical Center
4 Vegas attraction
5 City of Angels' "finest"
6 "This is a rush job!"
7 Author of "Heidi"
8 Western range
9 "I'm better than you" sort
10 Jessica in "Hitchcock"
11 Mexican missus
12 Deli appliance
13 Fired
21 Woodstock turn-on: Abbr.
22 Fast on one's feet
23 Satiric NBC show
28 Ordinal suffixes
29 Tube traveler
31 Trim a photo
33 "Absolutely!"
35 Value of S in "Words with Friends"
36 Despotic boss
37 "Over here . . ."
39 Songstress Eydie
40 Cantata cousin
41 Ready to be dubbed
44 Some microwaves
45 Evolved into
46 Of a heart chamber
47 Gets the hang of
49 Car ad letters
53 Sandwich-board words
54 Govt. security
55 End in ___ (unresolved)
57 "New York Times" sans-serif font
59 Newcastle river
60 Yawn inducer
61 Yard sale disclaimer
65 Jack of "Barney Miller"

SEIZE THE DAY by Pam Klawitter

Marlon Brando and Robert De Niro both won Oscars for portraying 33 Down.

ACROSS

1 Snoopy's flying wear
6 In-box junk
10 Crossword bird
14 Burj Dubai, notably
15 Diego's dwelling
16 Israeli airline
17 Do-re-mi
18 Blanco y Branco
19 Soffit locale
20 Cee
23 Dutch for "city"
24 They're out of this world
25 What fools do, proverbially
28 Bitter tasting
30 "That's disgusting!"
31 (Homophone of 20-A)
36 Nobelist Wiesel
38 "Exodus" hero
39 Succotash bean
40 (Homophone of 20-A)
45 Carter discovered his tomb
46 Drops down?
47 "___ Fables"
49 First-aid antiseptic
52 Tiny amount
53 (Homophone of 20-A)
57 Campbell in "House of Cards"
58 Road trip expense
59 Funky smells
62 Vein pursuits
63 Sunblock additive
64 Accrued a bar tab
65 News source in Moscow
66 Match makers
67 Hard to hold

DOWN

1 Divinity degree
2 Soft murmur
3 Way off base
4 Dog topper
5 Beside oneself
6 Cape Cod catch
7 Beach toy
8 Jack London novel "___ of the Sun"
9 It could run in the rain
10 Ariana Grande, for one
11 Buoy with joy
12 Poe's gaunt bird
13 Cards and Pirates
21 Where water became wine
22 Double-___ tourney
25 Wished one hadn't
26 Jamaican tangelo
27 Knife, slangily
28 Homestead Act's "160"
29 "Pet" plant
32 Mountain pool
33 "The Godfather" godfather
34 "My turn to bat!"
35 Finishes off
37 Spooky sensation
41 Bollywood princess
42 Noonday naps
43 Myanmar neighbor
44 Streakers in the night
48 Shore shoe
49 "The World ___ Enough" (1999)
50 "Parsifal" is one
51 Famous ___ Bar-B-Que
52 Some keys
54 You can dig it
55 Bunches
56 Author Morrison
60 Piña colada ingredient
61 Expert on bugs?

118 THEMELESS   by Harvey Estes
One non-alphanumeric character is needed for the answer grid.

ACROSS
1 FTD affiliate
8 Not so common
15 "Rhinoceros" dramatist
16 Buck in "Rise of the Planet of the Apes"
17 Dilapidated dwelling
18 "Marines' Hymn" city
19 Moody rock genre
20 Foe of Xena
22 Snapped
23 Pipe problems
25 Steamed (up)
26 Test of public opinion
30 Longtime Chicago maestro
31 Mattel boy toy
32 "Spark" singer Tori
36 Roundball stat
39 Teaching focus of old, ironically
41 Phillippe of "Brooklyn Nine-Nine"
42 Like a piece with two sharps
44 Arnold's farewell start
45 Part of many an address
49 Massage reactions
52 What saints are beyond
53 "Flashdance" hit
55 Cicero's garment
56 Larry O'Brien Trophy org.
59 Axes to grind
61 Charlemagne's foe

63 Sits unsteadily
64 May birthstone
65 Encroachments
66 Varlets

DOWN
1 Cashier
2 Fertile soil
3 Not taken in by
4 Pt. of AARP
5 Kibbutzniks
6 Fiddler beetle
7 Midwestern capital
8 Bilko's rnk.
9 Vito or Fredo
10 Melodic piece
11 Cheats, with "off"
12 Felt, for example
13 Songwriter Greenwich
14 Grammy winner Bonnie
21 Polio scientist
23 Gender-neutral word for Hispanic
24 Narrow valley
26 Winter Palace ruler
27 Flushed
28 Rick's old flame
29 Football's "Broadway Joe"
33 German noun gen.
34 "Beetle Bailey" barker
35 Pillow covering
37 Record of hours
38 Lose it
40 "So?"
43 Malicious gossip
46 Dairy designation
47 Less taut
48 1490s sailor to India

49 Precious strings
50 Rival of Bobby Jones
51 Visual putdown
54 Absorbed by
56 SEC overseer
57 Class ender
58 Added factors
60 Snake sound
62 Circumference segment

119 THEMELESS by Harvey Estes
You can get anything you want at 58/60 Across!

ACROSS

1 Where a surfer may click
5 Netman Rod
10 Auction stipulation
14 Quotation notation
15 A heap of energy?
17 Pass out
18 Overly protective mother/father (with 19-A)
19 See 18 Across
21 Stonewall
22 Show disgust
24 Adds color
25 Conclude by
26 Treat badly
30 Great strides
31 Coal locale
32 Relief of FDR
36 Surreal ending
37 Den piece
40 Journal unit
41 Leave in the text
43 Magritte or Russo
44 Conjure up
46 Ella in "Arsène Lupin"
48 They climb the walls
49 German spa city
52 Soft ice-cream servings
54 Monopoly avenue
58 Arlo Guthrie debut album (with 60-A)
60 See 58 Across
62 Vehicle with a turret
63 Bad way to be held by a judge
64 Highlands dialect
65 "Say no more!"
66 Rockets
67 Home paper

DOWN

1 Reading aid
2 All out
3 Paul Hornung's alma mater
4 Limb center
5 "Chicago Hope" actress
6 Bolted down
7 Tennessee team, for short
8 Put out
9 Costa ___
10 Not theoretical
11 Withhold release of
12 "The Girl ___ Behind Me"
13 Old workers without a retirement plan
16 Preakness entrants
20 "That's a lie!"
23 Pay attention
25 Ivy League team
27 "Fistful of Dollars" director
28 Like the least convincing excuses
29 Thurman of "Chambers"
33 "Whatever"
34 Hold water
35 "Jeepers Creepers" peepers
38 Corn starter
39 "On the Beach" novelist Shute
42 Angel's spot at Christmas
45 Popped in on
47 Kofi once of the UN
49 Baddie Badenov of cartoons
50 "Looks ___ everything"
51 "Saturday Night Fever" setting
53 Light bulb figure
55 Sounds of skepticism
56 Mars prefix
57 Monk of Lhasa
59 Timetable, slangily
61 "All Things Considered" ntwk.

THEMELESS by Justin Andrew

Pachira aquatica is the botanical name of 56 Across.

ACROSS

1 Constellation's second brightest
5 Cyberspace activity
9 Cassowary weapons
14 Result of a stellar collapse
16 Shop shaper
17 Cosmetic for blemishes
18 Showed curiosity
19 "Abbey Road" album cover sight
21 Get testy with
23 Meaning in a nutshell
24 Retraced one's steps
27 Foil-wrapped Hershey candy
28 Ram near a bull
29 Soap scent
31 Neville Longbottom's pet Trevor
32 Digs on the rich side of town
33 Skewer
37 Steps up?
38 Shrek's love
39 Low voices
43 Ferrari logo
45 NYC's Fifth and Sixth
47 Physiques
48 No-second-chance policy
51 "Is that true of us?"
52 Barrel jumper, e.g.
55 Ed in "The Gathering"
56 Welcome source of bills?
57 Stalks in the marsh
58 Mireille of "Hanna"
59 Saw

DOWN

1 "The Beeb"
2 "Can't Get It Out of My Head" band
3 Eastern African republic
4 Taken in as a full member
5 ___ new course
6 Juan's "What's up?"
7 Obi-Wan player
8 Pied-à-___
9 Definitive opus
10 Some Scots
11 A low-carb diet
12 From what source
13 Moor growth
15 Greek menu items
20 Painter Kokoschka
21 Kind of team
22 Franco in "Camelot"
25 "Braveheart" group
26 Carol trio
30 Going around in circles
32 Prado, to Madrilenians
33 Quartz, for one
34 Grooming article
35 With a wink and ___
36 Puts the kibosh on
37 London news agency
38 Lowly assistant
39 Church fundraiser
40 Objecting
41 Collected
42 Put one over on
44 Puts down
46 Cover with ectoplasm
49 Study of GDP and such
50 Nevada border city
53 Shoe width
54 Cherry or cranberry

121 THEMELESS by Justin Andrew

There's a museum displaying 38 Across in Nazareth, Pennsylvania.

ACROSS

1 Renault sedan
6 Chrysler engine
10 Brainstorming product
14 Margaret Cho, for one
15 Gomer's "anti"
16 Prepare to take off
17 Olympic swimmer Nall
18 Hood's honey
19 Tabloid couple
20 Used pickaxes
21 Go for
22 Good ending
23 Pointless games
26 "What, me worry?" is Neuman's
27 Snare and more
30 Retrospective writing
34 Shining example
36 This second
37 Not today, José
38 Noted steel-string acoustic guitars
40 Canary's mouth?
41 Lei Day greeting
42 This isn't o'er
44 Mantle was a great one
50 Meet event
52 Lowly laborer
53 1998 "Rear Window" star
54 Some
55 Sea that's now part desert
56 Credit card come-on
57 "Fanny" author
58 Deserve
59 Continuously
60 Church niche
61 Solomon's seal
62 Pastry shop supply

DOWN

1 Bogus offers
2 Like some coffee filters
3 Protein acid
4 A quart and a bit
5 One for the books?
6 Whistle stops
7 Self-server
8 Timid type
9 Coastal cove
10 Wandering
11 Health food sweetener
12 Flames that died out
13 Points on the range
24 "Two Women" star
25 "Pass!"
28 Barthel of tennis
29 Lead-pipe cinch
30 Playpen cry
31 Series terminal
32 Rabat residents
33 Hanging by a thread
35 Priceless violin
39 Pooh-pooh
40 Chance seller
43 Book bloopers
45 Pre-1917 rulers
46 Soprano Mitchell
47 Put off
48 Happening
49 Bagpipe parts
50 Indian chief?
51 Resting on

ACROSS

1 Docking place
5 "Full House" star Sokoloff
10 Oater sound effect
14 Like 16:9 monitors
16 Go hither and yon
17 Colonial druggist
18 Part of YSL
19 Bujold in "Anne of the Thousand Days"
20 "Stupid me!"
21 "Sesame Street" roomie
22 Stat for Corey Kluber
24 Dairy servings in little cups
26 Bram Stoker's "The ___ Path"
31 Cardiff language
32 "Girls" creator Dunham
33 French I verb
35 Wrench type
37 Peptide acid
39 Gist of the problem
40 Range accessory
41 "Au contraire!"
42 Cartel formed in 1960
44 Mireille of "World War Z"
45 Like George Carlin's weatherman
47 Nave crosser
49 Shuts tight
51 Monogram of Prufrock's creator
52 Enchanted girl of film
53 Org. in "Patriot Games"
55 Collision protection
60 Adele's "___ Ask"
61 Oscar-winning 1943 film
63 Driver's Ed student
64 Banned Orwell book
65 Vegas line
66 "Days of Our Lives" et al.
67 They lead to shootouts

DOWN

1 Mop asea
2 Surgery that sucks?
3 Venerated object
4 Buttigieg of South Bend
5 "You Cannot Be Serious" author
6 Pole-vaulter's path
7 Peer at a page
8 Bad Brown of song
9 All the same
10 Harassers who play the victim
11 Osculation location
12 Too too
13 Flies, e.g.
15 Less outgoing
23 Nolan Ryan, for nine years
25 Low, for one
26 Think out
27 Did over
28 Okayed, in a way: Brit.
29 Clarifies condescendingly
30 Blow one's top
34 "Your Movie Sucks" author
36 Cartoonist who drew Santa
38 Alley and Ooola
43 Honeydew relatives
46 Evergreens of New Mexico
48 Noel who played Lois Lane
49 Old defense pact
50 Honky-tonk instrument
54 Georgia's continent
56 Whole bunch
57 Sons of, in Hebrew
58 Building lot
59 Schools of ocean mammals
62 Current unit

123

The earliest type of 11 Down was called a "ten-wide."

ACROSS

1 Get in on a deal
5 Charity request
9 Deadens
14 Kindred spirits
16 Previously, old-style
17 Galápagos population segment
18 Explorer Sebastian
19 Give lots of backstory at once
20 Landing sites
21 Court order
22 Ferdinand, e.g.
23 Hawaii's Mauna ___
24 Tangy flavor
27 ___ for election
29 Gardener on screen
30 It may be narrow
33 Glenn of "The Walking Dead"
34 Bubbles behind boats
36 Close-encounter being
37 Ellen ___ Barkin
38 Fit to serve
39 Country estates
41 Range components: Abbr.
42 Awe-inspiring
44 Beyond beefy
46 Lit. hopefuls
47 Before, in the past
48 NIT org.
50 ___ Wall Street (2011 protest)
52 Inquiry with a fine-tooth comb
56 Oozes through
57 Approached
58 The blahs
59 The stuff you need
60 Walking, on an NBA court
61 Radon lacks it
62 Novel ending

DOWN

1 ___ spumante
2 High time
3 Gang domain
4 Mexican tequila brand
5 ___ Julius Caesar
6 Brief confession
7 HBO comedy about the politician Selina Meyer
8 Curve shape
9 Metrical foot
10 Way out there
11 Double-wide, for one
12 Advocates
13 Says "no worries" to
15 Matthew of "Weeds"
20 One-named Tejano singer
22 Run off
24 First five books of the Bible
25 Fleeting
26 Have a public tantrum
27 Ethiopia's Selassie
28 Chilling comment?
31 Lip-smacking
32 Area, meteorologically
35 Place for a stud
40 Halloween trickster
43 Blood poisoning, e.g.
45 Guy in a black hat
48 "Rad!"
49 One that gives up
51 "___ and away!"
52 Like useless batteries
53 "___ first you don't . . ."
54 Electrical measure
55 Its found in Celtic Woman songs
57 Medical ins. plan

A meringue dessert topped with fruit and whipped cream is named after 5 Down.

ACROSS

1 ___ San Lucas
5 Lay the groundwork
9 Helen's mother
13 Cheers heard at 1 Across
14 Skylit lobbies
16 Make-up item?
17 Hall of Champions org.
18 Scorpion secretion
19 Titular Verdi heroine
20 Home often carried on a yak's back
23 Big name in skin care
24 Conductors' pronouncement: Abbr.
25 BFF
28 Stark of House Stark
29 Asseverate
32 "Earth in the Balance" author
34 Bologna bigwig's country house
36 Spec at Victoria's Secret
39 Genre
40 Unappetizing leftover
41 Oligarch's weekend retreat
46 Venues for Aristophanes plays
47 Hairy armed Biblical hunter
48 Film ratings
51 Lat. or Lith., once
52 Sei school
54 Street race?
56 Palace of Versailles, e.g.
60 Stead
62 Lopez in "The Dirty Dozen"
63 Bryn ___ College
64 Sweet quaffs
65 Moth-___ (shabby)
66 Commencing on
67 Washington paper
68 Approximations: Abbr.
69 Guitarist Cline of Wilco

DOWN

1 Scammer
2 Nook
3 Conked with an errant curve ball
4 "August: ___ County"
5 Immortal Bolshoi prima ballerina
6 It runs 2,369 miles from ME to FL
7 Met soprano Berger
8 No-spin subatomic particles
9 "O! let me not be mad" speaker
10 Election Day sampling
11 Relationship of 9 Down to Goneril
12 "First, do no harm" org.
15 Author of "The Joy Luck Club"
21 Go ___ great length

22 Where J. Tarkanian coached
26 Woody Guthrie's son
27 Grand jeté, e.g.
30 Lena in "Hollywood Homicide"
31 "Booksmart" director
33 Prefix denoting 10 to the ninth power
34 By itself: Lat.
35 Noms de plume
36 Family business abbr.
37 Holstein mouthfuls
38 They're paid at park entrances
42 "Picnic" playwright
43 Former Gold Coast empire
44 Redemptions
45 Pantomine dance
48 Make happy
49 Leave base illegally
50 Mushroom house dwellers
53 Chanteuse Carmen
55 Universal soul, in Hinduism
57 Reddish brown
58 "Hamilton" and "Lion King"
59 Site for techies
60 Pass at Daytona
61 Last words of bachelorhood

125 COMICS CHARACTERS by Richard Shlakman

If you're doing a strip search, look for 20 Across at Camp Swampy.

ACROSS

1 Express Mail org.
5 Letters from a hostess
9 Slyly spiteful
14 Ornamental neckband
15 Antioxidant berry
16 Hammer in "Final Portrait"
17 "The Kite Runner" boy
18 Strap site
19 Hunts up
20 Dik Browne characters
23 Nikki Giovanni work
24 M ÷ IV
25 Mort Walker characters
32 Inner circle
33 Took a card
34 Sigh of delight
35 Billfold filler
36 Avarice
38 Shah Jahan's tomb site
39 It's pressed for cash
40 Faust sold his
41 Used a scope
42 Greg Evans characters
46 Feel strange
47 Gasteyer and Alicia
48 Al Capp characters
55 Stuff and nonsense
56 Nullify
57 Verdi's 1871 masterpiece
58 It grows down?
59 Genesis creation
60 Lute ridge
61 Must-haves
62 A handful
63 Cassidy's "Smallville" role

DOWN

1 Bonneville Flats site
2 AT&T Park locale
3 Self-righteous sort
4 Deicing tools
5 Jennifer's "Friends" role
6 Cabal's concoction
7 Aspen rival
8 Golf clubs brand
9 Borden's Elsie, e.g.?
10 Ring around a pupil
11 Revenuers
12 Pool-party torch
13 Referendum option
21 Boring routine
22 Wasn't oneself
25 Malawi native
26 Tomato swelling
27 NFL receiver Beckham
28 Three, in Torino
29 Volcanic spillage
30 Eight-___ shell
31 Migratory herring
32 Lignite, for one
36 Divine
37 Feel bad about
38 Ventilation provider
40 Surreptitious shooters
41 Saudi robes
43 Caught a few winks
44 Bicycle built for two
45 Whoever's available
48 ___-dieu (kneeler)
49 Campaign worker
50 Elect. day
51 Proto-___-European languages
52 Swampy area
53 Claudel's "Five Great" poems
54 Part of GORP
55 Hours in a Jupiter day

SISTER CITIES by John M. Samson
The term "twin towns" is more commonly used in the United Kingdom.

ACROSS

1 Cannabis
5 Hibernated
10 "___ corny as Kansas . . ."
14 Ending for pop
15 Tosca's lover
16 Verne's mad mariner
17 Sister city of Chicago
19 Earth clump
20 Get moving
21 Freshman math
23 Football's "Broadway Joe"
24 ___ mundi
25 Harmonica piece
27 Exceptional
30 Type of blue or bean
33 Generous order at the bar
35 "Harper's Bazaar" cover artist
36 ___ king
37 Special attention
38 ___ compos mentis
39 Beethoven Museum site
41 Plot over
43 Grass of greens
44 Backed with property, as a loan
46 Monetary unit of Cuba
48 Bleep
49 B vitamin
53 Strawberry's pie partner
56 Personalize a watch
57 Icicle's spot
58 Sister city of Cleveland
60 Opera-house level
61 One-fifth of a gram
62 Anon partner
63 Has it wrong
64 Signature melody
65 Wine grouping

DOWN

1 Vulnerable
2 Greta's role in "The Temptress"
3 Common saying
4 Election prelim
5 Cover thickly
6 Corset feature
7 "___ tu" (Verdi aria)
8 Gyro bread
9 Victor Herbert song
10 Thurible smoke
11 Sister city of Boston
12 Son of Venus
13 Scotch mixer
18 Blanchett in "Notes on a Scandal"
22 "New" homophone
26 Slobbered over
27 Twist the top off
28 Oceans
29 Good Friday's time
30 Arrests, slangily
31 South African succulent
32 Sister city of Los Angeles
34 Pelican State sch.
40 Old Testament book
41 Take back
42 Feathered
43 B&B guest
45 Narrow inlet
47 Make a contract official
50 Make a pumpkin face
51 Like Columbia's walls
52 Gets next to
53 Anatomical mesh
54 "Aquarius" musical
55 Listless
56 Physical, e.g.
59 Before, to bards

ACROSS

1 Prohibits
5 "Elmer Gantry" novelist
10 Kills, in mob slang
14 For one, casually
15 Bitter twist
16 Coropuna locale
17 Chinese take-out favorite
19 Unit of matter
20 Tapioca, for one
21 Hippie light fixture
23 Itsy-bitsy piece
25 Turkey Day veggie
26 Publisher Condé ___
29 Wallet items
31 Neptune's wife, for one
36 Chicken ___ reine
37 "Cold Mountain" soldier
39 Like a nebbish
40 "___ back"
43 "You've Really Got ___ On Me"
44 Gives a thumbs-down
45 Nonexplosive gunpowder?
46 Punch servers
48 Train alternative
49 Source of ethanol
50 Cartoon squeal
52 Normandy's "Capital of the Ruins"
54 Rose Bowl venue
59 His last words were, "The rest is silence"
63 FOX's "American ___"
64 Gorilla troop leader
66 Oil measure
67 Papuan woodcarvers
68 Waffles brand
69 Grand narrative
70 Pearl Krabs, for one
71 Katharine in "The Graduate"

DOWN

1 Quartet member
2 Date with a doctor: Abbr.
3 Best-selling author Roberts
4 Panache
5 Stage manager's concern
6 Make a fluff
7 Cashmere
8 Dental filling
9 Arboreous
10 Katy Perry's birthstone
11 Crumbly cheese
12 ___ bad to worse
13 Cellar pump
18 Barracks boss
22 Reparation
24 Occupation in "The Hucksters"
26 Like an oboe's sound
27 Kind of bet?
28 Lute of India
30 Term of respect in the Raj
32 He may cry foul
33 Sister of Terpsichore
34 Thumb-twiddler
35 "Positively 4th Street" singer
37 Certainly
38 Connecting link
41 Feeling peaked
42 Art collector, for example
47 Shilly-shally
49 Large wave
51 Jewish appetizer
53 Roman houshold god
54 Knight's backup
55 Sarah McLachlan hit
56 "Torch ___ Trilogy"
57 Utah ski resort
58 Award for Jennifer Lopez
60 Italian lake
61 Cardiology charts
62 Stats for Rocky
65 Batman actor Kilmer

128 T MINUS 4*   by Don Law
18 Across is often misspelled.

ACROSS

1 Vail and Vichy
5 Fairway hazards
10 Gush lava
14 Prefix for vision
15 Sepulcher sight
16 Kotb of the "Today Show"
17 Bellicose god
18 Alley Oop's love
19 Auditory
20 Iron Out or CLR, e.g.?*
22 Bart's bus driver
23 Dawn goddess
24 Cook in butter
26 Lacking diplomacy
31 It'll hold a bit
34 GI entertainer
35 Plumb
37 Remove a brooch
38 Bulgar or Croat
40 Aunt in "Lady and the Tramp"
42 "Aren't You ___ You're You"
43 Swimmer Ledecky
45 Obi-Wan's creator
47 "It's ___-brainer!"
48 They have pryer knowledge
50 Virginia City native
52 Aviator
54 Debussy's "Poissons ___"
55 Fisherman's ring wearer
57 Amtrak jacket?*
63 Gulf state
64 Some hotel lobbies
65 ___-Honey candy
66 Stonestreet of "Modern Family"
67 June birthstone
68 Has an interest
69 Colliery
70 "The Monuments Men" author
71 Breezed through a test

DOWN

1 See 10 Down
2 Where huayno music is heard
3 Heady drinks
4 Six performers
5 Breeches
6 Model T rivals
7 Frequently
8 Heaps
9 Jewelry beetle
10 Meteor (with 1 Down)
11 Itinerary for a pub crawl?*
12 Do some "Self" improvement
13 Baylor site
21 Maple trunk
25 Simba's grandmother
26 Mammoth teeth
27 Narnia lion
28 Outerwear cousin of a hair shirt?
29 "Kiss From a Rose" singer
30 Rugby formation
32 Congo vine
33 ___ a high note
36 Basketball center Fall
39 Cause for a PG-13 rating
41 Soccer foul
44 Prefix for dermis
46 Plane for small airfields
49 Shawl for Francisco
51 Lawrence's domain
53 Given a "PG-13"
55 Haiku, for one
56 Katz on "Dallas"
58 Cleo's handmaiden
59 Old money in Milan
60 Battery metal
61 Suffix for disk
62 Chancel cross

129 "TENNIS, ANYONE?" by Don Law
Jim Carrey played the role of 52 Across.

ACROSS

1 Insecticide brand
5 Spanish farewell
10 Steel girder
14 "___ sprach Zarathustra"
15 Indecent
16 Jackalope, for one
17 "Fiddler on the Roof" song
19 Brazil soccer great
20 Diet sheet group
21 Largest peninsula
23 Like red meat
24 Creepy
25 Dwell
28 Star groups
31 Dark clouds, perhaps
32 Right off the vine
33 Tide type
34 Israeli seaport
35 Party pancake
36 "The Godfather" composer
37 Race the engine
38 King Hamlet, on stage
39 Elton John song
40 Like some grapes
42 Clemson team
43 Word with "tooth" or "heart"
44 "Girl with a Rose" painter
45 Present but unseen
47 Cared for lovingly
51 Pierre's girlfriend
52 Pet detective of film
54 Item for Rapunzel
55 Tepee makeup
56 Muslim title
57 Shiva has three
58 St. Catherine's birthplace
59 "___ Island Line"

DOWN

1 Sloping passageway
2 Like Pegasus
3 Proportion words
4 Isolationism, for one
5 Revere
6 Varsi in "Peyton Place"
7 Bothers
8 Capri add-on
9 "Salt City" of New York
10 Pass on, as knowledge
11 Everly Brothers hit
12 "Volsunga Saga" king
13 Large, flightless bird
18 Flip decision?
22 Scratch test reaction
24 Churchill's "While England ___"
25 Airport sounds
26 Host a roast
27 Finishes a sentence
28 Salad green
29 Chopper blade
30 Some pens
32 "Dust of Snow" poet
35 Speedy cats
36 Make an impression
38 Valley
39 Eton collar material
41 Dorks
42 Mother with a Nobel prize
44 Baltimore gridder
45 Needlepoint fabric
46 Island in the Taiwan Strait
47 Grant (a point)
48 Sapporo sport
49 Omar's "House" role
50 Like Earth Hour
53 Fever reading, in old Rome

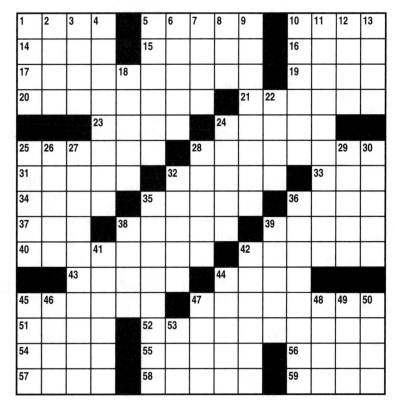

130 FORD MODELS by Tim Wagner
These models never worked for Eileen Ford's agency.

ACROSS

1 Turkey Day veggies
5 Diamond surface
10 Not nigh
14 "You're So ___": Simon
15 Adult insect stage
16 Admirably tricky
17 Way-out idea?
19 Hosea, in the Douay
20 Farsighted lady?
21 Interrogate, in a way
23 Delt neighbor
24 Beatle bride of 1969
25 Proposer's fear
29 "Jaws" sighting
31 Ultimate in degree
34 Go with the beau
35 Emulate Cicero
37 "My man!"
38 Torso muscles
39 Glove material
40 Increase sharply
41 Ostrich kin
42 Moosehead Lake location
43 Summer forecast word
44 Fleur-de-___
45 Security needs
46 Growth on a shaved head
48 Wrigley field?
50 Cartoonist Spiegelman
51 Mid-life decade
55 Retreat
59 Mine, to Jacques
60 Somerset Maugham novel (with "The")
62 Faust sold his
63 Pierre's parting
64 Restaurant fish
65 Drink too much
66 Clan divisions
67 Compact

DOWN

1 Designer Saint-Laurent
2 Peet Gynt's mother
3 Quiet creatures
4 Traffic jams
5 Cinco de Mayo party
6 Gig equipment
7 Ripken who played 2,632 consecutive games
8 Edwardian oath
9 Muscle quality
10 Capped seed
11 Certain nuclear weapon
12 Fit to finish?
13 Snorkeling locale
18 "___ porridge hot . . ."
22 Off-white
25 Keep at bay
26 Varnish resin
27 Research panel
28 Son of Prince William
29 Loses vigor
30 Meteor tail
32 Way through the woods
33 Mob
36 Stimpy's toon pal
39 Like an elegy
40 Least obvious
42 "The Drew Carey Show" role
43 Throws a discus
47 Sign of spring
49 Scrabble vowel pick
51 Fleet-footed
52 South Pacific tale
53 Times to remember
54 Libertine Marquis de ___
55 Ted Kooser, notably
56 Limburger quality
57 Jamaican hybrid fruit
58 Rain buckets
61 Compress a data file

CIVIL WAR SIDES by Tim Wagner
NASA astronaut Frank Borman was once president of 20 Across.

ACROSS

1 Non-recyclable can?
5 Ornamental buttons
10 Lustful look
14 Need an Anacin
15 Absolute
16 Laker star, casually
17 1961 Elvis Presley hit
19 "Rikki-Tikki-___" (Kipling story)
20 "Wings of Man" airline that ceased flying in 1991
21 Wandered off
23 Holbrook in "The Firm"
24 Corey in "License to Drive"
25 Barbary Coast country
29 Like most Olympic gymnasts
32 NFL QB Derek
33 Hourglass, e.g.
35 Suffix with road or hip
36 Baghdad news agency
37 Code character
38 Druggist's "thrice"
39 "Happy ___ are here . . ."
41 Cooperstown catcher
43 ___ majesté
44 Spotted
46 Took in, say
48 Olympic queen
49 "The Gods ___-begging" : Handel
50 Classic comic Coca
53 RSVP bad news
57 C-worthy
58 State flower of Texas
60 Edmonton loc.
61 Not inactive
62 Literary governess
63 "Get some sleep"
64 Davis in "Beetlejuice"
65 Parking garage feature

DOWN

1 Naive one
2 Pauley Pavilion locale
3 Sic
4 Ring in a crib
5 Bright at night
6 Junior city
7 Marathoner Pippig
8 Place for a teacher
9 Make like a snake
10 Gets possession of
11 Brains
12 Heart's desire
13 Markey of Tarzan films
18 Parliamentary shout
22 Hip-hop duo ___ Sremmurd
25 Essential amino ___
26 Hawaii's "Pineapple Island"
27 Weimaraner nicknames
28 Was a good Samaritan
29 Di- doubled
30 Gaggle members
31 Behaved humanly?
34 Space station launched in 1986
40 Kid's mom
41 Ashtray base, perhaps
42 Pursuit of the unknown?
43 Novice
45 Three, in Roma
47 Nancy Drew's dog
50 River through Munich
51 Vole look-alike
52 End of a threat
53 Harness lead
54 "The Longships" singer
55 Period for a prisoner or president
56 Course of action
59 All-around truck

62 ACROSS by David Van Houten
An amusing duty roster can be found below.

ACROSS

1 Brahma believer
6 Bent, for one
11 "___ sweet it is!"
14 Geometry calculations
15 Red-faced
16 Antagonism
17 IRS warrior?
19 Shaving goo
20 Tolkien creatures
21 Still-life object
22 "You're ___ water!"
24 Word with Timor or India
26 Monty Python songwriter Neil
28 What your 1040 deductions will hopefully do?
33 Get the soap out of
34 Crossed (out)
35 "I ___ bad moon rising . . .": CCR
36 Akashi accessory
37 Industrial cleaning cloth
41 Philippe of Belgium, e.g.
42 Letter before gamma
44 Mine line
45 Hamlet's foppish courtier
47 Inheritance levy on the sons of Adam?
51 Hebrew word for messenger
52 Fertilizer
53 Sun prefix
55 Rubik of cube fame
57 Word after tattle
61 Nickname of a Washington Cap

62 Final price
65 Candy with collectable containers
66 Start of school?
67 Give a speech
68 ". . . ___ I saw Elba"
69 Packing
70 Seafood garnish

DOWN

1 Mail opener?
2 "La La Land" song
3 Adjacent (to)
4 Camelot maidens
5 2019 Women's World Cup champion
6 Progress in the garden
7 Davis of "Petticoat Junction"
8 Sterling Cooper employee
9 Sabbath-on-Sat. sect
10 Nymph pursued by Pan
11 Bogart/Lupino film of 1941
12 Cookie bestseller
13 Caning memento
18 Sit (within)
23 Tortoise beaks
25 Pub drinks
27 Nothing, in Nogales
28 Oatmeal is a good source of it
29 Format a disk
30 Throw out
31 Pope who brought about the Great Schism
32 Secular

33 Annoying ___-calls
38 Sharpen
39 Grad school challenge
40 Word shouted at auctions
43 Vedic fire god
46 Prominence
48 "Sorry, ___ run!"
49 Caught some rays
50 Classic Camaro
53 Pandora's Box remnant
54 Word after what or who
56 Fair attraction
58 "Paradise Lost" character
59 Jared in "Dallas Buyers Club"
60 Paradise lost
63 Abbr. at SFO
64 Cyber-giggle

133 TERMS OF ENDEARMENT   by David Van Houten
The song at 17 Across can be heard in the film "Forrest Gump."

ACROSS

1 Rhône's source
5 Chinese calculators
10 Bar mitzvah site
14 Take during a riot
15 Art gallery
16 Cornbread
17 Jimmy Gilmer and the Fireballs hit
19 Lock opener?
20 Like durian
21 On to
23 You can lend it or bend it
24 Artsy-craftsy site
25 "Maybe This Time" musical
29 Peanut ___
32 Sci. class
33 Keep house
35 Cub legend Sandberg
36 Poke fun at
37 "Thank God ___ Country Boy"
38 1988 Meg Ryan film
39 Adams and Poehler
41 Affluent semirural area
43 Stones not to throw
44 Upholstery fabric
46 Mosque tower
48 Russian city on the Irtysh
49 Country reunited in 1990: Abbr.
50 Chance card in Monopoly
53 Facilitates
57 Do–fa bridge
58 Met pitcher in the 1986 World Series
60 "Currently serving" military status
61 Self-evident truth
62 Give off
63 Warning at Winged Foot
64 "Velvet Fog" vocalist Mel
65 Root beer brand

DOWN

1 Too
2 Clear partner
3 Walt Kelly possum
4 Rubberneck
5 Guaranteed
6 Scrooge exclamations
7 Fla. neighbor
8 ___-Cola
9 Old-school desk accessory
10 Less crowded
11 Beachcomber in "Dr. No"
12 "Render therefore ___ Caesar . . ."
13 Viking explorer Erikson
18 Belly laugh
22 Falcons, on the scoreboard
25 One of 24 in pure gold
26 Jungian "self"
27 Gen Xer's parent
28 Poetic between
29 Sleepyhead's need
30 Garden statue
31 Agent of ferment
34 Australian bird
40 Washington Senator Hall of Famer
41 Hamelin cry of fright?
42 A-list star
43 Like some dropped calls
45 They lead to U
47 Approach
50 Class-conscious one?
51 Wine prefix
52 Love letter sign-off
53 Ancient Dead Sea land
54 "Glee" city
55 Geraint's love
56 York and Pepper, briefly
59 Conductor Kabaretti

"THAT'S TAT!" by David Van Houten
The league at 49-A includes Superman, Batman, Aquaman, and Wonder Woman.

ACROSS

1 Nomadic shelter
5 Begged for
9 Ravi Shankar musical pieces
14 Audio engineer Bose
15 Move in an easy canter
16 Methuselah's father
17 Lake fish
18 "Star Trek" actor Eisenberg
19 "Watchmen" creator Alan
20 Downwind, at sea
21 Like L. Frank Baum's woodsman?
23 Cool and calm
25 Cravings
26 Netizen's need
28 Chihuahua, por ejemplo
33 "Encore!"
36 Nick and Nora's dog
38 Tear apart
39 Accountant's books
41 Loan
43 What Ctrl-Z is a hot key for
44 Parisian pronoun
46 Daisylike flower
47 Fiddled (with)
49 Justice League member
51 Teller of tales
53 Approached
57 Gershwin musical written just for kicks?
62 See 65 Across
63 Goldfinger
64 Nastase of tennis
65 Prefix meaning 62 Across
66 Play footsie
67 Computer name
68 ___-friendly
69 Blackthorn fruits
70 Looks over
71 Spare item

DOWN

1 Fiesta appetizers
2 "Some Enchanted Evening" singer
3 In the altogether
4 Ent pals?
5 Like Oscar
6 Alan heard in "Toy Story 4"
7 Watt and Joule, for two
8 Not too bright
9 Dilatory
10 Soon, to Shakespeare
11 Roughneck
12 It could be a lot
13 Outbuilding
22 Work the dough
24 Call-waiting signal
27 Whence daybreak
29 Garbage everywhere?
30 Em or Bea
31 Chuck-a-luck cubes
32 Nonpareil
33 Grad
34 Family hand-me-down
35 Tots up
37 Follow
40 It takes two to cross a circle
42 Flower holder
45 Life ___ (carefree existence)
48 Votes in
50 Kushner's "___ in America"
52 Line said to the audience
54 Actress Portia de ___
55 Computer key
56 Its homonym is its logo
57 Lummoxes
58 At capacity
59 The Magi, e.g.
60 Connemara locale
61 World's longest river

135 "ENOUGH, ALREADY" by David Van Houten
59 Across is the key to this theme.

ACROSS

1 Seafood entrée
6 Noted Champagne, familiarly
10 "Young Frankenstein" actress Garr
14 Wore away
15 "Try" singer
16 Training for a Trane technician
17 Rules for making a flour-based sauce?
19 Counting-out word
20 Brother of Edward and Charles
21 Graduates
23 "Psst!"
24 Desmond Morris book (with "The")
27 Chauffeur's coif?
31 Antithesis of better
35 Piece of office furniture
36 Samoan capital
37 German poet Mörike
39 Most undeniable
41 Mayfair elevator
42 Trail grooves
46 Shooting sport
47 What's the meaning of "perhaps"?
50 Came to understanding, in England
51 Duck dog
54 Puzzle
56 Staring fiercely
58 Actor Braeden
59 "Enough, already!"
62 "Dracula" heroine Harker
63 Lex Luthor's friend
64 Beginning
65 Shade close to cerulean
66 Accelerated nursing program
67 Reagan's attorney general

DOWN

1 Psalms interjection
2 Brom Bones' rival
3 Riotous
4 Olfactory stimulus
5 Public ___
6 Life-saving technique
7 Long, narrow inlet
8 Interlopes
9 Buick models
10 Universal attraction
11 Like two or four
12 Indian princess
13 Freezing
18 Blöthar's metal band
22 Delivery co.
25 Nanny's baby
26 Grandmother of Enos
28 Sword with a fuller
29 Shine partner
30 "The Simpsons" creator Groening
31 Join metal to metal
32 "Garfield" dog
33 "Dennis the Menace" dog
34 Like Voltaire plays, often
38 REM specialist, for one?
40 Pre-owned Honda motorcycle
43 Two-dot diacritics
44 China's "Great Lake"
45 Part of GPS
48 Opposite of pos.
49 Wampum unit
51 Run out
52 Heavenly ram
53 Midler in "Ruthless People"
54 Canal in a Springsteen song
55 Fashion designer Ricci
57 Single
58 One skilled in 6 Down
60 Impiety
61 Security org. at SFO

136 LOOK TWICE by Richard Silvestri
Don't cry "ow!" when solving this one.

ACROSS

1 Mystical deck
6 Jack Horner's find
10 Wild party
14 Isolated
15 Hydrant hookup
16 Treat with milk
17 Displayer of infants?
19 Take a little off the top
20 Church custodian
21 Predetermine
23 Power co. product
25 Copier need
26 Off the ship
30 Language of the Masses, once
33 Get high
34 Sound-related
35 CIA forerunner
38 Brawny hauler?
42 Well filler
43 Bent out of shape
44 Calculus calculation
45 Siesta sound
46 Subjoin
48 Two-faced deity
51 Sub ___ (secretly)
53 Three-syllable foot
56 Deodorant type
60 Bit of smoke
61 River, during flood season?
64 Bibliography abbr.
65 Position at sea
66 Wagnerian work
67 Broad valley
68 Cyclist's choice
69 "Delta Dawn" singer

DOWN

1 Folder projection
2 Word of woe
3 Ring wear
4 Figurine material
5 Professor, at times
6 Speech sound
7 Base or bass
8 Put to work
9 Trifling
10 Beacon Hill locale
11 "Catch-22" actor
12 Trawler equipment
13 Early war reporter
18 Swimming spot
22 Fence crossing
24 Bunch of grapes
26 Piedmont province
27 Before you know it
28 Bird of prey
29 Smeltery input
31 Uffizi disply
32 Pit contents
34 Place of worship?
35 Shrek, for one
36 Tommy's gun
37 Roe source
39 Washer cycle
40 El Dorado's lure
41 Kindergarten break
45 Limber
46 Date-indicating phrase
47 Ashen complexion
48 Had a chat
49 "West Side Story" role
50 Twangy
52 It may be tall
54 Loot
55 Floor unit
57 Bound along
58 Had to pay
59 Teen outcast
62 Gamboling place
63 Sun emanatiuon

137 IT ISN'T FARE by Richard Silvestri
We're guessing Rich is a committed carnviore.

ACROSS

1 Hold back
5 Corpsmen
11 Cornfield sound
14 This clue has oen
15 Camden Yards player
16 Hagen of the stage
17 Syllabus section
18 Like some windshields
19 Face Rocky
20 **Start of a quip**
23 Short spin
24 Years of note
25 Brother
28 Trusted counselor
32 Sound grate?
36 "First Blood" hero
38 Crew need
39 Caravan beast
40 Something to lend
41 **Middle of quip**
42 Greek marketplace
43 She honeymooned on Ork
44 Stage design
45 Dahomey, today
46 "The NeverEnding Story" author
47 Breakfast option
49 Caught
50 Long-snouted fish
52 Montreal's Place ___ Arts
54 **End of quip**
62 One of the Brady Bunch
63 Wagner heroine
64 Hard to find
65 Say, "What?"
66 Filter
67 Pizza place
68 The reason
69 Drunk as a skunk
70 Bog moss

DOWN

1 Usher's hand-back
2 Newcastle river
3 Grist for DeMille
4 Drive a roadster
5 Issue in a murder trial
6 Land of leprechauns
7 Bumper blemish
8 Teeny bit
9 Quick-witted
10 Passover meal
11 San Juan Hill setting
12 Lots
13 Ski application
21 It may be eidetic
22 Sale site
25 Bowling round
26 Arrested
27 Change a bill
29 One kind of pollution
30 Shocking weapon
31 Take the stump
33 Surounded by
34 ___-comic play
35 Undercover agent
37 No-goodnik
39 Suspension bridge supports
47 Monte ___ sandwich
48 It leads to a sum
51 Not quite right
53 Barbershop band
54 Blowout
55 Black as night
56 Word processing command
57 Mattress support
58 Emmy winner Falco
59 Roof feature
60 Side-by-side result
61 Canterbury's county
62 Mandible

ACROSS

1 Place for a gas grill
5 Bit of derring-do
9 Wine cellar fixtures
14 Skin-cream additive
15 Mascara target
16 Vote off the island, so to speak
17 Seedy lodging
19 Peaceful protest
20 Body art
21 Point of exasperation
23 Coffee bean variety
26 ___ Moines
27 Nightclub denizen
32 ___ facto
33 One of the Seven Dwarfs
34 Opposite of o'er
37 "___ say more?"
39 Highland cap
41 Had sore muscles
43 Judge played by Stallone
45 Fabric defect
47 Frosty coating
48 Teen overnighter
51 Ozone pollutant: Abbr.
54 Santa portrayer in "Elf"
55 Brings back on staff
57 Brings to an end
62 Good excuse
63 Somnambulate
66 Infant's ailment
67 Sized up
68 Jiffy ___
69 Potato dumpling
70 Take-out sign
71 Whole lot

DOWN

1 Balmy
2 Fitzgerald of jazz
3 Old geezer
4 Held on to
5 Gobsmacked
6 ___ de toilette
7 Grand Canyon pack animal
8 Broadway musical set in Oz
9 Interstate stop
10 Gyroscope part
11 Referenced
12 Oscar winner for "A Fish Called Wanda"
13 Drops in the mail
18 Mystery writer Tami
22 Confident assertion
24 Tons
25 Stomach settlers, in brief
27 Playwright ___-Manuel Miranda
28 Speaking-out page
29 App buyer
30 Network connections
31 Russian country home
35 Superhero role of Chris Hemsworth
36 Miami team
38 Leisure class
40 Countenance
42 Like some martinis
44 "No way, bro!"
46 Come before
49 Gathered together
50 Get ready
51 Wise remark?
52 Serious offender
53 Cook-off dish
56 Large wading bird
58 Leatherworking tools
59 First king of Israel
60 Hamburg river
61 Slant unfairly
64 Caustic cleaner
65 Sushi selection

139 END RHYMES by Harvey Estes
There are 1,200 varieties of 15 Across.

ACROSS

1 Tweet elite
11 Wine with a muscat flavor
15 Picnic fruit
16 Tommy's gun
17 Wind instrument
18 Potter's stick
19 Rel. school
20 Cancun coin
21 Land on Lake Victoria
23 Something to build on
24 Into pieces
25 Airbag activator
28 "New York Times" publisher Adolph
29 Deluge refuge
30 Hayley in "Pollyanna"
31 Church song
32 Commandment violation
33 Surveyor's map
34 Large and petite
35 1987 Masters winner Larry
36 Ring icon
37 Pampered, with "on"
38 Guys
39 Capitol Hill pol.
40 Makes a pick
41 Gets in the way of
42 Like rice and potatoes
44 Etta of old comics
45 Home of St. Francis
46 Glass opera "La Belle et la ___"
47 "I knew it!"
50 Hospital count
51 Cyber adolescent
54 Faucet malfunction
55 Conventional
56 Ice-cream brand
57 Equal and Splenda

DOWN

1 "Jabberwocky" opener
2 Drop off
3 Bit of news
4 Chairman pro ___
5 Equatorial clime
6 "Dixie" composer
7 Peanut Butter Cup inventor
8 Karen Carpenter, for one
9 Gout spot
10 Mass arrivals
11 Dam north of Lake Nasser
12 "Out of the way!"
13 Meat mallet
14 How Washington chose to cross the Delaware
22 Vane mover
23 Add gold to a mine
24 Played the part
25 Like roads after a landslide
26 Turkey food
27 Quite clear
28 Seeps slowly
31 Thurber fantasizer
34 Specious arguments
35 Jeff's cartoon pal
37 Scrip writers
38 Global thawing
41 Absolutely loathe
43 Takes gambles
44 New Hampshire city
46 Soft cheese for parties
47 "Miracle Mets" outfielder
48 Get wind of
49 Master-at-___
52 Crow call
53 Son of Prince Valiant

140 THEMELESS by Brian E. Paquin
The clue at 19 Across has its roots in the days of pay telephones.

ACROSS

1 Elucidates in a patronizing way
11 Short boxing shots
15 Epithet for Sammy Davis Jr.
16 Help out with a bank job
17 Living the dream
18 Type of bond, briefly
19 Dropped a dime
20 "For Your Eyes Only" singer
22 Outback bird
23 Sucrose and fructose
25 Pose
26 Stocking stuffer
29 Ra's realm
30 Hip-hop duo Kris ___
32 "Fiddler on the Roof" matchmaker
34 Serf
36 "Guardians of Ga'Hoole" birds
38 Hotel amenity
39 In a daze
42 Puccini opera
45 Athlete who cheats
46 Wonderment
48 Tries for a part
50 Radio range
51 Hits the pavement like a pumpkin
54 Emcee's aid
55 Root beer concoctions
57 "Breaking Storm" is one
60 Old MacDonald's spread
61 "Hammerin' Hank" of baseball
63 Nobelist author Wiesel
64 On the job
65 Targets of chin-ups
66 Cannons used to fend off pirates

DOWN

1 Rippled silk fabrics
2 Wong in "Shanghai Express"
3 Eighth rock from 29 Across
4 Ella's singing style
5 Tiny opening
6 Laundry units
7 Author Huxley
8 Getting slippery during winter
9 "Life Is Good" rapper
10 Navigate
11 Printer issues
12 Touches
13 Melissa on "Supergirl"
14 Tours of duty
21 Deserves, in a way
24 From the top
27 Govt. security
28 In the least favorable circumstance
31 Bump a bet
33 Brownie
35 Island on a river
37 Earth's crust layer
39 "Tres chic!"
40 Ready, willing, and able to deliver
41 Didst not exist
43 GM sports cars
44 Not lean
45 Coarse woolen cloth
47 Forever, to a poet
49 Aromas
52 "Fiddlesticks!"
53 Yea or nay follower
56 Iowa State city
58 Window frame
59 Guitar clamp
62 Airport posting

141 THEMELESS by Brian E. Paquin
Buffalo solvers will know the answer to 19 Down.

ACROSS
1 Eager to head home
7 Most wacky
14 Asserted
15 Corroded
16 The eyes have them
17 Weathervane bird
18 Pants measurement
19 "That's show ___!"
20 Study intensely
21 Masked swordsman of film
23 Partner of reason
24 Naval Academy mascot
28 Society column word
29 ___ maxima culpa
30 Project Blue Book concern
36 Decide to stop arguing
37 Visit a funeral home
38 ___-de-lance
39 Lucky strike
40 "___ Leaving Home": Beatles
41 Perturbs
44 Primary strategy
46 Squadron
47 Jungfrau pass
48 Toy boy
53 Cheetahs and cougars
55 Earned an Olympic podium spot
56 Quiver
57 Cork's country
58 "A no-brainer!"
59 Analyzes 39 Across

DOWN
1 Place for a timer
2 Cod catchers
3 White cheese
4 Desilu Studio founder
5 The Kraken, for one
6 "Inc." execs
7 Luigi's Nintendo sib
8 The full range
9 "In excelsis ___"
10 Sends packing
11 Journal jotting
12 Carpet cleaner
13 Mel of the Mel-Tones
14 Singer Grande, in fanzines
19 Kummelweck, for one
22 Bank recoveries
23 Summarize
24 Bean counter's standards, initially
25 Russian Orthodox saint
26 Well-ventilated
27 Links reservation
29 Courier cyclists
31 Spanish babies
32 1990s Oldsmobile model
33 Part of a foot
34 Soiree
35 Dick Tracy's love
41 Civvies
42 Like krypton
43 Cabinet contents
44 Parker in "Superman Returns"
45 Senatorial staffers
47 Cartoon frames
49 Big ball
50 "Ageless" skin moisturizer
51 Periscope part
52 Like Felix and Oscar
54 June draft org.
55 Ronan Farrow's mom

142 STARS AND STRIPES   by Mike Gifford
A good one to solve on June 14.

ACROSS

1 Mutter
5 Jimmy of "Sons of Anarchy"
10 Writing style
14 Miscellany
15 Balsam of "Mad Men"
16 Mayberry moppet
17 Creole dish
20 Look like
21 High-voltage sign
22 Facial tissue layer
23 Refer to
24 Blues singer Smith
28 Brief break
32 Marine mammal
33 Laborious task
34 Earth-friendly prefix
35 Second-largest land mammal
39 Suffix for president
40 Start of a count
41 Befuddle
42 Blown up
45 Wraps up
46 Brilliant move
47 CSA monogram
48 Miscreant
51 Learn by heart, in London
56 Strauss opus heard in "2001"
58 Fatal March day
59 Saturn's largest moon
60 Almanac period
61 Take these tests sitting down?
62 Bring to bear
63 Grand narrative

DOWN

1 Pressure unit
2 Away from the wind
3 Kitchen cover-ups
4 Japanese beef
5 Trotter's home
6 Masculine
7 Steppat in "Madeleine"
8 Mowry of "Instant Mom"
9 California zoo city
10 Center of Charlotte?
11 Put lipstick on ___
12 Riviera resort
13 Natty Bumppo's quarry
18 Darth Vader's side
19 It's put in banks
23 Sidekick
24 "Fame" singer
25 Phillips of "Star Trek: Voyager"
26 Moonshine machine
27 Collection
28 Hunter's cover
29 They're home on the range
30 Sorbonne is one
31 Valentine's Day dozen
33 Bo Peep's loss
36 Adjust to a standard
37 Immature
38 Shogun's capital
43 What passwords provide
44 Way to go
45 Dental anchor
47 Concrete support rod
48 Slugger's stats
49 Alan in "Paper Lion"
50 Woodpecker food
51 Remote button
52 Tampa Bay nine
53 Endoscopic focuses
54 Harry Potter's Patronus
55 Old Testament book
57 Veto

REDUPLICATIONS by Mike Gifford

58 Across is also the name of a popular 1960s dance.

ACROSS

1 Part of a doorframe
5 Molten rock
10 Guess from left field
14 First Dominican MLB manager
15 Hour after midnight
16 Knell
17 Haphazard
19 Sword with a button
20 Many eBay users
21 Passed, as time
23 Kung ___ chicken
24 Like many HGTV projects
25 Held fast
29 Simple sheds
33 Laughing birds
34 Domain
36 "Back in the ___": Berry
37 Twin of Ares
38 Panasonic subsidiary
39 Place for corn or baby
40 SF time
41 Louisiana marsh, e.g.
42 Nightclub charge
43 Barn lofts
45 Ancient city of Syria
47 Leaves in a cup
48 Battle of Britain heroes
49 Self-guided tour?
53 Looked the other way
57 Dragon's den
58 Essential details
60 Saxophone range
61 Toledo product

62 Sonority
63 Bill-blocking votes
64 Signature melody
65 Tip of Tinker Bell's wand

DOWN

1 Blockbuster movie of 1975
2 "You can't pray ___"
3 Defoe's Flanders
4 Where diamond clubs find relief
5 Missouri Compromise president
6 Cannes cordial flavoring
7 Type of hair goo
8 Gander gender
9 Univalent chemical group
10 Intervene
11 Inverted
12 Aweather antonym
13 Extorted
18 "My Ten ___ in a Quandary": Benchley
22 First rib donor
25 Hebrew "A"
26 Backs
27 Highfalutin
28 Horse-drawn carts
29 "Down low" shot
30 "Strange Magic" group
31 Willow twig

32 One born on a kibbutz
35 North Carolina river
38 Logger's tool
39 Offers solace to
41 Pig's wild cousin
42 Trolley sound
44 Paris tubes
46 Sock pattern
49 Liveliness
50 Inaugural ball, e.g.
51 "Meet Me ___ Louis" (1944)
52 Soft core
53 Gossip tidbit
54 National Guard concern
55 Where Enceladus is buried, in myth
56 Salon colorist
59 Placekicker's aid

144 PREVIEWS* by Roger & Kathy Wienberg
An original theme that reveals itself at 55 Across.

ACROSS

1 Acknowledged a fellow Wrangler driver
6 Rihanna song "Te ___"
9 Some Uno cards
14 "You win!"
15 June/December occurrences
17 Pizza order
18 Moccasin leather?
19 OneStep camera insert*
21 Put your foot down
22 DoD division
23 Do not disturb
27 Airbag, for one*
31 Not as bright
32 Walton of Walmart fame
33 1987 John Candy role
34 Welsh dish
38 Sgt. Bilko portrayer
41 Bitter beer
42 Cattle call
44 Stocking stuffer
45 Understood*
50 Video's counterpart
51 Victoria Island discoverer
52 Big brass
55 Preview
59 Step on it
62 Great guy?
63 Prima donna
64 Leaves in a bind?
65 Bottomless pit
66 Photo finishes
67 With cunning

DOWN

1 Citrus cloud formations
2 Distribute
3 Semisheer fabrics
4 Rollicking adventure
5 Whitetail or blacktail
6 Basketball stat
7 "Rainy Days and ___"
8 "Frozen" snowman
9 McCartney of fashion
10 Destiny
11 "That's gross!"
12 Louvre Pyramid architect
13 ID with two hyphens
16 Go downhill
20 Highway marker interval
24 Sassiness, slangily
25 Remus rabbit
26 Slippery swimmers
28 Little lie
29 Ol' Blue Eyes' monogram
30 Signal sender
34 Sitar music
35 Baseball family name
36 Part of AARP: Abbr.
37 Overtrump
39 Singer Rawls
40 Like some blinds
43 Bug
46 They work around the clock?
47 Kerfuffles
48 Provides food
49 Passing remarks?
53 Tropical palm
54 Bohemian
56 Biological duct
57 Comparison words
58 Nile reptiles
59 Extinct New Zealand bird
60 NYPD alert
61 Fundamental

JURY PANEL?* by Roger & Kathy Wienberg
The answer to the punny title can be found at 55 Across.

ACROSS

1 Hindu mystic
6 Spa sound
9 Figure-skating competition
14 How some securities are priced
15 Color TV pioneer
16 Radiant
17 Tend
19 Jeweler's eye
20 Bar stock
21 Like totem poles
22 Cosmetics giant
24 It's worth fighting for*
26 Kept score in cribbage
28 Block or stock follower
29 Crossword diagrams
30 Traffic infraction result
32 Screech
35 Community college offering*
39 Rubbish
40 Errant shot
41 Olympic marathoner's destination
42 Objector's word
43 "Ship of Fools" director
44 Just split*
50 Show disinterest
51 Wiener schnitzel
52 Statement ending in "or else"
54 Muhammad Ali's daughter
55 Jury panel?
58 Neck scarf
59 Daily grind
60 Bugs
61 Warms
62 Settle on
63 "Get Yer ___ Out!" (Stones album)

DOWN

1 Richard Edson's "Platoon" role
2 Global assn. with 164 members
3 Defender
4 Getting by
5 Where the Tigris and Euphrates meet
6 Pal of Threepio
7 Sour
8 Part of a guffaw
9 London's Crystal ___
10 Ancient marketplace
11 Common Feb. 14 text
12 Procedures to be learned
13 Borg, Edberg, or Wilander
18 Sponsor
21 Acquiesced
22 Newborn test score
23 Left-hand page
25 Olympic pool paths
27 Corner PC key
30 Conviction
31 Possessive pronoun
32 Pet mortuary device
33 Extend a driver's license
34 Hunger for
36 "Don't try to stop me!"
37 Violinist's gift
38 Ambiguous situation
42 Sheepish sounds
43 Golden State Warriors coach Steve
44 Pizzazz
45 Stamp out
46 City on the Mohawk River
47 License
48 Thoroughly enjoyed
49 Cause of Scarlett's fever?
53 Like French toast
55 Supporting
56 Thurman in "Jennifer 8"
57 Letter addenda letters

146 HAIRY PROBLEM by Roger & Kathy Wienberg
. . . and that hairy problem is at 60 Across.

ACROSS

1 Uber alternatives
6 Fool
9 Pound sounds
14 Past plump
15 Hoppy beer, for short
16 Battery pole
17 Yankee slugger Judge
18 Rapid transit?*
20 Some kisses or glances
22 Seduce
23 Gas station symbol since 1909*
25 Food stamp
28 Yarn
29 Snake along
31 Electrify
34 "Give it ___"
36 Repasts
37 Numerical suffix
38 Alpine feature*
41 Letter from Greece
42 It may be blank
44 Negative prefix
45 Similar
46 Ebay words
49 Goes downhill quickly
51 King toppers
52 List of starters and replacements*
57 Zenith
59 Protective coat
60 Hairy problem (and a hint to the theme*)
63 Love, Italian-style
64 Egg holders
65 Nest egg letters
66 Biological subdivision
67 Wizards

68 Epoch
69 Blissful spots

DOWN

1 Clink glasses
2 Let up
3 Photocopy
4 Keep from spreading
5 New York tribe
6 Broadcast news
7 Tipped over
8 Computer command
9 Type of stick
10 Not there yet
11 Person of interest . . . great interest
12 Shareable PC file
13 Steadfast
19 Lady's man
21 Strikeout king Ryan
24 Lily plant
26 Indian city
27 Incendiary crime
30 Little rascal
31 Electric car maker
32 Room at the top
33 "Hurry up!"
35 Part of BYOB
38 DC figure
39 Tag info
40 Crosses with loops
43 Don't hold your breath
45 Regretful
47 Upper hand
48 Frank
50 Period frozen in time
53 Peter of Paraguay
54 Single-handedly

55 What many incumbents do
56 It's a lock
58 Mayberry resident
60 Bottom line
61 Mom-and-pop org.
62 Diego or Antonio

147 GROUP THINK by Rob Gonsalves & Jennifer Lim
The Tree is the unofficial mascot of 28 Across.

ACROSS

1 Freeway exit
5 Wouldn't ___ a fly
9 News outlets, collectively
14 Moonfish
15 Continent with over 4 billion people
16 Turn away
17 DVR brand since 1999
18 Sets of points, in geometry
19 She played June in "Walk the Line"
20 Air Force Academy play group?
23 Killer whale
24 ___ polloi
25 Triangular Indian appetizer
28 Tiger Woods' alma mater
33 Getaway for fall guys?
35 502, in old Rome
36 Seeks answers
37 Mandela's party: Abbr.
38 Await settlement
39 Fish eggs
40 Amphibian military force?
44 Recommends in an ad
46 "The Tempest" King
47 Intelligent playfulness
48 Pest in a cloud
49 Grizzly gumshoe?
55 Chemistry lab tube
57 2018 film by Cuarón
58 It's sticky
59 Chris of "Jurassic World"
60 One logged in
61 Stone of cinema
62 Vice follower
63 French 101 verb
64 To the right, mapwise

DOWN

1 Military grp. on campus
2 Capital of Samoa
3 Dallas hoops team, for short
4 Prefab events for news crews
5 Dialed-down in Starbucks speak
6 Country of MA and PA?
7 Costa ___
8 Follow close behind
9 Leaves on an island
10 Notwithstanding
11 "Added" has three
12 Taxing org.
13 Gobbled down
21 Approximately
22 Text on a smartphone
25 Gaze intently
26 Burning desire?
27 Prepped for amplification
28 Certain camcorders
29 Folded fare with filling
30 Greek theater
31 Circus stages
32 Response to a negative taunt
34 Tag, e.g.
38 Mentored woman
40 Short opera solo
41 Quartet between Q and V
42 Exuberant display
43 Dieter's concern
45 Little big-eyed birds
48 Pyle of Mayberry
49 Go at it
50 Like 1+1=2
51 Flock of sparrows
52 ___ mater
53 Bacardi and Goslings
54 Place in Congress
55 Service for buying TV events
56 Intense anger

148 THEMELESS by Victor Fleming

16 Across is also a phrase uttered by Morocco in "The Merchant of Venice."

ACROSS

1 Auto garage invoice
9 "In Flanders Fields" poet
15 Job for a tween
16 Trick-taking card game
17 Bind together
18 "On-the-way" delivery service
19 R.E.M. vocalist Michael
20 Gene Roddenberry creation
22 The Greatest Generation (with 46-A)
25 Prov. on Hudson Bay
26 Hillock
27 Word that evolved from a 2-letter initialism
28 Swinging or sliding thing
29 Handbag monogram
30 Collared one
31 Nigerian secessionist state (1967–70)
33 Hiker's nosh
34 Word with ant or brat
35 Broadway restaurant
38 Brilliant stroke
39 "Do a good turn daily" org.
42 Sporty sunroof
43 "Death in Venice" author
44 French vineyards
45 "Lizzie McGuire" setting: Abbr.
46 See 22 Across
49 Menu option
51 Conductor from Mumbai
52 Baseball's "Little Giant"
53 Meredith Willson play (with "The")
56 Classic Jaguars
57 Cole Porter's "___ Goes"
58 Guard duty puller
59 Flapdoodle

DOWN

1 1992 Bobby Fischer opponent
2 Goes quickly
3 Kind of mouse
4 A go
5 McMahon who authored the Atomic Energy Act
6 Fahd ___ Abdul Aziz
7 Sign
8 Grandma's hand cleaner
9 Kind of support
10 A minor, e.g.
11 Confab
12 Economy hotel chain
13 One who transfers property
14 Richard Strauss opera
21 Rugby play
23 Busy bees
24 Fictional Cincinnati station
28 Ishiguro's "The Remains of the ___"
30 Polynesian paste
31 Full force
32 Small snip
33 Econ. stat
34 First-class
35 Place in Monopoly
36 One with a trainer
37 "Calvin and Hobbes" babysitter
38 Geico ad role
39 Nehru, for one
40 Shades of summer
41 WikiLeaks figure
43 Clubber Lang portrayer
44 Nativity scene
46 Dog soup, in diners
47 ___-craftsy
48 Lets out
50 Cairo Christian
54 Tres minus dos
55 Thesis beginning

149 PERMIAN PANTHERS CHRONICLE by Victor Fleming
A movie and a TV series were adapted from the book featured below.

ACROSS

1 Calyx components
7 Deadly lung disease
11 Hockley in "Titanic"
14 Showy shrub
15 Pre-Derby race
16 Latin lover's word?
17 **H.G. Bissinger book: Part1**
18 Found hilarious
20 Diminished
21 Inanity
22 **Book: Part 2**
24 ___ alai
27 Neither correlative
28 Org. that issues Known Traveler Numbers
29 Almond
31 Like space cadets
34 Home, informally
38 Craftsman's workplace
39 Spot for a Shih Tzu
40 "After Midnight" songwriter J.J. ___
41 Posted
42 Smug look
44 Lustful deity
45 Keats product
47 Full-house letters
49 Take, after taxes
50 **Book: Part 3**
56 Annuls
57 Before deadline
61 Salt source
62 **Book: Part 4**
63 Small dose?
64 Unrevealing garment
65 Light up
66 Assent of man
67 Poker penny
68 "Children of a ___ God" (1986)

DOWN

1 Strongbox relative
2 Rock band Better Than ___
3 Spanish nation?
4 Ehrenreich in "Solo"
5 Intro
6 Articulate
7 Mast pole
8 On ___ (hot)
9 TV show genre
10 Parsley bits
11 Salvation Army trainee
12 Accumulate
13 A bunch of, slangily
19 Beautify
21 Irritatingly high-pitched
23 Theophobiac's fear
24 Dempsey ring opponent Willard
25 Masseuse's target
26 Club for Inbee Park
30 As yet
32 Feng shui purpose
33 Energetic outbursts
35 Attain justly
36 Tart plum
37 Touchstone
42 Sunbathe
43 X-___ large
46 Explorer Vasco ___
48 Tense
50 Lip-smacking
51 Portly
52 Tortilla sandwiches
53 Kindle material
54 Clifftop home
55 Sews with an egg
58 Portuguese kings
59 Past deadline
60 Elias or Mikael of tennis
62 Be indisposed.

THEMELESS **by Harvey Estes**
13 Down is a member of both Rock & Roll and Country Music Halls of Fame.

ACROSS

1 Kind of squash or western
10 Nursery fixtures
15 Rent
16 Artist Matisse
17 Puts off
18 Weighed down
19 Hides
20 Epicure's activity
22 Student monitors at Hogwarts
25 "___ the news today . . .": Beatles
26 Where David slew Goliath
27 Poker-faced
29 Wallach and Whitney
32 Monsignor, for one
34 Rock trigram
35 Huffs and puffs
37 Rapace in "Skyfall"
38 White-plumed wader
40 UPS delivery: Abbr.
41 Danes, not from Denmark
44 Applications
45 "Make sure this gets done!"
47 Congressman Gowdy
49 Saw lumber
50 Beats badly
54 Regular's bar order
56 Book after Jonah
57 Amish transportation
58 Anno Domini alternative
61 Vis-à-vis exams
62 Togged up
63 Row in a bar
64 Like Wisteria Lane women

DOWN

1 Ernie's "forever" honor
2 Antithetical
3 Come to mind
4 Comic-Con, e.g.
5 Grimm witch killer
6 Ecology org.
7 Work with a shuttle
8 Lock
9 Bonnie Tyler's "___ Heartache"
10 Potassium ___ (KClO3)
11 Brought up
12 Wearing nappies
13 "I Want to Be Wanted" singer
14 Be a squealer
21 Competes
23 Deerstalker
24 Vocal passage
27 Serious lack
28 Have-___
29 Omar in "Traffik"
30 Scenic Chicago drive
31 On the whole
33 River of W China
36 "Cape Fear" director
39 Makeup for a goth dude
42 Stead
43 Previously, in poems
46 Muss
48 "Get Shorty" author Leonard
50 Mountain feature
51 Amtrak flyer
52 Insertion symbol
53 Slight variation
54 Yorke of Radiohead
55 Part of USNA
59 Base cops
60 Waze display

BEAVER WORK by Harvey Estes

42 Across is also the title of a Jean-Paul Sartre novel.

ACROSS

1 Stand up to
5 Noted planner of long trips
9 S&L units
14 Part of a Faulkner title
15 Lena of "Chocolat"
16 Linney in "The Details"
17 Long-distance lens
19 Hiked
20 Preferred plum?
22 Discussion group
23 West or east ender
24 Fed. Rx watchdog
26 Former Ford model
27 Part of a flight
30 Mrs. Smith's pan
32 Opera set in Cyprus
34 40 days in the spring
35 Harm from prudish attitudes?
40 Calvary letters
41 Monkeyshines
42 2006 hit song by Beck
45 Anjou alternative
46 Second afterthought abbr.
49 Type widths
50 Exec's degree
52 Lucrezia Borgia's brother
54 Most flooded floodgate?
58 Runway figure
59 Vulgar words are in this
60 Because of
61 Picked out of a lineup
62 Russian revolutionary Trotsky
63 Pound resident
64 Drifts off
65 Barry Humphries' Dame ___

DOWN

1 Like a restless sleep
2 Red Sox div.
3 Had a cow?
4 "I've got my ___ you!"
5 Paxton's 2018 mound feat
6 Plenty
7 Surfer's find
8 Battery part
9 They went to school
10 Stadium souvenirs
11 Your thing
12 Hot, online
13 Down in the mouth
18 Not lento
21 Big name in Dadaism
25 Initial stake
28 "On the Waterfront" director Kazan
29 Backup strategy
31 Stately grove
32 Mayberry detainee
33 Not taken in by
35 Jungle transport
36 1997 Kevin Kline comedy
37 Nader, notably
38 Unharmonious harmonies
39 "Les Misérables" feature
43 Put to work
44 Pappy Yokum's grandson
46 Broke down in school
47 A hydrogen atom has one
48 One-named Tejano singer
51 Les of Clinton's cabinet
53 Hackneyed
55 Prefix with physics
56 Kind of list
57 Like some dorms
58 "ER" roles, briefly

152 NO-NONSENSE PUZZLE by Sarah Daniels
38 Across was honored with a Best Actress Oscar for her role in that film.

ACROSS
1 Growing places
6 Dispatch an email
10 Voice of Simba on "The Lion Guard"
14 Place to connect in Chicago
15 Middle of a noted palindrome
16 Adams and Grant
17 Green one in the White House?
20 Change the locks
21 Horse course
22 Hester with an "A"
23 One who's no pro
24 Heavy balloon material?
25 Wandering researcher
31 Copycats
32 Clock finish
33 Take more than your share
35 URL letters
36 Do a hairdresser's job
38 Blanchett in "Blue Jasmine"
39 Lady's man
40 Tele finish
41 Kind of holiday or candle
42 Good-for-nothin' vampire?
46 Gulf of Maine island
47 Vegas cousin
48 Make an outstanding design?
51 Kind of cracker
52 Leathernecks' org.
55 One whose fame comes and goes?
58 Chalk out
59 Face-saving plant
60 You find them in math class
61 iPod file
62 Their boughs make bows
63 Blessed event

DOWN
1 Like some farewells
2 Ship-to-shore call
3 Rant companion
4 Medical scan
5 They're not perfect
6 Sewage tank
7 Boots one
8 Maiden name signifier
9 Measure out meds
10 1981 royal wedding figure
11 It's a bad sign
12 Vegas resort developer Steve
13 East of Spain?
18 Wolfs down
19 Ticked off
23 Pensioner's org.
24 Grass skirt accessories
25 Slangy denials
26 Decide to join
27 Part of MGM
28 "___ to Hold Your Hand": Beatles
29 Fourth orca ever captured
30 Name in the cereal aisle
34 Rowlands in "Gloria"
36 Word on a calendar page
37 They go on and on
38 Oscar-winning Pixar film
40 Workout focus
41 Accrued a bar bill
43 Speaking lovingly
44 Subjects of the queen
45 "Flip or Flop" project
48 Omar in "Traffik"
49 Prefix for drama
50 Muffin choice
51 Flat-bottomed boat
52 Lyft rival
53 Mattress holder
54 Screen door stuff
56 O'Neill sea play
57 Singer Grande, familiarly

153 NOWHERE TO GO by Sarah Daniels

Jim Henson's final performance as 20-A was a song segment taped on 11/21/89.

ACROSS

1 Tourist destination in India
5 Icy mishap
9 Sticks a fork in it
14 Apartment type
15 Fairytale opener
16 Partridge family
17 Sign of life
19 Loses it
20 Half an iconic Muppet duo
21 Uses the backspace key
23 Hester's "A"
28 Gold, in Gijon
29 React to pepper
30 Return requirement: Abbr.
33 Made tracks
37 "To ___ human": Pope
38 ISP of note
39 Maze predicament, or a hint to the theme
41 Cone front
42 Question from Judas
44 Buggy terrain
45 Ready for a long drive
46 Harass, in a way
48 Ringing words
50 Where to take a hike?
55 Source of steam
56 Lightbulb-shaped fruits
59 TV encore
62 Collect dirt, in a way
64 Rewrite the will
65 Sportscaster Collinsworth
66 Prom hairstyle, perhaps
67 Man cave dwellers
68 Phishing targets: Abbr.
69 "Over here!"

DOWN

1 Sign that you overdid it
2 One who gets around
3 Bicolored horses
4 Jam fruit
5 Cry out loud
6 Prepare to be knighted
7 Words of sympathy
8 Type of coup
9 Checked at the airport
10 It might pop up
11 Batter's stat
12 Samantha of "Full Frontal"
13 Part of GPS
18 Sign of sadness
22 Some Mercedes models
24 National flower of England
25 Short and sweet
26 Online read
27 Fix up the lawn
30 Garage door tracks
31 Trig function
32 Half a toolbox item?
34 Lily ___
35 Duke's URL suffix
36 Where thieves lie low
39 Base places
40 Astrophysicist deGrasse Tyson
43 Horace Greeley's newspaper
45 Worked out
47 "I really didn't want to know that!"
49 Hummus and such
51 Smart guys?
52 PRNDL choices
53 Sam of Watergate fame
54 O.K. Corral brothers
57 Fishing gear
58 Dick and Jane's dog
59 "Ultra cool!"
60 Outback denizen
61 Dewdney's "Llama Llama ___ Pajama"
63 State capital?

154

THEMELESS by Anna Carson

31 Across can also mean "a group disproportionate to the task."

ACROSS

1 Delight
10 Rio Grande tributary
15 How dogs chase their tails
16 First island mentioned in "Kokomo"
17 Makes marginal memos
18 Pigeonhole
19 PI played by Selleck
20 "I need it yesterday!"
22 Childcare writer LeShan
23 Suffix with concert
24 Stable stretch
26 Philanthropist Hogg
27 Penguin Crosby
28 Évian evening
29 Put the next server in place
31 Circus vehicle with too many passengers
35 Tejano star or moon goddess
36 Old Murano money
37 Verb for Popeye
39 Like a doily
40 Unit cost word
43 Paternal corn
46 Ready
48 Baby kangaroo
49 Jerry Stiller's son
50 "Star Trek" trigram
51 Application data
52 "Spring ahead" letters
55 Grain in scones
56 Gets steamy (with "up")
58 Compact
60 Hersey setting
62 Nothing at all to eat
64 Like bell-bottoms, now
65 Universal red-cell donor
66 The willies
67 Jeweler's inventory

DOWN

1 Rival of Florida State
2 Kofi, once of the UN
3 Pal of Pooh
4 Nobel Prize subj.
5 Discovered by accident
6 Jesus spoke it
7 Slugging avg., e.g.
8 Court declaration
9 "You bet!"
10 Touch to diagnose
11 The Big Band ___
12 Tenderized beef cut
13 Trait of a trained canine
14 Times of youthful innocence
21 Writer Oz
25 Inside view
28 Four-game World Series
30 Hard mixture
31 Lap siding
32 One watching what you say
33 Get one's bearings
34 Way cool
38 Naked Goya subject
41 Garfield's grub
42 Composer Dohnányi
44 Soldier IDs
45 Taunts
47 New Year's Day drink
52 "Mack the Knife" singer
53 Cask slat
54 Sorts
57 Volume unit
59 Endo opposite
61 FDR program
63 Mayor pro ___

155 THEMELESS by Anna Carson
The order of names at 36 Across was decided by a coin toss.

ACROSS

1 Hazard in old buildings
9 Some choral music
15 Presentation graph
16 Like some 20th-century music
17 Reptile that will leave you breathless
18 Firenze's land
19 One who does an about-face
20 Make drinkable
21 Pitch, in a sense
23 Oz's means of departure (with "hot")
29 Simple creature
30 Band leader of song
36 ___-Packard Company
38 Goes light
39 Base runners, at times
41 Morning prayers
42 Cough up the cash
44 Like a UFC cage
49 Haifa greeting
50 Distraction from the main issue
57 Seth Meyers specialty
58 Kind of fracture
59 "How dare you!"
60 Lands within lands
61 Way to go
62 Most pricey

DOWN

1 On ___ with
2 Trig function
3 Theodore Cleaver, to Wally
4 A word from Pilate
5 Restaurateur Toots
6 Darkens in the sun
7 Tough sledding
8 Hollywood hopeful's hope
9 Miss handle?
10 Hermione Granger's Patronus
11 Breakfast bread
12 Zhou of China
13 Follows closely
14 Shade of blue
22 Word after viva
23 Sounds from the masseur's room
24 "Da Doo Ron Ron" opening
25 "Somebody's Gotta Do It" host
26 Martin's role in "Ed Wood"
27 Early sib
28 No early birds
31 Healthy ___ ox
32 Ron Darling's former team
33 Area east of the Urals
34 Least of the litter
35 Cathedral nook
37 1982 sci-fi film with a 2010 sequel
40 Broadway hits
43 Easily bent
44 Davis of "Do the Right Thing"
45 Harry Potter's friend Cho
46 Snuffy Smith's son
47 Still kicking
48 Almost first family of 2000
51 Monopoly rollers
52 Gardner of mystery
53 Avenge an insult, perhaps
54 Center of activity
55 Fin change
56 Adam of "Batman"

156 THEMELESS by Harvey Estes
10 Down is also the name of a Clark Gable-Jean Harlow film.

ACROSS

1 Go nowhere in a hurry?
10 Dance in Rio
15 Spin for Odile
16 "Winter of Artifice" author Nin
17 Be a busybody
18 Control
19 Like Oxford graduation caps
20 "Nightwatch" network
21 Sea dog
22 Still
23 "Too rich for my blood!"
27 Logician's conjunction
29 Campfire sight
30 Source of some low notes
36 Carmaker Maserati
38 Prepares for action
39 Chemical weapon of WW1
41 Blade brand
42 Care beginning
43 Swine's confines
44 Kidney-shaped nut
48 Huge, like improvement
51 Islam's deity
52 Aid in advancement
57 Saint of Assisi
58 Not lopsided
59 Performer with lions
60 Little by little
61 Knocker's phrase
62 Showed disdain for

DOWN

1 Bar in a grill
2 "GoldenEye" singer Turner
3 They may be graphic
4 Denials
5 Arm-twisting
6 Chap
7 Castaway's site
8 Character in jokes about heaven
9 Upset, with "off"
10 1777 battle site
11 "He that hath ___, let him hear": Rev. 2:7
12 Ship in the news in 1898
13 Holds together
14 It's a good thing
22 Copperfield's second wife
23 News bit
24 Seat of the Inca Empire
25 Raggedy dolls
26 Editor's notation
28 Baltic port
30 Toss about
31 Sondheim's Sweeney
32 The neighbor's kid
33 Vino venue
34 "Certainly!"
35 Where you get in hot water
37 Two "me-too" words
40 Relented
43 Not so new
44 Desert vista
45 Words before once
46 Noisy impacts
47 Belly-dancing pants
49 "Tiny Alice" playwright
50 Kind of bar
52 Hula shakers
53 Brocaded fabric
54 Lacking depth and height
55 SEC overseer
56 Hanukkah gift

157 THEMELESS by Harvey Estes
34 Across is also a slang word for "dishwasher."

ACROSS

1 Obsidian source
8 Van Gogh painting technique
15 Home of The Big A stadium
16 Performance you can look up to
17 It has one government
19 Turnblad portrayer in "Hairspray"
20 2012 Super Bowl winners
21 Crunches tighten them
22 Density symbols
24 The RSV, e.g.
27 "Watchmen" network
28 De Becque of "South Pacific"
33 "The ___ Gave My Heart To": Aaliyah
34 Gem handler who takes a deep breath
36 Get in on a deal
37 Uninvited pool guests
38 "Later!"
39 New thoughts about old times, perhaps
41 Stewart of "Tennessee Waltz" fame
42 Code subject
43 Summer abroad
44 Mobilized force
45 Adriatic port
47 Overdramatic type
48 Places for mirrored balls
52 Full of wonder
57 Walk onto a movie set?
59 He spoke up in "Up"
60 Greet and seat
61 Some depot staff
62 Narratives with many levels?

DOWN

1 Like the Great Plains
2 Words before "about"
3 It flows from 1 Across
4 Legion of Honor members
5 It needs oxygen
6 Nobelist Bohr
7 Pass by
8 "At Seventeen" singer
9 Tenor role in "Porgy and Bess"
10 Beat the drum for
11 "The Thin Man" dog
12 Place for a guard
13 Signal on the road
14 Confesses, with "up"
18 Final minutes of a blowout game
23 Barrister Rumpole
24 Surfing "blade"
25 Like some circles
26 Susan's role on "Feud"
27 Hamburger ___
29 Screw gauge
30 Brown and others
31 Investigation finds
32 Lose ground
34 Family men
35 Serve you must repeat
40 "One of Us" singer Joan
44 Cisco's pal
46 Dahlia relative
47 Hike
48 Like the Marianas Trench
49 Prefix for China
50 Castor, for example
51 "___ la vie!"
53 Classical work
54 Cosmonaut Gagarin
55 Jay Gould's railway
56 Man caves
58 MLB taters

ACROSS

1 Pillow cover
5 Belmont bet
10 Barrow
14 Yarn
15 Hippo's home
16 Currier's partner
17 Cosmetics giant
18 Hahn of "Grey's Anatomy"
19 Blue Nile source
20 **"If everybody likes you, you're pretty dull."**
22 Frankenstein's helper
23 River to the Volga
24 "Take 2" author Gibbons
26 Hidden
31 Canned heat
34 Whole nine yards
35 Italian liner Andrea ___
37 Home of the Ewoks
38 High-five
40 Creamy dressing
42 Basil Fawlty, for one
43 Scheherazade's milieu
45 "Winter Song" singer McLachlan
47 Helm heading
48 Those who pose?
50 Esteemed, in Essex
52 "Good ___!": Charlie Brown
54 Droning beetle
55 October gem
57 **"Imitations only better the original."**
63 Golfer Didrikson
64 The varsity
65 "A Cat in Paris" burglar
66 Afflictions
67 Second Mrs. Trump
68 Manipulator
69 Pedicure focus
70 Barkin in "Tender Mercies"
71 Satisfy

DOWN

1 Pierce
2 Own
3 Oodles
4 One with a protégé
5 Preying figure
6 Old World old money
7 Tel ___
8 DeMille of Hollywood
9 Strikes out
10 Natives
11 **"Elizabeth Taylor is not beautiful, she is pretty—I was beautiful."**
12 Escalator inventor
13 Ruler of old
21 Scraped by
25 Palindromic saison
26 Alexander of "NCIS"
27 Greek name for Greece
28 **"I never laugh until I've had my coffee."**
29 Special times
30 Alice's cat
32 Alicia Keys hit
33 Spherical
36 Word form for "high"
39 Without equal
41 All-rounder
44 Radiology scan
46 Homeboy's turf
49 Bread seed
51 Its year is 84 Earth years
53 Like Alex Forrest's attraction
55 Final bio
56 ___ Alto
58 Keyboardist Saunders
59 Like drone bees
60 Card to swipe
61 "The Coldest Rapper" rapper
62 Smarting

HOLLYWOOD QUOTES II by John M. Samson
"I didn't back into being an actor, I was born one." —20 Across

ACROSS

1 Admission exams
5 Cardiff citizens
10 "Goodness me!"
14 Ukrainian port
15 A mission to remember
16 "Othello" role
17 Not working
18 Peak performance?
19 Kinnear in "You've Got Mail"
20 **"I had to let my ego go a long time ago."**
22 Jekyll's alter ego
23 Herbal quaff
24 Slow, to Mozart
26 Run through lines
31 Hammered home?
34 "Hail, Caesar!"
35 Conclusion lead-in
37 Pascal on "Narcos"
38 Lacrosse teams
40 Beet and carrot
42 Corn disease
43 Misjudged
45 Doldrums
47 Big diamond?
48 Engraving tool
50 Mercury and argon
52 Wild
54 Clark's "Smallville" friend
55 Ad hoc coalition
57 **"We come. We go. And in between we try to understand."**
63 Go postal
64 Follow a line
65 Like many sportscasts
66 Man or gal Friday
67 Heavy suit
68 Falco in "The Sopranos"
69 Cap-and-gowner
70 Mudlarks have muddy ones
71 Computer giant

DOWN

1 Glides along a piste
2 "Ritorna vincitor!" singer
3 Swiss patriot
4 Slim and trim
5 One for the road
6 "The Time Machine" people
7 Fill a hold
8 Nasal appraisal
9 "The Catcher in the Rye" boy
10 When New Wave peaked
11 **"I enjoy playing characters where the silence is loud."**
12 Like balsamic vinegar
13 Venetian palace resident
21 Slangy approval
25 Fuzzy surface
26 Expedia listings
27 "Ice Maiden" of tennis
28 **"I don't want to be in a fake war in a studio."**
29 Persnickety one
30 Strasbourg school
32 Spew forth
33 Fawns over
36 Inclusive abbr.
39 Chosen
41 Homes for the homeless
44 German article
46 Jolly Roger crewman
49 Highland plaid
51 Like Napoleon on Elba
53 Peter in "Beat the Devil"
55 Talk the talk
56 Feral abode
58 Roosevelt and Hoover
59 Sporran wearer
60 "The Counterfeiters" novelist
61 Devil's domain
62 Fly fishing need

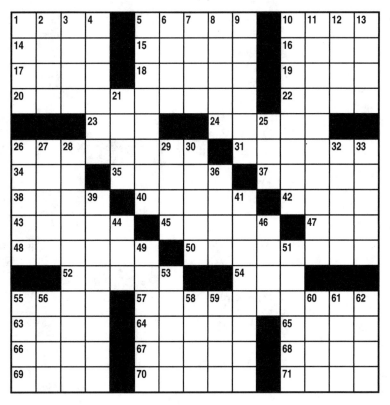

SELECTIVE AMNESIA   by Chris Carter

Percy Faith's instrumental of 46 Down was a #1 hit for nine weeks in 1960.

ACROSS

1 Vitamin C, for one
5 Be an alpinist
10 Golden State's Thompson
14 Krakatoa outflow
15 One with a rucksack
16 Film composer Schifrin
17 Like the Nefud
18 Met soprano Tokody
19 Bacchanal vessel
20 **Start of a quip (with "A")**
23 Noted bear island
24 Cunningham ballet
25 Kind of thief
28 Scoffs
32 United Kingdom, in verse
36 Praise
37 Do-over serve
38 Did a second-story job
40 ___ carte
41 Signs for good or bad
44 **Middle of quip**
47 End of an O'Neill title
49 Saint ___ and Nevis
50 Endoscopy focuses
52 Toughened up
56 **End of quip**
61 Place for a keystone
62 Aqua ___ (platinum dissolver)
63 Margaret Brown's "Goodnight ___"
64 Have the gumption
65 Adulterate
66 "The Neverending Story" author
67 Slide over
68 Fire evidence
69 Angler's spinner

DOWN

1 Interjection of regret
2 Film producer Ponti
3 Like many academic halls
4 Man Ray or Arp
5 Fraidy-cats
6 Disney friend of Stitch
7 Russian vodka brand
8 Table constellation
9 Orthodontic devices
10 It may be offered with a blessing
11 Place for an egg roll
12 "The Black Stallion" hero
13 Days long ago
21 Genus of pond frogs
22 Skye of "Say Anything . . ."
26 Thumbs-down voter
27 Sales booth
29 And others: Abbr.
30 Lucky streak
31 Dispatch
32 Coalition of a kind
33 DaVinci in "Mork & Mindy"
34 Technicality
35 His, in Colmar
39 Body shop proposal
42 Postal creed word
43 Embattled D-Day city
45 Quarterly magazine
46 "Theme From ___ Place"
48 Shoot-the-moon card game
51 Across the keel
53 "20/20" creator Arledge
54 Gradually break down
55 Fire-resistant fabric
56 Dog food brand
57 Siberian river
58 Oatmeal color
59 Exchange fee
60 Tennis drop shot

DIGITAL DISPLAY by John M. Samson
Alternate clue for 17 Across: "Where change is good."

ACROSS

1 "Toy Story" character
5 "It's ___" ("Let's shake on it")
10 RN's "at once!"
14 Greek theaters
15 Anatomical sac
16 Super!
17 1 Across and others
19 Head of Montreal
20 Mayor Lightfoot's predecessor
21 Truncate
23 Roker and Sharpton
24 "Go team!"
25 Most downy
29 Look for flaws
33 Bergman's "___ and Whispers"
34 Murray the K's medium
36 Irish sea god
37 Landers and Miller
38 Brunch fruit
39 Mineral that splits into sheets
40 Basenji or borzoi
41 Letter on a screen
42 Crack under pressure
43 Like Mayan pyramids
45 Grandiose
47 Monarch, to Monique
48 Ground groove
49 One of "the finest"
53 Wing flap
57 Before you know it
58 Hitchhike
60 Joe Orton Play
61 Andean abode
62 Throw out
63 Discontinued GM line
64 Touches down
65 They have mothers

DOWN

1 It stayed in Pandora's box
2 Take ___ view of (disapprove)
3 Big prefix
4 Captains of industry
5 Nun's superior
6 Two-part
7 Directional suffix
8 Makes a request
9 La Rue of oaters
10 Ancient Persian governor
11 Conform to a standard
12 White poker chip
13 "Not Another ___ Movie" (2001)
18 Noels
22 Bologna bear
25 Loads
26 "Ready ___, here . . ."
27 Ribs and chicken wings, e.g.
28 Boot bottom
29 Hero types
30 "Cities of the Interior" author
31 Beany's cartoon pal
32 Austin of tennis
35 "Open, sesame!" sayer
38 Tussaud's title
39 Made a difference
41 "Gladiator" is one
42 Prentiss in "The Stepford Wives"
44 Mortgage fees
46 "Survivor" sides
49 City once called Christiania
50 King's entertainer
51 Wrap-up abbr.
52 Daughter of Uranus
53 In the thick of
54 Frost coating
55 Viking war god
56 March Madness trophies
59 Tea brewer

162 "LET US BRAY" by Harvey Estes

Harvey was listening to "Donkey Serenade" when he thought this one up.

ACROSS

1 Arrange gracefully
6 Up to speed
10 Peace Nobelist Wiesel
14 Appian Way traveler
15 Sweet-talk
16 Hindu god of desire
17 Cheri in "Dumb and Dumberer"
18 Japanese attack word
19 Hoodwinks
20 Donkeys, e.g.
23 Teriyaki ingredient
24 "Odyssey" setting
25 Belief in Him
27 Support, when driving
28 Sportscaster Albert
32 Part of a designer name
33 Voice role for Robin Williams
34 Maze marking
35 Documentary on 20 Across running wild in 53 Across?
40 Aimee of "La Dolce Vita"
41 Bridges in movies
42 Milan opera house (with "La")
43 Moore of film
44 Business name abbr.
48 Council, perhaps
50 More handy
52 Eligible for soc. sec.
53 Fun City
57 "Hold on ___!"
59 Ahab, in a Ray Stevens song
60 Marvell's "___ Coy Mistress"
61 What to do
62 Tick off
63 Totally ridiculous
64 Ambulance personnel
65 Fabric choice
66 Group belief

DOWN

1 "Enough!"
2 Volleyballers do it
3 Don of "Cocoon"
4 Some winter wear
5 Pioneer computer
6 Play opening
7 Prosperous period
8 "Doctor Zhivago" heroine
9 Put on a pedestal
10 Hosp. test
11 Hits hard
12 Mere pretender
13 Patsy
21 When repeated, sings
22 Street-smart
26 Start of a selection process
29 "You can't teach ___ dog . . ."
30 Biathlon need
31 Scorpion secretion
33 Mini speedway racer
35 Standard payment
36 American icon
37 Brownie's exam
38 Regulation
39 Checking out
44 Ness target
45 Oliver Twist, for one
46 Fix, as brakes
47 Car radio button
49 "West Side Story" gang member
51 Al Yankovic parody about food
54 Joanie portrayer in "Happy Days"
55 "Jewel of the East Indies"
56 "Ha!"
58 Drafts: Abbr.

163 WORD DIVISION by Harvey Estes
9 Down can be found in "Cinderella."

ACROSS

1 "Wizard of the Sea" pirate
5 Vaults
10 Cup insert
14 Draft classification
15 Reproduce
16 "I Shot Andy Warhol" star Taylor
17 Warsaw agreement
18 Provide
19 Switch positions
20 AA, for example
23 Let
24 Declined a bid
26 Aunt in "Bambi"
27 Hoarder
31 23rd Greek letter
32 Italian wine city
34 Apple gismo
35 Spice made from nutmeg
36 Abound (with)
37 Let out
38 Mireille of "World War Z"
39 Part of an AA
42 Veer to the side
45 Trips up
46 Simon van ___ Meer
49 Build up
51 Hems and haws
52 Rendezvous request
54 Kitchen burners
56 Bowl or boat
57 Poetic tribute for 39 Across?
61 Jewish scroll
62 Pyromaniac's crime
63 And so
64 Greek war deity
65 C or D, e.g.
66 Compact Chevy pickup

DOWN

1 Keystone lawman
2 From one perspective
3 Trim
4 Spreadsheet item
5 Glasses not meant for drinking
6 "Alfred" composer
7 Everydog
8 Ample, to Mammy Yokum
9 Lady Tremaine, for one
10 Goes smoothly
11 Period from womb to tomb
12 Outdoors
13 Army guys
21 Pants problem
22 Morsel for a mare
23 Bog material
25 Subsides, with "down"
28 Force
29 Friend of Seinfeld
30 Varnish ingredients
33 "No doubt about it!"
35 Voice of Bugs
40 Take a sip of
41 Coveted quality
42 Revolutionary Emiliano
43 Key of all white notes
44 Aplenty
46 Mirage site
47 Come into existence
48 Trust
50 Movieplex drinks
53 Rob of "Melrose Place"
55 Deer guy
56 Arrow site
58 Bruins' great Bobby
59 Butterfield in "Ender's Game"
60 Physique, informally

164 ME, MYSELF, AND IDA by Richard Silvestri
12 Down is an ingredient in a Greek Tiger cocktail.

ACROSS
1 Sound of surprise
5 Brings up
10 Beginning
14 Jai follower
15 123 Sesame Street resident
16 Motown music
17 U.S. peanut butter rebranded for the Chinese market?
19 Visibility problem
20 Inspire with affection
21 Gawk at
23 At once
24 One of 100
26 Having a hangover?
28 It's a long story
30 A Rockefeller
33 Isn't anymore
36 Repeat from memory
38 Like a lot
39 Feels sore
41 Granite State sch.
42 Harris of "Grey's Anatomy"
43 Mark of excellence
44 2004 Oympics site
46 Put two and two together
47 Jet's home
49 In a snit
51 Syrian president
53 Diet plan
57 Meditation system
59 Drawer feature
61 Just
62 Occasion for proctors
64 High school course in Iceland?
66 Ocean motion
67 Cohort of Chapman and Cleese
68 Grades in the 70s
69 Not much
70 Field worker
71 Twelve Oaks neighbor

DOWN
1 Opens wide
2 Coeur d'___, Idaho
3 Prince of Darkness
4 Nursery rhyme merchant
5 Dress down
6 Notable time
7 Part of AD
8 Blue ___ Mountains
9 Main route?
10 French Open winner Barty
11 Soft drink for what's-his-name?
12 Anise-flavored liqueur
13 Took American
18 Helicopter parts
22 Woman in a garden
25 Appear at intervals
27 "Enchanted" Hathaway role
29 Cruise ship
31 "Metamorphoses" poet
32 Can't do without
33 Where it all comes out?
34 Recorded proceedings
35 Doo-wop group with nothing new to sing?
37 Not my, your, his, or her
40 Work units
42 "Turn! Turn! Turn!" songwriter
44 Reunion oldster
45 Name of 14 Popes
48 Make an inquiry
50 Call the shots
52 Bandana kin
54 Euripides tragedy
55 Church official
56 Tanzanian border lake
57 Epsilon follower
58 Ramp sign
60 Ill humor
63 Prescription, for short
65 Diesel on a set

165 ONE OF THE GUISE   by Richard Silvestri
Alternate clue for 39 Across: Voiceless consonants.

ACROSS

1 Something to do
5 H.S. exams
10 Bygone despot
14 In the know about
15 Islamic Almighty
16 Siberian river
17 Put one over on
18 "I'm not kidding"
19 Like the Mojave
20 Maher working pro bono?
22 Nothing special
23 High-___ (like some printers)
24 Take down a notch
26 Surety poster
30 Italian auto maker
32 Acrylic fabric
33 Take McGwire out of the starting lineup?
38 Unaided
39 Irrational numbers
40 Canal of song
41 Grand Bradbury?
43 Undercover operation
44 Beck's partner
45 Barbecue favorites
46 Stumble
50 Saratoga Springs, e.g.
51 Sheltered at sea
52 Little doing dirty impressions?
59 Ceremonial act
60 Think the world of
61 Shampoo additive
62 Mary Kay rival
63 Space leader?
64 Force user
65 Just say no
66 Split to unite
67 Jump on the ice

DOWN

1 Soybean extract
2 In a bit
3 Pull over
4 Flavorful nut
5 Play to the crowd
6 Oscar Madison types
7 "For ___ know . . ."
8 Do detective work
9 Wallops
10 Action group?
11 Round numbers
12 Bisciotti flavoring
13 Threat to homeowners
21 Old Age
25 Archaic verb ending
26 Anjou kin
27 Suffix with buck
28 Trials and tribulations
29 Textile machine
30 Wild
31 Famous 500
33 Oscar winner Ives
34 Apportion
35 Pavarotti piece
36 Curling place
37 They get tapped
39 Pacino film of 1983
42 Rocks in a glass
43 Obedience school command
45 Area of influence
46 Unit of capacitace
47 Drawing breath
48 Pretend
49 Really small
50 Throat ailment
53 Pastoral poem
54 Timberwolf
55 Indian chief
56 Holly plant
57 Spy writing
58 Third Reich salute

PROPER NAMES by Lee Taylor
Living up to your name can be a challenge, but not for these six.

ACROSS

1 In with
6 "I Love Rock 'n' Roll" singer Joan
10 Dance on 15 Across
14 Verboten
15 Honolulu locale
16 On a grand scale
17 He's a real go-getter
19 Couple in the news
20 One type of chart
21 "Smooth Operator" singer
22 Has had enough
24 Parking place
25 Hostile to
26 He's one to follow the leader
31 Songwriters' org.
35 Radiate
36 Genesis skipper
37 Feudal lord
38 Main and mizzen
40 Pay dirt
41 Like some statesmen
42 Jordan's capital
43 ___-Flush (bathroom cleaner)
45 Wind instrument?
46 Weeper of myth
47 He's a bit of a crybaby
49 Corn units
51 Super ending?
52 Katmai National Park location
55 Have a yen for
57 Actor's prompt
60 Hoagies
61 He's a Final Jeopardy! loser
64 Wheel support
65 Right-hand person
66 Hair-raising
67 Hammer head
68 Antarctic sea
69 Avoids carbs

DOWN

1 "Take ___ from me"
2 Nativity gift bearers
3 Bassoon cousin
4 Neither's partner
5 Beaucoup
6 "The Grapes of Wrath" family
7 Icicle site
8 Part of "GWTW"
9 City with a famous shroud
10 She's wary of her sticky-fingered guests
11 As far as
12 Creditor's claim
13 Vertex
18 Have a home-cooked meal
23 Like old bread
24 She tends to exaggerate often
25 Greek goddess of wisdom
26 Macho dude
27 Savory taste
28 Thingamajig
29 Perching places
30 Comedian Silverman
32 Chest wood
33 He may be undercover
34 Rosie of "Do the Right Thing"
39 Furtive sort
44 Menzel of "Wicked"
48 Trouble spot
50 Storm tracker
52 Pronto
53 Poshness
54 ___, Baker, Charlie . . .
55 Walks down the aisle
56 Flabbergasts
57 Give a hoot
58 Group of troups
59 Scratches (out)
62 Carnival city
63 Hibiscus necklace

167 "OH-OH!" by Pam Klawitter

38 Across was featured on a 2009 postage stamp designed by Matt Groening.

ACROSS

1 "No bet here!"
6 McEntire who was Colonel Sanders
10 Jackie of action films
14 Gossip spreader
15 Bit of dash
16 Campaign staffer
17 Common font
18 2016 campaign slogan: "Feel the ___!"
19 Mix it up
20 Gibberish
22 Word with open or pointy
23 Surgeons' milieus, briefly
24 Saturn neighbor
26 Does a tire adjustment
30 Jonathan on "Better Call Saul"
32 Japanese heavyweights
33 Swimming pool game of tag
37 Pearl Buck character
38 Blue-haired toon mom
39 Marked a ballot, perhaps
40 Head honcho in Juarez
42 Mix it up
43 End, for Etienne
44 Cantina dips
45 Al in "Paterno"
48 Early Tarzan portrayer
49 Fossey focus
50 Florida "tourist tree"
57 "The Daily Show" host Trevor
58 Big letters in genetics
59 Follow Amazon's course
60 Half of an old TV couple
61 Woodshop shaper
62 Sky blue
63 "Right on, brother!"
64 Faucet handle
65 Horseshoe ___

DOWN

1 Start of Popeye's credo
2 Home of Lima and llamas
3 Lively, on scores: Abbr.
4 Stick a fork in it
5 Wild West watering holes
6 Picture puzzle
7 K-5, briefly
8 Caustic comment
9 Tell the world
10 Bewitch
11 Make a play for
12 Goodbye, in Grenoble
13 "Big Bang Theory" types
21 PSAT takers
25 Old MGM rival
26 Irving's "___ of the Circus"
27 Little girl of old comics
28 Mosque official
29 Humorous "CLOSED" sign
30 Lofty places?
31 It sailed past Charybdis
33 Oahu neighbor
34 Big oafs
35 Headey on "Game of Thrones"
36 Bookie's quote
38 YSL or JFK
41 First name of a classic TV dog
42 Spaghetti sauce herb
44 ___-mo
45 Bamboo muncher
46 ". . . ___ lovely as a tree": Kilmer
47 "Stop it!"
48 Buddy who played Barnaby
51 Reverse a computer error
52 Minotaur's home
53 Chichén ___ (Mayan ruins)
54 Wood splitter
55 Roleo roll
56 Soccer match shouts

168 "PUT YOUR FOOT IN IT!" by Linda Gould

The northern terminus of the Appalachian Trail is located at 42 Across.

ACROSS

1 Curve in the road
5 Yale
10 Drink mentioned in "Lola"
14 Pastry bag wielder
15 Gives credit where credit is due
16 Covered-wagon beasts
17 Stuffing ingredient
19 Foo fighters
20 Flourish
21 Set forth
23 White bill in Monopoly
24 Likewise not
25 Candy nuts
29 Institutor
33 Daft
34 Ayn Rand's shrugger
36 Macaw in "Rio"
37 Bacon sizzle
38 Blooper
39 Think through
40 NRC predecessor
41 "All in ___ work!"
42 Katahdin, for one
43 James Bond actor
45 ___-cat
47 Come out on top
48 Thanksgiving mo. in Canada
49 Formidable foe
53 Rush of water
57 Feathered runners
58 Redundant term for a work shirker
60 Cartoonist Caniff
61 Sign of boredom
62 "Wouldn't ___ Nice?": Beach Boys
63 Olive genus
64 Stated further
65 General ___ chicken

DOWN

1 Butterhead lettuce
2 Neutral shade
3 Kind of do-well
4 First Regiment of Cavalry soldiers
5 Resounded
6 It may be taken out on a house
7 Ending for Carmel
8 Share the load
9 "Back in the ___": Beatles
10 Newspaper clipping
11 Dark azure
12 Thirteen Popes
13 Hatfield patriarch Devil ___
18 Laine of the Moody Blues
22 Weighty obligation
25 1942 Preakness winner
26 Hard case
27 Vodka–and–ginger beer drink
28 Microwave wrap
29 Dental forum thread?
30 Sampan mover
31 Serengeti antelope
32 Undersized
35 Give it a go
38 Childcare writer LeShan
39 "American Gothic" is one
41 Harding and Blyth
42 Keyboard timesaver
44 Forty winks
46 Lost heat
49 Sci-fi sub skipper
50 Pianist Gilels
51 Rick's "Casablanca" love
52 Diner "sugar"
53 British radial
54 Bog babies
55 Mount near the Dead Sea
56 "___ magnifique!"
59 General in "Man of Steel"

169 INSECT WORLD by Linda Gould
17 Across won the 1988 Tony Award for Best Play.

ACROSS

1 Diner dish
5 Tally
10 Bean used in falafel
14 Choral singing part
15 Carmichael of "Downton Abbey"
16 Wise to the plan
17 David Henry Hwang play
19 Wonder Woman's friend
20 Like Helvetica font
21 Freshwater mollusk
23 Forthwith, formerly
24 Slowly, at the Met
25 Ski downhill
28 Helena resident
31 Negotiated peace
32 Burrito bean
33 "Much ___ About Nothing"
34 Greet the judge
35 Ice-cream holders
36 Kith and kin
37 "A mouse!"
38 Also-ran
39 Poetry it's not
40 Hoosegow occupant
42 Looked for
43 Salamanders
44 Sean in "Gangster Squad"
45 Undergrad's goal
47 Canary's confines
51 Hamburg's river
52 Reputed aphrodisiac
54 Property claim
55 Instant
56 Shallowest Great Lake
57 "So that's it"
58 URLs
59 Has a good cry

DOWN

1 Amateur radio operators
2 Jessica in "Fantastic Four"
3 Flabbergast
4 Cajun condiment
5 Last Oldsmobiles made
6 "Dream Lover" singer Bobby
7 Hilary of "Lizzie McGuire"
8 WWW address
9 Loan installments
10 Cinco de Mayo party
11 Peanut butter and raisins on celery
12 Go to the polls
13 Like control freaks
18 Uptight
22 "Once more ___ the breech!"
24 Not a party person
25 Throat infection
26 Colonial news announcer
27 Colonial social event
28 One who digs hard rock
29 Small recipe amount
30 Opus for nine
32 Sits for a shoot
35 Challenges a will
36 Abdominal exercises
38 Rob of "Code Black"
39 Places to keep koi
41 Tranquil
42 Weekly TV show
44 ___-nez
45 Salad shop
46 New Haven team
47 Can of worms?
48 Bushy hairstyle
49 Smooth-spoken
50 They see things
53 Mexican political party

170 IN THE CARDS   by John M. Samson
A famous midtown Manhattan restaurant is named 34 Down.

ACROSS

1 Overseer
5 Taco sauce
10 Apple product
14 River of Rugby
15 Schematics
16 On your own
17 Move, realtor-style
18 Ear-relevant
19 Comparable (to)
20 Castle access
22 ___ noire
23 Lightning flash
24 Lop
26 Detain
29 Steal
32 Summer hrs. in CT
35 Met soprano Fleming
37 Blue-___ special
38 Obscene
40 Gives a hand to
42 Realty unit
43 Calvin of fashion
45 Country singer Travis
47 Sniggle
48 Had a feeling
50 Gets warmer?
52 Golden Horde member
54 Frisco footballers
58 West and Largo
60 1937 Triple Crown winner
63 Great deal
64 Flora and fauna
65 Unadulterated
66 Mood
67 Oil of wintergreen, e.g.
68 Blade of tempered steel
69 Nonpareil
70 Dragged
71 "Don't delete this"

DOWN

1 Troubadours
2 Open to view
3 From a close star
4 Made skiers happy
5 Glistened
6 His, in Paris
7 Cooking fat
8 Hose woes
9 In dreamland
10 Patron of Columbus
11 Lady Gaga hit
12 Hit terra firma
13 At an end
21 Boxer in "Cinderella Man"
25 Big kahuna
27 "Petite Ville" author
28 Ache for
30 Raison d'___
31 "Riverdance" dance
32 Benevolent brotherhood
33 Take-out sign
34 Adele album
36 Peace Nobelist Ducommun
39 Flood, e.g.
41 Word with gold or double
44 Trawl
46 Light haircut
49 "Mork & Mindy" actress
51 Wesley in "U.S. Marshals"
53 Former Russian first lady
55 Blow a gasket
56 Peep show
57 Wintry precip
58 Green Hornet's driver
59 North Carolina campus
61 OCS alternative
62 Suited to ___

ACROSS

1 Bare-bones
5 Religious denominations
10 Pro-adoption org.
14 Ben Gurion Airport is its hub
15 "Don't Know Why" singer Jones
16 Ragged part of a mountain
17 Rama's wife
18 "My hard drive crashed," e.g.
19 Donovan's daughter Skye
20 Like many B&B hosts
22 Three-sided sword
23 Part of SPCA
24 Kate Nelligan movie
26 Simultaneously
31 Med school graduate
34 Vein pursuit
35 Nest in the Rockies
37 Dobbin's negative?
38 Five-star
40 Obiter ___ (passing remarks)
42 "Smooth Operator" singer
43 1983 Indy 500 winner
45 Two-masted vessel
47 Hanoi lunar festival
48 Capital north of Tulsa
50 Descriptive of a rich dessert
52 Caspian region resident
54 Word before long or now
55 George Harrison's "Isn't It a ___"
57 Advice for one with a hangover
63 Cubic Rubik
64 Beat
65 "Abdul Abulbul ___"
66 "Messiah" chorus
67 Maternally related
68 New Rochelle campus
69 "White Christmas" star
70 Assigned stars on Amazon
71 "___ in Translation" (2003)

DOWN

1 Open weave
2 Italian filmmaker Petri
3 Hamelin undesirables
4 Slip by, as time
5 Seized
6 Orlando lake
7 Newborn's place
8 Postpone indefinitely
9 Police badge
10 Arts and ___
11 Pacify
12 What they raise in Cuba
13 Arthur of "Hoop Dreams"
21 Mite
25 Numerous centuries
26 Done for, slangily
27 Lake Minnetonka city
28 "Town Without Pity" singer
29 Karlsson of the NHL
30 Finely chopped, as potatoes
32 City near Brigham City
33 Clark in "GWTW"
36 Novel ending
39 The quick and the dead
41 Admitted to a group
44 Wanted poster abbr.
46 Rhodes in "Roots"
49 It's on the tip of your tongue
51 Particular
53 Massey in "Love Happy"
55 Scaler's goal
56 Comics pal of Nancy
58 Part of QED
59 Ferrara ducal family
60 Herman Melville book
61 Unwelcome beach sights
62 "Animal House" house

ACROSS

1 One of the Pillars of Islam
5 Tropical fruit
10 "Hurry up!"
14 MLB family name
15 Watergate senator
16 Lombardy lake
17 1967 PGA Championship winner
19 Like barn siding
20 "Gentlemen, start your ___!"
21 Pops up
23 Sonnet finale
24 "The ___ Love": R.E.M.
25 Go up the creek without a paddle?
27 Lunar landscape features
30 Korean rice liquor
33 Hidey-hole stockpile
35 Diving duck
36 Yale URL suffix
37 Joe's "Wise Guys" role
38 Caduceus org.
39 Dixie bread
41 Stone and Watson
43 City northeast of St. Etienne
44 Episcopal church government
46 Container weight
48 Dante's inferno
49 Ripped off
53 Hard work
56 "C'est magnifique!"
57 Talk wildly
58 Singer of the #1 hit "I Will Follow Him"
60 After a while
61 ___ Zagora, Bulgaria
62 Diane of "Law & Order: SVU"
63 Some apples or Apples
64 German steel city
65 Saturn and Mercury

DOWN

1 Underworld god
2 Stag
3 Sounds from Big Ben
4 Japanese self-defense method
5 Kind of map or code
6 Extinct ox
7 Director DuVernay
8 St. Lô river
9 "Alice Doesn't Live Here ___" (1974)
10 Bordeaux wines
11 Rod Stewart song
12 Curved molding
13 Auction bids
18 Yet again
22 Faline's mother in "Bambi"
26 Pappy Yokum's wife
27 Look at the answers
28 Riviera's San ___
29 Ballet lake
30 Former FIFA president Blatter
31 Smell
32 "Once a Thief" star
34 Dot partner
40 Gridiron teams
41 Third book in the "Twilight" series
42 "The Human Comedy" novelist
43 "Friends" star
45 Waikiki's ___ Wai Canal
47 Elisabeth of "Law & Order"
50 "J.J." of the NBA
51 "MacGyver" actor Dana
52 Writer Roald and actress Arlene
53 Disney World transport
54 Frog genus
55 "Why don't we?"
56 Brutish beast
59 It's in the pipeline

173 THEMELESS by Harvey Estes
41 Across is an anagram of "Tiger seen."

ACROSS

1 Dry cleaner?
8 Kind of deduction or bliss
15 Taking a break
16 Stress, in a way
17 Left speechless
18 Changed the subject
19 Geneva Convention concern
20 Blown away
21 Play with numbers
23 They say, "I believe not"
27 Brilliance
32 Break down
34 Mariner's friend in "Waterworld"
35 Layers in the barnyard
36 Insincere blows to the wrist
38 "Pictures ___ Exhibition"
39 Violinist Zimbalist
41 Park with 250,000 zebra
43 Does do's
45 Tennis officials
46 Connect with
48 IRA, e.g.
52 Strong connection
57 Pennsylvania's "A-Town"
58 Hose problem
59 Hard to discern
60 Give a name to
61 Mean bunch
62 Comes forward

DOWN

1 Old-style auxiliary verb
2 Gay Talese's "___ the Sons"
3 Curve on a score
4 Something to pitch
5 Set free
6 Wears out
7 Statuary support
8 Take off on
9 Like some 20th-century music
10 Adjust the buck, maybe
11 Steamed up
12 "Look what I did!"
13 All-inclusive
14 "Lucky Number" singer Lovich
22 Gene Simmons, by birth
23 Remains by the hearth
24 Ripping off
25 Dr. Frankenstein
26 Ford lemon
28 Woes for hose
29 Carved symbol
30 Send
31 Took to the station house
33 Ice-cream topping
37 Having feelings
40 Shower components
42 Recent arrival
44 Seal on a ring
47 Word of mock horror
48 Picks up
49 Enchanted girl of film
50 Mare's mate
51 Famous Amos
53 Pass over
54 Bowlers and such
55 Round house
56 Chicken in a basket

174

Astronomers use 17 Across as a term for the habitable zone around a star.

ACROSS

1 "Let's not be hasty" approach
11 It's only skin deep
15 Symbolic stories
16 When shadows are shortest
17 Fairy-tale bed tester
18 Do some housecleaning
19 GRE org.
20 Camera shop purchase
21 Taxed one
23 Bench item
24 An original Mouseketeer
25 Small songbirds
28 Big ref.
29 Jamaican guy
30 Strike site
31 Gives out
32 "Look inside" abbr.
33 Shredded side
34 Lounges around
35 Pal of Piglet
36 Toy soldier material
37 Got to
38 Put out
39 Legal rep.
40 Got an A on
41 Surpassed
42 Erne or tern
44 Split
45 Maestro Toscanini
46 Cole Porter's Indiana hometown
47 Data transmission letters
50 Animal shelter
51 Limit often set by parents
54 Quark's place
55 Strawberry desserts
56 Dietrich of "The Practice"
57 Economic comfort

DOWN

1 Carry on
2 Gobs
3 Trials and tribulations
4 Chaough of "Mad Men"
5 Nimbleness
6 Amazingly enough
7 Hive member
8 Commands to attack
9 Reaction to a rodent
10 Perfumery products
11 Marcus' role on "Black-ish"
12 "No, thanks!"
13 Up close and personal?
14 Deeply rooted
22 Hill builders
23 Aerie asset
24 Wasn't well
25 Picnic side dish
26 Analphabetic
27 Twelve Oaks, for one
28 Drifted off
31 In shock
34 Sport with face-offs
35 Put up
37 Just
38 Extinct
41 Special Forces headgear
43 Shave preceder
44 Smelling a rat
46 Old hands
47 Water barrier
48 Hook's bosun
49 Just in case
52 Two, in Klingon
53 River of Greenville, NC

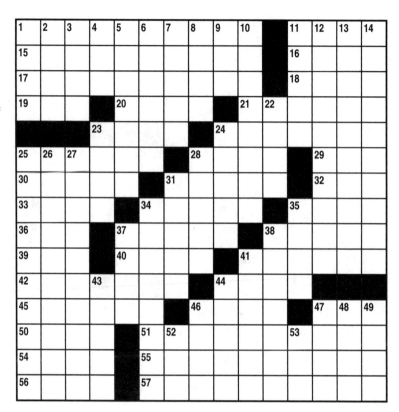

175 THEMELESS by Marie Langley
Colonial 15 Across was known as "the garden city of the East."

ACROSS

1 Tuscany wine
8 City on the Tigris
15 Former capital of Burma
16 Mideast national
17 Sidewalk rain catchers
18 Shake up
19 Least humble
20 Worked a wedding
21 Worms article
22 Inflatable item
24 Frida's friend
25 Clubs, of a sort
30 Cram into the overhead
31 Singer Grande, to fans
32 Lone Star coll.
34 Valiant son
35 How wizardry software works
39 Email address suffix
40 Start of a bedtime prayer
41 Har-___ tennis court
42 Pac 10 school
44 Instant
49 Object
51 Soviet security agcy.
52 Suffix with aqui
53 Air friction
55 Tennis court material
59 Decisively defeated
60 Go over again
61 Standoffishness
62 Decisive one
63 Made an attempt
64 Empty types?

DOWN

1 "Vampire in Brooklyn" director
2 Michener epic
3 Diamond unit
4 One mo' time
5 Zip
6 Duds
7 Marching together
8 Anise cookies
9 Dashiell Hammett dog
10 Persona ___ (welcome)
11 Polygamous groups
12 Of waste
13 Figurative narrative
14 Subside
23 Loan shark's activity
26 Checkroom item
27 Suffix for jumbo
28 "The Boxer" songwriter
29 Offshoots
33 Trim back
35 Record store?
36 Unattractive quality
37 Received enlightenment
38 Violinist Jean-___ Ponty
39 Exhausted
43 Ex-Raptor Bargnani
45 Hugh of "Tombstone"
46 In the recent past
47 Less messy
48 They replaced clotheslines
50 Cartoonist Trudeau
54 Collapsed
56 French I verb
57 They come out
58 Lit ___ (Eng. course)

176 THEMELESS by Harvey Estes
60 Across is the longest living land animal.

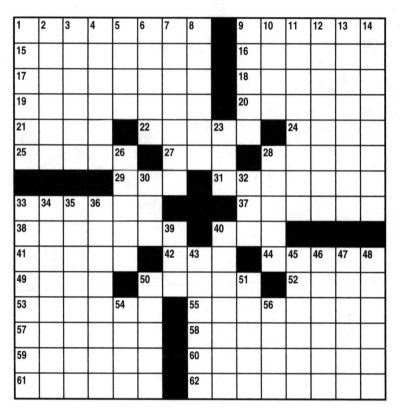

ACROSS

1 Quickie quiz
9 Become emotionally distant
15 Rake over the coals
16 #1 Oak Ridge Boys hit
17 Domed circular halls
18 Off track
19 Bob the Builder's team
20 Gets the idea
21 Land of Yeats
22 Orchestra section
24 Ten-speed, e.g.
25 Dated
27 Stir
28 Allen in "Game of Thrones"
29 All fired up
31 Cut at a slope
33 Horse malady
37 Blu-ray rays
38 Brisk movement
40 "___ folly to be wise"
41 Remove more moisture from
42 Gather intelligence
44 Early heat
49 Some big hearts
50 Sassy boy
52 To be, in Toulouse
53 Call at home
55 React to a blow
57 American gymnast Biles
58 Gives a right to
59 Jogged pages, e.g.
60 Galápagos reptile
61 Humans have 5 (or 6?)
62 Drive away

DOWN

1 Oscars' choice for "Sophie's Choice"
2 "But will it play in ___?"
3 Many John Wayne films
4 Battle breaks
5 Windshield feature
6 Lucas forest moon
7 Eye impolitely
8 Sent up a coin
9 Gives a hand
10 Additional
11 Sets set on them
12 Daisy product
13 Less friendly
14 Slickers' counterparts
23 DMV datum
26 Mournful ode
28 Command to a sailor
30 Tel Aviv's nat.
32 Biblical Samuel's mentor
33 Bugs
34 Nonrequired course
35 Municipal legislators
36 Competing narratives
39 City of Kirghizia
40 Headache helper
43 Pre-euro Spanish currency
45 Gymnast Mary Lou
46 Firenze's land
47 Take into custody
48 Flat fee payer?
50 Plants in the wrong place
51 Culture dish
54 Nudge with a joint
56 Where it's at

177 THEMELESS by Harvey Estes
27 Down could also mean "Be careful, dude!"

ACROSS

1 "The Nutcracker" dancer
10 Book with legends
15 Tough to budge
16 "Good job!"
17 Binary choice
18 Avalon, for one
19 Small batter's support
20 Pants problem
21 Rout
23 Cuts calories
25 Attacks on all sides
26 Dragon's nemesis
29 Trials and tribulations
31 Gunny's rank: Abbr.
32 Put forward
33 Score finales
34 Failed negotiation result
35 Red ink amount
36 "Air Music" composer
37 Richard in "An Officer and a Gentleman"
38 '50s campaign name
39 Like producing cornstalks
40 Transportation network
41 "I Won't Back Down" singer Petty
42 Opera set in Egypt
43 Sci-fi and such
44 Spiro's predecessor
46 Country sound
48 City near Rome
50 Light property
51 Debt memo
54 PR concern
55 Helping influences
58 Flies off the handle
59 Delicious source
60 Hagar's dog
61 Court-martial candidates

DOWN

1 Set-to
2 Shade of blue
3 Harass visually
4 A journalistic "W"
5 Went to Staten Island, perhaps
6 Southern poet Sidney
7 Put into effect, as a proposal
8 Jennings of "Jeopardy!" fame
9 "The Life of Henry James" author
10 Dental problem
11 Tough trips
12 Nordstrom section
13 Cutting-edge
14 She belts it out
22 Steel girder
23 Vat colors
24 Blasted with words
26 Quibble
27 "Eyes" at a heist
28 Gathering
30 Fehr of "Presidio Med"
33 Part of a parachute
36 "You Got It" singer Bonnie
37 Signal to leave
39 From the heart
40 Devoted subscriber
43 Charles de ___ Airport
45 Raring to go
47 Party managers
49 Somewhat
51 Memo phrase
52 Baltic Sea tributary
53 Functions
56 Boorish brute
57 Addams Family relation

178 SHIPBUILDING by Cindy Lather
43 Across is a Worcestershire sauce ingredient.

ACROSS

1 Prelaw test
5 Prologue follower
9 Hedgerow unit
14 Sold separately, as opposed to packaged
16 Jerry-built
17 Hall-of-Fame Black Hawk
18 Proprietor
19 Lamb's ma'am
20 Golfer Westwood
21 Betrothed
23 "¡___ favor, señor!"
24 Stirrup locale
25 Peerage member
29 Truth in ___ Act
33 Former NAACP leader Medgar
34 Spotted
36 Blackthorn fruit
37 Irish speech quality
38 Rundown
39 Musical step
40 Secular
41 "My Way" songwriter
42 Triplets share them
43 Small shoaling fish
45 Do a voice-over
47 One of two cards in a blackjack
48 Tween age
49 Female zoo cat
53 "___ Loves You": Beatles
54 2013 Justin Timberlake song
57 Florida horse city
58 Upper-lip line
61 Highlands loch

62 "Be that as it may . . ."
63 Vera Wang design
64 Pow!
65 Geritol ingredient

DOWN

1 Silicone spray, e.g.
2 K2's cap
3 Chartres cleric
4 Basin
5 Stick firmly
6 Inkling
7 Mideastern hill
8 At leisure
9 Ad campaign "hook"
10 Sirius XM Radio star
11 Ladder crosspiece
12 Plaintiff
13 First to fly over the South Pole
15 Sheer hose
22 On one's uppers
23 "General Hospital" setting
25 "Lost in Yonkers" aunt
26 Hawkish, in a sense
27 Thing of the past
28 Minute
29 French border lake
30 Finnish soprano Jokinen
31 Nine-piece combo
32 Sixth day of Christmas gift
35 It's milked in Tibet
38 Mariano Rivera stats

42 Grabby
44 Continental divides
46 "It don't mean ___ if it ain't got that swing . . ."
49 Snitched
50 Bakery artist
51 Became a donor
52 No friend of unions
53 Pair of oxen
54 Schussboomer's lift
55 Japanese stringed instrument
56 "Dulce et Decorum Est" poet
59 Hagen in "Key Largo"
60 ___ Lanka

179 TO COIN A PHRASE by Harvey Estes
A newly minted theme from a Carolina cruciverbalist.

ACROSS

1 "Satellite" singer Matthews
5 Fear, for one
9 Like some bulls
14 Ranks
16 Cell component
17 Discern the difference between
18 Highbrow
19 Adjective for the Sierra Club
21 Feeds a line to
22 Tall tale
23 Where a young king and queen rule
26 Poet Laureate Kooser
27 Animal pouch
29 Joy's cohost on "The View"
31 They may spin some yarns
34 Figure skater Lutz
35 Tacks on small hidden fees
39 Moral code
40 Wedding tributes
41 "Much obliged!"
43 Ramallah org.
44 Serena, to Venus
47 Lowly laborer
48 "___ and away!"
51 Carry on
52 Paris Agreement concern
56 Duck
58 Like a fisheye lens
59 Jack's twin on "Black-ish"
60 Stretched out
61 Triangle for Maria Callas
62 Slight progress
63 Eighty-six

DOWN

1 Sniff out
2 Means of access
3 Like tubas
4 "Less Than Zero" author Bret
5 Guitar device
6 Whatever it takes
7 Frost starter
8 Fruity-smelling compound
9 Kind of tense
10 "Old Line State" capital
11 Place for pockets
12 Big whoop
13 Null service
15 Eg. and Syr., once
20 Opposite of SSE
24 Small fry of '60s TV
25 Fail to see
27 Smidgen
28 Internet trigram
30 "Couldn't get out of it"
31 Cheapskate
32 Liver near the Mekong
33 Fastened with a pop
35 High wire safety gear
36 "Aren't ___ lucky one!"
37 Black-and-white medium
38 Kind of router or modem
42 Bottom line
44 Serenaded
45 English, to Evita
46 Mounts
49 Caressed like a collie
50 Scrabble vowel pick
51 Charged
53 Suggestion
54 Round rendering of Lincoln
55 "Macbeth" figure
56 State further
57 Nice life?

WINTRY CONDITIONS   by Cindy Lather
Grimhilde is the official name of the evil queen at 11 Down.

ACROSS

1 Sleeper ray's lack
5 Put in a pantheon
10 Cocoa powder amts.
14 Take an oath
15 Red-nosed "Sesame Street" character
16 "Don't bet ___!"
17 Nixon's 1977 TV interviewer
19 Chaplin's fourth wife
20 Hatfields, to McCoys
21 "Carefree ___": Lightfoot
23 Game fish
24 Contemptible
25 Source of Wagner's "Ring Cycle"
27 ___ or not (regardless)
31 River through Tours
34 "Breaking Bad" wife
36 Suffix for secret
37 Basics
38 Beckett's no-show
39 Spoon handle
40 "National Velvet" horse
41 Composer Copland
42 Like Tinker Bell
43 "The Ten Commandments" director
45 Wife of Uranus
47 "Fifty Shades Darker" heroine
48 Wrestler
52 Briefly sign
56 American, for one
57 Heckled
58 2016 Coen brothers film
60 "___ so sorry"
61 Show opener
62 Street blade
63 Florek of "Law & Order: SVU"
64 Car models
65 Freelancer's encl.

DOWN

1 Becomes a whiter shade of pale
2 An ex of Donald
3 King or Queen book, e.g.
4 Aquacade stars
5 Hold the fort
6 Fumbles a slow roller
7 "Odyssey" sea goddess
8 Sole mates?
9 Himalayan mystery
10 Like Papa Bear's porridge
11 The Evil Queen's stepdaughter
12 "If you like ___ coladas . . ."
13 Corset part
18 The "D" in LED
22 Jocundity
26 Love, Italian style
27 Off the mark
28 Top 40 member
29 Equalize
30 "Ratatouille" rat
31 "Dragnet" org.
32 Tony's cousin
33 Chris Evert's sobriquet
35 Stir
38 Gadot in "Justice League"
39 Like some stockings
41 Half a handball game
42 Prom queen's wear
44 Hospital worker with a residency
46 Altar vestments
49 Baryshnikov, familiarly
50 "Delta of Venus" author Nin
51 Backbone
52 Steamed
53 Exploding star
54 "Excuse me?"
55 "Lost Horizon" monk
56 Not aweather
59 "Eww-w-w-w!"

POSITIONAL PAPER by Karen Motyka
The ski resort at 4 Down is one of the largest in North America.

ACROSS

1 Ox-eyed goddess
5 Grieve
10 Ancient lyre
14 Voiced
15 Come to terms
16 Near-perfect score
17 Star's marquee position
19 Cartoon light bulb
20 George Costanza's mother
21 Hot breakfast
23 Stephen of "Bad Behavior"
24 Detente
25 Cowardly sneak
29 Apian way?
32 Vehicle for the high C's
33 Stonehenge worshiper
35 Cuddle and kiss in Hyde Park
36 Chaough of "Mad Men"
37 Barcelona bruin
38 Martini request
39 All-purpose trucks
41 ___ del Sol
43 Gather grain
44 Part of AMA
46 Emily Dickinson's hometown
48 Romance lang.
49 Knapsack
50 Of the stomach
53 Put in order
57 Stadium near Citi Field
58 Bean counter's concern
60 Ending for quip or hip
61 Great Lakes tribesmen
62 Middle East airline
63 Greet the villain
64 The Left Banke's "Walk Away ___"
65 Gig units

DOWN

1 Table d'___
2 Psyche's lover
3 Lost, in a way
4 Lake Louise Ski Resort locale
5 Common duck
6 Stare boorishly
7 New England sch.
8 City on the Truckee
9 Canceled out
10 Dr. Dolittle's patients
11 Rattlesnake
12 ___-Day vitamins
13 Tangible
18 Intestinal sections
22 Word ignored in indexing
25 Admitted fact
26 Mountain spur
27 Fries and slaw, e.g.
28 Want bad, with "over"
29 Regional life forms
30 Ephron and Charles
31 Exodus departure point
34 ___ Arizona Memorial
40 Childcare jobs
41 .45 or .22
42 "Band of Brothers" historian
43 Feasts royally
45 Corden's karaoke vehicle
47 "JAG" hero
50 It may require stitches
51 City of sparkling wine
52 Pear part
53 Suit to ___
54 Lake Nasser feeder
55 Black fly
56 Aquatic zappers
59 Bronze component

182 X'S OUT by Richard Silvestri

Alternate clue for 5 Down: Group that sang "I'll Never Find Another You."

ACROSS

1 Stage delivery
6 Off-color
10 Alternative to a taxi
14 Flip over
15 Declare
16 Emperor after Claudius
17 Cruise vehicle
18 Bundle in a barn
19 Pole or Croat
20 Extremely dark beers?
22 Otherwise
23 Musician's asset
24 Lingered on
26 Bounty
30 Literature Nobelist of 1936
32 Dumas dueler
33 Sleep soundly?
34 Polo Grounds great
37 The big house
38 Vice squad operations
39 Neutral hue
40 PC key
41 Tilting tool
42 Bed of nails user
43 Spring up
45 Spills the beans
46 Countenance
48 Crew need
49 Privy to
50 Criticisms of the garrison?
57 Social asset
58 More than miffed
59 Slave away
60 "My Way" composer
61 Aromatic compound
62 Speck
63 Word of comparison
64 Active ones
65 Gush out

DOWN

1 Chop meat
2 Fan favorite
3 Stellar spectacular
4 Idle of the Pythons
5 Some Quidditch players
6 Garage charge
7 Rescue mission, for short
8 "Champagne Music" man
9 Bedroom pieces
10 Open, in a way
11 Long hair on the tummy?
12 Rub out
13 Succumbed to wanderlust
21 Rotten
25 Make a bow
26 Hindu royal
27 List shortener
28 Big hits from Vanna?
29 ISP option
30 In safekeeping
31 Protuberance
33 Performed a cappella
35 Minuet movement
36 Chance to play
38 Lofty
39 Enjoy the buffet
41 Triangle side
42 Maidenhair, for one
44 Devilfish
45 Staples Center team
46 Of great importance
47 Senseless
48 Mink's kin
51 Approximately
52 Have value
53 Songwriter Blackwell
54 Something to fly
55 Something to fly
56 Deli side dish

LOST ART **by Richard Silvestri**
23 Across was the host of Miss America from 1980–1981.

ACROSS

1 Bit of wit
5 Energy source
10 Ledger listing
14 Eden evictee
15 Electric car company
16 State as fact
17 Triathlon vehicle
18 Modify
19 Area between hills
20 Protection from bees?
22 Run in park
23 TV Tarzan
24 Without a doubt
26 Free from impurities
30 Checkout annoyance
32 Give off
33 Alpha male?
38 Thin coin
39 Gets high
40 Tackle box item
41 Wrapper weight at the butcher's?
43 Prairie schooner
44 Phoenix five
45 Minimum
46 Element number 55
50 The aggregate
51 Let go
52 Wedding cake alternatives?
59 Six Flags attraction
60 LEM part
61 Wood-smoothing tool
62 Sorrowful cry
63 Split to be tied
64 Dermal opening
65 Camp sight
66 Body shop jobs
67 Presidential middle name

DOWN

1 Ring exchanges?
2 Fix text
3 "The Square Egg" author
4 Revenuers, for short
5 Firm
6 British tube
7 Last word of Missouri's motto
8 Smart guy?
9 Leopard's spots, e.g.
10 Michelangelo masterpiece
11 Give the slip to
12 Ball girl?
13 Out on a limb
21 Trait transmitter
25 Opposite of paleo-
26 Cardinal and others
27 Script direction
28 Be angry
29 Concept
30 Deceitful people
31 With regard to
33 Zen riddle
34 Defect
35 Really big
36 Archer of myth
37 Shipped off
39 Lost one's footing
42 Wildcats' sch.
43 In the pink
45 Warning lights
46 200 milligrams
47 Man without a country
48 Kind of chair
49 That is, to Tacitus
50 Change with the times
53 Sit on the throne
54 A party to
55 Family nickname
56 Object of adoration
57 Pound of poetry
58 Caught sight of

ACROSS

1 U.S. poet laureate Dove*
5 "The Sound of Music" heroine*
10 Kite attachment
14 Milks, in a way
15 The E of J.E.B. Stuart
16 City near the Yamuna River
17 Minimal tide type
18 Bumper sticker
19 Boat launch
20 Soprano Stratas
22 Petty tyrant
24 "Merry old" king
26 Sicily's highest peak
27 One of the Twelve*
30 Ichabod Crane's beloved*
34 Back in the day
35 Literary tribute
36 Poetic preposition
37 "Andy Capp" cartoonist Smythe
38 "Ready or ___ . . ."
39 Greeting to Gaius
40 Limonite, e.g.
41 "___ Italien": Strauss
44 Sit-ups tone them
47 Top of a scale
48 "Quantum of Solace" heroine*
50 Arnie Grape's brother*
52 Surfing mecca
53 Vaulted arch
54 Kind of price
57 Went around in circles
61 Open-mouthed
62 Wine bouquet
66 Togo capital
67 Dressing herb
68 Things to whistle
69 "Brokeback Mountain" heroine*
70 Duck genus
71 1964 Julie Andrews role*
72 Malicious

DOWN

1 Litter's littlest
2 "Uh, huh"
3 Sorry sight?
4 Dimension
5 Found gold in Tokyo 2020
6 Fear and wonder
7 Camcorder abbr.
8 Stevedore union
9 Elite athlete
10 Dental hygienist's concern
11 Lab gel
12 Hogwarts librarian Pince*
13 Arctic nomad
21 New York gallery district
23 Prefix for chamber
25 Sheepish she
26 Make do with
27 Wine region near Bordeaux
28 Where Plato shopped
29 Pole carving
31 Quite angry
32 "___ My Love": 5th Dimension
33 Insurance broker
41 Pik Tandykul's range
42 Howl like a wolf
43 Tre + tre
44 Back in the day
45 New Orleans' nickname (with "The")
46 Ski-Doo product
49 Public personae
51 Mass hysteria
54 Tabula ___
55 "A Visit From the Goon Squad" author
56 Academic gown
58 Captive of Hercules
59 Kenney of "Shameless"*
60 Butler or Martin*
63 Egg-nog spike
64 Naval CIA
65 Cooley or Gibson

185 NAMESAKES II* by John M. Samson
Letters within circles will reveal these namesakes.

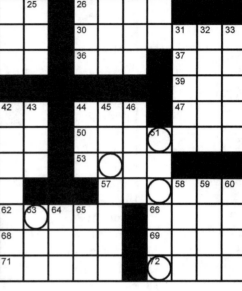

ACROSS

1 Hammock support
5 "The Audacity of Hope" author
10 Chihuahua coin
14 Eye greedily
15 Go by bicycle
16 It's smaller than a molecule
17 Cook spaghetti
18 Ibsen's Gabler
19 Potter's friend Lovegood
20 Bobolink relative
22 At an earlier time
24 Mezzo Rankin
26 Fat-free milk
27 Mrs. John Adams*
30 Knight-errant
34 June honoree
35 Hip dwelling
36 Whatever
37 Mine find
38 Sapporo sash
39 "Pioneer Woman" Drummond
40 Office PC hookup
41 Polar ___ cap
44 "Do something!"
47 To boot
48 "Baby" in "Dirty Dancing"*
50 Country singer Pride*
52 Aurist's concerns
53 Quote as an authority
54 Curtis of cosmetics*
57 Fashion designer Richie*
61 Mouthward
62 Plant with licorice-flavored seeds
66 Heaviest fencing sword
67 Earth
68 New York's Finger ___
69 Windmill blade
70 Renaissance patron
71 "Jungle Book" tiger ___ Khan
72 Dispatch

DOWN

1 Timber wolf
2 Frankenstein's aide*
3 DXXVI doubled
4 Fit in
5 She goes mad in "Hamlet"*
6 Spell-off
7 Append
8 More than miffed
9 Kodiak Islander
10 Fashion designer Picasso*
11 Vingt-___ (twenty-one)
12 Acoustic unit
13 Sharif of "Dr. Zhivago"
21 Take a bungee jump
23 Like crankcases
25 Honorary law deg.
26 Cruise ship amenity
27 Adidas founder Dassler
28 Elephant king
29 Menzel of "Frozen"
31 Home of golf's Blue Monster
32 Lead Belly's girl of song*
33 Far from well-off
41 2017 Peace Prize Nobelist
42 Kix and Trix
43 It makes a cat scat
44 Clemson's conference
45 Gunpowder inventors
46 Jacques who starred in "Mon Oncle"
49 Tease
51 Time out
54 Support stocking
55 Psyche's admirer
56 Café au ___
58 Translucent gem*
59 Daughter of Queen Amidala
60 Sorta fishy, sorta snaky
63 "Nope, not interested"
64 1952 campaign nickname*
65 Spanish 101 verb

186

"THAT'S HILARIOUS!" by Pam Klawitter
The clue at 49 Across refers to the United States.

ACROSS

1 Only Federalist president
6 Throw a fit
10 Cruise carrier
14 Rapper Shakur
15 Lena in "The Reader"
16 Let up
17 Of the highest status*
19 Song from "Rubber Soul"
20 Track events
21 K, at Kay Jewelers
22 Exit plan of sorts*
27 Drip edge
28 Showy meteor shower
29 Still on the shelf
31 Lily pad sitter
32 Arctic hoodie
35 Turkey carving tool*
40 Took stock during a riot
41 Hogwarts librarian Pince
43 Outback company
46 Negation
48 Subj. for new arrivals
49 21, as of July 17, 1984*
53 Build up
55 Work for nine
56 Throw a fit
57 It's found in clue* answers
62 They get in your hair
63 South Beach ___
64 Less readily available
65 Musk of SpaceX
66 Classic sneakers
67 Take a vow

DOWN

1 NFL passing stat
2 Eurythmics, e.g.
3 Many a download
4 Key a Kia, e.g.
5 Garlicky shrimp dish
6 Man of "Today"
7 High court name
8 Infomercial knife
9 Popular B.A. major
10 Sonic the Hedgehog's company
11 Bob or bun
12 Jordan neighbor
13 Bombarded
18 Necessity
21 Thompson of "SNL"
22 Keebler's Zoot, e.g.
23 Like arid land
24 Distant
25 Merkel or Bassett
26 Ankar native
30 Going downhill fast
32 Talk-radio legend Bell
33 When pigs fly over Flensburg
34 "Monk" affliction
36 Computer desk jumble
37 Go on the road
38 Arizona's Agua ___ River
39 Online read
42 You can buy it by the yard
43 Celebrex developer
44 FedEx alternative
45 City west of Austin
46 Lost power
47 Goes into
50 Navel sort
51 Barely beat
52 Works with needles
54 "Ode to a ___ Gun": S.N. Teed
57 Texting shrug
58 It's often dropped in surprise
59 Argentite, e.g.
60 New Zealand parrot
61 Drop the ball

187 THE SCOOP* by Pam Klawitter

55 Across won an Emmy for his performance in that film.

ACROSS

1 Go forth wearily
5 Part of an expiration notice
10 Candy Crush Soda Saga or Pokemon Go
13 Legendary "Cradle of Polynesia"
15 Fix a tot's shoe again
16 Lillie in "Thoroughly Modern Millie"
17 Wise guys*
19 DC player
20 Showed anxiety
21 Flickers
23 Rickman of "Harry Potter" movies
25 Almost
26 Fall orchard outing*
31 Blu the macaw's movie
32 What an oddball might draw
33 Ballpark figs.
37 Global supporter
39 Coral island
40 Android Artoo-___
41 "Cinderella" affair
42 Where slop is served
44 Car financing fig.
45 Becomes hostile toward*
48 Tidbit on a toothpick
51 Spreadsheet filler
52 Across the pond
55 "Tuesdays with Morrie" star
59 Popular symbols on March 14th
60 The scoop (and what's found in clue* answers)
62 Gathered dust
63 Saltine brand
64 Buffs up
65 Storm front
66 Millay and Ferber
67 Plains people

DOWN

1 "Hey, you!"
2 Flimsy, excuse-wise
3 Muscat's home
4 Shark fin
5 Bit of browser history
6 Calls, at the poker table
7 Carve in stone
8 Scanty attire
9 They're always agreeable
10 Capp's Li'l guy
11 Round gem
12 Country's Cline
14 Cut down on intake
18 Make adjustments
22 Kiddie-lit "Maniac"
24 Vitamin found in lean meat
26 One from 3 Down
27 Baba ganouj go-with
28 Viewpoint barometer
29 Mountaineers challenges
30 iPhone feature
34 Getz of jazz
35 First-class
36 Pigeonhole
38 Union spot
40 Ancestry.com tool
42 Primped
43 Equal, to Etienne
46 Buy a bigger place
47 Defiant response to "You are not!"
48 Thicket of trees
49 Some running shoes
50 Twiggy digs
53 AARP member?
54 "Come in and ___ spell"
56 Peak of the Alpes
57 Nickname for a Belted Galloway cow
58 Big Board initials
61 Russian affirmatives

188 WEED CONTROL   by Linda Gould
As every good Hogwarts student knows, a bezoar is a useful 9 Down.

ACROSS
1 Examine volumes
5 Buddhist shrine
10 Bubble bowl, e.g.
14 "Downton Abbey" maid
15 Ratio sign
16 City S of Moscow
17 First home
18 The Fugees' "Ready ___"
19 Meadow lands
20 **Start of a quip**
23 "___ homo!": Pilate
24 Leave it to beavers
25 Military courtesy
28 Zimbabwe, previously
33 Book of Mormon book
34 Fashionable
35 Embassy VIP
36 **More of quip**
40 Former Mideast alliance
41 Queensberry ___
42 Misfortunes
43 Takes for granted
45 Persistently annoy
47 Do likewise
48 Mazar in "GoodFellas"
49 **End of quip**
57 Free-verse rhyme scheme?
58 Ninja Turtles cohort April
59 "___ Most Unusual Day"
60 Din
61 Reunion attendee
62 The Big Easy acronym
63 Ward of "House"
64 Dionysian reveler
65 Hockey enforcer

DOWN
1 Hornpipe's kin
2 Icelandic work that influenced Tolkien
3 From scratch
4 Ballerina
5 Torch holder
6 "The Velvet Fog" Mel
7 Bone near the biceps
8 Like Job's turkey
9 Poison counteracter
10 Remote button
11 Linear calculation
12 NFL coach Payton
13 "Let It Go" singer in "Frozen"
21 UN Day mo.
22 "Been there, done that" feeling
25 Monopolize
26 At hand, poetically
27 Peter in "The Raven"
28 Saratoga summer events
29 Rustic dwellings
30 Offshore silhouettes
31 Jay Sean hit "___ Yours"
32 Humiliate
34 In fine fettle
37 Vent like Etna
38 A good many
39 Dropping in on
44 Bullock of "The Blind Side"
45 "Catch-22" novelist
46 ___ Dhabi
48 Lacy mat
49 Pantry lineup
50 Reed in a pit
51 Suffix for period
52 Sicilian summer resort
53 Offshoot
54 Opening soccer score
55 Where the Storting meets
56 Bread of Mumbai

189 DO THE MATH I by John M. Samson
Can you figure out what X is?

ACROSS

1 Horrified sound
5 ___ casino (seafood dish)
10 Emperor prior to 1917
14 Culture-dish medium
15 Make payment
16 The Phantom's horse
17 X + 100 − 18 = ___
19 Holiday times
20 Venus, but not Serena
21 Cold is one but hot is not
23 NYC's first subway line
24 A student may take one out
25 Remarkable
29 Start-up's need
32 Landed on
33 Bunk option
35 Yoked instrument
36 Request on bended knee
37 Tic-___-toe
38 German grandma
39 Noises heard in a bowl
41 14th of Adar
43 Prune
44 Rolle and Williams
46 Permissive
48 Time past
49 "___ for Gumshoe": Grafton
50 Internet browser button
53 Rhetoricians
57 What little things mean?
58 (X × 2) − 49 = ___
60 Union label?
61 LuPone role
62 Madras monarch
63 Elton John's "___ While You Learn"
64 "Lorna Doone" setting
65 Turnstile feature

DOWN

1 Spanky's group
2 Exchange fee
3 Castle material
4 What chartists do
5 Waterford product
6 Bit of eye makeup?
7 Lille buddy
8 Diminutive
9 Like the Milky Way
10 Hit ___ on the head
11 X + 45 + 15 = ___
12 Hawkish deity
13 Hudson Yards developer
18 Hollywood's Hatcher
22 Trim the tree
25 Buffalo wing?
26 Courtroom responses
27 (X × 4) − 24 = ___
28 Yoga position
29 Film producer DeMille
30 Shimerman in "Deep Space 9"
31 Left one's feet
34 Sherman's "hell"
40 Abbreviate
41 De-wrinkled
42 "When Harry Met Sally. . ." star
43 Norway's Seven ___ Waterfall
45 ". . . ___ he rode out of sight"
47 Island west of Sumatra
50 "The Dog Problem" playwright
51 "Pure ___" (1950 jazz album)
52 Active place
53 Conductor Klemperer
54 Shape of "The Big A"
55 Clinton's DOJ head
56 Pique period
59 VII doubled

ACROSS

1 Head shots
5 Beau
10 Benchmarks: Abbr.
14 "The Fifth Son" author Wiesel
15 Honolulu porch
16 Biblical pronoun
17 $(X \times 3) + 7 =$ ___
19 The Auld Sod
20 $X - 6 + 1 =$ ___
21 Headlined
23 Sitter's creation
24 Doctor documents
25 One looking for acceptance
29 Therapist
32 Lummox
33 Jet engine sounds
35 Sister of Ares
36 Mount where Aaron died
37 Draw a bead on
38 Publicity
39 "Pas de Deux" artist
41 Electric guitar wood
43 Andean ancient
44 Frank Barone's son
46 Brian in "Foul Play"
48 Pirouette
49 Fair and Milne
50 Bugs with wheels
53 Cirque du Soleil performer
57 Saxophonist Coltrane
58 $X - 40 + 7 =$ ___
60 "I eat what ___": Carroll
61 Refinement
62 "Madagascar" lion
63 Boutique department
64 Completed
65 Musical silence

DOWN

1 Mutt's pal
2 Hawaiian nobility of yore
3 "Back to the Future" bully
4 Put down roots
5 Unexpected success
6 French bread
7 "Life of Pi" director Lee
8 Root words?
9 Litter members
10 Clinically clean
11 $(X \times 3) + 6 =$ ___
12 "Paradise Lost" illustrator
13 Litigated
18 Diary duration
22 "The Piano" pianist
25 Akin to Mars orange
26 Native plant life
27 $(X \times 2) - 7 =$ ___
28 Polar explorer Amundsen
29 Locked and loaded
30 Out of ___ (not together)
31 Hungarian wine
34 Facilitate
40 Recycling bin fill
41 An original Mouseketeer
42 Underwent chemical change
43 To such an extent
45 Jed Clampett's wealth source
47 ___ a soul (none)
50 Pouring limit
51 Bed of roses
52 The Ugly Duckling, for one
53 Penny-___
54 Ill humor
55 Monopoly has 17
56 WhatsApp message
59 Apocryphal book: Abbr.

ACROSS

1 Rimrock
5 Dame Nellie of Covent Garden
10 Champagne brand
14 Impressionist
15 Traction improver
16 "___ Love Her": Beatles
17 $X + 2^2 + 47 =$ ___
19 Control (with "in")
20 They speak louder than words
21 Windpipe
23 Champigny-___-Marne
24 Former Expos manager
25 Keep in check
29 Eavesdropping device
32 "The Angry Hills" novelist
33 Fashionable dinner hour
35 Not in operation
36 Scathing review
37 Entrance line
38 Uncooked
39 Intestinal divisions
41 Had supper
43 Blow-out
44 City opposite Windsor
46 Dwelt
48 It has banks in Belgium
49 Garment loathed by PETA
50 Badminton official
53 Unbridle
57 "Enemies: A Love Story" star
58 **What each X stands for**
60 Peace Nobelist Myrdal
61 Breaks, at the ranch
62 He was, to Caesar
63 Dance music
64 Obscure
65 Anthroponym

DOWN

1 Tortilla dough
2 Saga
3 Blue message
4 Gallery exhibitors
5 Four-time U.S. Open winner
6 "___ Coming": Three Dog Night
7 Limb
8 Thai banknote
9 What pheromones do
10 "Father of Radio"
11 $X + 77 + 12 =$ ___
12 "Desperate Housewives" divorcée
13 Ginger on "Gilligan's Island"
18 "___ Mother Should Know": Beatles
22 GA neighbor
25 One of Santa's reindeer
26 Cape for Francis
27 $X + 7^2 + 19 =$ ___
28 Legal
29 See-through
30 Send over the moon
31 Like Taylor and Burton in 1975
34 Grease pump
40 Weaponry stock
41 Tells actors how to act
42 Shelter
43 9/11 heroes
45 Kaput, to Keats
47 Philippines archipelago
50 "And let the welkin ___": Shak.
51 La femme
52 Where David slew Goliath
53 2018 Masters winner
54 Magician's word
55 Carpet line
56 "Ben-Hur" costumer designer
59 June in "Henry & June"

THEMELESS by Harvey Estes
The loser of the war at 33 Across was Edison.

ACROSS

1 Tips off
6 Turns up the boom box
10 Deli side dish
14 About
15 Break down
16 Rich source
17 Agape, maybe
18 Weltschmerz
20 Drop off
21 Send forth
23 Acted piggish
24 Raider QB nicknamed "The Snake"
26 Investor who acquires distressed firms (with 27-A)
27 See 26 Across
29 Went lickety-split
30 Frisky fishers
31 Italian thing
33 "War of the Currents" winner
34 Dash
35 Sees to the future
40 Pacific country
42 Keg feature
43 1966 Beatles concert site
47 With 49 Across, it's not about competence
49 See 47 Across
51 Relating to a roof
52 Dated
53 Ratio phrase
54 Disney monkey
55 Glow under a black light
57 Hall's rock partner
59 1040, e.g.
60 "While ___ it . . ."
61 Teatime treat
62 Malaysia's Chin ___ Caves Temple
63 Their habits aren't bad
64 Homestead Act's "160"

DOWN

1 Wood paneling
2 Gloss
3 Makes further adjustments
4 Uey from SSE
5 Mind comparison
6 Spinning
7 Track trial
8 Thimblerig thing
9 Bean shoots
10 Biases unfairly
11 Secure, as in a safe
12 Stick
13 Did a garden chore
19 Up to
22 Ft. or yd., e.g.
25 Jessica in "Hitchcock"
26 Brandy bottle letters
28 Get a winter coat
32 Matt Dillon's horse
34 Bapt. or Meth.
36 Old money of Italy
37 Washing machine part
38 Attention getter
39 Engraving instruments
41 Fab Four manager
42 Part of a deck chair
43 Shows scorn
44 Like some Easter bunnies
45 Bear
46 Where teams like to play
48 Sports surprises
50 Place for a stud
53 Confident phrase
56 Laura Bush's alma mater
58 UVA's conference

20 Across had a successful career in vaudeville prior to that TV role.

ACROSS

1 Tree with papery bark
6 Crooked
10 Jazz technique
14 D-Day beach
15 Place that deals with flats, perhaps
17 Intelligence seekers
18 Influence peddler
19 Willy Loman's field
20 She played Jed Clampett's mother-in-law
21 iPhone travel option
23 Gift to a diva
24 Tidied the lawn
28 First two words of "Travelin' Man"
29 Hipster eyewear
34 Italy artery
35 Fred's portrayer on "Sanford"
37 Blue bloods
38 Where to find prices
39 Place for a pad
40 Eyeball
42 Port vessel
43 Throat opening
45 "Yea large . . ."
47 Presidential campaign focus areas
53 Flowering house plant
56 SeaWorld show
57 Harrowing
58 Couldn't stomach
59 One to follow
60 They point forward
61 Thin fastener
62 Odo portrayer Auberjonois
63 Good going down

DOWN

1 Start of a dance
2 Inability to perform
3 Conductor, for example
4 Nest din
5 Major headaches
6 Les of Clinton's cabinet
7 "I don't see it"
8 "Water Music" composer
9 Question variety
10 Ogled
11 "Buffalo" Bill
12 Circle statistic
13 Fork-tailed bird
16 Soft kid
22 Hearth waste
25 Approaches slowly, with "toward"
26 Promise to tie the knot
27 Biblical auxiliary
28 Gets under the skin of
30 Mahershala in "True Detective"
31 Pitcher Dean, familiarly
32 Nice beach season
33 Dr. of literature
36 Continued to shovel out
41 Cheap insult
44 Celebration of deliverance
46 ___ Mama cocktail
48 Sweeney Todd's blade
49 Roaring group
50 Stuff in a closet
51 Top BSA rank
52 In a froth
53 Starchy food
54 Aviation pioneer Sikorsky
55 Emeril's Big Easy restaurant

ACROSS

1 Paddock flyswatters
11 Links hazard
15 Hopping mad
16 Corleone leader
17 Purchasing power factor
18 Follower of John
19 Bring to trial
20 Admonition to a child
22 Father and son
23 Minor spasms
25 Start of Virginia's motto
26 Peer Gynt's mother
27 One of the seven virtues
31 Plots a course
33 Drop a dime
34 Georgia's Lake ___ Thurmond
36 Factions
37 Military dog of cartoons
39 Dogpatch family name
41 Gregorius of baseball
42 IRS form
44 Colombian coins
46 "Who am ___ judge?"
47 English counties
49 Ruling
51 Syllables of laughter
52 D.C. lobby group
54 Ark. neighbor
55 Meet
56 Slicing request
58 More on the edge
62 Confession of mendacity
64 Couple on the Sistine Chapel
66 Tomato variety
67 Copied
68 Leave as is
69 Dirt farmer's "dirt"

DOWN

1 Asimov's Seldon
2 In full flower
3 Line on a map
4 Alley challenges
5 Digs out
6 Temporary shelter array
7 Duke is in it
8 Words after bring or pass
9 Airport fleet
10 Like a vista
11 Depression org.
12 Shakespeare historical play
13 Corroborated
14 9/10 of the law
21 "Jim Dean of Indiana" singer
24 Barber belt
27 Part of a sight
28 Conspire
29 Now
30 Like oxen pulling a plow
32 Facilitate
35 ___ Nacional del Prado
38 Finish'd
40 Drink without alcohol
43 Part of DOD
45 Rest in the choir loft
48 Arid expanse
50 Warm-weather shoe
53 Kind of vinegar
57 Viticultural valley
59 Caterpillar hair
60 Odd opposite
61 He played Fred the junkman
63 Absorb, as a loss
65 "Boys of Summer" org.

195 THEMELESS by Alyssa Brooke
"Popular Mexican dishes" would be another clue for 30 Down.

ACROSS

1 Personal appearance
5 Cried a river
9 Religion of Bangladesh
14 Put aside
16 Hite of sexuality
17 Ankle concealers
18 Final straw
19 Put in chains
20 What you may pay through
22 Turns in
23 Packing a wallop
24 Nonschool diploma
25 Tells tales
26 Beginning of life, initially
28 Grate stuff
31 Broke the news
32 Art Deco name of fame
33 Switch to a new track
34 "Hoo" preceder
35 Atoll girl in "Waterworld"
36 Just right
37 Brochette
38 Kind of pusher or trail
39 Finish'd
40 Make tracks
41 Court target
42 Unhealthy color
44 Goes crazy
48 Less calm
49 Cut off
50 "Over There" composer
51 2006 Spike Lee movie
53 Brittany port
54 What Ray was to Jamie Foxx
55 Arizona sights
56 "Calm down . . ."
57 Tar on deck

DOWN

1 Roger Bannister, e.g.
2 Combined
3 Surrealist Max
4 Asleep at the switch
5 Drove drunkenly
6 Fish-eating eagles
7 First-class GI?
8 Frequent flyer
9 Specks on a map
10 Polish
11 Slightly sour candy
12 Alexander the Great's tutor
13 Pass out
15 Most lean
21 Broke ground
25 Sarge's superior
27 Den denizen
28 Regarding
29 Where loafers lie idle?
30 Mexican sandals
31 Use a keyboard
32 Pottery workers
35 Daily soap offering
37 Kind of gin
40 Prehistoric tools
41 In an upbeat way
43 Asian capital
44 Organizational aids
45 Mead subject
46 "What's ___ about, Alfie?"
47 Palindromic principle
48 SDI concern
52 2019 Miss America Franklin

196 "PLAY BALL!" by Cindy Lather

In 2018, 5 Down was inducted into the Country Music Hall of Fame.

ACROSS

1 Faithful
5 "42nd Street" number
10 Mountain ridges
14 Don't put these on
15 Vatican cape
16 Fish with a pudgy name
17 He collars the collarless
19 Collette of "Hostages"
20 Furtiveness
21 Shots
23 "Love Story" composer Frances
24 On the nose
25 Leaves the premises
29 Squad car
33 Marble type
34 Flower part
36 Peg from Fluff
37 Muskellunge relative
38 Contrapuntal opus
39 Jewish wedding dance
40 Dot on the Seine
41 Ill-fated Genesis city
42 Half-hearted
43 Political TV events
45 Tickles one's fancy
47 Begum's mate
48 "___ so it goes"
49 Capt. Edward Smith's ship
53 Came up with
57 Tiny hill builders
58 Carnivorous marsh plant
60 Air Force One VIP
61 Wipe clean
62 Telephone, slangily
63 LPGA great Pak
64 Set of cultural values
65 Suffix with smack

DOWN

1 Dandiprats
2 Prison problem
3 Lobby for
4 Grow rapidly
5 Country legend West
6 Foot area
7 ___-jongg
8 "Waiting for the Robert ___"
9 Medieval menial
10 Sea-bottom dwellers
11 Brief layovers
12 Duchess Kate, to Archie
13 Slugger stats
18 Winged
22 Artificial
25 Tasteless
26 Deft
27 Mixture for a springform pan
28 Skims along
29 Grass cluster
30 Pumpernickel source
31 Like King's "It"
32 Auditions for a part
35 Word with many moons?
38 Cornwallis, to Washington
39 Vexatious problem
41 Rizzo of "Mad Men"
42 Ideology
44 Graf's love match?
46 Emcee's opening word
49 Military funeral sound
50 Memo words
51 "___ what you mean"
52 Snappish
53 Itself, in Latin
54 Viking god
55 Saarinen of Gateway Arch fame
56 Honey Ryder's Bond film
59 "Bad idea"

197 ROUNDBALL RELATED by Cindy Lather
24 Across is the provincial symbol of Quebec.

ACROSS

1 Columbo's employer
5 See the light
10 "Excuse me . . ."
14 Albany's canal
15 Banks of baseball
16 "O ___ Mio"
17 What the NBA and NFL have in common
19 Potting material
20 Monotonous
21 Houdini did it
23 Magna ___ laude
24 Fleur-de-___
25 Consoled
29 Undesirable fan
33 A-team, e.g.
34 Constantly shifting
36 Nobelist UN agcy.
37 Plentiful
38 Arkansas mountains
39 Kitchen foil
40 "___ Got a Feeling": Beatles
41 TD Garden, for one
42 Italian word for "milk"
43 Counteracted
45 Weight room exercises
47 Martian craft
48 Ordinal suffix
49 Intensify
53 Excel
57 Sponge feature
58 Bullseye location
60 No ifs, ___ . . .
61 Smith's "Aladdin" role
62 Big biceps, slangily
63 Shift gears
64 Changes one's story
65 "The Blind ___" (2009)

DOWN

1 Bridle hand
2 "Video" singer India.___
3 Patchy in color
4 Easily broken
5 Bean, e.g.
6 Soho statue
7 "Wheel of Fortune" buy
8 Tick off
9 Highlands loch
10 Lay siege to
11 They're worn under wedding gowns
12 Art historian Faure
13 Spock's Vulcan mind-___
18 "Irma la ___" (1963)
22 Cuneiform medium
25 European finch
26 Drab color
27 Waikiki whistleblowers
28 In a fog
29 Razor sharpener
30 "For shame!"
31 Please a bunch
32 On the ___ (in trouble)
35 Bobbsey twin
38 Mispickel, e.g.
39 Ablutions
41 At the pinnacle
42 River in "The Divine Comedy"
44 One way to begin
46 SEAL recon rifles
49 Canned meat
50 Perfect one's skills
51 Microsoft Web browser
52 Must-have
53 Miner's way in
54 Manicurist's case
55 Move merchandise
56 Irish Gaelic
59 See 7 Down

198 THEMELESS by Brian E. Paquin
41 Across is also the name of a Peter & Gordon song.

ACROSS

1 Winter fishing abodes
7 Big name in power tools
13 More energized
15 1920 racehorse legend
16 Painting technique used by Van Gogh
17 Railroad city of Pennsylvania
18 Corn cob
19 Close kin, briefly
20 Cosmetics company of London
21 Glitch
23 Novice
25 Jacques Rogge's org.
27 Female ruff
28 Fencing foils
33 Acted immediately
37 Wheel turner
38 By hook or by crook
40 Real estate unit
41 Bareback rider of Coventry
42 Wingdings
44 Tennis shot that is smashed
45 Peeper, poetically
46 "Sorry, we're ___"
49 Puppy sounds
52 Kudos
56 Minor objection
58 Actress Carrere
59 Gandhi's title
60 Counting calories
62 Frank, to Jesse
63 Stamp in "Superman II"
64 Stork relatives
65 Dad-burned

DOWN

1 The Cambridge Five, e.g.
2 Leader of the "Masters of the Universe"
3 Real estate experts
4 Busy worker in Apr.
5 Bite-size candy
6 Take hold
7 ___ Lama
8 Steak au poivre, e.g.
9 Hockey stick, slangily
10 Missing at role call
11 Side street
12 Waiter's burden
14 1998 All-Star Game MVP
15 "Possibly . . ."
22 Forgot the umbrella
24 Eccentric ones
26 Hospital asst.
29 Blot up
30 Putting on display
31 Geog. stat.
32 Aventis Pasteur products
33 Kill time
34 Start of a fable
35 Olive of comics
36 Brit. Isle
39 Odometer reset
43 Lambaste
47 Lemon partners
48 Ate in style
50 Gun, to a gangster
51 Fully filled
52 Prefix meaning "both"
53 Engine part, briefly
54 Golfer K.J. ___
55 Workout targets
57 Reid in "American Pie"
61 Reading room

199

ACROSS

1 Alastair in "A Christmas Carol"
4 Military core group
9 L x W
13 End of a countdown
14 Benefit
15 "Death Be Not Proud" poet
17 "___ be a pleasure!"
18 Like simplex printing
20 Candy brand
22 Country singer Faith
23 Apteryx relative
24 Ambassador
25 Quark's "DS9" cousin
26 College celeb
27 Jacob's twin
28 Kaput
29 Pine Tree State
30 Bookcases with trick latches hide these
33 Drudgery
34 Brando quote from "On The Waterfront"
40 "You've got the wrong person!"
41 Glacial snow
42 Bo Derek film
43 Movie sets
44 Coin with 118 ridges
45 Cass and Michelle of music
46 "Xanadu" group
47 "Otello" baritone
48 A+ givers
49 Jet lag causes
52 Roman crowd?
53 Part of a drum set
54 "The Prime of Miss Jean Brodie" director
55 "Pioneer Woman" Drummond
56 Black fly
57 "Downton Abbey" daughter
58 Botch things up

DOWN

1 Evening galas
2 Acute
3 Hospital heliport lander
4 Mudville goat
5 Rara ___
6 Speed-skater Jansen
7 Quite correct
8 Financial forecasting pattern
9 Broadband connection
10 French chess piece
11 Native (to)
12 Windflower
16 Elicits
19 Plumber's joint
21 Pepperidge trees
25 Antics
26 Crowdfunding alternative
28 Valuable horse
29 Salsa singer Anthony
31 Perry's creator
32 Took a bus
34 Coves
35 Partner of heating
36 Footstool
37 Fancy cabinet
38 More hair-raising
39 More mouthy
44 "Lah-di-___!"
45 German wine region
47 "Rhyme Pays" rapper
48 Smallest size at Starbucks
50 Victorian, e.g.
51 Yak

ACROSS

1 Pinball penalty
5 Watch displays
9 Responds to insults
14 Fragrance
15 Went down
16 Hand out
17 Darth's daughter
18 Acadia, today
20 Class that isn't dirt poor?
22 Mireille of "The Killing"
23 Title clerk job
27 Join up
30 Got in the game
31 Island necklace
32 Reef resident
33 Boone nickname
34 Pole, for one
35 Hand-waving, for one
38 Submarine sinker
39 Auction stipulation
40 Tattoo remover
41 D.C. lobby group
42 Parentheses, for example
43 Some sodas
44 Lickety-split
46 When repeated, Mork's sign-off
47 Shifted
52 Shakespeare's would-be horse trader?
55 Minimal haircut
56 Sci-fi moon
57 Stare at
58 Fork feature
59 Didactic storyteller
60 Guitarist Lofgren
61 Inside track found in three answers

DOWN

1 Bridge payment
2 Conception
3 Tender ender
4 Apple, for one
5 Michael of "Highway to Heaven"
6 Does a folk dance
7 Seedy joint
8 Sports page feature
9 Kind of cow
10 Bridges of "Airplane!"
11 Flight stat.
12 Luau paste
13 RR terminal
19 Trump dossier compiler
21 Cookbook author Prudhomme
24 Treat badly
25 More handy
26 Philanthropic folks
27 Shrimp dish
28 Sea off Sicily
29 Jim Carrey role
30 "Quo ___?"
33 Approach from above
34 Oscar, e.g.
36 Sauce type
37 David's weapon
42 Black key by B
43 Those in waiting
45 Cold response?
46 Noel who played Lois Lane
48 Leslie Caron role
49 Wanting water
50 Tub stain
51 Hook's ally
52 Stephen of "Breakfast on Pluto"
53 Suffix with nectar
54 Accts. of interest

HOW DO YOU LEARN TO PLAY SCRABBLE? by Harvey Estes
. . . every letter bit helps.

ACROSS

1 Hit hard
5 Birch of Indiana
9 Confidence games
14 Alice's Restaurant patron
15 Think it over
16 SE Asian capital
17 "Don't move!"
19 ". . . then again, I could be wrong"
20 **Answer to title question: Part 1**
22 Mercury and Saturn
23 GPS display: Abbr.
24 **Answer: Part 2**
27 Ralph Kramden's buddy
32 Early lessons
33 Social surroundings
35 1945 battle site, briefly
36 Oil can letters
37 **Answer: Part 3**
38 Kate McKinnon show
39 Words before believer
40 Put in piles, say
41 Caroline of "Sabrina, the Teenage Witch"
42 Fruity wine drinks
44 **Answer: Part 4**
45 Stretch of history
46 Salon creation
48 **Answer: Part 5**
55 Swan relative
56 Honest intentions
57 "Ragged Dick" author
58 Fork over, with "up"
59 Ad award
60 Narrow cuts
61 Does in the forest
62 Trueheart of comics

DOWN

1 Fifth Avenue landmark
2 Two-toned cookie
3 Brooklyn Dodgers pitcher Labine
4 Russian coins
5 Dangerous dog
6 Guadalajara good-bye
7 Pained cry
8 Monitor's beat
9 Fail, currently?
10 Life line
11 Paquin of "The Piano"
12 Emotional state
13 Pose for a picture
18 Places to shape up
21 Frank's partner in the comics
24 Rationale
25 President from Illinois
26 Indian ___
27 Red Muppet dolls
28 Paris fashion house
29 Campbell of "Martin"
30 Mortgage payer
31 "Dunkirk" director
33 Cardinal who wore #6
34 "___ Wonderful Life" (1946)
37 The Outer Banks, e.g.
41 Bend with a prism
43 Prepare
44 Archaic "willingly"
46 Big bill
47 More unusual
48 ___ weevil
49 Boo-Boo's buddy
50 "Omigosh!"
51 Top-of-the-line
52 Get under one's skin
53 Elisha of elevators
54 Greek P's
55 Pump product

TRIPLE TRIPLE STACK by Bonnie L. Gentry
8 Down got its nickname from the University of Nebraska athletic teams.

ACROSS

1 Detergent's target
5 Work together, as organisms
10 D-Day boats
14 Pelvic bones
15 "... a penny, ___ a pound"
16 Suited to ___
17 Compost item
18 Poke
19 Subtle suggestion
20 Printout of heartbeats
21 Easy basket
22 Dadaist painter Max
23 Put a stop to
25 Color of fall leaves
27 Dodger legend Hodges
28 Big Foot's "feet"
29 Dry bath
30 Lego inventor Christiansen
31 Oklahoma natives
32 MIT and RIT
33 ___ XING
34 Tomato variety
35 Boundary-marking post
36 Gadfly
37 Grappler's goal
38 Snail trail
39 Western Australia capital
40 Given the thumbs-up
41 Boudin ingredient
42 Words of empathy
43 Last word in "America the Beautiful"
44 Brain passages
45 Richmond trucking company
46 Car gadget for iPods
48 Compound found in fertilizers
50 Part of BMI
51 Jefferson, briefly
52 All-stops train
53 Letterhead image
54 Comfort
55 Numbers on baseball cards
56 ___'acte
57 Eyelid swelling
58 "Hamilton" actress Benton
59 Flushing Meadows stadium

DOWN

1 Antitheses
2 1965 Dave Clark Five hit
3 Game that kids fall for
4 Minuscule amount
5 NYC-based bank
6 Optimistically
7 Springarn Medal recipient
8 Nebraska nickname
9 Have a bite of
10 Garland's "cowardly" costar
11 Vice-squad tactics
12 What a universal tester tests
13 Got even
21 Miss Trueheart of "Dick Tracy"
22 Cenozoic and Mesozoic
24 Be apparently true
26 Düsseldorf duck
35 Thin incision
36 Chest muscles
38 Lose ground in the standings
39 Dockside platform
47 Crystal-gazer's words
49 "You're something ___!"
52 Leary's trip ticket
53 Cow pasture

203 STACK 'EM UP!   by Bonnie L. Gentry
China is the biggest market for the cars at 38 Across.

ACROSS

1 Waze, for one
4 1972 Olympics site
11 1970 Jackson 5 chart topper
14 Wine bottle word
15 One showing disdain
16 Gob
17 Camp bed
18 Double-check the sum
19 Har-___ tennis court
20 Calendar col. heading
22 Siegfried's sigh
23 Pentathlon items with guarded tips
25 1980 NFL MVP Brian
26 To be, to Henri
27 Plant used in herbal remedies
28 Rural route
30 Full, and then some
31 Reluctant assent
32 Curling surface
33 Every picture tells one
34 QB's throw, completed or not
35 Tart plums
37 Boardroom VIP
38 French cars
40 Muddle or confuse
43 Patellae
44 Corleone's circle
45 Atomic absorption units
46 Ovid's 152
48 Overly inquisitive one
49 The NBA's Hawks, on a scoreboard
50 Sharpens one's appetite
51 Hosp. brain readout
52 Type of French salad
55 Suffer from symptoms
56 Word from a cheerleader
57 Now and forever
58 Take in the sights
59 Onetime JFK lander
60 Floating island, e.g.
61 Shape traced during a slalom

DOWN

1 Nos. on statements
2 They're off limits
3 Hang tough
4 Much of E. Europe, once
5 Serve that can't be returned
6 Clambake competitions
7 Hardly type-A types
8 Where to sign, often
9 "Let's Dance" singer Chris
10 More ___ (approximately)
11 "Now hear this!"
12 Just the essentials
13 Holy wars
21 Come again
24 Clover's family
26 EMT destinations
29 Ignition insert
33 Runs like a rabbit
35 The S in ASPCA: Abbr.
36 Percolate
39 In medias ___
41 Bald-faced statement
42 Was worthy of
47 Man and Wight, e.g.
50 Painful skin bump
53 Suffix for krypton
54 Hong Kong: Abbr.

ACROSS

1 Edinburgh toppers
5 Congeal
9 Borden's "saleslady"
14 Jacob's brother
15 Raise
16 Deviates
17 "When my family goes camping our___"
20 Cappelletti and farfalle, e.g.
21 Nicholas II, e.g.
22 "What ___ the odds?"
23 School support org.
25 Musical syllable sung by Nanki-Poo
26 Dissenting votes
27 "I eat only oats and barley. I'm ___"
33 Expressed sorrow
34 Sign before Virgo
35 Former Priceline bidding service: Abbr.
37 Valley known for its vineyards
38 Fixed fight
41 Slaughter of baseball fame
43 Like Buckingham Palace
45 Rapace in "Skyfall"
46 When a Joisey milkman gets up?
47 "I prefer escargot because ___"
51 Nimoy, to pals
53 "Cry ___ River"
54 Numbered hwy.
55 Gumby creator Clokey
56 Bollywood film costume
58 Shoe part
63 "I went to the photo shop hoping someday my ___"
66 It's not always common
67 "___ do for now"
68 Premed subj.
69 Whodunit award
70 Curling, e.g.
71 Entreats

DOWN

1 Short-term worker
2 East of the Urals
3 Eucharist rite
4 Tallow source
5 Watch parts
6 Oahu souvenir
7 Hops kiln
8 "Valse ___": Sibelius
9 Chicago carrier
10 Gettysburg general
11 Home of the Spurs
12 Opening notes
13 Slalom curves
18 Engrossed
19 Ancient ointment
24 "The murmur of ___ . . .": Dickinson
27 Have or hold
28 Minimum range tide
29 Presidential plenary power
30 Secret storage
31 "What a ___ hooey!"
32 Follett's "___ the Needle"
36 Mallet game
39 Suffix for gland
40 Gumdrop, e.g.
42 Barrett of Pink Floyd
44 Cute rodent
48 Soho socials
49 Insect with pincers
50 Watch over
51 Trivial slip
52 Took a wrong turn
57 Very tiny amount
59 Picket line crosser
60 Timbre
61 Online reading
62 "The Secret Life of ___" (2016)
64 CIA cousin
65 Einstein's birthplace

205

THEMELESS by Gene Newman
The answer at 8 Down is also its capital.

ACROSS

1 Scythe sweep
6 Brylcreem application
9 Legwear item
13 Shimmering fabric
14 Smallest size at Starbucks
15 Allege
16 Municipal laws
18 Jury member
19 A thousand smackers
20 Think-tank flashes
22 Behavioral quirk
23 Melody
24 Get through a rough patch
32 Revival site
33 Like a valedictory
34 A close one is scary
35 Perform
36 ___ this earth (otherwordly)
38 Bad review
39 "Common Sense" author
42 Madrid lady of rank
43 Phoenix team
44 Dissident factions
47 Rocky peak
48 Very casual hair style
49 Myopic
55 Balneotherapy site
58 "Queen of Jazz"
59 Great Depression queues
61 California Breed guitarist
62 Brothers at the O.K. Corral
63 Digital funds
64 Gin flavoring
65 Start-up loan org.
66 Indian mercenary

DOWN

1 One pollution result
2 Had on
3 A gofer, maybe
4 Prefix for angle
5 Creeping Charley look-alike weed
6 Start of a winter mo.
7 Positive response
8 Republic of Guinea-___
9 British term for "almost worthless"
10 Ham's word
11 Appear
12 Drops a pop-up
14 Watson and Crick research target
17 Ancient Greek magistrate
21 Sardine containers
22 "The Alienist" network
24 Summary
25 Up to
26 Succumb to the elements
27 UF athlete
28 "I knew it all ___!"
29 Accept enthusiastically
30 "I Love You" singer Faith
31 Sawbucks
32 Base music
37 Cultivated
40 Fertilizer component
41 Adam's grandson
43 Dine
45 Ancient Israel had twelve
46 Scads
49 The latest
50 Carrier to the Holy Land
51 The smaller sax
52 Seize
53 Jason's patroness
54 Spigot
55 Center's delivery
56 Tampico coin
57 Cinderous
60 NASA lunar discovery

206

THEMELESS by Clarence Tyler
Uber and Lyft are examples of companies that make 23 Across possible.

ACROSS

1 Like Pandora's music
9 Swipes a card?
15 Constitution component
16 Kohlrabi kin
17 Hearty entrée
18 Town of an animal-friendly saint
19 Instant beginning
20 Pool need
22 Chess piece
23 Market with short-term hires
27 Priest from the East
28 Double-dealing
29 Port of Brazil
30 Books reviewer
33 Sports figure
34 Caper
35 It rests in a cradle
37 Oktoberfest locale
38 Still there
39 Rowlands of "The Notebook"
40 IRA type
41 Painter Kahlo
42 Kingsley title role
44 Absorbs, with "up"
45 Likely to arouse interest
49 Health org.
50 A handful of
51 Penetrating reed
52 Some Scots
54 Tennis racket metal
58 Clown specialties
59 Move over

60 Like lacework
61 Principal player in "Grease"

DOWN

1 Parsley piece
2 "Lemon Tree" singer Lopez
3 Put in the sack again
4 Was worthy of
5 Latin I verb
6 Wharton degree
7 South African golfer
8 Home of Lions and Tigers
9 Keach of Hammer fame
10 Walrus feature
11 Hems and haws
12 Cel mates
13 Presley or Boothe
14 Rob Reiner's mock rock band
21 Check fig.
24 Plane name
25 Jazz combo, maybe
26 Straight up, at P.J. Clarke's
27 Obsidian source
29 Southwestern tribe
30 American cousin of 32 Down
31 Peace that began with Caesar Augustus
32 Ristorante courses
34 Reba's realm, for short
36 Dumb joke source
37 Julie of "Dexter"
39 Many a newspaper name

42 It comes in sticks
43 Wrinkle remover
45 Heifer handle
46 "Fun, Fun, Fun" car
47 Put up
48 Mocha's country
50 Faith fraction
53 Repentance necessity
55 "Bye Bye Birdie" scripter Brecher
56 Inventor's monogram
57 Robot in "Ex Machina"

THEMELESS by Clarence Tyler
27 Down is derived from the Greek words meaning "wise" and "foolish."

ACROSS

1 Supreme leader?
5 Handle
9 Digs among the trees
14 Where a castle may be found
16 Speculate
17 Cyber visits
18 Not shiny
19 Foot with three parts
20 Put up
22 The Police et al.
24 Leads
25 Stands in a studio
28 Snaps on a field
30 1989 Civil War flick
31 Cause of spilling ink?
32 Jim and Tammy's old club
34 Chain in Hannibal's way
35 Kind of manual
36 Siena "See ya!"
37 Unknown degree
38 Western shooter
39 Drops off
40 Hangs in there
42 Small shot
43 Like some classic movies
44 Replay option
46 Similar compounds
48 Appropriate to your product
52 Golfer Stupples
53 Canvas conveyer, at times
55 Correct
56 Dilute
57 Takes a load off
58 Trade punches
59 Camp Swampy canine

DOWN

1 Strahan's former cohost
2 Son of Judah
3 Sweeping story
4 Noble rods
5 Kind of center
6 "You're ___ talk!"
7 Basilica bench
8 Highland dialect
9 Wakes up
10 "Texas Tommy" dance move
11 It's hard to take
12 Lower 48 connector
13 Cries out for
15 Too
21 Small fry
23 Multiplex count
25 Richard in "Love Me Tender"
26 Still
27 Junior college "seniors"
29 "Fatha" Hines
31 Oil company in Ottawa
33 Series set on an island
35 Family name at Indy
36 Grand Canyon river
38 Calculator figures
39 Dues payer
41 Sing the blues
42 Deliberate
43 Frakes role on "Star Trek"
45 "Little" girl of Harvey Comics
47 Fellers need 'em
49 Plenty
50 Colorful salamander
51 Bond foe
54 "Alexander Hamilton" genre

208

"Fly" on Season 3 of "Breaking Bad" is one example of a 44 Across.

ACROSS

1 Poor box contents
5 They're Big at Mickey D's
9 Stone size
14 Hoodwink
15 Earthenware jar
16 Site of conflict
17 Relating to a joint
19 Tennis player Gilles
20 Film writer
21 "___ the Body Electric": Whitman
22 They're open to debate
24 Advisors to POTUS
25 Uncomfortable neckwear
28 Rudely sarcastic
32 Flow-control device
35 Drop off
36 Prescriptions data
37 Lounge about
38 Commemorating
40 Kind of artery
41 Like some voyages
42 Tigers of the SEC
44 TV series chapter filmed cheaply
51 Tee, e.g.
53 Running the show
54 Port of Brazil
55 Become familiar with
56 Out on a limb
57 Insurance grps.
58 Julia Louis-Dreyfus comedy series
59 Docking locales
60 Rolls-Royce whitewall
61 Highland dialect

DOWN

1 Pull ___ one (trick)
2 Spanish city or poet
3 Stop on the road
4 Leave in shame
5 Is grieved by
6 Pogo's pal Albert, for one
7 Bracelet attachment
8 Painter Andrea del ___
9 "Hit me" sites
10 Alexander the Great's tutor
11 Temporary recovery
12 Shortly, long ago
13 Zesty flavor
18 "The Cider House Rules" Oscar winner
23 Travel guide list
26 Cinders of old comics
27 Do a spokesperson's job
28 Sink or ___
29 Stroller pusher
30 Hypertension medication, perhaps
31 Roll-on item
33 "For the Boys" org.
34 Bike attachment
36 Cautionary advice
39 Really irritates
40 Archaeological sites
43 Life partner
45 Feathery
46 Other side
47 Martin of "Roxanne"
48 Select from the menu
49 Promotes spoilage?
50 Bolt and hitch
51 Break under strain
52 Moon ring

209

22 Across is the second most-visited home in the U.S. after the White House.

ACROSS

1 Puccini heroine
6 It may be gripping
10 "Take this!"
14 Betsy Wetsy's toy company
15 Pre-Columbian Peruvian
16 Turn over the ice
17 Toddlers
19 Some hosp. staff
20 Don't bother
21 Salad cheese
22 Tennessee landmark
24 New Orleans bread loaf
28 Aussie girl
31 "Tangled" composer Menken
32 Back
34 Choral section
35 Vulcan mind-___
36 Paid to get in
38 They're dubbed
39 Spoke for the flock
41 Take
42 Years ago
43 Lined up
45 Provided that
47 Plants thought to repel bugs
49 Sound purchase?
51 Being sympathetic with
56 Pearl Buck heroine
57 Cruise lodging
58 Dust Bowl refugee
59 "Don't Throw Bouquets ___"
60 Weaver portrayer on "ER"
61 Popeye and Bluto
62 Spidery spinnings
63 "___ Evil" (Mia Farrow film)

DOWN

1 Cash drawer
2 Garfield housemate
3 Bristle
4 Cable syst.
5 Cite as fact
6 Infringing upon
7 Extremely naive
8 It's part of the act
9 Oil holders
10 Hold for The Undertaker
11 Hastening delivery
12 Let out
13 "Frozen" queen
18 Catwoman Kitt
23 "You can't fool me!"
24 Bodyguard in "Diamonds Are Forever"
25 "___ and hungry look": Shak.
26 Big bash
27 Marks for attention
29 Spanish poet Garcia ___
30 Pack carriers
33 Goes off
37 Cut
40 Anonymous last name
44 Capital on the Vistula
46 Egyptian god of the dead
48 Susan's role on "Feud"
49 Amusing lark
50 Chase of "Now, Voyager"
52 Zip
53 Outta here
54 Certain Feds
55 ___ buco

210 TWO ARE BETTER THAN ONE   by Pam Klawitter
A prize named after 71 Across is awarded to editorial cartoonists.

ACROSS

1 Like overcooked pasta
5 Generic pup name
9 Armed greetings
13 Dumbbell
15 Iron and Stone
16 Great weight
17 Jell-O shapers
18 Permanent result
19 Art that is skin-deep
20 Steep ski run
23 Most people
24 Narrow choice
27 Tall NBAers: Abbr.
30 Two-dimensional shape
34 Bluesy Bonnie
36 Go with the wind
37 "___ for Peril": Grafton
38 They'll bring you down
41 Future residents
43 Spaniard's sun
44 ___ Nostra
46 Funeral hymn
47 Winter warmer-upper menu item
51 Roomy hotel rms.
52 Any minute now
53 On the money
55 Baseball two-fer (and a hint to the theme)
61 Culmination
64 Modest poker hand
65 Perform an axel
66 Surf sound
67 Jalopy ding
68 Roomy family ride

69 Spam generators
70 Metal rock group
71 Tweed's caricaturist

DOWN

1 Life partner?
2 Pop star, at times
3 Kunis of "Bad Moms"
4 Many NPR downloads
5 Spa amenity
6 Tropical lizards
7 Skin suffix
8 Peace Prize city
9 Stadium purchase
10 Stubbs of "Sherlock"
11 Prepare for a total rehab
12 Hissing sound
14 "You should be ashamed!" sounds
21 "What's the ___?"
22 Did a bit of carpentry
25 Grint who played a Weasley
26 Way across the water
27 Market disaster
28 Don't-do-it list
29 Bridge over the Grand Canal
31 Keg insert
32 Christmas tree
33 Scrabble one-pointers
35 Electronic music genre
39 Milne joey
40 Opposite of NNE
42 Wrong

45 Barbershop girl of song
48 Software specialists
49 Applies, as influence
50 Cheer-y word
54 Pool opening?
56 High hairstyle
57 Boxer in "Cinderella Man"
58 Arp art
59 Pilot's guesses
60 Figure on a Monopoly card
61 Hedge fund whiz, briefly
62 Dove sound
63 Yoga accessory

211 IN CONCLUSION by Pam Klawitter
"Little Women" was written in 44 Down.

ACROSS

1 Crown for 59 Across
6 House front?
10 "Fish" or "Bones"
14 Tossed in
15 It's in the air
16 Main website page
17 Discontinue business for good
20 You might sling it in a diner
21 Play on words
22 Finish a romance
23 DC lobby for seniors
25 Quaint oath
27 "Please come and see me!"
33 Lariat wielder
34 Vixen's home
35 Earth goddess
37 Ballerina's pivot
38 Approvals
42 UK lexicon
43 Blade name
45 Ump's call
46 Haunting
48 Suspend factory output
52 "Varsity Blues" actor Scott
53 Sparkling wine from Italy
54 Line winder
57 Word in a New Year's song
59 Snow Queen in "Frozen"
63 Words to a whiner
66 Ending for appease
67 Fictional mark of shame
68 MacDowell of "Love After Love"
69 Bothers
70 Chinese menu possessive
71 Avian abodes

DOWN

1 Dash gadget
2 It's just a notion
3 Courtroom figures: Abbr.
4 Mold the Play-Doh again
5 Gator tail in the drink aisle
6 Aggravating internet ads
7 Where Eve got snakebit
8 Raiders in longships
9 Scat syllable
10 A big bash
11 Stove overhang
12 Luxury hotel chain
13 Compass point
18 Nashville stage concert
19 Udder protuberance
24 Magical opening
26 Fellow
27 Mexicali miss: Abbr.
28 Comb feature
29 "Parsifal" is one
30 "___ Apollo": Keats
31 Kiwi language
32 "Old MacDonald" refrain
36 Yemeni port
39 Spanish soup
40 Smith and Jones
41 Chip off the old flock
44 Orchard House family
47 Aigner of fashion
49 Magnesium silicate
50 Headquarters of 12 Down
51 Letters on a meat label
54 640 acres: Abbr.
55 Boy, to Brutus
56 Sound from the sty
58 High hair
60 Hats, slangily
61 Huffy state
62 A month of Sundays
64 Scrap of food
65 Golfer Poulter

212 GOING TO GREAT LENGTHS by John M. Samson
The number at 38 Down hangs in the rafters of The Garden in Boston.

ACROSS

1 Stylish
5 Violin's predecessor
10 Furtive glimpse
14 Foolhardy
15 Hebrew alphabet starter
16 Shah Jahan's tomb site
17 Italian wine city
18 Not as friendly
19 Insect terrorizer, in ads
20 Everything (with "the")
23 Like Lucy's red hair
24 ___ Poke caramel bar
25 Batman's butler
28 Connection
33 Lead on
34 Parking regulator
35 Strands in a lab
36 1967 hit by the Who
40 iPad card
41 Go from two to four lanes
42 Prefix for watts
43 New driver, usually
45 Helix
47 Kenya neighbor: Abbr.
48 "Quickly!" in the ER
49 Mind-boggling distance
56 ___ Nostra
57 "Copperhead Road" singer Steve
58 Muleta charger
59 Crossbow arrow
60 Inventor Howe
61 Toward the mouth
62 "Peter Pan" pirate
63 Necessities
64 "And Still" singer McEntire

DOWN

1 Avian crop
2 ___ browns
3 "And that's all there ___ it!"
4 UNICEF concern
5 Poured
6 Spanish epic hero
7 "I'll ___ touch!"
8 Sport whose participants are masked
9 Pacifica, for one
10 Captain Flint, for one
11 Major Hoople's epithet
12 Dwarf planet discovered in 2005
13 Tablet
21 Kind of contact
22 Sleepyhead's need
25 Most-wanted members
26 Charles Darnay's love
27 Bowling unit
28 Send to a specialist
29 Prince William's alma mater
30 Work shirker
31 Major European lake
32 Like SpongeBob's voice
34 Ancient Persian
37 Scythe strip
38 Dave Cowens' retired number
39 Mimic
44 Render invalid
45 Emphasize
46 Ballet step
48 Green course
49 Moose order: Abbr.
50 ". . . here on Gilligan's ___ "
51 Flash Gordon's alma mater
52 Birthplace of Billy Blanks
53 Diminished (with "off")
54 Doha native
55 Bat-eared Jedi trainer
56 "The Young and the Restless" network

ACCORDING TO AMBROSE . . .   by John M. Samson
"The Devil's Dictionary" is the source of the definition below.

ACROSS

1 Cherry variety
5 Injure
9 Scrub, NASA-style
14 Maleficent
15 Filled cookie
16 Madagascar monkey
17 Basketball center Fall
18 "Mother of Russian Cities"
19 Amplify
20 **Lawyer definition: Part 1**
23 Has a vision
24 "The Gift of the ___": O. Henry
25 Department heads
28 Maryland naval site
32 Barbell boosters
33 Principle
34 Faddish 1990s disc
35 Adam's grandson
36 Dixie breakfast dish
37 Ambivalent
38 Novelist Radcliffe
39 "Braveheart" groups
40 Not these
41 Girl Scouts cookie
43 **Definition: Part 3**
44 "Land of a Million Elephants"
45 Paraphernalia
46 **Definition: Part 2**
53 "Hasta la vista"
54 Feast of Esther month
55 Minute interstice
56 Investigate
57 "Slumdog Millionaire" city
58 Erstwhile
59 Black Friday lures
60 More, to minimalists
61 Extinct

DOWN

1 Congressman O'Rourke
2 Russian martyr Susanin
3 Chagall Museum site
4 Actor's portfolio photos
5 Virginia Tech team
6 Seed integuments
7 Virginia dance
8 Symphony sections
9 "If you insist!"
10 Propeller cap
11 Fail to include
12 Bustle
13 Hammock holder
21 "Ol' Man River" composer
22 eHarmony connections
25 Hoodwink
26 Auburn dye
27 In the crowd
28 Person
29 Thread holder
30 Backs, anatomically
31 Veep that resigned
33 Boer War region
36 Melancholy
37 The ostrich, for one
39 Articles in contracts
40 "Prik khing" cuisine
42 Apartment recess
43 Aquarium favorites
45 Growls
46 Scoundrels
47 Fresh thought
48 Babbling brook
49 Microsoft web browser
50 Second to ___
51 Whale that's a dolphin
52 "Don't ___ the trolls"

214

TLDR* by Harvey Estes

A response to a wordy text message can be found in clue* answers.

ACROSS

1 Moore's "Arthur" costar
9 Town of St. Francis
15 Common oater climax
16 Rising sports star
17 Unbelievably favorable*
19 Tennis instructor
20 Pig repast
21 Leaning a bit
22 ___ de mots (pun)
23 Gallery of London
25 Enforcement power*
33 Where Spartacus revolted
34 Fall mo.
35 Go off course
36 Directive at work
37 Figure-skating competition
39 Sit to be shot
40 Previously, in poems
41 One side in the Pro Bowl
42 Salami selection
43 Tossed and turned all night*
48 Ending with switch
49 Metro area
50 Jackson Jr. in "Den of Thieves"
53 2012 Ben Affleck film
55 Versus: Abbr.
58 Become aware of through print media*
62 In a cutting way
63 Short bon mot
64 At leisure
65 Some cold-blooded killers

DOWN

1 Santa Fe hrs.
2 Stack acronym
3 Former queen of Jordan
4 NASA cancellation
5 Ike's WW2 command
6 Less binding
7 "The Bourne Identity" author
8 "What's ___ you?"
9 NYPD notice
10 Sword case
11 Soft seat
12 Icon inscription
13 Motown music
14 Opening words of "Da Doo Ron Ron"
18 Decide on
22 Toronto ballplayer, for short
24 Off-road travelers, briefly
25 Did a lawn job
26 Funny Cheri
27 "A Boy ___ Sue"
28 Shine, in some ads
29 Temporarily put aside
30 Téa of "Spanglish"
31 Firebug's crime
32 Bring about
37 Part of UTEP
38 Financially solvent
39 Basilica bench
42 Chew the fat
44 Must
45 Hiking paths
46 University of Oregon home
47 Well-mannered
50 "___ put it another way . . ."
51 House position
52 Part of an espionage name
54 Greek consonants
55 Early Ron Howard role
56 Ivy League team
57 ___-à-porter
59 Bill, the "Science Guy"
60 Gran Paradiso, e.g.
61 AARP members

Alternate clue for 18 Across: "End a three-minute round."

ACROSS

1 Soda insert
6 One of the three bears
10 Permission request
14 Busy hub airport
15 Son of Adam and Eve
16 In the sack
17 Yacht club site
18 Jog one's memory
20 **Start of a riddle**
22 Detective Spade
23 Stimpy's bud
24 Spanish affirmatives
27 Cherry stone
29 Midafternoon, on a sundial
30 Sunblock letters
33 **More of riddle**
37 Anakin Skywalker's daughter
38 Court
39 "Othello" conspirator
40 **End of riddle**
45 Some urban railways
46 "Guitarzan" singer Stevens
47 Low boggy land
48 Suffix with absorb
49 Oriental skillet
50 Morrison of the Doors
52 **Answer to riddle**
60 Be that as it may
61 It's a given
63 Take to the trail
64 Art deco designer
65 Moola
66 Not mint
67 Coup target
68 Violate a traffic law

DOWN

1 Weep aloud
2 Become less tense
3 Allergic reaction
4 Met highlights
5 Lost it
6 Links numbers
7 To some degree
8 Phnom ___, Cambodia
9 Setting of Camus' "The Stranger"
10 Log home
11 Help out
12 Dudley Do-Right's love
13 Goofing off
19 Had dinner at home
21 Poker declaration
24 Figure out
25 Sondheim's "___ Pretty"
26 Evokes feelings in
28 Local nonstudent
29 "See ya!"
30 Black Panther Bobby
31 Druid, for one
32 Fall event
34 "Morning ___ Broken"
35 Pal of Pooh
36 Adjective for Abner
41 Swift literary device
42 Iconic symbol of Oakland
43 Part of an eerie experience
44 Cracker shapes
49 Plied with port, perhaps
51 Mistaken identity, e.g.
52 Surfer's paradise
53 Inflammatory ending
54 Erie or Huron
55 Hind's mate
56 Kett of the comics
57 Pedal pushers
58 Beggar's-___ (sticky seeds)
59 Long ago, long ago
62 Club with resort villages

THEMELESS by Theresa Yves
"Presents" doesn't seem to be the right answer at 64 Across.

ACROSS

1 Dis
11 Flamingos do it
15 Artificial locks
16 Mayberry cell dweller
17 Alpine disasters
18 Win in a walk
19 Baum canine
20 Nice warm season
21 They're grumpy, some say
23 Read hastily
24 Amount to pay
26 Z ___ zebra
27 Angry display
28 "Heart of Georgia" city
30 Social gathering
34 Osaka drama
36 Hot issue
37 Beat the drum for
39 Scarlet bird
41 Order (around)
42 Tom Sawyer's sib
44 In an uncouth way
45 White elephant graveyard?
47 Shakers and others
49 Diminished by
50 Math class, briefly
51 Catches on to
55 Heart valve
57 Way off
58 Team components
59 ___ Nostra
60 Sydney landmark
63 Currently airing
64 Sight under a Christmas tree
65 A little progress

66 Back in the day

DOWN

1 "___ Life": Sinatra
2 2005 Anne Hathaway movie
3 Roundup rope
4 DuPont acrylic fiber
5 New Deal prog.
6 Jobs with little work
7 Trojan War hero
8 Truman's secretary of state
9 Fiddle-de-___
10 Canadian gas brand
11 Talk that doesn't make sense
12 Post–Manhattan Project time
13 Cheap fiction
14 Armchair athlete's channel
22 Hasty escape
25 Brisk pace
27 Suit to a tee
29 ___ a soul (none)
30 "Dancing Queen" group
31 Fancy-free partner
32 Temporary family member
33 Lab helper, e.g.
35 "The Bridge" poet
38 Frisbee, for one
40 Greek consonants
43 Overwhelms aurally
46 CBS forensic drama
48 Bordeaux wine
51 Mawkish

52 Radiate, as charm
53 "War of the Currents" winner
54 Look of disdain
55 Rock type
56 Clone
61 Pandowdy, for one
62 Ship designation

217 THEMELESS by Theresa Yves

The aggressive racing style of 18 Across earned him his "Intimidator" epithet.

ACROSS

1 Sprays defensively
6 Bay Area law group
10 Bubbly wine
14 Chinese leader Zhou ___
15 Both sides of an issue
17 Castor and Pollux
18 1998 Daytona 500 winner
19 With 31 Across, colonial representatives
21 Dedicated lines
22 Egyptian symbol
23 Start to play
24 Murder
25 Prevaricate
26 Wrong-and-right field
28 "Now ___ it!"
29 Parts of floats
31 See 19 Across
33 Bounders
36 Plug away
37 With 54 Across, political party in-fighting
41 Items in red
45 Part of DAR
46 Stable sections
49 Before, in the past
50 Hindu royal
51 Fancy
52 Out of the wind
53 Mellow
54 See 37 Across
57 "Jane Eyre" era
59 Not in
60 Trattoria salad
61 Execrate
62 Costner character
63 Chevy LUV successor
64 Comes down

DOWN

1 Spineless cacti
2 Madonna's costar in "Evita"
3 Made metallic sounds
4 Who to root for in a sci-fi war
5 Juan's "You bet!"
6 Address
7 Beside oneself
8 They're often columned
9 Fox's "X-Files" partner
10 Canine care org.
11 "A Christmas Carol" protagonist
12 Fireside drinks
13 Where campers sleep?
16 Senators' org.
20 Turner of American history
24 Solemn song
26 Genesis man
27 "Live from New York!" show
30 Ghana's chief city
32 Mercury and Saturn
34 MLB injured reserves, briefly
35 Swift, for example
37 Saharan train
38 "Just think!"
39 Says no to
40 Give off
42 James of "The Defenders"
43 Serious betrayal
44 Rain makers
47 "#9 Dream" singer
48 Fall back
52 Jordanian seaport
54 Dandy
55 Portfolio components
56 Box for practice
58 Seventh notes

218 THEMELESS by Marie Langley
There's a mini-theme at 22 and 43 Across.

ACROSS

1 Some hieroglyph images
5 Ending with chick
9 NBC fantasy/crime drama
14 Good, in Grenoble
15 Story source?
16 Abdominal protrusion
17 Former Dodge model
18 Out in the afternoon?
20 Barack's 2012 opponent
21 Result of a spinal
22 Marvel film of 2018
24 "Works for me!"
25 Eraser type
29 Arabian, for one
30 Pan's attendants
33 Biddeford, ME school
34 Simple housing
35 Put a strain on
36 Turn over
37 Uplifting lines
38 Curmudgeonly
39 Fiona's love
40 "Holy" brat
42 Belle of the old West
43 Film genre of 22 Across
48 Wipe out
51 Rival of Jimmy and Bjorn
52 Places of indoor starlight
53 When it snows, it goes
54 Reserved
55 Rock's Jethro
56 Epiphany kings
57 Loses a coat
58 Manages, with "out"
59 On a crossing

DOWN

1 Enola Gay payload
2 Likeness
3 Five feet of lines
4 They tell
5 Joe Btfsplk's creator
6 Princess Charlotte's grandmother
7 Eroded, with "away"
8 Arp contemporary
9 Underground group
10 Grint of "Harry Potter" films
11 "That a fact?" reply
12 ___ Cooper
13 Prefix with bucks
19 Present
23 A little butter?
26 Resistance fighters
27 1992 Steven Seagal film
28 Like a lamb
29 Scotch measure
30 Way off
31 Rose of rock
32 Slangy turn
35 Battleship feature
36 Magnetism
38 Tones down
39 "The Simpsons" disco guy
41 Fell from the sky
42 Baseball stats
44 Address Congress
45 Father of Fuad II of Egypt
46 Of service
47 Kind of blitz
48 Waffles no more
49 Boring
50 Cottage site

219 THEMELESS by Marie Langley
44 Down was added to the Oxford English Dictionary in 2018.

ACROSS

1 Prefix for watts
5 All-night bash
9 McCain running mate
14 Lou Gehrig's nickname
16 "Prince Valiant" princess
17 Stenographers take it
18 Covers ground
19 Yarmulke, for one
20 School break
21 VCR input
22 Powers a trike
23 Put up a new steeple?
27 Seehorn in "Better Call Saul"
29 Holiday helper
32 Some petty officers
33 Half scores
34 Café au ___
36 Start of a legal conclusion
37 Unit price word
38 Bedroom slipper
39 Rollerblader
41 Poor grade
42 City south of Moscow
43 B'nai B'rith symbol
45 Gooey goody
47 "Blue Ribbon" beer
51 Monopoly avenue
52 Steep
55 You might shed it
56 Aleutian Islands locale
57 "Mama Tried" singer Haggard
58 Parallel ___ (alternate realities)
59 Sought answers
60 Chap
61 Past time

DOWN

1 In the thick of
2 Eleniak of "Baywatch"
3 Travel mug's cousin
4 Nonmusical horn
5 Campus cadet org.
6 Song for Scotto
7 Brandy letters
8 Nevertheless, poetically
9 Played like Pan
10 Menu option
11 Good sense
12 Basically
13 Cherry Island's loch
15 Admiral in a McCartney song
20 Catalog anew
22 Very fast tempo
24 Earthshaking
25 Pen dweller
26 Clarification beginning
28 Arthur ___ Courage Award
29 Cuddly Muppet
30 Nobelists, e.g.
31 Office aide
35 Like Poe's heart
40 Plunder
44 Irritable at dinnertime
46 On TV
48 Low pitch hitter?
49 Take the tiller
50 Rib
51 Crimson Tide, for short
52 Choice list
53 Uninteresting
54 Bank of Paris
56 Homie

THAT TIRED FEELING   by Chris Carter
Total points scored are factors of 27 Down.

ACROSS

1 Driver in "Lincoln"
5 Lengthy yarns
10 Rowling's Beedle, e.g.
14 The Kinks hit of 1970
15 Partner of Lois or Lewis
16 Reverse curve
17 **Start of a quip**
20 Pollen bearers
21 Exception to a trend
22 Avena sativa
23 Heredity's helix
24 Blankety-blank type
28 Skullcaps
32 Caen's river
33 Personal attendant
35 "The Confessions of ___ Turner"
36 **More of quip**
40 Fermented beverage
41 Cook's paste
42 Continental prefix
43 School assignments
45 Hay fever cause
48 The Liberty Tree, for one
49 Shop ___ you drop
50 Steamed Mexican dishes
54 Papal domain
58 **End of quip**
60 "Cogito, ___ sum": Descartes
61 Sky-blue
62 Snakeless isle
63 Dork
64 St. Andrews, for one
65 Tot's cry

DOWN

1 Mendicant's request
2 Parts of DIY
3 Alan in "Bridge of Spies"
4 Frivolity fund
5 Patchouli et al.
6 "Sad to say . . ."
7 Funny bit
8 Quarter
9 Like beauty, proverbially
10 Quiver holder
11 From the Turkish meaning "chief"
12 Lively barn dance
13 Disavow
18 Coveted role
19 Hyundai model
24 LOL cousin
25 Papal scarf
26 Baxter and Meara
27 Some sports bets
28 More gloomy
29 ___ time (soon enough)
30 Tsunami kin
31 Was part of the SRO crowd
34 Completed a course
37 God of medicine
38 Dull bluish-gray color
39 Honeymooner
44 Triton, for one
46 Does penance
47 Apply gold leaf
50 In that case
51 Thun river
52 Cath. prelate
53 1970s rocker Quatro
54 Listen
55 Evening, in Roma
56 Vance Air Force Base city
57 Volcano near Messina
59 Groan getter

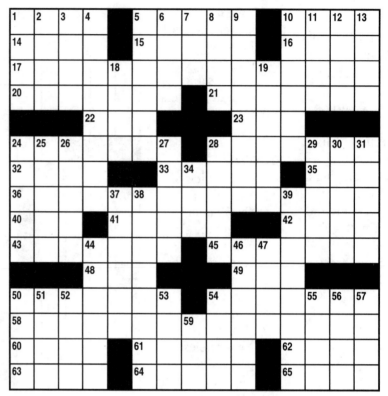

221 WORDS FROM SUPERMAN by John M. Samson
. . . and those words can be found in three long answers.

ACROSS

1 Cough syrup amts.
5 Bookstore must
10 Some factories contribute to it
14 Injure
15 Like Nathan Hale
16 Bluegrass banjoist Scruggs
17 Melville title
18 It starts when diciembre ends
19 In addition
20 Scheduled to be talked about
23 Identify in a Facebook pic
24 Stephen in "Guinevere"
25 Did lookout duty
29 Nielsen count
33 Exeunt ___ (stage direction)
34 Tuneful Tori
36 LXX divided by X
37 Creedence Clearwater Revival hit
41 After taxes
42 Kid-lit detective ___ the Great
43 Take care of
44 Incline (to)
47 Awakened suddenly
49 Fork lift?
50 Howl or bark
51 Alee
60 Apple, to Apple
61 Take ___ on balls (walk)
62 Once ___ lightly
63 ___-à-porter (ready-to-wear)
64 Within the Arctic Circle
65 Extraordinary
66 "Peter Pan" character
67 Ones looking ahead
68 Body covering

DOWN

1 Poe's "___ Art the Man"
2 Corn porridge
3 Faculty member
4 With fewer wrinkles
5 Stake-driving tool
6 Hägar and Helga's daughter
7 Needle apertures
8 The arch, in Paris
9 Thrive
10 Balanced plank
11 French Sudan, today
12 ". . . ___ they say"
13 "A View to a Kill" director
21 Joe's friend in "Midnight Cowboy"
22 Get the point
25 Solvent
26 Louvre Pyramid architect
27 Blackflies
28 Zeus visited her as a shower of gold
29 Member of a select crowd?
30 Chris in the Tennis Hall of Fame
31 Get the suds out of
32 Did a vinyl house job
35 Summer hrs. in Colorado
38 Loosens belts
39 Caseharden: Var.
40 Beaver dam building, e.g.?
45 Mescaline source
46 Galoot
48 Iron pigments
51 Where lederhosen are worn
52 Computer virus
53 "The Morning Watch" novelist
54 One of the winds
55 Like drone bees
56 Anastasia's father, e.g.
57 Drago in "Rocky IV"
58 Claudius I's successor
59 Took a card

ACROSS

1 Kind of beer
5 "This won't hurt ___!"
9 Sam of "Ben Casey"
14 Ben Affleck movie
15 Fizzy drink
16 Gawked at
17 Has a tab
18 Lou Grant's paper
19 Harass relentlessly
20 Like quests to find King Solomon's treasure?
23 Divided evenly
24 They loop the Loop
25 "Is that true about me?"
28 Teen faves
32 Bridge of song
34 Craig's cruise ship company?
38 Black, in Bordeaux
39 Contemporary of Virgil
40 Loved ones
42 Become frayed
43 Tangy pie flavor
45 Admirable flaw, like caring too much?
47 Mortar accessory
49 Get wind of
50 Swine's confines
51 Cher, to Chaz
53 Deuce followers
57 Device for calling back the sommelier?
61 Sites for dates
64 All-night party
65 Can't stand
66 New York strip alternative
67 Fed. agents
68 "Frozen" queen
69 Sends a selfie, for example
70 Rustler's target
71 Secluded corner

DOWN

1 Ruth's mother-in-law
2 "Desert Fox" Rommel
3 PR person
4 It lets in the light from above
5 Regarding
6 "Star Trek" collective
7 "Gotcha"
8 Columns with data
9 First lady Lady Bird
10 Worked up
11 Kind of shot
12 Marshy area
13 Byrnes of "77 Sunset Strip"
21 Kind of language
22 Not in the pink
25 It may be bid
26 Fable feature
27 Like krypton
29 On in years
30 Gladly
31 Kind of mail
33 Once in a while
34 Blows
35 Turn inside out
36 Spock portrayer Leonard
37 Flying fisher
41 Poseidon's province
44 Luthor and Zod, to Superman
46 Herr's mate
48 Make moos
52 Gaiety
54 Nationality prefix
55 "That's a lie!"
56 Quarterback's play
57 Check for a flat?
58 Driver's license datum
59 Even once
60 Give a little
61 Polo Grounds hero Mel
62 Vigoda of "Barney Miller"
63 Fenway squad, for short

EARLY BLOOMERS   by Linda Gould
48 Down is a song from "The Lion King."

ACROSS

1 Of the flock
5 Excessively energetic
10 Jay Gould's railway
14 Alan in "Bridge of Spies"
15 Hubbard in "Akeelah and the Bee"
16 Romance novelist Roberts
17 Denim short shorts
19 Imperialist of yore
20 What Stoics lack
21 Chapel Hill collegian
23 French possessive adjective
24 Dorothy Gale's creator
25 Auto pioneer Ransom
28 Topeka natives
31 450 in old Rome
34 Mexican muralist Rivera
36 Third canonical hour
37 Corey in "The Lost Boys"
39 Effie Klinker's friend Mortimer
41 Anthropologist Fossey
42 Chicago planetarium
44 Somniphobiac's fear
46 ___ and run
47 Emmy category
49 God with a crested helmet
51 Since Hector ___ pup
52 Stable fathers
56 One with a trainer
59 Gull
61 ___ deGrasse Tyson
62 Starred, in a sense
64 Jacques in "Jour de fête"
65 Aerobic exercise program
66 Prefix for "trillion"
67 One of the Baldwin brothers
68 Em and Bee
69 Galway Bay islands

DOWN

1 Bearing freight
2 Square of San Francisco
3 ___ savant
4 MLB All-Star Starlin
5 "The Devil made ___ it": Flip Wilson
6 "Make ___ for it!"
7 Aerialist Wallenda
8 Tracy Lauren Marrow's stage name
9 Melon with a yellow rind
10 Gung-ho
11 "Indian Love Call" operetta
12 "Dies ___"
13 Father of Tiger Woods
18 Road sign
22 Companion of rave
26 Trash-talk
27 Get the feeling
28 Home to Samsung
29 "March Madness" org.
30 Shipped
31 Libya neighbor
32 Man Ray's art
33 Beyond reproach
35 It's used to spike hair
38 Sparkling auto paint type
40 "___ Rosenkavalier"
43 Greet the judge
45 "My Cousin Vinny" star
48 "Hakuna ___"
50 Spanish snooze
53 Capt. Picard's #1
54 "If ___ wiz there was . . .": E.Y. Harburg
55 Four-door car
56 Square column
57 Cyan shade
58 Rebekah's firstborn
59 Card balance
60 Aphrodite's son
63 X, at times

224

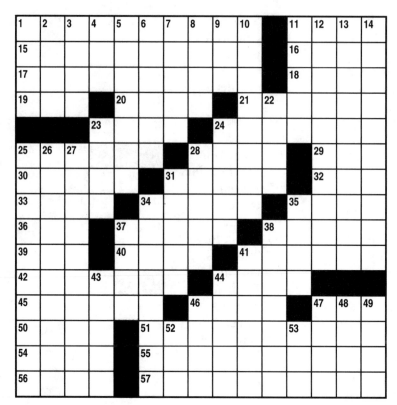

ACROSS

1 Veiled political message
11 "Aida" quartet
15 Ready for whatever
16 Make spiffy
17 Runs the show
18 Message starter
19 Curve shape
20 Personal quirks
21 Goolagong of tennis
23 Flirty gesture
24 Ouzo flavoring
25 Interjecting
28 Sloth, e.g.
29 Accts. of interest
30 Word after nothing
31 Like the SATs
32 Shaver
33 Means: Abbr.
34 Bad spells
35 Hipster jargon
36 View from the Riviera
37 Punished via the wallet
38 Not the first recording
39 Eroded, with "away"
40 Mary Kay rival
41 Puts in a serious mood
42 More lowdown
44 Needy's need
45 Render harmless
46 Salon sound
47 Autumn mo.
50 Ivy League team
51 It cools you off and wakes you up
54 Blow off steam
55 Pulse taker, at times
56 Pushing the envelope
57 Like lands ravaged by wildfires

DOWN

1 Measured amount
2 Burden of proof
3 Hoodwinks
4 "___ is me!"
5 In trouble
6 Brom Bones's creator
7 "Fetch" missile
8 Flip
9 "Chi-Raq" director Spike
10 Concentrated extracts
11 "So long" from Seville
12 Tissue type or joining word
13 Lost the football
14 440 relay team, e.g.
22 Contended
23 Sports column?
24 Got ready to fire
25 Everyone was named after them
26 Meshed perfectly
27 Getting off subject
28 Member of Santa's team
31 Gist
34 Collective mentality
35 Apple cofounder
37 Blond
38 Score a film
41 Deli machine
43 Pleasing to the palate
44 "___ it goes . . ."
46 Vassal of yore
47 "Think nothing ___!"
48 Sign away
49 Drove (off)
52 Give a nod to, perhaps
53 Scale notes

225 CLASSICAL ELEMENT   by Karen Motyka
. . . and that element can be found at 35 Down.

ACROSS

1 Bests
5 "___ Grows in Brooklyn" (1945)
10 "___ that's your game!"
14 Component
15 One of Hawthorne's seven
16 Fall through
17 Invoice from Mr. Fix-It
19 Gift from Prometheus
20 Voldemort portrayer
21 Pain-relief pill
23 Expected in
24 Clip-___ (some bow ties)
25 Kerry's 2004 running mate
29 Victory margins at the track
33 Dudley in "Arthur"
34 Mainlander at a luau
36 Turned tail
37 Antarctic explorer
38 Crickets
39 Text-removal mark
40 Wing that can't flap
41 Celebrity chef Guy
42 Throw with might
43 California's state tree
45 Polly's request
47 Anthony Hopkins' title
48 Concourse abbr.
49 Repeated song section
53 Some walking sticks
57 "Dies ___" (requiem hymn)
58 Backyard recliners
60 Coconut fiber
61 Sonneteer's Muse
62 Render speechless
63 ___ d'oeuvres
64 One who likes long lines
65 Swiss cheese holes

DOWN

1 Epsom Downs surface
2 Coldplay's "___ Love"
3 Meerschaum
4 Norm
5 "Ditto!"
6 File extensions
7 DH's stat
8 Jazz vocalist Fitzgerald
9 Stork's supper
10 In the ___ (soon to come)
11 Cousin of a highlight
12 Apple assistant
13 "The Tourist" author Steinhauer
18 Habituate
22 Corn cake
25 Small live coal
26 "The Five Orange Pips" author
27 London held the first one in 1851
28 Make confetti
29 Spock's forte
30 Jolly pair?
31 Reduce by 50%
32 Facial grimace
35 Classical element found in four long answers
38 Urshela of baseball
39 Trim down
41 ". . . my kingdom ___ horse!": Shak.
42 Ruthless
44 Circuit creators
46 Spite
49 Calorific
50 Suffix for smack
51 Intestine divisions
52 Horse seizer
53 Bump ___ (meet)
54 Megalopolis
55 Level and plumb
56 Payroll IDs
59 Cambodia's Angkor ___

THEMELESS   by Matthew Sewell
Boxing and four-man bobsled were the events won by 55 Across.

ACROSS

1 Optician's eye-catching display?
11 Stop up
15 Vigorously denounce via social media
16 Elder care?
17 1991 Genesis hit
18 Skateboard component
19 Safety features behind home plate
20 Catching the sunrise, maybe
22 Start-up co. investors
23 Phone bill category
27 Jump starter?
31 Incendiary
32 "Beowulf" characters
33 Dunderhead
34 Polynesian drink
35 "This ___ my first rodeo"
36 Stream buildups
37 Map fig.
38 Juristic exam
39 Applies
40 It makes a martini "dirty"
41 Sluggishness
43 Devilkin
44 Skyline point
45 Sue (for)
46 "Sign me up!" types
48 Guerilla garb
52 Animation
55 Only person to win a gold medal at both Summer and Winter Olympic Games
57 Put down by sending up
58 Article 1, Section 5 derivation
59 Enlightened
60 Got across a different way

DOWN

1 Influence
2 Purple-brown shade
3 Homme d'___ (statesman)
4 Games, in a bad sense
5 "Rizzoli & Isles" airer
6 Carry away
7 Storm warnings
8 Nathan with three Tonys
9 Members of the slow food movement?
10 "Game of Shadows" subject
11 Key team personnel
12 Word from German for "salmon"
13 Permalink, e.g.
14 "Goodness gracious!"
21 Map fig.
22 VCR tape format
24 Accentuated
25 Devotion to St. Jude
26 Japanese garden material
27 Nonessentials
28 Brown shade
29 Passed on, in a sense
30 Query with an elbow jab
31 Metaphorical area of expertise
33 Accepting a delivery label?
36 Most uncivil
40 Snare
42 Base abbr.
43 Zeroes
45 Boyle of the NHL
47 "The Awakening" heroine
48 Cherished, in Catania
49 "Just ___ feeling . . ."
50 Like all Wabash College students
51 Having only length, briefly
52 Mercedes rival
53 Milne marsupial
54 Word with a curled lip
56 Sea floor burrower

227 THEMELESS by Raymond Young

The duo at 50 Across were 2019 Four Continents gold medalists.

ACROSS

1 Pull a chair up to
6 Fed note
11 Unknown posters
16 St. Teresa's birthplace
17 Bony prefix
18 Holy book read right to left
19 House paint
20 Liz of "Girly Sound"
21 "Thanks, mon ami!"
22 Edgar Bergen dummy
23 Bed of greens
24 Small terrier
25 Like some dogfights
27 "Hogwash!"
29 Gift to a cinephile
32 The Incredible Hulk's stalker
36 Ace of Base music genre
41 Dozen Scrabble vowels
42 Huevos ___ (Spanish egg dish)
43 Missile with many warheads
44 Some Deco prints
45 Copier brand
46 Malificent portrayer
47 Ward of "Sisters"
48 Kiddie puzzles
49 Jib roller
50 Madison Chock's ice-dancing partner
52 Ink and studs
53 First-name-only gathering
55 Dirty rat
59 Seeps slowly
64 Strip of equipment
65 Deck with a Queen of Wands
68 Cézanne's "yellow"
69 "___ Needs to Know": Shania Twain
70 Queen of DC Comics
71 Employable
72 1994 Indy 500 winner
73 Pause in the rain
74 Dispatched
75 Sneaks a look
76 Severus of Slytherin
77 "Lapis Lazuli" poet

DOWN

1 Marc Anthony's music
2 Grand Duke of Moscow (1325–1332)
3 Solution strength
4 Quick on the uptake
5 Offshore havens, e.g.
6 On deck
7 C, naturally
8 Leaning print: Abbr.
9 Carrie Fisher role
10 "She Walks in Beauty" poet
11 It's swiped at banks
12 Karaoke liability
13 Hatch of Utah politics
14 Classical guitar inlay
15 Like showroom cars
26 Dodo's class
28 Some August births
30 It's spoken in Salamanca
31 Allstate covers them
32 Attorney general under Reagan
33 Prelate's title: Abbr.
34 "___ Pass": Uris
35 Rated G
37 "This Side of Paradise" protagonist
38 Nabisco's ___ Wafers
39 Messenger of yore
40 Court foe of King
42 Converted warship
45 Feline kennels
46 Reality court show
48 Goat sounds
49 "Happy Days" character
51 Wisconsinites
52 Habitat
54 Started a hobby
55 Dracula's curfew
56 Two ___ (NHL line rush)
57 Heeded the alarm
58 9,000
60 "Enfantines" composer
61 "A Dog of Flanders" novelist
62 Like Camels in a pack
63 Cold temperature range
66 Church corner
67 "All Time High" singer Coolidge

228 SUPER SUNDAY STARS by Mike Gifford
24 Across appears in "Harry Potter and the Order of the Phoenix."

ACROSS

1 Major European lake
6 Stole
11 Ne plus ___
16 Cash register inserts
17 Neon fish
18 Glacial pinnacle
19 Puccini songs
20 MVP of Super Bowl XXVIII
22 Fairy-tale rescuees
24 Hermione Granger's Patronus
25 Index omission
26 In the matter of
27 California river
28 Big name in faucets
29 General pardon
32 ___ gratia artis
33 Film noir, for one
34 Syndicate heads
35 "___ in Heaven": Clapton
37 Louvre oeuvre
38 "Do it, ___ will!"
39 Mystique
40 Baseball bird
44 Judicial bench
46 Weapons stockpile
48 Spanish Steps city
49 Firehouse trucks
51 Affirmative votes
52 Basque separatist group
53 Boxing official
54 Meet at the door
56 Cupid
57 Put on the books
60 Ox genus
61 Harvard spoof
63 Nothing
64 John Mason's namesake
65 Clambake veggie
66 Of yore
67 Karloff or Johnson
69 Elaine in "Autumn in New York"
72 MVP of Super Bowl XVIII star
75 Central Florida city
76 County Clare town
77 Mild cigar
78 Dolphin sense
79 Mislays
80 "Wham!"
81 Tour de France stage

DOWN

1 Toward the mouth
2 "A Doll's House" heroine
3 MVP of Super Bowl XLVI
4 Stemware
5 Strengths
6 Roomy hotel rms.
7 Fashion line
8 Prefix for sphere
9 PEN members
10 Starbucks orders
11 Stalin's empire
12 "Apollo 13" vehicle
13 Sea god with a conch shell
14 More or less
15 Samara, for one
21 Address book no.
23 NFL Hall-of-Famer Ronnie
28 Parking ___
29 InDesign company
30 Capone's archenemy
31 College classes
32 Unpaid debts
33 "Despicable Me" villain
36 "___ for Alibi": Grafton
37 Half and half
40 Swiss university city
41 MVP of Super Bowl XXIV
42 Childish retort
43 Harbor longings
45 Approximately
46 Doughboys of WW1
47 "Baled Hay" humorist
50 Basketball "trophy"
54 Nairobi Trio member
55 Finesse
56 Brandy flavor
57 Cloisonné surface
58 Japan's 1998 Olympics site
59 Hangs tinsel, e.g.
60 First Family member in 2010
62 Bummed out
64 Alcott's "___ Boys"
67 Kiss
68 Duelist's challenge
69 President in "The Hunger Games"
70 Play pat-a-cake
71 Leporidae member
73 French co.
74 Handel's "___ e Leandro"

229 "FIDDLER ON THE ROOF" MASH-UPS   by Betty Lopez
... and all these mash-ups feature Broadway title songs.

ACROSS

1 Like Niagara Falls
6 Bar assoc. member
9 New York strip alternative
14 Game-show hosts
16 Ride a Deere
17 Straw hat
18 Ancient Greek city
19 Song about Quixote dreaming of wealth? (with 35-A & 70-A)
20 Joker portrayer Cesar
21 Song about Norma Desmond's ascent and fall?
24 Art deco illustrator
25 Fourbaggers, in MLB
26 Fuel up
27 Helm location
28 "L.A. Law" star Susan
29 Fairy tale figure
30 Orr org.
32 Off the wall
33 Future mother-in-law's song for her daughter's fiancé? (with 61-A)
35 See 19 Across
37 Frozen carbon dioxide
40 "Diff'rent Strokes" actress Charlotte
42 Banished people
46 Part of ROM
47 Poker face
50 Kind of base
51 Geeky
53 Linen or denim
54 Four-letter words, sometimes
55 Red Book author
56 Fun, for short
58 Berliner's article
60 Wide size
61 See 33 Across
67 Helmet add-on for TV
68 Mystery story pioneer
69 Eighth mo.
70 See 19 Across
78 Remove a coat lining, perhaps
79 Make heady
80 Port on the Seine
81 Sandy spots on the links
82 You better not call me this
83 Hate the thought of
84 That girl's
85 Venus de Milo, essentially
86 Swirling water

DOWN

1 Slipped (up)
2 In need of refining
3 Hardly enough
4 ___ Haute, Indiana
5 Tibetan legend
6 Off the mark
7 Soybean dish
8 Bale binder
9 Tugboat sound
10 Ritchie Valens hit (with "La")
11 Moor of a Verdi opera
12 Gave courage to
13 Ate into
15 Ambled with oomph
17 Fellow Masons
22 Proof part
23 Right in the head
29 Word after post or ad
31 Roman law
33 Gregorius of baseball
34 Siberian river
35 Cried a river
36 Elton John musical
37 Oil container
38 Of the kidneys
39 Swift brute
41 Tumult
43 Sooner alternative
44 Lucy's sidekick
45 Letter enc.
48 Behold, in old Rome
49 "Um, pardon me"
52 Sound system components
54 Fencing phrase
57 Flaubert heroine
59 Start of Popeye's credo
62 TV censoring devices
63 God of medicine
64 "That's cheating!"
65 Flood-prone areas
66 Tune out
70 Naomi's daughter-in-law
71 About, in memos
72 Antidrug honcho
73 Straight up
74 Start for space or plane
75 Helped with a line
76 Pin part
77 Pop artist Warhol

230 LOST VICTORY   by Anna Carson
11 Across is the nickname of pitcher Mike Mussina.

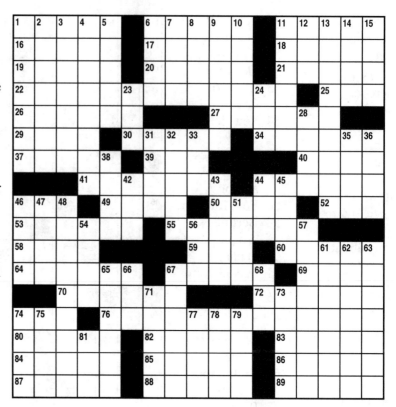

ACROSS

1 Dog in a Viking helmet
6 Settings for company
11 Archie's dimwitted pal
16 Kitchen utensil
17 Tibetan holy men
18 Borders on
19 Way to go
20 Put into law
21 Cubes
22 Device for generating suffixes?
25 Ins. letters
26 Orders
27 Kind of inspection
29 Blanchett of "The Gift"
30 Aerial defense acronym
34 Not seeing eye to eye
37 Villain in "The Lion King"
39 Nancy's "Rhoda" role
40 "Never heard ___"
41 With 55 Across, inn beverage to cry over?
44 "Friends, Romans . . ." speaker
46 Hindu title
49 It takes the cake
50 SEC overseer
52 Title for Oedipus
53 Fine point
55 See 41 Across
58 Response to a joke, with "it"
59 Kevin in "Footloose"
60 ___ d'Alene
64 Danish, e.g.
67 Meccas for shoppers
69 It connects to the wrist
70 Having butterflies
72 Haunted house reaction
74 Sigma's follower
76 Relative with a navel nickname?
80 Fiber source
82 Basilica sections
83 Some are canned
84 Handed over
85 Dorothy, to Em
86 Kilmer simile phrase
87 In a snit
88 "Here, try some!"
89 Stalks in the marsh

DOWN

1 Sound of a sudden stop
2 High time
3 Learned
4 Reserved
5 Lott of Mississippi
6 Skelton's Kadiddlehopper
7 "The English Patient" nurse
8 Apple of a sort
9 Crispy snacks
10 His wife was a Duke
11 Achieved success
12 Sci-fi contemporary of Ani
13 Loudly and painfully
14 Hold back
15 It's pumped in Canada
23 Fed. oversight group
24 Gov't. code breakers
28 Traffic jam sound
31 Like Nestor
32 Fictional Italian town
33 Stanford rival, briefly
35 Break bread
36 Charon's river
38 "Cat On ___ Tin Roof"
42 Wall greenery
43 "C'mon in!"
44 Tiny battery
45 Popeye Doyle, for one
sympathized with?
46 Cutting sound
47 Baltic capital
48 Hockey teams?
51 Coin of the realm
54 Question at an assassination
56 Brother's title
57 It isn't pitched well
61 1968 hit by the Turtles
62 Like the naked eye
63 An African king
65 Put right
66 "I'm so glad!"
67 Reason for glasses
68 IRS ID
71 Hardly any
73 Groucho Marx prop
74 A social grace
75 "The Morning Watch" novelist
77 Draws on
78 Religious faction
79 Shrink reaction
81 Cur curer

INTERNAL NOTE   by Anna Carson
32 Across was Jimmy Buffett's first Top 40 hit single.

ACROSS

1 Plot piece
5 Zodiac crustacean
9 From the outset
16 Hood sticker
17 Makeover
18 More dear
19 Lug
20 Autumn birthstone
21 Camera type
22 Oliver's "grueling" request
25 Half score
26 Mouth off to
27 Trojan Horse, e.g.
28 Put a halt to
29 Physical exertion
32 1974 Jimmy Buffett song
35 Vintage wheels
36 Popular vegan food
38 Arcade name
39 "How sweet ___"
41 Bump off
44 Heaps of, slangily
48 Bearing a close resemblance
52 Choral section
53 "The best is ___ come!"
54 No idea start
55 Part of ROM
58 Years on end
60 Lance of justice
61 The deity, in theology
66 Codgers
68 Hangup
69 Top spot
70 Have the lead
71 New Age music pioneer
72 Worker who doesn't commute
77 Puffed up
79 Zootopia mayor
80 Golden State valley
81 Chinese, e.g.
82 "I agree"
83 Sticks to the pool players
84 Bed occupants
85 Match parts
86 Tip

DOWN

1 Vino region
2 Dog with a blue-black tongue
3 Maid of song
4 Still
5 Like the bus in Paul Simon's "At the Zoo"
6 Bank takebacks
7 Figure skater Rippon
8 Ravel composition
9 Puts side by side
10 Ancient vessel
11 Like some print
12 I, in Innsbruck
13 Ran amuck
14 One-named '90s singer
15 In vogue
23 Cutting
24 Not talking
29 Susan's Emmy-winning role
30 Kind of position
31 Impose (on)
32 Undemanding
33 Look at hotties in a bar
34 Mother-in-law of Ruth
37 Yankovic parody of Jackson's "Bad"
40 High-wind source
42 Comfy shirt
43 Fragrant substance
45 Lerner and Loewe's "A Hymn ___"
46 Shade of gray
47 Supplement
49 "Interesting"
50 Letters before Z
51 "The Book of Love" group (with "The")
56 Greenhorn
57 Trace impurities
59 Bridge coup
61 Prestidigitation exclamation
62 Model path
63 Old Apple laptops
64 "Oy" follower
65 Elevates
67 Saturate
70 Tallyho, e.g.
72 Gin type
73 Spare item
74 Honeymoon isle
75 Tournament type
76 It may be rigged
78 Court cry

BIRTHSTONES by Brenda Cox

46 Across finished first in that race, but was disqualified for interference.

ACROSS

1 Nucleus of potential leaders
6 Stacy who played Mike Hammer
11 Jamaican black magic
16 The Doctor, for one
17 Eclipse shadow
18 Supermodel Evangelista
19 Respond to a prompt
20 Rolling Stones song about a groupie
22 Sackcloth and ashes
24 Houston hitter
25 Japanese apricot
26 Century-old cookie
27 Indian export
28 Scholarship criterion
29 "Where We Go from Here" author
32 Fred Flintstone's pal
34 High academic degs.
35 Picasso's prop
37 Chesapeake Bay features
41 Drama genre with many fans?
42 "Horsefeathers!"
43 Manhattan eatery of the '50s
44 Valuable finds underground
46 2019 Kentucky Derby horse ___ Security
48 Nautilus captain
49 "___ Don't Eat Quiche": Feirstein
51 Trygve's UN successor
52 Recruit or deal
53 Math machines
54 Anne in "The Best of Enemies"
56 India ___ ale
57 "Saturday Night Fever" clubs
59 Sang lustily
61 Smack on the mouth
64 McKellen of movies
65 Passed with flying colors
66 Bart's granddad
67 It might be hooked to an outrigger
69 Embassy staffer
72 USS Arizona Memorial site
75 Strong aversion
76 Place for a hibachi
77 Northern Ireland city
78 Culture dish
79 In the middle of
80 Bread baking, e.g.
81 Narrative poem

DOWN

1 NFL QB Derek
2 "Hard ___!" (nautical order)
3 Landmark seen from Waikiki Beach
4 Jukebox stock
5 Heart of the meal
6 Honshu seaport
7 Apteryx relative
8 "The Name of the Game" group
9 Part of LCD
10 Mad party figure
11 Stick around the kitchen?
12 "___ for Burglar": Grafton
13 Provide (with)
14 "There Is Nothin' Like ___"
15 Made a bundle on the farm
21 Heaviest natural element
23 Piqued
28 Racket-string fiber
29 Madam of the casa
30 Venerated
31 Clingy wrap
32 Happens to, in Camelot
33 Treebeard is one
36 Red or White team
38 Yellow brick road's end
39 Enchilada relative
40 Packed away
43 It's nothing
45 Snowmobiles
46 Deliverer
47 "Big" burger
50 Hosp. diagnostic
54 Medal presenter
55 Quod ___ faciendum
56 Made, as a case
58 Home of the loonie and toonie
60 Sea-bottom dwellers
61 Capital of Korinthos?
62 Fun house girder?
63 Former cousin of NATO
67 Target of a snake
68 River near Barcelona
69 Stark in "Game of Thrones"
70 Overthrow
71 Dr. Skoda of "Law & Order"
73 ___ Tin Tin
74 Agatha Christie's "N ___?"

233 VOCAL COACH'S COMMENT by Richard Silvestri
The song at 66 Down comes from "Damn Yankees."

ACROSS

1 Like the Vikings
6 Some nerve
11 Nancy with 48 LPGA wins
16 On the nose
17 University city of India
18 See eye to eye
19 **Start of a vocal coach's comment**
22 It's taken into account
23 Engraving tool
24 Moreover
25 Completely botch
27 Parliamentary vote
30 Draw for a moth
33 Give the go-ahead
35 Tribal symbol
37 Promises to pay
38 Black-and-tan ingredient
39 Sounds of dismay
40 Painter van Eyck
41 Abandoned
42 Sow chow
43 **Middle of comment**
49 Prop for Sherlock
50 Major happening
51 Chatroom chuckle
52 Easter tradition
55 The way things are going
56 Out of control
57 Far from fresh
58 Meat in chili
59 Vigor
60 Little rascal
61 Mimic
62 MGM motto starter
63 Prom crowd
66 "Heart" singers
71 **End of comment**
75 Bad spell?
76 For all to hear
77 "Stormy Weather" composer
78 A Dutch master
79 Tall and lean
80 Gettysburg victor

DOWN

1 Classic soft drink
2 Farm team
3 Whole bunch
4 Primal therapy sounds
5 Ageless, in verse
6 Piece of work
7 Frost, e.g.
8 Shipping unit
9 QB stat
10 Inexperienced
11 Science classrooms
12 Fairy tale villain
13 Equitably divided
14 Comic strip cry
15 Snore symbol
20 Proof windup
21 Deviate, at sea
25 Hill of song
26 Development division
28 Craving
29 Typesetting spaces
30 Viti Levu's island group
31 Bank negotiation
32 Godmother, often
33 Put things right
34 In need of editing, perhaps
35 Salmon kin
36 Klutz's comment
38 Skiing surface
39 Pineal ___
41 Digression
42 Part of the act
44 October birthstone
45 On a plane?
46 Bark beetle victims
47 Derisive laugh
48 City on the Humboldt
52 Last Greek consonant
53 PIN reader
54 State of bliss
55 Keg feature
56 No-frills
58 Share billing
59 Chapman of the Pythons
61 MSNBC rival
62 Hill resident
64 End of a threat
65 First family's home
66 Comfy and cozy
67 "Christian Science Monitor" founder
68 Neighbor of Ark.
69 Rush
70 Lang follower
71 IV units
72 On a date
73 Key st.
74 It's not free of charge

234 FOUR TOPS   by Bonnie L. Gentry
The tune at 65 Across started as a 19th-century social dance in England.

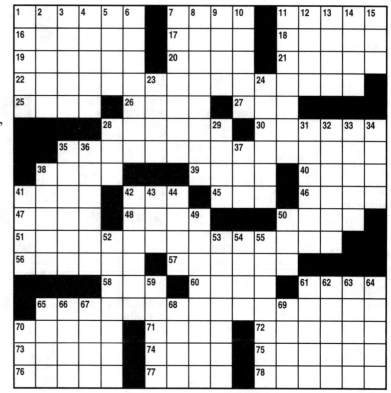

ACROSS

1 Talks smack to
7 StubHub parent
11 Big kerfuffle
16 Put a match to
17 West Coast gas station chain
18 Lagoon entry
19 Ad campaign "hook"
20 Deer parasite
21 Gets warm, so to speak
22 Contrary to what common sense would suggest
25 Boozers
26 "Bohemian Rhapsody" ender
27 Open-mic night hosts
28 Pulpit figure
30 Reacts to fireworks
35 "What's inside" list
38 Cobb in "On the Waterfront"
39 Seventh-inning stretchers
40 Operate a combine
41 Items in a Londoner's pantry
42 "Your Feet's Too Big" lyricist Benson
45 ___ Miguel
46 Some restaurant waiting areas
47 "There ___ time like the present"
48 Reinhart on "Riverdale"
50 "The Square Egg" author
51 Poolside footwear
56 Come clean
57 Watch others dance
58 PhD holders
60 Jodie Foster's "Little Man ___"
61 ___ out (determine)
65 Jack-in-the-box tune
70 Diameter fractions
71 Billion : giga- :: trillion : ___
72 Fill with fury
73 The NCAA's Huskies
74 Break-in take
75 Not spontaneous
76 Chinese menu claim
77 Editor's change of heart
78 Printer cartridges

DOWN

1 Harrow blades
2 Cold weather quarters
3 Shovelnose nose
4 Astrological chart divisions
5 Vermont, to Veronique
6 Gambia's only neighbor
7 Gradually deplete
8 Execute successfully
9 ID no. on a bank statement
10 Li'l Abner's family name
11 Doesn't say outright
12 "The ___ Love": R.E.M.
13 Patron saint of Norway
14 Roll-call response
15 Sobriety org.
23 Pink table wine
24 Response to a doubter
28 Peter Pan sandwich
29 Some clock radios
31 Like some teas and medicines
32 Athletic shoes
33 Early name in arcade games
34 Six make a fl. oz.
35 Roland Garros sport
36 "___ Fables"
37 "___ Carousel": Hollies
38 Stocking thread
41 Minor quarrel
42 Belonging to the sports elite
43 God, in Genoa
44 Source of Evian water
49 "For real?"
50 Parked it
52 Figure-falsifying
53 Not moving
54 Pay attention to
55 90° left, when facing north
59 Moulton and Rogen
61 Cling wrap
62 Gas bill info
63 Bob of the "Silver Bullet Band"
64 Snowmobiles
65 Rabanne of fashion
66 Lamar who married a Kardashian
67 They're knocked down in alleys
68 Straphanger's need
69 Ecto- opposite
70 Compete in a sprint

235 "I" PROBLEM   by Jim Leeds
Finding one's niche in life can be frustrating.

ACROSS

1 Stare at from across the room
5 Leftover part
10 Pistachio's family
15 Scotch brand
16 Anaya in "Wonder Woman"
17 Carefee refrain
18 As a prospector I found many a stream that looked promising, ___
21 Yeun of "The Walking Dead"
22 Basic beliefs
23 Door sign
25 News feature
27 Sack opener?
28 Galway Bay site
29 Glasgow gal
31 Popular drink order?
33 Ed in "JFK"
34 Control tower datum: Abbr.
35 I tried farming over in Dijon, however I couldn't ___
38 "See other side": Abbr.
39 Bee-related
40 Two make a fly
41 Forrest Gump's game
43 Believing in one God
48 Big time
49 Case load?
50 Cenozoic is the current one
51 I once got a job modeling shoes, but was let go.
56 They told me I ___ Early space station
57 Acclimate: Var.
58 Steinbeck's middle name
59 Cathedral projection
60 French 101 verb
61 Anguished sound
62 Dick's veep
65 Lusterless
66 Fork-tailed bird
67 Children's author Lindgren
70 I once worked in a diner, but was fired after a customer ended up ___
75 Knotted scarf
76 Toon with numerous bad hare days
77 River of 1,575 miles
78 Avuncular storyteller
79 "If I Ran the Zoo" author
80 "The Bronx Zoo" author

DOWN

1 Oodles
2 Touch on
3 Sam in "Nixon"
4 Cutlery
5 Solar System dwarf planet
6 151, in the Forum
7 Color that suits Santa?
8 ___ Arbor
9 Copper coatings
10 Philatelic item
11 Starbucks dispensers
12 Minorca's capital
13 Processed bauxite
14 Party person
19 Gumshoe
20 Service song
24 Dweeb
26 Russian leader
27 MLB commissioner (1969–84)
28 Colorado resort park
29 Reindeer herdsman
30 Choir voices
32 "Guys only" party
33 Basketball stat unit
35 "Breakfast at Tiffany's" author
36 "Once ___ midnight dreary . . ."
37 Ultrasound images
42 Bluegrass, for one
43 Cruz and Nugent
44 Tests by lifting
45 Provisional
46 Rainbow goddess
47 Give a hang
49 Former German capital
51 Roundup target
52 Dovish
53 Conjecture
54 Captain von Trapp
55 Indian River fruits
59 Crafty
61 Running battles?
63 Skating competition
64 56-A successor
66 Ten Commandments word
68 Suffix for angel
69 Remove a typo
71 Channel for old films
72 World Cup cheer
73 Campus on Lake Superior
74 "For ___ a jolly good . . ."

236 PENNY LANE by Fred Piscop
In 2018, it costs the U.S. Mint 2.06 cents to make a penny.

ACROSS

1 Castaway's signal
6 Muslim holy war
11 Superior beef
16 Clark's partner in exploration
17 Launch an insurrection
18 Bird who was quoted
19 ___-jazz (Coltrane genre)
20 Freak out
21 Emmy or Edgar
22 You could get it for a penny, once
25 Financially secure
26 Long, long time
27 Judge to be
28 Museum attraction
29 With ___ breath
32 Cherry variety
36 Read the UPC of
39 First zodiac sign
40 French Provincial, e.g.
41 You could get it for a penny, once
44 Blake's "Gossip Girl" role
45 "Heidi" peak
46 Itty-bitty
47 Lobbyist's target
48 Cleveland hoopster, briefly
49 Water park fixtures
51 You could get it for a penny, once
55 Stuck in muck
56 Brownies group
57 ___-book exam
58 Taken in, in a way
59 ___ Alaska
60 Played for a fool
62 iPhone image
64 Inning ender
65 "I figured so!"
68 You could get it for a penny, once
74 Ned who composed "Miss Julie"
75 Container with slats
76 Far from unwitting
77 Reader's download
78 Tin Pan ___
79 Committed to
80 Stop pedaling
81 Wins in a laugher
82 Gain popularity on Facebook

DOWN

1 Diamond defects
2 Flood-preventing barrier
3 Keep vigil for
4 Bathtub residue
5 "America's Mermaid" Williams
6 Kyoto's land
7 "La La Land" song
8 Like two of a dog's legs
9 "Think again, pal!"
10 Cracks a cryptogram
11 Talk gibberish
12 Natural brown pigment
13 Lendl with 94 singles titles
14 "A ___ formality!"
15 Terminus
23 Young 'un
24 Soccer card color
28 Hard-working Aesopian character
29 Auto grille cover
30 Word before quotes or guitar
31 Olympic skier Ligerty
33 Polar covering
34 Generic
35 Carved, as an image
36 Cramps, e.g.
37 Sheepdog
38 Shoot for the moon
39 The Red Baron, e.g.
40 Remove text
42 Blew away
43 Guitar innovator ___ Paul
44 Lawn-patching material
47 Gloppy fare
50 Inhabitants
51 Object of Indy's quest
52 Shad delicacy
53 Fish-and-chips fish
54 Pantheon member
56 Transporter of liquid hydrogen
59 Respond to a bad call
60 Atlanta, to Delta
61 "It's about time!"
63 Celestial snowball
64 Toes the line
65 Quartz variety
66 HOMES lake
67 Add a rider to
68 Foolish sort
69 Prima donna's solo
70 Folkie who sang of Alice
71 Bengay, e.g.
72 Sch. near the Rio Grande
73 Fancy pitcher
74 Camcorder abbr.

ACROSS

1 Piece of paper
6 Refrain syllables
11 Scots toss it
16 Bakery lure
17 Sound studio work
18 On ___ (when challenged)
19 "Norwegian Wood" instrument
20 Roomy dress
21 "Casablanca" actor
22 Clobbered
23 Spinner on the roof
24 "My sentiments exactly"
25 College basketball strategy
28 Bullring bravo
29 Salt Lake City player
30 Convoy
35 Seven Sisters school
38 Early feminist Lucretia
42 Toll area
43 Tennis great Nastase
44 Lampshade shade
45 1939 Boris Karloff movie
50 Soothsayer's sighting
51 Film credit
52 All worked up
53 Fashion
54 People at terminals
56 Set things right
57 Word on a towel
58 Party member
60 An ex-con might report to one
70 Insurance workers
71 Light gas
72 "Where ___ has gone before . . ."
74 Group of eight
75 Quiet, in the choir
76 Still in the game
77 Geoffrey of fashion
78 Polyphonic song
79 Punt propeller
80 Official scorer's decision
81 Nap noise
82 The way things are going

DOWN

1 Back talk
2 Seal a pie
3 Snow blower blade
4 Valuable violin
5 ( ), for short
6 See the world
7 Connects mentally
8 Type of acid
9 Hotel supply
10 Bunyan cutter
11 Port holder
12 Wise words
13 Wee Scot
14 Sea eagles
15 View anew
24 Kind of proposition, in logic
26 Bed on wheels
27 Navel formation?
30 Derby site
31 Sportscast feature, briefly
32 Worked with wicker
33 Endangered layer
34 UK fliers
36 He goes for the gold
37 Kind
38 NY Rangers division
39 Indian, for one
40 Commonplace
41 Readied the banjo
46 Gift basket contents
47 Martini partner
48 Bath brew
49 Tend the kiddies
55 Clergyman who "watched birds"?
56 "Mad" fellow
57 How some try
59 Significant
60 Examine closely
61 Drag participant
62 Dark brown fur
63 Lotto kin
64 Winner over Secretariat at Saratoga
65 "Keen!"
66 Not fitting
67 Vermilion, for one
68 Rousseau classic
69 Shade of black
73 Dweeb
75 Times in want ads

238 "WHERE IS HE?" by Bruce Venzke
The 1955 Kentucky Derby winner is named 11 Across.

ACROSS

1 Armada members
6 Online marketing
11 Cashless deals
16 "Park" near Stanford
17 Señor's mark
18 Calf-length pants style
19 Heap praise upon
20 Sing in the Crosby manner
21 Gain succulence
22 **Start of a quote by Hannah Gadsby**
25 Performs perfectly
26 Wolflike
27 Taking the stage, say
31 Deliver a verdict
33 Subtle radiance
34 Clever device
39 Drummer Krupa
40 Brief beachwear
43 Some are cultured
45 Brit. military award
46 **More of quote**
49 Stomach-crunching focus
52 Agony aunt's specialty
53 Idle scribble
57 Hogwarts graduation gift
59 Lower-Jersey sights?
61 Vicuna fleece
62 One with "I" trouble
64 Armful for Moses
67 Maury on "Maury"
69 Persian Gulf resident
71 **End of quote**
77 Mimickers
78 Goof off
79 Like an eggplant
80 It often follows vice
81 Open area in a forest
82 "For a Few Dollars More" director
83 Capital item
84 "Oklahoma" aunt
85 eHarmony connections

DOWN

1 Saw-billed duck
2 Prefix meaning "six"
3 Abbr. in many airport names
4 Slog along wearily
5 "See ya later!"
6 Dropping acid, in a way
7 Austrian alpine region
8 Baseball family
9 Much-admired celebrity
10 Court rival of McEnroe
11 Knee boo-boo
12 Relinquishing (rights)
13 Tacked on
14 Most middle-schoolers
15 Prefix meaning "Chinese"
23 ___ Tomé
24 Zipped along
27 Talk casually
28 Garçon's assent
29 Rile
30 Guileless one
32 Stutz contemporary
35 Ladybug's lunch
36 Make a runway safer
37 PlayStation user
38 Stammering sounds
41 2019 Miss America Franklin
42 Up the creek
44 Highway warning sign
47 Karaoke machine insert
48 Plymouth Rock, for one
49 Impress mightily
50 They're played at funerals
51 Flimflams
54 Nanny goat
55 Property unit
56 Trains in the Loop
58 Heterogeneous
60 Speech defect
63 Occupies, as a table
65 Hubbub or hullabaloo
66 Kind of wallet
68 Row between neighbors
69 "The Goldbergs" actor George
70 "All kidding ___ . . ."
71 Glowing flow
72 Go round and round
73 Eye membrane
74 Carbon coating
75 Eat formally
76 Literary tributes

MEDICAL CENTER   by Justin Andrew
The symbol of this "medical center" is the staff of Aesculapius.

ACROSS

1 Gave the twice-over
6 In a frenzied state
10 Ascribe
16 Laissez-___
17 Andy Kaufman sitcom
18 Small tower
19 Place for bargain hunters
21 State of secrecy
22 Make an offer
23 Point in the right direction
24 Maine sinking spot
25 Seasonal employee
26 Waistband
27 Blue material
28 Geologic time unit
30 Put on the floor
33 Talk trash
36 Ring fighter
39 Pained cry
40 Cop of '70s and '80s TV
41 Two tablets, maybe
43 Replay option
45 Rough stuff
46 Vote of dissent
49 Reunion site
51 Like some crunchy vegetables
52 Prop for the Tin Man
53 Snake charmer's pet
54 Matches a poker bet
56 Vantage point
58 Goneril's dad
60 Followed
64 German river to the North Sea
65 Join forces
67 Makeover
68 Bedside noise
70 Honey drink
73 Band's job
74 First of England's Stuart kings
76 Andre of the courts
78 "The Addams Family" cousin
79 Northernmost state
80 Columbus' flagship
82 Went bad
83 Mayberry kid
84 In the midst of
85 Knights' mounts
86 Cold feet
87 Turf war sides

DOWN

1 Unconventional
2 Telescope pioneer
3 Abetted with mendacity
4 Pitching stat
5 Some records or cars
6 On the line
7 Utilize solar energy?
8 Team components
9 "C'est Si Bon" singer Eartha
10 Reacted to a mosquito bite
11 Disney film set in China
12 Condition
13 Dipper over our heads
14 Young adult
15 Sundance's Place
20 Astronomical altar
27 Stops on a line
29 Homer Simpson's neighbor
31 Courteous consent
32 Earthenware jar
34 Tegan's duet partner
35 Distort
37 Kind of motel
38 Scandinavian capital
40 "M*A*S*H" locale
42 Skull and crossbones, e.g.
44 Come together
46 Back of the neck
47 Jump for Tara Lipinski
48 Paraguay tea
50 Kind of code or rug
55 "To ___ With Love"
57 Holm of "All About Eve"
59 Black Sea country
61 Lower shackle
62 Film work
63 Some military IDs
65 Threesomes
66 Be a bother
69 Popped the question
71 Butterfield of "Ender's Game"
72 "Joltin' Joe," for short
74 Jelly containers
75 Oodles
76 Starting on
77 Get an eyeful
81 Medical group at the center of 5 answers

240 STATIONERY AMOUNT   by Alyssa Brooke
The clue for 73 Down contains a homophone hint to the riddle answer.

ACROSS

1 Game with men that are queens
6 Pottery finish
11 Get straight
16 On the up-and-up
17 Desert havens
18 Lose ground
19 "Family Ties" mom
20 Cricket sound
21 Threw a party for
22 Peak for Heidi
23 **Start of a riddle**
26 IRA type
28 Toledo's lake
29 Hun king
30 Parting words
32 World's largest tennis stadium
34 "Shiny Happy People" band
35 **More of riddle**
41 Shriners in hospitals
42 Fast also-ran
43 Rice University team
47 Get a bead on
48 Strong point
49 Do detective work
50 Ball balancers
51 Civil Rights' activist Parks
52 City south of Salem
53 **End of riddle**
57 '60s radical org.
60 Ward's role on "Wagon Train"
61 Trojan Horse, e.g.
62 Herman Munster's car
64 Starchy veggie
66 Uneven hairdo
70 **Answer to riddle**
74 Access ending
75 Crows
76 On your toes
77 Provide with gear
79 Flat top
80 Like a nervous Nellie
81 Radiant glows
82 Orbital periods
83 Couldn't stand
84 Like slippery rocks

DOWN

1 Go over
2 "You there?"
3 "Cleopatra" backdrop
4 Auntie, to dad
5 Goulash, for example
6 Soapbox racers
7 "Chicago Hope" actress Christine
8 LP half
9 Zip
10 Sports award
11 Proves false
12 Put up
13 Empty talk
14 Nutritionist Davis
15 Utter chaos
24 Will VIPs
25 Turtle Bay locale
27 "Nonsense!"
31 Proclivity
32 Trunk lines
33 Nemesis of Tinkerbell
35 "Beat it!"
36 "Would ___ to you?"
37 Seward Peninsula port
38 Wind-tunnel sound
39 Hard to bear
40 Shoe pieces
44 Afflictions
45 "WKRP" actress Anderson
46 What some writers work on
48 Raised area on a neck
49 Grade school math
52 Piano exercise
54 Gives a hand to
55 Type of offense in football
56 Went off
57 Neglected
58 Official mandate
59 Arid expanse
63 Pilot's OK
64 All tuckered out
65 Analyze, as a sentence
67 What little hands indicate
68 Met highlights
69 Styne/Sondheim musical
71 Scout's recitation
72 Boxer's problem
73 1 quire = 1/20 of this
78 Quid pro ___

241 TECHNO MUSIC ARTIST by Harvey Estes

A twist on a saying mistakenly attributed to Maya Angelou.

ACROSS

1 Spectrum producer
6 Practical literary genre
11 Oompa Loompas' boss
16 "Ray" star Foxx
17 "Are you calling me ___?"
18 Reserved
19 Circus prop
20 Designer Oscar de la ___
21 Denial phrase
22 **Start of a quote by 65 Across**
25 Seasonal air
26 Stadium portal
27 Dermal blemish
30 Dogpatch diminutive
32 Rented togs
33 Pink-slip
37 "There Will Be Blood" preacher
38 Like "The Bible" in 1966
41 Water tester
42 **More of saying**
45 Search thoroughly
46 Household inspection target
47 Enjoys indolence
48 Lunes or Martes
50 Something fishy
51 Artificial locks
52 **More of saying**
56 **More of saying**
60 1 or 11, in 21
61 Heads off
63 Scott of "Happy Days"
64 Bill-blocking word
65 Children's author ___ Walsh Anglund
67 Forest protectors
69 Upper hand
70 **End of saying**
73 "Nice job!"
75 Harangue
76 Ryan of "Pippin"
79 Showed to the foyer
80 Of late
81 Skinflint
82 Where to wear a spat
83 U-turn from NNW
84 Change in Chile

DOWN

1 Overnight duds
2 Tat opener
3 Hacker's cry
4 Mum
5 Paris underground
6 Unyielding pol
7 It's sold in sticks
8 Tokay, for one
9 Skin designs
10 Arboreal ape
11 You watch it on a diet
12 "Yesterday" and "Tomorrow"
13 Time coming and going?
14 King on Skull Island
15 Naval direction
23 Sub stations
24 Hack fleet
27 Signs of disuse
28 Trump impersonator Baldwin
29 "Little Caesar" gangster
31 "The Merry Widow" composer
32 Chevrolet truck model
34 All-inclusive expression
35 Traffic pylon
36 Tavern inventory
38 Smokehouse process
39 "What would you have ___?"
40 Mottled feline
43 Autobahn car
44 Sweeping yarn
49 Where Plato shopped
51 Houdini's birth name
52 Uris novel, with "The"
53 Bio system start
54 Osprey
55 Fall, for example
56 Kidvid dinosaur
57 Peel
58 Reagan was president of this
59 Needle feature
62 Tom-toms' counterparts
63 Pete Best was one
66 "On the Beach" writer Shute
68 Eats (at)
69 Chilling
71 Fine-tune
72 Spineless one
73 Troop grp.
74 Sought office
77 Prefix with con
78 EMT destinations

LEGAL ADVICE   by Richard Silvestri
The humorous quip below is attributed to Steve Landesberg.

ACROSS

1 "Poet in New York" poet
6 Bad writers
11 Volkswagen model
16 Great quantity
17 Gland, in combinations
18 Visitor to earth
19 Four-alarm dish
20 Queue before Q
21 Admixture
22 **Start of a quip**
25 Word of warning
26 Eastern discipline
27 Duct
30 Poetic preposition
31 Shakespeare, for one
33 Angel dust, initially
36 Got out
39 Call from a cradle
40 Aberdeen accent
41 Put on
42 Assume an attitude
43 Admiral Andrea
44 **Middle of quip**
47 Andrews and Moran
48 Begin the bidding
49 Carol starter
50 Familiar sound
51 Fully attentive
52 Racket
53 Slump in the middle
54 Disraeli, e.g.
55 Couple
56 GRE takers
57 Dietary concern
58 Like state dinners
61 **End of quip**
68 Sing like a bird
69 Honey badger
70 "Gate City of the West"
71 Not as good
72 What "veni" means
73 Wanders about
74 Day one
75 Dependable
76 Superman, to Lex Luthor

DOWN

1 Scotch water?
2 Dos cubed
3 Keep in check
4 Biblical spy
5 Licorice flavoring
6 Flagpole rope
7 Regard highly
8 Use a thurible
9 Speed unit
10 Former frosh
11 Poked in the ribs
12 Terry of the theater
13 Railroad wood
14 Campsite sight
15 Partnership word
23 Like Norfolk jackets
24 Pound or Stone
27 Evening service
28 Columbia River city
29 Fish preparation
31 Tidal area
32 Grace period?
33 Sticklers
34 Backwoods beast
35 Rorem's "5 ___ for the Young"
37 Winery process
38 Iron-pumper's pride
39 Sacred music
40 "A Different World" star
42 Little pointer
43 Absurdist art movement
45 Sow's mate
46 Strauss opera
51 Memorization method
52 Went sour
54 Gelcap alternative
55 "The Sound of Music" song
57 Quiz answer
58 Prenatal
59 Earlier, in verse
60 Wheels of misfortune?
61 De-crease
62 Gentlemen
63 Speaker in Cooperstown
64 Baja bite
65 Basilica center
66 Noah's eldest son
67 No sweat
68 Computer base

243

THEMELESS by Brian E. Paquin

17 Across is also the title of a Frank Sinatra–Gene Kelly musical.

ACROSS

1 Sneeze response
8 The ultimate in friends
16 Gloat
17 Out and about
19 Wigging out
20 Got carried away
21 Shoulder of the road
22 Places in a schedule
23 Propeller head
25 Verb ending
26 Done in steps
30 "___ rang?"
32 Instagram pic
38 Used a tined tool
39 Schoolyard retort
41 Tornado's rider
42 One who ogles
43 Type
44 Trees with large acorns
46 Facing courageously
48 Banquets
49 Experiencing the outdoors
50 Baseball's "Say Hey Kid"
51 Dark, poetically
53 Doldrums
54 Adds gold to a mine
56 Replay feature
57 Felt
59 Peacock network
60 Agree to a proposal
61 Ad ___
63 Owl sound
65 Colloquial
71 Move the ball down court
76 Devoted fan
77 Phone for a pizza
78 Biblical division
79 Going down the highway
80 Letter writing and calligraphy, e.g.
81 Varsity letter location

DOWN

1 Furled face part
2 Potter's friend Lovegood
3 Paypal's parent
4 Dated letter opener
5 Not painted
6 Objected to
7 Key key
8 Italy's shape
9 Green, in a way
10 Curtails
11 "___ a crowd!"
12 Retirement places?
13 Mthly expense
14 Flintstones' Doozy
15 Loretta of "M*A*S*H"
18 Evenings, briefly
24 Bombing (on stage)
26 Historic starter
27 Unit of fodder
28 "Suburgatory" actrress Malin
29 Highest-ranking angels
31 Flaky
33 Pound of poetry
34 In a vague way
35 Boisterous college student
36 Pesky
37 Goddess of the dawn
39 Minor dents
40 Follows orders
43 Relatives
45 High points
47 Head holder?
48 Notched bar
49 James Corden's network
50 Rob Manfred's org.
52 Negative responses
55 Olden
56 Was unused
58 Greg's TV friend
60 Heartache
62 River dweller
64 Bad smells
65 Final ending
66 Pistol fight
67 ___ jure (by law)
68 Chooses
69 Castle protector
70 Picture tubes
72 Lugosi in "Black Friday"
73 Canterbury chap
74 Pedigree
75 Dilbert's job, briefly

244

THEMELESS by Victor Fleming

12 Down might be considered a mondegreen of 5 Down.

ACROSS

1 Branch of Islam
7 Costly error
17 Keep, as a promise
18 Shell game odds, to the naive
19 Incorporate
20 First lady who lived to be 97
21 Eucalyptus eaters
22 Dither
23 Court scores
24 Construction area
26 Alvarado in "The Babe"
28 Marshal under Napoleon
29 Bridge expert
32 Antibiotic target
34 Webzines
36 Challenge for a Jeep Wrangler
39 Cultural
42 Long-plumed bird
43 Piggy bank opening
45 Hollis and Keach
47 Gemini rocket
48 Cybercommerce
50 Stiff-backed
51 Trending upward
53 Contrarian
54 1960 Wimbledon champ Fraser
55 Piano pieces
57 Bar soap alternative
59 Goes bonkers
61 Geraint's wife
62 Needle point
63 TV show featuring Gil Grissom
66 "New York Times" font
68 Concrete chunk
70 Titleholder
72 Twelfth month in Haifa
74 Nod off
78 Desperation strategy
80 Corrigenda
81 Starry-eyed one?
82 "How Do I Love Thee?" is one
83 Perspicacity
84 Trump texts

DOWN

1 "Hamlet" auth.
2 Itinerant traveler
3 "Casablanca" heroine
4 They're adorable
5 Moral path, figuratively
6 Syndicate member
7 Fishing floats
8 Concerning
9 Will
10 Swing late, e.g.
11 Savings acct. entry
12 Repaired quiver item
13 Sound of impact
14 "Avalon" actor Mueller-Stahl
15 "The Family Circus" cartoonist
16 Teeny-tiny
25 Adjective for an oak leaf
27 Washington sluggers
29 Sorrowful, in verse
30 Window occupant of song
31 Least vacillating
33 Fictional falcon's home
35 Certain trapper
37 Brainiac
38 Backache pills
40 Glacial epoch
41 Frank Sinatra song
44 Parishioner's pledge
46 Engraved pillar
49 Pride Lands group
52 Overdrive, e.g.
56 Surveils
58 "Not in my ___ dreams"
60 Strauss opera
63 Carbonated drinks
64 Buckle opener
65 Orch. member
67 Tackle box options
69 Shouldered
71 Raison d'___
73 USPS deliveries
75 Wind down
76 Dele negator
77 Beanery sign
79 Wind up

THEMELESS by Harvey Estes

Chris Hemsworth played the title character at 50 Down.

ACROSS

1 "Star Trek" assimilators
5 Amusement park features
10 Mason of "The Goodbye Girl"
16 Two-toned treat
17 Concerning
18 Marc Antony, for example
19 Watch 12 episodes in 24 hours
21 Set off
22 Responded to a bad call
23 A-list notable
25 Deep chasm
26 High-hatters
28 Milky
30 Simon van ___ Meer
31 Polish partner
32 Birthright seller
33 Turkish title
36 Nora Ephron's "___ Got Mail"
37 Fertilizer compounds
39 Taking umbrage
42 Star in "M*A*S*H"
43 Will Kane's showdown time
44 Re or so
45 Bows of females
50 Befell
54 Flagg's striped poster person
55 Politico Mo
56 Sorbonne summer
57 Vomit Comet org.
58 Zilch
59 Alternatives to Macs
62 Seismic events
64 Long John Silver's quest
66 Trouble
68 Dalai Lama's city
70 Stuffed to the gills
71 Newspaper VIP
73 Boast masquerading as modesty
75 Call it a day
76 Prefix for Rome's country
77 Comparable to
78 Take stock of
79 Shades
80 Ice cream brand

DOWN

1 Went for apples
2 Baltimore ballplayer
3 "Nude in the Sun" painter
4 Fetch
5 How celery is usually served
6 Like some volcanoes
7 Couldn't stand
8 Letter-ending abbr.
9 Isle of exile
10 Joe's "Wise Guys" role
11 Generator part
12 Jewish scholar
13 Holiday at home
14 Part of an appetizer?
15 Torah chests
20 He made light work
24 Foundation
27 Starchy veggie
29 Women's rights pioneer
34 Romantic adventure
35 Used one of the five W's
36 Streisand title role
38 Textile trademark
39 When prompted
40 Wellspring
41 Shuts down an unresponsive program
46 Capitol Hill contingent
47 Storywriter Dinesen
48 Canvas site
49 Chartbuster
50 Title character in a 2012 Snow White film
51 Cute
52 Window piece
53 Pretty follower
59 Foul-smelling
60 Like noisy floorboards
61 Marsh greenery
63 Loosen the ropes
65 Pine marten
66 Mother of Ares
67 Fruity coolers
69 Place for a moonroof
72 Scale tones
74 Aragón article

246

THEMELESS by Harvey Estes

42 Down became "in the year of our Ford" in "Brave New World."

ACROSS

1 French Revolution figure
6 Penelope of "Vanilla Sky"
10 Quiver carrier
16 Sydney landmark
18 "Cut out the shenanigans!"
19 Hen-and-chickens milieu
20 Hereafter
21 Number one seeker online
22 Old PC program
23 Before, in the past
24 Island necklace
25 Name of 12 Popes
26 Where it's priced to move
28 Ward of "Sisters"
30 Pine products
32 Asian prefix
33 Theda Bara's nickname
37 Skin designs, for short
39 Not recorded
41 Wall decorator
44 TV interference of the '50s
45 Wednesday namesake
46 One-million link
47 Standing on Twitter
50 Rocker Brian
51 Drops the curtain on
53 Raines on screens
54 Brew packets
56 Went by horse
57 Dr. Dolittle's Dab-Dab
58 Eyelid ailment
59 Changes colors
61 What we eat
63 Totally blown away
67 Like some donuts
69 In the sack
73 Cinnabar, for example
74 Doc's org.
75 Dorm VIPs
76 Invite yourself in for a shot
78 Mud hole
80 Ink spillers
81 Apply oil
82 Climactic conclusion
83 Betrays discomfort
84 Auction stipulation
85 Actress Pfeiffer

DOWN

1 Gourmet mushrooms
2 Orbital point
3 Pistol's kick
4 Synagogue cabinets
5 Touch base on a fly
6 Greek island
7 Least polite
8 Web surfer
9 Kind of Buddhist
10 Can't stomach
11 Brand of peanut butter cup
12 Half of a ballroom dance
13 Suspect
14 "Have you lost your ___ mind?"
15 Zellweger of "Chicago"
17 Spydom name
22 Gets out of shape
26 Cannes coin of old
27 Missile housing
29 "___ Maria"
31 In danger of being lost
34 Gallery objects
35 Copied a cat
36 Opera overtures
38 Like Caroline of song
40 Mireille of "World War Z"
41 Place on piles
42 Words used in dating
43 Police van
48 1961 Heston role
49 Doris of "Pillow Talk"
52 Rank competitors
55 "Luck, ___ lady tonight . . ."
60 Worry free
62 Edible paste
64 Sylvan
65 Fancy fur
66 Historic Kennedy-Nixon event
67 Fleshy fruit
68 Hurls invectives
70 Sonny and son Chaz
71 "___, Brute?"
72 Like a rotunda
76 Corp. VIP
77 "Let It ___": Everly Brothers
79 Snapshot
80 Handheld computer, briefly

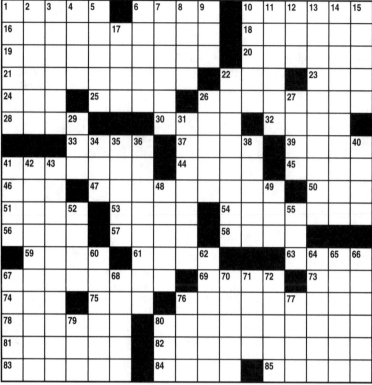

ACROSS

1 Pointed remarks
6 When repeated, a Pacific port
10 Lightly sprayed
16 "Scary Movie" actress
17 "Voice of Israel" author
18 Off the trail
19 Gas-grill option
21 John of "A Fish Named Wanda"
22 Writing a few letters
23 Purity units
24 Second start
25 Eyeball covers
26 Used stopwatches
27 Rebounding, with "off"
29 "Oh, brother!"
30 Has bills
33 Jolie of "Girl, Interrupted"
35 Home to many a Constable and Turner
36 Quell the concerns of
40 Capricious (with 46-A)
42 "NCIS" actor Joe
43 Malia's sister
45 Take the floor
46 See 40 Across
48 Backs out in the harbor
49 El Prado paintings, e.g.
50 Dole out
53 At the ready
54 Rebuffs
55 Yachting cup
60 Thickens, as cream
62 "Star Trek" counselor
63 Ready to be eaten
64 Queued up
66 Trust in
68 More nasty
69 While being somewhere else
70 Where to load some BBs
71 "Brothers & Sisters" matriarch
72 With regard to
73 Necklace parts
74 Torah scroll containers
75 Strong suit

DOWN

1 Dull
2 Like Schönberg's music
3 Image receiver
4 Englishman
5 "Spanish Eyes" ayes
6 Apple preparation
7 Pare down
8 Gets heavier
9 Earth's pull, briefly
10 Woolen coat
11 Religion of the Koran
12 Strong, silent kind, for example
13 Barely stay afloat
14 All-star game side
15 Easter egg solutions
20 Normal IV fluid
26 C&W singer Tucker
28 Chocolate substitute
29 Ho Chi ___ City
31 Hawke in "Juliet, Naked"
32 Looks for
34 Roundup rope
36 City on the Nile
37 Tower of faith
38 Headquarters of Intel
39 Flunkies
41 Fall blossom
43 Goes it alone
44 Cobblers' tools
47 Signals to Revere
48 Rathskeller stock
51 A lot of London?
52 Lab slide items
56 "Couldn't tell ya"
57 Chopper
58 Apply oil to
59 House on the Hill
61 Ahead of the game
62 Drift
64 Apple product
65 Sedaka or Simon
66 "True Colors" actress Merrill
67 Like many who sign

ACROSS

1 "The Lady of the Lake" author
6 Dermatologist's concern
10 Senior snubber
16 Sci-fi "home team"
17 Off-key
18 Artillery position
19 Carnegie Hall auditorium namesake
21 "An Inconvenient Truth" narrator
22 One-level dwelling
23 Pass unnoticed
24 Twist an arm
25 Rap sheet data
27 Costner character
28 Took a gander
30 Step part
32 Lush vegetation
37 Text message menu option
40 Seine feeder
44 Van Gogh painted here
45 Burt Ward role
46 TV studio sign
47 III, to Icarus
48 Cracker consumer
49 Reserved
50 Peter of "Casablanca"
51 First words in "Ozymandius"
52 They may be closed
53 Coke variety
55 Jazz pianist Hines, to fans
57 Steam bath attire
62 TV commercial
64 Asian environmental disaster
69 Set down
70 Wall intersection
72 Distribute differently
74 Ed of "Modern Family"
75 "Beat it!"
76 Crunch maker
77 "Tell me ___ haven't heard!"
78 Put to the grindstone
79 Prize
80 Wear down
81 Kind of manual

DOWN

1 Provoke
2 Basso Siepi
3 Syracuse team
4 Shipping inquiry
5 RPM dial
6 Furrier John Jacob
7 Heart, in le Havre
8 Hot Lips Houlihan, for one
9 Soaring seafood lovers
10 Court star
11 Beach scavenger
12 Chief engineer's responsibilty
13 On the fritz
14 Belgrade residents
15 Low cards
20 It's thrown by trash talkers
26 Rapunzel's golden stair
29 Hillary's high point
31 Pacino flick
33 Track vehicle
34 Eagerly anticipate
35 Part of UHF
36 Brings up
38 Mississippi bank deposit
39 "Orinoco Flow" singer
40 Secure with lines
41 Bates' wife on "Downton Abbey"
42 Brazil has the world's largest
43 Where "Mom" can be found
54 San Marino surrounder
56 "The Cotton Club" setting
58 Nuts
59 Role for Julia
60 Emergency transportation
61 Spirited mounts
62 Teatime treat
63 Servings of corn
65 Secret language
66 "Madam Secretary"
67 Less risky
68 Ewing matriarch
71 "Vogue" competitor
73 Surfing mecca

249 MAN OF STEAL by Richard Silvestri
The quip below is attributed to Liverpool comedian Ken Dodd.

ACROSS

1 Sale caveat
5 Cy Young winner Saberhagen
9 Draft pick
12 Hologram creator
17 Mining bonanza
18 River through Leeds
19 Artist's specialty?
20 Moderate
21 "Simon Says" player
22 Ectomorphic
23 Luggage marker
24 Bad kids
25 **Start of a quip**
29 Fateful March date
30 Thing in a thole
31 Spur
32 Aerie baby
35 Outfielder's asset
36 Lodged soldiers
40 Out of this world
41 Avis nest eggs
42 Ristorante wine
43 MPG raters
44 Peri's "Frasier" role
45 Akeelah Anderson's forte
47 Flathead ___
49 Space Needle city
52 Put into service
53 Tong-wielders of yore
54 **Middle of quip**
58 Stood up against
61 Feel bad about
62 Louisville Slugger stickum
66 Single-handedly
67 Gave solace to
70 "Boola Boola" singer
71 Winter worry
72 Hebrides island
73 Word of honor
74 Cranium contents
76 Very
79 Get one's goat
80 Made a big stink
81 Like the Karakum
82 Jelly holder
83 Have the earmarks of
84 **End of quip**
92 Frontier dwelling
93 "March Madness" trophy
94 Out of port
95 Spinner on the roof
96 Leave the depths
97 Break bread
98 "Hud" Oscar winner
99 Mary Kay rival
100 Strips of wood
101 Hog haven
102 Feint on the ice
103 Advance

DOWN

1 Jai follower
2 Last year's frosh
3 Fresh thought
4 Obsequious
5 It fronts a backboard
6 Small brooks
7 War of 1812 battle site
8 Time-related
9 Part player
10 Good earth
11 Attractive
12 Of the lips
13 Rub away
14 Car from Trollhattan
15 Rebuke from Julius
16 Take five
26 First place?
27 Gretna Green beret
28 Court plea, for short
32 Head set?
33 Sunburn soother
34 Great Pyramid site
35 Pennsylvania, in D.C.
36 IQ researcher
37 Two years in the House
38 Olympic blade
39 Four Seasons hit
41 Andre Agassi autobiography
42 Workbench item
45 Iditarod entry
46 Downhill racers
47 Check the barcode
48 Formally hand over
50 Romulus or Remus
51 Of whom I sing?
53 Kin of op. cit.
55 O. Henry trademark
56 Sandwich choice
57 Gush out
58 Bonkers
59 French fashion magazine
60 "The Sign of ___": Doyle
63 Sitar wood
64 Get caught in ___
65 Orange skin
67 Brewskis
68 How not to pitch in softball
69 Deli delicacy
72 Sacred bird of Egypt
74 Bone to pick
75 Elimination
77 Devil-may-care
78 Cara and Castle
79 Napa Valley vessel
80 Entertain in style
82 Harbor wall
83 Snake in the grass
84 Myth ending
85 "Gone With the Wind" setting
86 Somewhat
87 Vegan's no-no
88 Crystal-ball words
89 Go on a tirade
90 Privy to
91 Take care of

250 DIVINE INTERVENTION   by Pam Klawitter
7 Down is a 2019 Presidents Cup captain.

ACROSS

1 Benny's dog in "Rent"
6 They end up in hot water
13 Bros
18 More unique
19 Brisk tempo
20 Watering hole
21 "Billy Madison" setting
23 Stupefy
24 How some work is done
25 Arizona plants
27 One on the left, briefly
29 "Whew! They finally left!"
34 Sound engineer Bose
38 Letter flourish
40 Feasible, as a plan
41 ___ dressing
43 Like a March hare
44 They showed up
47 Big chunk of NASA's budget
50 Mirthful states
51 Jewish ascetic of yore
52 Giggle
54 "Trust in Me" singer James
55 "Enough already!"
60 South Texas river
64 Speak out against
65 Telescope support
70 Prompt again
72 Words from one who has it made
76 "Gentlemen Prefer Blondes" author
78 Jones of Wall Street
79 Chris in "American Pie"
80 ___-know basis
81 Jazz pianist Marsalis
83 Planes in the no-fly zone?
84 Poker, for one
88 Grafton's "___ for Noose"
90 Ike's autobiography
91 Body snatchers
96 Blu in "Rio"
100 Winged protector
104 "___ Oe" ("Blue Hawaii" song)
105 "Moonlighting" hero
106 United competitor
107 Shrewd
108 "NCIS: Los Angeles" star
109 Dost speak

DOWN

1 Brand of corn starch
2 Richard of "Home Improvement"
3 Personal pension funds
4 Fill-in worker
5 Ready to fight
6 La Brea find
7 2012 Open Championship winner
8 Ready-to-wear fashion name
9 Acting for
10 Disco name ender
11 Pun reaction
12 Work a puzzle
13 Gliding effortlessly
14 Noah's second son
15 Carli Lloyd's World Cup team
16 Broadway's "Les ___"
17 Albany–NYC dir.
22 Unbeatable pair
26 Locale for a wasp nest
28 Viral GIF
29 Hospital helper
30 Punchbowl emptier
31 Red as ___ (humiliated)
32 Wintry forecast
33 Role in "The Gondoliers"
34 South African fox
35 Garmin products
36 Baleful word
37 Tortoise/hare contest
39 Batman foe al Ghul
42 Mezzo Yun ___
44 District
45 Faculty mem.
46 Friend's pronoun
48 2013 Senate Majority Leader
49 Plaintiff's reps.
53 OT book
56 Presidential power
57 Popular smart speaker
58 Showy June flower
59 Journey
60 Dennis of "NYPD Blue"
61 Zellweger in "Miss Potter"
62 Wintry forecast
63 One-up
66 Pandora's escapees
67 Slapstick staples
68 "Think nothing ___!"
69 Man caves
71 Gradually destroys
73 Warming the bench
74 It shines over Sonora
75 Doppelganger
77 Big oaf
81 "Bam!" shouter
82 Make one's mark
85 Rapinoe of soccer
86 Casa Mila architect
87 Carne ___ (roasted meat)
89 Herring relatives
92 Prime window seat
93 Far from fetching
94 "Why don't we?"
95 Lattice piece
96 Fleetwood ___
97 ___ king
98 Take in
99 Philip of "Kung Fu"
101 Brit. military award
102 Electric atom
103 Film director Lee

251 A HANDY PUZZLE by Patti M. Walker
Raphus cucullatus is the scientific name of 33 Across.

ACROSS

1 It springs eternal
5 Pack down
9 Projects for beavers
13 Lush surroundings?
17 Keats pieces
18 March Madness gp.
19 Once-great inland sea
20 "How sad!"
21 Fonzie's flame on "Happy Days"
24 Flat payment
25 Bollywood locale
26 Seagull relatives
27 Demolishes
29 "It's on me!"
32 Gardener's target
33 Ill-fated bird
36 1963 Johnny Cash hit
39 Sault-Marie link
42 Loses one's way
43 Sword with a fuller
44 ___ in "Oscar"
45 Manuscript sheet
47 Reply from a stubborn Scot
48 Bit of wit
49 Compare
51 Ivy League school
52 Pool table top
54 Remain hidden
55 Genetic strands
56 Postmenopausal gain
61 Get a bellyful
63 Hauled off
64 Sweater letter
67 Say it and mean it
68 Qatar natives
69 Spa sounds
72 Kind of hall or room
73 Part of LCD
75 That, in Tijuana
76 Topflight
77 Mall map word
78 Novelist Clancy
79 Speaker's prompts
82 Treaty topic
83 Disney goldfish
84 "Only the Lonely" singer
86 GPS treasure hunt discoveries
89 Bit part
91 Two-time loser to Ike
95 City in the Rust Belt
96 Digital sport
100 Scads
101 Tombstone marshal
102 Gunn of "Breaking Bad"
103 Webzine
104 Port sediment
105 Sugar bowl team?
106 Team Bench played for
107 "___ Sadie": Beatles

DOWN

1 Pueblo people
2 Valhalla VIP
3 Await action
4 Arctic natives
5 Cause of a big bang
6 Pressure lead-in
7 "Thaïs" composer
8 FedEx delivery
9 Duchamp's movement
10 Father of Antiope
11 Scratch or dent
12 Not so fast
13 Made like Godiva
14 Guinness on screen
15 Seeding
16 Fast fliers, once
22 Cry in the stands
23 Taurus, e.g.
28 Unseen hazard
30 Kilmer subject
31 Clothing mishaps
32 Get a clue
33 Man caves
34 Tough test
35 Superstar roster
37 Frustrated
38 Puts on an act
39 Jack Sprat, vis-à-vis his wife
40 Ike Turner's ex
41 Extensive periods
46 "Queen of All Media"
48 Buddy's hillbilly role
49 Met boxes
50 Radio's PBS counterpart
53 Cake sections
54 Bonnet holder
57 Reagan baggage tag letters
58 Texas border town
59 Clean the slate
60 "Men in Black" extras
61 Shaker contents
62 Chevy subcompact
65 Report card's span
66 They can't be beat
69 On the wing
70 "You ___": Lady Gaga
71 Collectible toy truck
74 Do a flooring job
76 Flying competition?
77 Takes care of
80 Tetley competitor
81 You may part with it
83 Mating game
85 Muffin morsel
86 2006 Stephen King novel
87 Island group off New Guinea
88 Name as a source
89 Brusque
90 Rock blasters?
92 Gin rickey garnish
93 "Lizzie Borden took ___ . . ."
94 Pop of rock
97 Chewbacca's friend
98 Final curtain
99 Airline from Stockholm

252

BLACK-TIE AFFAIR by Bruce Venzke
The author of the quip below is a legendary billiards player and hustler.

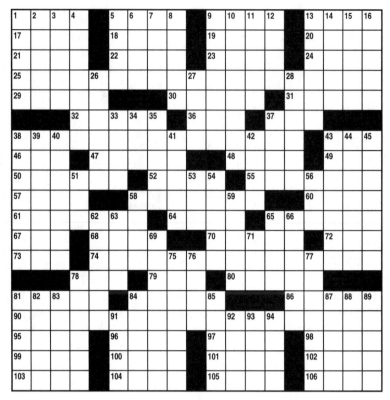

ACROSS

1 Mideast carrier since 1948
5 Furnace fuel
9 Dorsey in "Django Unchained"
13 Kon-Tiki Museum locale
17 Interested look
18 Half an old radio team
19 Opposite of "yup"
20 Mental aptitude
21 Ashtray sight
22 40-day observance
23 Sundance Kid's girl
24 "Eso ___" (Paul Anka hit)
25 **Quip: Part 1**
29 Gem feature
30 Put on the skillet again
31 Letter-shaped girders
32 Reunion in Dallas, e.g.
36 The Black Keys, e.g.
37 Vague amount
38 **Quip: Part 2**
43 Start-up government loan org.
46 Debussy subject
47 Fibula and femur neighbor
48 Deuce follower
49 Tidbit for War of Will
50 Downtown rd.
52 "First Take" network
55 Load software
57 Soup pasta
58 **Quip: Part 3**
60 "Lost ___ Mancha" (2002 documentary)
61 1970 John Wayne western
64 Maine river
65 Michael of "Bonanza"
67 Miller in "Kiss Me Kate"
68 Room for Ricardo
70 Room at the top?
72 Hooch hound
73 Alternative to JFK
74 **Quip: Part 4**
78 Daneyko of hockey
79 Tiny fraction of a joule
80 Official language of India
81 First blond Bond
84 Like a cheering crowd
86 Inventor Singer
90 **End and source of quip**
95 Major Hoople's expletive
96 Assess
97 Georgetown athlete
98 Chain with links?
99 Sleek, in car talk
100 Scrapping
101 "GoldenEye" villain Trevelyan
102 Chanteuse Horne
103 Speaker of baseball
104 Inventory syst.
105 Cartoon clown
106 Groucho's last wife

DOWN

1 Treble clef letters
2 Carmichael of "Downton Abbey"
3 Montezuma, notably
4 "Chow time, everybody!"
5 Colombian cartel city
6 Red sky, for some
7 King on Skull Island
8 Spanish 101 verb
9 A member of our group
10 Smartphone company
11 In a proper way
12 Receive, as benefits
13 Dick Vitale's catchphrase
14 Michael Kay's catchphrase
15 Microsurgery tool
16 Secret targets
26 Does a cocky walk
27 Prefix meaning "foot"
28 White sale goods
33 Pearl Jam's "Last ___"
34 Kan. neighbor
35 French farewell
37 Sharing a family tree
38 Wicked
39 Getting close to
40 Petrified Forest state
41 Malt-drying kilns
42 Hippie's "Got it!"
43 Blankety-blank type
44 Phileas Fogg's transport
45 Six Flags Over Georgia site
51 ___-pros (discontinue legally)
53 Community school org.
54 Battery type
56 Tenth anniversary gift
58 ___ sci
59 Gunslinger's tally
62 Ontario port
63 Rheinland road
65 Bank security
66 GMC SUV
69 Pre-dinner drink
71 Prefix with pod or cycle
75 Characterized by
76 First governor of the 49th state
77 Poorly manage a cabinet position?
78 Youngsters, informally
81 Skirt the rules
82 Pianist Williams
83 Early name in arcades
84 Italian violin
85 Sobering process, for short
87 Showed satisfaction
88 Do a makeup job?
89 Senate-hearing station
91 Tennis great Steffi
92 Recital piece
93 Courtroom cry
94 Sandwich that crunches

253 GOOD INTEL by Bruce Venzke
A classic comedian shares a great observation with us.

ACROSS

1 Mormon State flower
5 Toolbar heading
9 Brute
12 Joe's "Midnight Cowboy" pal
17 Thieves' take
18 It's sold in bars
19 Clinton cabineteer Aspin
20 Honey Boo Boo
21 Lake that I-90 runs along
22 Union Pacific property
24 Arch supports?
25 **Quote: Part 1**
27 Briefly
29 Far from fragrant
30 "And every third word ___ . . .": Shak.
32 Serengeti herd
33 Attack dog command
37 Houdini feat
39 **Quote: Part 2**
46 Spitfire fliers: Abbr.
47 Amanda in "Syriana"
48 Emulates the weasel
49 "Lean ___" (1989 film)
50 Juliet's sigh
53 Saint, in Lisbon
55 Like straight shooters
57 Hess and Breckinridge
58 **Quote: Part 3**
61 Kukla's puppet pal
62 Painter who influenced Picasso
64 Screener's org.
65 Upshot
66 It might be square
67 Initiate the betting
70 Canis lupis
72 "Gidget" actress Sandra
73 **Quote: Part 4**
78 City on the Rio Grande
79 Metrical feet
80 Chew on like a dog
84 Construction item
86 2009 Peace Nobelist
90 One in no hurry to retire
92 **Source of quote**
96 Sigmoid curves
97 Hangar site
99 Misery causes
100 Coffee-break hour
101 Lion's prey
102 Like pawn-shop items
103 Roman known as "The Elder"
104 Buoy one's spirits
105 Alvin York's rnk.
106 Front-page stuff
107 Tae ___ do

DOWN

1 Bundle of 83 Down
2 Bogart's "High Sierra" role
3 Kind of trip
4 John Grisham's alma mater
5 Phone, slangily
6 Jack in "The Comancheros"
7 "Star Wars" twin
8 "Too Fat ___": Yankovic
9 Waikiki's ___ Wai Canal
10 Tapered cigar
11 Canadian gas choice
12 Grappler in the sticks
13 Lanai greeting
14 Accipter nail
15 Bergen's Mortimer
16 Firing ovens
23 "TMZ" subject
26 Do some paper work
28 Diner offering
31 "The jig ___!"
34 Banjo adjunct
35 Barely manage, with "out"
36 U.S. Attorney General (1985–88)
38 Kicked up a notch
39 Olympian Retton
40 Lame excuse
41 Wawrinka of tennis
42 Muddies the water
43 Encompass
44 Spammer, e.g.
45 Strike out (without swinging)
46 "Creepshow" director
51 Atlanta transit option
52 Jargon suffix
54 Literary adverb
56 Garden shed item
58 Put finishing touches on
59 Martha's Vineyard, e.g.
60 Model Campbell
63 Unexcited about
65 Leeway
68 Doing online business
69 Government crash gp.
71 "Be prepared" org.
74 "I haven't a clue!"
75 Be a pack rat
76 Cousin of a bassoon
77 Nine iron of old
80 Grand
81 Father of Austin Powers
82 Gemini program rocket
83 Major grain
85 Brother of Linus and Lucy
87 Attorney modifier
88 Very, musically
89 "Happy Days" actor Williams
91 Comics
93 Medicinal unit
94 Eurasian duck
95 Classic sneakers
98 Daily grind

REWRITES by Pam Klawitter

The son of 46 Across is an acclaimed actor.

ACROSS

1 Tabloid target
6 Unfortunately . . . (with 42-A)
11 Mexican revolutionary (1879–1919)
17 "Centipede" maker
18 E.L. James' Anastasia
20 Noah's debarkation site
21 Frank McCourt book about his Italian cooking?
23 Empty-nester
24 Madeira Mrs.
25 State police unit
27 Low in pitch
28 Org. that regulates explosives
31 Not good
34 Base neutralizer
36 Fielding book about a London milkmaid?
41 Tucson campus
42 See 6 Across
43 Keyboard key
44 "Pygmalion" playwright
46 Former Yale president and MLB commissioner
49 7-Eleven rival
51 Name on a combine
52 Naval spy org.
53 Cruet contents
55 Toss into the mix
56 Dan Brown book about fiendish hidden agendas?
60 PIN point
62 Cup won by the St. Louis Blues in 2019
63 Nor. neighbor
64 "I Will Not Be Broken" singer
66 Creek at Augusta National
67 Devoted student of Splinter
72 Australian outback
73 "Shrek" release date
74 Roadside bomb
75 Apple relative
76 John Green book on a failing autocracy?
82 Jerky source
83 Siren, for one
84 Great Leap Forward initiator
85 Bookbinding job
88 Babette's brother
90 Maiden name signifier
92 Do a bomb squad job
94 Stephen King book about a citrus tree?
100 Painter del Sarto
101 Conger, for one
102 Decathlete Thompson
103 They raise dough
104 "To ___ human . . ."
105 "Washington Post" ezine

DOWN

1 "East of Eden" brother
2 Zeta follower
3 Part of UNLV
4 Memorable times
5 Weigh-station vehicle
6 Garmin reading
7 One-time connectors
8 Obliterate
9 "Argo" setting
10 Fútbol cheer
11 Use a microwave
12 Largest peninsula
13 Heaven on earth
14 Olympian hawk
15 Brown shades
16 LL.B. holder
19 That, en español
22 Newborn's need
26 Biblical verse
28 Put ___ in someone's ear
29 Enterprise counselor
30 World Cup org.
32 ___ Helens, WA
33 Town near Santa Barbara
35 Atlanta-based health org.
37 Matt in "The Great Wall"
38 Clinched (with "up")
39 Birds of the pampas
40 Play place
45 Tie the knot
47 High anxiety
48 Pinball term
49 Cellar stock
50 "Show Boat" cap'n
51 Totally drench
53 Valley coursed by a stream
54 Sandbox comeback
56 Electricity eschewers
57 Skating rink wear
58 Slow-moving sort
59 Apogean tides
60 Certain trader
61 Tight as a drum
65 Super Bowl XX winners
67 "The Great" saint
68 Part of NEA
69 Paper purchase
70 Olympic swimmer Torres
71 Roughly speaking
73 West in "Klondike Annie"
74 Whole number
77 Travis in "Zootopia"
78 Bit of a laugh
79 Where delivery trucks often park
80 Russo in "Nightcrawler"
81 Political shifts
85 Outback "howdy!"
86 It may be dotted
87 T-bone stamp
89 Some NFL linemen
91 It flies over the Holy Land
93 Dogpatch matriarchs
95 L.L.Bean rival
96 Golf's "Big Easy"
97 Pier group, in brief
98 New York swinger?
99 Kind of contact

255 SMALL CHANGE by Pam Klawitter
11 Down is also the national flower of England.

ACROSS

1 Takes an oath
6 Like Cirque du Soleil performers
12 Soda-shop treats
17 Support a church
18 "Absolutely not!"
19 It's assumed
20 Looking back on a Georgia vacation?
22 "Biloxi Blues" playwright
23 Tiny Hanna-Barbera superhero
24 Feature of the fastidious
26 Dead or alive: Abbr.
29 Whisk, e.g.
31 Find a purpose for
32 Father of Greek tragedy
34 Fountain nymph
37 Motor City union
40 Smooth sailing
41 Authorization to go nuclear?
46 Borders on
48 "Low Bridge" mule
49 They often seal the deal
50 Unfortunate occurrence
52 Little bit
55 Position of pressure
56 Norma Desmond et al.
59 ___ as a ghost
63 Command to a boxer
64 Sudden upswings
69 Where to go downhill fast
71 GI grub
73 Break down in English class
74 Sides in the rabbit dispute?
78 LPGA golfer Hataoka
79 When temps rise on the Riviera
80 High-strung one
81 Hospital dessert
83 Winter coat
85 Put on a pedestal
88 Some RIP graduates
89 "Land of the Hummingbird"
94 Made an effort
96 Workers on the Hill
97 Zootopia mayor sworn to tell the truth?
102 Nats, but not gnats
103 Subject to a late fee
104 "Christine" hero
105 Bluish-gray
106 Unwelcome burdens
107 Big name in chicken

DOWN

1 PIN point
2 Point on a GPS?
3 Non-Rx
4 Horse halter
5 Put in the pen
6 Salesman of the stage
7 Desktop array
8 "Dirty" drink
9 Leading referral org.
10 Utopian spot
11 USA's national flower
12 A galleon has three
13 Flared dress style
14 Cuba libre ingredient
15 Georgia O'Keeffe's retreat
16 Scammer targets
18 Red Skull, to Captain America
21 Recurrent theme
25 Book reviewers
26 First-stringers
27 Abu ___
28 First baseman Aguilar
30 Thai language
33 Hazlitt of "Murder, She Wrote"
35 A keeper keeps it
36 Hawaiian howdy-do
37 Combined, in Calais
38 Off the coast
39 270° on the compass
42 2008 James Patterson thriller
43 Wild plums
44 Red condiment: Var.
45 EMT destinations
47 "Taste the Bass" singer
51 Unlike Franklin's inventions
53 "Animal Kingdom" network
54 "Same here"
57 Like coriander
58 One new in the field
59 ". . . even ___ speak"
60 32-card bidding game
61 It might be barbed
62 Nobelist ___ Gobind Khorana
65 Frog genus
66 Shred cheese
67 "Ah, Wilderness!" role
68 Lennon and Penn
70 Gullible guy
72 Fencer's cry
75 Capital of Cuba
76 Aptitudes
77 Sicilian 7
82 Eye maliciously
83 Lethargic
84 Draco Malfoy's mother
86 Give off, as confidence
87 Planet with the longest day
89 Beach souvenirs
90 Small channel
91 Invention impetus
92 Chihuahua chow
93 Zoologist Fossey
95 "Finding Nemo" heroine
98 Letters for Buckeyes
99 Short reply
100 Andalusian uncle
101 Mrs. octopus

256 GOOD AND PLENTY   by Robert H. Wolfe
A sweet theme from a veteran vet and puzzler.

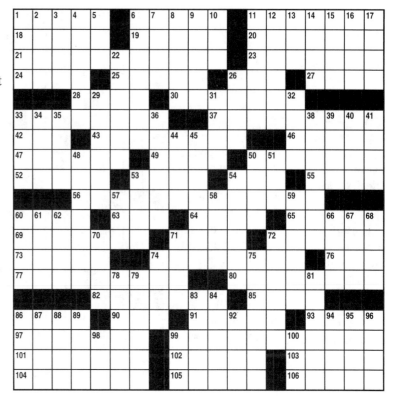

ACROSS

1 Labradoodle color
6 Unwelcome summer cloud
11 After the fact
18 Major artery
19 Aqua ___ (gold dissolver)
20 Dessert request
21 Closing credits of a 1982 Hoffman film?
23 Part of some splits
24 Greek gathering place
25 Rattle bunkmates
26 Paraffin
27 Badger's den
28 Señora's home
30 Hall in "Martial Law"
33 Flops from Harvey?
37 College taverns in Worcester, Mass.?
42 It's between Telescopium and Norma
43 "All in the Family" character
46 Rajah's consort
47 Steamy
49 Rocker Jett
50 Scandalize
52 Finale
53 Coal quantities
54 New Jersey cape
55 Dummy
56 Busses from Barbara?
60 Go out with
63 Over there
64 Went up the creek
65 "___ Triste": Sibelius
69 Wolfs down
71 One lax with the facts
72 Clinton who ran against Madison
73 Bypass
74 Sentry
76 Common Market letters
77 Bergen's cheesy one-liners?
80 The Bambino, when a bambino?
82 Cannoli filling
85 A pulpwood
86 Ditto
90 ___ Moines
91 Pass a resolution
93 Radiate
97 South Carolina college
99 Vänern salmon, for one?
101 Platinum Nirvana album
102 Concave omphalos
103 Maria in "Thank You for Smoking"
104 Obtuse to the max
105 French cathedral city
106 Felix, compared to Oscar?

DOWN

1 Lloyd Webber musical
2 Dig for truffles
3 Buck, smack, or switch closure
4 Onset
5 Suffix for Michael
6 One of the Windwards
7 Sleuth Wolfe
8 Athenian assembly place
9 Mosaic master
10 Slugger Fasano
11 Milkshake fruit
12 Panacea
13 Office PC linkup
14 Iowa State U. city
15 Hit the sauce
16 Do some "Self" improvement?
17 Can ding
22 Published
26 Braze
29 Think highly of
31 Radar reading
32 Gumbo veggie
33 Win for Magnus Carlsen
34 Meteorite element
35 A shortening
36 New Brunswick city
38 Wood cutter on wheels
39 Champion skater Miki
40 Fly fishing need
41 Muralist friend of Dali
44 Use a strop
45 Romp
48 Tried again in court
50 Ticket-order encl.
51 Scheldt feeder
53 General ___ chicken
54 Leaf's central vein
57 Crown Royal, for one
58 16-time Gold Glove pitcher Jim
59 Singer "Champagne" King
60 Frisbee
61 "Eso Beso" singer
62 Lanky
66 In ___ of (rather than)
67 Proofer's "save"
68 Make art with acid
70 Almost 10 trillion kms.
71 Fast time?
72 Account entries
74 Some low-budget hotels, for short
75 They're changed by UK nannies
78 Apple drinks
79 Venezuelan cat
81 Lowered a sail
83 Brindled
84 Gland: Comb. form
86 Beyond sarcastic
87 "A Chorus ___"
88 Zap with a phaser
89 Afleet Alex's dinner
92 Norse god of art
94 Bland
95 Homophone of "I'll"
96 God with a belt of strength
98 "Peppermint Twist" singer Joey
99 Part of RSVP
100 "Succession" network

257 NUMBERS GAME by Robert H. Wolfe

23 Across is the subject of a 2011 documentary "The Eye Has to Travel."

ACROSS

1 Indian silk center
6 Russian Empire successor
10 Air France retirees
14 Temple mascot
17 Thick chunks
18 Microwave
19 "1984" superstate
21 2008 Liam Neeson film
22 Hipbones
23 "Vogue" editor Diana
24 **Start of a quip**
27 Caribbean fruit
28 Vampire repellent
29 Chilled
32 Jack or jenny
33 Freshly
37 Quarry product
38 It's sung at Scotiabank Arena
40 **Quip continues**
46 Really cracks up
47 Sister of Helios
48 Did a farrier's job
49 Buffet-table fuel
53 Added bonus
57 So yesterday
58 **Quip continues**
62 ___ Lanka
63 Boundless
64 Iditarod Trail racer
65 Parrilla of "Once Upon a Time"
67 "Yabba dabba ___!"
69 New Jersey skater
73 **Quip continues**
81 Generally
82 "O Sole ___"
83 Popular insecticide
84 Off-road wheels
87 Public display
88 Revival cries
90 Whigham of "Boardwalk Empire"
92 **End of quip**
98 First Norman king of England
101 Didgeridoo, for one
102 The sea, to Neptune
103 Pamela in "Superhero Movie"
104 Other
105 Stand up
106 After taxes
107 Robert Baratheon, for one
108 Cask sediment
109 Pie nut

DOWN

1 Cold duck's kin
2 Metal waste
3 Rice liquor
4 Help a yegg
5 "Morning Joe" network
6 Even
7 It separates Malaysia and the Philippines
8 Loses traction
9 Peruse
10 Time for a wake-up call
11 Fish packed in mustard
12 Tokyo Big Board: Abbr.
13 Canonized mlle.
14 2018 U.S. Open winner
15 "Sideways" side topics
16 Stows in holds
20 Resembling
25 Switch back
26 Place
30 Volt, e.g.
31 Author LeShan
33 Cribside chorus
34 Zip
35 Greek vowel
36 "For what reason?"
38 "Wish Tree" artist
39 Capp and Capone
41 Queue after Q
42 City light
43 Kaput
44 2018 "Star Wars" film
45 Quaint
50 Honshu mount
51 NFL linemen
52 Kook
53 Sticker on an apple
54 "___ for Lawless": Grafton
55 "Disgusting!"
56 Dilapidated
58 "If ___ the Zoo": Dr. Seuss
59 Cannes film
60 "___ the opinion that . . ."
61 Poll finding
62 ___-mo
66 "I get it!"
67 Edited out
68 Keats specialty
70 London's Old ___
71 "Odyssey" sea nymph
72 "Spy Story" author Deighton
74 Carrier letters
75 29-member NATO org.
76 "Ain't gonna happen!"
77 Operating
78 Dunk
79 Ralph of "The Reader"
80 Morrison or Tennille
84 Egyptian dam
85 "To ___ own self . . .": Shak.
86 South African grassland
88 "Fixing ___": Beatles
89 Binding cord
91 Flagon filler
93 "___-Shaped Room": Lynne Reid Banks
94 Parrot beak feature
95 Secular
96 Ingrid's classic 1942 role
97 Mutant superheroes
99 Get one's goat
100 "Softly ___ Leave You"

258 WHY THEY WERE FIRED by Pam Klawitter
63 Down is believed to be the world's oldest desert.

ACROSS

1 Wikipedia tidbit
5 One with a dash-cam
8 Bit of slime
12 It rises and falls with the times
15 Czech river
16 BP subsidiary
17 Part of OJ
18 It might come before long
19 The songwriter was fired because he . . .
22 Speck on the River Sprint
23 Cakewalk
24 Dr. Hartman of "Family Guy"
25 Some draft picks
26 The banker . . .
31 Type of alliance
32 Black Sea port
33 Border range
37 Peeples of pop
38 Like fireplace logs
41 Sets off
43 Zany
46 Mother of Hermes
48 Christian monogram
49 What a keeper keeps
50 Where Baldwin is Trump
51 Disorderly sort
54 Removes from power
56 The cab driver . . .
59 Frank topper, for short
61 Romano relative
62 Like some music
66 Clarke in "Frankenstein"
67 Put in stitches
69 Where Anna met the king
70 Sleuth played by Bogart
71 Aircraft's approach
75 Not kosher
77 Ronan Farrow's mom
78 Mixed and social
79 Split the difference
81 Scottish cuisine vis-à-vis Japanese
84 The baker . . .
88 VFW members
91 Iliac opening
92 Campfire stories
93 Stonemason's tool
94 The ceiling fan installer . . .
99 Wash partner
100 Wet bars?
101 Expressed surprise
102 Soccer star Lavelle
103 Salon opening
104 Eyelid problem
105 Op opener
106 Goal in musical chairs

DOWN

1 Chosen ___
2 Honolulu's ___ Wai Canal
3 "God Friended Me" network
4 Take care of
5 Holey footwear
6 Vocal group
7 "The Black Cat" author
8 Everglades python
9 Bookish lot
10 Fall shade in Falmouth
11 Queen in "The Lion King"
12 Work a cure
13 Warmest Great Lake
14 Polar Bear's team
16 Tees off
17 Stunned
20 Like Tacko Fall
21 Make one's way
25 Gillette razor
26 Snowbird
27 Group in labor
28 Genuine they're not
29 Early Greeks.
30 Summer wear
34 In the fight
35 Part of a focus group?
36 Phishing catch
39 Mrs. George Clooney
40 Famed film fish
42 "Well, alrighty then"
44 Cuzco native
45 Bumbling inspector of film
47 NBA legend Gilmore
52 Spicy brew
53 Viking of comics
55 Word on the corner
57 El Paso school
58 Dog owner's command
59 Popular smoothie ingredient
60 He's the Lone Ranger
63 West African desert
64 Bid word?
65 Get smart
66 "2001" and "2010" studio
68 Remove by cleaning
72 Tango moves
73 New England vacation spot, familiarly
74 Styles and Connick
76 "Curses! ___ again!"
80 Sweater letters
82 Back to square one
83 They're stunning
85 Kind of router bit
86 Rarin' to go
87 Some steak requests
88 Still-life subject
89 Email kisses
90 Holidays in Hue
94 Sancho's mount
95 Frantic letters
96 Anonymous surname
97 2019 World Cup champion
98 Favorite

ZOOLOGY TERMS?   by Pam Klawitter
The leg lamp at 1 Down can be seen in "A Christmas Story."

ACROSS

1 "Frozen" Olaf's carrot
5 Caniff who drew Steve Canyon
9 Headed to court
13 Sticky stuff
17 Tighten text
18 Part of DOE: Abbr.
19 "Tonight Show" theme composer
20 Sea almost dammed to death
21 Loose reins for free-roaming mustangs?
24 A disease, when doubled
25 Texts in real-time
26 Rikki-Tikki-Tavi, for one
27 Bring delight to
28 Sal in "Giant"
29 Half of GIGO
32 Pile in the laundry room
35 Rod not spared in obedience school?
39 PC handle
40 Fighters of rock
42 Took a wrong turn
43 Put on Netflix
44 Cause of a zoo quarantine?
48 Sum it up
49 Rodriguez of "Miss Bala"
50 Part of UCLA
51 Bobolink, for one
53 Lemon scrapings
54 Crossword clue heading
55 Roman 61
56 Predecessors to smartphones, briefly
58 Popular brand of mandarins
61 Boat color in an Edward Lear poem
63 TGIF segment
66 All over again
67 ___-50 (German sniper rifle)
69 Simian saloons?
71 RR stop
72 Salami selection
74 "Insecure" star Issa
75 Flock response
76 School for bigmouths?
79 "Foiled again!"
81 Shanghai or Singapore
82 Get a chuckle out of
84 Havana homes
87 They're always popping up
89 Company that sells Souls
92 Runner's challenge
93 Plus-size beachwear?
96 Biblical animal namer
97 "The Rescuers" alligator
98 Chicago mayor Lightfoot
99 Smell of smoke
100 Vet charges?
101 Gain counterpart
102 Jimmy Buffett's "Son of ___ of a Sailor"
103 Meadows for munching

DOWN

1 Soft drink formerly with a leg lamp logo
2 "Hamilton" star Leslie
3 Dubbed ones
4 They're out of this world
5 Breakfast fruits
6 Overly foolish
7 "Hands off, that's mine!"
8 Group in "Jeopardy!"

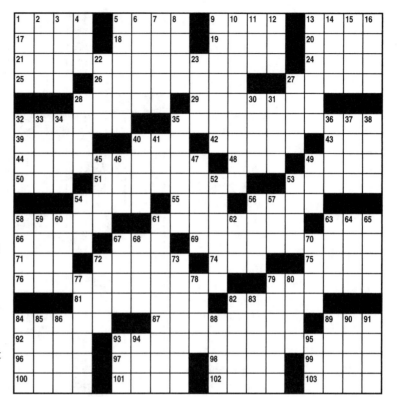

9 McMuffin type
10 Robert Morris junior, e.g.
11 Barely make, with "out"
12 Courtroom figs.
13 Saved until later
14 Quarter
15 Audition prize
16 Nobelist Ducommun
22 Bahrain bigwig
23 On wheels, in dinerese
27 "Drat!"
28 Dawn, poetically
30 Founder of Richmond, Virginia
31 Took off on
32 Sagan or Sandburg
33 Seis y dos
34 Luau adornments
35 Extra-base hit
36 Rostrum
37 Laundry room detritus
38 Ballpark stats
40 "The Last Jedi" hero
41 .gov alternative
45 Barcelona bears
46 It's given at a wedding
47 Early riser's wake-up hr.
49 Some radios
52 Hardships
53 Off-the-wall
54 Part of DJIA
56 Toy from China
57 Dicey start
58 It's slung in the diner
59 Thesis opener
60 Type of year
61 Concert drummers?
62 It's in your makeup
63 Alpo shelfmate
64 Ancestry.com chart
65 Some ID thefts
67 Prefix meaning "10"
68 Piece of cake
70 Without a stitch
72 Doesn't hang around
73 Timed perfectly
77 Job follower
78 Sevier Lake locale
79 "SNL" alumna Jane
80 Khrushchev's concern
82 Periodic table figs.
83 Paris underground
84 Bloke
85 Campaign staffer
86 Mattress support
88 Ricardo's room
89 Replaceable body part
90 Name in home furnishings
91 Seeks info
93 Blow up in the lab: Abbr.
94 Sign of summer
95 Browser bookmark

ACROSS

1 Get in line
5 Seafarer's saint
9 Hist. or Eng.
13 Does a checkout job
17 Skin-cream additive
18 Pond duck
19 Venture capital?
20 Dr. Dre contemporary
21 **Start of a quote from 98 Across**
23 Cupid
24 Boarding site
25 Most sudsy
26 Fed. loan agency
27 Adept in
29 Let the dog run free
31 Feels the heat
33 Retired Concordes
36 Sneaking a look
38 Sound heard in a herd
39 **More of quote**
45 Hip-hop duo ___ Sremmurd
46 "The Waste Land" poet
47 "Toni Erdmann" director Maren
48 Some radio hobbyists
49 "Unbelievable" techno-funk band
50 Waiter at Le Cinq
52 Org. twitted in "Sicko"
54 **More of quote**
62 Q&A center
63 Cut into
64 Run from the law
65 Retired
68 Evildoer in Tolkien tales
71 "Heard ___ Love Song": Marshall Tucker Band
72 "Madagascar 3" jaguar
73 **End of quote**
78 Lady of Esp.
79 Like California's Highway One
80 Holiday lodgings
81 "Monty Python" cast member
83 Double curves, e.g.
88 Win-win
89 Telethon hosts
91 Rakes over the coals
95 Minnesota pro
96 Canis lupis
98 **Oft-quoted catcher**
99 6.2-mile run
100 Fanning in "3 Generations"
101 "Beauty ___ the eye . . ."
102 Some dishes
103 AAA and AARP
104 Monopoly card
105 "Over here . . ."
106 Sabin's vaccine rival

DOWN

1 Child of the streets
2 Vienna Boys' Choir voice
3 Waterloo setting
4 Olympic group in red, white, and blue
5 Mertz or Merman
6 Pad papers
7 Atlanta transit system
8 Like Father William
9 What Jerry drove in "Seinfeld"
10 Like Zorro in "The Legend of Zorro"
11 Band that sang "TCB"
12 Skin-care brand
13 Racist
14 College life
15 Cry to lovebirds in the park?
16 Western wear
22 Tax type
26 "Kung Fu Panda 2" villain
28 "Three Sisters" sister
30 Accurate
32 Informant's wear
33 Toss haphazardly
34 "Likewise!"
35 Plagiarism
37 NASA walk, for short
40 One with a strict diet
41 Large African antelope
42 Like a screened-in porch
43 Model wife of 20 Across
44 Spring event
51 Loretta Lynn, ___ Webb
52 Scene of conflict
53 Veteran's pride
55 "If I Only ___ Brain"
56 Quavering sounds
57 Table d'___
58 Doctor documents
59 NBA Hall-of-Famer Baylor
60 Wilson of "The Office"
61 Online reads
65 Approve
66 Loan shark's customer
67 Sending through cyberspace
68 Milky birthstone
69 Take after
70 Shelter offering
74 "JAG" spin-off
75 Sang from Mont Blanc
76 Drew Brees aerial
77 Mugs
82 Hits on the noggin
84 Industrialist Perot
85 Auspices
86 House coat?
87 Diplomat's HQ
90 For both sexes, in a way
92 Seal killer
93 Pechora's mountains
94 Piece of work
97 Cheer for Real Sociedad
98 High-pitched bark

LARGE AND IN CHARGE by Bruce Venzke and Victor Fleming
60 Across is also the title of a 1965 hit by the Shangri-Las.

ACROSS

1 Pathfinding puzzle
5 Baltusrol sport
9 Pierre's papa
13 Shock jock who retired in 2018
17 Jack in "The Way West"
18 Lasting leader?
19 Way not to run
20 ___ Hashanah
21 Hardly a low-hanging fruit?
23 Top of the salsa hit charts?
25 Halvah seed
26 Laura in "Deep Impact"
28 Año opener
29 Working title of "Tangled"
31 Prefix for sphere
33 Alpha swine?
36 Supervisor of the latrine detail?
41 Like aspirin
42 Crack a tough nut
45 Coin with 118 ridges
46 ___-Pei dog
47 Etc. kin
49 It's done through one's teeth
51 Macnee's "The Avengers" costar
53 Subj. for a green card holder
54 Logging camp contest
56 Piccadilly statue
58 Earthy and then some
60 Cubmaster?
64 Noteworthy trip
66 Disney lioness
67 Principled
70 The way
71 The Untouchables, e.g.
73 Tears
76 Cream type
77 Harem spots
79 Movie beekeeper
81 "Golden Boy" dramatist
83 El Dorado's lure
84 Lama?
87 Oceanographer?
89 Angry (with "off")
90 Inherit
93 Liquid glyceride
96 Walking papers
97 Worked on a hole
101 Cheddar wheel, e.g.?
104 Dean of academic disciplines?
106 Writer Dinesen
107 Summer salad
108 Moisés of baseball
109 Cat in "Peter and the Wolf"
110 Light shades
111 Dated letter opener
112 Dele killer
113 UFC octagon

DOWN

1 Big Apple team
2 Medicinal plant
3 Debugs, in a way
4 Puts in jail
5 Hereditary source
6 In vitro items
7 Soviet Union founder
8 Trapp Family butler
9 Like woodie station wagons
10 Some Australian fowl
11 "Deep Space Nine" Ferengi
12 Scratch out a living
13 Some patches
14 Pout
15 "Ready Now, Anytime, Anywhere" org.
16 "Amscray!"
22 Eastern nannies
24 San ___ (Riviera resort)
27 Book before Esth.
30 Unfair?
31 Regard highly
32 Old Navy parent
33 Great Trek trekker
34 David Rabe's "Good for ___"
35 Scamp
37 Make public
38 Where coats are left
39 Dish that's "slung"
40 Paris hub
43 Competitor
44 Former Astros' Field
48 Vintner's "mud"
50 Succeed
52 Saipan neighbor
55 Malt kiln
57 Pope who confronted Attila the Hun
59 Lt. saluters
61 Coy
62 It's often shadowed
63 Straight, e.g.
64 Expectant exclamation
65 Diana's tragic love
68 Atmosphere
69 "Dianetics" author Hubbard
72 Miss-named
74 Smallest size at Starbucks
75 All-Star athlete
78 Comedy routines, in slang
80 Has sworn off
82 Gourdlike instrument
85 Phnom ___
86 Kicker's asset
88 Skiing category
91 "Last of the Red Hot ___"
92 Elevate
93 Final notice?
94 Bart's sib
95 Alaska's first governor
96 Ruler over Tolstoy
98 Cold-smoked salmon
99 Webzine
100 "Been there, ___ that!"
102 Sulfur symbol
103 Photographer Linnetz
105 Montana, for one

DATING APPROPRIATELY   by Theresa Yves
A good one for couples to solve on date night.

ACROSS

1 Marvin of Motown
5 Absolutely positive
9 Della's angel
13 Zipcar parent
17 Bath's county
18 High point
19 Spanish for "stop"
20 Gave for a bit
21 Where to take an antedate?
23 Where to take a liquidate?
25 Cussed out
26 Elevator cage
28 Alms receptacle
29 Location identifier
30 Models A and T
32 Rel. school
33 Frilly
36 Pennsylvania coal city
38 "Man and Superman" playwright
42 Miscalculate
43 Where to take a mandate?
47 It gets picked out
48 I problem
49 Cavalry weapon
50 Whacks sharply
51 Emmy winner Arthur
52 WBO wins
53 Drescher of "The Nanny"
54 Skewed view
55 Part of ABA
56 Where to take a target date?
62 Orthodox counterpart
64 Asian capital
65 Burdens of proof
68 Mayberry jailbird
69 Leaning to the side
71 Drive-___ teller
72 Kind of law
75 Cookbook meas.
76 Et cetera
79 Samuel Adams namesake
80 Swimsuit model Kang
81 Kind of teeth
82 "Look at Me, I'm Sandra ___"
83 Ends of letters
84 Gate-crash, e.g.
86 Blood poisoning, e.g.
89 Andy of "Taxi"
91 "You cheated!"
94 Where to take a double date?
96 Where to take a stardate?
98 Vaccine developer
99 Creative spark
100 Nautical adverb
101 "Not ___ many words"
102 X, on a greeting card
103 Until all hours
104 Skip a turn
105 "The Hippopotamus" poet

DOWN

1 Spaces between teeth
2 State positively
3 Opera soprano Watanabe
4 Juice
5 Long tales
6 ___ the crack of dawn
7 "Losing My Religion" band
8 One with will power
9 Watering holes
10 "Evil Woman" band
11 Obey the red light
12 Arias, e.g.
13 Sounds the klaxon
14 Do or die, e.g.
15 Absorbed by
16 Where Thetis dipped Achilles
22 Weight training unit
24 Author of "Al Aaraaf"
27 Oodles
30 Caleb Carr novel (with "The")
31 Rabbit in "The Secret Life of Pets"
33 Vichyssoise veggie
34 Xena's horse
35 Brisk repartee
36 Swing time
37 Benefit
39 Kit seller
40 Type of code
41 Tear's companion
43 In regards to
44 Bounce off
45 Novelist Calvino
46 City on the Ruhr
57 Party thrower
58 Spruce up
59 Survived
60 Assumed appearances
61 Wheel-worn ways
62 Tomato variety
63 Series ender
66 Asteroid in "Ender's Game"
67 Phoenix team
69 "Betsy's Wedding" director
70 They croak when they get older
73 "See ya!"
74 "Par avion" letters
77 Snuggles down
78 Apotheosize
84 Large pieces
85 Narrow waterway
87 Mary Ridenbaugh title character
88 Greeted and seated
89 River bridged in a 1957 film
90 Has a bug
92 Macbeth's burial isle
93 "Love Hangover" singer
94 Condescending cluck
95 Oil can letters
96 Fortune
97 "My bad!"

263 EQUALITY ON THE HILL   by Theresa Yves

55 Across was the first female to hold federal office in the U.S.

ACROSS

1 Sask. cops
5 Cook's smidgen
9 Rifle range report
13 Dwindles
17 Historic spans
18 "Not again!"
19 Skin moisturizer
20 Two-part
21 Blown weapon
22 Hiss at
23 Knock off
24 Words after stick
25 Many an exec
26 **Start of a quote from 55 Across**
29 Stroll along
31 Spiritual path
32 Grant's successor
33 **More of quote**
36 Test pilot Chuck
40 Comic actress Charlotte
42 Washday chore
43 Fajita filler
44 Lunch-counter order
45 Alf and others
46 Go sparking
48 Felt (for)
49 Certain constellation star
50 Half a rum cocktail
52 Redeem
54 Pentagon people, informally
55 American suffragist (1880–1973)
58 Camelot curse
60 "Laramie" and others
61 Make do with
62 Not all there
63 More subtle
64 Make tiny knots
66 Hiker's word
69 Grill event
70 Yeltsin or Johnson
71 He danced in "Silk Stockings"
74 Nonprofessional sports org.
75 Puts up
77 **More of quote**
78 Moves toward
80 Alley of Moo
82 Collect bit by bit
83 **End of quote**
89 Collection
90 Like a top
91 Horse course
92 Naomi's daughter-in-law
93 Hearty swallow
94 Nathan of "Penny Dreadful"
95 Rip apart
96 Hose hue
97 Not fancy at all
98 River near Dunkirk
99 Uno + dos
100 Noticed
101 Watched intently

DOWN

1 Rhode Island's state tree
2 Chesapeake Bay cake ingredient
3 African storks
4 L.A. clock setting
5 School for martial arts
6 Interruption starter
7 Blessed event, perhaps
8 "Stormy Weather" singer
9 Attorney General under Bush/Trump
10 Helm location
11 Chips and dip, e.g.
12 Take the lead
13 Uplift spiritually
14 Succotash veggie
15 Tub additives
16 Gin fruit
26 Merge metals
27 Whichever
28 Carefree episode
30 Home-care worker
34 "Desert Fox" Rommel
35 Idaho neighbor: Abbr.
37 "Drawing Hands" lithographer
38 Wanting water
39 Oscar winner Davis
41 They precede thetas
47 Like some rays
48 Daisy or sunflower
49 Dessert cheese
50 "What would you have ___?"
51 Small batteries
53 Bear witness (to)
54 They have ISBNs
55 Cellist du Pré
56 Black, in Bordeaux
57 Off your rocker
58 Isle near Corsica
59 Lose it
63 Briefly
65 "What a relief!"
66 Secluded spot
67 Townie relative
68 In the tempestuous years
70 Muppet in saddle shoes
72 Liner's leaders
73 Best effort
76 Last word in "If"
77 Spiff (up)
79 In search of
81 Brutish bosses
83 Devout
84 Even once
85 Gregory House's trademark
86 GM car of yore
87 Infinitive with a circumflex
88 Steer clear of
93 "___ sells seashells . . ."

ACROSS

1 Use Comet, e.g.
6 Pabst beer brand
12 Quesadilla go-with
17 "Common Sense" pamphleteer
18 Part of a crown canopy
19 "I'll have another!"
20 Count Rugen's dueler turns blue?
22 Photo finish
23 Golf date?
24 "___ Rides Again" (1939)
26 Sullivan had a "really big" one
27 Catch in a web
29 Toon squeals
31 Diagon Alley purchases
34 Seagoing Raveloe weaver?
40 Year in Uruguay
41 Leafstalk angle
43 Statue in St. Peter's
44 Nobelist UN agency
45 Cocktail shaker accessory
48 Palindromic "before"
49 Part of Dig'em Frog's cereal name
51 Entrance for Garfield
52 Skirt features
54 Hockey feints
55 Chesapeake Ripper's reading desk?
58 Haste product
60 Theaters
61 Ancient Greeks
64 Swear it's so
66 Cariou in "About Schmidt"
67 Viking
68 MTA stop
69 Oddballs
71 Say "It ain't so!"
72 Scroll and Key member
73 Scheming foe of Lord Voldemort?
76 Begin contemporary
78 Listen to
79 Thruway exit
82 He has a goldfish named Dorothy
85 Shrimp dish
88 Words of emphasis
92 Yes-man
94 Tom Robinson's lawyer getting cold feet?
96 Come to terms
97 Take back
98 Milk prefix
99 L'chaim, e.g.
100 Starts off
101 Elvis expression

DOWN

1 Archerfish do it
2 It plays a supporting role
3 Uber offering
4 One way to stand
5 Starts off
6 Sure sign of success
7 Cucumber climber
8 Iterate
9 Whitehorse's tribe
10 Songwriter Axton
11 "I've heard enough!"
12 Uncle seen in stripes
13 1992 Wimbledon winner
14 Stucco support
15 Web destination
16 Back to square one
18 Treasury agents
21 Mantra words
25 "Lapis Lazuli" poet
28 Saudi province
30 "The Honeymooners" family
31 Paper ___
32 Hand holder's payment
33 Guiding light?
35 Times for showers
36 Pedro's lucky number?
37 Also known as
38 Sommer of screendom
39 Bay of Whales sea
41 In due time
42 Desertlike
46 You can make it or break it
47 "Say Anything . . ." star
48 Barkin in "The New Normal"
50 1972 John Denver album
52 Has the most marbles
53 Boxy-looking Toyota
56 "You'll Never Get Rich" schemer
57 Fashion designer Burch
58 Tide's place
59 Kofi ___ Annan
62 Kiara's leonine mother
63 Steamy state
65 Hits the bottle
67 Spongy ball
70 Jay Leno collects these
71 Shortfall
74 Colossus of ___
75 They're up for discussion
76 Enjoys the roses
77 Way in Rome
80 Providence campus
81 Boxer's comment
82 Coup d'___
83 57 Down's double-T, e.g.
84 Wilson of "Matilda"
86 Exactly (with "to")
87 ___ Helens, WA
89 Ending for confer
90 Part of a Parisian play
91 God of Norse mythology
93 "But then again . . ."
95 Skip-Bo cousin

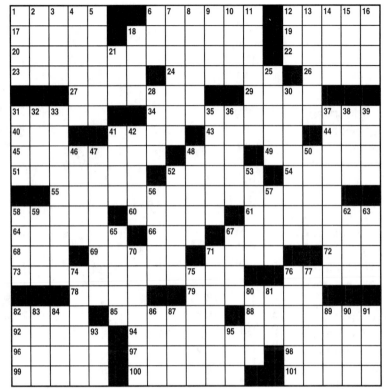

265 STRANGE CROSSINGS by Emma Avery
68 Across is the only state motto written in Spanish.

ACROSS

1 Windex window targets
6 Hockey stat
12 Enya's music
18 Anonym
19 "Seriously?"
20 "Trainwreck" director
21 What you get when you cross a centipede with a parrot?
23 "Moulin Rouge!" heroine
24 Eyelid woe
25 Weigh station sight
26 "OED" listings
28 "Smells like ___ Spirit": Nirvana
29 Car club founded in 1902
31 Texas Hold'em stake
33 Scandal sheets
35 . . . an Andean condor with a grasshopper?
39 Rain cats and dogs
40 "Mamma Mia!" number
43 Places in the heart
44 Takes on a mortgage
46 Low-budget prefix
48 Early computer language
50 Gallery head
52 Craggy crest
53 Rogue and Sentra
57 Troubled state
58 . . . an electric eel with a sponge?
61 Candle ingredient
64 Georgia neighbor
65 "Tapestry" label
68 Motto of Montana
70 "We Were Soldiers" setting
73 "Disgusting!"
74 A sacrament
78 Abandon détente
79 Balaam's mount
80 A place for numbers?
82 . . . an owl with a goat?
84 "Ugly Betty" magazine
85 Potpourri: Abbr.
86 Facebook chuckle
87 Madlyn in "A Majority of One"
90 Mother of the Titans
92 Furniture giant
94 Toronto gas brand
98 Treat aquarium water
100 . . . a razorbill with a triggerfish?
103 More stale
104 Hit the big time
105 Hogwarts School professor
106 Gets smart with
107 Comes down hard?
108 What some can't take

DOWN

1 Lumber mill equipment
2 Surveyor's reference
3 Needing a shampoo
4 Lose a bundle
5 FICA benefit
6 Johnson of "Laugh-In"
7 Nautical charts
8 Dry-eye solutions
9 Unkind word for kind
10 Hit the dirt at home
11 Chinook salmon
12 Bahamas cruise stop
13 Org. concerned with wetlands
14 "Sanford and Son" setting
15 "___ is like kissing your sister"
16 Flown the coop
17 Bremner in "Wonder Woman"
22 Twin of Jacob
27 Orchard nightmare
30 Slightly cracked
32 Har-___ clay court
34 "The Quiet American" author
35 Sword grip
36 "___ Sing America": Hughes
37 Airedale alert
38 In a frenzy
39 PC suffix
40 Fish served meunière
41 A place for numbers?
42 Do a mailroom job
45 Reverend's residence
47 "The Hollow Man" novelist
49 End of a wise simile
51 Persian Gulf emirate
54 "Starlight Express" footwear
55 It's a wrap
56 SALT weapon
58 Stallone and Stone
59 Gets a move on
60 Fuselage fastener
61 Commencement wear
62 SFO postings
63 Heads for London?
65 ___ even keel
66 "Phooey!"
67 Small-screen award
69 Sleep disrupter
71 Architect Goldfinger
72 "Madam Secretary" star
75 Hawaiian tuna
76 "Absolutely not!"
77 Place for an ace
81 Lawn tools
83 Where Goliath met his match
84 Arby's slogan: "We have the ___"
85 Taj of blues
87 "Phooey!"
88 Queen of Olympus
89 "The Haj" author
91 Doctrines
93 Garage quotes: Abbr.
95 "American Dad!" dad
96 Sapphire's mo.
97 Heavy metal?
99 Giveaway shirt
101 Fruit drink
102 Kyrgyzstan city

266 THEMELESS by Peter Wentz
25 Across can be heard in the films "Speed" and "The Doors."

ACROSS

1 Initial repulsion, quantified
10 Region of industrial decline
18 Funeral procession, often
19 One skilled in Muay Thai
20 Idiot boxes
21 Piece of cake
22 Simple approvals
23 Result of a levee break
24 Liturgical vestment
25 "O Fortuna" composer
26 Baton passing event
28 Mountain ash
30 Roosevelt's coin
32 La Salle of "One Hour Photo"
33 Pink's "God Is ___"
34 Medieval musician
37 Madrilenian Mrs.
40 A real go-getter
42 Avena sativa
44 Surpassed
46 "Let the Music Play" singer
49 Garciaparra of baseball
50 In the real world
53 They go to blazes
54 Stay clear of
55 Hot time at the Louvre
56 Kellogg's subsidiary
58 Ticket checker
60 Pesky little thing
61 Big N' Tasty predecessor
63 Dance in 3/4 time
65 They can see well
67 "Rumor has it . . ."
68 "Excelsior!"
70 Sixfold
72 They troupe for the troops
73 Poet Plath
77 "Equal Rites" heroine
78 "Let's talk things over sometime"
80 Michelle of the LPGA
82 Hawk at the ballpark
83 One of Pac-Man's pursuers
85 Dot in an archipelago
87 About the time of
88 SPECTRE villain
90 TV watchdog
92 Eleniak of "Baywatch"
94 Part of DMV
95 Canadian liqueur
98 Coadjutant
100 1977 hit for Bob Welch
101 History is written in it
102 Thickened a lawn
103 Miata or Corvette, e.g.

DOWN

1 Cabin fever complaint
2 CIA domain
3 "80's Ladies" singer
4 Watch chain
5 ___-craftsy
6 Bra size
7 Knight's tunic
8 Tune from Beethoven's Ninth
9 Put another patch on
10 Omani coin
11 Golden State school
12 Sun spot?
13 Hole in the TV Guide sched.
14 Close and personal
15 Expedited USPS service
16 Viking explorer Erikson
17 Not kosher
19 Reeves in "Replicas"
27 Jordan seaport
29 Even if, to a poet
30 Broadband connection
31 Travel plan
33 Way to a man's heart?
35 Heads of France
36 Gig for Olympic skaters
38 "Do you ___? Over"
39 Space sellers
41 Semi with a bulldog ornament
43 For a bit
45 PBS film series
47 Place for a conspiracy theorist
48 Troopers and Ascenders
50 Unfortunate ending
51 Works on a zinc plate
52 UPS Store rival
57 First president of the Czech Republic
59 Prepare the board
62 Back muscle
64 Quiz answers
66 LVII x VIII
69 Carpenter's tool
71 Pony up
74 Lush with growth
75 Joss stick
76 AC converter
79 Fleetwood and Jagger
81 "Yes, indeed"
84 Alicia Keys hit
86 Was a bounder?
87 Beehive division
88 Salon specialist
89 Contraption man Goldberg
90 Bonnie in "Bonnie and Clyde"
91 Shared a link with
93 Little foxes
96 Carrie in "Creepshow"
97 "Hang 'Em High" hero
99 Bigelow product

267 THEMELESS by Harvey Estes

The first 18 Across was invented by Ezra J. Warner in 1858.

ACROSS

1 Wolverine player Jackman
5 Door part
9 Neighbor of Minn.
13 Hawk in the bleachers
17 State of Browns and Reds
18 Kitchen gadget
20 Noted lab assistant
21 Prison escape route, at times
24 Louise's partner in crime
25 Christopher of "Superman"
26 Pasture plot
27 Bark like a chihuahua
28 Makeup maker Lauder
29 Scale notes
30 Sinbad's milieu
33 Part of ROM
35 Bk. of the Pentateuch
37 Guys
40 Fools
42 Boy in "The Lorax"
45 Lopsided win
47 Grimm villain
48 Involving dispute
51 Razor product
52 Innocent and Clement
54 Kept adding
55 Banned refrigerant
56 Magnum ___
58 2 in a 100
59 Kentucky frontier nickname
60 Ground Zero hero
63 FedEx Cup org.
64 Citrus mixer
67 "CHiPs" star
68 Mrs. lobster
69 Summer refresher
70 Monk's title
71 Determined the age of an artifact
74 Roofing sealant
75 Supercilious one
77 Cut short
78 Round sound
79 Three R's supporter
81 Lease period, often
82 Capo di tutti capi
83 Colorful trout
86 White House souvenir
87 Big bash
91 Behaves willfully
92 Outsmarted
94 Marked down
95 Pick out
96 "Are you calling me ___?"
97 Bad guy
98 Ear part
99 Patriot Ross
100 Readied for release

DOWN

1 Party thrower
2 "I don't think so"
3 Taunting remark
4 With intensity
5 Manage to find the funds for
6 Rhine feeder
7 Took in
8 Puts an edge on
9 Taffeta ___
10 Destitute
11 Autumn mo.
12 Stuffed to the limit
13 Passport stamps
14 "My stars!"
15 NASA cancellation
16 Pulled
19 Amanda of "Syriana"
22 Eastern bigwigs
23 Former defense pact
30 Hit the brakes
31 And so
32 Flight information display
34 For one
36 "Voice of Israel" author
37 Front-desk worker
38 Mark replacer
39 Oliver's partner
41 Voyeur
42 Lineman's workplace
43 Fire escape
44 Henry Purcell opera
46 Sounded an alarm
49 Garfield's vet
50 Battle of the Alamo general
53 Poison ivy's family
55 Well-known
57 1978 Co-Nobelist for Peace
59 Chopped up
60 G-men and T-men
61 Currently airing
62 Like cigarette boats
64 Engine measures
65 Big bargain
66 James ___ Jones
72 Dog holder
73 One-time link
76 Royal Society of Literature medal
78 Dwarf tree
80 Shabby treatment
82 Ate a formal meal
83 Hanger holder
84 Dull discomfort
85 Astra car
88 Kind of office
89 Rival of Jimmy and Bjorn
90 Made a right turn
92 "Terrif!"
93 Sec

268

BOOK BEGINNINGS* by John M. Samson
In 1986, Cleveland set a Guinness record by releasing 1.5 million 67 Across.

ACROSS

1 Came out with
5 Scapegrace
10 Milk whey
15 Kate of "House of Cards"
19 Cronyn in "Lifeboat"
20 Virginia Tech athlete
21 Maui neighbor
22 "Sunday Night Baseball" analyst
23 "-zoic" periods
24 "Nadja" actress Löwensohn
25 Astronauts Bean and Shepard
26 Salon makeup?
27 1998 Stephen King novel*
29 Bud buy*
31 Wind harp
32 "I feel like ___ man!"
34 Cider purchase
35 Sternward
36 Causes of misery
38 Rolls-___ Wraith
40 Pronouncements
43 Glossy alternative
44 Haggard
45 Auxiliary verb
48 ___ au Haut, Maine
49 Bike helmet option
50 "The Full ___" (1997)
51 Acoustic guitar genre
52 Mustangs of Dallas
53 "Just you wait!"*
55 Atlanta's subway system
56 Islands off Scotland
58 Vietnam War chopper
59 Whistling rodent
60 Abhorred
61 The Doctor, for one
63 Be in stitches
64 Relief pitcher
66 Hazy memory
67 Birthday party buys
70 Awkward brutes
71 Park residences*
74 Aloha garland
75 Snow Queen of Arendelle
76 Phony
77 Date before ides
78 "Beowulf" beverage
79 UC Santa Barbara mascot
80 Something to stake
81 Scent, in Sussex
82 Quebec peninsula
83 Waze suggestion
84 Exploits
85 Line from "Wayne's World"
86 Published
89 Tree trunk
90 At a greater distance
94 Keep watch*
97 Selfie stick go-with*
100 Minnesota state bird
101 Assume
102 Quran chapter
103 McGregor in "Big Fish"
104 Non-PC suffix
105 "Awake and Sing!" dramatist
106 Andean grazer
107 Nits to pick
108 Visionary
109 Opus for nine
110 Former UAR member
111 Apportion

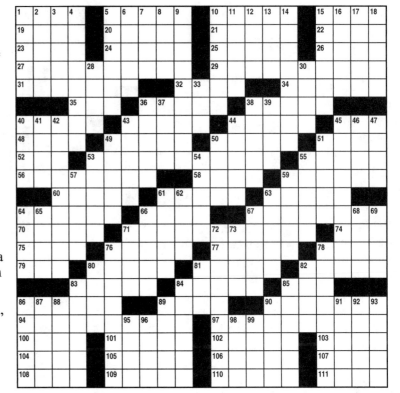

DOWN

1 Lola Delaney's dog
2 Angelic glows
3 Stage after pupa
4 Abandoned
5 Month before Adar
6 Emoticon "eyes"
7 Comparable (to)
8 "You Will Be ___": Faith Hill
9 Revolting group in "The Wizard of Id"
10 Melrose and Peyton
11 NBC legal drama (1986–94)
12 Jenna Bush's "___ Story"
13 Rational
14 Dislike of women
15 Monument stone
16 About to faint
17 Bull-riding venue
18 Embellish
28 World Cup org.
30 Almanac entry
33 No, in Cape Town
36 Sunbathes
37 Director Egoyan
38 Composer Newman
39 "Three up, three down" results
40 Spoon's eloper
41 "Woe ___!"
42 19th hole at Quail Hollow*
43 Like a stick in the mud
44 "Bridge Complete" author
45 Space-time "shortcuts"*
46 Anne Murray's voice
47 Card game for three
49 "Star Wars" villain
50 Pouty look
51 1996 Coen brothers film
53 Tiny biters
54 Emulate a dervish
55 Batters
57 Jamaican religion
59 "GQ" target audience
61 "Thriller" is one
62 Director Buñuel
63 Debussy opus
64 Geppetto's goldfish
65 Act indolent
66 "Casablanca" star's nickname
67 A little something extra
68 Low high tide
69 Onion rings, e.g.
71 That's not funny
72 Ad infinitum
73 Jolly Roger captain
76 Cudgel
78 "The Silencers" hero
80 Like many dorms
81 Lamp fuel
82 Trail mix
83 Narrow rug
84 Unassuming
85 Handwerker of hot dog fame
86 TNT series "Rizzoli & ___"
87 London weight
88 French river of 300 miles
89 Uncouth bully
90 Bowling unit
91 Ex-Raider Long
92 Put on the books
93 Betty in "Nurse Betty"
95 Offset
96 Seaport of 110 Across
98 West Point mascot
99 "11 Harrowhouse" director Avakian

269 BEGINNING OF BOOKS* by John M. Samson
Alternate clue for 29 Across: Black Friday leftover

ACROSS

1 Kind of bargain
5 "Heartbreak ___": Presley
10 Uncle Sam has one
15 Avoid socially
19 Egg roll location
20 Fall off
21 Lassitude
22 Poi source
23 "The ___ Gave My Heart To": Aaliyah
24 Counter, in a debate
25 Lady Gaga's sign
26 Solar flare measures
27 Exercise outfit*
29 Abrupt way to quit*
31 "Suits me to ___!"
32 Green science: Abbr.
34 Novelist Beattie
35 Roof beam
38 Baseball's "Bad Henry"
40 Fruity dessert
45 They might be giants
46 Wiggle open, as with a bar
47 Edie of "Nurse Jackie"
48 Modern art?
49 Large crucifix
50 Pause sign
51 Nick in "Cape Fear"
52 Portico in Greek architecture
53 Relative of the osprey
54 Toronto's waterfront*
56 Olympics legend Jesse
57 Had importance
59 Tabriz locale
60 Product of Bordeaux
61 Oahu transport
62 Tomorrow's catcher
64 Infant's woe
65 They're picked up in alleys
67 Nolin of "Sheena"
68 Prairie State
71 Constellation Ara
72 What Hillary won in 2016*
75 ___ trial basis
76 "Jabberwocky" creature
77 Leary in "Wag the Dog"
78 Redbone and Uris
79 Airline to Ben Gurion
80 Burgundy burro
81 Silenced a hinge
82 Chateaux river
83 It's part of the act
84 Ecdysiast
86 Fredo Corleone's brother
87 Household duties
88 Fam. tree member
89 Ed Sheeran song
90 Sparkle
91 Reunion time on campus*
96 Depot*
102 King or Arkin
103 USWNT star Rapinoe
104 Rhône tributary
105 Horse voiced by Rocky Lane
106 Unique fruit of Jamaica
107 Truly love
108 Claire in "Temple Grandin"
109 Seaplane stop
110 Member of the flock
111 Schlepped
112 Eat at the shore
113 James in "Misery"

DOWN

1 Furrow the field
2 Singer Del Rey
3 Still-life subject
4 Lively
5 Novelist Lee
6 Like many offensive linemen
7 Dana perfume
8 Sewing case
9 Colbert's predecessor
10 Source of light
11 Register
12 Indigo plant
13 Bemoaned
14 Map calculation
15 Buffet warmer
16 "___ the herald angels . . ."
17 Strong temptation
18 Like Cyrano?
28 Beehive State natives
30 Make in reverse
33 Playfully demure
35 "Sky Music" composer
36 Coin of Tel Aviv
37 Beginning of books (and a hint to clue* answers)
38 Used a scope
39 These slugs have shells
40 Alaskan governor in 2008
41 Female voice
42 Office oasis*
43 Surveillance vehicle
44 Fermenting fungus
46 Told gags
47 Initial venture
50 Feels concern
51 Honshu hub
52 Rustic gallant
54 Hansen's disease sufferer
55 Subject to ebbs and flows
56 Golfer Schniederjans
58 Hebrew body of law
60 Team Unitas played for
62 Not so hot?
63 Stigma
64 Replica
65 Roosevelt and Teasdale
66 Celebrate Arbor Day
67 One beyond hope
68 "99.44% pure" soap
69 Ditsy
70 Yard events
72 Hawaiian volcano goddess
73 Right next to
74 Dobbin's restraint
77 Worker at the United Nations
79 Part of LEI
81 Fuel price setter, for short
82 Allie's fiancé in "The Notebook"
83 1979 exiled Irani
85 Peaceful
86 Like some confessions
87 Idle colleague
89 Double-headed drum
90 Made a blooper
91 Big winnings, in slang
92 Russian Orthodox saint
93 Algeria neighbor
94 "Love ___": Beatles
95 "___ a Woman": Ray Charles
97 Emperor prior to 1917
98 Greek goddess of wine
99 Stellar bear
100 Ward of "House"
101 Tree of life locale

270 CHAIRMAN OF THE BOARD* by Elizabeth C. Gorski
... and this chairman loved solving crosswords in ink.

ACROSS

1 Earth tone
7 Mark Harmon series
11 Slower, musically
14 "Around the Horn" network
18 Mollycoddle
19 Near eternity
20 Punk rock subgenre
21 Tom Cruise's daughter
22 "We have no rules here"*
28 Make very happy
25 1976 Heart hit
27 Former Bills QB
29 Nut in a rich cookie
30 Leggy shore bird
33 Some Oscar Night gowns
35 Phone button
36 Gotham address*
40 "Diners, Drive-Ins and Dives" host
41 Hayes at Iwo Jima
42 OED entries
43 Lesedi La ___ diamond
44 Sparkling, like morning grass
46 Covered with soft hair
48 Eldest son of Isaac
50 Jared in "Blade Runner 2049"
51 Blankenship on "Mad Men"
52 Personal rights org.
53 Bowling venue
55 Classical lyric poem
57 Sooner than later
58 "Them's the breaks ..."*
60 Cope with change
61 Stop-___ traffic
62 Cardinal point
63 Highway choice?*
65 In a bad way
67 Comic Atkinson
70 Rains hard
72 Start of a bridal rhyme*
77 Barbecue bar
78 Ibsen's Gabler
79 Veep after Chaney
80 ___ about (circa)
81 Hanoi festival
82 Composer Bacharach
83 Conga feature
84 Florentine painter
86 Uses a snake
88 Dart about
90 Criterion: Abbr.
91 Pretoria's loc.
92 ___ kabob
93 Buzz Aldrin's 1969 request?*
97 Prefix for derm
98 At hand
99 Swamp emanation
100 Tusk carving
102 Like vines
104 Syracuse stadium
108 Change schools
109 Chairman of the Board
112 It's not right
113 Prefix for eminent
114 Titicaca locale
115 Personal history
116 Conductor Klemperer
117 Pulled off
118 Citi Field nine
119 Fixate

DOWN

1 Mt. Rushmore's state
2 Skye of "Moonglow"
3 Word origin: Abbr.
4 Spendable salary
5 Osaka drama
6 Tropical blackbird
7 Disprove
8 Ducklike bird
9 America hit
10 Start of a hissy fit?
11 Casual statement
12 Apple Store purchases
13 Forum robe
14 One on the outs?
15 Cooler on a July day*
16 Barking rodent
17 Pinta's partner
23 Sunburned areas
24 "Danny Boy" valley
26 "Mamma Mia" song
29 Swedish knife
31 Wedding day promises
32 Trying times
34 Atomic particle
36 Bite, puppy-style
37 Conductor Kunzel
38 Half a Washington city
39 Fay in "King Kong"
40 Gala
44 When folks retire
45 Paul in "Gigantic"
47 Emulate Joey Chestnut
48 Keebler's Ernie, e.g.
49 Appeared so
50 Snip (off)
54 Kitten caboodles
55 Childcare writer LeShan
56 Antes up
57 "On a different matter ..."
59 Cabo ___ Lucas
60 Nursery sounds
61 Cockpit stat
64 Singer Sumac
66 Hands and feet
67 Run before V
68 Common knowledge
69 Elphaba's practice*
71 August hrs. in Philly
73 Poetic praise
74 Emcee's job
75 "Uh-uh"
76 Pun reaction
78 Grant or Laurie
79 Dentist's concern
82 Chests
83 Bearer of green fruit
85 "Ditto" in a footnote
87 Lambasted
88 "Orinoco ___": Enya
89 Fleur-de-___
90 Doesn't leave
93 Like bell-bottoms
94 Countdown term
95 Sty cry
96 Bordello bosses
98 Dear, to Henri
100 Normandy city
101 Haight-Ashbury law gp.
103 Skin bump
105 Plains Amerind
106 3-D hospital scans
107 Mousketeer wear
109 Lebanese pol. party
110 Texter's "As I see it"
111 Bobolink beak

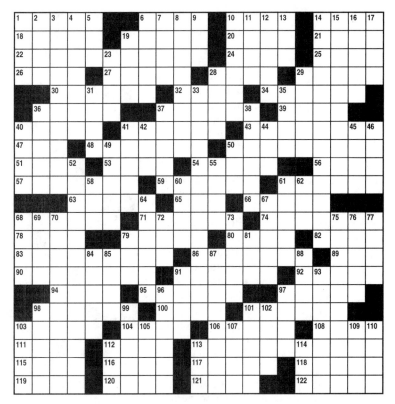

ACROSS

1 Liniment targets
6 Marriage or bar mitzvah
10 Ward of "House"
14 Cognac category
18 Mount Katahdin's state
19 Navel variety
20 Taxi alternative
21 Yours, in France
22 2018 Lady Gaga film*
24 Cornbread
25 Hubbard of Scientology
26 "The Supernatural Man" essayist
27 Mannheim river
28 Give credit where credit's due?
29 American plan inclusions
30 Tracey in "A Dirty Shame"
32 Construction piece
34 Angola's capital
36 "___ man's life is a tedious one": Shak.
37 Spanish shout of joy
39 Terse denial
40 Catty
41 Insert more film
43 Lacking opportunity
47 Behavioral quirk
48 Collision type
50 Intrigue
51 March Madness gp.
53 Platter
54 Egg size
56 "Manhattan Mary III" artist
57 Have no tickets left
59 Coin of the realm
61 Element in an atomic clock
63 Milk prefix
65 Pink Floyd founder Barrett
66 Leaves on the side?
68 Pinpoint
71 Lorraine of "The Sopranos"
74 Dish for Garfield
78 Fertile Crescent denizen
79 Bush Supreme Court appointee
80 Busted
82 "___ be surprised!"
83 Intrudes
86 Unique occurrence
89 Actor Essandoh
90 Sky-blue
91 Rival of Athens
92 Whitman and Frazier
94 Name dropped by TASS in 2014
95 Reformation Wall city
97 Gusty
98 Anthony Trollope biographer
100 Differ
101 Saint Agnes, e.g.
103 Benjamin in "Coco"
104 At the summit of
106 It may hold a lot of weight
108 Silent clown
111 Lacoste
112 "Alright, I get it now"
113 2009 Heather Graham film*
115 Ron Howard film
116 Pantheon city
117 Funerary stands
118 Talking Stick, for one
119 Rx amount
120 Bounces like a buoy
121 Church recess
122 Geranium, e.g.

DOWN

1 Barrister Clooney
2 Juan's home
3 "The Lion King" is one
4 Empowered
5 Short homily
6 Apply by massaging
7 Marvin Gaye's "Let's Get ___"
8 Lever in a trunk
9 Still, to Shakespeare
10 "Excellent!"
11 Deep black
12 Andy Murray's former coach
13 Exist
14 2010 Jessica Alba film*
15 Noted Cremonese luthier
16 Alley Oop's wife
17 Bowling targets
19 Job-safety org.
23 Cookbook author Rombauer
28 ___ up (ailing)
29 Kiri Te Kanawa, e.g.
31 Ogler's look
33 Puzzle honoree and star of clue* films
35 Potentially insulting, for short
36 Way to pack fish
37 Baldwin and Guinness
38 Saws
40 Amtrak stops: Abbr.
41 "Nick of Time" Grammy winner Bonnie
42 Triage ctrs.
44 Vane reading
45 Rebuke to a backstabber
46 Consider
49 Draw forth
50 Calendar abbr.
52 2009 Sandra Bullock film*
55 Outlet letters
58 Feedbag morsel
60 Pre-college exam
61 Mild cigar
62 ___ in "easy"
64 Like an eclair
67 Honolulu stadium
68 Secular
69 "Her ___" ("Miss Saigon" song)
70 Clamdiggers
72 ___ Tin Tin
73 Glass work?
75 Like Megan Rapinoe?
76 Off one's rocker
77 Big fusses
79 Actor Butterfield
81 East, to Heinrich
84 Editorial bias
85 Architect Saarinen
87 Flotilla member
88 Ninny
91 Cinch
93 No longer
96 Brings out
97 South Carolina's state bird
98 Words to live by
99 "Yippee!"
101 Skier Phil
102 Regrettably
103 Raised
105 Pyramid of Cheops, e.g.
107 Mediocre grades
109 Bistro handout
110 Historic times
112 Celestial sphere
113 TV schedule abbr.
114 Joke

ACROSS

1 Act greedily, in a way
5 A boldface type
10 Letter writer to Santa
15 "She's Gotta Have It" girl
19 Klebb of SPECTRE
20 "All in the Family" character
21 Dangerous elephant
22 German auto pioneer
23 "So be it!"
24 1499 marble masterpiece
25 Call off a mission
26 Altar approach
27 Coquilles St.-Jacques ingredient*
29 9-to-9er*
31 Patagonian ___
32 "Beautiful Freak" band
34 "+" thing
35 BBC documentary "The ___ of Man"
38 ___ nest (hoax)
40 Thundered
45 "Robert's ___ of Order"
46 UFC star McGregor
47 Acted human
48 "Get!"
49 "Vaya con ___"
50 McQuewick on "Entourage"
51 Adroitly eschew
52 City in western Belarus
53 Giant with 511 homers
54 Signal caller*
56 Abbatial headdress
57 Run through
59 Bolger's "Wizard of Oz" role
60 Arms, Las Vegas style
61 Kefauver of 1950s politics
62 They're fired but never hired
64 Alternative to contacts
65 A first banana
67 "I'm in the ___ for Love"
68 "Cloud Atlas" star
71 "Elements of Algebra" author
72 Merlin's apprentice*
75 Indignation
76 Minor melee
77 Ketchup company
78 Dummy positions
79 "Ghostbusters" character
80 "Prince Valiant" character
81 Airport summonses
82 Lesser of two ___
83 "Centric" lead-in
84 Do another hitch
86 Talking Stick, for one
87 Babylonian love goddess
88 Alpine flower?
89 1980s pesticide
90 "Cough up" in poker
91 Arts and crafts chain*
96 Preakness pacesetters
102 Word form of "thought"
103 "Downton Abbey" extras
104 Mosey along
105 Trough locale
106 "Pants on fire" guy
107 Choo designs
108 More mannerly
109 Raindrop cake ingredient
110 "Our treat!"
111 "Space Is the Place" jazzman
112 Snoop Dogg's discoverer
113 ___ majesté

DOWN

1 Pâté de foie ___
2 Borghese Villa locale
3 Befuddled
4 Blarney Castle ghosts
5 Break camp
6 "Swan Lake" temptress
7 Phnom Penh cash
8 "Break ___ me gently"
9 Mom's prom hat?
10 Barely advances
11 Bindle carriers
12 Aviation pioneer Sikorsky
13 Hide and sneak
14 Thoroughly cleaned a car
15 "Ain't gonna happen!"
16 Fiery gem
17 Dolly of "Hello, Dolly!"
18 Le Carré spy Leamas
28 "Just Married" sign accompaniments
30 Cargo bay
33 Suffix for chariot
35 A Cyrano quality
36 Hotel room upgrade
37 Solar drying device*
38 "Live and Let Die" star
39 Med school subj.
40 Wrestler Lesnar
41 Phantom of Broadway
42 Stereotypical hero*
43 Pillow stuffing
44 Sweet things
46 Terrence McNally's "Master ___"
47 J.J. on "Good Times"
50 Less ambiguous
51 Adjacent to
52 "I, Claudius" machinator
54 2022 World Cup host
55 Griffis in "Runaway Jury"
56 Chiffonlike
58 "Drop It Low" singer Dean
60 Lorenzo of "Falcon Crest"
62 Does a laundry job
63 "I want it all!" types
64 SoHo studios
65 French film award
66 Beyond the fringe
67 "Bain à la Grenouillère" painter
68 Edison contemporary
69 Icelandic coin
70 Granada gentleman
72 Cocoa cups
73 Where the Lost Boys are found
74 Remained prone
77 Mexican ___ dog
79 Airy
81 "Family Feud" option
82 The Big Band ___
83 Idaho motto start
85 "Gomer Pyle, U.S.M.C." star
86 Actress Milano
87 "Come ___ at once!"
89 Less inept
90 "Damn Yankees" composer
91 Big Island's biggest city
92 Norse god of war
93 Boyfriend
94 Diamond Head locale
95 Laker star, casually
97 Islamic chieftain
98 Multiple choice choices
99 Savant
100 Longoria and Mendes
101 Waterless

273 SPICE OF LIFE by Brenda Cox
A variety of words and clues can be found within this culinary creation.

ACROSS

1 Action break
5 Ersatz chocolate
10 Debate subject
15 File extensions
19 Out of the cove
20 Aquatic mammal
21 Fielding flub
22 "Collect $200 after passing Go," e.g.
23 Veggies that roll
24 Stellar events
25 Going ___ a minute
26 Fan favorite
27 What "D" means to numismatists
29 Wise counsel
31 Spacewalks
32 Middle East gulf
34 "Après ___ le déluge": Louis XV
35 Beseeched
38 Choreographer de Mille
40 Put back
45 Adjective for sandalwood
46 Glissade
47 Cliff dwelling
48 "Promoting decent work for all" agcy.
49 1040 IDs
50 "Canterbury Tales" pilgrim
51 ___ du Louvre
52 Aim at the barcode
53 "As is" location
54 Iron Man's love interest
56 Sit still, at sea
57 Biting canines
59 Ring holders
60 Trial balloon
61 "Mary Tyler Moore Show" spinoff
62 Backbiting
64 Cereal can become this
65 They're played at ballparks
67 "House of Cards" actress Kate
68 Aimed at
71 Like dad jokes
72 John Cleese TV role
75 "Exotic" singer Sumac
76 Maple seeds
77 "___ la vista, baby!"
78 Martini option
79 Botanical sacs
80 "1-2-3" singer Barry
81 "Big" star
82 Brigitte's brother
83 Arctic Ocean drifters
84 Amazes
86 Back-room plotters
87 Minibus
88 Dropout's deg.
89 "Jour de Fête" director
90 Cracow citizen
91 Butter up
96 Best friend of Jem and Scout
102 Great Plains tribe
103 Suffix for fraud
104 A plumber may unclog it
105 "___ on Down the Road"
106 Tom Brady aerial
107 Powerball, for one
108 Down the hatch
109 Accreted
110 "___ a Lady": Tom Jones
111 Flatware item
112 Insolvent
113 Regatta athletes

DOWN

1 "Adam-12" org.
2 Suit beneficiary
3 "Hobson's Choice" director
4 "The Hangover" setting
5 Hotelier Hilton
6 Collider units
7 Father of Norah Jones
8 "Casablanca" escape route city
9 Chance spectator
10 Acts the coquette
11 Financial guru Suze
12 Holier-than-thou type
13 Love of Hercules
14 Boston dessert
15 "Jeopardy!" fodder
16 Lamborghini parent
17 Special interest group
18 Campania river
28 Roulette bet
30 Banana label
33 "A Raisin in the Sun" star Ruby
35 Sew big stitches
36 "A Modest Proposal" is one
37 "Gilligan's Island" castaway
38 "A" in Tel Aviv
39 Hand out
40 "The defense ___!"
41 "No ___ Para Mi": EYA hit
42 "Sounder" star
43 Make jubilant
44 Angel, in some cases
46 Nasal partitions
47 "Here Comes Santa Claus" singer
50 About one-ninth of an orchestra
51 Castle circler
52 "Dog Day Afternoon" event
54 Indiana's state flower
55 "He loves me" piece
56 Long-limbed
58 "Macbeth" attendant
60 Métier
62 Fills roles
63 "Ah! Perfido!" is one
64 Balm
65 Florida citrus city
66 "Inside the Actors Studio" topics
67 Conceals
68 "Dancing With the Stars" move
69 Party boss?
70 "Blondie" dog
72 Parade group
73 Verboten
74 "Iacta ___ est": Caesar
77 Tough kids to babysit
79 Hyde, to Jekyll
81 Vietnam War chopper
82 Spare-tire material
83 Nike rival
85 Grimm witch
86 Box
87 Bench of baseball
89 "Kemo Sabe" utterer
90 Applied (oneself)
91 "Cheese it, the ___!"
92 Rainbow Bridge state
93 Soccer star Lavelle
94 Cockeyed
95 Block a bill
97 "Dies ___" (medieval hymn)
98 Past deadline
99 ___ avis (nonpareil)
100 Bohemian river
101 Puts in stitches

274

88 Across was played by Native Americans as early as 1100 AD.

ACROSS

1 Walker Cup sport
5 Ancient Hebrew measure
10 Links water hazard
14 "Daily Bruin" reader
19 Thought-provoking page
20 Dry red table wine
21 Hyalite
22 Developmental stage
23 **Start of a quip**
27 Goof
28 Dean of "Songland"
29 Like a total solar eclipse
30 Pore over again
31 Encountered
33 "Drop this!" editorially
34 Aleutian island
35 **Part 2 of quip**
42 10k finish line
45 "Red ___ in the Sunset"
46 Out ___ limb
47 Samba city, familiarly
48 Lizard with a dewlap
51 Colonoscopy concern
53 Small sheepdogs
57 Burrito filling ingredient
59 Set-to
61 Spirited meeting?
62 Like an EF5 tornado
63 Santiago locale
65 Slightly colored
66 **Part 3 of quip**
70 Siberian plain
75 Hullabaloo
76 Metrical foot
82 Covers with mail
83 2016 Super Bowl MVP Miller
84 Asia Minor, e.g.
86 Stick-and-ball game
88 Top grade
91 Mite
92 Utilize
93 Rose fruit
95 Unleash upon
97 Fireside stack
98 **Part 4 of quip**
105 Potpourri
106 Free electrons
107 Like Peters Glacier
111 Cut some slack
114 Libation with sushi
115 Unoriginal
117 In the past
118 **End of quip**
122 Tow truck in "Cars"
123 Source of dates
124 Disentangle
125 Pride of lions
126 Fourth Estate
127 A month of Sundays
128 Dr. Dre's buds
129 Myrmecology study

DOWN

1 Office runner
2 "I Puritani" is one
3 Take in
4 New Deal pres.
5 Spanish song translated as: "It's You"
6 They retired Dennis Rodman's number
7 Haberdashery stock
8 Nearly shut
9 Solo in "Solo"
10 Area folks
11 Mexican packsaddle
12 Crinkly cabbage
13 Blighted tree
14 Surprise outcomes
15 Rosy-cheeked toddler
16 Do ablutions
17 With the fleet
18 Bully's target, often
24 Headey on "Game of Thrones"
25 Like formalwear
26 Commedia dell'___
32 Be creative
33 Big name in Round Rock
34 Nanjing nanny
36 Acapulco appetizer
37 Löwenbräu logo
38 Test request
39 Rubber gasket
40 Wednesday, to Fester
41 Medicated
42 Conical tent
43 Opposed, to Jed Clampett
44 Thames boat
49 Sine qua ___
50 Carbuncle, for one
52 Vainglory
54 Baltic state
55 Souvenir of Hawaii
56 Souvenir of Hawaii
58 Suffix for rocket
60 Like Father Time
63 Wedgwood product
64 ". . .___ just my Bill"
67 Make known
68 "Hamilton" actress Phillipa
69 "Chat" novelist McCarthy
70 French toast
71 Take-out item
72 Mic holder
73 "___ nada, senor!"
74 What Jack Hughes turned in 2019
77 RSA political party
78 Book before Proverbs
79 Wallaroo
80 Snail without a shell
81 Agency based in Moscow
84 Deposits
85 Duped twin in Genesis
87 "Am-scray!"
89 "Daily" Metropolis paper
90 Reduced
94 Readily influenced
96 Surveying tool
99 Between-meal bites
100 Buses tables
101 "Sooey!" reply
102 Honest Abe's family
103 Exhilarates
104 Salvador the Surrealist
108 Donna of fashion
109 Binky Urban, notably
110 Bumps on stumps
111 Like overcooked pasta
112 Dorsey in "The Blind Side"
113 Elbe tributary
114 Hose problem
115 Mother Hubbard's lack
116 "A Bug's Life" princess
119 Org. concerned with dioxin
120 Crux of the matter
121 Dent Medal's org.

ONE FOR THE ROAD   by Lou Sabin

"Levelheaded society member?" would be another clue for 72 Across.

ACROSS

1 Kerouac's "generation"
5 "Hägar the Horrible" dog
10 Shrub with red berries
15 "Out!"
19 Faith Hill's voice
20 Sunbathing spot
21 Chorus syllables
22 Pueblo Indian
23 Bountiful harvest*
25 Convicted unfairly*
27 "Hamlet" setting
28 Guzzle
30 Big man on campus
31 Up for payment
32 Spoils a parade
33 Voldemort's title
35 Chic clique
39 "How are you ___?"
40 Picks on
44 Tart
45 Sweater pattern*
47 Tout's offering
48 Twelve sharp
49 Kipling's "Rikki-Tikki-___"
50 Utah ski resort
51 Language written from right to left
52 Feeling malaise
53 Centerpiece site*
57 Denomination
58 Saved from ruin
60 Wack jobs
61 Ice-fishing tools
62 Chair designer Charles
63 Bark beetle, e.g.
64 Snow White and friends
65 Waco campus
67 Martini onion
68 Underscores
71 Wrench type
72 Not one to circle the globe*
74 Year in Henry III's reign
75 X-acto cut
76 Philistine
77 Pro votes
78 Come up short
79 Geologic time frame
80 Send via messenger*
84 Grossglockner locale
85 Wine servers
87 Zebrula dams
88 Plucky
89 Las Vegas casino
90 Missouri tributary
91 Spanish Main cargo
92 Nonplus
95 Lorelei, for one
96 Historic bomber of WW2
101 West Virginia industry*
104 Over-the-shoulder look*
106 Very involved with
107 Scorch
108 Rubber gasket
109 Airport walkway
110 Profound
111 Summoned electronically
112 Insolvent
113 She-sheep

DOWN

1 Golfer Didrikson
2 Last Hebrew month
3 Bread machines?
4 Roan African antelope
5 Bamboo shoot
6 Abalone shell
7 Arles auxiliary
8 Brazil carnival city
9 Part of a schooner's rigging
10 Orchestra section
11 Nizhni Tagil's peaks
12 What Santa gets a lot of
13 Berlin's "___ Alone"
14 One for the road (and a hint to clue* answers)
15 Dig discoveries
16 Cryptography study
17 Top
18 In apple-pie order
24 Stopped
26 OWN founder
29 Fondue ingredient
32 Bird from a blue egg
33 Cappuccino cousin
34 Scourge of penguins
35 Joplin at Woodstock
36 Oregon state park
37 Public transit of Philly*
38 Confession topic
39 Playwright Rabe
40 Breed's and Bunker
41 Wise to urban ways*
42 Large sea duck
43 Taters
45 Rose stems
46 Israeli mount
49 Grambling mascot
51 Primal impulses
53 Pythias' friend
54 Glory in
55 Jeter's former manager
56 Amtrak express train
57 More fetching
59 Gentleman's gentleman
61 The Pentagon covers 34
63 Male Amish feature
64 ___ side of the coin
65 Diamond thefts?
66 Parcel out
67 Drags along
68 Eye sores
69 Grizabella's creator
70 Kooky
72 Peter in "Easy Rider"
73 Shiny black
76 Adriatic resort
78 Murphy Brown's show
80 Sultan's palace area
81 Popped up
82 Like the White Rabbit
83 Applies a patch
84 Blog pest
86 Belt
88 Dazed
90 Hint of color
91 Upturned, as a box
92 Vitamin C, for one
93 Cooked through
94 See regularly
95 Audition for "The Voice"
96 Sedgwick of Warhol films
97 Bern river
98 Chew like a beaver
99 Wile E. Coyote's supplier
100 Slangy agreements
102 Where to get a WWW address
103 Long of "NCIS: Los Angeles"
105 Infuriation

ACROSS

1 Novak Djokovic, for one
5 Gofer's task
11 Songwriter Silverstein
15 Chopin's paramour
19 Shawkat of "Arrested Development"
20 Cat on the prowl
21 Folk knowledge
22 "The potted physician"
23 Bikini Bottom monarch
25 Fish bait
27 Acts the Muse
28 "In the Heart of the Sea" ship
30 Ball of fire
31 "The eye is not satisfied with ___": Eccles.
32 It runs in Vermont
33 Quadruple ___ loop
34 McGrew in a Service poem
35 Facebook friends
38 "Batman v Superman" villain
39 Man about ___
40 Burnt pigment
43 They're eaten green
45 Auburn dye
46 Half a vise
49 Lincoln and Ford
50 Vietnamese hub
51 Candlestick ___
52 "Pipe down!"
54 Merchandise ID
55 Carnivorous plant
58 Basilica section
59 Pep-rally blazes
61 Composer Speaks
62 Finneran's "Downton Abbey" role
64 End of Ripley's slogan
65 "I Know Why the ___ Bird Sings"
67 Invitee
68 Structural harm
70 "And so . . ."
71 Ireland's wailers
74 "Casablanca" escape-route city
75 Honors for horror films
79 College near Albany, NY
80 "Thanks, mon ami!"
82 "The Haunting" heroine
83 Admonishes
84 "Dirty Harry" org.
85 Colubrine letter
86 Yo-yo part
88 "20,000 Leagues Under the Sea" author
89 Like crocodile tears
90 Aoudad dads
91 eBay offer
92 Flight part
94 Andean tuber
97 Start of MGM's motto
98 "Stop filming!"
99 "___ than a junkyard dog . . ."
103 Contended
105 ___ metabolic rate
107 Password partner
109 Kansas state symbol
111 Winged Liberty Head coin
113 "Thought" word form
114 Court plea, briefly
115 Stressed type
116 0-shaped
117 Bar-tacks
118 Liquidate
119 Add an explanation to
120 Highlands loch

DOWN

1 Colombian monkeys
2 NYC subway route
3 Car wash cycle
4 Woodwind instrument
5 Come to light
6 "Clue" clue
7 Axle-breakers
8 Tempe campus
9 Big Island goose
10 Prom rentals
11 Stephen King's Doctor
12 "Balloon Boy," for one
13 Flub
14 Anticlimax
15 Already cut, as lumber
16 "Get ___ of this!"
17 "Bates Motel" mother
18 "Buffy the Vampire Slayer" extra
24 SF gridder
26 "The Lion King" villains
29 Kenny G's instrument
33 Toy truck maker
36 Eris is a dwarf one
37 Skull cavity
38 Explorer Erikson
39 Towel material
40 Gauchos of the Big West
41 Fierce shark
42 "Grenade" singer
44 Def in "Showtime"
45 Loathed
46 Home of T. Woods
47 Bat-eared fox
48 "At what time?"
50 Good guys
51 Goober or Gomer
53 Stringent
55 Actor Rhames
56 Access Facebook
57 Beats and beats
60 Pittance
63 "Catfish Row" resident
65 Pitiless
66 Field: Comb. form
67 January birthstone
68 Cupola
69 Enyo's companion
70 Cultural values
71 Jersey homes
72 Actor Omar
73 Camp
76 Chemistry 101 models
77 Blown away
78 1812 happening
81 Mount Carmel locale
84 Susan in "About Ray"
87 Forgives
88 Folic acid is one
89 Aflame
91 It often goes to school
93 Arbitrarily fine
94 Palm Springs, for one
95 Adjective for OPEC oil
96 Vice President in 1972
98 "Brady Bunch" mom
100 Artless
101 Peel and Roberts
102 Angling gear
104 NORAD trackees
105 Brontë pen name
106 Jared in "Blade Runner 2049"
107 "Daily Bruin" publisher
108 Red diamonds
110 "Ah, me!"
112 Ben in "Ben"

SMALL-SCREEN SIDEKICKS by Linda Gould
53 Across is regarded to be an expert in the "art of doing nothing."

ACROSS

1 ["Omigosh!"]
5 Adds to the kitty
10 Les Halles locale
15 Airport curb queue
19 Pueblo pot
20 Coin of the ___
21 A-listers
22 Ice-cream cookie
23 Takeoff artist
24 Deadly African snake
25 Playwright Spewack
26 Vex
27 Gilligan was his sidekick
29 Rocket J. Squirrel's sidekick
31 "Animal Farm" and others
32 Camelot contest
34 Belittles
35 "___ for Fugitive": Grafton
36 "/" to a kegler
38 About the eye
40 "Absinthe" artist
43 Didst reside
44 Had a bawl
45 "P" as in Ptolemy
48 October gem
49 Chester of "Gunsmoke"
50 A boring person might have one
51 Natterjack
52 Quill point
53 Spongebob's sidekick
55 Keyboard timesaver
56 Auditioned for Wes Craven?
58 Markedly similar
59 Zero
60 Acquire (debt)
61 "Eek!" evoker
63 Perez or O'Donnell
64 Adjust beforehand
66 Former capital of Italy
67 Turned turtle
70 Lollapaloozas
71 Richie Cunningham's sidekick
74 2018 Gary Oldman film
75 Fanning in "Maleficent"
76 Prefix for graphic
77 Its day is longer than its year
78 Suit option
79 "Spellbound" contest
80 Apartment types
81 Hip-huggers
82 Sordid
83 Thrifty
84 Discoveries
85 London brume
86 From time immemorial
89 Cherry variety
90 Pride member
94 Kermit the Frog's sidekick
97 Lucy Ricardo's sidekick
100 "Ma Belle ___" (1970 hit)
101 Acts as agent provocateur
102 Sabbatical
103 Banyan, for one
104 Bristol loc.
105 Marco Island bird
106 Eminem's "No One's ___"
107 Knell
108 Start of a Cockney toast
109 Batik artists
110 "Hold all my ___"
111 Six-days-a-week airline

DOWN

1 "The Men Who Stare at ___" (2009)
2 "A" as in Athens
3 Wintry precip
4 Wagner's last opera
5 Mailer's "___ of the Night"
6 Bimonthly tides
7 Pipe tool
8 Dresden river
9 Wisenheimer
10 Rockette?
11 Aboriginal Alaskan
12 Babbling brook
13 "___ never fly!"
14 Salt source
15 Fine brandy
16 Armenian river
17 "A Change in Me" singer
18 Cobbler's stock
28 Letang of the NHL
30 Footnote abbr.
33 NYC's first subway line
36 Prince Valiant's Singing ___
37 Prefix for cure or cab
38 In-house publication
39 Berth place
40 Grandees
41 Grandiose
42 Xena's sidekick
43 Granny, often
44 "Aww" evoker
45 Jack Benny's sidekick
46 Fabled also-ran
47 "Ewww" inducer
49 A to Z
50 Starts the Q&A
51 Hoglike herbivore
53 Meadowlands races
54 "Lilo & Stitch" setting
55 Closefisted one
57 Eventuate
59 Bays
61 Kitchen handwear
62 ". . . ___ I'm told"
63 "Concentration" puzzle
64 Naval Academy freshman
65 Principle
66 A bit bonkers
67 Monopoly payments
68 Occasional dummy
69 Jury ___
71 Unit of loudness
72 Like Billy Graham's ministry
73 Go one's way
76 Contemplated
78 Literary sketch
80 Colombian city
81 Matman's win
82 Unhappy end
83 Cheats
84 Flawless goods
85 TurboTax clientele
86 ___ worse than death
87 Pvt. Pyle
88 "Salon" or "Slate"
89 Cotton bundler
90 Raze
91 "Captain Blood" star Flynn
92 Memorial pillar
93 Hungarian conductor (1897–1970)
95 Hobgoblin
96 "My Left Foot" setting
98 Honduras port
99 Concert venue

STARTING PLAYERS   by Scott Atkinson
. . . and these starters all have something in common.

ACROSS

1 "Chestnuts roasting ___ open fire . . ."
5 1980s legal drama
10 "Up and ___!"
14 Provoke
19 Osso ___
20 City SSE of Gainesville
21 Sitar music
22 Letter-shaped fasteners
23 "Top Gun" role
26 New Orleans gridder
27 Bottled Alpine water
28 Look after
29 Flyer on a string
31 Scott in a Supreme Court case
32 Gin mixer
33 QB's pocket protectors
35 "Where the Wild Things Are" author
37 Children's nature periodical
45 Historic opening?
48 Where Hamlet saw a ghost
49 Leveling tool
50 Protagonist
52 FINRA predecessor
53 Puller of many cars
56 Ratite bird
57 George M. Cohan biopic
61 Crimson Tide's conference
62 Command to Fido
63 Egg ___ yung
64 Plains tribe
65 Pre-college exam
66 Pink stomach soother, for short
70 Returns pro
72 How Reuben is sandwiched
74 Backyard party torch
77 Macbeth's burial place
79 "Slippery" tree
81 Pitch a fit
85 Syllable in a bray
86 FDR and J.P. Morgan were once its members
91 Nonprofit URL suffix
92 Resident doctor
93 Fishing rod attachment
94 Thanksgiving side
95 Katmandu resident
97 Having a ball at the mall
100 Catch forty winks
101 Really irksome sort
106 Stage platforms
107 Ban Ki-moon's alma mater
108 Palm Springs, for one
112 Furry companions
114 Valley
116 Thompson and Watson
120 "Elder" or "Younger" Roman writer
121 Somber notices
123 Performed as expected
126 "Wonderfilled" cookies
127 "Like ___ not . . ."
128 Register
129 Paris evening
130 Egypt's Mubarak
131 IRS IDs
132 Like attics
133 Palimony payers

DOWN

1 ___ d'art
2 New, in Nicaragua
3 Muscle protein
4 "You cheated!"
5 Record keeper
6 German expletives
7 Lacking punctuality
8 Toward the sheltered side
9 Like Aleppo or Homs
10 Musical based on "Exodus"
11 What to do at the beep
12 "I" problem
13 "Goin' Gone" singer Kathy
14 Two per qt.
15 Stunned
16 Idiosyncrasy
17 American quarterly
18 Founded: Abbr.
24 Andes ancient
25 Salk vaccine target
30 Give rise to
34 Mountainside debris
36 One of NASCAR's Allison brothers
38 Hawaiian honker
39 Tickled
40 "Put a tiger in your tank" company
41 Free from
42 Japanese fencing sport
43 Home to Hercules' lion
44 Spew forth
45 ___ ed class
46 Harvest
47 Haliaeetus albicilla
51 Animal discovered in 1900
54 Chihuahua cat
55 A party to
58 Barely make, with "out"
59 "What's up, ___?"
60 Easy strider
65 Soul singer Sledge
67 Walrus or seal
68 "Nothing ___" ("Easy peasy")
69 Some time ago
71 Father's robe
73 "So's ___ old man!"
74 Skimpy swimsuit
75 "Able was ___ saw Elba"
76 Beer blasts
78 Goodyear headquarters
80 Shape-shift
82 ___ Bator, Mongolia
83 Cougar
84 Recipe amt.
86 Tartan garments
87 "Brokeback Mountain" cowboy
88 Parrot beak segment
89 Wail
90 "Waiting for the Robert ___"
96 Jennifer on "The Morning Show"
98 Put a wing on
99 Baffled
102 Swashbuckling Dumas character
103 Keys in lochs
104 Egyptian Christian
105 Baseball's "Mr. Tiger"
109 Plains Nation
110 Concave navel
111 Methods: Abbr.
112 Hunny-loving bear
113 River of Aragón
115 Harrow rival
117 Carte du jour
118 Book before Romans
119 Proofer's countermand
122 FICA benefit
124 Hesitant sounds
125 Suffix for vision

ACROSS

1 Highlands hillside
5 Good buddies with handles
10 Bruno ___ shoes
15 History
19 Church tower fixture
20 Potential officer
21 Shaped like Humpty Dumpty
22 North Korean rocket
23 Tortilla chip dip
25 Surprise classroom events
27 Service do-overs
28 Toy pistol
30 Straightens a hose
31 Where hangers hang
34 Roller-coaster feature
35 Nobel novelist Morrison
36 European cheer
37 Augusta National, for one
39 3 in 1,000
41 "Sk8er ___": Avril Lavigne
42 Blind a peregrine
43 Industry magnate
45 Raga instrument
49 Duel invitation
51 Flimsy
53 Total accuracy
56 Award given J.K. Rowling
58 Stephen in "The Musketeer"
60 Mambo's cousin
61 Iberian river
62 In a total fog
65 Astronomy chart
67 Keaton film
69 It runs in Vermont
70 Musical duo first seen in an "SNL" sketch
74 Grant-in-___
75 Bears or Cubs
77 Bit of progress
78 "Wheel of Fortune" name
80 Sicilian landmark
81 Precipitousness
84 Baggage tag at Stuttgart
85 Astronaut Swigert's alma mater
86 Textile dealer of old, slangily
89 Butterine
91 Gaelic girl
95 Slippery as ___
96 Square-dance group
98 "A-Tisket, A-Tasket" singer
100 "How now brown cow?" reply
101 Spud sieves
104 Victorian bedmaker
107 NY Knicks' home
110 Sound measure
111 Grammy winner for "Believe"
112 Shake down
113 Cousins of 60 Across
115 Muskmelon
117 Pianist Maisenberg
118 Gallivant
120 Nadir
124 Ground-floor apartment
125 "Excellent!"
126 More exact
127 Derby winner Lil ___
128 Mueller report releaser
129 10-point type
130 Celestial giant
131 Snack

DOWN

1 Daisy ammo
2 "Groovy!"
3 "Praise the Lord!"
4 Ex-Yankee catcher Howard
5 IV units
6 Ovine cry
7 Cabinet dept.
8 Defective directive
9 Run an errand, say
10 Clean a spill
11 Mary Kay rival
12 House party?
13 It's sold in bars
14 "No idea at all"
15 "The Godfather" author
16 WW2 beachhead
17 Tortoise feature
18 Calais cup
24 NHL stats
26 Most unfriendly
29 "___ or go home"
32 "Maid of Athens, ___ part": Byron
33 Chinook salmon
35 Prime-time time
37 Showtime parent
38 Emilia in "Game of Thrones"
39 Actress Pitts
40 Fathered
44 Lethargic states
46 Abolitionist Harriet
47 "Take the ___": Ellington
48 Fleming in "Spellbound"
50 "The Bells" poet
52 Curious George's creators
54 Faded away
55 Wild boar's home
57 Hoggett's pet pig
59 Brian Eno's genre
62 Kansas motto ender
63 Highland wear
64 Bob SquarePants, e.g.
65 Poison elder
66 Son of Aleta
68 Invitation initials
71 Cowardly Lion portrayer
72 Cowardly Lion harasser
73 Apollo Theater locale
76 Less lively, party-wise
79 Feel strange
82 Breakers break here
83 Tic ___ (breath mints)
85 Sea-Dweller watch company
87 Elevator pioneer Otis
88 Dell support group
90 Czech-German river
92 Almond cordial
93 "C'est la vie!"
94 Nursery product
97 Dance, drama, etc;
99 Pal of Threepio
102 Not refined
103 Enrich spiritually
105 Shady spots
106 Like lava streams
107 Work for a high schooler
108 Model Hiatt
109 Crystal-___ (seer)
111 Training staff
114 Boris Godunov, e.g.
115 Popular site for 88 Down
116 ___ above the rest
119 News agcy. in Boca Raton
121 New Zealand parrot
122 "It's sooo cold!"
123 [Shrug]

ACROSS

1 "Mares eat ___ and . . ."
5 Former Belgian coin
10 Future tulips
15 Spud buds
19 Squander
20 "The Rocket" of tennis
21 American chameleon
22 Tweed caricaturist
23 Bacchanal "whoopee!"
24 Add one's two cents
25 Sturdy chiffon
26 Minutes
27 Frozen ropes, in baseball lingo*
29 Stray hunter*
31 "Or how about . . ."
32 "Am I my brother's keeper?" speaker
34 Rip to pieces
35 Caught a bug
36 Nonreactive
38 Navy decoration
40 French royal line
43 Close in "Mary Reilly"
44 Idiosyncrasy
45 Mr. Ed's bed
48 Pamplona cheers
49 Aquatic dragonfly larva
50 Tabloids
51 Unwanted patio growth
52 Take off the top
53 What Brits call "crisps"*
55 ___ manner born
56 Banished, in a way
58 Snoopy's former owner
59 Barbershop foam
60 Cat Nation people
61 Used a prie-dieu
63 Dakota abode
64 Airport holding areas
66 Poet Angelou
67 2018 Stanley Cup champions
70 Beyond repair

71 Dugout fixture*
74 "Wall Street Journal" cofounder
75 "___ Rhythm"
76 Change tenants
77 Ship of fuels
78 "Big" prefix
79 Lets touch this
80 Like Swiss cheese
81 Corrodes
82 Delaware statesman
83 ___ and services
84 The Pentagon covers 34
85 Cubs group
86 Insist upon
89 RN's imperative
90 Like a links course
94 Cape Canaveral neighbor*
97 Decathlete, at times*
100 Piece of work
101 Hogwarts student Macmillan
102 Midtown establishment
103 Tabula ___
104 "Familiar" sound
105 "Bennie and the Jets" singer John
106 "101" title word
107 "Benevolent and Protective Order"
108 Jean ___ perfume
109 An anagram for siren
110 Large perennial
111 Throw in the towel

DOWN

1 ÷ symbols
2 "Future Shock" author Toffler
3 "Who Framed Roger Rabbit" extras
4 Darlings
5 Wallpaper pattern
6 Double-quick
7 Tel ___
8 Aloha goose
9 Musical buildup
10 Highwayman
11 Alliance
12 Drawn-out

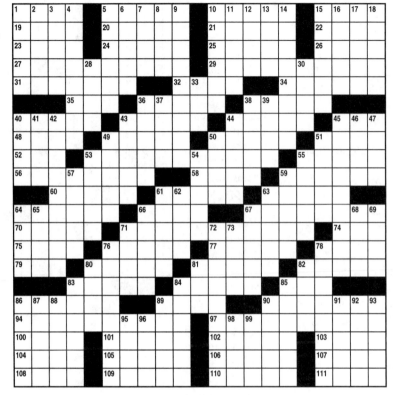

13 Ad hoc coalition
14 Ottawa hockey team
15 Legislates
16 Nantucket vessel
17 Lauder of Fifth Avenue
18 "Act Naturally" singer
28 Shoulder muscle
30 "Honey do" list item
33 Queen Aleta's son
36 24-book epic
37 Sans mixer
38 Mea ___
39 Tears
40 Wintery
41 First-aid plant
42 Spicy stew*
43 JFK boarding areas
44 Patchwork ___
45 Short-fused (and a hint to theme answers)
46 "A Hard Road To Glory" author
47 1914 Belgian battle line

49 Staff members
50 "Both Sides" artist Collins
51 A Bach work
53 "CSI" evidence
54 "C" on a calculator
55 "Mountain cow" of Belize
57 "Are you in ___?"
59 Ben-Hur's mother was one
61 Sagal in "Sons of Anarchy"
62 "Can't do it, Sasha"
63 The stuff of legends
64 Analogous
65 Squire-to-be
66 "GQ" target audience
67 2007 Super Bowl winners
68 Theater section
69 Kind of song or dive
71 Use a blowtorch
72 Matrimony prelude
73 Where the Aisne ends
76 Barq's beverage

78 Medieval musician
80 "Fiddler on the Roof" dance
81 "Heartbreak Hotel" label
82 Bridges in "Norma Rae"
83 "The King's Speech" king
84 Plato's birthplace
85 Arrange for battle
86 One fell on Chicken Little
87 "Casa de Mi Padre" heroine
88 Aramis, for one
89 Grafting shoot
90 Opposite of lenient
91 High speed train of Rome
92 Work stations
93 Eradicate
95 Oilman Halliburton
96 Not for
98 Sharpen
99 David Rabe's "Good for ___"

ACROSS

1 "Helicopter" band ___ Party
5 Civil War nurse Barton
10 Because
15 Dollop
19 Astronomer Beebe
20 "King Lear" role
21 Bearded sheep
22 Etc. relative
23 "Toe" of the Arabian Peninsula
24 Eric Trump's mother
25 Our, in Paris
26 Tax-free bond
27 1937 Triple Crown winner*
29 GPA booster*
31 Hits the books
32 Earl of tea
34 Went sour
35 "Old" and "road" endings
36 "And you, Miss, are no lady!" speaker
38 "Alice in Wonderland" pastries
40 Admission need, slangily
43 Backcomb
44 "Miss Saigon" hero
45 Pentagon org.
48 Ghostbuster Spengler
49 Culture dish
50 Bad actor at the rodeo
51 Moon over Marseille
52 Cockney abyss
53 Kind of frosting*
55 Italian lawn bowls
56 Trivial
58 Opposed to aweather
59 Arabian Sea vessel
60 Like whitecaps
61 Kalahari bushman
63 "The Dark Knight ___" (2012)
64 "La Cerveza Más Fina" brew
66 40-decibel unit
67 Globetrotters' opponents
70 "I knew it all ___!"
71 Gridiron protection*
74 Dubai locale
75 Johnnycake
76 Part of SWAK
77 Renée Fleming solos
78 A tug may tow it
79 Table scrap
80 Think out loud
81 Beyond breezy
82 Mating game
83 Baby boxer
84 Deep thinkers
85 Roadwork sign
86 "Make yourself ___!"
89 "Winter Song" pianist
90 "Puh-leeze!"
94 Make callous*
97 Ragtime dance*
100 "Bound for Glory" singer
101 Rainforest vine
102 French pewter
103 Crafty
104 Biblical pronoun
105 Bittern relative
106 Not quite mashed
107 Baylor rival
108 Scout housing
109 "La Vita Nuova" poet
110 Bobrun runners
111 Voicemail prompt

DOWN

1 Forehead features
2 Paul in "Stateside"
3 Hokkaido city
4 Like the loonie or toonie
5 "CSI" concerns
6 Jeans label
7 Seaweed extract
8 Frog genus
9 Pain reliever
10 When Ramadan ends
11 Bitter twist
12 Naldi of silent movies

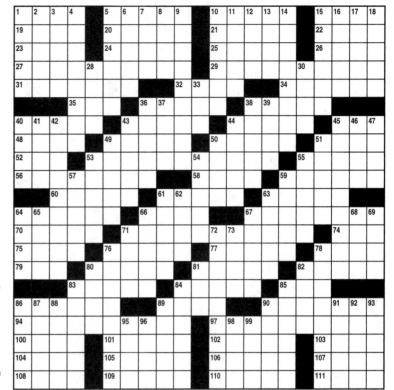

13 "B.C." character Clumsy ___
14 "I Sing the Body ___": Whitman
15 Arboreal primates
16 180° manuever
17 Parsonage
18 Applied (oneself)
28 Take a loss?
30 "Three up, three down" results
33 Numbered rd.
36 Mark down, in a way
37 Rough up
38 "Just One of ___ Things"
39 "A-Hunting We Will Go" composer
40 Like Lake Tanganyika
41 Exotic tangelo
42 Weather map line (and a hint to theme answers)
43 Itsy-bitsy
44 Mail carriers have one
45 Spring roll dip*

46 "___ I Had a Secret Love"
47 Venison
49 ___ ballerina
50 Banjo player Fleck
51 Introvert
53 "The Trolley Song" sound
54 Veronica of "Hill Street Blues"
55 Headquartered
57 Half a shortbread cookie
59 "Tony n' ___ Wedding"
61 Snare feature
62 Load to bear
63 Square accounts
64 Guitar bar
65 Swan genus
66 Aglitter
67 Corn porridge
68 "Land of a Million Elephants"
69 Adds a border to a quilt
71 Cut class
72 Marmee's "little women"
73 Enya's language

76 Challenged a verdict
78 Faster way
80 "Yipe!"
81 Jupiter's composition
82 Tennis court surface
83 Adjust beforehand
84 Chamber on the Hill
85 Passes bills
86 Caan of "Hawaii Five-0"
87 Apt rhyme for "stash"
88 White as a sheet
89 Principle
90 Schussed
91 Muse for a troubadour
92 Jewish star
93 Classic Jaguar model
95 Baltic seaport
96 "Aw, gee!"
98 One of two Monopoly cards: Abbr.
99 Hambletonian, e.g.

282 THEMELESS by Steve Russell
Disputes with England over 71 Down triggered the Hundred Years' War.

ACROSS

1 Virgin Galactic craft
10 Remove barnacles, e.g.
16 Triathlon leg
20 Distinguish
21 Service area
22 Barrie pooch
23 Up and down, e.g.
24 Runoff place
25 Baltic Sea tributary
26 Bugged
27 Paramaribo is its capital
28 Necklace bauble
29 Brit. word ref
30 Nimble
31 Singer Campbell
33 Hindu title
34 Track-and-field event
38 Like some homes
40 Record making
42 Like a dark street
43 Political party managers
44 New Yorker, for one
47 Wawrinka of tennis
48 Prison blades
49 Miscue on the mound
50 Heaps of, slangily
51 Thunderbird Park sight
53 Rigor ___
55 Small fry
56 Ladybugs, to aphids
57 "So sorry"
59 House flip
60 Noblewoman
62 Tickles pink
67 "Apollo 13" actor
69 "Goosebumps" series author
70 Chews the fat
74 Biblical dancer
75 Current gossip
77 Fit out
79 Merlot and Malbec
80 Visits the mall
81 "___ stands now . . ."
82 Divert
84 Pulls the cover from
85 Beginning, slangily
86 Squirm
87 Best of seven, e.g.
89 Overlong sentences
90 Suffix for Israel
91 Melissa Gilbert's sister
94 It crosses Hollywood
95 Lepidopterist's tool
96 Cartoonist who drew Santa
98 "Bewitched" actor Dick
100 Prince Andrew's daughter
105 Potluck choice
106 Calculator figure
107 Absolutely adore
108 ___-Day vitamins
109 One of the Barrymores
110 Semitones and microtones
111 Celebration suffix
112 Tongue-lashing
113 Sound judgment

DOWN

1 Cry to a thief
2 Amorous skunk Le Pew
3 Weisshorn's chain
4 Coagulate
5 Remove tactfully
6 Steeple toppers
7 Couldn't abide
8 Steamed up
9 Parts of qts.
10 Napes
11 Powder paper: Rx
12 Shankar of sitar
13 Taking off on
14 Like the Botany Bay colony
15 Periodic table entry
16 Uppity sort
17 Begins with gusto
18 Whole hog
19 New Orleans celebration
27 Oozes through
30 Ambition
32 December air
34 Light housecoat
35 Talk like James Earl Jones
36 Puts on the agenda
37 Kubrick's art
38 Actor Collins
39 Parts of Santa costumes
41 Yonkers race
43 Grinch victims
45 Choral section
46 Birthday suit
48 Goes over the limit
49 Puts to sleep
52 It's as good as a miss
53 Madame Tussaud
54 Tests the air
57 Salon works
58 Snow Queen in "Frozen"
60 Lost color
61 Wears down
63 Arrive at
64 Relates with
65 Naval standard
66 Brief arguments
68 Rhodes of "Roots"
69 Weightlifting units
70 Hear about
71 Eleanor's region of France
72 Colonial legislators
73 Spill the beans
75 Proverbial crowd
76 Gardeners' tools
78 Good buddies
80 John, Paul, or George
83 Ocean condiment
84 Great Dane color pattern
85 Eavestroughs
88 Made uniform
89 Brought in
92 Hub-to-rim lines
93 Intense devotion
95 "Awesome!"
97 "___ Old Black Magic"
99 Rowlands of "The Notebook"
100 U2 frontman
101 Exhibit wanderlust
102 Psychologist Pavlov
103 Elmer Fudd collectibles
104 Limerick language
107 Band booking

There's a museum named for 20 Across in Henning, Tennessee.

ACROSS

1 Luau dancewear
10 Smug smiles
16 Big ref.
20 "Roots" author
21 Packing a wallop
22 Dorsey of "Queen Sugar"
23 Captives
24 "Songs in ___": Keys album
25 "Doctor Zhivago" heroine
26 Wrangler's rope
27 Basso profundo, e.g.
29 Grand Opry center
30 Dirt clump
31 Averse to compromise
35 "New Attitude" singer Patti
37 Put down
41 Playwright Chekhov
43 Take up residence
44 "Sweet Emotion" band
47 Spiritual advisors
49 Moon goddess
50 "Breaking Bad" protagonist
51 Woodwind section
53 Olympian goal
55 Ore carrier
56 "There's ___ every crowd!"
58 Pulls down
60 Espresso cup
62 "Touché" sayer
64 Brings to ruin
66 Exclusive
67 Many an interstate
69 Crawls, e.g.
71 Below wholesale
76 Coll. subj.
78 Dance instructor's topics
80 Like a vista
81 Mentally acute
86 Mattress supports
88 "___ la vista, baby!"
89 Popular Japanese seafood
90 Rises dramatically
92 Dragnet
94 Bowed instrument
95 Salon strokes
97 Tough to climb
99 Boiling mad
101 Petruchio's prowess
103 Overact
105 Orrery orbs
106 Temple, for one
108 Bank account holder
111 Macbeth's burial isle
112 Sundial hour
114 Rathskeller mug
115 Pipsqueak
120 Tiny terror
121 Mischievous imp
123 Sword lily
126 Not taken in by
127 Olympic skater Eric
128 Part of Oceania
129 At no time, poetically
130 State emphatically
131 Nowadays

DOWN

1 "___, Caesar!"
2 Wrist bone
3 Repeated services
4 Electric guitars, slangily
5 Hides from view
6 Neb. neighbor
7 ___-de-la-Cité
8 Christopher in "The Aviator"
9 Cicely in "Sounder"
10 Layout concern
11 What a rolling stone gathers?
12 "Bring ___ pray you . . .": Shak.
13 City in "Folsom Prison Blues"
14 Small hill
15 Mill site
16 Fellini's "sweet life"
17 "Do tell!"
18 Southern region
19 Apple, for one
28 Brick Pollitt's mom
32 Verne submariner
33 Illegal inducement
34 Like some Pamplona runners
36 Physique, informally
37 Took to the airport, e.g.
38 Shoe against a stake
39 Francis or Dahl
40 Become aware of
42 Art studio subjects
45 Sticky-tongued critter
46 Deli offerings
48 Apia is its capital
52 "The ___ of Kilimanjaro"
54 Rhythmic cadences
57 More recent
59 Jimmy of "Buff City Law"
61 Show the ropes
63 Futurities
65 Refine ore
68 Fluctuates wildly
70 Preps for a bout
72 Baking powder, e.g.
73 Last-minute NFL kick
74 Not participate in
75 Hustles tickets
77 Under, poetically
79 "Now!" in the OR
81 Eartha Kitt hit
82 Glinda portrayer in "The Wiz"
83 Cross off the list
84 Suction pump
85 Hate the thought of
87 Took the Stanley Cup in four
91 Campus stretch
93 French composer Édouard
96 Lorne Michaels show
98 Scout shelter
100 Beswick in "Thunderball"
102 Kyoto companion
104 "The City in the Sea" poet
107 "Great Scott!"
117 Word after who or what
109 Greek "S"
110 Narrow waterway
113 Eye part
116 Causes of moans and groans
117 Word after who or what
118 Bring crashing down
119 College prep exam
122 Chemical suffix
124 Bavarian peak
125 Patriotic woman's org.

284 LEADING LADIES by Jean Peterson

In 1971, Tricia Nixon married Edward Cox in the 29 Across.

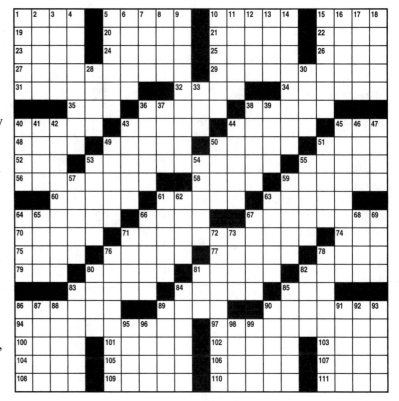

ACROSS

1 Torah cabinets
5 Musical org.
10 Gay Nineties footwear
15 Helgenberger of "China Beach"
19 Postflop hold'em bet
20 Antelope with lyre-shaped horns
21 Burgundy wine
22 Earth Hour subj.
23 Vaulted arch
24 Close, in verse
25 Actress Milicevic
26 Driftwood carrier
27 Deadly nightshade
29 Site of Presidential ceremonies
31 Joined
32 Steps to the Ganges
34 Liam in "Kinsey"
35 Kang of "The Mentalist"
36 Matriculate
38 Laughs heartily
40 Sierra Nevada lake
43 Swell up
44 ___ Domingo
45 Procedural query
48 "Walk Like ___": Four Seasons
49 Like snap beans
50 Seawater barrier
51 "Downton Abbey" countess
52 "Glee" coach
53 Jonas Nightingale, for one
55 Manila ___
56 Prevent from happening
58 Ireland, in songs
59 Only just
60 Skunk
61 Hip-hop headwear
63 Pale purple bloom
64 Make up
66 Hatcher in "Tomorrow Never Dies"
67 En masse
70 Games guru Edmond
71 Payment extension
74 Moody rock genre
75 Emotional poetry
76 Speed skater Hughes
77 Navratilova rival
78 Trident-shaped letters
79 Bentley in "The Hunger Games"
80 Cheaply ornate
81 Curling rock
82 Paperless pups
83 Food from a blender
84 Like Virginia hams
85 Sherman's "hell"
86 Story setting
89 Gilpin of "Frasier"
90 Roasts corn
94 Day for pranks
97 Elsie the Cow's necklace
100 Facial expression
101 Capital of Morocco
102 Andean ancient
103 Alan in "The Aviator"
104 Prefix for chamber
105 Susan Lucci's daytime role
106 Tomb marker
107 Slip through the cracks
108 Watermelon discard
109 Will in "Blue Bloods"
110 Roughs up
111 Jane in a Brontë novel

DOWN

1 PostScript creator
2 Seth in "The Guilt Trip"
3 Prepared to be dubbed
4 Type of key
5 Garland for Caesar
6 Church council
7 Lower Normandy capital
8 Chester ___ Arthur
9 Writer's block?
10 Coil
11 Do an about-face
12 Duck genus
13 Muscle fitness
14 Become sluggish
15 They run in London taxis
16 Litmus reddeners
17 Calgary Stampede, for one
18 First American in orbit
28 Indy winner Luyendyk
30 Prefix for dynamic
33 Flying off the shelf
36 Top of the heap
37 Bagel, at ten
38 Baltimore gridder
39 Nonesuch
40 Wrigley Field covering
41 Señorita's love
42 Heidi Klum facial feature
43 One with a train
44 MLB commissioner (1998–2015)
45 Symbol of a maiden's dream
46 Soviet grain center
47 On one's guard
49 ___ célèbre
50 Zhivago's inspiration
51 Tiffany weight
53 Champagne glass
54 Hair-raising
55 Washed out
57 Hibachi glowers
59 Racist
61 Honey
62 Large-toothed whale
63 River of Orléans
64 Heavyset dog
65 Took the bus
66 Baseball deal
67 How things are going
68 Irradiate
69 "The Hunger Games" director
71 Gorilla ___
72 Lab glass
73 Bacchanal "whoopee!"
76 Happy-go-lucky
78 Buy
80 Aquatic bird
81 Prefix for charge
82 Painter Chagall
83 Showing anguish
84 Jai-alai baskets
85 "___ World" (1992)
86 Lorenzo of "Falcon Crest"
87 Air views
88 Minotaur's island
89 Spot
90 Choir song
91 "Roots" author
92 Large sea duck
93 Severus of Slytherin
95 Shell movers
96 Final bio
98 Pier at a wall's termination
99 NHL penalty killer

LEADING MEN   by Jean Peterson
Alternate clue for 67 Across: Round that Ali stopped Ron Lyle.

ACROSS

1 Maine shipyard city
5 Curved sports basket
10 Surrey racecourse site
15 For fear of
19 Bushy hairdo
20 Storage spot
21 German soprano Lehmann
22 "Sesame Street" regular
23 Agitate
24 River or wine
25 George Sand, for one
26 Roe in "Madam Secretary"
27 1940s teenybopper
29 Silly behavior
31 Music players
32 Just out of the pool
33 Talk-show lineup
34 Conservative TV channel
35 Say "nolo," say
38 Outpouring
40 "You're ___ a surprise!"
43 Many a newspaper
44 Buds
45 GRF's successor
48 Like gallows humor
49 Hourly
50 Foamy
51 Number crunching
52 Greek letter
53 "You'll see!"
55 "___ bleu!"
56 Gobi Desert locale
58 "___ old chap!"
59 Lulu
60 Wombat relative
61 Seafaring
63 Leg
64 Bring into accord
66 Big name in pineapples
67 Junior grade
70 Rides thermals
71 Cartes du jour
74 Shoe size
75 Nelson, for one
76 ___ Dog cocktail
77 Civilian clothes
78 "I" preceders
79 Bugling deer
80 Esther in "Maude"
81 Hair-raising
82 Find out bit by bit
83 Five-O
84 Rectory
85 "___ you serious?"
86 Be of service
89 Cross type
90 Piled up
94 Hamburger meat
97 Last second
100 Kind of master
101 Footnote daggers
102 Triton's milieu
103 "La Dolce Vita" locale
104 Track shape
105 NFL QB Rodgers
106 ___ Carlo
107 "Jurassic World" hero
108 Painter Magritte
109 Spork feature
110 Fed the kitty
111 NL East ball club

DOWN

1 Nasty remarks
2 "Come, Watson, the game's ___ !"
3 Choctaw, e.g.
4 Hal in "The Firm"
5 Nancy Drew's father
6 Societal standards
7 Pixy ___ candy
8 Spork feature
9 Box-elder genus
10 In hog heaven
11 Barnstormer
12 Modelesque
13 Disney snowman
14 Hatred of marriage
15 Sobieski in "Joan of Arc"
16 Figures in "Teutonic Mythology"
17 Spiffy
18 Awards for "The Lion King"
28 One Earth orbit
30 On the ___ (not speaking)
32 Method
35 Arctic coat
36 Payne of One Direction
37 Donna Douglas role
38 Disreputable
39 Baby sharks
40 Literary footnote
41 Peacekeeping alliance
42 Heart-to-heart discussion
43 Andrea ___ (ill-fated liner)
44 Barrier reef makeup
45 Platform dive
46 French 101 verb
47 "The Way of Love" singer
49 Berry with a Best Actress Oscar
50 2000 NL home run champ
51 Pont du Marché river
53 Ghostly sounds
54 Henry VIII's eight
55 Verona white wine
57 Watermelon's family
59 Deauville darling
61 Nick in "The Ridiculous 6"
62 Friend in need
63 Primary ticket
64 Queens stadium eponym
65 Dupe
66 Doozy
67 Mrs. Doubtfire
68 Robe of office
69 Violinist Hilary
71 East European
72 Sign of trouble
73 Objects of PETA protests
76 Butter up
78 Hydrogen has just one
80 Go for broke
81 Évian water
82 Golden Slam winner in tennis
83 Capricious
84 "___ Mr. Right" (1987)
85 Made amends for
86 Emmy hopeful
87 Remove an imperial
88 Singer Boyle
89 Raptor's nail
90 Pursue the puck
91 Plains Indian
92 "The Lego Movie" hero
93 Faculty heads
95 Lift over snow
96 Chair designer Aarnio
97 Famed Copenhagen restaurant
98 Toolbar symbol
99 Former meter coin

MARGARINE OF ERROR   by Harvey Estes
A riddle low in saturated fat.

ACROSS

1 Bracelet attachment
6 Heavy horns
11 Place for a mobile
15 Slips on
19 Bart's old man
20 Father of the Pleiades
21 Cry of frustration
22 Place for a run
23 **Start of a riddle**
25 Meyer in "Saw"
26 Rowlands in "Gloria"
27 Amigo
28 Hit the hay
29 French film
30 Toast opener
31 Siberian plains
33 **More of riddle**
37 Insurgent
39 Jimmy Nelson dummy
40 Dirt-cheap
41 Panzer protection
44 Orb-related
46 Spanish affirmatives
47 Part of mph
48 **More of riddle**
54 This could be a lot
55 Oodles
56 Trifle
57 Barkley nickname
60 Pick four, for one
61 John Wayne Airport code
62 "Cool beans!"
65 Sporty Mazda
66 **More of riddle**
71 Hostile state
72 Arborio and basmati
73 Rita in "Fifty Shades Freed"
74 1971 McCartney album
76 Patriot's place
77 Recycling receptacle
78 Abnormal food craving
80 The L.A. Sparks org.

81 **End of riddle**
87 "Good Will Hunting" setting
90 Delivery people, briefly
91 Totally befuddled
92 Fence stakes
93 Whole
96 Dreaded tsar
97 Between the lines
100 **Start of riddle answer**
103 Rug near a tub
107 Caesar's land
108 Lou Gehrig's 1,888
109 Striped herbivore
111 Suffix for Brooklyn
112 Cubist Rubik
113 Brisbane bud
114 **End of answer**
117 Nothing, in Monaco
118 Apropos of
119 Tex of "Looney Tunes" fame
120 Wading bird
121 A real eye sore
122 Fehr of "Presidio Med"
123 Time trials, e.g.
124 Mezzanine sights

DOWN

1 Chocolate pieces
2 Lite
3 Enough and then some
4 Wait partner
5 Magician in "The Tempest"
6 "Frank Sinatra Has a Cold" author
7 Lone Star school
8 Wooer of Olive Oyl
9 Smallish batteries
10 U-turn from NNW
11 Systemize
12 Massive mammal
13 Urban renewal target area
14 Drag queen's wear

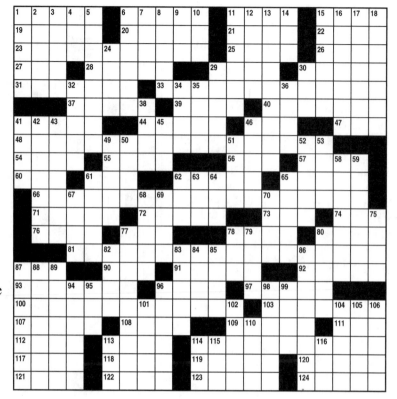

15 Impromptu bookmark
16 Have in common with
17 Emmy winner Fabray
18 Freddy Krueger, for one
24 Commoner
29 Nick Saban, e.g.
30 Irate, with "up"
32 Unmetered language
34 NFL Hall-of-Famer Ronnie
35 Ready for press
36 Awed response
38 Canis lupis
41 Man of Oman
42 Draws back
43 Bond's drink of choice
45 Construct, with "up"
46 Social climber
49 Tot watcher
50 Put in stitches
51 "Miss Peaches" James
52 "High Flying, Adored" musical

53 "You bet!"
58 Like the Arc de Triomphe flame
59 Due
61 Where Stevenson wrote "Catriona"
62 Former U.S. capital
63 Meadow mother
64 Patient sounds
65 Moriarty's hitman
67 Slippery swimmers
68 Court orders
69 "Say it ___ so!"
70 Prefix for drama
75 Kind of transit or hysteria
77 Piano of piano bars
78 Grand ___ ("Evangeline" setting)
79 "___ first you don't . . ."
80 Fury
82 Days of old
83 The privileged
84 State, in St. Lô
85 "Money ___ object"

86 Famous last words?
87 Complains sotto voce
88 Come into
89 Maura of "ER"
94 Ulster county
95 Filmmaker DuVernay
96 Destitute
98 Westminster and St. Mary's
99 NFL quarterback Derek
101 Beyond the fringe
102 Montezuma, for one
104 Anne in "Awakenings"
105 Gold Cup race place
106 "Dawson's Creek" characters
110 Irregular French verb
113 "O Sole ___"
114 Limbo need
115 Charlottesville school
116 Appomattox figure

287 CONNECTING WATERWAYS by Harvey Estes
There's a theme revealer at 120 Down.

ACROSS

1 Royal Portrush hazard
5 Thermometer site
9 Gobble, with "down"
14 Looks elated
19 Calorie-laden
20 Lawn application
21 Comic-strip Viking
22 Nostalgia stimulus
23 Jazz singer James
24 Supersonic weapon
25 Reserved
26 Get stuck
27 Time for card exchanges
31 Saint from Ávila
32 Landline phone piece
36 "The Handmaid's Tale" author
39 Anesthetized
44 Exploit
45 Indistinct complaints
47 Emulates Delilah
48 Three-card game
50 Young Darth
51 Worry for srs.
53 "The Man From U.N.C.L.E." star
55 Trial run
57 Reservations
59 AOL, e.g.
60 In groups
61 Lapel label
63 Birds and apes, e.g.
66 "The ___ Around Us": Carson
67 Kid of jazz
68 "The Night Watch" painter
73 Snake sound
76 Negative vote
77 Fix a pump
78 Latin step
82 At fever pitch
84 Green prefix
86 First lady's son
88 Spree site
89 Regulator of escaping gas
93 Locality
95 Joplin work
96 Archaeological sites
97 Take part in a plot reversal?
99 Island south of Martinique
101 Audio systems, for short
102 Campaign from town to town
104 Slight
105 Annual volume
108 Simple shelters
110 Golden Ball awardee
118 Choir section
121 Gulf ship
122 Obsidian source
123 November catchword
124 Musical show
125 Neighbor of Vatican City
126 Meadow group
127 "My stars!"
128 Phobias
129 Gives a backhand
130 Formal letter intro
131 Morse marks

DOWN

1 Bien beginning
2 Novelist ___ Mae Brown
3 When the action starts
4 Not really there
5 Uniform color
6 Chapel figure
7 Ford oval, e.g.
8 Tough opponents
9 Beyond repair
10 Permission request
11 One mo' time
12 Go lickety-split
13 Most current
14 Heights in the Mideast
15 Bridges in "Airplane!"
16 Off the wall
17 Artificial locks
18 Get a load of
28 Biblical pronouns
29 Consumerist Ralph
30 Jerry Stiller, to Ben
33 Serenaded
34 "Sanford and Son" aunt
35 Diminutive
36 Cherished cello
37 On pitch
38 Slap target, at times
40 Exchanged words
41 Braque and Picasso
42 Deck quartet
43 Maryland athlete, for short
46 Squat
48 Ethnic group of Borneo
49 Nice affirmative
52 Tend to the pudding
54 Zig or zag
56 Swabbie
58 Mudbath spot
62 Sheer quality
64 Signs up
65 JFK's predecessor
66 Shows contempt
69 London rainwear
70 Govt. broadcaster
71 Goya's duchess
72 "Miss Saigon" setting
73 K2 guide
74 Marvin Gaye's "___ Healing"
75 Sharp divide
79 Tour de France winner Pantani
80 Selma in "The Fog"
81 Chlorine's pool target
83 Copper-toned
84 Even a single time
85 ___ Crunch cereal
87 "Take the high road"
90 John Deere line
91 Winery sight
92 Name on a bomber
94 Star in Perseus
98 Increases threefold
100 Not backed up
102 ___ mitzvah
103 Neighbor of Zambia
106 Cyrano's love
107 Attendance count
109 "Over my dead body!"
111 Bowed instrument
112 "Summer and Smoke" heroine
113 Group of leopards
114 Java vessels
115 Cartoon bear
116 Coup d'___
117 Cincinnati team
118 Pet shop sound
119 Appomattox figure
120 Waterway that connects 5 theme answers

288 ENTOMOLOGY STUDY   by Linda Lather
Alternate clue for 53 Across: Master Po's young student on "Kung Fu."

ACROSS

1 "Absolutely!"
5 Gain altitude
10 "Can you do me a ___?"
15 Sorvino in "Summer of Sam"
19 "East of Eden" girl
20 A form of defamation
21 Slobber over
22 Driver in "Lincoln"
23 Wellington or Napoleon
24 Dispatch vessel
25 Debutante dance of Paris
26 Hirschfeld hidden name
27 Scarlett's "Avengers: Endgame" role
29 Faulkner novel
31 Ditz
32 Pluto, for one
34 "Ghostbusters" goops
35 "LOTR" tree
36 Rolex logo
38 Begrimes
40 Cy Young winner Martinez
43 Make butter
44 Apollo's birthplace
45 Good, in street talk
48 Grand Ole ___
49 Rodeo horse
50 One of the Seven Sages
51 Ginormous
52 Grazing ground
53 Crème de menthe drink
55 Aquarium favorite
56 Decriminalize
58 Bemoans
59 "Il Penseroso" poet
60 Speak pompously
61 Monsoonal
63 Honorific
64 "Gunsmoke" star
66 River of northern Germany
67 Penned
70 Elevator shoes
71 Annual Scripps event
74 To and ___
75 Cracow citizen
76 Scuffle
77 Zebrula dams
78 Buttonhole, say
79 "Animal Farm" setting
80 Send payment
81 Top bunk
82 "The Highwayman" poet
83 "America's Drive-In"
84 "Shop 'til you drop" episode
85 Cul-de-___
86 Feign
89 Italian rice
90 Pakistan's largest city
94 Equipment for a Twenty20 game
97 Like the U.S. Navy's reserve fleet
100 Poi base
101 Person, place, and thing
102 ___ meridian
103 Cut off
104 Warning to heed
105 Welsh dog
106 Pitchpipe user
107 Sicilian spa
108 Ginger pirate of Disneyland
109 Actress Barkin
110 Computerniks
111 Truman's was Fair

DOWN

1 "___ Dabba Do!"
2 "Don Carlos" princess
3 Like Victoria Falls
4 Breeding place
5 Assault, bear-style
6 Angry
7 "As before" in footnotes
8 "You've Made ___ Very Happy"
9 Welding tool
10 Gravlax fish
11 "___ Melancholy": Keats
12 High court returns
13 "American Sniper" setting
14 Aspect of paranoia
15 Fox sci-fi series
16 "Hands down" is one
17 Canadian jazz singer ___ Lee
18 Stockpile
28 "Stray and play" casino game
30 Maladies
33 Admit (with "up")
36 Selected
37 Box-score column at Fenway
38 Tennis legend Monica
39 Swan genus
40 Market research tool
41 Duelist's blade
42 Ziggy Marley album
43 The Twist was one
44 "Snow White" miner
45 "Dolphin kick" stroke
46 Field: Comb. form
47 Author Koontz
49 Original Ryder Cup team
50 Pirouetted
51 "Aloha!"
53 Sandwich ___
54 Balcony window
55 Pledge a tenth
57 Mountain spur
59 Tick cousins
61 Butler of fiction
62 1968 folk album
63 Yam or 100 Across
64 Grossglockner et al.
65 Uprising
66 About the eye
67 "Hollywood Squares" answer
68 Lake that borders four states
69 Ellipsis trio
71 Prefix for precious
72 Off-the-cuff
73 Mane location
76 Send up the river
78 Commonly named
80 Stone Age weapon
81 Happy days
82 First capital of Japan
83 What's base
84 Joins a jam session
85 Cutlass cousins
86 "Cattle call" respondent
87 Scaffolding
88 Discharged
89 Coloratura's pride
90 Cambodia's ___ Rouge
91 Carbon copy
92 Auburn dye
93 Utopian
95 Cat's-paw
96 Ives in "Cat on a Hot Tin Roof"
98 "It's either them ___!"
99 Spork feature

289 MR. ROY G. BIV   by Linda Lather

71 Across is also the name of a 2006 Vernor Vinge novel.

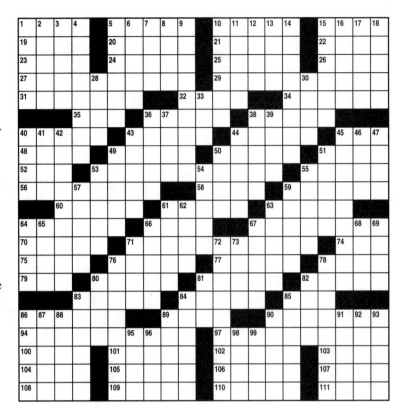

ACROSS

1 "Braveheart" group
5 Statement nos.
10 "Boston Legal" matters
15 "My Life" singer Billy
19 News-story grabber
20 Gown fabric
21 Abhorrence
22 "A Room With a View" view
23 As to
24 Playful prank
25 Montreal subway
26 "All About That ___": Meghan Trainor
27 Duke Ellington classic
29 Bobby Vinton hit
31 Detonate
32 Sweet Sixteen org.
34 Acts the coquette
35 "About when" inits.
36 Angry with
38 Find repugnant
40 Oklahoma college town
43 Place for a crown
44 Oscar winner Mirren
45 It breaks 24/7
48 "Eureka!" moments
49 Kind of vinegar
50 Smiled for a selfie
51 Former times
52 "Here's ___ in your eye!"
53 2017 Cardi B song
55 "Hit it!"
56 Annual checkup
58 Inedible cake
59 Whence zombies emerge
60 1998 Apple debuts
61 Mookie of baseball
63 "The Godfather" enforcer Luca
64 Highest North American peak
66 "Anti-art" movement
67 Back-stabbers
70 Indian cuisine dish
71 Where gold may be found?
74 Mauna ___
75 Utah's "Family City USA"
76 Sermon from Buddha
77 Plainsong
78 Stars of 7 Down
79 Signal approval
80 Practiced a trade
81 Square one
82 Brownie bunch
83 Recovered
84 Royal edicts
85 Yak genus
86 Provisional
89 "___ all due respect . . ."
90 Kodiak Islander
94 Envies
97 Neighbor of Newark
100 Raccoon's resting place
101 Hawkeye
102 "Buffy the Vampire Slayer" extra
103 Festive soiree
104 "Jimmy Crack Corn" singer
105 Barrel strip
106 Bar buy
107 Anon companion
108 Minimal change
109 Ulee's gold
110 Adds to the kitty
111 Passes for a spiker

DOWN

1 Weather, for short
2 Tanglewood site
3 ___ in the bucket
4 Uncalled-for
5 Anisimova of tennis
6 "___ Nast Traveler"
7 Queens stadium
8 Sine field
9 NFL defensive unit
10 Warfare
11 "A Passage to India" heroine
12 In ___ (undisturbed)
13 Chartres river
14 Ironed out
15 Laker great Abdul-___
16 Med school exams
17 Eventuate
18 Comes up short
28 Letter before kappa
30 Downtown sign
33 Golf, for one
36 Relating to structure
37 Supermodel Wek
38 "Belling the Cat" author
39 Shaped glass
40 Pack down
41 "No can do"
42 Chris de Burgh song (with "The")
43 Exemplar of greed
44 Guadalajara greetings
45 Purple wildflower
46 "I Am Not My Hair" singer
47 Deep desires
49 Strep bacteria
50 "The ___ thickens"
51 Agent of ferment
53 Bagel's cousin
54 Pub sign abbr.
55 Shoulder knot
57 Toady talk
59 "American Gothic" painter Wood
61 "Father of Television"
62 David Rabe's "Visiting ___"
63 Sportscaster Musburger
64 Raid rival
65 Currency since 1999
66 Old hat
67 Romanov royals
68 Elective at VPI
69 Merit badge holder
71 Make a mess of
72 Eight-faced solids
73 "Are you kidding?"
76 Like bayous
78 Rubdowns
80 Coloratura Lily
81 Rest one's dogs
82 One killed Adonis
83 Crème de la crème
84 Albert in "Tom Jones"
85 Fair-haired chaps
86 Anne Frank's hideout
87 Slider
88 Wooden tableware
89 Act the drunk driver
90 Observe Yom Kippur
91 Jack of hearts
92 Shoelace tip
93 Closes in
95 Prefix for tiller
96 Actor McGregor
98 One billion years
99 Corn disease

290 THEMELESS by Elizabeth C. Gorski

64 Across composed over 600 works before his untimely death at age 35.

ACROSS

1 Spicy tea
5 Pirate's drink
9 Writing surface
13 "Goldberg Variations" composer
19 Man of the haus
20 Notes after "do"
21 McCartney's "___ Cor Meum"
22 Yellow Teletubby
23 Pinnacle
24 Mideast gulf
25 Monument Valley's region
27 Reggae relative
28 Yani of the LPGA
29 Modern leader?
30 Fancy neckwear
31 Tightly packed
33 "Someone ___ Dream": Faith Hill hit
35 Louisiana hrs.
37 Toy (with)
39 Nobelist Curie
41 BLT spread
42 Feedbag bit
45 "Damn Yankees" vamp
46 Daughter of Lear
47 Coerces
50 Oft-torn knee part, for short
51 Berlioz's "___ in Italy"
52 Sit-up targets
53 Islamic leader
54 "Rats!"
56 Cracks down
59 Colombian city
60 "Done!"
62 "Park" where Google was founded
63 Less loony
64 "Die Zauberflöte" composer
71 "Girl Holding ___": Peale
72 Sun, for one
73 Wife of Zeus
74 Sitarist Shankar
75 2014 animated film starring Surly the Squirrel
79 In danger
83 Supreme Theban deity
85 Guitar master Paul
86 Labor groups
88 Plymouth privy
89 Relating to one's profession
91 "Histoires" composer
92 Custard tart
93 Train chasers
94 Detail, briefly
95 Central Florida city
96 Hooded snake
97 Korea founder Ki ___
98 Egypt's Gamal ___ Nasser
100 Ruth's retired number
102 Photographer Adams
106 "The Chronic" rapper
108 Vowel group
110 Office machine
113 "Swan Lake" footwear
115 Many charity gps.
116 "Carpe ___!"
117 Mumford in "Fifty Shades Darker"
118 Start of a Cockney toast
119 Quitter's word
120 Concerning
121 Most recent
122 Forever ___ day
123 "Born Free" lioness
124 Drudge

DOWN

1 "New Yorker" cartoonist Addams
2 "Darn!"
3 Armored animal
4 Anger
5 Centre Court surface
6 Savior
7 Portent
8 Fizzy mixer
9 Render harmless
10 Paris school
11 Rabbit tails
12 2015–16 NBA Coach of the Year
13 "Selena" actress, to fans
14 New York summer racing venue
15 Proscribes
16 Actor Guinness
17 "___ nome" ("Rigoletto" aria)
18 Biblical verb
26 Chocolate source
28 Stick with a kick
32 Mound stat
34 Big name in Swiss chocolate
36 Mesh
37 Envelope part
38 Scottish lake
40 Awestruck
41 Enterprise navigator
42 "Interview With History" author Fallaci
43 More sizable
44 Fun run souvenir
46 Connie's "Nashville" role
47 Totally full
48 Steak choice
49 Palace in Seville
51 Katherine of "27 Dresses"
55 Disconnected
57 Brainy
58 "Holy cow!"
61 Foot part
63 Varieties
64 Red Baron, for one
65 Psychic in "Ghost"
66 Paramours
67 Erse
68 Choreographer de Mille
69 North Sea tributary
70 Intended
75 Infield covers
76 Kickapoo Joy ___
77 All in all
78 Jessica of "7th Heaven"
80 "Don't worry about me . . ."
81 Fly high
82 Hawaiian coffee
84 Antsy
87 Keynote speeches
90 Garden invaders
92 Nemesis
95 "Friday Night Lights" setting
96 French vineyard
98 Prettify
99 Dog show category
101 Shade-loving plant
102 First victim
103 Beyoncé's "Lion King" role
104 Bellagio bandit
105 "Night" author Wiesel
107 Saturn satellite
109 Equal, in Amiens
111 Flying-related
112 Marvel superheroes
114 Hanoi holiday
116 Party tray bowlful

291 NOT-SO-NERVOUS NELLIE by Elizabeth C. Gorski

Fret and live happily ever after.

ACROSS

1 Private line?
6 Decree
10 Famous shock jock
14 TiVo products
18 Stand ___ foot (do a yoga pose)
19 Plus
21 "GQ" publisher Condé ___
22 Magic stick
23 Season as desired
25 The other way around
27 **Nellie's quip: Part I**
29 ___-pitch softball
30 Summer camp craft
31 Opt
34 Result in
38 **Quip: Part II**
42 Enterprise helmsman
43 Prudential Center site
47 Fan setting
48 Tiny fraction of a min.
49 **Quip: Part III**
52 Carpenter's gizmo
54 Rickey Henderson's original team
55 Oriole's home
56 Eye-popping paintings
61 Hairy
62 Office PC hookup
63 Ando who directed "Blue"
65 "___ Rewind" (Jack Black film)
68 **Quip: Part IV**
71 Peck away at
72 Earn
74 Crock pot top
75 Put it on the line?
77 Intuit
78 Still snoozing
80 Straightens matted hair
83 Overhauled
85 **Quip: Part V**
87 "C'est Si Bon" singer
91 Women's ___
92 Spiritual truths
93 Words of accusation
94 **Quip: Part VI**
97 "Domani" singer Julius
99 "The ___ See You": Chris Montez
100 1986 Indy 500 winner
103 Big time
104 **Quip: Part VII**
113 Cruiser's quarters
115 Tanqueray drink
116 Flap
117 Hathaway in "The Hustle"
118 Prophetic signs
119 First ruler of Normandy
120 Lemon candy
121 Peace Nobelist Eisaku
122 Formerly, once
123 "Amo, amas, I love ___": O'Keeffe

DOWN

1 Carrot on a snowman
2 Stay ___ even keel
3 Cry at an auction
4 Like many JFK flights
5 Check again
6 1980 Anne Bancroft film
7 "Vidi" translated
8 NAACP part
9 Aquarium favorite
10 Visible
11 Water carrier
12 "Semper Paratus" org.
13 One-dish meal
14 Linger over
15 Shakespearean creeps
16 Hosp. staffers
17 Protestant rel.
20 Threefold
24 Munch Museum site
26 Locked horns
28 Break this to scramble
32 Revolutionary Guevara
33 Sleuth, in slang
34 D-Day transport
35 Cash abroad
36 Shawkat of "Arrested Development"
37 Bowling variation
39 Shakespeare title opener
40 Early years
41 Personal ad shorthand
43 Cancún boy
44 Result
45 Backed (out of)
46 Compact Cadillac
50 "M*A*S*H" character
51 Nita of the silents
52 Baseball flags
53 Queens, for one
55 "No, laddie"
57 More roly-poly
58 Pop the question
59 Sorority letter
60 Pewter component
62 iPhone screen
64 "___ dance, don't . . ."
65 Air gun ammo
66 Before, to Keats
67 Thanksgiving Day guests
69 Free (of)
70 Worshiper's contribution
73 Tennis player Petrova
76 Creek at Augusta National
79 Butterhead lettuce
80 Tabloid topic
81 Opposite of exo-
82 Pepper and Bilko, e.g.
84 Bridge expert Culbertson
85 Busy, busy, busy
86 "Dalla ___ pace" (Mozart aria)
87 "Miss Saigon" heroine
88 1945 battle site, for short
89 An ill wind that blows no good
90 Osprey perch
92 Agana's island
95 Bank of Paris
96 Start of Juliet's plaint
97 Piercing
98 "Peer Gynt" dancer
101 Grisham's "___ To Kill"
102 Introvert
103 Steinbeck's middle name
105 Noteworthy time periods
106 Anagram name of Nora
107 Page-ending abbr.
108 Cheerleader's audience
109 Plane, for one
110 "Lost ___ Mancha" (2002 documentary)
111 Art supplies
112 Noncoms
113 Avg.
114 Round Table knight

292 VOICE CAST by Eva Finney
42 Down is also the voice of Fluke in "Finding Dory."

ACROSS

1 One of a Rice Krispies trio
5 Sine's reciprocal, for short
10 Clown costume
15 Sparkling wine
19 Medically induced state
20 Concerning the acreage
21 Prop for Ed Ruscha
22 Rarely seen bills
23 Annoy
24 Celestial table
25 Nickname of Scotland's capital
26 Gabriel's instrument
27 Voice of Bo Peep in "Toy Story"
29 Voice of Rapunzel in "Tangled"
31 Popular perennials
32 Ending for old or young
34 Tendency to get angry
35 Famous Bruin blueliner
36 Displayed openly
38 "Dirigo" state
40 Playground sight
43 Conflagration crime
44 Chiromancers read them
45 Title for David Beckham
48 It's often tanned
49 Gem of the Mountains
50 Flight seating option
51 Toy block
52 River of Switzerland
53 Voice of Donkey in "Shrek"
55 Meant to be
56 Squirmed
58 Court action
59 Dance wear
60 Bred winners?
61 Like the game, to Holmes
63 Not terribly important
64 KP utensil
66 Donegal island
67 City on the Gulf of Mexico
70 Hooter's hatchling
71 Voice of Elsa in "Frozen"
74 Joke
75 Bird bills
76 "Unforgettable" singers
77 Fugard's "A Lesson From ___"
78 Carte du jour
79 Noted period
80 Quiz-show group
81 Speak slowly
82 Coloratura's pride
83 Chance taker
84 Mattress name
85 Wino
86 Bach cantata highlight
89 Shade of raw linen
90 Get down on bended knee
94 Voice of Diego in "Ice Age"
97 Voice of Pops in "The Secret Life of Pets"
100 Bath waters
101 Atlas extra
102 Trotsky's sentence
103 "Cheers" beer drinker
104 Bean of India
105 Saw edge
106 Cordoned (off)
107 Markedly similar
108 Calls on
109 Greatly please
110 Part of Ringo's set
111 Places to graze

DOWN

1 Bit for a quilt, maybe
2 Ghost town population
3 Protein acid
4 Poetic retraction
5 Yellowstone vehicle
6 Dunkable snacks
7 Email status
8 Brooklyn Bridge river
9 "Saved by the Bell" set
10 Rained cats and dogs
11 Police car feature
12 V ___ Victor
13 Get better
14 Kindergarten break
15 Where charity begins
16 Dive like an osprey
17 2000 World Series manager
18 Tall tennis pro
28 Rock of Cashel locale
30 Part of YMCA
33 Maximum rating, often
36 Uniform trim
37 Flushing stadium
38 Maria Sharapova's nickname
39 McDonald of the LPGA
40 "Pygmalion" playwright
41 His pants aren't really on fire
42 Voice of Chief Bogo in "Zootopia"
43 Did some math
44 Calibrated tube
45 Voice of Pumbaa in "The Lion King"
46 "___ Around": Beach Boys
47 Reactor parts
49 Vagrant
50 Dinosaur voiced by Raymond Ochoa
51 Nigerian metropolis
53 White wading bird
54 Broadway's "Once ___ Mattress"
55 Championship match
57 Mentor of Buffy Summers
59 A bicycle's built for two
61 Mermaid voiced by Jodi Benson
62 Ballpark figures
63 "___ tov!"
64 Corn cake
65 Aquarius vessel
66 Brando's drama coach
67 Like Kilimanjaro's peaks
68 Piquancy
69 Fit of fever
71 Skye in "XOXO"
72 Moss-troopers
73 Mideast airline
76 Sweet girl of song
78 Matronly
80 Make the grade
81 "___ Rosenkavalier"
82 Bond villain Klebb
83 Accomplishments
84 Father Time's symbol
85 Leave the Union
86 President during the XYZ Affair
87 Ziegfeld offering
88 ___ fell swoop
89 Standing tall
90 Haying machine
91 Bring on reminiscences
92 Ceramics powder
93 Canticles
95 Hydroxyl compound
96 "The Thin Man" dog
98 Neuron appendage
99 Thatching palm

293 BIRTHDAY PARTIES by Eva Finney
"Happy Birthday to everyone having birthdays this year!"

ACROSS

1 Liquid asset
5 Music of the '40s
10 Saying
15 Basics
19 Domain
20 Singer whose birthday is May 5
21 Lay back
22 It'll put you into a lather
23 Sound from Sarabi
24 Join the poker game
25 Like ___ on a log
26 Vocal quality
27 Actress whose birthday is April 15
29 Actress whose birthday is October 1
31 Fez features
32 Land in el mar
34 Diminished.
35 Scene site
36 Martinique volcano
38 Whale food
40 Needed liniment
43 Noted pumpkin eater
44 "You Light Up My Life" singer
45 Golf great Venturi
48 Envisages
49 Irene in "Zorba the Greek"
50 Contract conditions
51 Running behind
52 Senator Amidala's love
53 Actress whose birthday is June 22
55 Number of hills, in Roma
56 Where jockeys mount up
58 Little bit
59 Remained firm
60 Midwest tribe
61 Card balances
63 "Hair" choreographer
64 "Jean" songwriter
66 Rhodes of "Roots"
67 Ethereal quality
70 Waldorf ___
71 Singer whose birthday is December 31
74 Rally yell
75 "___ walks into a bar . . ."
76 LED part
77 Pursued busily
78 Spirit
79 Chairman pro ___
80 "Lucky" aviator
81 Chance and Koontz
82 Peter in "The Dream Team"
83 Puts on Angie's
84 "___ Mrs. Smith" (2005)
85 Ecclesiastic robe
86 Like Spider-Man
89 Rank or file
90 Drop of liquid
94 Singer whose birthday is January 25
97 Singer whose birthday is November 23
100 Cheat
101 Build a fire under
102 TaylorMade products
103 Labored breath
104 Between engagements
105 Mulligrubs
106 Local theaters
107 "Picnic" playwright
108 Rorschach ___
109 Bridges
110 Seed cover
111 Sense of smell

DOWN

1 Inverted "v" mark
2 Chocolate shop lure
3 Clothing lines
4 Hounds
5 Volcanic rock
6 Goes over copy
7 Two-dollar window transactions
8 Mishmash
9 Out of pocket
10 Fit for farming
11 Paget in "Love Me Tender"
12 French possessive
13 Willing to try
14 Clears up
15 Like Leo
16 Help over a fence
17 Camp vessel
18 Fork out
28 Garden trespasser
30 Up to snuff
33 Spanish 101 verb
36 Elizabethan diarist
37 Catchall abbr.
38 Country divided in 1948
39 Win going away
40 Stat!
41 John in "Bumblebee"
42 Model whose birthday is June 1
43 Picnic sites
44 Red veggies
45 Singer whose birthday is October 25
46 Novel ending
47 Scholarship criterion
49 Walnut relative
50 Sulky race
51 Ascertain
53 Made a green faster
54 Bone of the lower leg
55 Way up
57 Bible version
59 Prepare mozzarella
61 Fashion plate
62 Coastal eagle
63 London newspaper
64 Sports medicine degree
65 Batting backstop
66 Wiseguys
67 "I've got half ___ to . . ."
68 Spinnaker
69 Brake part
71 By ___ of (due to)
72 Gum flavor
73 ___ Bator
76 Bridge plays
78 Makeshift lock picker
80 2019 Super Bowl
81 "Forgot About ___": Eminem
82 Special-interest group
83 Lucy of nursery rhyme
84 Unlikely donors
85 "Charmed" actress Milano
86 Nail biting, e.g.
87 Say "somethin' "?
88 Moon valleys
89 Mike in "The Hangover"
90 "The Balcony" playwright
91 Heavenly combiner
92 Pulmonary pair
93 Floral Lauder perfume
95 Surgeon General under Reagan
96 "Rooster Cogburn" heroine
98 "Dies ___"
99 High court returns

ADOLESCENT AUGMENTATION   by Harvey Estes
The answer to the riddle sounds like the opposite of a term for "old money."

ACROSS

1 Like some champagne glasses
7 Most kindly
13 Morally upright
20 Likely to change
21 Queued up
22 Farmers' market buy
23 Like music without a key
24 Male companion
25 Meteorological effects
26 **Start of a riddle**
28 **More of riddle**
29 Gets hard
30 Exercise accessory
31 "Friends in Low Places" singer
35 Netanyahu's nickname
36 "Shut up!"
38 Narrow walk
42 **More of riddle**
48 Lamprey lurer
49 AC unit
50 Lao-tse's "way"
51 By-the-book
52 Great Salt Lake, e.g.
56 Cooking meas.
57 Depp's "Finding Neverland" role
58 Sch. subj.
59 Clubs, e.g.
60 Hairy twin in Genesis
62 Arno crosser
63 Back-to-school mo.
65 **More of riddle**
68 Where to find Munch work
71 Dogpatch denizen Hawkins
73 Circus cries
74 Min. parts
76 VIP on the Hill
77 Amerindian language
79 Debate side
80 Feeling fine
82 Spare change
83 Make an offer
84 Eccentricity
86 Strip away, as confidence
87 **More of riddle**
93 Large-scale
94 Leaves the premises
95 CEO, often
96 Presidential middle name
97 Night class subj.
98 "Hey, over here!"
102 **End of riddle**
106 **Answer to riddle**
111 Went around
113 Became eligible for repentance
114 Dirty mind locale
115 Most accessible
116 Hebrew speaker
117 TV pal of Jerry and George
118 Sleeve adornments
119 Noah of "The Daily Show"
120 Eradicate

DOWN

1 Second features?
2 Shaping tool
3 Ashcan's target
4 Adds color
5 Jack in "The Comancheros"
6 Mark the boundaries of
7 Lingerie item
8 Part of an OK
9 Shrewd
10 Slangy suffix
11 Like salt in water
12 Afternoon time
13 Air quality org.
14 One who works in a cab
15 Israeli dances
16 Teen fave
17 Bent lock
18 Antioxidant berry
19 "___ we forget . . ."
27 Clark, to Lombard
32 Recovers from a workout
33 From the keg
34 Estefan's eight
35 Cow pads
36 Army NCO
37 Paper promise
38 Mexican map word
39 Cyberbullying, e.g.
40 Asian language
41 In good health
42 Houdini's birth name
43 For this reason
44 Earth, for one
45 Three R's supporter
46 Knicks org.
47 Buck heroine
53 Refused to budge
54 Contribute to the birth of
55 DDE's WW2 sphere
56 "Pravda" news provider
57 Muck up
60 Royal educator
61 Librarian's admonition
62 Ready, in Rouen
64 Rides
66 Lumberjack
67 "Anchors Aweigh" org.
69 3-time U.S. Open winner
70 Well-pitched
72 Cook's smidgen
75 Planter's needs
77 Rip-off
78 New Rochelle college
79 Word used in dating
80 Frozen dessert
81 Season opener
83 False god in Judges
84 ___ kwon do
85 R.E.M.'s former label
88 Himalayan height
89 Less friendly
90 One over limit
91 Sky bear
92 In up to one's neck
96 Actress Pfeiffer
98 "She loves me" decider
99 Composer Erik
100 Pheromone
101 Wish count
102 Lang of Smallville
103 In charge of
104 Linguist Chomsky
105 Young lady
107 "My treat!"
108 A coll. is part of it
109 Emphatic no
110 Wield the scepter
112 Some NFL linemen
113 Atlantic crosser of old

AFTERNOON OF A FAUNA   by Harvey Estes
. . . with apologies to Claude Debussy.

ACROSS

1 Rice dish
6 Soldier's stir
10 Achilles, e.g.
14 Get through to
19 Stradivari's mentor
20 Magazine section
21 Crude cartel
22 Perk
23 Piece with staggered melodies
24 Stick in the fridge
25 Straight up
26 Loser to Truman
27 Egregious act of corvine cleansing?
31 Spanish hero, with "El"
32 Brit breaks
33 Go separate ways
34 Sci-fi author Arthur
38 Biographical focus
40 Vehicle for new vehicles
44 Fresh Pony Express shift?
48 "What a relief!"
49 "SVU" rapper
50 Half of the Odd Couple
51 U.K. member
52 Hit, in the Bible
54 "Of ___ Sing"
56 Comedian Allen
57 Trial copies
60 Slumlord's declaration?
61 Hospital work
63 Willingly
64 Screen lines
66 Wasteful legislation that's almost laughable?
71 Betraying woe
72 Lacking bumps
73 R.E.M.'s "The ___ Love"
74 Dos follower
75 Served soup
77 CD's offering
78 Site of many Goyas
83 Very affordable jewelry
85 Crude material
86 Soda insert
88 Anticipatory nights
89 TV spots
90 Institiution for aspiring bass vocalists?
95 Unwrap in a hurry
97 Brontë heroine
98 John's "Grease" costar
99 Town on the Thames
100 Hot pie place
102 Kleenex layer
103 Bugs in Adam and Eve's garden?
112 Nostalgic trend
113 Not sloppily
114 Cafeteria worker
115 Wined and dined
117 All gone
118 Earthenware jar
119 "The Court Jester" star
120 For the birds
121 Commercials
122 Knocks on the door
123 Toots of crosswords
124 Ukrainian city

DOWN

1 Logger's boot
2 Apple product
3 Turner of Tinseltown
4 On the summit of
5 Like Morris the Cat
6 Across-the-board
7 Drumbeat succession
8 Bit of news
9 Try to make the team
10 Accord maker
11 Tools for duels
12 Like Hitchcock's window
13 Gardener of song
14 "Serve One Another" org.
15 Brings to bear
16 "That's ___-edged sword"
17 Hands at sea
18 Bales fescue
28 Connect with
29 Coral habitat
30 Lot in life
34 Word after "lit" at college
35 Walesa of Polish politics
36 Helm location
37 Mortgage consideration
38 More frilly
39 Mosque figure
40 It survived Symplegades
41 "Airport" novelist
42 Wayne's world?
43 Puts an edge on
45 "CHiPs" star
46 This point forward
47 Switch words
53 Small sum
55 Too sentimental
57 Accumulated, with "up"
58 Head-on
59 Not loco
62 Brother of Seth
63 Tears down
65 Record problem
66 Easter event
67 Texas oil city
68 Take a load off
69 Find on a dig
70 Bill of bluegrass
71 Irish patron, briefly
76 Bump off
77 "Like ___ not"
79 Altered mtge.
80 Tel ___–Jaffa
81 Boston Marathon winner Linden
82 Job conditions org.
84 You can feel them
86 Loan sharks
87 "Mrs. Dalloway" author
91 Well-informed about
92 Impeachment trial juror
93 Can unit
94 Take off
96 Have second thoughts
100 Take too much off the top
101 Tiny amounts
102 Bluffer's game
103 Vein contents
104 Sow's opposite
105 "Suffice ___ say . . ."
106 1970 hit by the Kinks
107 Biblical skipper
108 Donald Duncan's toy
109 PBS science show
110 Raise a sweat
111 House position
116 Inherited chain

296 THEMELESS by Harvey Estes

20 Across was a line used by Ross Perot in his 1992 presidential campaign.

ACROSS

1 Ham operator skill
10 Cramps, e.g.
16 Plumbing passage
20 "Spill it!"
21 Length of service
22 Way to come
23 Modernizes
24 Harvest machine
25 Superman's alter ego
26 Back-to-back
27 Martini item
29 Spiral notebook feature
31 Start of a legal conclusion
33 Met performance
35 Subject to limitations
36 Company dinnerware
39 Isolated from the crowd
42 Messing of "Will and Grace"
43 Time-consuming
44 Black suit
46 "Dude!"
47 Land in the lake
48 Beast that bore Balaam
49 Sheepskin holders
50 Cool off, as a fad
53 Matches a poker bet
54 Grow up
56 Pride's place
57 Wooden piece
59 Speak sharply to
60 Makes one's own
63 Shashlik sticks
68 Loosen a corset
69 In a state of mental collapse
71 Crown material
72 Equivocates.
74 Tomcat in "Cats"
75 City in NW Italia
76 Moulton or Rogen
78 Air homophone
79 Good place for cruising
81 Off-rd. transports
85 Coat with flour
87 Composes
88 "I ___ lineman for the county . . ."
89 Online discussions
91 "___ you serious?"
92 Creek, for one
93 Tommy's gun
94 Matisse or Rousseau
95 Cough syrup measure
98 Stalks in the marsh
99 Tide movement
101 Press pass, e.g.
102 Apply, as a patch
105 Hard laborers
107 Metabolism type
109 Milestone locale
113 Ticket to ride
114 Concern of some agencies
116 Debt-ridden
118 Roasting place
119 Fleecy fabric
120 Perching bird
121 Musical based on "La Bohème"
122 Odometer increments
123 The Flash, notably

DOWN

1 Bog down
2 Blood moon, to some
3 Capetown currency
4 Easing off the gas
5 #1 Oak Ridge Boys hit
6 Stop
7 Hall's "Maneater" partner
8 Dr. of the rap world
9 Pump name in Ottawa
10 Barber pole feature
11 In a pet
12 Oxygen eschewer
13 Chow down
14 Horse show
15 Cursive curlicue
16 Lethargy
17 Like the coyote melon
18 Needle dropper
19 Petitions
28 Chops (off)
30 Center of Caesar's boast
32 "Doonesbury" cartoonist
34 High hair
36 Stops talking
37 Shout of adoration
38 Set up for service
40 Delivery drs.
41 Balls hit out of bound
44 Like the lunar surface
45 Back muscle
49 Adorns
50 Disapprove of
51 Properly pitched
52 Stop and smell the roses
55 Words before arms
56 Fairway bend
58 Dovetails
61 Trial evidence
62 Remarks, in slang
64 Political district
65 Dubai, for one
66 Appointed again
67 "Just do it" and more
70 Bailiwicks
73 Classic guitar, briefly
77 "California, ___ Come"
80 Deacon's wear
81 Deeply desired
82 "The Star-Spangled Banner" ending
83 Jackson successor
84 Vociferous
86 Sue Grafton's "D"
87 ___-Magnon
90 Be a squealer
92 Cicero's garment
93 Fax users
96 Stop the flow of
97 Vermicelli et al.
98 Emulated Simba
100 Insinuate
103 Degauss a tape
104 Retrogressing
106 Garage event
108 Puckered pair
110 Stand in line
111 "Alfred" composer
112 River of Flanders
115 RN's assistant
117 Nod off

WEEK LINKS   by Victor Fleming

Another clue for 33 Down would be: 1972 hit song.

ACROSS

1 No walk in the park
5 Two-time loser to Ike
10 "George of the Jungle" elephant
14 Canoeing site
18 Dust Bowl refugee
19 Having gotten on
20 Russian river
21 Epiphanies
22 American evangelist (1862–1935)
24 Corrida shouts
25 Boutique department
26 A single bite
27 Furance fans
29 Tale that goes on and on
30 Major works
32 Neighborhood of Make-Believe monarch
34 Early computer
36 "The Hobbit" actor Turner
39 Pilfered booty
40 Detective Inspector on "Endeavour"
43 Fashion designer Ecko
44 Bentley in "The Hunger Games"
47 Nomology study
48 Mexican homes
49 Embarrassed
50 '80s Chrysler models
52 Tribe for whom a state is named
53 Buddy-buddy
55 Paid admission
56 "Desert Fox" Rommel
57 Sunporches
59 Get excited
61 Grill favorites
62 Morticia's daughter
66 Detour
69 Cause of death in "A Quiet Place"
70 ". . . old woman who lived ___"
74 "If ___ could kill!"
75 Saucy
76 Pie nut
78 That muchacha
79 Ice-fishing tool
80 Cuprite, e.g.
81 "It ___ hit me yet"
83 Spasms
84 Buddy, slangily
85 Viking Ship Museum city
87 Consort of 32 Across
90 "Ice Age" sabertooth
91 Spur wheel
92 Where the euphoric walk
93 Top pick of the first MLB draft (1965)
97 Birthplace of Penélope Cruz
100 Nasty, as a mood
101 Choose paper over plastic?
104 Guise
108 Sharp personal criticism
109 Washbasin
110 "Looking For Mr. Goodbar" Oscar nominee
112 African hartebeest
113 "Understood"
114 "Rise" trumpeter
115 Like the Nefud
116 It's bought in bars
117 Tree home
118 Up the ante
119 Like jungle vines

DOWN

1 Homemade Halloween costume
2 Similar
3 Ruffle the feathers of
4 Shoulder muscles
5 Adjoins
6 Presentee
7 Young kiltie
8 Oman resident
9 Pastoral writing
10 Strand at a chalet
11 Dame Mirren
12 Swampy tract
13 Look like
14 Skips town
15 In the future
16 Roo's mom
17 Bar exam unit
19 Per se
23 Bother with barking
28 Approval
31 On the fresh side
33 2019 box-office hit
34 Odist's Muse
35 Handrail support
37 First lady McKinley
38 "___ Kapital"
40 Annual shot targets
41 Bruin in the Rose Bowl
42 Dorm staff, briefly
43 Dispensed
44 Guitar pedal
45 Composer Satie
46 Payroll dept. IDs
49 Pro___
51 Leafy vegetable
53 Where media reps gather
54 "Angels in America" concern
55 "Inner City Blues" musician
58 Not sleeping
59 Cut a bit to fit
60 Head for Vegas?
61 Capital of Yemen
63 Felipe's first month
64 Needing liniment
65 Judicial opinions
66 Sing, so to speak
67 "Not on ___ life!"
68 Okefenokee Swamp critter
71 Supermodel Klum
72 "Alley Oop" character
73 Walk in the park
75 Marchlike dance
76 Writing attributed to David
77 Minnesota twins?
81 Turn left
82 "___ you serious!?"
83 Economic conflict
86 Visits briefly
87 Veggie burger bean
88 Sped toward
89 Kwanzaa principle
90 Guide to the heavens
91 Shuttlecock whacker
93 Corrodes
94 Block house
95 "Bewitched" aunt
96 Units of force
98 Cathedral sections
99 Eminem mentor
102 General wear?
103 Kind of hoop
105 Seneca tutored him
106 Banana peel mishap
107 Countercurrent
111 Prefix with glottis

298 BOARD MEMBERS by Eva Finney

53 Across is listed "vulnerable" on the IUCN Red List of Threatened Species.

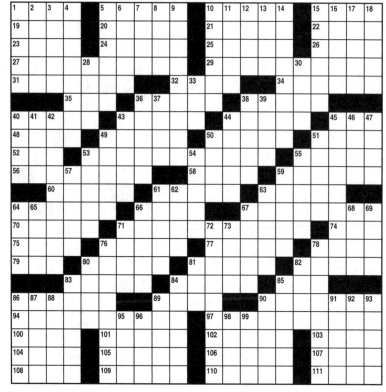

ACROSS

1 Islamic commander
5 Drink noisily
10 Made like a crow
15 "Oy!"
19 Rat cousin
20 Tippy craft
21 Pontiff's garb
22 Insulting tip
23 ___-washed jeans
24 Player
25 Eton, to Harrow
26 Sugar source
27 "___ to Buffalo" ("42nd Street" song)
29 State dessert of Florida
31 Cinco de Mayo fare
32 Guadalajara cheers
34 Let off steam
35 Rotter
36 Apple gadget
38 Cause of black ice
40 Housing for nuns
43 Argue in court
44 Snellen eye ___
45 Uzbek, prev.
48 Nippy
49 Asian cobra
50 Like bathwater
51 Tres plus cinco
52 Cenozoic ___
53 Himalayan cat
55 Norwegian toast
56 Paper parts
58 Blanchett in "Elizabeth"
59 Too flattering
60 Mardi Gras group
61 Dr. Austin portrayer on "Chicago Hope"
63 Troop encampment
64 Cruise ship quarters
66 "It Must Be Him" singer
67 NYC's Avenue of the ___
70 Maria's "West Side Story" friend
71 Wonderland character
74 ___ Dhabi
75 Read carefully
76 ___ and the Pacemakers
77 Page of "Inception"
78 Sitcom horse
79 Culminate
80 Lacking zest
81 Showy perennial
82 Conroy's "The Prince of ___"
83 Puts in order
84 Solemnly promise
85 D'Amato who trained 93 Down
86 "Long Day's Journey Into Night" playwright
89 Apple waste
90 Like the best wallets?
94 One way to ride a horse
97 Peter Venkman's portrayer
100 Sharpens cheddar
101 Water wheel
102 Danny's "Taxi" role
103 Mireille on "Hanna"
104 Polite guy
105 Took some courses?
106 Economics curve
107 Word form for "Chinese"
108 Anna's sister in "Frozen"
109 Tot's bedtime request
110 Clairvoyants
111 Spotted

DOWN

1 "Belay!"
2 Starbucks order
3 Hipbone
4 Ashamed
5 Attacked El Capitan
6 Football features
7 Golden Rule preposition
8 It's over the attic
9 Punch holes in
10 Doozy
11 Lady Gaga's sign
12 Like perms
13 Mideast airline
14 FedEx notification
15 Mark over a vowel
16 Was a bounder?
17 "It's the Hard-Knock Life" musical
18 Noble mount
28 Celebrity chef Bobby
30 Speak with
33 Long-lasting light
36 Aardvark features
37 French eye
38 Go halfsies
39 "Dragnet" org.
40 "Pocket rockets" in poker
41 Put to sleep, so to speak
42 "Take these broken wings . . ." song
43 Prostrate
44 Ring-tailed critter
45 Pebble Beach course record?
46 Smoke and mirrors
47 ___-poly
49 Has down pat
50 Quarrel
51 Striped zoo animal
53 City near Florence
54 An earth tone
55 Stylish
57 Like some dad jokes
59 Black-and-tan mug
61 Nixon defense secretary
62 Pretentiously hip
63 Fireplace bit
64 Boy Wonder's wear
65 In a while
66 Comedian Rock
67 Better equipped
68 "One clover, and ___ . . .": Dickinson
69 Beer, slangily
71 Turned on the waterworks
72 Takes after
73 Utah ski resort
76 Leis
78 Paramour
80 Crimson Tide rivals
81 Aurora borealis reaction
82 Nobelist from Cape Town
83 Noontime ritual in Tijuana
84 High school honey
85 Rink spins
86 Kansas river
87 Brexit Party's Farage
88 Wonderlands
89 More cunning
90 Leaflet
91 Banks of baseball
92 Lyons river
93 Boxing's "Iron Mike"
95 Parts of DIY
96 SPECTRE villain
98 Orchid genus
99 Olympic sled

ACROSS

1 Captain's position
5 The Pineapple Isle
10 See 7 Down
15 Mizzen, e.g.
19 Auricular
20 They make chemists see red?
21 Festoon
22 Anon companion
23 Catch some rays
24 Hackneyed
25 Unreasoning fear
26 Trident part
27 1976 Kool & the Gang hit
29 Nickname of Ernie Els
31 Space Needle city
32 Novel by Herman Melville
34 Aerial photography craft
35 Ending for talk or pant
36 Office runner
38 Dull and dismal, to Donne
40 Bat one's eyes
43 Toddler's word
44 Twist in "Oliver Twist"
45 Dorothy Parker, e.g.
48 Cut off
49 "Shrek" princess
50 Clown prop
51 Tatting fabric
52 Hrs. in Quebec
53 Robert Frost poem
55 Pottery class projects
56 They're on the ball?
58 Overly smarmy
59 They're worth seeing
60 Swiss mathematician (1707–83)
61 Well-marbled
63 More than ache
64 Chock-full
66 Miss Universe wear
67 Ten cubed
70 Brotherly love
71 Roads less traveled
74 "My dear fellow"
75 Spot for an address
76 About half of all humans
77 Physically ejects
78 It may be before one's time
79 Northeast ending
80 Moroccan hub
81 Scacchi or Garbo
82 Muscular power
83 Grew dim
84 Not quite wasted
85 IV units
86 Nautilus relatives
89 Lilith portrayer on "Cheers"
90 Apple pie order
94 1943 Triple Crown winner
97 "Marnie" actress
100 Was a snitch
101 Third from the Sun
102 Kondopoga's lake
103 ___ avis
104 End of a threat
105 Ballot listing
106 Everglades bird
107 P&L preparers
108 Industrial giant
109 Ore-Ida's ___ Tots
110 Offshore silhouettes
111 Charlie Brown flies one

DOWN

1 Guthrie's "___ Lullaby"
2 Bivouac stop
3 Simile center
4 "I'm a Survivor" singer
5 Wrappers on cans
6 Make ___ for (advocate)
7 French fashion house (with 10-A)
8 Reliever Ottavino
9 Land in the Irish Sea
10 "Jurassic Park" predator
11 British Columbia neighbor
12 Volcano apex
13 Corn holder
14 Minor event
15 Celestial streaker
16 For the birds
17 Intuit
18 Deuce toppers
28 Cancel a dele
30 White rhinoceros color
33 "Marry ___ Little"
36 They're often grouped with services
37 Prefix for present
38 How deadpan humor is delivered
39 Sub base?
40 Kind of market
41 Unsalvageable
42 By and large
43 Forty-niner
44 It's "kicking" Sicily
45 Sink
46 "Law & Order: SVU" star
47 Thomas Hardy heroine
49 Honored in a big way
50 One of the "M*A*S*H" cast
51 Nigerian seaport
53 Bench-clearer
54 Fans of the Cure
55 McAfee target
57 Sugar cubes
59 They're fired but never hired
61 Characteristic
62 Puts in a request
63 Eta follower
64 Alaska's state gem
65 Culture medium
66 First course
67 On a short fuse
68 Nest of pheasants
69 Teen sleuth Nancy
71 Nursling
72 78 Down sinkers
73 Has regrets
76 Crystal-clear
78 German battleship of WW2
80 Lost in thought
81 Male cat
82 Union pariah
83 "Sir Duke" singer
84 Kind of ball
85 Spiked shoes
86 Quarterfinalists, e.g.
87 Puts on ice
88 City NW of Muskogee
89 Oscar winner Davis
90 Illusionist Criss
91 Zebra giraffe
92 Purge, Pied Piper–style
93 Clean the slate
95 Rube Goldberg's Palooza
96 Eram, eras, ___
98 Meryl's "Holocaust" role
99 Ethereal prefix

300 BIG APPLE HOT SPOT   by Pam Klawitter
. . . and that hot spot can be found at 69 Across.

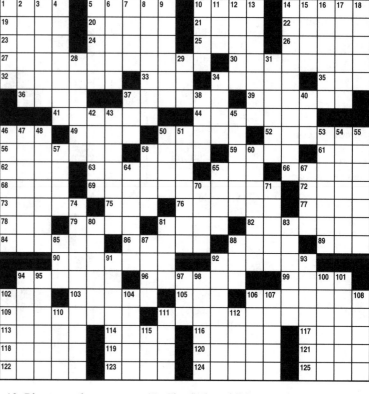

ACROSS

1 SpaceX partner, at times
5 Red rice of India
10 Wild guess
14 Throws in the cards
19 Compost bin filler
20 Think tank output
21 Silver finish?
22 Blockhead
23 Lint catcher
24 Darlings
25 Carpet layer's measurement
26 ___-Dame de Paris
27 Crafter's JPEG logo
30 Academy of ___ in the Fields
32 Exploit
33 "Ready" follower
34 Arthur ___ Doyle
35 Zodiac sun sign
36 Bob Dylan's "Gates of ___"
37 Instead (of)
39 Sumac symptoms
41 Greek god of terror
44 Casual Friday discard
46 French riot-control org.
49 "La La Land" song
50 VP Agnew
52 Corrodes
56 Apprentice
58 Flock of mallards
59 "Cosmos" author Sagan
61 It's crossed in boats
62 Periodic table fig.
63 Sugar or flour, e.g.
65 Nonverbal agreement
66 Vacationer's co-op
68 They rarely pass the bar
69 Big Apple hot spot
72 Ever so many
73 Blue Jay pitching great Dave
75 Ding-a-ling
76 Closing time for many parks
77 Oompah sounder
78 Knighted actor McKellen
79 Christian rel.
81 Hopping John ingredients
82 Conference handout
84 Platitude
86 Online greeting
88 Mother of Hermes
89 Hot time in Le Havre
90 Offtrack tire changers
92 Talk-radio feature
94 Mouse
96 Begrudged
99 Salon request
102 God, in Vatican City
103 Wee nips of Scotch
105 Schumann's "Fantasy ___ Major"
106 Cause of a blackout
109 Nepotistic appointee
111 Gadget to increase efficiency
113 Conductor Leinsdorf
114 Surmounting
116 Mexican newspaper
117 ___-Seltzer
118 Rocky ridge
119 African hartebeest
120 Drawn-out attack
121 Reba ___ McEntire
122 Eastern Canadian provinces (with "The")
123 Part of ASAP
124 Fronton fare
125 Father of 41 Across

DOWN

1 Refrain from
2 Make it big
3 Prepped a house for sale
4 Had high hopes
5 King with a gilt complex
6 "River Lea" singer
7 11 am and 3 pm, in London
8 Highland wear
9 Verbally attack
10 Make a trade
11 Road sealant
12 Playground comeback
13 Cool dude of the '50s
14 UK rival of "The Wall Street Journal"
15 Sign of a gas leak
16 Stuart of kiddie lit
17 Flat-bottomed rowboats
18 Shorthand specialist
28 Catch a podcast
29 2001, in movie credits
31 Topic
34 Cardholder on stage
37 Free electron
38 Chisholm Trail town
40 ___ up (miffed)
42 Start of a courtroom conclusion
43 E.B. White's "elixir of quietude"
45 Swiss Miss products
46 It stands the test of time
47 Check the addition
48 "Great" Duvall role
50 Fifth notes
51 News conference
53 ___ mile
54 Stunt pilot
55 Like most Olympic gymnasts
57 "The Bachelor" handout
58 Small barracuda
60 Endocrine gland
64 Class clown
65 "Call the Midwife" roles
67 Extreme dislike
70 Campus hub
71 Cybercommerce
74 No longer in fashion
80 "Great" czar
81 Man who would be queen?
83 ___ d'hôtel
85 Cost-of-living fig.
87 Cyclic trio
88 One in a red state?
91 Forerunners of 44 Across
92 Patron saint of music
93 State of total bliss
94 GMC pickup
95 ___-than-thou
97 By way of
98 Back a business
100 Roofer's gun
101 Touch with a feather
102 Alice's adventure, for one
104 Words of agreement
106 Disco suffix
107 Sits around
108 Does a casino job
110 When Hamilton sings "My Shot"
111 Era or epoch
112 Minute pt. of a minute
115 Granada gold

ANSWERS

FOREWORD

I	C	E	D		G	C	H	A	T		S	O	F	T
P	A	N	E		O	H	A	R	E		C	R	A	W
O	P	T	S		J	E	T	T	A		I	O	T	A
D	E	E	P	S	I	X			S	N	O	P	E	S
			R	O	E		M	B	A		E	R	R	
A	G	I	T	A	T	I	O	N		C	R	O	C	S
W	O	N		S	O	X	X	O	N	E	A	D	A	Y
A	U	G		O	N	O	X	X	I	S		U	R	L
K	L	E	E	N	E	X	O	O	P	S		C	E	P
E	D	I	C	T		E	L	I	S	A	B	E	T	H
	T	O	W		D	E	L		R	E	S			
S	C	H	N	O	Z			T	O	Y	C	A	R	S
O	R	E	O		A	S	I	A	N		A	T	O	P
B	E	R	M		P	E	N	N	E		M	I	L	A
S	E	X	Y		S	A	C	K	S		E	E	L	S

1

S	P	A	D	E	S		P	E	O	N		S	A	G
K	I	M	O	N	O		O	A	H	U		C	U	E
I	N	P	U	T	S		P	R	O	M		O	N	E
		B	R	O	K	E	N	H	E	A	R	T	S	
M	I	S	T	Y		L	Y	E		R	I	N	S	E
A	T	M	S		P	I	E	R	R	O	T			
C	S	I		F	O	N	D		O	U	C	H	E	S
H	O	T	W	I	R	E		P	I	N	H	O	L	E
O	N	H	I	R	E		H	A	L	O		N	I	X
		P	E	S	T	E	R	S		L	O	D	E	
S	T	E	E	P		A	I	S		A	I	R	E	D
L	O	N	D	O	N	B	R	I	D	G	E			
A	R	E		K	A	L	E		D	A	S	H	E	S
B	A	M		E	T	E	S		A	T	T	I	R	E
S	H	Y		R	O	T	S		Y	E	O	M	E	N

2

C	H	O	I	R		A	W	L		S	M	I	T	E
H	O	R	N	E		C	O	Y		K	O	R	A	N
O	R	A	N	G	E	H	U	E		A	B	O	U	T
P	S	T		E	V	E	N		S	T	I	N	T	S
S	T	E	R	N	E		D	O	W	E	L			
		E	C	R	U		S	I	D	E	B	A	R	
H	E	A	V	Y		D	E	A	N		L	I	M	O
A	X	L	E		A	D	A	G	E		I	D	E	S
T	I	E	R		P	E	T	E		K	E	E	N	E
S	T	E	E	P	E	R		S	A	N	G			
		W	U	R	S	T		S	E	E	S	A	W	
A	R	M	O	R	Y		H	A	H	A		E	T	A
L	O	I	R	E		N	I	C	E	D	E	R	B	Y
F	O	R	M	S		E	R	R		E	V	I	A	N
A	T	E	S	T		O	D	E		D	A	N	T	E

3

P	U	F	F	S		F	E	M		T	R	O	O	P
A	K	I	T	A		A	M	A		H	E	N	N	A
T	R	A	D	I	T	I	O	N		U	M	B	E	R
H	A	S		L	I	T	T	L	E	G	I	R	L	S
S	I	C	S		T	H	E	Y	D		S	E	A	L
		N	O	T	S	O			I	N	S	A	N	E
E	S	A	U		C	H	I	C	O		K	E	Y	
		T	E	A	F	O	R	T	W	O				
S	T	S		D	R	O	N	E		O	M	A	R	
H	O	L	D	E	M			P	R	I	Z	E		
O	B	O	E		O	M	A	N	I		T	A	L	K
E	L	E	C	T	R	I	C	I	T	Y		L	E	E
P	A	G	E	R		S	T	E	A	M	H	E	A	T
A	M	I	N	E		D	O	C		C	E	A	S	E
C	E	N	T	S		O	R	E		A	N	S	E	L

4

S	A	N	E	R		P	E	G	S		N	A	P	E
E	C	O	L	E		E	D	I	E		A	R	A	L
T	H	U	M	B	D	R	I	V	E		R	E	D	S
S	E	N	S	O	R		T	E	S	T	C	A	S	E
			O	O	H		T	A	O	S				
K	N	U	C	K	L	E	D	O	W	N		S	O	S
N	O	N	O		L	E	E		S	A	T	I	R	E
O	L	D	E	R		L	I	L		L	O	R	A	X
T	I	E	D	U	P		S	I	S		N	E	N	E
S	E	R		P	A	L	M	S	P	R	I	N	G	S
			P	E	S	O		P	I	E				
E	S	P	R	E	S	S	O		R	I	O	T	E	D
A	H	O	Y		K	E	P	T	O	N	H	A	N	D
R	O	L	O		E	R	I	E		I	N	T	O	A
P	E	E	R		Y	S	E	R		N	O	I	S	Y

5

S	P	C	A		G	A	S	P		A	G	N	E	W
A	L	U	G		E	C	H	O		P	R	O	L	E
T	A	B	H	U	N	T	E	R		P	E	R	I	L
S	T	E	A	D	I	E	D		T	E	E	M	E	D
			D	U	D		L	E	A	N				
S	H	A	D	E	S		C	H	A	R	A	D	E	S
T	U	D	O	R		P	E	A	S		R	A	V	I
E	L	A	N		T	E	N	S	E		R	I	O	T
E	L	M	O		R	O	S	A		P	O	L	K	A
P	O	S	T	P	O	N	E		S	A	W	Y	E	R
			E	L	L	Y		B	T	U				
T	U	N	N	E	L		D	I	A	L	O	G	U	E
A	N	I	T	A		W	O	R	K	S	H	I	F	T
T	U	N	E	S		A	R	T	E		I	G	O	T
A	M	O	R	E		R	A	H	S		O	I	S	E

6

N	O	A	H		C	H	E	R	T		A	H	A	B
O	M	N	I		R	A	C	E	R		N	A	R	A
R	O	T	C		A	R	R	A	U		A	N	N	S
M	O	S	C	O	W	M	U	L	E		T	K	O	S
			U	A	L		M	U	S	H	Y			
S	A	P	P	H	I	R	E		P	E	E	P	E	R
A	D	A		U	N	B	A	R		A	M	A	L	E
R	A	I	L		G	I	G	O	T		A	N	S	A
A	N	N	A	N		S	E	L	I	G		K	I	D
H	O	K	I	E	R		R	E	P	L	A	Y	E	D
			I	D	L	E	R		P	U	B			
B	U	L	B		J	U	N	G	L	E	B	I	R	D
O	L	L	A		E	M	I	L	E		O	B	I	E
O	N	E	C		C	O	N	O	R		T	E	T	E
M	A	R	K		T	R	A	P	S		S	T	A	R

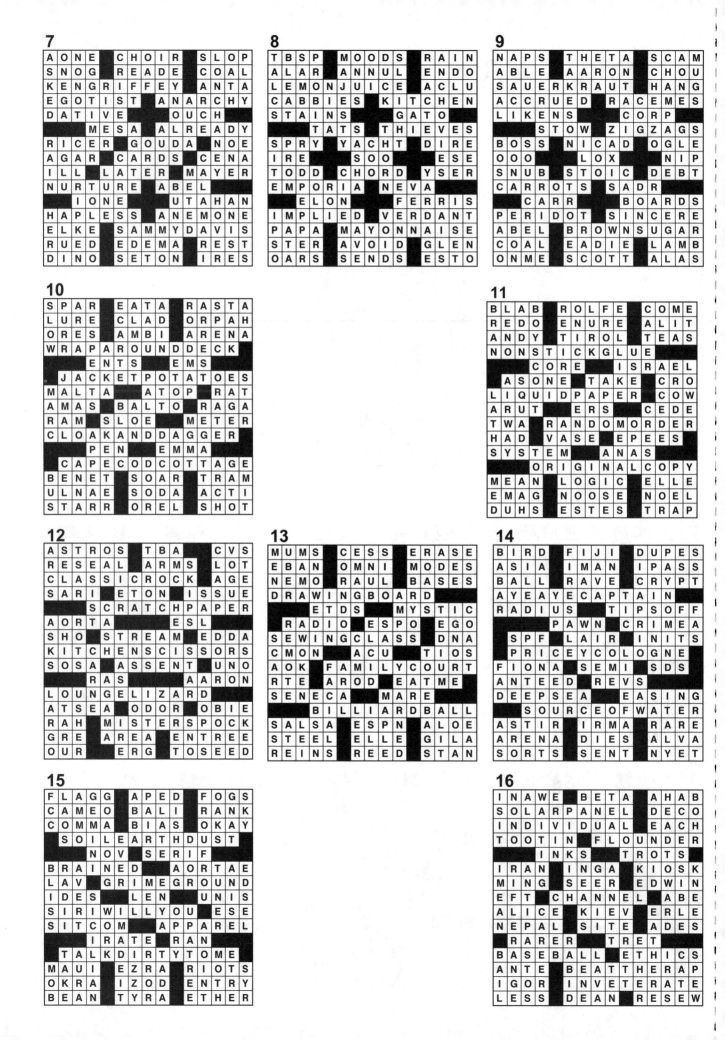

7

A	O	N	E		C	H	O	I	R		S	L	O	P
S	N	O	G		R	E	A	D	E		C	O	A	L
K	E	N	G	R	I	F	F	E	Y		A	N	T	A
E	G	O	T	I	S	T		A	N	A	R	C	H	Y
D	A	T	I	V	E			O	U	C	H			
			M	E	S	A		A	L	R	E	A	D	Y
R	I	C	E	R		G	O	U	D	A		N	O	E
A	G	A	R		C	A	R	D	S		C	E	N	A
I	L	L		L	A	T	E	R		M	A	Y	E	R
N	U	R	T	U	R	E		A	B	E	L			
		I	O	N	E			U	T	A	H	A	N	
H	A	P	L	E	S	S		A	N	E	M	O	N	E
E	L	K	E		S	A	M	M	Y	D	A	V	I	S
R	U	E	D		E	D	E	M	A		R	E	S	T
D	I	N	O		S	E	T	O	N		I	R	E	S

8

T	B	S	P		M	O	O	D	S		R	A	I	N
A	L	A	R		A	N	N	U	L		E	N	D	O
L	E	M	O	N	J	U	I	C	E		A	C	L	U
C	A	B	B	I	E	S		K	I	T	C	H	E	N
S	T	A	I	N	S			G	A	T	O			
			T	A	T	S		T	H	I	E	V	E	S
S	P	R	Y		Y	A	C	H	T		D	I	R	E
I	R	E			S	O	O			E	S	E		
T	O	D	D		C	H	O	R	D		Y	S	E	R
E	M	P	O	R	I	A		N	E	V	A			
		E	L	O	N			F	E	R	R	I	S	
I	M	P	L	I	E	D		V	E	R	D	A	N	T
P	A	P	A		M	A	Y	O	N	N	A	I	S	E
S	T	E	R		A	V	O	I	D		G	L	E	N
O	A	R	S		S	E	N	D	S		E	S	T	O

9

N	A	P	S		T	H	E	T	A		S	C	A	M
A	B	L	E		A	A	R	O	N		C	H	O	U
S	A	U	E	R	K	R	A	U	T		H	A	N	G
A	C	C	R	U	E	D		R	A	C	E	M	E	S
L	I	K	E	N	S			C	O	R	P			
			S	T	O	W		Z	I	G	Z	A	G	S
B	O	S	S		N	I	C	A	D		O	G	L	E
O	O	O			L	O	X			N	I	P		
S	N	U	B		S	T	O	I	C		D	E	B	T
C	A	R	R	O	T	S		S	A	D	R			
		C	A	R	R			B	O	A	R	D	S	
P	E	R	I	D	O	T		S	I	N	C	E	R	E
A	B	E	L		B	R	O	W	N	S	U	G	A	R
C	O	A	L		E	A	D	I	E		L	A	M	B
O	N	M	E		S	C	O	T	T		A	L	A	S

10

S	P	A	R		E	A	T	A		R	A	S	T	A
L	U	R	E		C	L	A	D		O	R	P	A	H
O	R	E	S		A	M	B	I		A	R	E	N	A
W	R	A	P	A	R	O	U	N	D	D	E	C	K	
			E	N	T	S			E	M	S			
	J	A	C	K	E	T	P	O	T	A	T	O	E	S
M	A	L	T	A			A	T	O	P		R	A	T
A	M	A	S		B	A	L	T	O		R	A	G	A
R	A	M		S	L	O	E			M	E	T	E	R
C	L	O	A	K	A	N	D	D	A	G	G	E	R	
			P	E	N			E	M	M	A			
	C	A	P	E	C	O	D	C	O	T	T	A	G	E
B	E	N	E	T		S	O	A	R		T	R	A	M
U	L	N	A	E		S	O	D	A		A	C	T	I
S	T	A	R	R		O	R	E	L		S	H	O	T

11

B	L	A	B		R	O	L	F	E		C	O	M	E
R	E	D	O		E	N	U	R	E		A	L	I	T
A	N	D	Y		T	I	R	O	L		T	E	A	S
N	O	N	S	T	I	C	K	G	L	U	E			
			C	O	R	E			I	S	R	A	E	L
	A	S	O	N	E		T	A	K	E		C	R	O
L	I	Q	U	I	D	P	A	P	E	R		C	O	W
A	R	U	T			E	R	S			C	E	D	E
T	W	A		R	A	N	D	O	M	O	R	D	E	R
H	A	D		V	A	S	E		E	P	E	E	S	
S	Y	S	T	E	M			A	N	A	S			
		O	R	I	G	I	N	A	L	C	O	P	Y	
M	E	A	N		L	O	G	I	C		E	L	L	E
E	M	A	G		N	O	O	S	E		N	O	E	L
D	U	H	S		E	S	T	E	S		T	R	A	P

12

A	S	T	R	O	S		T	B	A			C	V	S
R	E	S	E	A	L		A	R	M	S		L	O	T
C	L	A	S	S	I	C	R	O	C	K		A	G	E
S	A	R	I		E	T	O	N		I	S	S	U	E
			S	C	R	A	T	C	H	P	A	P	E	R
A	O	R	T	A				E	S	L				
S	H	O		S	T	R	E	A	M		E	D	D	A
K	I	T	C	H	E	N	S	C	I	S	S	O	R	S
S	O	S	A		A	S	S	E	N	T		U	N	O
			R	A	S					A	A	R	O	N
L	O	U	N	G	E	L	I	Z	A	R	D			
A	T	S	E	A		O	D	O	R		O	B	I	E
R	A	H		M	I	S	T	E	R	S	P	O	C	K
G	R	E		A	R	E	A		E	N	T	R	E	E
O	U	R			E	R	G			T	O	S	E	E	D

13

M	U	M	S		C	E	S	S		E	R	A	S	E
E	B	A	N		O	M	N	I		M	O	D	E	S
N	E	M	O		R	A	U	L		B	A	S	E	S
D	R	A	W	I	N	G	B	O	A	R	D			
			E	T	D	S			M	Y	S	T	I	C
	R	A	D	I	O		E	S	P	O		E	G	O
S	E	W	I	N	G	C	L	A	S	S		D	N	A
C	M	O	N			A	C	U			T	I	O	S
A	O	K		F	A	M	I	L	Y	C	O	U	R	T
R	T	E		A	R	O	D		E	A	T	M	E	
S	E	N	E	C	A			M	A	R	E			
			B	I	L	L	I	A	R	D	B	A	L	L
S	A	L	S	A		E	S	P	N		A	L	O	E
S	T	E	E	L		E	L	L	E		G	I	L	A
R	E	I	N	S		R	E	E	D			S	T	A	N

14

B	I	R	D		F	I	J	I		D	U	P	E	S
A	S	I	A		I	M	A	N		I	P	A	S	S
B	A	L	L		R	A	V	E		C	R	Y	P	T
A	Y	E	A	Y	E	C	A	P	T	A	I	N		
R	A	D	I	U	S			T	I	P	S	O	F	F
			P	A	W	N		C	R	I	M	E	A	
	S	P	F		L	A	I	R		I	N	I	T	S
P	R	I	C	E	Y	C	O	L	O	G	N	E		
F	I	O	N	A		S	E	M	I		S	D	S	
A	N	T	E	E	D		R	E	V	S				
D	E	E	P	S	E	A		E	A	S	I	N	G	
	S	O	U	R	C	E	O	F	W	A	T	E	R	
A	S	T	I	R		I	R	M	A		R	A	R	E
A	R	E	N	A		D	I	E	S		A	L	V	A
S	O	R	T	S		S	E	N	T		N	Y	E	T

15

F	L	A	G	G		A	P	E	D		F	O	G	S
C	A	M	E	O		B	A	L	I		R	A	N	K
C	O	M	M	A		B	I	A	S		O	K	A	Y
	S	O	I	L	E	A	R	T	H	D	U	S	T	
			N	O	V		S	E	R	I	F			
B	R	A	I	N	E	D			A	O	R	T	A	E
L	A	V		G	R	I	M	E	G	R	O	U	N	D
I	D	E	S			L	E	N		U	N	I	S	
S	I	R	I	W	I	L	L	Y	O	U		E	S	E
S	I	T	C	O	M			A	P	P	A	R	E	L
			I	R	A	T	E		R	A	N			
	T	A	L	K	D	I	R	T	Y	T	O	M	E	
M	A	U	I		E	Z	R	A		R	I	O	T	S
O	K	R	A		I	Z	O	D		E	N	T	R	Y
B	E	A	N		T	Y	R	A		E	T	H	E	R

16

I	N	A	W	E		B	E	T	A		A	H	A	B
S	O	L	A	R	P	A	N	E	L		D	E	C	O
I	N	D	I	V	I	D	U	A	L		E	A	C	H
T	O	O	T	I	N		F	L	O	U	N	D	E	R
			I	N	K	S		T	R	O	T	S		
I	R	A	N		I	N	G	A		K	I	O	S	K
M	I	N	G		S	E	E	R		E	D	W	I	N
E	F	T		C	H	A	N	N	E	L		A	B	E
A	L	I	C	E		K	I	E	V		E	R	L	E
N	E	P	A	L		S	I	T	E		A	D	E	S
		R	A	R	E	R		T	R	E	T			
B	A	S	E	B	A	L	L			E	T	H	I	C	S
A	N	T	E		B	E	A	T	T	H	E	R	A	P
I	G	O	R		I	N	V	E	T	E	R	A	T	E
L	E	S	S		D	E	A	N		R	E	S	E	W

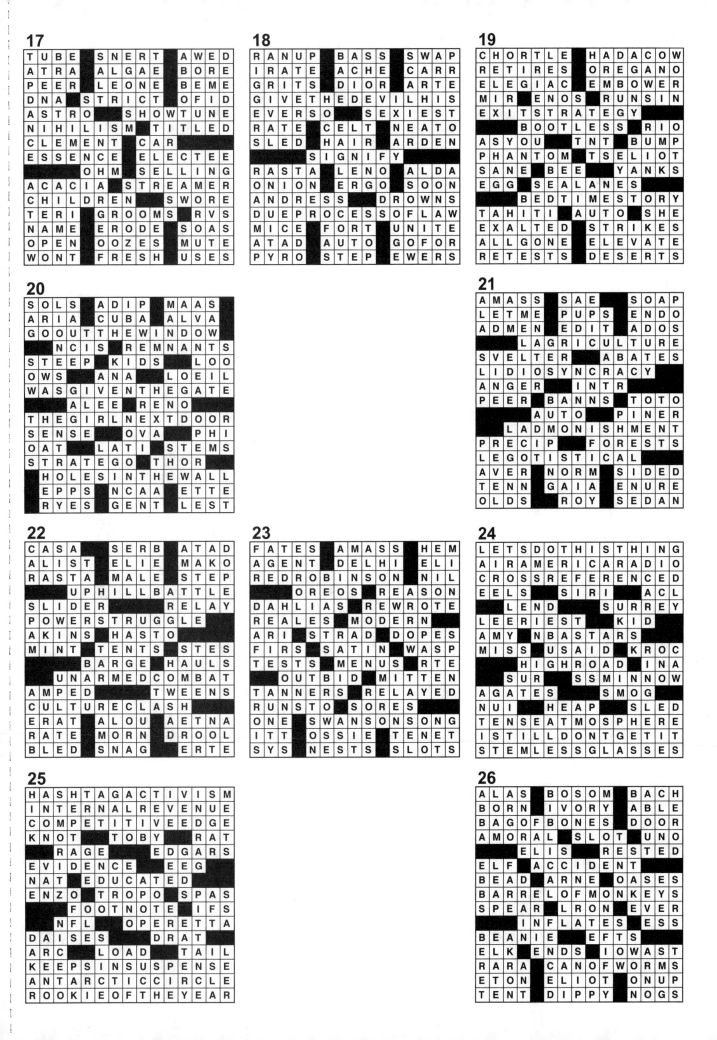

17

```
TUBE SNERT AWED
ATRA ALGAE BORE
PEER LEONE BEME
DNA STRICT OFID
ASTRO SHOWTUNE
NIHILISM TITLED
CLEMENT CAR
ESSENCE ELECTEE
OHM SELLING
ACACIA STREAMER
CHILDREN SWORE
TERI GROOMS RVS
NAME ERODE SOAS
OPEN OOZES MUTE
WONT FRESH USES
```

18

```
RANUP BASS SWAP
IRATE ACHE CARR
GRITS DIOR ARTE
GIVETHEDEVILHIS
EVERSO SEXIEST
RATE CELT NEATO
SLED HAIR ARDEN
SIGNIFY
RASTA LENO ALDA
ONION ERGO SOON
ANDRESS DROWNS
DUEPROCESSOFLAW
MICE FORT UNITE
ATAD AUTO GOFOR
PYRO STEP EWERS
```

19

```
CHORTLE HADACOW
RETIRES OREGANO
ELEGIAC EMBOWER
MIR ENOS RUNSIN
EXITSTRATEGY
BOOTLESS RIO
ASYOU TNT BUMP
PHANTOM TSELIOT
SANE BEE YANKS
EGG SEALANES
BEDTIMESTORY
TAHITI AUTO SHE
EXALTED STRIKES
ALLGONE ELEVATE
RETESTS DESERTS
```

20

```
SOLS ADIP MAAS
ARIA CUBA ALVA
GOOUTTHEWINDOW
NCIS REMNANTS
STEEP KIDS LOO
OWS ANA LOEIL
WASGIVENTHEGATE
ALEE RENO
THEGIRLNEXTDOOR
SENSE OVA PHI
OAT LATI STEMS
STRATEGO THOR
HOLESINTHEWALL
EPPS NCAA ETTE
RYES GENT LEST
```

21

```
AMASS SAE SOAP
LETME PUPS ENDO
ADMEN EDIT ADOS
LAGRICULTURE
SVELTER ABATES
LIDIOSYNCRACY
ANGER INTR
PEER BANNS TOTO
AUTO PINER
LADMONISHMENT
PRECIP FORESTS
LEGOTISTICAL
AVER NORM SIDED
TENN GAIA ENURE
OLDS ROY SEDAN
```

22

```
CASA SERB ATAD
ALIST ELIE MAKO
RASTA MALE STEP
UPHILLBATTLE
SLIDER RELAY
POWERSTRUGGLE
AKINS HASTO
MINT TENTS STES
BARGE HAULS
UNARMEDCOMBAT
AMPED TWEENS
CULTURECLASH
ERAT ALOU AETNA
RATE MORN DROOL
BLED SNAG ERTE
```

23

```
FATES AMASS HEM
AGENT DELHI ELI
REDROBINSON NIL
OREOS REASON
DAHLIAS REWROTE
REALES MODERN
ARI STRAD DOPES
FIRS SATIN WASP
TESTS MENUS RTE
OUTBID MITTEN
TANNERS RELAYED
RUNSTO SORES
ONE SWANSONSONG
ITT OSSIE TENET
SYS NESTS SLOTS
```

24

```
LETSDOTHISTHING
AIRAMERICARADIO
CROSSREFERENCED
EELS SIRI ACL
LEND SURREY
LEERIEST KID
AMY NBASTARS
MISS USAID KROC
HIGHROAD INA
SUR SSMINNOW
AGATES SMOG
NUI HEAP SLED
TENSEATMOSPHERE
ISTILLDONTGETIT
STEMLESSGLASSES
```

25

```
HASHTAGACTIVISM
INTERNALREVENUE
COMPETITIVEEDGE
KNOT TOBY RAT
RAGE EDGARS
EVIDENCE EEG
NAT EDUCATED
ENZO TROPO SPAS
FOOTNOTE IFS
NFL OPERETTA
DAISES DRAT
ARC LOAD TAIL
KEEPSINSUSPENSE
ANTARCTICCIRCLE
ROOKIEOFTHEYEAR
```

26

```
ALAS BOSOM BACH
BORN IVORY ABLE
BAGOFBONES DOOR
AMORAL SLOT UNO
ELIS RESTED
ELF ACCIDENT
BEAD ARNE OASES
BARRELOFMONKEYS
SPEAR LRON EVER
INFLATES ESS
BEANIE EFTS
ELK ENDS IOWAST
RARA CANOFWORMS
ETON ELIOT ONUP
TENT DIPPY NOGS
```

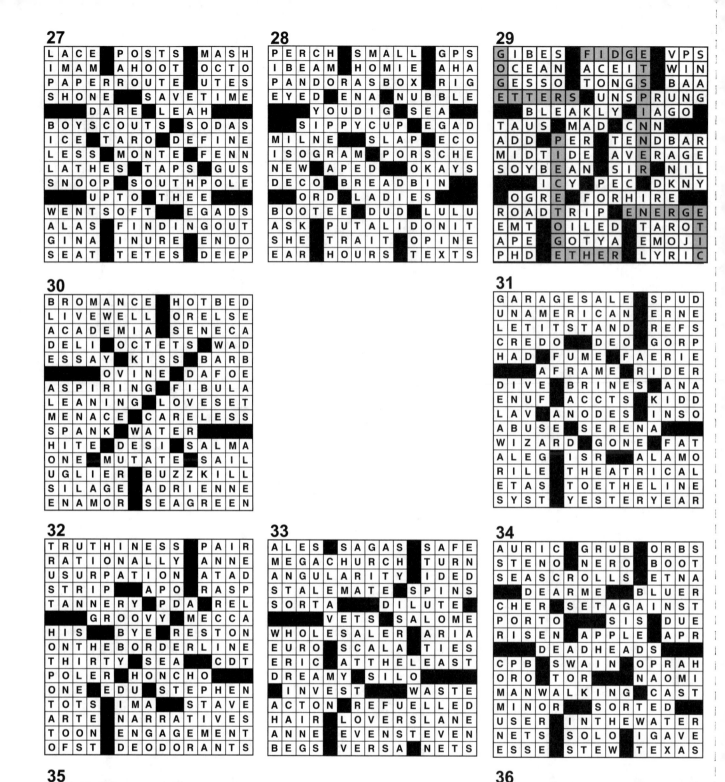

27

LACE · POSTS · MASH
IMAM · AHOOT · OCTO
PAPERROUTE · UTES
SHONE · · SAVETIME
· · DARE · LEAH ·
BOYSCOUTS · SODAS
ICE · TARO · DEFINE
LESS · MONTE · FENN
LATHES · TAPS · GUS
SNOOP · SOUTHPOLE
· · UPTO · THEE ·
WENTSOFT · EGADS
ALAS · FINDINGOUT
GINA · INURE · ENDO
SEAT · TETES · DEEP

28

PERCH · SMALL · GPS
IBEAM · HOMIE · AHA
PANDORASBOX · RIG
EYED · ENA · NUBBLE
· · YOUDIG · SEA ·
· SIPPYCUP · EGAD
MILNE · SLAP · ECO
ISOGRAM · PORSCHE
NEW · APED · OKAYS
DECO · BREADBIN ·
· ORD · LADIES · ·
BOOTEE · DUD · LULU
ASK · PUTALIDONIT
SHE · TRAIT · OPINE
EAR · HOURS · TEXTS

29

GIBES · FIDGE · VPS
OCEAN · ACEIT · WIN
GESSO · TONGS · BAA
ETTERS · UNSPRUNG
· BLEAKLY · IAGO ·
TAUS · MAD · CNN ·
ADD · PER · TENDBAR
MIDTIDE · AVERAGE
SOYBEAN · SIR · NIL
· ICY · PEC · DKNY
· OGRE · FORHIRE ·
ROADTRIP · ENERGE
EMT · OILED · TAROT
APE · GOTYA · EMOJI
PHD · ETHER · LYRIC

30

BROMANCE · HOTBED
LIVEWELL · ORELSE
ACADEMIA · SENECA
DELI · OCTETS · WAD
ESSAY · KISS · BARB
· · OVINE · DAFOE
ASPIRING · FIBULA
LEANING · LOVESET
MENACE · CARELESS
SPANK · WATER · ·
HITE · DESI · SALMA
ONE · MUTATE · SAIL
UGLIER · BUZZKILL
SILAGE · ADRIENNE
ENAMOR · SEAGREEN

31

GARAGESALE · SPUD
UNAMERICAN · ERNE
LETITSTAND · REFS
CREDO · DEO · GORP
HAD · FUME · FAERIE
· AFRAME · RIDER
DIVE · BRINES · ANA
ENUF · ACCTS · KIDD
LAV · ANODES · INSO
ABUSE · SERENA · ·
WIZARD · GONE · FAT
ALEG · ISR · ALAMO
RILE · THEATRICAL
ETAS · TOETHELINE
SYST · YESTERYEAR

32

TRUTHINESS · PAIR
RATIONALLY · ANNE
USURPATION · ATAD
STRIP · APO · RASP
TANNERY · PDA · REL
· GROOVY · MECCA
HIS · BYE · RESTON
ONTHEBORDERLINE
THIRTY · SEA · CDT
POLER · HONCHO ·
ONE · EDU · STEPHEN
TOTS · IMA · STAVE
ARTE · NARRATIVES
TOON · ENGAGEMENT
OFST · DEODORANTS

33

ALES · SAGAS · SAFE
MEGACHURCH · TURN
ANGULARITY · IDED
STALEMATE · SPINS
SORTA · · DILUTE ·
· · VETS · SALOME
WHOLESALER · ARIA
EURO · SCALA · TIES
ERIC · ATTHELEAST
DREAMY · SILO · ·
· INVEST · · WASTE
ACTON · REFUELLED
HAIR · LOVERSLANE
ANNE · EVENSTEVEN
BEGS · VERSA · NETS

34

AURIC · GRUB · ORBS
STENO · NERO · BOOT
SEASCROLLS · ETNA
· DEARME · BLUER
CHER · SETAGAINST
PORTO · · SIS · DUE
RISEN · APPLE · APR
· DEADHEADS ·
CPB · SWAIN · OPRAH
ORO · TOR · NAOMI
MANWALKING · CAST
MINOR · SORTED ·
USER · INTHEWATER
NETS · SOLO · IGAVE
ESSE · STEW · TEXAS

35

SLID · ABLE · AGREE
EURO · CROP · WEIRD
LAIR · CINE · LOONY
FUSSBUDGET · RTES
· ERSE · SAGS ·
SESTET · APPLIQUE
ALT · TORIO · PAULA
GOIN · MOTET · NATS
APRON · OCTAL · DRE
NETWORTH · KANSAS
· HARE · SEGO ·
GREY · FLAPDOODLE
REPOS · AFRO · DREW
ABOUT · LOEW · LATE
BATTY · OXEN · EGON

36

CORP · UNAGI · BLAH
AMAL · NYLON · AONE
LOSANGELES · LUNA
COPYCAT · SUNDIAL
· FIT · · LOWS ·
ACCUSED · NATIVES
PHIL · DETER · NIDE
ION · · FRA · LIX
NICE · COATS · ALTE
GRIDDLE · HARNESS
· NALA · · LID ·
CONSIST · BOORISH
LEAN · SANANTONIO
ANTE · ICING · ISMS
NOIR · CONGA · DOSE

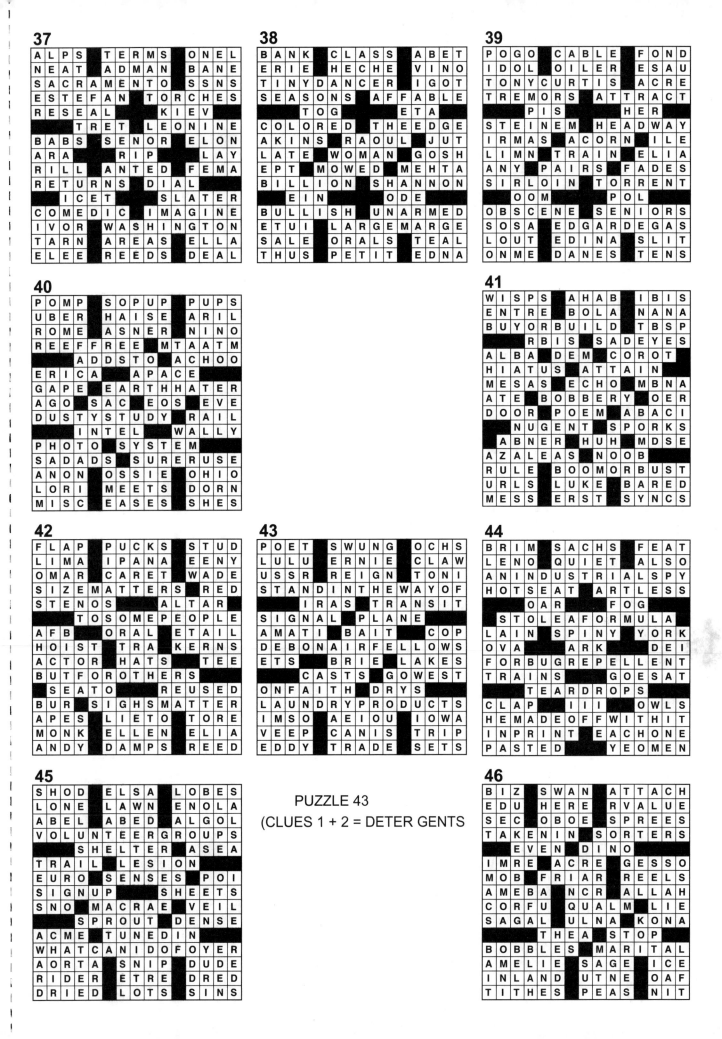

37

```
A L P S   T E R M S   O N E L
N E A T   A D M A N   B A N E
S A C R A M E N T O   S S N S
E S T E F A N   T O R C H E S
R E S E A L     K I E V
    T R E T   L E O N I N E
B A B S   S E N O R   E L O N
A R A     R I P     L A Y
R I L L   A N T E D   F E M A
R E T U R N S   D I A L
  I C E T     S L A T E R
C O M E D I C   I M A G I N E
I V O R   W A S H I N G T O N
T A R N   A R E A S   E L L A
E L E E   R E E D S   D E A L
```

38

```
B A N K   C L A S S   A B E T
E R I E   H E C H E   V I N O
T I N Y D A N C E R   I G O T
S E A S O N S   A F F A B L E
    T O G     E T A
C O L O R E D   T H E E D G E
A K I N S   R A O U L   J U T
L A T E   W O M A N   G O S H
E P T   M O W E D   M E H T A
B I L L I O N   S H A N N O N
  E I N       O D E
B U L L I S H   U N A R M E D
E T U I   L A R G E M A R G E
S A L E   O R A L S   T E A L
T H U S   P E T I T   E D N A
```

39

```
P O G O   C A B L E   F O N D
I D O L   O I L E R   E S A U
T O N Y C U R T I S   A C R E
T R E M O R S   A T T R A C T
    P I S     H E R
S T E I N E M   H E A D W A Y
I R M A S   A C O R N   I L E
L I M N   T R A I N   E L I A
A N Y   P A I R S   F A D E S
S I R L O I N   T O R R E N T
  O O M       P O L
O B S C E N E   S E N I O R S
S O S A   E D G A R D E G A S
L O U T   E D I N A   S L I T
O N M E   D A N E S   T E N S
```

40

```
P O M P   S O P U P   P U P S
U B E R   H A I S E   A R I L
R O M E   A S N E R   N I N O
R E E F F R E E   M T A A T M
    A D D S T O   A C H O O
E R I C A   A P A C E
G A P E   E A R T H H A T E R
A G O   S A C   E O S   E V E
D U S T Y S T U D Y   R A I L
  I N T E L   W A L L Y
P H O T O   S Y S T E M
S A D A D S   S U R E R U S E
A N O N   O S S I E   O H I O
L O R I   M E E T S   D O R N
M I S C   E A S E S   S H E S
```

41

```
W I S P S   A H A B   I B I S
E N T R E   B O L A   N A N A
B U Y O R B U I L D   T B S P
    R B I S   S A D E Y E S
A L B A   D E M   C O R O T
H I A T U S   A T T A I N
M E S A S   E C H O   M B N A
A T E   B O B B E R Y   O E R
D O O R   P O E M   A B A C I
  N U G E N T   S P O R K S
  A B N E R   H U H   M D S E
A Z A L E A S   N O O B
R U L E   B O O M O R B U S T
U R L S   L U K E   B A R E D
M E S S   E R S T   S Y N C S
```

42

```
F L A P   P U C K S   S T U D
L I M A   I P A N A   E E N Y
O M A R   C A R E T   W A D E
S I Z E M A T T E R S   R E D
S T E N O S     A L T A R
    T O S O M E P E O P L E
A F B   O R A L   E T A I L
H O I S T   T R A   K E R N S
A C T O R   H A T S   T E E
B U T F O R O T H E R S
  S E A T O   R E U S E D
B U R   S I G H S M A T T E R
A P E S   L I E T O   T O R E
M O N K   E L L E N   E L I A
A N D Y   D A M P S   R E E D
```

43

```
P O E T   S W U N G   O C H S
L U L U   E R N I E   C L A W
U S S R   R E I G N   T O N I
S T A N D I N T H E W A Y O F
    I R A S   T R A N S I T
S I G N A L   P L A N E
A M A T I   B A I T   C O P
D E B O N A I R F E L L O W S
E T S   B R I E   L A K E S
    C A S T S   G O W E S T
O N F A I T H   D R Y S
L A U N D R Y P R O D U C T S
I M S O   A E I O U   I O W A
V E E P   C A N I S   T R I P
E D D Y   T R A D E   S E T S
```

44

```
B R I M   S A C H S   F E A T
L E N O   Q U I E T   A L S O
A N I N D U S T R I A L S P Y
H O T S E A T   A R T L E S S
    O A R     F O G
  S T O L E A F O R M U L A
L A I N   S P I N Y   Y O R K
O V A   A R K   D E I
F O R B U G R E P E L L E N T
T R A I N S   G O E S A T
  T E A R D R O P S
C L A P   I I I   O W L S
H E M A D E O F F W I T H I T
I N P R I N T   E A C H O N E
P A S T E D   Y E O M E N
```

45

```
S H O D   E L S A   L O B E S
L O N E   L A W N   E N O L A
A B E L   A B E D   A L G O L
V O L U N T E E R G R O U P S
  S H E L T E R   A S E A
T R A I L   L E S I O N
E U R O   S E N S E S   P O I
S I G N U P     S H E E T S
S N O   M A C R A E   V E I L
  S P R O U T   D E N S E
A C M E   T U N E D I N
W H A T C A N I D O F O Y E R
A O R T A   S N I P   D U D E
R I D E R   E T R E   D R E D
D R I E D   L O T S   S I N S
```

PUZZLE 43
(CLUES 1 + 2 = DETER GENTS

46

```
B I Z   S W A N   A T T A C H
E D U   H E R E   R V A L U E
S E C   O B O E   S P R E E S
T A K E N I N   S O R T E R S
    E V E N   D I N O
I M R E   A C R E   G E S S O
M O B   F R I A R   R E E L S
A M E B A   N C R   A L L A H
C O R F U   Q U A L M   L I E
S A G A L   U L N A   K O N A
    T H E A   S T O P
B O B B L E S   M A R I T A L
A M E L I E   S A G E   I C E
I N L A N D   U T N E   O A F
T I T H E S   P E A S   N I T
```

47

Y	O	D	E	L		S	E	N	T		C	A	S	A
A	L	A	M	O		A	V	I	A		A	L	E	C
M	A	L	E	V	O	L	E	N	T		L	E	E	R
	F	I	R	E	D	O	N		T	A	L	E	S	E
		G	L	E	N		L	O	T	S				
M	A	B	E	L	S		P	O	O	R	I	D	E	A
A	L	L			F	R	E	E	A	G	E	N	T	
R	O	E	S		C	R	O	W	D		N	A	S	H
C	H	A	P	L	A	I	N	S				L	U	O
O	A	K	R	I	D	G	E		T	A	S	T	E	S
			E	C	I	G		M	U	T	T			
I	S	R	A	E	L		E	A	R	T	I	P	S	
R	A	I	D		L	O	N	G	F	E	L	L	O	W
A	N	T	E		A	U	D	I		S	T	E	A	K
N	E	E	R		C	R	O	C		T	S	A	R	S

48

M	A	M	A		D	E	I	S	M		H	A	R	E
A	L	A	R		E	T	A	P	E		Y	N	O	T
C	O	M	M	O	N	C	L	O	D		E	N	T	E
S	T	E	A	L	T	H		T	O	W	N	I	E	S
			M	L	I				R	A	E			
F	A	D	E	I	N	S		R	O	E		S	O	V
A	L	I	N	E		C	R	O	O	N		S	U	I
B	E	A	T		T	A	E	B	O		A	N	I	S
E	R	R		L	I	N	G	O		R	I	O	J	A
R	O	Y		O	P	T		T	E	A	R	G	A	S
		Q	B	S					I	N	B			
S	O	U	R	S	O	P		O	L	D	R	O	S	E
K	N	E	E		O	U	T	R	E	B	A	N	K	S
I	T	E	S		L	E	A	S	E		K	Y	A	T
M	O	N	T		A	R	G	O	N		E	X	T	S

49

E	R	R	S		A	B	C	S		M	O	I	S	T
F	E	A	T		R	E	A	P		A	R	M	I	E
F	A	I	R	T	R	A	D	E		R	E	P	L	Y
E	L	S	I	E		U	S	E	D	T	O			
C	L	E	A	T	S		D	I	I		O	L	E	
T	Y	S		R	O	T	A		S	N	I	P	E	S
			R	A	S	H	D	E	C	I	S	I	O	N
I	O	W	A		U	A	L			N	E	N	E	
S	N	A	P	J	U	D	G	M	E	N	T			
M	A	R	T	I	N		E	S	T	O		P	S	T
S	T	Y		G	O	D		A	V	I	A	T	E	
		A	S	S	E	R	T		A	R	L	E	N	
E	R	I	C	A		S	H	O	C	K	W	A	V	E
B	E	D	E	W		K	E	E	P		I	C	E	T
B	E	A	R	S		S	O	D	A		N	E	S	S

50

A	M	A	H		P	A	R	K	A		S	T	E	P
M	A	L	A		A	R	I	A	N		O	H	N	O
M	R	M	I	D	N	I	G	H	T		R	E	N	O
O	C	A	R	I	N	A		N	E	U	T	R	A	L
			L	A	E				R	E	O			
D	E	P	E	N	D	S		M	E	G	R	Y	A	N
A	R	O	S	E		C	H	U	T	E		A	L	E
T	O	W	S		I	R	O	N	S		S	L	O	E
E	S	D		S	T	O	I	C		C	A	W	E	D
S	E	E	T	H	E	D		H	A	R	N	E	S	S
			R	H	O			B	U	D				
R	E	P	R	E	S	S		E	A	S	I	E	S	T
A	L	U	I		K	I	S	S	T	H	E	S	K	Y
T	I	F	F		I	R	A	T	E		G	A	I	N
S	O	F	T		M	E	D	E	S		O	I	S	E

51

B	O	O	P		M	A	S	T		P	R	I	A	M
E	A	V	E		Y	U	L	E		H	E	L	L	O
S	T	E	T		S	T	U	N		I	N	E	P	T
T	H	R	E	E	T	O	E	D	S	L	O	T	H	S
			R	B	I			P	I	I				
R	E	S	P	E	C	T		R	E	P	R	E	S	S
E	L	C	A	R		H	A	I	R			L	A	P
M	O	U	N	T	A	I	N	G	O	R	I	L	L	A
A	P	B			S	N	A	G		O	N	I	O	N
P	E	A	N	U	T	S		S	L	O	V	E	N	S
			E	R	A			I	S	O				
P	E	R	E	G	R	I	N	E	F	A	L	C	O	N
R	A	I	S	E		S	E	N	T		V	E	R	A
O	R	L	O	N		P	A	C	E		E	D	A	M
S	P	E	N	T		S	L	E	D		D	E	L	E

52

S	N	I	P	E		M	A	S	C		C	A	L	M
T	I	D	A	L		A	M	O	R		O	L	E	A
E	L	L	Y	M	A	Y	C	L	A	M	P	E	T	T
W	E	E	D	E	R	S		D	N	A	T	E	S	T
				A	R	I		G	E	N	X			
L	I	V	Y		A	V	E	R	Y	B	R	O	W	N
O	N	E		P	L	A	N		A	E	R	I	E	
F	I	N	A	L		N	E	T		E	L	O	P	E
A	G	O	R	A			R	O	A	R		N	E	D
T	O	M	M	Y	H	Y	A	T	T		C	O	R	Y
			P	O	O	L		A	M	I				
P	R	O	N	E	T	O		G	R	A	N	G	E	R
S	A	M	A	N	T	H	A	M	I	C	E	L	L	I
S	C	A	M		I	O	W	A		A	M	A	I	N
T	Y	N	E		P	O	E	T		W	A	D	E	D

53

D	R	A	M		T	I	G	H	T		S	W	A	P
H	O	M	E		O	N	I	C	E		H	A	L	O
S	P	E	A	K	O	F	T	H	E	D	E	V	I	L
	E	S	T	A	T	E	S			R	E	E	S	E
			T	A	S			S	K	I	S			
T	E	L	L	I	T	T	O	T	H	E	H	A	N	D
O	R	A	T	E		B	E	A	R		L	O	O	
L	I	P	S		S	T	E	R	N		M	E	N	U
E	K	E		A	L	A	S		F	A	X	E	S	
T	A	L	K	L	I	K	E	A	P	I	R	A	T	E
			E	T	T	E		R	A	N				
A	G	R	E	E			I	G	U	A	N	A	S	
S	A	Y	P	R	E	T	T	Y	P	L	E	A	S	E
T	I	N	E		L	I	S	L	E		V	A	S	E
A	L	E	R		F	O	Y	E	R		E	A	S	E

54

T	A	M	A	L	E	S		T	E	A	P	O	T	S
O	C	A	N	A	D	A		E	R	R	A	T	I	C
P	O	R	T	R	A	I	T	P	A	I	N	T	E	R
P	L	I	E	S		D	U	E	S		G	O	T	A
L	Y	N	D	O	N		R	E	E	F		M	A	P
E	T	E		N	A	S	T		D	E	F	A	C	E
S	E	R	F		P	O	L	I		T	A	N	K	S
			O	Y	S	T	E	R	B	A	R			
D	I	S	C	O		O	D	O	R		E	R	I	Q
U	N	L	I	K	E		O	N	E	S		U	N	U
S	S	E		O	N	T	V		L	A	O	T	S	E
T	H	E	M		T	R	E	S		L	A	T	H	E
M	A	K	E	A	R	E	S	O	L	U	T	I	O	N
O	P	E	N	S	E	A		B	E	T	H	E	R	E
P	E	R	U	S	E	D		S	E	E	S	R	E	D

55

N	O	M	O	P	H	O	B	I	A		W	A	D	S
A	N	A	L	G	E	S	I	C	S		O	L	I	N
R	E	D	A	S	A	B	E	E	T		E	L	M	O
C	A	E	N		V	O	N	D	A		S	T	E	W
			A	I	R		T	I	N		H	A	Y	
B	A	C	K	M	E	N		E	R	O	D	E	D	
E	C	L	I	P	S	E		A	E	R	A	T	O	R
A	C	A	N						M	I	Z	E		
R	E	V	E	N	U	E		R	A	D	O	M	E	S
	S	I	R	E	N	S		E	M	I	N	E	N	T
S	S	E		T	L	C		T	U	X				
H	I	R	T		E	A	S	E	L		A	M	A	D
O	B	I	E		A	P	P	L	E	J	U	I	C	E
E	L	S	E		R	E	E	L	T	O	R	E	E	L
S	E	T	S		N	E	W	S	S	T	A	N	D	S

56

A	M	O	S		R	A	I	S	E		B	M	W	S
T	A	K	E	P	A	R	T	I	N		L	E	A	N
V	I	L	L	A	N	E	L	L	E		U	L	N	A
S	M	A	L	L	T	A	L	K		R	E	B	E	C
			L	E	S			D	A	M	A	S	K	
P	A	W	N	E	D		L	O	O	K	A	T		
E	L	I	O	T		B	E	T	T	E	R	O	F	F
C	A	D	S		J	O	D	I	E		L	A	R	A
K	N	E	E	P	A	N	T	S		W	I	S	E	R
			S	T	E	R	E	O		C	A	N	T	E	R
A	S	C	O	T	S			O	A	K				
L	O	R	N	A		E	G	G	B	E	A	T	E	R
O	R	E	O		K	I	L	L	I	N	G	E	V	E
I	R	E	S		G	R	E	E	N	S	A	L	A	D
S	Y	N	E		B	E	N	D	S		R	E	N	O

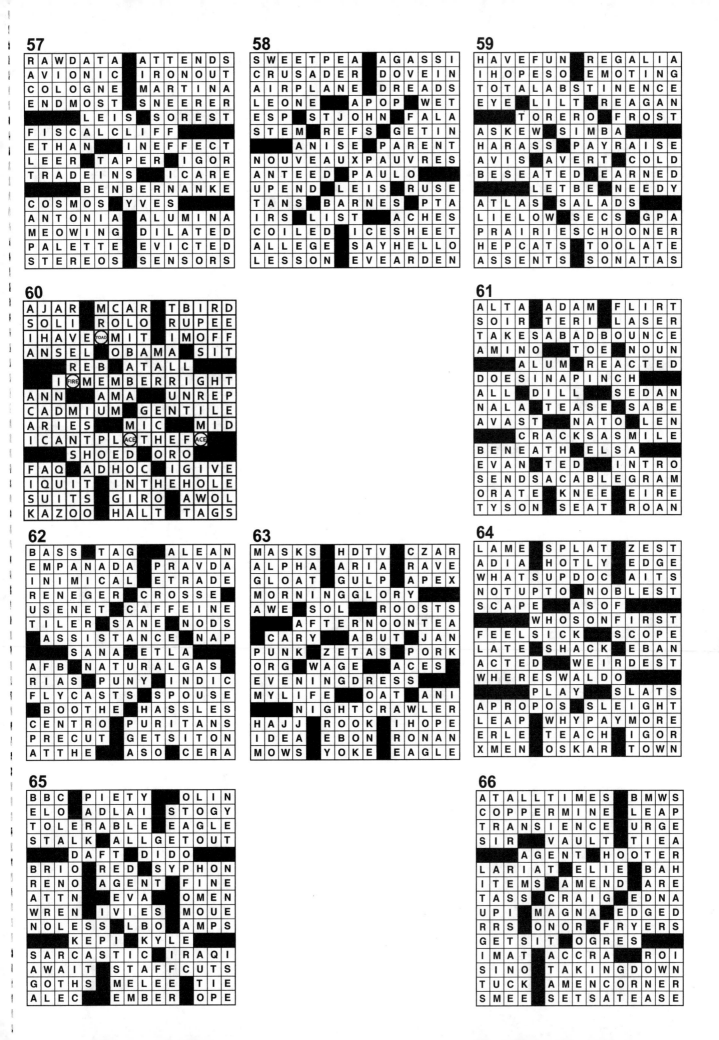

57

R A W D A T A		A T T E N D S
A V I O N I C		I R O N O U T
C O L O G N E		M A R T I N A
	L E I S		S O R E S T
F I S C A L C L I F F	
E T H A N		I N E F F E C T
L E E R	T A P E R	I G O R
T R A D E I N S		I C A R E
	B E N B E R N A N K E
C O S M O S		Y V E S
A N T O N I A		A L U M I N A
M E O W I N G		D I L A T E D
P A L E T T E		E V I C T E D
S T E R E O S		S E N S O R S

58

S W E E T P E A		A G A S S I
C R U S A D E R		D O V E I N
A I R P L A N E		D R E A D S
L E O N E	A P O P		W E T
E S P	S T J O H N	F A L A
S T E M	R E F S	G E T I N
	A N I S E		P A R E N T
N O U V E A U X P A U V R E S
A N T E E D		P A U L O
U P E N D	L E I S	R U S E
T A N S	B A R N E S	P T A
I R S	L I S T	A C H E S
C O I L E D		I C E S H E E T
A L L E G E		S A Y H E L L O
L E S S O N		E V E A R D E N

59

| H A V E F U N | | R E G A L I A |
| I H O P E S O | | E M O T I N G |
| T O T A L A B S T I N E N C E |
E Y E	L I L T		R E A G A N
	T O R E R O		F R O S T
A S K E W		S I M B A	
H A R A S S		P A Y R A I S E
A V I S	A V E R T	C O L D
B E S E A T E D		E A R N E D
	L E T B E		N E E D Y
A T L A S		S A L A D S	
L I E L O W	S E C S	G P A
P R A I R I E S C H O O N E R
H E P C A T S		T O O L A T E
A S S E N T S		S O N A T A S

60

A J A R	M C A R		T B I R D
S O L I	R O L O		R U P E E
I H A V E (TOAD) M I T	I M O F F
A N S E L		O B A M A	S I T
	R E B	A T A L L	
I (FIRE) M E M B E R R I G H T
A N N		A M A		U N R E P
C A D M I U M		G E N T I L E
A R I E S		M I C		M I D
I C A N T P L (ACE) T H E F (ACE)
	S H O E D		O R O	
F A Q	A D H O C	I G I V E
I Q U I T		I N T H E H O L E
S U I T S	G I R O	A W O L
K A Z O O	H A L T	T A G S

61

| A L T A | A D A M | F L I R T |
| S O I R | T E R I | L A S E R |
| T A K E S A B A D B O U N C E |
A M I N O		T O E	N O U N
	A L U M	R E A C T E D
D O E S I N A P I N C H	
A L L	D I L L		S E D A N
N A L A	T E A S E	S A B E
A V A S T		N A T O	L E N
	C R A C K S A S M I L E
B E N E A T H		E L S A	
E V A N	T E D		I N T R O
S E N D S A C A B L E G R A M
O R A T E	K N E E	E I R E
T Y S O N	S E A T	R O A N

62

B A S S		T A G		A L E A N
E M P A N A D A		P R A V D A
I N I M I C A L		E T R A D E
R E N E G E R		C R O S S E
U S E N E T		C A F F E I N E
T I L E R	S A N E	N O D S
	A S S I S T A N C E	N A P
	S A N A		E T L A	
A F B	N A T U R A L G A S
R I A S	P U N Y	I N D I C
F L Y C A S T S		S P O U S E
	B O O T H E		H A S S L E S
C E N T R O		P U R I T A N S
P R E C U T		G E T S I T O N
A T T H E		A S O	C E R A

63

M A S K S		H D T V		C Z A R
A L P H A		A R I A		R A V E
G L O A T		G U L P		A P E X
M O R N I N G G L O R Y	
A W E	S O L		R O O S T S
	A F T E R N O O N T E A
C A R Y		A B U T		J A N
P U N K	Z E T A S		P O R K
O R G	W A G E		A C E S
E V E N I N G D R E S S	
M Y L I F E		O A T	A N I
	N I G H T C R A W L E R
H A J J	R O O K	I H O P E
I D E A	E B O N	R O N A N
M O W S	Y O K E	E A G L E

64

L A M E	S P L A T	Z E S T
A D I A	H O T L Y	E D G E
W H A T S U P D O C	A I T S
N O T U P T O	N O B L E S T
S C A P E		A S O F	
	W H O S O N F I R S T
F E E L S I C K		S C O P E
L A T E	S H A C K	E B A N
A C T E D		W E I R D E S T
W H E R E S W A L D O	
	P L A Y		S L A T S
A P R O P O S		S L E I G H T
L E A P	W H Y P A Y M O R E
E R L E	T E A C H	I G O R
X M E N	O S K A R	T O W N

65

B B C	P I E T Y		O L I N
E L O	A D L A I	S T O G Y
T O L E R A B L E	E A G L E
S T A L K	A L L G E T O U T
	D A F T	D I D O	
B R I O	R E D	S Y P H O N
R E N O	A G E N T	F I N E
A T T N	E V A	O M E N
W R E N	I V I E S	M O U E
N O L E S S	L B O	A M P S
	K E P I	K Y L E	
S A R C A S T I C	I R A Q I
A W A I T	S T A F F C U T S
G O T H S	M E L E E	T I E
A L E C	E M B E R	O P E

66

A T A L L T I M E S	B M W S
C O P P E R M I N E	L E A P
T R A N S I E N C E	U R G E
S I R	V A U L T	T I E A
	A G E N T	H O O T E R
L A R I A T	E L I E	B A H
I T E M S	A M E N D	A R E
T A S S	C R A I G	E D N A
U P I	M A G N A	E D G E D
R R S	O N O R	F R Y E R S
G E T S I T	O G R E S	
I M A T	A C C R A	R O I
S I N O	T A K I N G D O W N
T U C K	A M E N C O R N E R
S M E E	S E T S A T E A S E

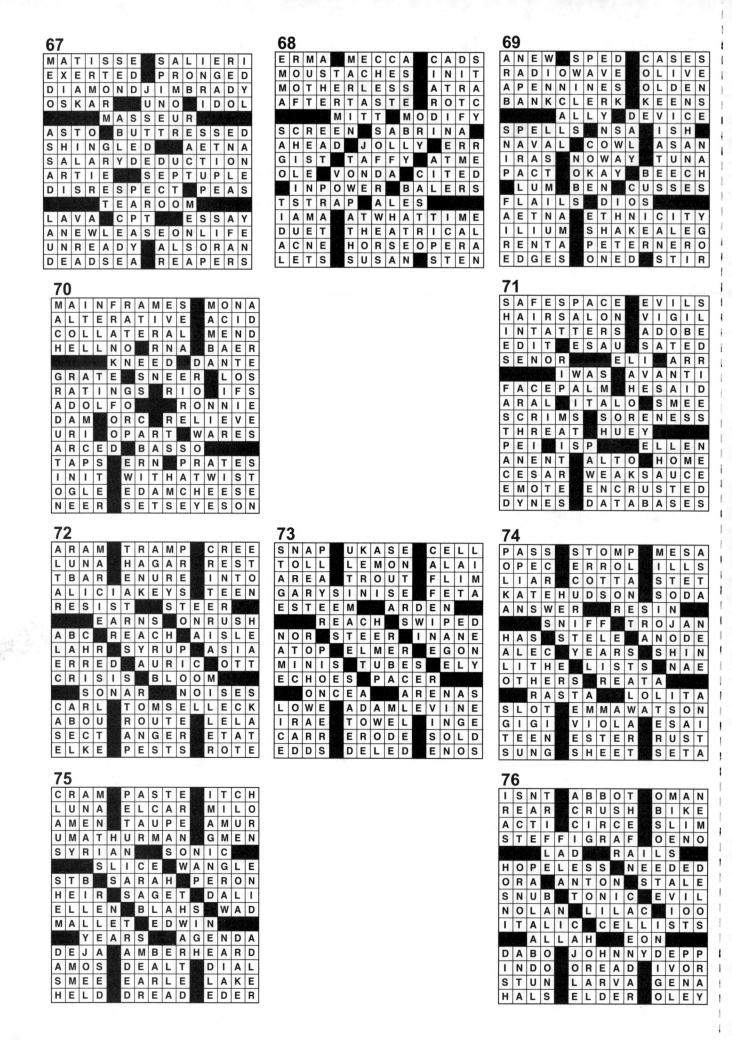

67

```
M A T I S S E ■ S A L I E R I
E X E R T E D ■ P R O N G E D
D I A M O N D J I M B R A D Y
O S K A R ■ ■ U N O ■ I D O L
■ ■ ■ M A S S E U R ■ ■
A S T O ■ B U T T R E S S E D
S H I N G L E D ■ ■ A E T N A
S A L A R Y D E D U C T I O N
A R T I E ■ ■ S E P T U P L E
D I S R E S P E C T ■ P E A S
■ ■ T E A R O O M ■ ■
L A V A ■ C P T ■ E S S A Y
A N E W L E A S E O N L I F E
U N R E A D Y ■ A L S O R A N
D E A D S E A ■ R E A P E R S
```

68

```
E R M A ■ M E C C A ■ C A D S
M O U S T A C H E S ■ I N I T
M O T H E R L E S S ■ A T R A
A F T E R T A S T E ■ R O T C
■ ■ M I T T ■ M O D I F Y
S C R E E N ■ S A B R I N A ■
A H E A D ■ J O L L Y ■ E R R
G I S T ■ T A F F Y ■ A T M E
O L E ■ V O N D A ■ C I T E D
■ I N P O W E R ■ B A L E R S
T S T R A P ■ A L E S ■ ■
I A M A ■ A T W H A T T I M E
D U E T ■ T H E A T R I C A L
A C N E ■ H O R S E O P E R A
L E T S ■ S U S A N ■ S T E N
```

69

```
A N E W ■ S P E D ■ C A S E S
R A D I O W A V E ■ O L I V E
A P E N N I N E S ■ O L D E N
B A N K C L E R K ■ K E E N S
■ ■ A L L Y ■ D E V I C E
S P E L L S ■ N S A ■ I S H
N A V A L ■ C O W L ■ A S A N
I R A S ■ N O W A Y ■ T U N A
P A C T ■ O K A Y ■ B E E C H
■ L U M ■ B E N ■ C U S S E S
F L A I L S ■ D I O S ■ ■
A E T N A ■ E T H N I C I T Y
I L I U M ■ S H A K E A L E G
R E N T A ■ P E T E R N E R O
E D G E S ■ O N E D ■ S T I R
```

70

```
M A I N F R A M E S ■ M O N A
A L T E R A T I V E ■ A C I D
C O L L A T E R A L ■ M E N D
H E L L N O ■ R N A ■ B A E R
■ ■ ■ K N E E D ■ D A N T E
G R A T E ■ S N E E R ■ L O S
R A T I N G S ■ R I O ■ I F S
A D O L F O ■ R O N N I E
D A M ■ O R C ■ R E L I E V E
U R I ■ O P A R T ■ W A R E S
A R C E D ■ B A S S O ■ ■
T A P S ■ E R N ■ P R A T E S
I N I T ■ W I T H A T W I S T
O G L E ■ E D A M C H E E S E
N E E R ■ S E T S E Y E S O N
```

71

```
S A F E S P A C E ■ E V I L S
H A I R S A L O N ■ V I G I L
I N T A T T E R S ■ A D O B E
E D I T ■ E S A U ■ S A T E D
S E N O R ■ E L I ■ A R R
■ ■ I W A S ■ A V A N T I
F A C E P A L M ■ H E S A I D
A R A L ■ I T A L O ■ S M E E
S C R I M S ■ S O R E N E S S
T H R E A T ■ H U E Y ■ ■
P E I ■ I S P ■ E L L E N
A N E N T ■ A L T O ■ H O M E
C E S A R ■ W E A K S A U C E
E M O T E ■ E N C R U S T E D
D Y N E S ■ D A T A B A S E S
```

72

```
A R A M ■ T R A M P ■ C R E E
L U N A ■ H A G A R ■ R E S T
T B A R ■ E N U R E ■ I N T O
A L I C I A K E Y S ■ T E E N
R E S I S T ■ S T E E R ■ ■
■ E A R N S ■ O N R U S H
A B C ■ R E A C H ■ A I S L E
L A H R ■ S Y R U P ■ A S I A
E R R E D ■ A U R I C ■ O T T
C R I S I S ■ B L O O M ■
■ S O N A R ■ N O I S E S
C A R L ■ T O M S E L L E C K
A B O U ■ R O U T E ■ L E L A
S E C T ■ A N G E R ■ E T A T
E L K E ■ P E S T S ■ R O T E
```

73

```
S N A P ■ U K A S E ■ C E L L
T O L L ■ L E M O N ■ A L A I
A R E A ■ T R O U T ■ F L I M
G A R Y S I N I S E ■ F E T A
E S T E E M ■ A R D E N ■
■ ■ R E A C H ■ S W I P E D
N O R ■ S T E E R ■ I N A N E
A T O P ■ E L M E R ■ E G O N
M I N I S ■ T U B E S ■ E L Y
E C H O E S ■ P A C E R ■
■ O N C E A ■ A R E N A S
L O W E ■ A D A M L E V I N E
I R A E ■ T O W E L ■ I N G E
C A R R ■ E R O D E ■ S O L D
E D D S ■ D E L E D ■ E N O S
```

74

```
P A S S ■ S T O M P ■ M E S A
O P E C ■ E R R O L ■ I L L S
L I A R ■ C O T T A ■ S T E T
K A T E H U D S O N ■ S O D A
A N S W E R ■ R E S I N ■
■ ■ S N I F F ■ T R O J A N
H A S ■ S T E L E ■ A N O D E
A L E C ■ Y E A R S ■ S H I N
L I T H E ■ L I S T S ■ N A E
O T H E R S ■ R E A T A ■
■ R A S T A ■ L O L I T A
S L O T ■ E M M A W A T S O N
G I G I ■ V I O L A ■ E S A I
T E E N ■ E S T E R ■ R U S T
S U N G ■ S H E E T ■ S E T A
```

75

```
C R A M ■ P A S T E ■ I T C H
L U N A ■ E L C A R ■ M I L O
A M E N ■ T A U P E ■ A M U R
U M A T H U R M A N ■ G M E N
S Y R I A N ■ S O N I C ■
■ ■ S L I C E ■ W A N G L E
S T B ■ S A R A H ■ P E R O N
H E I R ■ S A G E T ■ D A L I
E L L E N ■ B L A H S ■ W A D
M A L L E T ■ E D W I N ■
■ Y E A R S ■ A G E N D A
D E J A ■ A M B E R H E A R D
A M O S ■ D E A L T ■ D I A L
S M E E ■ E A R L E ■ L A K E
H E L D ■ D R E A D ■ E D E R
```

76

```
I S N T ■ A B B O T ■ O M A N
R E A R ■ C R U S H ■ B I K E
A C T I ■ C I R C E ■ S L I M
S T E F F I G R A F ■ O E N O
■ ■ L A D ■ R A I L S ■
H O P E L E S S ■ N E E D E D
O R A ■ A N T O N ■ S T A L E
S N U B ■ T O N I C ■ E V I L
N O L A N ■ L I L A C ■ I O O
I T A L I C ■ C E L L I S T S
■ A L L A H ■ E O N ■
D A B O ■ J O H N N Y D E P P
I N D O ■ O R E A D ■ I V O R
S T U N ■ L A R V A ■ G E N A
H A L S ■ E L D E R ■ O L E Y
```

77

C	U	F	F		S	U	M	A	C		A	V	O	W
A	L	L	I		O	V	I	N	E		R	I	P	E
S	N	A	G		M	E	N	S	A		K	N	I	T
K	A	T	H	Y	B	A	T	E	S		A	D	E	S
S	E	T	T	E	R			L	E	O	N	I		
			S	L	E	D	S		D	E	S	E	R	T
B	I	T		P	R	A	M	S		D	A	S	H	Y
I	D	O	L		O	D	I	U	M		S	E	E	K
R	E	M	I	T		A	L	L	A	N		L	E	E
D	O	C	K	E	T		E	U	L	E	R			
		R	E	L	I	C			A	T	H	E	N	S
F	A	U	N		C	A	R	L	Y	S	I	M	O	N
O	D	I	E		K	N	E	E	S		N	O	L	O
L	A	S	S		L	A	N	A	I		O	T	T	O
D	Y	E	S		E	L	E	N	A		S	E	E	P

78

M	O	T	H		S	T	R	A	P		D	U	M	B
O	R	E	O		W	H	O	L	L		I	S	E	E
C	E	L	L		A	E	A	E	A		S	A	M	E
H	A	L	L	E	B	E	R	R	Y		R	I	O	T
A	D	S	O	R	B			T	E	N	O	N		
			W	A	I	S	T		R	I	B	B	O	N
H	A	J		S	E	O	U	L		L	E	O	N	E
E	L	K	S		S	U	N	U	P		S	L	A	W
L	O	R	A	X		R	E	N	E	E		T	N	T
L	E	O	N	I	D		R	E	E	V	E			
		W	I	V	E	S			R	I	D	G	E	S
M	A	L	T		S	A	M	E	L	L	I	O	T	T
A	R	I	A		E	T	U	D	E		C	O	H	O
R	E	N	T		R	I	S	E	S		T	E	A	K
C	A	G	E		T	E	E	N	S		S	Y	N	E

79

T	A	N	G		L	E	A	S	T		R	E	A	P
U	S	E	R		I	N	D	I	A		E	M	M	A
M	I	L	A		G	N	A	R	L		S	M	U	G
S	A	L	M	A	H	A	Y	E	K		P	Y	R	E
			P	S	T			S	E	N	O	R		
L	I	B	A	T	I	O	N		D	E	N	O	T	E
A	M	I		I	N	T	E	L		A	S	S	A	M
B	A	L	L		G	R	O	O	M		E	S	S	E
O	G	L	E	D		A	N	S	E	L		U	S	N
R	E	M	O	R	A		S	T	R	E	A	M	E	D
		U	T	U	R	N			C	I	D			
S	E	R	A		M	A	R	K	H	A	R	M	O	N
P	U	R	R		I	V	A	N	A		O	O	N	A
O	R	A	D		E	A	T	E	N		I	D	E	S
T	O	Y	S		S	L	E	E	T		T	E	S	T

80

B	O	S	C		D	U	N	S	T		N	O	G	S
E	L	L	I		E	L	O	P	E		A	S	A	P
A	G	A	R		P	A	L	I	N		U	C	L	A
R	A	Y	C	H	A	R	L	E	S		S	A	L	T
			L	A	R			S	E	D	E	R		
M	A	J	E	S	T	I	C		D	R	A	W	E	R
O	D	O		H	E	L	O	T		U	T	I	L	E
L	A	H	R		D	I	N	A	H		E	L	L	A
A	N	N	E	X		A	C	R	E	S		D	I	P
R	O	L	L	E	D		H	E	L	P	L	E	S	S
		E	A	S	E	D			S	E	E			
P	A	N	T		N	A	O	M	I	W	A	T	T	S
R	A	N	I		I	R	W	I	N		N	O	R	A
E	R	O	O		A	L	E	C	K		O	M	I	T
P	E	N	N		L	A	N	A	I		N	A	M	E

81

S	O	B	S		P	O	S	S	E		I	D	E	S
O	G	R	E		E	L	E	N	A		M	E	T	E
C	L	A	P		C	O	R	E	R		A	M	O	R
K	E	I	T	H	U	R	B	A	N		G	I	N	A
O	R	D	E	A	L			D	E	N	I	M		
			T	R	I	T	E		D	O	N	O	R	S
E	L	K		D	A	R	L	A		S	E	O	U	L
M	E	A	T		R	E	B	E	C		D	R	N	O
I	N	T	R	A		T	O	R	A	H		E	E	E
L	A	Y	E	R	S		W	I	F	E	S			
		P	A	N	I	C			F	R	A	C	A	S
C	H	E	T		G	R	A	C	E	S	L	I	C	K
H	A	R	I		H	E	N	R	I		I	L	I	E
I	N	R	E		T	E	T	O	N		N	I	D	E
P	A	Y	S		S	L	I	C	E		E	A	S	T

82

J	A	V	A		R	E	E	D	S		S	T	U	B
A	L	E	G		E	L	L	E	N		T	I	R	E
M	A	R	A		M	A	U	N	A		U	N	I	T
B	E	N	S	T	I	L	L	E	R		D	A	S	H
			S	A	N			B	E	G	E	T		
B	E	W	I	L	D	E	R		D	A	N	U	B	E
I	R	A		L	E	V	E	E		S	T	R	O	M
P	A	L	S		D	E	M	M	E		S	N	O	B
O	T	T	E	R		N	A	I	V	E		E	N	E
D	O	D	G	E	R		P	R	E	P	A	R	E	D
		I	M	P	E	L			R	I	N			
I	L	S	E		M	I	L	E	Y	C	Y	R	U	S
M	A	N	N		A	M	E	N	D		O	U	S	T
A	N	E	T		K	E	N	Y	A		N	E	N	E
S	A	Y	S		E	S	S	A	Y		E	D	A	M

83

C	A	S	H		S	T	E	A	L		D	A	T	A
A	N	T	E		N	I	E	C	E		E	M	U	S
S	T	A	R		O	R	R	I	S		T	A	N	K
T	I	G	E	R	W	O	O	D	S		A	N	A	S
			T	A	B			S	O	L	I	D		
M	A	J	O	R	I	T	Y		R	O	N	A	L	D
E	D	O		E	R	R	E	D		T	E	P	E	E
D	A	H	L		D	I	N	E	D		D	E	N	T
A	G	N	E	W		S	T	R	E	W		E	T	E
L	E	D	G	E	R		A	N	C	E	S	T	O	R
		E	A	T	U	P			A	B	C			
I	S	N	T		D	A	V	I	D	B	O	W	I	E
N	A	V	E		E	R	A	S	E		N	E	S	T
F	R	E	E		S	E	R	I	N		E	A	S	T
O	A	R	S		T	R	Y	S	T		S	L	O	E

84

A	D	A	M	S	A	L	E		L	S	A	T	S	
P	I	N	I	O	N	E	D		E	L	R	O	P	O
B	E	T	A	W	A	V	E		T	I	N	P	A	N
S	T	E	M		K	A	M	A		G	I	A	N	T
	I	F	I	R	A	N	T	H	E	Z	O	O		
M	A	R	V	I	N			S	I	T				
A	N	A	I	S		S	E	A	R		P	R	A	M
C	A	T	C	H	A	N	D	R	E	L	E	A	S	E
E	T	T	E		T	A	X	I		E	E	R	I	E
			I	M	P			B	A	R	E	S	T	
C	R	O	W	D	S	U	R	F	I	N	G			
R	E	L	I	C		P	A	R	A		R	E	F	I
O	N	E	D	A	Y		N	O	N	T	O	X	I	C
C	E	T	E	R	A		I	T	C	O	U	P	L	E
	W	A	R	D	S		S	H	A	M	P	O	O	S

85

H	A	N	S	O	M		W	O	R	D	L	E	S	S
E	Q	U	I	N	E		I	B	E	R	I	A	N	S
R	U	N	N	E	L		N	O	M	A	T	T	E	R
B	A	C	K	S	L	I	D	E		W	H	I	R	S
			C	H	O	P	S		S	E	N	D		
G	A	L	L	O	W	S	H	U	M	O	R			
E	L	I	O	T			I	R	O	N		A	S	K
M	I	N	G		S	P	E	N	D		A	R	E	A
S	A	T		C	E	I	L		E	N	A	C	T	
		B	R	A	N	D	L	O	Y	A	L	T	Y	
	F	R	A	U		N	O	N	E	T				
P	E	E	L	E		O	O	P	S	S	O	R	R	Y
I	W	I	L	L	N	O	T		T	O	M	A	T	O
P	E	N	A	L	I	Z	E		A	R	I	S	E	S
P	R	E	D	A	T	E	S		R	E	C	A	S	T

86

M	A	R	S		M	S	G	T		J	E	S	T	S
A	L	U	M		B	A	L	E		U	N	T	I	E
N	O	M	I	N	A	T	O	R		P	A	U	L	A
S	E	P	T	A		U	R	N		I	M	P	E	L
			H	U	R	R	Y		S	T	E	E	D	S
G	E	E		R	O	N		R	I	E	L			
U	R	A	N	U	S		B	E	G	R	I	M	E	S
M	I	R	A		E	A	R	T	H		N	O	V	A
P	E	N	U	M	B	R	A		I	N	G	L	E	S
			S	E	A	T		D	N	A		T	S	E
V	A	L	E	R	Y		L	O	G	I	C			
I	L	I	A	C		I	O	U		V	E	N	U	S
B	A	N	T	U		S	U	B	G	E	N	E	R	A
E	M	E	E	R		I	S	L	E		T	A	S	S
S	O	D	D	Y		T	E	E	M		S	R	A	S

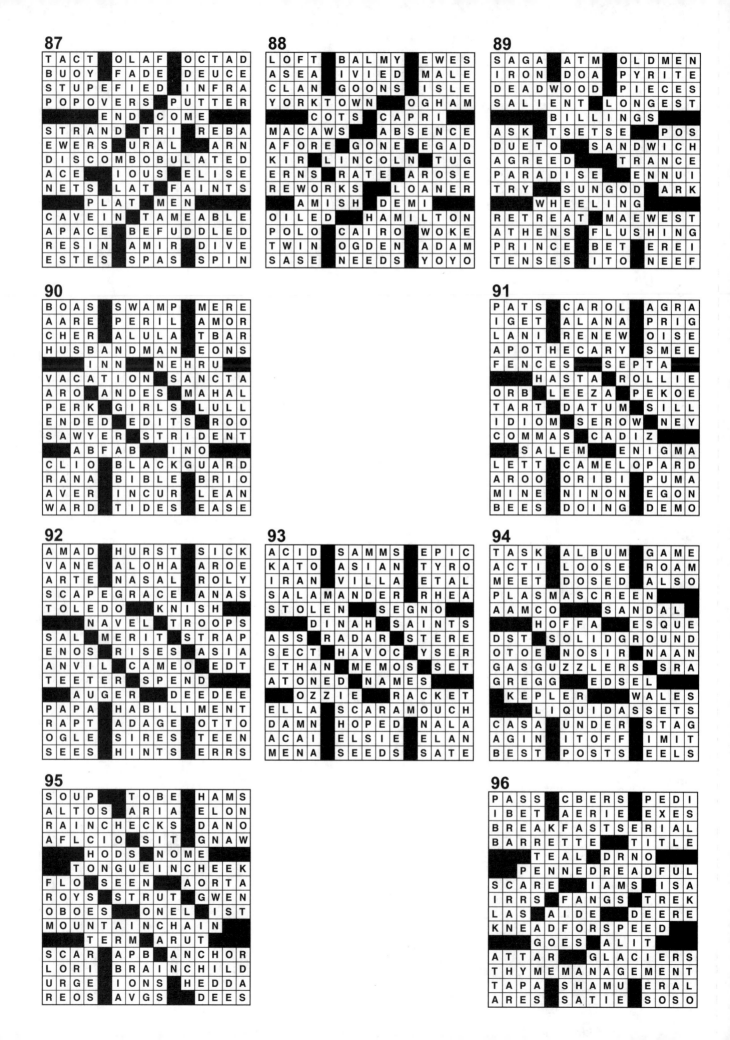

87

T A C T · O L A F · O C T A D
B U O Y · F A D E · D E U C E
S T U P E F I E D · I N F R A
P O P O V E R S · P U T T E R
· · · E N D · C O M E · · ·
S T R A N D · T R I · R E B A
E W E R S · U R A L · · A R N
D I S C O M B O B U L A T E D
A C E · I O U S · E L I S E
N E T S · L A T · F A I N T S
· · · P L A T · M E N · · ·
C A V E I N · T A M E A B L E
A P A C E · B E F U D D L E D
R E S I N · A M I R · D I V E
E S T E S · S P A S · S P I N

88

L O F T · B A L M Y · E W E S
A S E A · I V I E D · M A L E
C L A N · G O O N S · I S L E
Y O R K T O W N · O G H A M
· · C O T S · C A P R I · ·
M A C A W S · A B S E N C E
A F O R E · G O N E · E G A D
K I R · L I N C O L N · T U G
E R N S · R A T E · A R O S E
R E W O R K S · L O A N E R
· · A M I S H · D E M I · ·
O I L E D · H A M I L T O N
P O L O · C A I R O · W O K E
T W I N · O G D E N · A D A M
S A S E · N E E D S · Y O Y O

89

S A G A · A T M · O L D M E N
I R O N · D O A · P Y R I T E
D E A D W O O D · P I E C E S
S A L I E N T · L O N G E S T
· · · B I L L I N G S · · ·
A S K · T S E T S E · · P O S
D U E T O · · S A N D W I C H
A G R E E D · · · T R A N C E
P A R A D I S E · · E N N U I
T R Y · S U N G O D · · A R K
· · W H E E L I N G · · ·
R E T R E A T · M A E W E S T
A T H E N S · F L U S H I N G
P R I N C E · B E T · E R E I
T E N S E S · I T O · N E E F

90

B O A S · S W A M P · M E R E
A A R E · P E R I L · A M O R
C H E R · A L U L A · T B A R
H U S B A N D M A N · E O N S
· · · I N N · N E H R U · ·
V A C A T I O N · S A N C T A
A R O · A N D E S · M A H A L
P E R K · G I R L S · L U L L
E N D E D · E D I T S · R O O
S A W Y E R · S T R I D E N T
· · A B F A B · I N O · ·
C L I O · B L A C K G U A R D
R A N A · B I B L E · B R I O
A V E R · I N C U R · L E A N
W A R D · T I D E S · E A S E

91

P A T S · C A R O L · A G R A
I G E T · A L A N A · P R I G
L A N I · R E N E W · O I S E
A P O T H E C A R Y · S M E E
F E N C E S · S E P T A · ·
· · H A S T A · R O L L I E
O R B · L E E Z A · P E K O E
T A R T · D A T U M · S I L L
I D I O M · S E R O W · N E Y
C O M M A S · C A D I Z · ·
· · S A L E M · E N I G M A
L E T T · C A M E L O P A R D
A R O O · O R I B I · P U M A
M I N E · N I N O N · E G O N
B E E S · D O I N G · D E M O

92

A M A D · H U R S T · S I C K
V A N E · A L O H A · A R O E
A R T E · N A S A L · R O L Y
S C A P E G R A C E · A N A S
T O L E D O · K N I S H · ·
· · N A V E L · T R O O P S
S A L · M E R I T · S T R A P
E N O S · R I S E S · A S I A
A N V I L · C A M E O · E D T
T E E T E R · S P E N D · ·
· · A U G E R · D E E D E E
P A P A · H A B I L I M E N T
R A P T · A D A G E · O T T O
O G L E · S I R E S · T E E N
S E E S · H I N T S · E R R S

93

A C I D · S A M M S · E P I C
K A T O · A S I A N · T Y R O
I R A N · V I L L A · E T A L
S A L A M A N D E R · R H E A
S T O L E N · S E G N O · ·
· · D I N A H · S A I N T S
A S S · R A D A R · S T E R E
S E C T · H A V O C · Y S E R
E T H A N · M E M O S · S E T
A T O N E D · N A M E S · ·
· · O Z Z I E · R A C K E T
E L L A · S C A R A M O U C H
D A M N · H O P E D · N A L A
A C A I · E L S I E · E L A N
M E N A · S E E D S · S A T E

94

T A S K · A L B U M · G A M E
A C T I · L O O S E · R O A M
M E E T · D O S E D · A L S O
P L A S M A S C R E E N · ·
A A M C O · · S A N D A L ·
· · H O F F A · · E S Q U E
D S T · S O L I D G R O U N D
O T O E · N O S I R · N A A N
G A S G U Z Z L E R S · S R A
G R E G G · E D S E L · · ·
· K E P L E R · · W A L E S
· · L I Q U I D A S S E T S
C A S A · U N D E R · S T A G
A G I N · I T O F F · I M I T
B E S T · P O S T S · E E L S

95

S O U P · T O B E · H A M S
A L T O S · A R I A · E L O N
R A I N C H E C K S · D A N O
A F L C I O · S I T · G N A W
· · H O D S · N O M E · ·
· · T O N G U E I N C H E E K
F L O · S E E N · A O R T A
R O Y S · S T R U T · G W E N
O B O E S · O N E L · I S T
M O U N T A I N C H A I N · ·
· · T E R M · A R U T · ·
S C A R · A P B · A N C H O R
L O R I · B R A I N C H I L D
U R G E · I O N S · H E D D A
R E O S · A V G S · D E E S

96

P A S S · C B E R S · P E D I
I B E T · A E R I E · E X E S
B R E A K F A S T S E R I A L
B A R R E T T E · T I T L E
· · · T E A L · D R N O · ·
· · P E N N E D R E A D F U L
S C A R E · I A M S · I S A
I R R S · F A N G S · T R E K
L A S · A I D E · D E E R E
K N E A D F O R S P E E D ·
· · G O E S · A L I T · ·
A T T A R · · G L A C I E R S
T H Y M E M A N A G E M E N T
T A P A · S H A M U · E R A L
A R E S · S A T I E · S O S O

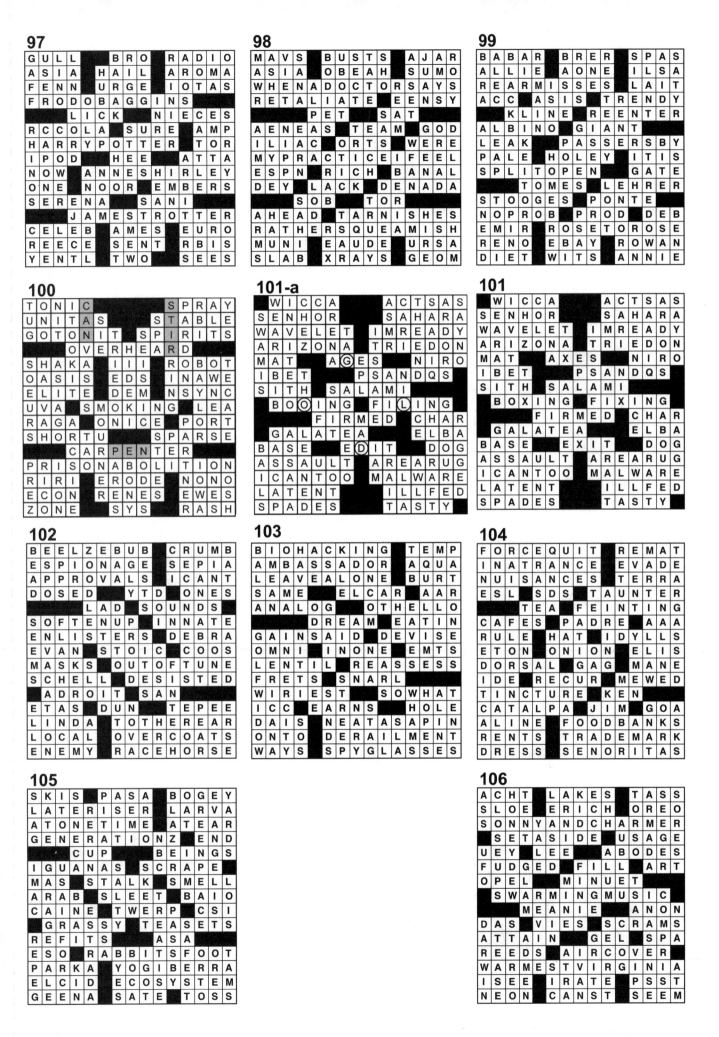

107

S	O	F	A		C	A	S	T	S		K	H	A	N
O	V	A	L		E	N	T	R	Y		I	A	G	O
B	E	R	L	I	N	W	A	I	L		N	I	N	O
S	N	E	E	R	S	A	T		L	A	D	L	E	S
		Y	O	U	R		V	A	M	O	O	S	E	
M	A	S	O	N	S		F	O	B	O	F	F		
A	L	L	O	Y		C	A	L	L	S		F	O	P
S	T	E	P		S	H	U	T	E		G	A	M	E
T	O	A		H	E	L	L	S		L	O	M	A	N
	Z	E	A	L	O	T		D	I	N	E	R	S	
S	T	E	R	I	L	E		T	I	E	D			
A	R	B	O	R	S		D	O	G	O	O	D	E	R
T	O	A	D		F	A	I	L	I	N	L	O	V	E
I	L	I	E		O	C	T	E	T		A	M	E	N
E	L	L	S		R	E	S	T	S		S	E	N	T

108

H	A	R	P		R	A	T	S	O		O	W	L	S
O	L	O	R		O	R	A	T	E		T	H	O	U
W	A	T	E	R	M	E	L	O	N		T	I	M	E
L	E	S	S	E	E	S		L	O	C	A	T	E	D
		U	A	R			A	W	E					
S	H	A	M	P	O	O		P	O	T	A	B	L	E
L	O	P	E	S		F	A	L	S	E		R	E	N
I	M	P	S		S	T	R	U	T		M	E	A	D
N	E	L		A	T	E	A	M		S	O	A	V	E
G	R	E	A	T	E	N		B	R	A	N	D	E	D
		C	R	O			U	H	S					
E	N	I	G	M	A	S		K	N	I	T	T	E	D
N	O	D	E		S	T	R	A	W	B	E	R	R	Y
O	M	E	N		A	L	O	H	A		R	A	S	A
S	E	R	T		D	O	N	N	Y		S	P	E	D

109

S	T	E	P		N	A	M	E	D		S	K	O	L
I	A	G	O		O	P	E	R	A		E	E	R	O
B	R	O	W	N	B	E	T	T	Y		R	Y	A	N
S	A	N	D	A	L	S		E	S	T	E	L	L	E
			E	V	E			O	N	I				
D	E	A	R	E	S	T		F	O	R	E	M	A	N
E	X	P	E	L		A	N	I	T	A		E	T	E
L	A	P	D		S	T	I	L	T		S	P	A	S
I	L	L		S	H	E	L	L		B	U	I	L	T
S	T	E	A	M	E	R		S	E	A	B	E	E	S
		C	L	U			D	R	J					
G	A	R	A	G	E	S		D	I	R	E	C	T	S
E	R	I	N		C	H	E	E	S	E	C	A	K	E
L	I	S	I		H	E	L	L	O		T	R	O	T
T	A	P	S		O	A	K	E	N		S	A	S	S

110

M	A	L	E		L	O	C	A	L		S	M	O	G
A	N	O	N		E	M	I	L	Y		P	Y	L	E
U	N	F	O	R	G	I	V	E	N		A	F	A	R
D	E	T	R	O	I	T		E	N	G	R	A	V	E
		M	A	O			A	S	I					
O	S	B	O	R	N	E		A	D	V	E	R	B	S
V	I	R	U	S		A	G	R	E	E		L	E	T
I	M	A	S		P	R	E	E	N		S	A	G	A
N	O	V		R	I	P	E	N		C	A	D	E	T
E	N	E	M	I	E	S		A	C	O	L	Y	T	E
		H	A	L			A	R	I					
S	T	E	L	L	A	R		T	R	A	V	A	I	L
C	O	A	L		C	A	S	A	B	L	A	N	C	A
O	G	R	E		H	Y	D	R	O		T	I	E	D
W	A	T	T		E	S	S	E	N		E	L	S	E

111

R	A	S	H		C	A	R	P	S		J	E	M	S
A	S	H	E		O	S	O	L	E		A	R	I	P
W	H	E	N	C	A	E	S	A	R		N	I	D	E
D	A	R	N	E	L		A	N	I	S	E	T	T	E
A	M	P	E	R	E	S		E	N	T	E	R	E	D
T	E	A	R	O	S	E	S		S	A	Y	E	R	S
A	D	S		C	U	T	S		D	R	A	M		
			T	H	E	S	E	N	A	T	E			
	S	W	A	B		S	P	A	S		B	O	A	
S	P	A	R	E	S		S	K	I	M	P	I	N	G
A	L	L	H	A	I	L		E	S	C	O	L	A	R
D	I	L	E	M	M	A	S		E	X	C	I	S	E
I	N	M	E		B	R	O	K	E	L	O	O	S	E
S	E	A	L		A	C	T	I	I		N	U	I	T
T	S	P	S		S	H	O	A	T		O	S	S	O

112

T	A	B	S		S	T	E	E	R		O	C	T	A
U	T	A	H		H	O	N	D	A		B	R	O	M
B	L	U	E	H	A	W	A	I	I		E	Y	R	E
A	I	M	L	E	S	S		E	N	T	R	I	E	S
		T	N	T			K	O	N					
A	R	S	E	N	A	L		S	P	O	N	G	E	D
T	I	A	R	A		A	S	H	E	S		G	T	O
O	L	D	S		A	N	T	I	C		M	A	N	E
N	E	B		N	I	G	E	R		M	A	M	A	S
E	D	U	C	A	T	E		E	V	E	R	E	S	T
		T	R	Y			I	N	G					
A	R	T	I	S	A	N		E	N	L	A	R	G	E
F	O	R	M		S	O	B	S	T	O	R	I	E	S
R	O	U	E		A	L	A	M	O		E	T	A	S
O	D	E	S		P	A	T	E	N		T	A	R	O

113

H	I	N	T		S	L	E	P	T		S	H	O	O
O	R	E	O		C	I	G	A	R		I	A	N	S
S	M	I	L	E	Y	F	A	C	E		E	P	E	E
T	A	L	E	N	T	E	D		M	A	G	P	I	E
		R	A	H	S		A	B	B	E	Y			
R	E	L	A	T	E		T	A	L	C		H	A	W
E	L	I	T	E		T	I	R	E	S		O	N	A
P	A	G	E		S	Y	N	O	D		R	U	G	S
E	T	H		N	O	L	A	N		B	E	R	E	T
L	E	T		A	C	E	S		H	A	S	S	L	E
	B	R	I	A	R		L	A	S	T				
O	N	E	I	L	L		D	E	S	E	R	T	E	R
B	E	A	N		L	A	U	G	H	L	A	U	G	H
I	S	M	S		E	L	L	I	E		I	N	G	E
E	S	S	E		D	O	L	T	S		N	A	S	A

114

S	H	E	W		A	M	A	N		M	A	S	T
M	A	L	E		M	A	F	I	A		A	S	H	Y
O	L	O	R		P	L	A	N	B		K	N	A	P
G	O	N	E	A	S	T	R	A	Y		E	E	R	O
		M	U	S			S	C	A	R	E	S		
L	A	P	T	O	P		B	O	S	C	S			
A	R	E	A	S		L	A	T	E	S	T	A	R	T
W	E	A	K		B	O	R	I	S		I	R	I	S
S	E	R	E	N	A	D	E	S		K	N	I	C	K
		A	F	T	E	R		A	N	K	L	E	S	
H	I	R	S	C	H		A	L	E					
O	N	I	T		M	I	D	D	L	E	E	A	S	T
G	A	G	A		A	D	E	L	E		M	I	K	E
A	N	O	N		T	O	K	A	Y		M	R	E	D
N	E	R	D		S	E	I	S		A	Y	E	S	

115

S	L	O	W		A	L	A	S		G	A	S	P	S
C	A	R	A		D	E	L	E		R	I	P	U	P
A	D	A	G	E	O	F	M	A	J	O	R	I	T	Y
M	E	L		A	R	T	S		O	U	S	T	S	
		F	R	E	T		N	A	N	A				
S	E	M	I	P	R	O	S	A	N	D	C	O	N	S
I	N	I	T	S		C	H	I	S		L	O	P	
C	O	T	S		H	O	U	S	E		V	E	T	O
E	K	E		C	A	L	F		P	A	T	I	O	
M	I	S	C	H	I	E	F	O	F	S	T	A	F	F
	E	E	R	S		B	A	A	S					
A	I	L	E	D		C	T	R	L		A	D	S	
A	N	T	I	S	O	C	I	A	L	M	E	D	I	A
I	N	A	N	E		A	T	I	E		S	A	N	G
M	A	L	E	S		N	Y	N	Y		S	M	E	E

116

A	P	B	S		L	A	S	T	S		B	E	S	S
D	U	E	T		A	S	P	E	N		I	S	L	A
E	N	T	R		P	A	Y	T	O		E	P	I	C
	C	H	I	L	D	P	R	O	O	F	L	O	C	K
S	T	E	P	S		I	N	T	L		S	E	E	
N	U	S		D	E	B		E	C	A	R	D		
L	A	D	S		T	R	O	O	P	E	R			
	L	A	U	G	H	I	N	G	S	T	O	C	K	
	R	O	S	T	E	R	S		P	O	N	G		
B	A	L	E	R		E	T	A		N	E	E		
E	T	E		M	E	T	A		P	A	C	E	S	
C	R	A	T	E	A	N	D	B	A	R	R	E	L	
A	I	R	Y		T	O	R	O	S		I	R	I	S
M	A	N	N		A	T	A	R	I		A	T	N	O
E	L	S	E		T	E	W	E	S		L	O	G	O

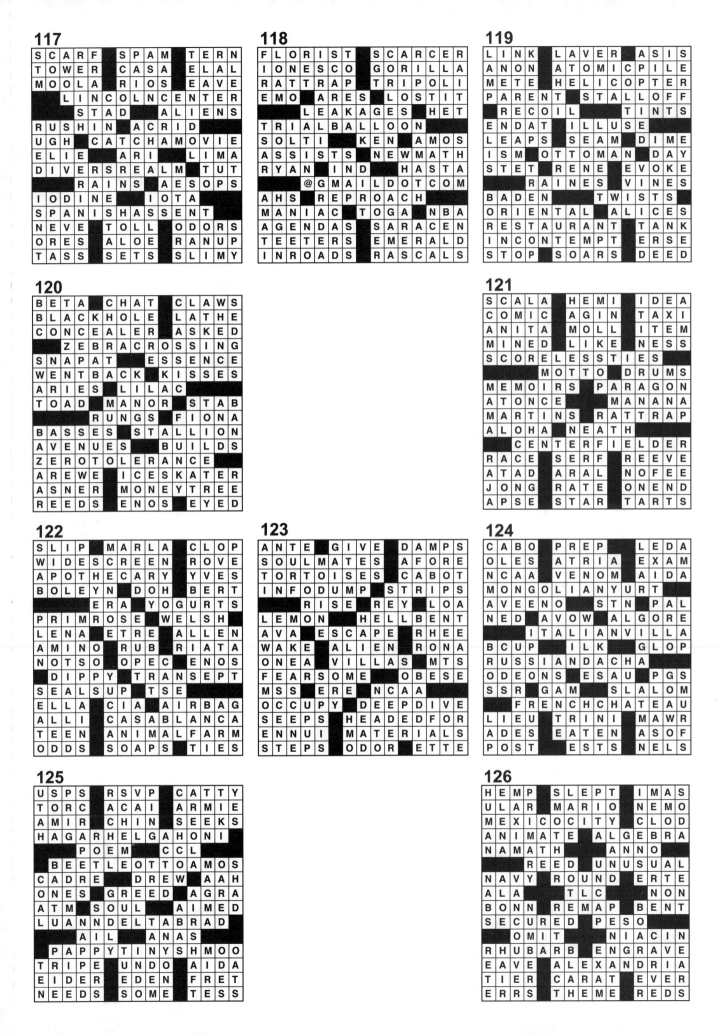

117

S	C	A	R	F		S	P	A	M		T	E	R	N
T	O	W	E	R		C	A	S	A		E	L	A	L
M	O	O	L	A		R	I	O	S		E	A	V	E
	L	I	N	C	O	L	N	C	E	N	T	E	R	
		S	T	A	D		A	L	I	E	N	S		
R	U	S	H	I	N		A	C	R	I	D			
U	G	H		C	A	T	C	H	A	M	O	V	I	E
E	L	I	E		A	R	I		L	I	M	A		
D	I	V	E	R	S	R	E	A	L	M		T	U	T
		R	A	I	N	S		A	E	S	O	P	S	
I	O	D	I	N	E		I	O	T	A				
S	P	A	N	I	S	H	A	S	S	E	N	T		
N	E	V	E		T	O	L	L		O	D	O	R	S
O	R	E	S		A	L	O	E		R	A	N	U	P
T	A	S	S		S	E	T	S		S	L	I	M	Y

118

F	L	O	R	I	S	T		S	C	A	R	C	E	R
I	O	N	E	S	C	O		G	O	R	I	L	L	A
R	A	T	T	R	A	P		T	R	I	P	O	L	I
E	M	O		A	R	E	S		L	O	S	T	I	T
	L	E	A	K	A	G	E	S		H	E	T		
T	R	I	A	L	B	A	L	L	O	O	N			
S	O	L	T	I		K	E	N		A	M	O	S	
A	S	S	I	S	T	S		N	E	W	M	A	T	H
R	Y	A	N		I	N	D		H	A	S	T	A	
		@	G	M	A	I	L	D	O	T	C	O	M	
A	H	S		R	E	P	R	O	A	C	H			
M	A	N	I	A	C		T	O	G	A		N	B	A
A	G	E	N	D	A	S		S	A	R	A	C	E	N
T	E	E	T	E	R	S		E	M	E	R	A	L	D
I	N	R	O	A	D	S		R	A	S	C	A	L	S

119

L	I	N	K		L	A	V	E	R		A	S	I	S
A	N	O	N		A	T	O	M	I	C	P	I	L	E
M	E	T	E		H	E	L	I	C	O	P	T	E	R
P	A	R	E	N	T		S	T	A	L	L	O	F	F
	R	E	C	O	I	L		T	I	N	T	S		
E	N	D	A	T		I	L	L	U	S	E			
L	E	A	P	S		S	E	A	M		D	I	M	E
I	S	M		O	T	T	O	M	A	N		D	A	Y
S	T	E	T		R	E	N	E		E	V	O	K	E
		R	A	I	N	E	S		V	I	N	E	S	
B	A	D	E	N		T	W	I	S	T	S			
O	R	I	E	N	T	A	L		A	L	I	C	E	S
R	E	S	T	A	U	R	A	N	T		T	A	N	K
I	N	C	O	N	T	E	M	P	T		E	R	S	E
S	T	O	P		S	O	A	R	S		D	E	E	D

120

B	E	T	A		C	H	A	T		C	L	A	W	S
B	L	A	C	K	H	O	L	E		L	A	T	H	E
C	O	N	C	E	A	L	E	R		A	S	K	E	D
	Z	E	B	R	A	C	R	O	S	S	I	N	G	
S	N	A	P	A	T		E	S	S	E	N	C	E	
W	E	N	T	B	A	C	K		K	I	S	S	E	S
A	R	I	E	S		L	I	L	A	C				
T	O	A	D		M	A	N	O	R		S	T	A	B
		R	U	N	G	S		F	I	O	N	A		
B	A	S	S	E	S		S	T	A	L	L	I	O	N
A	V	E	N	U	E	S		B	U	I	L	D	S	
Z	E	R	O	T	O	L	E	R	A	N	C	E		
A	R	E	W	E		I	C	E	S	K	A	T	E	R
A	S	N	E	R		M	O	N	E	Y	T	R	E	E
R	E	E	D	S		E	N	O	S		E	Y	E	D

121

S	C	A	L	A		H	E	M	I		I	D	E	A
C	O	M	I	C		A	G	I	N		T	A	X	I
A	N	I	T	A		M	O	L	L		I	T	E	M
M	I	N	E	D		L	I	K	E		N	E	S	S
S	C	O	R	E	L	E	S	S	T	I	E	S		
			M	O	T	T	O		D	R	U	M	S	
M	E	M	O	I	R	S		P	A	R	A	G	O	N
A	T	O	N	C	E			M	A	N	A	N	A	
M	A	R	T	I	N	S		R	A	T	T	R	A	P
A	L	O	H	A		N	E	A	T	H				
	C	E	N	T	E	R	F	I	E	L	D	E	R	
R	A	C	E		S	E	R	F		R	E	E	V	E
A	T	A	D		A	R	A	L		N	O	F	E	E
J	O	N	G		R	A	T	E		O	N	E	N	D
A	P	S	E		S	T	A	R		T	A	R	T	S

122

S	L	I	P		M	A	R	L	A		C	L	O	P
W	I	D	E	S	C	R	E	E	N		R	O	V	E
A	P	O	T	H	E	C	A	R	Y		Y	V	E	S
B	O	L	E	Y	N		D	O	H		B	E	R	T
			E	R	A		Y	O	G	U	R	T	S	
P	R	I	M	R	O	S	E		W	E	L	S	H	
L	E	N	A		E	T	R	E		A	L	L	E	N
A	M	I	N	O		R	U	B		R	I	A	T	A
N	O	T	S	O		O	P	E	C		E	N	O	S
	D	I	P	P	Y		T	R	A	N	S	E	P	T
S	E	A	L	S	U	P		T	S	E				
E	L	L	A		C	I	A		A	I	R	B	A	G
A	L	L	I		C	A	S	A	B	L	A	N	C	A
T	E	E	N		A	N	I	M	A	L	F	A	R	M
O	D	D	S		S	O	A	P	S		T	I	E	S

123

A	N	T	E		G	I	V	E		D	A	M	P	S
S	O	U	L	M	A	T	E	S		A	F	O	R	E
T	O	R	T	O	I	S	E	S		C	A	B	O	T
I	N	F	O	D	U	M	P		S	T	R	I	P	S
	R	I	S	E		R	E	Y		L	O	A		
L	E	M	O	N		H	E	L	L	B	E	N	T	
A	V	A		E	S	C	A	P	E		R	H	E	E
W	A	K	E		A	L	I	E	N		R	O	N	A
O	N	E	A		V	I	L	L	A	S		M	T	S
F	E	A	R	S	O	M	E		O	B	E	S	E	
M	S	S		E	R	E		N	C	A	A			
O	C	C	U	P	Y		D	E	E	P	D	I	V	E
S	E	E	P	S		H	E	A	D	E	D	F	O	R
E	N	N	U	I		M	A	T	E	R	I	A	L	S
S	T	E	P	S		O	D	O	R		E	T	T	E

124

C	A	B	O		P	R	E	P		L	E	D	A
O	L	E	S		A	T	R	I	A		E	X	A	M
N	C	A	A		V	E	N	O	M		A	I	D	A
M	O	N	G	O	L	I	A	N	Y	U	R	T		
A	V	E	E	N	O		S	T	N		P	A	L	
N	E	D		A	V	O	W		A	L	G	O	R	E
		I	T	A	L	I	A	N	V	I	L	L	A	
B	C	U	P		I	L	K		G	L	O	P		
R	U	S	S	I	A	N	D	A	C	H	A			
O	D	E	O	N	S		E	S	A	U		P	G	S
S	S	R		G	A	M		S	L	A	L	O	M	
	F	R	E	N	C	H	C	H	A	T	E	A	U	
L	I	E	U		T	R	I	N	I		M	A	W	R
A	D	E	S		E	A	T	E	N		A	S	O	F
P	O	S	T		E	S	T	S		N	E	L	S	

125

U	S	P	S		R	S	V	P		C	A	T	T	Y
T	O	R	C		A	C	A	I		A	R	M	I	E
A	M	I	R		C	H	I	N		S	E	E	K	S
H	A	G	A	R	H	E	L	G	A	H	O	N	I	
		P	O	E	M		C	C	L					
	B	E	E	T	L	E	O	T	T	O	A	M	O	S
C	A	D	R	E		D	R	E	W		A	A	H	
O	N	E	S		G	R	E	E	D		A	G	R	A
A	T	M		S	O	U	L		A	I	M	E	D	
L	U	A	N	N	D	E	L	T	A	B	R	A	D	
	A	I	L		A	N	A	S						
	P	A	P	P	Y	T	I	N	Y	S	H	M	O	O
T	R	I	P	E		U	N	D	O		A	I	D	A
E	I	D	E	R		E	D	E	N		F	R	E	T
N	E	E	D	S		S	O	M	E		T	E	S	S

126

H	E	M	P		S	L	E	P	T		I	M	A	S
U	L	A	R		M	A	R	I	O		N	E	M	O
M	E	X	I	C	O	C	I	T	Y		C	L	O	D
A	N	I	M	A	T	E		A	L	G	E	B	R	A
N	A	M	A	T	H			A	N	N	O			
			R	E	E	D		U	N	U	S	U	A	L
N	A	V	Y		R	O	U	N	D		E	R	T	E
A	L	A			T	L	C			N	O	N		
B	O	N	N		R	E	M	A	P		B	E	N	T
S	E	C	U	R	E	D		P	E	S	O			
			O	M	I	T		N	I	A	C	I	N	
R	H	U	B	A	R	B		E	N	G	R	A	V	E
E	A	V	E		A	L	E	X	A	N	D	R	I	A
T	I	E	R		C	A	R	A	T		E	V	E	R
E	R	R	S		T	H	E	M	E		R	E	D	S

127

```
BANS . LEWIS . OFFS
APOP . IRONY . PERU
SPRINGROLL . ATOM
STARCH . LAVALAMP
. IOTA . YAM . . .
NAST . IDS . NEREID
ALA . INMAN . NERDY
SPRINGAHEADFALL
AHOLD . NIXES . TEA
LADLES . BUS . CORN
. EEK . STLO . . .
PASADENA . HAMLET
IDOL . SILVERBACK
PINT . ASMAT . EGGO
SAGA . WHALE . ROSS
```

128

```
SPAS . TRAPS . SPEW
TELE . RELIC . HODA
ARES . OOOLA . OTIC
RUSTBUSTER . OTTO
. EOS . SAUTE . . .
TACTLESS . BRIDLE
USO . ERECT . UNPIN
SLAV . SARAH . GLAD
KATIE . LUCAS . ANO
SNOOPS . MONTANAN
. FLIER . DOR . . .
POPE . RAILBLAZER
OMAN . ATRIA . BITO
ERIC . PEARL . INTO
MINE . EDSEL . ACED
```

129

```
RAID . ADIOS . IBAR
ALSO . DIRTY . MYTH
MATCHMAKER . PELE
PROTEINS . ARABIA
. RARE . SCARY . .
RESIDE . CLUSTERS
OMENS . FRESH . LOW
ACRE . CREPE . ROTA
REV . GHOST . LEVON
SEEDLESS . TIGERS
. SWEET . RENI . .
LATENT . CARESSED
AMIE . ACEVENTURA
COMB . HIDES . EMIR
EYES . SIENA . ROCK
```

130

```
YAMS . FACET . AFAR
VAIN . IMAGO . CUTE
ESCAPEPLAN . OSEE
SEERESS . DEBRIEF
. LAT . ONO . . . .
REFUSAL . FIN . NTH
ELOPE . ORATE . BRO
PECS . SUEDE . SOAR
EMU . MAINE . HUMID
LIS . IDS . STUBBLE
. GUM . . ART . . .
FORTIES . PULLOUT
AMOI . RAZORSEDGE
SOUL . ADIEU . SOLE
TOPE . SEPTS . TRIM
```

131

```
BUTT . STUDS . OGLE
ACHE . TOTAL . BRON
BLUEHAWAII . TAVI
EASTERN . STRAYED
. HAL . HAIM . . .
ALGERIA . TEENAGE
CARR . TIMER . STER
INA . DIT . . . TER
DAYS . BERRA . LESE
SIGHTED . ALTERED
. HERA . GOA . . .
IMOGENE . REGRETS
SOSO . BLUEBONNET
ALTA . ASTIR . EYRE
REST . GEENA . RAMP
```

132

```
HINDU . GRASS . HOW
AREAS . RUDDY . IRE
TAXMANOFWAR . GEL
ENTS . EWER . INHOT
. EAST . INNES . .
. FILLTHETAXBILL
RINSE . XED . SEEA
OBI . SHOPRAG . ROI
BETA . ORE . OSRIC
ORIGINALSINTAX
. ANGEL . UREA . .
HELIO . ERNO . TALE
OVI . TAXINCLUDED
PEZ . TRADE . ORATE
ERE . ARMED . LEMON
```

133

```
ALPS . ABACI . SHUL
LOOT . SALON . PONE
SUGARSHACK . ANTI
ODOROUS . AWAREOF
. EAR . ETSY . . .
CABARET . ALLERGY
ANAT . DWELL . RYNE
RIB . IMA . . . DOA
AMYS . EXURB . GEMS
TABARET . MINARET
. OMSK . GER . . .
POORTAX . ENABLES
REMI . RONDARLING
ONEC . AXIOM . EMIT
FORE . TORME . DADS
```

134

```
TENT . PLED . RAGAS
AMAR . LOPE . ENOCH
PIKE . ARON . MOORE
ALEE . TINSKINNED
SEDATE . YENS . . .
. MODEM . ESTADO
AGAIN . ASTA . RUIN
LEDGERS . ADVANCE
UNDO . ATOI . ASTER
MESSED . FLASH . .
. LIAR . NEARED
OFTEEISING . BONE
AURIC . ILIE . OSTE
FLIRT . DELL . USER
SLOES . EYES . TIRE
```

135

```
SCROD . CRIS . TERI
ERODE . PINK . HVAC
LAWOFGRAVY . EENY
ANDREW . ALUMNI .
HEY . NAKEDAPE . .
. . DRIVERSPERM
WORSE . DESK . APIA
EDUARD . SUREST .
LIFT . RUTS . SKEET
DEFINEMAYBE . . .
. REALISED . LAB
. ENIGMA . AGLARE
ERIC . JUSTDROPIT
MINA . OTIS . ONSET
TEAL . BSNA . MEESE
```

136

```
TAROT . PLUM . BASH
ALONE . HOSE . OREO
BABYSHOWER . SKIM
. SEXTON . DESTINE
. . ELEC . TONER
ASHORE . LATIN . .
SOAR . AURAL . OSS
TOWEROFSTRENGTH
INK . IRATE . AREA
. SNORE . APPEND
JANUS . ROSA . . .
ANAPEST . ROLLON
WISP . WILDFLOWER
ETAL . ALEE . OPERA
DALE . GEAR . REDDY
```

137

```
S T E M   M E D I C S   C A W
T Y P O   O R I O L E   U T A
U N I T   T I N T E D   B O X
B E C O M I N G A V E G A N
      R E V       E R A
F R A   M E N T O R   R A S P
R A M B O   O A R   C A M E L
A N E A R   I S A   A G O R A
M I N D Y   S E T   B E N I N
E N D E   C E R E A L   G O T
      G A R       D E S
  B I G M I S S E D S T E A K
J A N   I S O L D E   R A R E
A S K   S T R A I N   O V E N
W H Y   S O T T E D   P E A T
```

138

```
D E C K   F E A T   R A C K S
A L O E   L A S H   E X I L E
F L O P H O U S E   S I T I N
T A T T O O     W I T S E N D
      A R A B I C A   D E S
L O U N G E L I Z A R D
I P S O   D O C   N E A T H
N E E D I   T A M   A C H E D
  D R E D D   R I P   H O A R
    S L U M B E R P A R T Y
C F C   E D A S N E R
R E H I R E S     C E A S E S
A L I B I   S L E E P W A L K
C O L I C   E Y E D   L U B E
K N I S H   D E L E   S L E W
```

139

```
T W I T T E R A T I   A S T I
W A T E R M E L O N   S T E N
A N E M O M E T E R   W A N D
S E M   P E S O   U G A N D A
      S I T E   A S U N D E R
I M P A C T   O C H S   A R K
M I L L S   M O T E T   S I N
P L A T   S I Z E S   M I Z E
A L I   D O T E D   D U D E S
S E N   O P T S   D E T E R S
S T A R C H Y   K E T T
A S S I S I   B E T E   A H A
B E D S   S C R E E N A G E R
L E A K   M A I N S T R E A M
E D Y S   S W E E T E N E R S
```

140

```
M A N S P L A I N S   J A B S
O N E C O O L C A T   A B E T
I N P A R A D I S E   M U N I
R A T T E D O N   E A S T O N
E M U   S U G A R S   S I T
S A N T A   S U N   K R O S S
  Y E N T E   P E A S A N T
    O W L S   W I F I
  O U T O F I T   T O S C A
D O P E R   A W E   R E A D S
U H F   S P L A T S   M I C
F L O A T S   S E A S C A P E
F A R M   H E N R Y A A R O N
E L I E   A T O N E S P O S T
L A T S   W A T E R H O S E S
```

141

```
  O N B A S E   M A D D E S T
A V E R R E D   A T E I N T O
R E T I N A S   R O O S T E R
I N S E A M   B I Z   C R A M
      Z O R R O   R H Y M E
G O A T   N E E   M E A
A L I E N S P A C E C R A F T
A G R E E T O D I S A G R E E
P A Y O N E S R E S P E C T S
      F E R   O R E   S H E S
M I F F S   P L A N A
U N I T   C O L   G I G O L O
F E L I N E S   M E D A L E D
T R E M B L E   I R E L A N D
I T S E A S Y   A S S A Y S
```

142

```
T A L K   S M I T S   H A N D
O L I O   T A L I A   O P I E
R E D B E A N S A N D R I C E
R E S E M B L E   D A N G E R
      P L Y   C I T E
B E S S I E   B R E A T H E R
O T T E R   S L O G   E C O
W H I T E R H I N O C E R O S
I A L   E E N Y   A D D L E
E N L A R G E D   C L O S E S
    C O U P   R E L
R A S C A L   M E M O R I S E
B L U E D A N U B E W A L T Z
I D E S   T I T A N   Y E A R
S A T S   E X E R T   S A G A
```

143

```
J A M B   M A G M A   S T A B
A L O U   O N E A M   T O L L
W I L L Y N I L L Y   E P E E
S E L L E R S   E L A P S E D
    P A O       D I Y
A D H E R E D   L E A N T O S
L O O N S   R E A L M   U S A
E R I S   S A N Y O   C R I B
P S T   B A Y O U   C O V E R
H A Y M O W S   P A L M Y R A
    T E A       R A F
E G O T R I P   I G N O R E D
L A I R   N I T T Y G R I T Y
A L T O   S T E E L   T O N E
N A Y S   T H E M E   S T A R
```

144

```
W A V E D   A M O   S K I P S
I L O S E   S O L S T I C E S
S L I C E   S N A K E S K I N
P O L A R O I D F I L M
S T E P   N S A   L E T B E
  S A F E T Y F E A T U R E
    D I M   S A M   D E L
R A R E B I T   S I L V E R S
A L E   L O W   T O E
G O T T H E P I C T U R E
A U D I O   R A E   T U B A
  M O V I E T R A I L E R
M A K E H A S T E   S C O T T
O P E R A S T A R   P A G E S
A B Y S S   O P S   S L Y L Y
```

145

```
S W A M I   A A H   P A I R S
A T P A R   R C A   A G L O W
L O O K A F T E R   L O U P E
  L I Q U O R   C A R V E D
A V O N   N O B L E C A U S E
P E G G E D   A D E
G R I D S   F I N E   C R Y
A S S O C I A T E D E G R E E
R O T   M I S S   A R E N A
  B U T   K R A M E R
E Q U A L S H A R E   Y A W N
C U T L E T   T H R E A T
L A I L A   P E E R G R O U P
A S C O T   R U T   G E R M S
T H A W S   O P T   Y A Y A S
```

146

```
T A X I S   A S S   Y E L P S
O B E S E   I P A   A N O D E
A A R O N  (R)I V E R R A F(T)
S T O L E N   L E A D O N
(T)E X A C O S T A(R)   U S D A
      T A L E   S L I T H E R
T A S E   A G O   M E A L S
E T H  (S)N O W C A(P)   R H O
S T A R E   N O N   A K I N
L I K E N E W   S K I S
A C E S  (D)E(P)T H C H A(R)(T)
    A P O G E E   S E A L E R
S P L I T E N D S   A M O R E
U T E R I   I R A   G E N U S
M A G E S   E O N   E D E N S
```

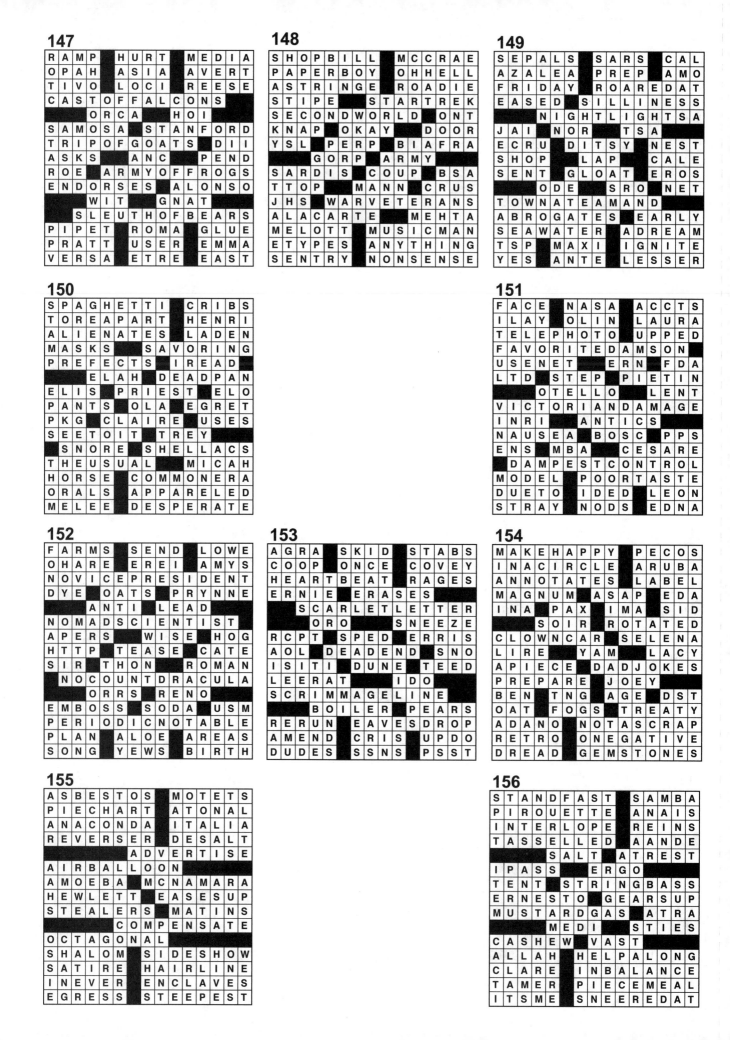

147

```
R A M P   H U R T   M E D I A
O P A H   A S I A   A V E R T
T I V O   L O C I   R E E S E
C A S T O F F A L C O N S
    O R C A   H O I
S A M O S A   S T A N F O R D
T R I P O F G O A T S   D I I
A S K S   A N C   P E N D
R O E   A R M Y O F F R O G S
E N D O R S E S   A L O N S O
    W I T   G N A T
  S L E U T H O F B E A R S
P I P E T   R O M A   G L U E
P R A T T   U S E R   E M M A
V E R S A   E T R E   E A S T
```

148

```
S H O P B I L L   M C C R A E
P A P E R B O Y   O H H E L L
A S T R I N G E   R O A D I E
S T I P E     S T A R T R E K
S E C O N D W O R L D   O N T
K N A P   O K A Y   D O O R
Y S L   P E R P   B I A F R A
  G O R P   A R M Y
S A R D I S   C O U P   B S A
T T O P   M A N N   C R U S
J H S   W A R V E T E R A N S
A L A C A R T E   M E H T A
M E L O T T   M U S I C M A N
E T Y P E S   A N Y T H I N G
S E N T R Y   N O N S E N S E
```

149

```
S E P A L S   S A R S   C A L
A Z A L E A   P R E P   A M O
F R I D A Y   R O A R E D A T
E A S E D   S I L L I N E S S
    N I G H T L I G H T S A
J A I   N O R   T S A
E C R U   D I T S Y   N E S T
S H O P   L A P   C A L E
S E N T   G L O A T   E R O S
    O D E   S R O   N E T
T O W N A T E A M A N D
A B R O G A T E S   E A R L Y
S E A W A T E R   A D R E A M
T S P   M A X I   I G N I T E
Y E S   A N T E   L E S S E R
```

150

```
S P A G H E T T I   C R I B S
T O R E A P A R T   H E N R I
A L I E N A T E S   L A D E N
M A S K S   S A V O R I N G
P R E F E C T S   I R E A D
    E L A H   D E A D P A N
E L I S   P R I E S T   E L O
P A N T S   O L A   E G R E T
P K G   C L A I R E   U S E S
S E E T O I T   T R E Y
  S N O R E   S H E L L A C S
T H E U S U A L   M I C A H
H O R S E   C O M M O N E R A
O R A L S   A P P A R E L E D
M E L E E   D E S P E R A T E
```

151

```
F A C E   N A S A   A C C T S
I L A Y   O L I N   L A U R A
T E L E P H O T O   U P P E D
F A V O R I T E D A M S O N
U S E N E T   E R N   F D A
L T D   S T E P   P I E T I N
    O T E L L O   L E N T
V I C T O R I A N D A M A G E
I N R I   A N T I C S
N A U S E A   B O S C   P P S
E N S   M B A   C E S A R E
  D A M P E S T C O N T R O L
M O D E L   P O O R T A S T E
D U E T O   I D E D   L E O N
S T R A Y   N O D S   E D N A
```

152

```
F A R M S   S E N D   L O W E
O H A R E   E R E I   A M Y S
N O V I C E P R E S I D E N T
D Y E   O A T S   P R Y N N E
    A N T I   L E A D
N O M A D S C I E N T I S T
A P E R S   W I S E   H O G
H T T P   T E A S E   C A T E
S I R   T H O N   R O M A N
  N O C O U N T D R A C U L A
  O R R S   R E N O
E M B O S S   S O D A   U S M
P E R I O D I C N O T A B L E
P L A N   A L O E   A R E A S
S O N G   Y E W S   B I R T H
```

153

```
A G R A   S K I D   S T A B S
C O O P   O N C E   C O V E Y
H E A R T B E A T   R A G E S
E R N I E   E R A S E S
  S C A R L E T L E T T E R
  O R O   S N E E Z E
R C P T   S P E D   E R R I S
A O L   D E A D E N D   S N O
I S I T I   D U N E   T E E D
L E E R A T   I D O
S C R I M M A G E L I N E
  B O I L E R   P E A R S
R E R U N   E A V E S D R O P
A M E N D   C R I S   U P D O
D U D E S   S S N S   P S S T
```

154

```
M A K E H A P P Y   P E C O S
I N A C I R C L E   A R U B A
A N N O T A T E S   L A B E L
M A G N U M   A S A P   E D A
I N A   P A X   I M A   S I D
  S O I R   R O T A T E D
C L O W N C A R   S E L E N A
L I R E   Y A M   L A C Y
A P I E C E   D A D J O K E S
P R E P A R E   J O E Y
B E N   T N G   A G E   D S T
O A T   F O G S   T R E A T Y
A D A N O   N O T A S C R A P
R E T R O   O N E N E G A T I V E
D R E A D   G E M S T O N E S
```

155

```
A S B E S T O S   M O T E T S
P I E C H A R T   A T O N A L
A N A C O N D A   I T A L I A
R E V E R S E R   D E S A L T
        A D V E R T I S E
A I R B A L L O O N
A M O E B A   M C N A M A R A
H E W L E T T   E A S E S U P
S T E A L E R S   M A T I N S
        C O M P E N S A T E
O C T A G O N A L
S H A L O M   S I D E S H O W
S A T I R E   H A I R L I N E
I N E V E R   E N C L A V E S
E G R E S S   S T E E P E S T
```

156

```
S T A N D F A S T   S A M B A
P I R O U E T T E   A N A I S
I N T E R L O P E   R E I N S
T A S S E L L E D   A A N D E
    S A L T   A T R E S T
I P A S S   E R G O
T E N T   S T R I N G B A S S
E R N E S T O   G E A R S U P
M U S T A R D G A S   A T R A
    M E D I   S T I E S
C A S H E W   V A S T
A L L A H   H E L P A L O N G
C L A R E   I N B A L A N C E
T A M E R   P I E C E M E A L
I T S M E   S N E E R E D A T
```

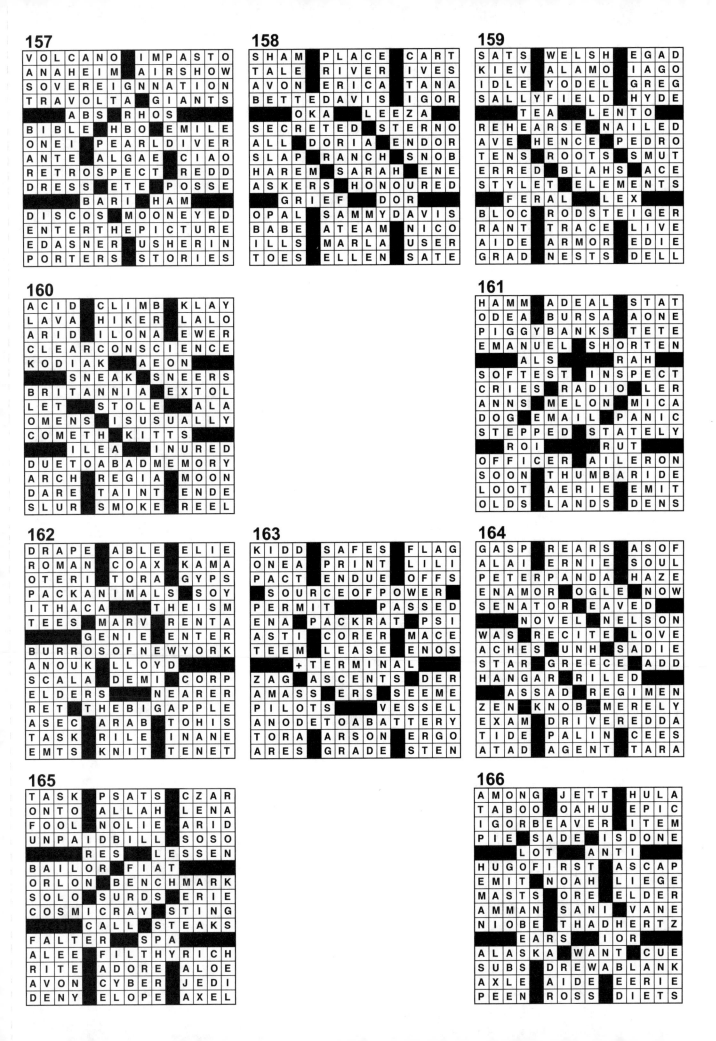

157

```
VOLCANO  IMPASTO
ANAHEIM  AIRSHOW
SOVEREIGNNATION
TRAVOLTA  GIANTS
    ABS  RHOS
BIBLE HBO  EMILE
ONEI  PEARLDIVER
ANTE  ALGAE  CIAO
RETROSPECT  REDD
DRESS  ETE  POSSE
    BARI  HAM
DISCOS  MOONEYED
ENTERTHEPICTURE
EDASNER  USHERIN
PORTERS  STORIES
```

158

```
SHAM  PLACE  CART
TALE  RIVER  IVES
AVON  ERICA  TANA
BETTEDAVIS  IGOR
    OKA  LEEZA
SECRETED  STERNO
ALL  DORIA  ENDOR
SLAP  RANCH  SNOB
HAREM  SARAH  ENE
ASKERS  HONOURED
    GRIEF  DOR
OPAL  SAMMYDAVIS
BABE  ATEAM  NICO
ILLS  MARLA  USER
TOES  ELLEN  SATE
```

159

```
SATS  WELSH  EGAD
KIEV  ALAMO  IAGO
IDLE  YODEL  GREG
SALLYFIELD  HYDE
    TEA  LENTO
REHEARSE  NAILED
AVE  HENCE  PEDRO
TENS  ROOTS  SMUT
ERRED  BLAHS  ACE
STYLET  ELEMENTS
    FERAL  LEX
BLOC  RODSTEIGER
RANT  TRACE  LIVE
AIDE  ARMOR  EDIE
GRAD  NESTS  DELL
```

160

```
ACID  CLIMB  KLAY
LAVA  HIKER  LALO
ARID  ILONA  EWER
CLEARCONSCIENCE
KODIAK  AEON
    SNEAK  SNEERS
BRITANNIA  EXTOL
LET  STOLE  ALA
OMENS  ISUSUALLY
COMETH  KITTS
    ILEA  INURED
DUETOABADMEMORY
ARCH  REGIA  MOON
DARE  TAINT  ENDE
SLUR  SMOKE  REEL
```

161

```
HAMM  ADEAL  STAT
ODEA  BURSA  AONE
PIGGYBANKS  TETE
EMANUEL  SHORTEN
    ALS  RAH
SOFTEST  INSPECT
CRIES  RADIO  LER
ANNS  MELON  MICA
DOG  EMAIL  PANIC
STEPPED  STATELY
    ROI  RUT
OFFICER  AILERON
SOON  THUMBARIDE
LOOT  AERIE  EMIT
OLDS  LANDS  DENS
```

162

```
DRAPE  ABLE  ELIE
ROMAN  COAX  KAMA
OTERI  TORA  GYPS
PACKANIMALS  SOY
ITHACA  THEISM
TEES  MARV  RENTA
    GENIE  ENTER
BURROSOFNEWYORK
ANOUK  LLOYD
SCALA  DEMI  CORP
ELDERS  NEARER
RET  THEBIGAPPLE
ASEC  ARAB  TOHIS
TASK  RILE  INANE
EMTS  KNIT  TENET
```

163

```
KIDD  SAFES  FLAG
ONEA  PRINT  LILI
PACT  ENDUE  OFFS
  SOURCEOFPOWER
PERMIT  PASSED
ENA  PACKRAT  PSI
ASTI  CORER  MACE
TEEM  LEASE  ENOS
  +TERMINAL
ZAG  ASCENTS  DER
AMASS  ERS  SEEME
PILOTS  VESSEL
ANODETOABATTERY
TORA  ARSON  ERGO
ARES  GRADE  STEN
```

164

```
GASP  REARS  ASOF
ALAI  ERNIE  SOUL
PETERPANDA  HAZE
ENAMOR  OGLE  NOW
SENATOR  EAVED
    NOVEL  NELSON
WAS  RECITE  LOVE
ACHES  UNH  SADIE
STAR  GREECE  ADD
HANGAR  RILED
    ASSAD  REGIMEN
ZEN  KNOB  MERELY
EXAM  DRIVEREDDA
TIDE  PALIN  CEES
ATAD  AGENT  TARA
```

165

```
TASK  PSATS  CZAR
ONTO  ALLAH  LENA
FOOL  NOLIE  ARID
UNPAIDBILL  SOSO
    RES  LESSEN
BAILOR  FIAT
ORLON  BENCHMARK
SOLO  SURDS  ERIE
COSMICRAY  STING
    CALL  STEAKS
FALTER  SPA
ALEE  FILTHYRICH
RITE  ADORE  ALOE
AVON  CYBER  JEDI
DENY  ELOPE  AXEL
```

166

```
AMONG  JETT  HULA
TABOO  OAHU  EPIC
IGORBEAVER  ITEM
PIE  SADE  ISDONE
    LOT  ANTI
HUGOFIRST  ASCAP
EMIT  NOAH  LIEGE
MASTS  ORE  ELDER
AMMAN  SANI  VANE
NIOBE  THADHERTZ
    EARS  IOR
ALASKA  WANT  CUE
SUBS  DREWABLANK
AXLE  AIDE  EERIE
PEEN  ROSS  DIETS
```

167

```
I P A S S . R E B A . C H A N
Y E N T A . E L A N . A I D E
A R I A L . B E R N . S T I R
M U M B O J U M B O . T O E D
. . . O R S . U R A N U S . .
A L I G N S . B A N K S . . .
S U M O S . M A R C O P O L O
O L A N . M A R G E . E X E D
N U M E R O U N O . B L E N D
. . F I N I S . S A L S A S .
P A C I N O . . E L Y . . . .
A P E S . G U M B O L I M B O
N O A H . R N A S . E T A I L
D E S I . A D Z E . A Z U R E
A M E N . M O E N . F A L L S
```

168

```
B E N D . E L I H U . C O L A
I C E R . C I T E S . O X E N
B R E A D H E E L S . U F O S
B U R G E O N . P R O P O S E
. . . O N E . . . N O R . . .
A L M O N D S . F O U N D E R
L O O N Y . A T L A S . B L U
S S S S . E R R O R . P L A N
A E C . A D A Y S . M O U N T
B R O S N A N . S C A R E D Y
. . W I N . . . . O C T . . .
N E M E S I S . T O R R E N T
E M U S . L A Z Y L O A F E R
M I L T . S N O R E . I T B E
O L E A . A D D E D . T S O S
```

169

```
H A S H . A D D U P . F A V A
A L T O . L A U R A . I N O N
M B U T T E R F L Y . E T T A
S A N S E R I F . M U S S E L
. . . A N O N . L E N T O . .
S C H U S S . M O N T A N A N
T R U C E . P I N T O . A D O
R I S E . C O N E S . C L A N
E E K . L O S E R . . P R O S E
P R I S O N E R . S O U G H T
. . N E W T S . P E N N . . .
D E G R E E . B I R D C A G E
E L B E . S P A N I S H F L Y
L I E N . T R I C E . E R I E
I S E E . S I T E S . S O B S
```

170

```
B O S S . S A L S A . I P A D
A V O N . P L A N S . S O L O
R E L O . A U R A L . A K I N
D R A W B R I D G E . B E T E
S T R E A K . S E V E R . . .
. . D E L A Y . P I L F E R
E D T . R E N E E . P L A T E
L E W D . D E A L S . A C R E
K L E I N . T R I T T . E E L
S E N S E D . N E A R S . . .
. . T A T A R . N I N E R S
K E Y S . W A R A D M I R A L
A L O T . B I O T A . P U R E
T O N E . E S T E R . E P E E
O N E R . R A C E D . S T E T
```

171

```
M E R E . S E C T S . S P C A
E L A L . N O R A H . C R A G
S I T A . A L I B I . I O N E
H O S P I T A B L E . E P E E
. . . S O C . E L E N I . . .
T O G E T H E R . D O C T O R
O R E . A E R I E . N E I G H
A O N E . D I C T A . S A D E
S N E V A . K E T C H . T E T
T O P E K A . D E C A D E N T
. . I R A N I . E R E . . .
P I T Y . S L E E P I T O F F
E R N O . W O R S T . A M I R
A M E N . E N A T E . I O N A
K A Y E . R A T E D . L O S T
```

172

```
H A D J . G U A V A . C M O N
A L O U . E R V I N . L A G O
D O N J A N U A R Y . A G E D
E N G I N E S . E M E R G E S
S E S T E T . . O N E I . . .
. . S W I M . C R A T E R S
S O J U . C A C H E . S M E W
E D U . . M O E . . . A M A
P O N E . E M M A S . L Y O N
P R E L A C Y . T A R E . . .
. H E L L . . . R O B B E D
T R A V A I L . O O H L A L A
R A V E . P E G G Y M A R C H
A N O N . S T A R A . N E A L
M A C S . E S S E N . C A R S
```

173

```
D U S T M O P . M A R I T A L
O N L E A V E . I T E R A T E
S T U N N E D . M O V E D O N
T O R T U R E . I N A D A Z E
. . . M U S I C A L . . .
A T H E I S T S . L U S T E R
S H E D T E A R S . E N O L A
H E N S . S L A P S . A T A N
E F R E M . S E R E N G E T I
S T Y L E S . L I N E S M E N
. . T I E I N T O . . .
N E S T E G G . K I N S H I P
A L T O O N A . L E A K A G E
B L U R R E D . E N T I T L E
S A D I S T S . S T E P S U P
```

174

```
W A I T A N D S E E . A C N E
A L L E G O R I E S . N O O N
G O L D I L O C K S . D U S T
E T S . L E N S . E A R N E R
. . V I S E . A N N E T T E
P I P I T S . D I C T . M O N
A L L E Y . D O L E S . E N C
S L A W . L A Z E S . P O O H
T I N . F A Z E D . D O U S E
A T T . A C E D . B E S T E D
S E A B I R D . L E F T . . .
A R T U R O . P E R U . D S L
L A I R . S C R E E N T I M E
A T O M . S H O R T C A K E S
D E N A . E A S Y S T R E E T
```

175

```
C H I A N T I . B A G H D A D
R A N G O O N . I S R A E L I
A W N I N G S . S T A R T L E
V A I N E S T . C A T E R E D
E I N . . E G O . A M I G O
N I G H T S P O T S . S T O W
. . A R I . U T E P . A R N
. A U T O M A G I C A L L Y
O R G . N O W I . T R U . .
U C L A . N A N O S E C O N D
T H I N G . K G B . . F E R
W I N D A G E . R E D C L A Y
O V E R R A N . I T E R A T E
R E S E R V E . A R B I T E R
E S S A Y E D . N E S T E R S
```

176

```
S P O T T E S T . D E T A C H
T E A R I N T O . E L V I R A
R O T U N D A S . A S T R A Y
E R E C T O R S . L E A R N S
E I R E . R E E D S . B I K E
P A S S E . A D O . A L F I E
. . . L I T . B E V E L E D
H E A V E S . . L A S E R S
A L L E G R O . T I S . . .
R E D R Y . S P Y . T R I A L
A C E S . W H E L P . E T R E
S T R I K E . S E E S T A R S
S I M O N E . E N T I T L E S
E V E N E D . T O R T O I S E
S E N S E S . A L I E N A T E
```

177

```
S N O W F L A K E █ A T L A S
P I G H E A D E D █ B R A V O
A L L O R N O N E █ S E D A N
T E E █ R I P █ L I C K I N G
█ █ █ D I E T S █ B E S E T S
S L A Y E R █ W O E S █ S G T
P O S E D █ C O D A S █ W A R
L O S S █ R O R E M █ G E R E
I K E █ E A R E D █ R O A D S
T O M █ A I D A █ G E N R E S
H U B E R T █ T W A N G █ █ █
A T L A N T A █ H U E █ I O U
I M A G E █ T A I L W I N D S
R A G E S █ A P P L E T R E E
S N E R T █ D E S E R T E R S
```

178

```
L S A T █ A C T I █ S H R U B
U N B U N D L E D █ L O U S Y
B O B B Y H U L L █ O W N E R
E W E █ L E E █ E N G A G E D
█ █ █ P O R █ E A R █ █ █ █ █
B A R O N E T █ L E N D I N G
E V E R S █ E Y E D █ S L O E
L I L T █ S E A M Y █ T O N E
L A I C █ A N K A █ G E N E S
A N C H O V Y █ N A R R A T E
█ █ █ A C E █ T E N █ █ █ █ █
T I G R E S S █ S H E █ T K O
O C A L A █ C U P I D S B O W
L E V E N █ A T A N Y R A T E
D R E S S █ B A N G █ I R O N
```

179

```
D A V E █ C A P E █ P A P A L
E V A L U A T E S █ A N O D E
T E L L A P A R T █ S N O O T
E N V I R O N M E N T A L █ █
C U E S █ Y A R N █ P R O M
T E D █ S A C █ W H O O P I
█ █ █ S P O O L S █ A L O I S
N I C K E L S A N D D I M E S
E T H I C █ T O A S T S █ █ █
T H A N K S █ P L O █ S I S
S E R F █ U P U P █ R A N T
█ █ C L I M A T E C H A N G E
A V O I D █ W I D E A N G L E
D I A N E █ E L O N G A T E D
D E L T A █ D E N T █ T O S S
```

180

```
F I N S █ D E I F Y █ T S P S
A V O W █ E R N I E █ O N I T
D A V I D F R O S T █ O O N A
E N E M I E S █ H I G H W A Y
S A L M O N █ █ █ L O W █ █ █
█ █ █ E D D A █ W H E T H E R
L O I R E █ M A R I E █ I V E
A B C S █ G O D O T █ S T E M
P I E █ A A R O N █ T E E N Y
D E M I L L E █ G A I A █ █ █
█ █ A N A █ █ █ M A T M A N
I N I T I A L █ A I R L I N E
R O D E █ H A I L C A E S A R
E V E R █ E M C E E █ S H I V
D A N N █ M A K E S █ S A S E
```

181

```
H E R A █ M O U R N █ A S O R
O R A L █ A G R E E █ N I N E
T O P B I L L I N G █ I D E A
E S T E L L E █ O A T M E A L
█ █ █ R E A █ █ █ T H A W █ █
D A S T A R D █ B E E L I N E
A R I A █ D R U I D █ S N O G
T E D █ █ O S O █ █ D R Y
U T E S █ C O S T A █ R E A P
M E D I C A L █ A M H E R S T
█ █ I T A L █ █ █ B A G █ █
G A S T R I C █ A R R A N G E
A S H E █ B O T T O M L I N E
S T E R █ E R I E S █ E L A L
H I S S █ R E N E E █ S E T S
```

182

```
L I N E S █ L E W D █ U B E R
A D O R E █ A V E R █ N E R O
M O V I E █ B A L E █ S L A V
B L A C K B O C K S █ E L S E
█ █ █ E A R █ S T A Y E D █ █
R E W A R D █ O N E I L L █ █
A T H O S █ S N O R E █ O T T
J A I L █ R A I D S █ E C R U
A L T █ L A N C E █ F A K I R
█ █ E M E R G E █ L E T S O N
V I S A G E █ █ O A R █ █ █
I N O N █ F O R T K N O C K S
T A C T █ I R A T E █ T O I L
A N K A █ E S T E R █ I O T A
L E S S █ D O E R S █ S P E W
```

183

```
J E S T █ S T E A M █ D E B T
A D A M █ T E S L A █ A V E R
B I K E █ A L T E R █ V A L E
S T I N G B L O C K █ I D L E
█ █ █ E L Y █ I N D E E D █ █
R E F I N E █ L I N E █ █ █
E X U D E █ K I N G O F H E S
D I M E █ S O A R S █ L U R E
S T E A K T A R E █ W A G O N
█ █ █ S U N S █ F E W E S T
C E S I U M █ A L L █ █ █ █
A X E D █ B R I D A L P I E S
R I D E █ L U N A R █ A D Z E
A L A S █ E L O P E █ P O R E
T E N T █ D E N T S █ A L A N
```

184

```
R I T A █ M A R I A █ T A I L
U S E S █ E W E L L █ A G R A
N E A P █ D E C A L █ R A M P
T E R E S A █ █ S A T R A P
█ █ █ C O L E █ E T N A █ █
M A T T H E W █ K A T R I N A
E G O █ O D E █ E R E █ R E G
D O T █ █ █ █ █ █ █ A V E
O R E █ A U S █ A B S █ T E N
C A M I L L E █ G I L B E R T
█ █ M A U I █ O G E E █ █ █
R E T A I L █ █ E D D I E D
A G O G █ A R O M A █ L O M E
S A G E █ T U N E S █ A L M A
A N A S █ E M I L Y █ M E A N
```

185

```
L I M B █ O B A M A █ P E S O
O G L E █ P E D A L █ A T O M
B O I L █ H E D D A █ L U N A
O R I O L E █ █ S O O N E R
█ █ N E L L █ S K I M █ █ █
A B I G A I L █ P A L A D I N
D A D █ P A D █ A N Y █ O R E
O B I █ █ █ █ █ █ █ R E E
L A N █ I C E █ A C T █ A N D
F R A N C E S █ C H A R L E Y
█ █ E A R S █ C I T E █ █ █
H E L E N E █ █ N I C O L E
O R A D █ A N I S E █ E P E E
S O I L █ L A K E S █ S A I L
E S T E █ S H E R E █ S L A Y
```

186

```
A D A M S █ R A G E █ S H I P
T U P A C █ O L I N █ E A S E
T O P R A N K I N G █ G I R L
█ █ █ █ M E E T S █ K A R A T
E S C A P E R O U T E █ D E E
L E O N I D █ █ U N S O L D
F R O G █ A N O R A K █ █ █
█ E L E C T R I C K N I F E
█ █ █ L O O T E D █ I R M A
S U B A R U █ █ D E N I A L
E S L █ D R I N K I N G A G E
A M A S S █ N O N E T █ █ █
R A N T █ I N S I D E J O K E
L I C E █ D I E T █ R A R E R
E L O N █ K E D S █ S W E A R
```

187

```
P L O D . U S E B Y . A P P
S A M O A . R E T I E . B E A
S M A R T A L E C K S . N A T
T E N S E D . S H I M M E R S
. . A L A N . N E A R L Y . .
A P P L E P I C K I N G . . .
R I O . S T A R E S . E S T S
A T L A S . C A Y . D E T O O
B A L L . P I G P E N . A P R
. . . T U R N S A G A I N S T
C A N A P E . D A T A . . . .
O V E R S E A S . L E M M O N
P I S . I N S I D E S T O R Y
S A T . Z E S T A . T O N E S
E S S . E D N A S . O T O E
```

188

```
R E A D . S T U P A . V A S E
E D N A . C O L O N . O R E L
E D E N . O R N O T . L E A S
L A W S O N M A R I J U A N A
. . E C C E . D A M . . . . .
S A L U T E . R H O D E S I A
E N O S . H A U T E . A M B
W E R E E N A C T E D V I A A
U A R . R U L E S . I L L S
P R E S U M E S . H A S S L E
. . A P E . D E B I . . . .
J O I N T R E S O L U T I O N
A B C D . O N E I L . I T S A
R O A R . U N C L E . N O L A
S E L A . S A T Y R . G O O N
```

189

```
G A S P . C L A M S . T S A R
A G A R . R E M I T . H E R O
N I N E T Y N I N E . E V E S
G O D D E S S . I L L N E S S
. . I R T . L O A N . . . .
S P E C I A L . C A P I T A L
A L I T . L O W E R . L Y R E
B E G . T A C . O M A
R A H S . P U R I M . S N I P
E S T H E R S . L E N I E N T
. . Y O R E . G I S . . . .
R E F R E S H . O R A T O R S
A L O T . S I X T Y S E V E N
B L U E . E V I T A . R A N I
E A R N . D E V O N . S L O T
```

190

```
J A B S . S P A R K . S T D S
E L I E . L A N A I . T H O U
F I F T Y E I G H T . E I R E
F I F T E E N . S T A R R E D
. . L A P . E D I T . . . .
O F F E R E R . A N A L Y S T
C L O D . R O A R S . E N Y O
H O R . A I M . I N K
E R T E . A L D E R . I N C A
R A Y M O N D . D E N N E H Y
. . S P I N . A A S . . . .
B E E T L E S . A C R O B A T
R A V I . T W E N T Y F I V E
I S E E . T A S T E . A L E X
M E N S . E N D E D . R E S T
```

191

```
M E S A . M E L B A . M O E T
A P E R . C L E A T . A N D I
S I X T Y E I G H T . R E I N
A C T I O N S . T R A C H E A
. . S U R . A L O U . . . .
C O N T R O L . S C A N N E R
U R I S . E I G H T . I D L E
P A N . C U E . R A W
I L E A . D I N E D . F E T E
D E T R O I T . R E S I D E D
. . Y S E R . F U R . . . .
R E F E R E E . R E L E A S E
O L I N . C L U E N U M B E R
A L V A . T A M E S . E R A T
R E E L . S H A D E . N A M E
```

192

```
W A R N S . A M P S . S L A W
A N E N T . W E E P . L O D E
I N A W E . H E A R T A C H E
N O D . E M I T . O I N K E D
S T A B L E R . V U L T U R E
C A P I T A L I S T . S P E D
O T T E R S . C O S A . . .
T E S L A . P E P . P L A N S
. . P E R U . S P I G O T
S H E A . P O P U L A R I T Y
C O N T E S T . P A L A T A L
O L D H A T . I S T O . A B U
F L U O R E S C E . O A T E S
F O R M . I M A T . S C O N E
S W E E . N U N S . A C R E S
```

193

```
B I R C H . A W R Y . S C A T
O M A H A . S H O E S T O R E
S P I E S . P E R S U A D E R
S A L E S . I R E N E R Y A N
A I R P L A N E M O D E . . .
. R O S E S . . E D G E D
I M A . S H A D E S . A R N O
R E D D . E L I T E . T A G S
K N E E . S I Z E U P . V A T
S T R E P . . S O B I G
. . P U R P L E S T A T E S
C I N E R A R I A . S H A M U
A G O N I Z I N G . H A T E D
R O L E M O D E L . O M E N S
B R A D . R E N E . T A S T Y
```

194

```
H O R S E T A I L S . T R A P
A P O P L E C T I C . V I T O
R E A L I N C O M E . A C T S
I N D I C T . N O N O . H E S
. . T I C S . S I C . A S E
C H A S T I T Y . C H A R T S
R A T . S T R O M . S I D E S
O T T O . Y O K U M . D I D I
S C H E D . P E S O S . I T O
S H I R E S . D E C I S I O N
H A S . P A C . O K L A . .
A P T . T H I N . T E N S E R
I L I E . A D A M A N D E V E
R O M A . R E P L I C A T E D
S T E T . A R A B L E L A N D
```

195

```
M I E N . W E P T . I S L A M
I N R E S E R V E . S H E R E
L O N G P A N T S . L I M I T
E N S L A V E . T H E N O S E
R E T I R E S . P O T E N T
. . G E D . L I E S . D O B
A S H E S . T O L D . E R T E
S H U N T . Y O O . E N O L A
T O A T . S P I T . P A P E R
O E R . F L E E . R I M . .
. S A L L O W . L O S E S I T
I T C H I E R . I S O L A T E
C O H A N . I N S I D E M A N
B R E S T . T I T L E R O L E
M E S A S . E A S Y . S A L T
```

196

```
T R U E . D A M E S . O S A R
A I R S . O R A L E . C H U B
D O G C A T C H E R . T O N I
S T E A L T H . E F F O R T S
. . L A I . . A P T . .
V A C A T E S . C R U I S E R
A G A T E . C A L Y X . T E E
P I K E . F U G U E . H O R A
I L E . S O D O M . T E P I D
D E B A T E S . P L E A S E S
. . A G A . . A N D . .
T I T A N I C . I D E A T E D
A N T S . S U N P I T C H E R
P R E S . E R A S E . H O R N
S E R I . E T H O S . E R O O
```

197

```
L A P D . L E A R N . A H E M
E R I E . E R N I E . S O L E
F I E L D G O A L S . S O I L
T E D I O U S . E S C A P E D
. . . C U M . . . L I S .
S O L A C E D . S T A L K E R
E L I T E . A N T S Y . I L O
R I F E . O Z A R K . W R A P
I V E . A R E N A . L A T T E
N E G A T E D . P R E S S E S
. U F O . . . E T H .
S H A R P E N . A C H I E V E
P O R E . D E A D C E N T E R
A N D S . G E N I E . G U N S
M E S H . E D I T S . S I D E
```

198

```
S H A C K S . . D E W A L T
P E P P I E R . M A N O W A R
I M P A S T O . A L T O O N A
E A R . S I B . Y A R D L E Y
S N A G . N E W B I E . .
. I O C . R E E . E P E E S
L O S T N O T I M E . A X L E
O N E W A Y O R A N O T H E R
A C R E . L A D Y G O D I V A
F E S T S . L O B . O R B .
. . C L O S E D . Y I P S
A C C L A I M . N I T . T I A
M A H A T M A . O N A D I E T
B R O T H E R . T E R E N C E
I B I S E S . . D A N G E D
```

199

```
S I M . C A D R E . A R E A
O N E . A V A I L . D O N N E
I T D . S I N G L E S I D E D
R E E S E S . H I L L . E M U
E N V O Y . S T O L . B M O C
E S A U . S H O T . M A I N E
S E C R E T E N T R A N C E S
. . . G R U N T W O R K .
I C O U L D A H A D C L A S S
N O T M E . N E V E . O R C A
L O T S . D I M E . M A M A S
E L O . I A G O . D O N O R S
T I M E C H A N G E S . I I I
S N A R E . N E A M E . R E E
. G N A T . S Y B I L . E R R
```

200

```
T I L T . L C D S . S L A P S
O D O R . A L I T . A L L O T
L E I A . N O V A S C O T I A
L A N D E D G E N T R Y . .
. . E N O S . D E E D I N G
S I G N O N . V I E D . L E I
C O R A L . D A N L . S L A V
A N I M A T E D G E S T U R E
M I N E . A S I S . L A S E R
P A C . A R C S . L I T E R S
I N H A S T E . N A N U . .
. . C H A N G E D G E A R S
R I C H A R D I I I . T R I M
E N D O R . O G L E . T I N E
A E S O P . N I L S . E D G E
```

201

```
S O C K . B A Y H . S C A M S
A R L O . I D E A . H A N O I
K E E P S T I L L . O R N O T
S O M E P E O P L E R E A D .
. . . C A R S . R T E .
B O O K S . E D N O R T O N
A B C S . M I L I E U . I W O
S A E . B U T M O S T . S N L
I M A . A S S O R T . R H E A
S A N G R I A S . L E A R N
. . E R A . C O I F . .
B Y T I L E A N D E R R O R
G O O S E . G O O D F A I T H
A L G E R . A N T E . C L I O
S L I T S . D E E R . T E S S
```

202

```
D I R T . C O A C T . L S T S
I L I A . I N F O R . A T E E
R I N D . T A R R Y . H I N T
E K G . T I P I N . E R N S T
C E A S E . O C H E R . G I L
T I R E S . S A U N A . O L E
O T O E S . I N S T S . P E D
P L U M . S T A K E . P E S T
P I N . S L I M E . P E R T H
O K D . L I V E R . I C A R E
S E A . I T E R S . E S T E S
I T R I P . N I T E R . I N C
T H O S . L O C A L . L O G O
E A S E . S T A T S . E N T R
S T Y E . D E N E E . A S H E
```

203

```
A P P . S A P P O R O . A B C
C R U . S C O R N E R . T A R
C O T . R E T O T A L . T R U
T H U R S . A C H . E P E E S
S I P E . E T R E . S E N N A
. B A C K R O A D . S A T E D
. I G U E S S O . . I C E
S T O R Y . A T T . S L O E S
C E O . . C I T R O E N S .
A D D L E . K N E E C A P S
M A F I A . R A D S . C L I I
P R I E R . A T L . W H E T S
E E G . N I C O I S E . A I L
R A H . E T E R N A L . S E E
S S T . D E S S E R T . E S S
```

204

```
T A M S . C L O T . E L S I E
E S A U . R E A R . L E A N S
M I S E R Y I S I N T E N T S
P A S T A S . T S A R . A R E
. . P T A . T R A . N O S
O N A S T A B L E D I E T .
W E P T . L E O . N Y O P
N A P A . S E T U P . E N O S
. P O S H . O L A . O I L Y
. I H A T E F A S T F O O D
L E N . M E A . R T E .
A R T . S A R I . I N S T E P
P R I N T S W O U L D C O M E
S E N S E . I T L L . A N A T
E D G A R . G A M E . B E G S
```

205

```
S W A T H . . D A B . H O S E
M O I R E . D E M I . A V E R
O R D I N A N C E S . P E E R
G E E . B R A I N S T O R M S
. . T I C . . A I R . .
. R U N T H E G A U N T L E T
T E N T . O R A L . S H A V E
A C T . N O T O F . . P A N
P A I N E . D O N A . S U N S
S P L I N T E R G R O U P S
. . T O R . . M O P . .
N E A R S I G H T E D . S P A
E L L A . B R E A D L I N E S
W A T T . E A R P . E C A S H
S L O E . S B A . S E P O Y
```

206

```
S T R E A M E D . S T E A L S
P R E A M B L E . T U R N I P
R I B R O A S T . A S S I S I
I N A N . . R A C K . M A N
G I G E C O N O M Y . L A M A
. . D E C E I T . N A T A L
C P A . S T A T . C A V O R T
H A N D S E T . B A V A R I A
E X T A N T . G E N A . S E P
F R I D A . G A N D H I . .
S O P S . B U Z Z W O R T H Y
A M A . S O M E . . O B O E
L A S S E S . T I T A N I U M
A N T I C S . T R A V E R S E
D A I N T Y . E V E A R D E N
```

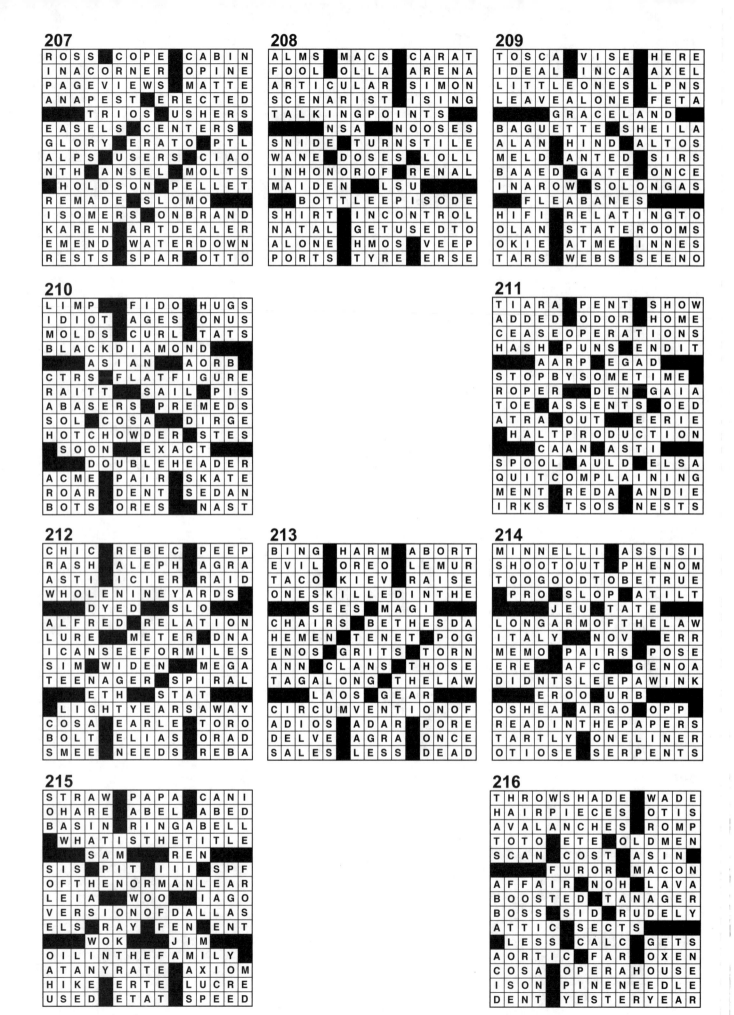

207

```
R O S S   C O P E   C A B I N
I N A C O R N E R   O P I N E
P A G E V I E W S   M A T T E
A N A P E S T   E R E C T E D
    T R I O S   U S H E R S
E A S E L S   C E N T E R S
G L O R Y   E R A T O   P T L
A L P S   U S E R S   C I A O
N T H   A N S E L   M O L T S
  H O L D S O N   P E L L E T
R E M A D E   S L O M O
I S O M E R S   O N B R A N D
K A R E N   A R T D E A L E R
E M E N D   W A T E R D O W N
R E S T S   S P A R   O T T O
```

208

```
A L M S   M A C S   C A R A T
F O O L   O L L A   A R E N A
A R T I C U L A R   S I M O N
S C E N A R I S T   I S I N G
T A L K I N G P O I N T S
    N S A   N O O S E S
S N I D E   T U R N S T I L E
W A N E   D O S E S   L O L L
I N H O N O R O F   R E N A L
M A I D E N     L S U
  B O T T L E E P I S O D E
S H I R T   I N C O N T R O L
N A T A L   G E T U S E D T O
A L O N E   H M O S   V E E P
P O R T S   T Y R E   E R S E
```

209

```
T O S C A   V I S E   H E R E
I D E A L   I N C A   A X E L
L I T T L E O N E S   L P N S
L E A V E A L O N E   F E T A
      G R A C E L A N D
B A G U E T T E   S H E I L A
A L A N   H I N D   A L T O S
M E L D   A N T E D   S I R S
B A A E D   G A T E   O N C E
I N A R O W   S O L O N G A S
    F L E A B A N E S
H I F I   R E L A T I N G T O
O L A N   S T A T E R O O M S
O K I E   A T M E   I N N E S
T A R S   W E B S   S E E N O
```

210

```
L I M P   F I D O   H U G S
I D I O T   A G E S   O N U S
M O L D S   C U R L   T A T S
B L A C K D I A M O N D
    A S I A N   A O R B
C T R S   F L A T F I G U R E
R A I T T   S A I L   P I S
A B A S E R S   P R E M E D S
S O L   C O S A   D I R G E
H O T C H O W D E R   S T E S
  S O O N   E X A C T
  D O U B L E H E A D E R
A C M E   P A I R   S K A T E
R O A R   D E N T   S E D A N
B O T S   O R E S   N A S T
```

211

```
T I A R A   P E N T   S H O W
A D D E D   O D O R   H O M E
C E A S E O P E R A T I O N S
H A S H   P U N S   E N D I T
    A A R P   E G A D
S T O P B Y S O M E T I M E
R O P E R   D E N   G A I A
T O E   A S S E N T S   O E D
A T R A   O U T   E E R I E
  H A L T P R O D U C T I O N
    C A A N   A S T I
S P O O L   A U L D   E L S A
Q U I T C O M P L A I N I N G
M E N T   R E D A   A N D I E
I R K S   T S O S   N E S T S
```

212

```
C H I C   R E B E C   P E E P
R A S H   A L E P H   A G R A
A S T I   I C I E R   R A I D
W H O L E N I N E Y A R D S
    D Y E D   S L O
A L F R E D   R E L A T I O N
L U R E   M E T E R   D N A
I C A N S E E F O R M I L E S
S I M   W I D E N   M E G A
T E E N A G E R   S P I R A L
    E T H   S T A T
  L I G H T Y E A R S A W A Y
C O S A   E A R L E   T O R O
B O L T   E L I A S   O R A D
S M E E   N E E D S   R E B A
```

213

```
B I N G   H A R M   A B O R T
E V I L   O R E O   L E M U R
T A C O   K I E V   R A I S E
O N E S K I L L E D I N T H E
    S E E S   M A G I
C H A I R S   B E T H E S D A
H E M E N   T E N E T   P O G
E N O S   G R I T S   T O R N
A N N   C L A N S   T H O S E
T A G A L O N G   T H E L A W
    L A O S   G E A R
C I R C U M V E N T I O N O F
A D I O S   A D A R   P O R E
D E L V E   A G R A   O N C E
S A L E S   L E S S   D E A D
```

214

```
M I N N E L L I   A S S I S I
S H O O T O U T   P H E N O M
T O O G O O D T O B E T R U E
  P R O   S L O P   A T I L T
    J E U   T A T E
L O N G A R M O F T H E L A W
I T A L Y   N O V   E R R
M E M O   P A I R S   P O S E
E R E   A F C   G E N O A
D I D N T S L E E P A W I N K
    E R O O   U R B
O S H E A   A R G O   O P P
R E A D I N T H E P A P E R S
T A R T L Y   O N E L I N E R
O T I O S E   S E R P E N T S
```

215

```
S T R A W   P A P A   C A N I
O H A R E   A B E L   A B E D
B A S I N   R I N G A B E L L
  W H A T I S T H E T I T L E
    S A M     R E N
S I S   P I T   I I I   S P F
O F T H E N O R M A N L E A R
L E I A   W O O   I A G O
V E R S I O N O F D A L L A S
E L S   R A Y   F E N   E N T
    W O K   J I M
O I L I N T H E F A M I L Y
A T A N Y R A T E   A X I O M
H I K E   E R T E   L U C R E
U S E D   E T A T   S P E E D
```

216

```
T H R O W S H A D E   W A D E
H A I R P I E C E S   O T I S
A V A L A N C H E S   R O M P
T O T O   E T E   O L D M E N
S C A N   C O S T   A S I N
    F U R O R   M A C O N
A F F A I R   N O H   L A V A
B O O S T E D   T A N A G E R
B O S S   S I D   R U D E L Y
A T T I C   S E C T S
  L E S S   C A L C   G E T S
A O R T I C   F A R   O X E N
C O S A   O P E R A H O U S E
I S O N   P I N E N E E D L E
D E N T   Y E S T E R Y E A R
```

217

```
M A C E S | | S F P D | | A S T I
E N L A I | P R O A N D C O N | |
S T A R S | | E A R N H A R D T
C O N T I N E N T A L | | O D E
A N K H | | A C T I | | D O I N
L I E | E T H I C S | | I G E T
S O D A S | | C O N G R E S S |
| | C A D S | | S L O G | | |
C I R C U L A R | | D E B T S |
A M E R | S T A L L S | | E R E
R A J A | | I D E A | | A L E E
A G E | F I R I N G S Q U A D |
V I C T O R I A N | | P A S S E
A N T I P A S T O | | A B H O R
N E S S | | S T E N | | R A I N S
```

218

```
A S P S | | A D E E | | G R I M M
B I E N | | L I A R | | O U T I E
O M N I | C A T N A P P I N G |
M I T T | A N E S T H E S I A |
B L A C K P A N T H E R | | |
| I M H I P | | A R T G U M
S T E E D | F A U N S | | U N E
H U T S | T A X E D | | C E D E
O D E | S U R L Y | | S H R E K
T E R R O R | | S T A R R | |
| A F R O F U T U R I S M | |
O B L I T E R A T E | | I L I E
P L A N E T A R I A | | S L E D
T A K E N | | T U L L | M A G I
S H E D S | | E K E S | A S E A
```

219

```
M E G A | | R A V E | | P A L I N
I R O N H O R S E | | I L E N E
D I C T A T I O N | | P A V E S
S K U L L C A P | R E C E S S
T A P E S | | | P E D A L S |
| | R E S P I R E | | R H E A
E L F | Y E O M E N | | T E N S
L A I T | I R E S T | | E A C H
M U L E | S K A T E R | | D E E
O R E L | M E N O R A H | | |
| E C L A I R | | | P A B S T
B A L T I C | | M A R I N A T E
A T E A R | | B E R I N G S E A
M E R L E | | U N I V E R S E S
A S K E D | | D U D E | | Y O R E
```

220

```
A D A M | | S A G A S | | B A R D
L O L A | | C L A R K | | O G E E
M I D D L E A G E I S W H E N
S T A M E N S | | A N O M A L Y
| | O A T | | D N A | | | |
S O A N D S O | | B E A N I E S
O R N E | | V A L E T | | N A T
M A N Y A G E T U P A N D G O
A L E | P U R E E | | E U R O
L E S S O N S | | R A G W E E D
| | E L M | | T I L | | | |
T A M A L E S | | H O L Y S E E
H A S G O T U P A N D W E N T
E R G O | A Z U R E | | E R I N
N E R D | | L I N K S | | D A D A
```

221

```
T S P S | | S H E L F | | S M O G
H A R M | | L O Y A L | | E A R L
O M O O | | E N E R O | | E L S E
U P F O R D I S C U S S I O N
| | T A G | | | R E A | | |
S I G H T E D | | V I E W E R S
O M N E S | A M O S | | V I I
U P A R O U N D T H E B E N D
N E T | | N A T E | | N U R S E
D I S P O S E | | R O U S T E D
| | E A T | | | C R Y | | |
A W A Y F R O M T H E W I N D
L O G O | | A B A S E | | O V E R
P R E T | | P O L A R | | R A R E
S M E E | | S E E R S | | K N O W
```

222

```
N E A R | | A B I T | | J A F F E
A R G O | | S O D A | | O G L E D
O W E S | | T R I B | | H O U N D
M I N E B O G G L I N G | | |
I N T W O | | | E L S | | A M I
| | I D O L S | | L O N D O N
J E N N Y L I N E | | N O I R E
O V I D | | D E A R S | | W E A R
L E M O N | | F I N E F A U L T
T R O W E L | | L E A R N | |
S T Y | | M O M | | A D I N S
| | R E W I N E B U T T O N
O A S E S | | R A V E | | H A T E
T B O N E | | T M E N | | E L S A
T E X T S | | H E R D | | N O O K
```

223

```
L A I C | | M A N I C | | E R I E
A L D A | | E R I C A | | N O R A
D A I S Y D U K E S | | T S A R
E M O T I O N | | T A R H E E L
N O T R E | | | B A U M | | |
| | O L D S | | K A N S A N S
C D L | D I E G O | | T E R C E
H A I M | S N E R D | | D I A N
A D L E R | S L E E P | | E A T
D A Y T I M E | | A R E S | |
| | W A S A | | | S I R E S
A T H L E T E | | D E C E I V E
N E I L | | A S T E R I S K E D
T A T I | | T A E B O | | T E R A
A L E C | | A U N T S | | A R A N
```

224

```
D O G W H I S T L E | | A C T S
O N Y O U R T O E S | | D O U P
S U P E R V I S E S | | I N R E
E S S | T I C S | | E V O N N E
| | | W I N K | A N I S E E D
A D D I N G | V I C E | | C D S
D O I N G | | T I M E D | | T O T
A V G S | | H E X E S | | J I V E
M E R | F I N E D | | C O V E R
A T E | A V O N | | S O B E R S
N A S T I E R | | A L M S | |
D I S A R M | | S N I P | | O C T
E L I S | | I C E D C O F F E E
V E N T | | N U R S E S A I D E
E D G Y | | D E F O R E S T E D
```

225

```
T O P S | | A T R E E | | O H S O
U N I T | | G A B L E | | F A I L
R E P A I R B I L L | | F I R E
F I E N N E S | | A S P I R I N
| | D U E | | | O N S | | |
E D W A R D S | | L E N G T H S
M O O R E | | H A O L E | | R A N
B Y R D | | G R I G S | | D E L E
E L L | F I E R I | | H E A V E
R E D W O O D | | C R A C K E R
| | S I R | | | A R R | | |
R E F R A I N | | I N S E C T S
I R A E | L A W N C H A I R S
C O I R | | E R A T O | | S T U N
H O R S | | A C T O R | | E Y E S
```

226

```
S P E C T A C L E S | | P L U G
P U T O N B L A S T | | L O R E
I C A N T D A N C E | | A X L E
N E T S | | U P E A R L Y | |
| | | V C S | | R O A M I N G
F R I G H T | | A G I T A T O R
R U N E S | | C L O D | | K A V A
I S N T | | S I L T S | | E L E V
L S A T | | U S E S | | B R I N E
L E T H A R G Y | | R A S C A L
S T E E P L E | | B E G | | |
| | | J O I N E R S | | C A M O
B R I O | | E D D I E E A G A N
M O C K | | S E N A T E R U L E
W O K E | | T R A N S L A T E D
```

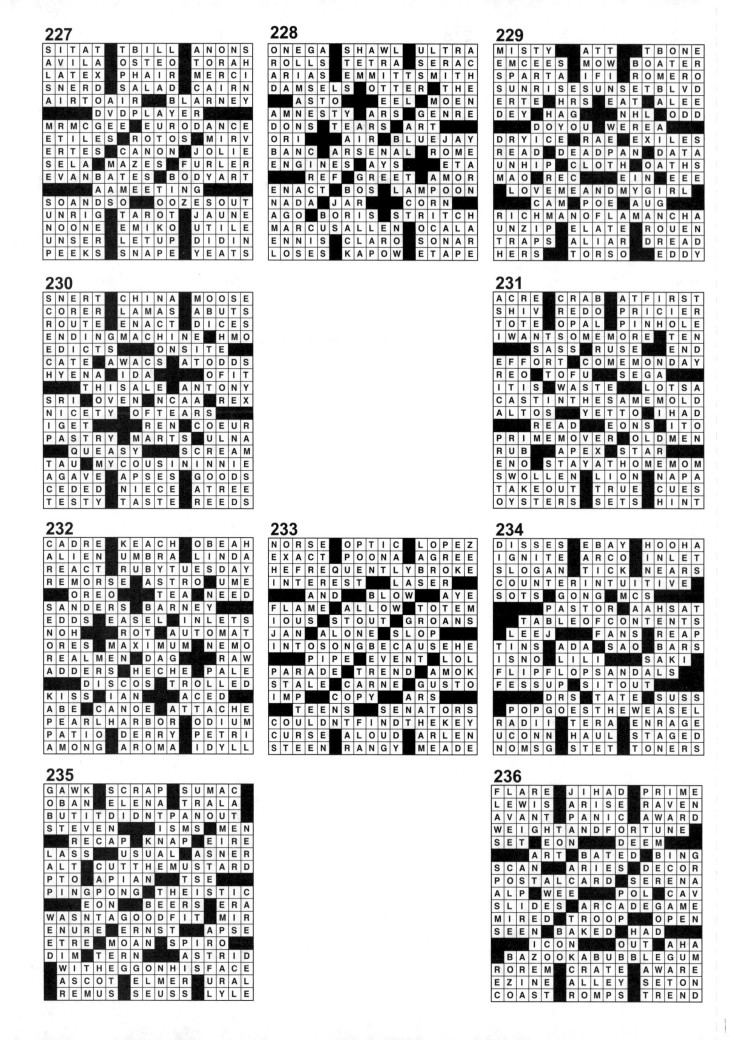

227

```
S I T A T   T B I L L   A N O N S
A V I L A   O S T E O   T O R A H
L A T E X   P H A I R   M E R C I
S N E R D   S A L A D   C A I R N
A I R T O A I R     B L A R N E Y
        D V D P L A Y E R
M R M C G E E   E U R O D A N C E
E T I L E S   R O T O S   M I R V
E R T E S   C A N O N   J O L I E
S E L A   M A Z E S   F U R L E R
E V A N B A T E S   B O D Y A R T
        A A M E E T I N G
S O A N D S O   O O Z E S O U T
U N R I G   T A R O T   J A U N E
N O O N E   E M I K O   U T I L E
U N S E R   L E T U P   D I D I N
P E E K S   S N A P E   Y E A T S
```

228

```
O N E G A   S H A W L   U L T R A
R O L L S   T E T R A   S E R A C
A R I A S   E M M I T T S M I T H
D A M S E L S   O T T E R   T H E
    A S T O   E E L   M O E N
A M N E S T Y   A R S   G E N R E
D O N S   T E A R S   A R T
O R I   A I R   B L U E J A Y
B A N C   A R S E N A L   R O M E
E N G I N E S   A Y S     E T A
    R E F   G R E E T   A M O R
E N A C T   B O S   L A M P O O N
N A D A   J A R     C O R N
A G O   B O R I S   S T R I T C H
M A R C U S A L L E N   O C A L A
E N N I S   C L A R O   S O N A R
L O S E S   K A P O W   E T A P E
```

229

```
M I S T Y     A T T     T B O N E
E M C E E S   M O W   B O A T E R
S P A R T A   I F I   R O M E R O
S U N R I S E S U N S E T B L V D
E R T E   H R S   E A T   A L E E
D E Y   H A G   N H L     O D D
    D O Y O U     W E R E A
D R Y I C E   R A E   E X I L E S
R E A D   D E A D P A N   D A T A
U N H I P   C L O T H   O A T H S
M A O   R E C   E I N     E E E
    L O V E M E A N D M Y G I R L
    C A M   P O E   A U G
R I C H M A N O F L A M A N C H A
U N Z I P   E L A T E   R O U E N
T R A P S   A L I A R   D R E A D
H E R S   T O R S O   E D D Y
```

230

```
S N E R T   C H I N A   M O O S E
C O R E R   L A M A S   A B U T S
R O U T E   E N A C T   D I C E S
E N D I N G M A C H I N E   H M O
E D I C T S     O N S I T E
C A T E   A W A C S   A T O D D S
H Y E N A   I D A     O F I T
    T H I S A L E   A N T O N Y
S R I   O V E N   N C A A   R E X
N I C E T Y   O F T E A R S
I G E T     R E N   C O E U R
P A S T R Y   M A R T S   U L N A
    Q U E A S Y     S C R E A M
T A U   M Y C O U S I N I N N I E
A G A V E   A P S E S   G O O D S
C E D E D   N I E C E   A T R E E
T E S T Y   T A S T E   R E E D S
```

231

```
A C R E     C R A B   A T F I R S T
S H I V     R E D O   P R I C I E R
T O T E     O P A L   P I N H O L E
I W A N T S O M E M O R E     T E N
        S A S S   R U S E     E N D
E F F O R T   C O M E M O N D A Y
R E O   T O F U     S E G A
I T I S   W A S T E     L O T S A
C A S T I N T H E S A M E M O L D
A L T O S     Y E T T O   I H A D
        R E A D     E O N S   I T O
P R I M E M O V E R   O L D M E N
R U B   A P E X   S T A R
E N O   S T A Y A T H O M E M O M
S W O L L E N   L I O N   N A P A
T A K E O U T   T R U E   C U E S
O Y S T E R S   S E T S   H I N T
```

232

```
C A D R E   K E A C H   O B E A H
A L I E N   U M B R A   L I N D A
R E A C T   R U B Y T U E S D A Y
R E M O R S E   A S T R O   U M E
    O R E O     T E A   N E E D
S A N D E R S     B A R N E Y
E D D S   E A S E L   I N L E T S
N O H   R O T   A U T O M A T
O R E S   M A X I M U M   N E M O
R E A L M E N   D A G     R A W
A D D E R S   H E C H E   P A L E
    D I S C O S   T R O L L E D
K I S S   I A N     A C E D
A B E   C A N O E   A T T A C H E
P E A R L H A R B O R   O D I U M
P A T I O   D E R R Y   P E T R I
A M O N G   A R O M A   I D Y L L
```

233

```
N O R S E   O P T I C   L O P E Z
E X A C T   P O O N A   A G R E E
H E F R E Q U E N T L Y B R O K E
I N T E R E S T   L A S E R
    A N D     B L O W   A Y E
F L A M E   A L L O W   T O T E M
I O U S   S T O U T   G R O A N S
J A N   A L O N E   S L O P
I N T O S O N G B E C A U S E H E
    P I P E   E V E N T   L O L
P A R A D E   T R E N D   A M O K
S T A L E   C A R N E   G U S T O
I M P   C O P Y     A R S
    T E E N S   S E N A T O R S
C O U L D N T F I N D T H E K E Y
C U R S E   A L O U D   A R L E N
S T E E N   R A N G Y   M E A D E
```

234

```
D I S S E S   E B A Y   H O O H A
I G N I T E   A R C O   I N L E T
S L O G A N   T I C K   N E A R S
C O U N T E R I N T U I T I V E
S O T S   G O N G   M C S
        P A S T O R   A A H S A T
T A B L E O F C O N T E N T S
L E E J   F A N S   R E A P
T I N S   A D A   S A O   B A R S
I S N O   L I L I     S A K I
F L I P F L O P S A N D A L S
F E S S U P   S I T O U T
        D R S   T A T E   S U S S
P O P G O E S T H E W E A S E L
R A D I I   T E R A   E N R A G E
U C O N N   H A U L   S T A G E D
N O M S G   S T E T   T O N E R S
```

235

```
G A W K   S C R A P   S U M A C
O B A N   E L E N A   T R A L A
B U T I T D I D N T P A N O U T
S T E V E N   I S M S   M E N
    R E C A P   K N A P   E I R E
L A S S   U S U A L   A S N E R
A L T   C U T T H E M U S T A R D
P T O   A P I A N     T S E
P I N G P O N G   T H E I S T I C
    E O N   B E E R S   E R A
W A S N T A G O O D F I T   M I R
E N U R E   E R N S T   A P S E
E T R E   M O A N   S P I R O
D I M   T E R N   A S T R I D
    W I T H E G G O N H I S F A C E
A S C O T   E L M E R   U R A L
R E M U S   S E U S S   L Y L E
```

236

```
F L A R E   J I H A D   P R I M E
L E W I S   A R I S E   R A V E N
A V A N T   P A N I C   A W A R D
W E I G H T A N D F O R T U N E
S E T   E O N   D E E M
        A R T   B A T E D   B I N G
S C A N   A R I E S   D E C O R
P O S T A L C A R D   S E R E N A
A L P   W E E   P O L   C A V
S L I D E S   A R C A D E G A M E
M I R E D   T R O O P   O P E N
S E E N   B A K E D   H A D
    I C O N     O U T   A H A
B A Z O O K A B U B B L E G U M
R O R E M   C R A T E   A W A R E
E Z I N E   A L L E Y   S E T O N
C O A S T   R O M P S   T R E N D
```

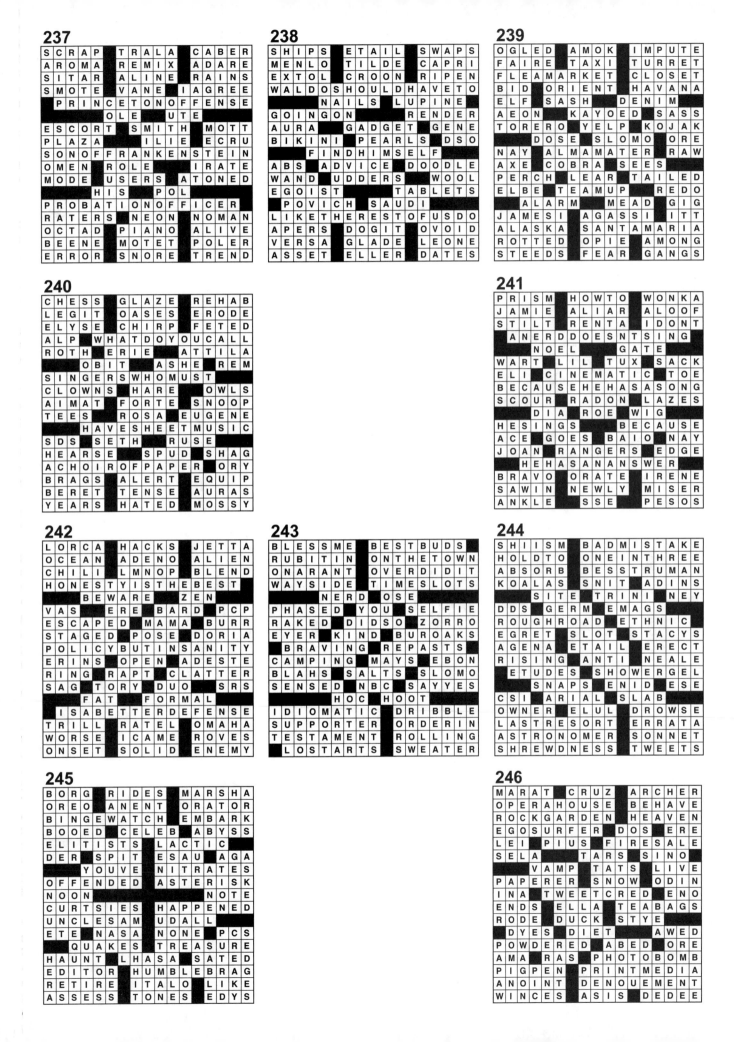

237

S	C	R	A	P		T	R	A	L	A		C	A	B	E	R
A	R	O	M	A		R	E	M	I	X		A	D	A	R	E
S	I	T	A	R		A	L	I	N	E		R	A	I	N	S
S	M	O	T	E		V	A	N	E		I	A	G	R	E	E
	P	R	I	N	C	E	T	O	N	O	F	F	E	N	S	E
			O	L	E				U	T	E					
E	S	C	O	R	T		S	M	I	T	H		M	O	T	T
P	L	A	Z	A		I	L	I	E		E	C	R	U		
S	O	N	O	F	F	R	A	N	K	E	N	S	T	E	I	N
O	M	E	N		R	O	L	E			I	R	A	T	E	
M	O	D	E		U	S	E	R	S		A	T	O	N	E	D
			H	I	S				P	O	L					
P	R	O	B	A	T	I	O	N	O	F	F	I	C	E	R	
R	A	T	E	R	S		N	E	O	N		N	O	M	A	N
O	C	T	A	D		P	I	A	N	O		A	L	I	V	E
B	E	E	N	E		M	O	T	E	T		P	O	L	E	R
E	R	R	O	R		S	N	O	R	E		T	R	E	N	D

238

S	H	I	P	S		E	T	A	I	L		S	W	A	P	S
M	E	N	L	O		T	I	L	D	E		C	A	P	R	I
E	X	T	O	L		C	R	O	O	N		R	I	P	E	N
W	A	L	D	O	S	H	O	U	L	D	H	A	V	E	T	O
			N	A	I	L	S			L	U	P	I	N	E	
G	O	I	N	G	O	N			R	E	N	D	E	R		
A	U	R	A		G	A	D	G	E	T		G	E	N	E	
B	I	K	I	N	I		P	E	A	R	L	S		D	S	O
	F	I	N	D	H	I	M	S	E	L	F					
A	B	S		A	D	V	I	C	E		D	O	O	D	L	E
W	A	N	D		U	D	D	E	R	S			W	O	O	L
E	G	O	I	S	T					T	A	B	L	E	T	S
	P	O	V	I	C	H		S	A	U	D	I				
L	I	K	E	T	H	E	R	E	S	T	O	F	U	S	D	O
A	P	E	R	S		D	O	G	I	T		O	V	O	I	D
V	E	R	S	A		G	L	A	D	E		L	E	O	N	E
A	S	S	E	T		E	L	L	E	R		D	A	T	E	S

239

O	G	L	E	D		A	M	O	K		I	M	P	U	T	E
F	A	I	R	E		T	A	X	I		T	U	R	R	E	T
F	L	E	A	M	A	R	K	E	T		C	L	O	S	E	T
B	I	D		O	R	I	E	N	T		H	A	V	A	N	A
E	L	F		S	A	S	H		D	E	N	I	M			
A	E	O	N		K	A	Y	O	E	D		S	A	S	S	
T	O	R	E	R	O		Y	E	L	P		K	O	J	A	K
			D	O	S	E		S	L	O	M	O		O	R	E
N	A	Y		A	L	M	A	M	A	T	E	R		R	A	W
A	X	E		C	O	B	R	A		S	E	E	S			
P	E	R	C	H		L	E	A	R		T	A	I	L	E	D
E	L	B	E		T	E	A	M	U	P		R	E	D	O	
		A	L	A	R	M		M	E	A	D		G	I	G	
J	A	M	E	S	I		A	G	A	S	S	I		I	T	T
A	L	A	S	K	A		S	A	N	T	A	M	A	R	I	A
R	O	T	T	E	D		O	P	I	E		A	M	O	N	G
S	T	E	E	D	S		F	E	A	R		G	A	N	G	S

240

C	H	E	S	S		G	L	A	Z	E		R	E	H	A	B
L	E	G	I	T		O	A	S	E	S		E	R	O	D	E
E	L	Y	S	E		C	H	I	R	P		F	E	T	E	D
A	L	P		W	H	A	T	D	O	Y	O	U	C	A	L	L
R	O	T	H		E	R	I	E			A	T	T	I	L	A
			O	B	I	T			A	S	H	E		R	E	M
S	I	N	G	E	R	S	W	H	O	M	U	S	T			
C	L	O	W	N	S		H	A	R	E			O	W	L	S
A	I	M	A	T		F	O	R	T	E		S	N	O	O	P
T	E	E	S		R	O	S	A		E	U	G	E	N	E	
	H	A	V	E	S	H	E	E	T	M	U	S	I	C		
S	D	S		S	E	T	H		R	U	S	E				
H	E	A	R	S	E			S	P	U	D		S	H	A	G
A	C	H	O	I	R	O	F	P	A	P	E	R		O	R	Y
B	R	A	G	S		A	L	E	R	T		E	Q	U	I	P
B	E	R	E	T		T	E	N	S	E		A	U	R	A	S
Y	E	A	R	S		H	A	T	E	D		M	O	S	S	Y

241

P	R	I	S	M		H	O	W	T	O		W	O	N	K	A
J	A	M	I	E		A	L	I	A	R		A	L	O	O	F
S	T	I	L	T		R	E	N	T	A		I	D	O	N	T
	A	N	E	R	D	D	O	E	S	N	T	S	I	N	G	
			N	O	E	L				G	A	T	E			
W	A	R	T		L	I	L		T	U	X		S	A	C	K
E	L	I		C	I	N	E	M	A	T	I	C		T	O	E
B	E	C	A	U	S	E	H	E	H	A	S	A	S	O	N	G
S	C	O	U	R		R	A	D	O	N		L	A	Z	E	S
			D	I	A		R	O	E		W	I	G			
H	E	S	I	N	G	S				B	E	C	A	U	S	E
A	C	E		G	O	E	S		B	A	I	O		N	A	Y
J	O	A	N		R	A	N	G	E	R	S		E	D	G	E
	H	E	H	A	S	A	N	A	N	S	W	E	R			
B	R	A	V	O		O	R	A	T	E		I	R	E	N	E
S	A	W	I	N		N	E	W	L	Y		M	I	S	E	R
A	N	K	L	E			S	S	E			P	E	S	O	S

242

L	O	R	C	A		H	A	C	K	S		J	E	T	T	A
O	C	E	A	N		A	D	E	N	O		A	L	I	E	N
C	H	I	L	I		L	M	N	O	P		B	L	E	N	D
H	O	N	E	S	T	Y	I	S	T	H	E	B	E	S	T	
			B	E	W	A	R	E			Z	E	N			
V	A	S		E	R	E		B	A	R	D		P	C	P	
E	S	C	A	P	E	D		M	A	M	A		B	U	R	R
S	T	A	G	E	D		P	O	S	E		D	O	R	I	A
P	O	L	I	C	Y	B	U	T	I	N	S	A	N	I	T	Y
E	R	I	N	S		O	P	E	N		A	D	E	S	T	E
R	I	N	G		R	A	P	T		C	L	A	T	T	E	R
S	A	G		T	O	R	Y		D	U	O		S	R	S	
			F	A	T			F	O	R	M	A	L			
	I	S	A	B	E	T	T	E	R	D	E	F	E	N	S	E
T	R	I	L	L		R	A	T	E	L		O	M	A	H	A
W	O	R	S	E		I	C	A	M	E		R	O	V	E	S
O	N	S	E	T		S	O	L	I	D		E	N	E	M	Y

243

B	L	E	S	S	M	E		B	E	S	T	B	U	D	S	
R	U	B	I	T	I	N		O	N	T	H	E	T	O	W	N
O	N	A	R	A	N	T		O	V	E	R	D	I	D	I	T
W	A	Y	S	I	D	E		T	I	M	E	S	L	O	T	S
				N	E	R	D			O	S	E				
P	H	A	S	E	D		Y	O	U		S	E	L	F	I	E
R	A	K	E	D		D	I	D	S	O		Z	O	R	R	O
E	Y	E	R		K	I	N	D		B	U	R	O	A	K	S
	B	R	A	V	I	N	G		R	E	P	A	S	T	S	
C	A	M	P	I	N	G		M	A	Y	S		E	B	O	N
B	L	A	H	S			S	A	L	T	S		S	L	O	M	O
S	E	N	S	E	D		N	B	C		S	A	Y	Y	E	S
				H	O	C			H	O	O	T				
I	D	I	O	M	A	T	I	C		D	R	I	B	B	L	E
S	U	P	P	O	R	T	E	R		O	R	D	E	R	I	N
T	E	S	T	A	M	E	N	T		R	O	L	L	I	N	G
	L	O	S	T	A	R	T	S		S	W	E	A	T	E	R

244

S	H	I	I	S	M		B	A	D	M	I	S	T	A	K	E
H	O	L	D	T	O		O	N	E	I	N	T	H	R	E	E
A	B	S	O	R	B		B	E	S	S	T	R	U	M	A	N
K	O	A	L	A	S		S	N	I	T		A	D	I	N	S
			S	I	T	E		T	R	I	N	I		N	E	Y
D	D	S		G	E	R	M		E	M	A	G	S			
R	O	U	G	H	R	O	A	D			E	T	H	N	I	C
E	G	R	E	T		S	L	O	T		S	T	A	C	Y	S
A	G	E	N	A		E	T	A	I	L		E	R	E	C	T
R	I	S	I	N	G		A	N	T	I		N	E	A	L	E
	E	T	U	D	E	S		S	H	O	W	E	R	G	E	L
S	N	A	P	S		E	N	I	D		E	S	E			
C	S	I		A	R	I	A	L		S	L	A	B			
O	W	N	E	R		E	L	U	L		D	R	O	W	S	E
L	A	S	T	R	E	S	O	R	T		E	R	R	A	T	A
A	S	T	R	O	N	O	M	E	R		S	O	N	N	E	T
S	H	R	E	W	D	N	E	S	S		T	W	E	E	T	S

245

B	O	R	G		R	I	D	E	S		M	A	R	S	H	A
O	R	E	O		A	N	E	N	T		O	R	A	T	O	R
B	I	N	G	E	W	A	T	C	H		E	M	B	A	R	K
B	O	O	E	D		C	E	L	E	B		A	B	Y	S	S
E	L	I	T	I	S	T	S		L	A	C	T	I	C		
D	E	R		S	P	I	T		E	S	A	U		A	G	A
			Y	O	U	V	E		N	I	T	R	A	T	E	S
O	F	F	E	N	D	E	D		A	S	T	E	R	I	S	K
N	O	O	N									N	O	T	E	
C	U	R	T	S	I	E	S		H	A	P	P	E	N	E	D
U	N	C	L	E	S	A	M		U	D	A	L	L			
E	T	E		N	A	S	A		N	O	N	E		P	C	S
			Q	U	A	K	E	S		T	R	E	A	S	U	R	E
H	A	U	N	T		L	H	A	S	A		S	A	T	E	D
E	D	I	T	O	R		H	U	M	B	L	E	B	R	A	G
R	E	T	I	R	E		I	T	A	L	O		L	I	K	E
A	S	S	E	S	S		T	O	N	E	S		E	D	Y	S

246

M	A	R	A	T		C	R	U	Z		A	R	C	H	E	R
O	P	E	R	A	H	O	U	S	E		B	E	H	A	V	E
R	O	C	K	G	A	R	D	E	N		H	E	A	V	E	N
E	G	O	S	U	R	F	E	R		D	O	S		E	R	E
L	E	I		P	I	U	S		F	I	R	E	S	A	L	E
S	E	L	A			T	A	R	S		S	I	N	O		
			V	A	M	P		T	A	T	S		L	I	V	E
P	A	P	E	R	E	R		S	N	O	W		O	D	I	N
I	N	A		T	W	E	E	T	C	R	E	D		E	N	O
E	N	D	S		E	L	L	A		T	E	A	B	A	G	S
R	O	D	E		D	U	C	K				S	T	Y	E	
	D	Y	E	S			D	I	E	T			A	W	E	D
P	O	W	D	E	R	E	D		A	B	E	D		O	R	E
A	M	A		R	A	S		P	H	O	T	O	B	O	M	B
P	I	G	P	E	N		P	R	I	N	T	M	E	D	I	A
A	N	O	I	N	T		D	E	N	O	U	E	M	E	N	T
W	I	N	C	E	S		A	S	I	S		D	E	D	E	E

247

BARBS · PAGO · MISTED
OTERI · EBAN · ASTRAY
ROTISSERIE · CLEESE
INITIALING · KARATS
NANO · LIDS · TIMED
GLANCING · MAN · OWES
ANGELINA · TATE
ASSURE · ANYWAYTHE
SPANO · SASHA · SPEAK
WINDBLOWS · STERNS
ARTE · ALLOCATE
NEAR · NOS · AMERICAS
CLOTS · TROI · DONE
INLINE · DEPENDUPON
MEANER · INABSENTIA
AIRGUN · NORA · ANENT
CLASPS · ARKS · FORTE

248

SCOTT · ACNE · AGEIST
TERRA · SOUR · GUNNER
ISAACSTERN · ALGORE
RANCHHOUSE · SLIPBY
URGE · ARRESTS · NESS
PEERED · RISER
VERDURE · ERASE
MARNE · ARLES · ROBIN
ONAIR · IOTAS · POLLY
ONICE · LORRE · IMETA
RANKS · CLASSIC
FATHA · TOWELS
SPOT · ARALSEA · ALIT
CORNER · REALLOCATE
ONEILL · GOFLYAKITE
NESTLE · ONEI · HONED
ESTEEM · TIRE · USERS

249

ASIS · BRET · ALE · LASER
LODE · AIRE · CON · ABATE
APER · SLIM · TAG · BRATS
IHAVEKLEPTOMANIABUT
IDES · OAR · GOAD
EAGLET · ARM · BILLETED
ALIEN · OVA · VINO · EPA
ROZ · SPELLING · SCREW
SEATTLE · USE · ICEMEN
WHENITGETSBAD
DEFIED · RUE · PINETAR
ALONE · CONSOLED · ELI
FLU · IONA · VOW · BRAIN
TERRIBLY · VEX · REEKED
ARID · JAR · SEEM
ITAKESOMETHINGFORIT
CABIN · NET · ASEA · VANE
ARISE · EAT · NEAL · AVON
LATHS · STY · DEKE · LEND

250

AKITA · TEABAGS · CHUMS
RARER · ALLEGRO · OASIS
GRAMMARSCHOOL · AMAZE
ONSPEC · AGAVES
DEM · ALONEATLAST
AMAR · SERIF · VIABLE
SALAD · MAD · ATTENDEES
SPACERESEARCH · GLEES
ESSENE · TEHEE · ETTA
GIVEITAREST
FRIO · DECRY · TRIPOD
RECUE · THISISTHELIFE
ANITALOOS · DOW · KLEIN
NEEDTO · ELLIS · SSTS
ZEROSUMGAME · NIS
ATEASE · GHOULS
MACAW · GUARDIANANGEL
ALOHA · ADDISON · DELTA
CANNY · NIALONG · SAYST

251

HOPE · TAMP · DAMS · BARS
ODES · NCAA · ARAL · ALAS
PINKYTUSCADERO · RENT
INDIA · SKUAS · WRECKS
MYTREAT · WEED
DODO · RINGOFFIRE · STE
ERRS · EPEE · OAS · FOLIO
NAE · JEST · LIKEN · PENN
SLATE · HOLEUP · RNAS
MIDDLEAGESPREAD
SATE · CARTED · THETA
AVER · ARABS · AAHS · REC
LEAST · ESO · FINE · HERE
TOM · INDEXCARDS · ARMS
CLEO · ORBISON
CACHES · CAMEO · ADLAI
ERIE · THUMBWRESTLING
LOTS · EARP · ANNA · EMAG
LEES · ANTS · REDS · SEXY

252

ELAL · COKE · OMAR · OSLO
GAZE · AMOS · NOPE · HEAD
BUTT · LENT · ETTA · BESO
DRESSINGAPOOLPLAYER
FACET · REFRY · IBARS
ARENA · DUO · ANY
INATUXEDOISLIKE · SBA
MER · TIBIA · ADIN · OAT
MAINST · ESPN · INSTALL
ORZO · PUTTING · INLA
RIOLOBO · SACO · LANDON
ANN · SALA · ATTIC · SOT
LGA · WHIPPEDCREAMONA
KEN · ERG · HINDI
CRAIG · AROAR · ISAAC
HOTDOGMINNESOTAFATS
EGAD · RATE · HOYA · IHOP
AERO · ATIT · ALEC · LENA
TRIS · FIFO · BOZO · EDEN

253

SEGO · HELP · APE · RATSO
HAUL · OLEO · LES · ALANA
ERIE · RAILCARS · SOLES
ALLMENMAKE · FORSHORT
FETID · ALIE · ELANDS
SICEM · ESCAPE
MISTAKESBUTMARRIED
RAF · PEET · POPS · ONME
OROMEO · SAO · ETHICAL
MYRAS · MENFIND · OLLIE
ELGRECO · TSA · RESULT
ROOT · OPEN · LOBO · DEE
OUTABOUTTHEMSOONER
ELPASO · IAMBI
GNAWAT · IBAR · OBAMA
NIGHTOWL · REDSKELTON
OGEES · AIRDROME · ILLS
TENAM · GNU · USED · CATO
ELATE · SGT · NEWS · KWON

254

CELEB · SADTO · ZAPATA
ATARI · STEELE · ARARAT
LASAGNEASHES · PARENT
SRA · TROOP · BASSY
ATF · IMMORAL · ACID
BRIDGETJONESSDAIRY
UOFA · SAY · ESC · SHAW
GIAMATTI · WAWA · DEERE
ONI · VINEGAR · ADD
ANGLESANDDEMONS
ATM · STANLEY · SWE
RAITT · RAES · LEONARDO
BUSH · MMI · IED · PEAR
THEFAULTINOURTSARS
BEEF · ENTICER · MAO
GLUER · FRERE · NEE
DISARM · THEGREENLIME
ANDREA · SEAEEL · DALEY
YEASTS · ERRIS · SLATE

255

AVOWS · LIMBER · MALTS
TITHE · NOCANDO · ALIAS
MACONMEMORIES · SIMON
ATOMANT · NEATNESS
ADJ · UTENSIL · USE
THESPIS · NAIAD · UAW
EASE · FISSIONLICENSE
ABUTS · SAL · NOTARIES
MISHAP · IOTA · HOTSEAT
FALLENSTARS
ASWHITE · STAY · SURGES
SKIAREAS · MRE · PARSE
WARRENFACTIONS · NASA
ETE · TYPEA · GELATIN
ICE · ELEVATE · EES
TRINIDAD · EXERTED
AIDES · LIONUNDEROATH
NLERS · PASTDUE · ARNIE
SLATY · ONUSES · TYSON

256

CREAM · GNATS · BELATED
AORTA · REGIA · ALAMODE
TOOTSIEROLL · NINEPIN
STOA · SNORE · WAX · SETT
CASA · ARSENIO
MILKDUDS · CLARKBARS
ARA · MEATHEAD · RANEE
TORRID · JOAN · SLANDER
ENDER · TONS · MAY · DOLT
HERSHEYKISSES
DATE · YON · WADE · VALSE
INHALES · LIAR · DEWITT
SKIRT · SENTINEL · EEC
CANDYCORN · BABYRUTH
RICOTTA · PINE
ALSO · DES · ADOPT · EMIT
CITADEL · SWEDISHFISH
INUTERO · INNIE · BELLO
DENSEST · LYONS · ODDER

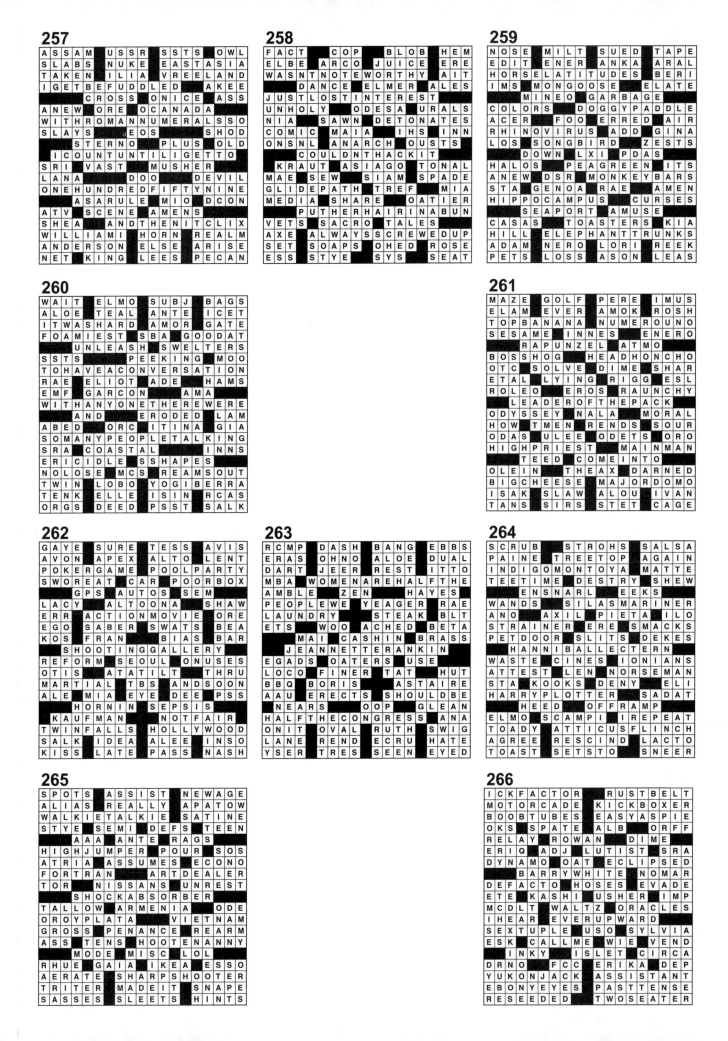

257

```
A S S A M | U S S R | S S T S | O W L
S L A B S | N U K E | E A S T A S I A
T A K E N | I L I A | V R E E L A N D
I G E T B E F U D D L E D | A K E E
    C R O S S | O N I C E | A S S
A N E W | O R E | O C A N A D A
W I T H R O M A N N U M E R A L S S O
S L A Y S | E O S | S H O D
S T E R N O | P L U S | O L D
I C O U N T U N T I L I G E T T O
S R I | V A S T | M U S H E R
L A N A | D O O | D E V I L
O N E H U N D R E D F I F T Y N I N E
A S A R U L E | M I O | D C O N
A T V | S C E N E | A M E N S
S H E A | A N D T H E N I T C L I X
W I L L I A M I | H O R N | R E A L M
A N D E R S O N | E L S E | A R I S E
N E T | K I N G | L E E S | P E C A N
```

258

```
F A C T | C O P | B L O B | H E M
E L B E | A R C O | J U I C E | E R E
W A S N T N O T E W O R T H Y | A I T
D A N C E | E L M E R | A L E S
J U S T L O S T I N T E R E S T
U N H O L Y | O D E S A | U R A L S
N I A | S A W N | D E T O N A T E S
C O M I C | M A I A | I H S | I N N
O N S N L | A N A R C H | O U S T S
C O U L D N T H A C K I T
K R A U T | A S I A G O | T O N A L
M A E | S E W | S I A M | S P A D E
G L I D E P A T H | T R E F | M I A
M E D I A | S H A R E | O A T I E R
P U T H E R H A I R I N A B U N
V E T S | S A C R O | T A L E S
A X E | A L W A Y S S C R E W E D U P
S E T | S O A P S | O H E D | R O S E
E S S | S T Y E | S Y S | S E A T
```

259

```
N O S E | M I L T | S U E D | T A P E
E D I T | E N E R | A N K A | A R A L
H O R S E L A T I T U D E S | B E R I
I M S | M O N G O O S E | E L A T E
    M I N E O | G A R B A G E
C O L O R S | D O G G Y P A D D L E
A C E R | F O O | E R R E D | A I R
R H I N O V I R U S | A D D | G I N A
L O S | S O N G B I R D | Z E S T S
    D O W N | L X I | P D A S
H A L O S | P E A G R E E N | I T S
A N E W | D S R | M O N K E Y B A R S
S T A | G E N O A | R A E | A M E N
H I P P O C A M P U S | C U R S E S
S E A P O R T | A M U S E
C A S A S | T O A S T E R S | K I A
H I L L | E L E P H A N T T R U N K S
A D A M | N E R O | L O R I | R E E K
P E T S | L O S S | A S O N | L E A S
```

260

```
W A I T | E L M O | S U B J | B A G S
A L O E | T E A L | A N T E | I C E T
I T W A S H A R D | A M O R | G A T E
F O A M I E S T | S B A | G O O D A T
    U N L E A S H | S W E L T E R S
S S T S | P E E K I N G | M O O
T O H A V E A C O N V E R S A T I O N
R A E | E L I O T | A D E | H A M S
E M F | G A R C O N | A M A
W I T H A N Y O N E T H E R E W E R E
    A N D | E R O D E D | L A M
A B E D | O R C | I T I N A | G I A
S O M A N Y P E O P L E T A L K I N G
S R A | C O A S T A L | I N N S
E R I C I D L E | S S H A P E S
N O L O S E | M C S | R E A M S O U T
T W I N | L O B O | Y O G I B E R R A
T E N K | E L L E | I S I N | R C A S
O R G S | D E E D | P S S T | S A L K
```

261

```
M A Z E | G O L F | P E R E | I M U S
E L A M | E V E R | A M O K | R O S H
T O P B A N A N A | N U M E R O U N O
S E S A M E | I N N E S | E N E R O
    R A P U N Z E L | A T M O
B O S S H O G | H E A D H O N C H O
O T C | S O L V E | D I M E | S H A R
E T A L | L Y I N G | R I G G | E S L
R O L E O | E R O S | R A U N C H Y
    L E A D E R O F T H E P A C K
O D Y S S E Y | N A L A | M O R A L
H O W | T M E N | R E N D S | S O U R
O D A S | U L E E | O D E T S | O R O
H I G H P R I E S T | M A I N M A N
    T E E D | C O M E I N T O
O L E I N | T H E A X | D A R N E D
B I G C H E E S E | M A J O R D O M O
I S A K | S L A W | A L O U | I V A N
T A N S | S I R S | S T E T | C A G E
```

262

```
G A Y E | S U R E | T E S S | A V I S
A V O N | A P E X | A L T O | L E N T
P O K E R G A M E | P O O L P A R T Y
S W O R E A T | C A R | P O O R B O X
    G P S | A U T O S | S E M
L A C Y | A L T O O N A | S H A W
E R R | A C T I O N M O V I E | O R E
E G O | S A B E R | S W A T S | B E A
K O S | F R A N | B I A S | B A R
    S H O O T I N G G A L L E R Y
R E F O R M | S E O U L | O N U S E S
O T I S | A T A T I L T | T H R U
M A R T I A L | T B S | A N D S O O N
A L E | M I A | E Y E | D E E | P S S
    H O R N I N | S E P S I S
K A U F M A N | N O T F A I R
T W I N F A L L S | H O L L Y W O O D
S A L K | I D E A | A L E E | I N S O
K I S S | L A T E | P A S S | N A S H
```

263

```
R C M P | D A S H | B A N G | E B B S
E R A S | O H N O | A L O E | D U A L
D A R T | J E E R | R E S T | I T T O
M B A | W O M E N A R E H A L F T H E
A M B L E | Z E N | H A Y E S
P E O P L E W E | Y E A G E R | R A E
L A U N D R Y | S T E A K | B L T
E T S | W O O | A C H E D | B E T A
M A I | C A S H I N | B R A S S
J E A N N E T T E R A N K I N
E G A D S | O A T E R S | U S E
L O C O | F I N E R | T A T | H U T
B B Q | B O R I S | A S T A I R E
A A U | E R E C T S | S H O U L D B E
N E A R S | O O P | G L E A N
H A L F T H E C O N G R E S S | A N A
O N I T | O V A L | R U T H | S W I G
L A N E | R E N D | E C R U | H A T E
Y S E R | T R E S | S E E N | E Y E D
```

264

```
S C R U B | S T R O H S | S A L S A
P A I N E | T R E E T O P | A G A I N
I N D I G O M O N T O Y A | M A T T E
T E E T I M E | D E S T R Y | S H E W
    E N S N A R L | E E K S
W A N D S | S I L A S M A R I N E R
A N O | A X I L | P I E T A | I L O
S T R A I N E R | E R E | S M A C K S
P E T D O O R | S L I T S | D E K E S
    H A N N I B A L L E C T E R N
W A S T E | C I N E S | I O N I A N S
A T T E S T | L E N | N O R S E M A N
S T A | K O O K S | D E N Y | E L I
H A R R Y P L O T T E R | S A D A T
    H E E D | O F F R A M P
E L M O | S C A M P I | I R E P E A T
T O A D Y | A T T I C U S F L I N C H
A G R E E | R E S C I N D | L A C T O
T O A S T | S E T S T O | S N E E R
```

265

```
S P O T S | A S S I S T | N E W A G E
A L I A S | R E A L L Y | A P A T O W
W A L K I E T A L K I E | S A T I N E
S T Y E | S E M I | D E F S | T E E N
    A A A | A N T E | R A G S
H I G H J U M P E R | P O U R | S O S
A T R I A | A S S U M E S | E C O N O
F O R T R A N | A R T D E A L E R
T O R | N I S S A N S | U N R E S T
    S H O C K A B S O R B E R
T A L L O W | A R M E N I A | O D E
O R O Y P L A T A | V I E T N A M
G R O S S | P E N A N C E | R E A R M
A S S | T E N S | H O O T E N A N N Y
    M O D E | M I S C | L O L
R H U E | G A I A | I K E A | E S S O
A E R A T E | S H A R P S H O O T E R
T R I T E R | M A D E I T | S N A P E
S A S S E S | S L E E T S | H I N T S
```

266

```
I C K F A C T O R | R U S T B E L T
M O T O R C A D E | K I C K B O X E R
B O O B T U B E S | E A S Y A S P I E
O K S | S P A T E | A L B | O R F F
R E L A Y | R O W A N | D I M E
E R I Q | A D J | L U T I S T | S R A
D Y N A M O | O A T | E C L I P S E D
    B A R R Y W H I T E | N O M A R
D E F A C T O | H O S E S | E V A D E
E T E | K A S H I | U S H E R | I M P
M C D L T | W A L T Z | O R A C L E S
I H E A R | E V E R U P W A R D
S E X T U P L E | U S O | S Y L V I A
E S K | C A L L M E | W I E | V E N D
    I N K Y | I S L E T | C I R C A
D R N O | F C C | E R I K A | D E P
Y U K O N J A C K | A S S I S T A N T
E B O N Y E Y E S | P A S T T E N S E
R E S E E D E D | T W O S E A T E R
```

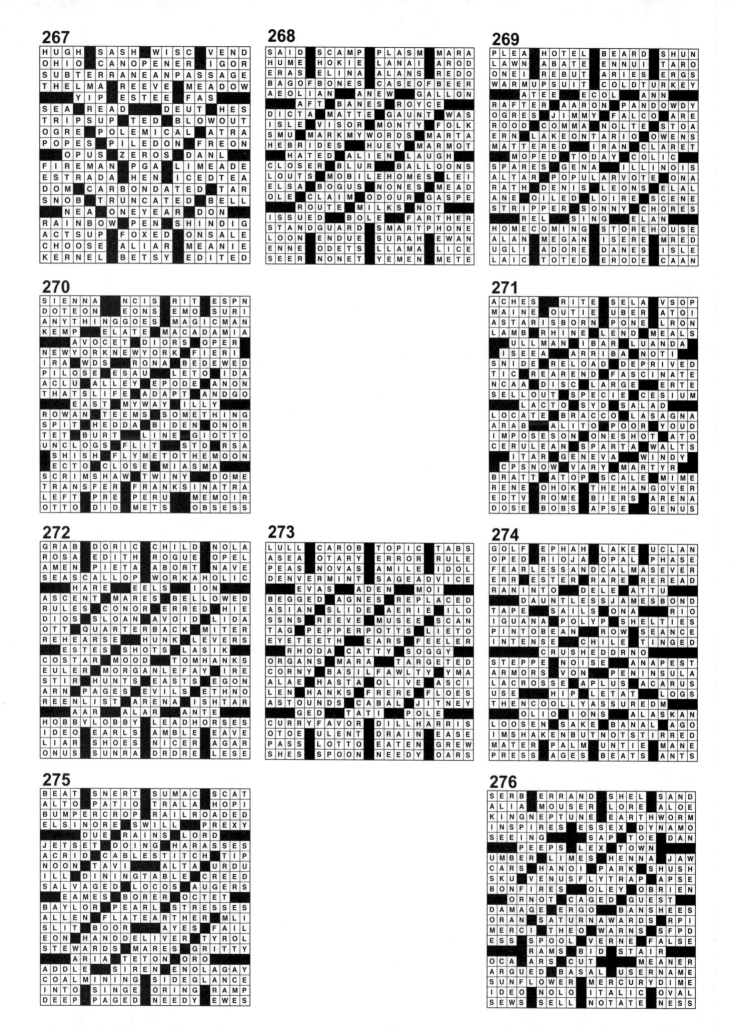

277

| | | | | | | | | | | | | | | | | | | | |
|G|A|S|P| |A|N|T|E|S| |P|A|R|I|S| |C|A|B|S|

GASP · ANTES · PARIS · CABS
OLLA · REALM · ELITE · OREO
APER · MAMBA · BELLA · GALL
THESKIPPER · BULLWINKLE
SATIRES · TILT · ABASES
FIS · SPARE · OPTIC
DEGAS · DWELT · CRIED · RHO
OPAL · GOODE · AUGER · TOAD
NIB · PATRICKSTAR · MACRO
SCREAMED · AKIN · CIPHER
INCUR · MOUSE · ROSIE
PRESET · LIRA · REVERSED
LULUS · POTSIEWEBER · TAU
ELLE · PHOTO · VENUS · VEST
BEE · COOPS · PANTS · DIRTY
CANNY · FINDS · FOG
AGEOLD · BING · LIONESS
FOZZIEBEAR · ETHELMERTZ
AMIE · ROILS · LEAVE · TREE
TENN · EGRET · ILLER · TOLL
ERES · DYERS · CALLS · ELAL

278

ONAN · LALAW · ATEM · PIQUE
BUCO · OCALA · RAGA · TNUTS
JETFIGHTERPILOT · SAINT
EVIAN · SEETO · KITE · DRED
TONIC · OLS · SENDAK
RANGERRICKMAGAZINE
PRE · ELSINORE · EVENER
HERO · NASD · ENGINE · EMU
YANKEEDOODLEDANDY · SEC
SPEAK · FOO · OTOE · PSAT
PEPTO · CPA · ONRYE
TIKI · IONA · ELM · ERUPT
HEE · KNICKERBOCKERCLUB
ORG · INTERN · REEL · YAMS
NEPALI · ONASPREE · NAP
GIANTPAININTHENECK
RISERS · SNU · OASIS
PETS · DALE · EMMAS · PLINY
OBITS · METEXPECTATIONS
OREOS · ITOR · ENTER · NUIT
HOSNI · SSNS · DUSTY · EXES

279

BRAE · CBERS · MAGLI · PAST
BELL · CADET · OVOID · UNHA
SALSASAUCE · POPQUIZZES
LETS · CAPGUN · UNCOILS
CLOSET · LOOP · TONI · OLE
COUNTRYCLUB · ZEROES
BOI · SEEL · TITAN · SITAR
SLAP · WEAK · GOSPELTRUTH
OBE · REA · RUMBA · EBRO
ATSEA · SKYMAP · BIRDMAN
SAP · BLUESBROTHERS · AID
PROTEAM · INROAD · VANNA
ETNA · HASTE · STR · RPI
RAGMERCHANT · OLEO · LASS
ANEEL · OCTET · ELLA · MOO
RICERS · CHAMBERMAID
MSG · SONE · CHER · EXTORT
CHACHAS · CASABA · OLEG
JAZZAROUND · ROCKBOTTOM
ONEA · SUPER · TRUER · ETEE
BARR · ELITE · SSTAR · NOSH

280

OATS · FRANC · BULBS · EYES
BLOW · LAVER · ANOLE · NAST
EVOE · OPINE · NINON · ACTA
LINEDRIVES · DOGCATCHER
INSTEAD · CAIN · TATTER
ILL · INERT · CROSS
CAPET · GLENN · QUIRK · HAY
OLES · NAIAD · PULPS · MOSS
LOP · POTATOCHIPS · TOTHE
DEPORTED · LILA · LATHER
ERIES · KNELT · TEPEE
APRONS · MAYA · CAPITALS
KAPUT · WATERCOOLER · DOW
IGOT · RELET · OILER · MEGA
NET · HOLEY · RUSTS · BIDEN
GOODS · ACRES · DEN
ASSERT · STAT · SEASIDE
COCOABEACH · SHOTPUTTER
ONER · ERNIE · HOTEL · RASA
RING · ELTON · INTRO · ELKS
NATE · REINS · PEONY · LOSE

281

BLOC · CLARA · SINCE · LUMP
RETA · REGAN · URIAL · ETAL
OMAN · IVANA · NOTRE · MUNI
WARADMIRAL · SNAPCOURSE
STUDIES · GREY · TURNED
IES · RHETT · TARTS
DUCAT · TEASE · CHRIS · DOD
EGON · PETRI · BRONC · LUNE
ELL · CREAMCHEESE · BOCCE
PIDDLING · ALEE · TANKER
FOAMY · NOMAD · RISES
CORONA · SONE · GENERALS
ALONG · SHOULDERPAD · UAE
PONE · AKISS · ARIAS · SCOW
ORT · OPINE · GUSTY · CHESS
PUPPY · SAGES · SLO
SCARCE · TESH · SPAREME
CASEHARDEN · TURKEYTROT
OCHS · LIANA · ETAIN · CAGY
THEE · EGRET · RICED · UTEP
TENT · DANTE · SLEDS · TONE

282

SPACESHIP · SCRAPE · SWIM
TELLAPART · CHAPEL · NANA
OPPOSITES · RAVINE · ODER
PESTERED · SURINAM · BEAD
OED · DEFT · GLEN · SRI
DISCUS · PREFAB · NOTING
UNLIT · WHIPS · EASTERNER
STAN · SHIVS · BALK · LOTSA
TOTEMPOLE · MORTIS · TOTS
ENEMIES · PARDONME
RESALE · PEERESS · ELATES
EDHARRIS · RLSTINE
GABS · SALOME · THELATEST
EQUIP · REDS · SHOPS · ASIT
TURNASIDE · BARES · GITGO
WIGGLE · SERIES · RUNONS
ITE · SARA · VINE · NET
NAST · SARGENT · BEATRICE
DISH · ADDEND · GOAPEOVER
ONEA · LIONEL · INTERVALS
FEST · TIRADE · GOODSENSE

283

HULASKIRT · SMIRKS · DICT
ALEXHALEY · POTENT · OMAR
INTERNEES · AMINOR · LARA
LASSO · VOICE · OLE · CLOD
UNBENDING · LABELLE
SLANDER · ANTON · MOVEIN
AEROSMITH · GURUS · DIANA
WALT · OBOES · MEDAL · TRAM
ONEIN · EARNS · DEMITASSE
FENCER · DOOMS · SOLE
FREEWAY · SWIMS · ATALOSS
ECON · STEPS · SCENIC
CLEAREYED · SLATS · HASTA
EELS · SOARS · TRAWL · VIOL
SNIPS · STEEP · STEAMEDUP
TAMING · HAMUP · PLANETS
SHIRLEY · DEPOSITOR
IONA · III · STEIN · TWERP
BRAT · SPRITE · GLADIOLUS
ONTO · HEIDEN · MELANESIA
NEER · ASSERT · ATPRESENT

284

ARKS · ASCAP · SPATS · MARG
DONK · NYALA · PINOT · ECOL
OGEE · ANEAR · IVANA · TIDE
BELLADONNA · ROSEGARDEN
ENTERED · GHAT · NEESON
TIM · ENROL · ROARS
TAHOE · BLOAT · SANTO · HOW
AMAN · CRISP · LEVEE · CORA
ROZ · FAITHHEALER · PAPER
PRECLUDE · ERIN · BARELY
LOUSE · DORAG · LILAC
CREATE · TERI · TOGETHER
HOYLE · GRACEPERIOD · EMO
ODES · CLARA · EVERT · PSIS
WES · GAUDY · STONE · MUTTS
PUREE · CURED · WAR
LOCALE · PERI · PARCHES
APRILFOOLS · DAISYCHAIN
MIEN · RABAT · INCAN · ALDA
ANTE · ERICA · STELE · SEEP
SEED · ESTES · HARMS · EYRE

285

BATH · CESTA · EPSOM · LEST
AFRO · ATTIC · LILLI · ELMO
ROIL · RHINE · ALIAS · EVAN
BOBBYSOXER · TOMFOOLERY
STEREOS · WET · GUESTS
OAN · PLEAD · SPATE
INFOR · DAILY · CHUMS · JEC
DARK · HORAL · SOAPY · MATH
ETA · MARKMYWORDS · SACRE
MONGOLIA · ISAY · CORKER
KOALA · NAVAL · SHANK
ATTUNE · DOLE · ELEVENTH
SOARS · BILLSOFFARE · IOA
HOLD · SALTY · MUFTI · EFGH
ELK · ROLLE · EERIE · GLEAN
FIFTY · MANSE · ARE
ASSIST · TAU · STACKED
CHUCKSTEAK · NICKOFTIME
TASK · OBELI · OCEAN · ROMA
OVAL · AARON · MONTE · OWEN
RENE · PRONG · ANTED · NATS

286

CLASP · TUBAS · CRIB · DONS
HOMER · ATLAS · OHNO · OVAL
IFPEOPLEUSE · DINA · GENA
PAL · SLEPT · CINE · HERES
STEPPES · OLEOFORHEALTH
REBEL · ODAY · CUTRATE
ARMOR · OPTIC · SIS · PER
REASONSBUTTHENTHEY
ACRE · ALOT · TOY · VEEP
BET · SNA · NEATO · MIATA
DIEANYWAYWHATDOTHEY
ENEMY · RICES · ORA · RAM
SILO · BIN · PICA · WNBA
SAYATTHEIRFUNERALS
MIT · OBS · ATSEA · PALES
UNITARY · IVAN · TACIT
THEYVEGONETOA · BATHMAT
TERRA · RUNS · ZEBRA · ESE
ERNO · MATE · BUTTERPLACE
RIEN · INRE · AVERY · HERON
STYE · ODED · RACES · SEATS

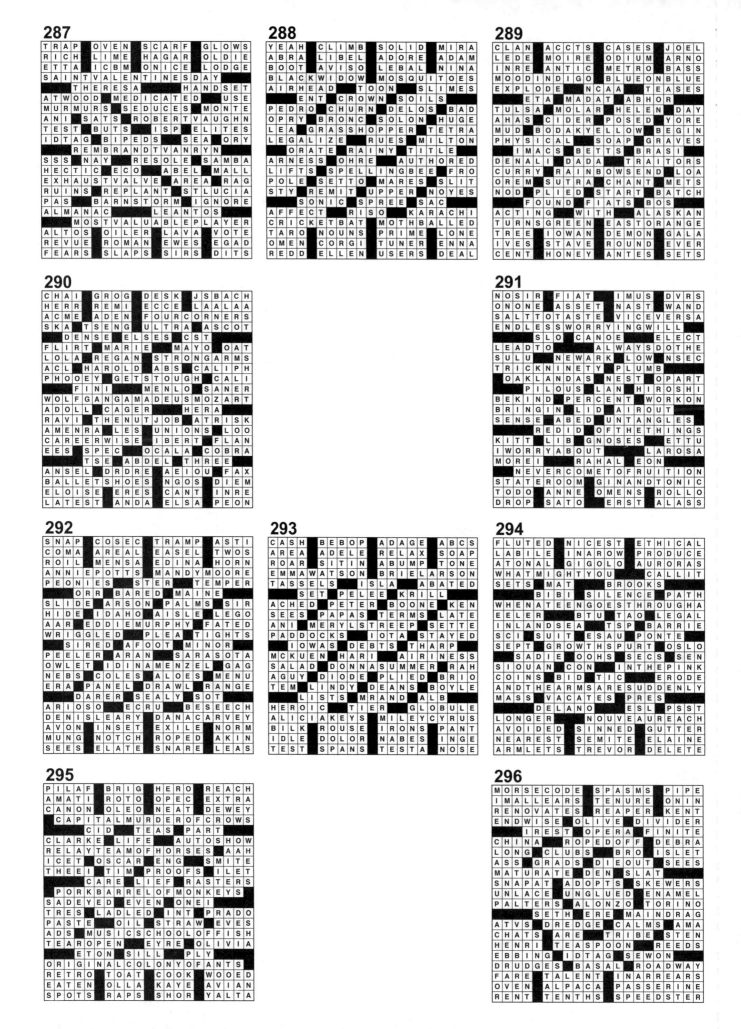

287

T	R	A	P		O	V	E	N		S	C	A	R	F		G	L	O	W	S

TRAP OVEN SCARF GLOWS / RICH LIME HAGAR OLDIE / ETTA ICBM ONICE LODGE / SAINTVALENTINESDAY / THERESA HANDSET / ATWOOD MEDICATED USE / MURMURS SEDUCES MONTE / ANI SATS ROBERTVAUGHN / TEST BUTS ISP ELITES / IDTAG BIPEDS SEA ORY / REMBRANDTVANRYN / SSS NAY RESOLE SAMBA / HECTIC ECO ABEL MALL / EXHAUSTVALVE AREA RAG / RUINS REPLANT STLUCIA / PAS BARNSTORM IGNORE / ALMANAC LEANTOS / MOSTVALUABLEPLAYER / ALTOS OILER LAVA VOTE / REVUE ROMAN EWES EGAD / FEARS SLAPS SIRS DITS

288

YEAH CLIMB SOLID MIRA / ABRA LIBEL ADORE ADAM / BOOT AVISO LEBAL NINA / BLACKWIDOW MOSQUITOES / AIRHEAD TOON SLIMES / ENT CROWN SOILS / PEDRO CHURN DELOS BAD / OPRY BRONC SOLON HUGE / LEA GRASSHOPPER TETRA / LEGALIZE RUES MILTON / ORATE RAINY TITLE / ARNESS OHRE AUTHORED / LIFTS SPELLINGBEE FRO / POLE SETTO MARES SLIT / STY REMIT UPPER NOYES / SONIC SPREE SAC / AFFECT RISO KARACHI / CRICKETBAT MOTHBALLED / TARO NOUNS PRIME LONE / OMEN CORGI TUNER ENNA / REDD ELLEN USERS DEAL

289

CLAN ACCTS CASES JOEL / LEDE MOIRE ODIUM ARNO / INRE ANTIC METRO BASS / MOODINDIGO BLUEONBLUE / EXPLODE NCAA TEASES / ETA MADAT ABHOR / TULSA MOLAR HELEN DAY / AHAS CIDER POSED YORE / MUD BODAKYELLOW BEGIN / PHYSICAL SOAP GRAVES / IMACS BETTS BRASI / DENALI DADA TRAITORS / CURRY RAINBOWSEND LOA / OREM SUTRA CHANT METS / NOD PLIED START BATCH / FOUND FIATS BOS / ACTING WITH ALASKAN / TURNSGREEN EASTORANGE / TREE IOWAN DEMON GALA / IVES STAVE ROUND EVER / CENT HONEY ANTES SETS

290

CHAI GROG DESK JSBACH / HERR REMI ECCE LAALAA / ACME ADEN FOURCORNERS / SKA TSENG ULTRA ASCOT / DENSE ELSES CST / FLIRT MARIE MAYO OAT / LOLA REGAN STRONGARMS / ACL HAROLD ABS CALIPH / PHOOEY GETSTOUGH CALI / FINI MENLO SANER / WOLFGANGAMADEUSMOZART / ADOLL CAGER HERA / RAVI THENUTJOB ATRISK / AMENRA LES UNIONS LOO / CAREERWISE IBERT FLAN / EES SPEC OCALA COBRA / TSE ABDEL THREE / ANSEL DRDRE AEIOU FAX / BALLETSHOES NGOS DIEM / ELOISE ERES CANT INRE / LATEST ANDA ELSA PEON

291

NOSIR FIAT IMUS DVRS / ONONE ASSET NAST WAND / SALTTOTASTE VICEVERSA / ENDLESSWORRYINGWILL / SLO CANOE ELECT / LEADTO ALWAYSDOTHE / SULU NEWARK LOW NSEC / TRICKNINETY PLUMB / OAKLANDAS NEST OPART / PILOUS LAN HIROSHI / BEKIND PERCENT WORKON / BRINGIN LID AIROUT / SENSE ABED UNTANGLES / REDID OFTHETHINGS / KITT LIB GNOSES ETTU / IWORRYABOUT LAROSA / MOREI RAHAL EON / NEVERCOMETOFRUITION / STATEROOM GINANDTONIC / TODO ANNE OMENS ROLLO / DROP SATO ERST ALASS

292

SNAP COSEC TRAMP ASTI / COMA AREAL EASEL TWOS / ROIL MENSA EDINA HORN / ANNIEPOTTS MANDYMOORE / PEONIES STER TEMPER / ORR BARED MAINE / SLIDE ARSON PALMS SIR / HIDE IDAHO AISLE LEGO / AAR EDDIEMURPHY FATED / WRIGGLED PLEA TIGHTS / SIRED AFOOT MINOR / PEELER ARAN SARASOTA / OWLET IDINAMENZEL GAG / NEBS COLES ALOES MENU / ERA PANEL DRAWL RANGE / DARER SEALY SOT / ARIOSO ECRU BESEECH / DENISLEARY DANACARVEY / AVON INSET EXILE NORM / MUNG NOTCH ROPED AKIN / SEES ELATE SNARE LEAS

293

CASH BEBOP ADAGE ABCS / AREA ADELE RELAX SOAP / ROAR SITIN ABUMP TONE / EMMAWATSON BRIELARSON / TASSELS ISLA ABATED / SET PELEE KRILL / ACHED PETER BOONE KEN / SEES PAPAS TERMS LATE / ANI MERYLSTREEP SETTE / PADDOCKS IOTA STAYED / IOWAS DEBTS THARP / MCKUEN HARI AIRINESS / SALAD DONNASUMMER RAH / AGUY DIODE PLIED BRIO / TEM LINDY DEANS BOYLE / LISTS MRAND ALB / HEROIC TIER GLOBULE / ALICIAKEYS MILEYCYRUS / BILK ROUSE IRONS PANT / IDLE DOLOR NABES INGE / TEST SPANS TESTA NOSE

294

FLUTED NICEST ETHICAL / LABILE INAROW PRODUCE / ATONAL GIGOLO AURORAS / WHATMIGHTYOU CALLIT / SETS MAT BROOKS / BIBI SILENCE PATH / WHENATEENGOESTHROUGHA / EELER BTU TAO LEGAL / INLANDSEA TSP BARRIE / SCI SUIT ESAU PONTE / SEPT GROWTHSPURT OSLO / SADIE OOHS SECS SEN / SIOUAN CON INTHEPINK / COINS BID TIC ERODE / ANDTHEARMSARESUDDENLY / MASS VACATES PRES / DELANO ESL PSST / LONGER NOUVEAUREACH / AVOIDED SINNED GUTTER / NEAREST SEMITE ELAINE / ARMLETS TREVOR DELETE

295

PILAF BRIG HERO REACH / AMATI ROTO OPEC EXTRA / CANON OLEO NEAT DEWEY / CAPITALMURDEROFCROWS / CID TEAS PART / CLARKE LIFE AUTOSHOW / RELAYTEAMOFHORSES AAH / ICET OSCAR ENG SMITE / THEEI TIM PROOFS ILET / CARE LIEF RASTERS / PORKBARRELOFMONKEYS / SADEYED EVEN ONEI / TRES LADLED INT PRADO / PASTE OIL STRAW EVES / ADS MUSICSCHOOLOFFISH / TEAROPEN EYRE OLIVIA / ETON SILL PLY / ORIGINALCOLONYOFANTS / RETRO TOAT COOK WOOED / EATEN OLLA KAYE AVIAN / SPOTS RAPS SHOR YALTA

296

MORSECODE SPASMS PIPE / IMALLEARS TENURE ONIN / RENOVATES REAPER KENT / ENDWISE OLIVE DIVIDER / IREST OPERA FINITE / CHINA ROPEDOFF DEBRA / LONG CLUBS BRO ISLET / ASS GRADS DIEOUT SEES / MATURATE DEN SLAT / SNAPAT ADOPTS SKEWERS / UNLACE UNGLUED ENAMEL / PALTERS ALONZO TORINO / SETH ERE MAINDRAG / ATVS DREDGE CALMS AMA / CHATS ARE TRIBE STEN / HENRI TEASPOON REEDS / EBBING IDTAG SEWON / DRUDGES BASAL ROADWAY / FARE TALENT INARREARS / OVEN ALPACA PASSERINE / RENT TENTHS SPEEDSTER

```
HARD  ADLAI  SHEP  LAKE
OKIE  ABOARD NEVA  AHAS
BILLYSUNDAY  OLES  MENS
ONETASTE  BLOWERS  SAGA
   OPUSES  KINGFRIDAY
 ENIAC  AIDAN  LOOT
FREDTHURSDAY  MARC  WES
LAWS  CASAS  RED  KCARS
UTE  PALSY  GATE  ERWIN
SOLARIA  ELATE  STEAKS
   WEDNESDAYADDAMS
BYPASS  NOISE  INASHOE
LOOKS  PERT  PECAN  ESA
AUGER  ORE  HASNT  TICS
BRO  OSLO  SARASATURDAY
 SOTO  ROWEL  ONAIR
RICKMONDAY  MADRID
UGLY  PAYCASH  PRETENSE
SLAM  SINK  TUESDAYWELD
TORA  ISEE  ALPERT  ARID
SOAP  NEST  RAISE  ROPY
```

```
AMIR  SLURP  CAWED  ALAS
VOLE  CANOE  ORALE  CENT
ACID  ACTOR  RIVAL  CANE
SHUFFLEOFF  KEYLIMEPIE
TAMALES  OLES  VENTED
  CAD  CORER  SLEET
ABBEY  PLEAD  CHART  SSR
COLD  KRAIT  SOAPY  OCHO
ERA  SNOWLEOPARD  SKOAL
SECTIONS  CATE  SMARMY
 KREWE  LAHTI  ETAPE
CABINS  CARR  AMERICAS
ANITA  WHITERABBIT  ABU
PORE  GERRY  ELLEN  MRED
END  VAPID  ASTER  TIDES
 SORTS  SWEAR  CUS
ONEILL  STEM  FATTEST
SIDESADDLE  BILLMURRAY
AGES  NORIA  LOUIE  ENOS
GENT  DINED  ENGEL  SINO
ELSA  STORY  SEERS  SEEN
```

```
HELM  LANAI  RICCI  MAST
OTIC  ACIDS  ADORN  EVER
BAKE  BANAL  PANIC  TINE
OPENSESAME  THEBIGEASY
SEATTLE  OMOO  DRONES
 IES  GOFER  DREAR
FLIRT  MOMMA  IRONY  WIT
LONE  FIONA  STILT  LACE
EST  MENDINGWALL  VASES
ATHLETES  OILY  SIGHTS
 EULER  FATTY  THROB
JAMMED  SASH  THOUSAND
AGAPE  BACKSTREETS  SIR
DAIS  MALES  OUSTS  BIDE
ERN  RABAT  GRETA  SINEW
 WANED  TIPSY  CCS
OCTOPI  BEBE  ALAMODE
COUNTFLEET  DIANEBAKER
TOLD  EARTH  ONEGA  RARA
ELSE  SLATE  EGRET  CPAS
TSAR  TATER  SAILS  KITE
```

```
NASA  MATTA  STAB  FOLDS
ORTS  IDEAS  WARE  IDIOT
TRAP  DEARS  AREA  NOTRE
DIGITAL[TIMES]TAMP  STMARTIN
OVERUSE  AIM  CONAN  LEO
 EDEN  INLIEU  ITCHES
 DEIMOS  NECKTIE
CRS  IRAN  SPIRO  EATSAT
LEARNER  SORD  CARL  TEE
ATNO  STAPLE  NOD  [TIMES]HARE
SOTS  TIMESSQUARE  ATON
STIEB  NUT  SUNSET  TUBA
IAN  EPIS  PEAS  NAMETAG
CLICHE  ECARD  MAIA  ETE
 PITCREW  CALLIN
SHINER  ENVIED  TINT
DIO  DRAMS  INC  AIRRAID
RELATIVE[TIMES]AVINGDEVICE
ERICH  ATOP  ELSOL  ALKA
ARETE  TORA  SIEGE  NELL
MARI[TIMES]SOON  TACOS  ARES
```

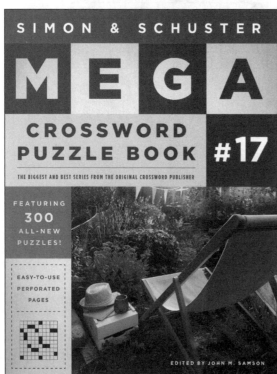